Chapter 6 Arkansas Valley

$4.00

MT. ELBERT

TWIN LAKES

DAYTON

LEADVILLE

EVERETT

GRANITE

BEAVER CITY

GEORGIA BAR

VICKSBURG

WINFIELD

ROCKDALE

COTTONWOOD PASS

HARVARD CITY

BUENA VISTA

SOUTH PARK

HIGHWAY 24 285

TINCUP

TINCUP PASS

HORTENSE

NATHROP

IRON CITY

ALPINE

MT. PRINCETON HOT SPRINGS

WHITEHORN

ALPINE TUNNEL

ST. ELMO

ROMLEY

TURRET

CALUMET

HANCOCK

SHAVANO

HIGHWAY 24

PITKIN

GARFIELD

MONARCH

HARTVILLE

ARBOURVILLE

MAYSVILLE

HIGHWAY 50

SALIDA

CLEORA

PONCHA SPRINGS

MONARCH PASS

←SAGUACHE

HIGHWAY 285

CANON CITY →

$8.00

VICTOR, ITS DUMPS AND THE AJAX MINE

Stampede to Timberline

THE GHOST TOWNS AND MINING CAMPS
OF COLORADO

WRITTEN AND ILLUSTRATED BY

MURIEL SIBELL WOLLE

Revised and Enlarged

SAGE BOOKS

THE SWALLOW PRESS INC.
CHICAGO

First Edition
  1st Printing, July 1949
  2nd Printing, October 1949
  3rd Printing, December 1949
  4th Printing, May 1950
  5th Printing, April 1952
  6th Printing, July 1954
  7th Printing, February 1957
  8th Printing, April 1959
  9th Printing, October 1962
10th Printing, April 1965
11th Printing, April 1967
12th Printing, February 1969
13th Printing, August 1971

Second Edition
Revised and Enlarged
June 1974

Sage Books are published by
The Swallow Press Incorporated
1139 South Wabash Avenue
Chicago, Illinois 60605

ISBN 0-8040-0282-7
LIBRARY OF CONGRESS CATALOG CARD NUMBER 74-6940

Dedicated to all hard-rock miners
of Colorado, who since 1859 supplied
the material for this book.

Preface

Perhaps it is strange that someone brought up in a big eastern city, completely ignorant of mining and all that goes with it, should willingly abandon the east and become steeped in the history of pioneer Colorado. And perhaps it is equally strange that from a single mountain drive such an absorbing hobby was born. As the result of one ride, I dedicated myself to recording pictorially the mining towns of the state before they disappeared, or before those which are still active were "restored" past all semblance of their past glory; and almost without knowing it, I was also deep in history.

During the twenty-two years that I have been engaged on this project I have covered the mountain areas of the state and have visited two hundred and forty mining communities. A few of them are thriving towns today, but most of them are living in the past or have quietly fallen asleep. Others have completely disappeared and their sites can be found with difficulty. Even when I knew of the existence of all of these places I could not visit them without a companion, for I am enough of a Coloradan by now to know that one does not go into the mountains alone. Many of the places visited were miles from a highway on old roads which no one traveled or were at the end of dead-end trails.

Most of my historical research was done in the State Historical Society, the Western History Collection of the Public Library and the Bureau of Mines, all in Denver; The Western State College library in Gunnison, the University of Colorado library in Boulder and the public library of Silverton. Newspaper files consulted at length include the Central City *Register-Call*, the Leadville *Herald-Democrat* and the Gunnison *News-Champion*, to all of whose editors I express my thanks. This search has been aided by six University of Colorado Research grants which have enabled me to procure a student chauffeur to drive me on extended and unpredictable trips.

The following persons contributed to the project, either by serving as "chauffeur" or by accompanying me on my quest. Names of many of these people appear in individual chapters, without any attempt at characterization, and I have taken the liberty of using their first names, chiefly to avoid the necessity of saying "he" and "she" repeatedly. Merrill Beckwith, Boyd Brown, Dan Mackay, Jane Dyde Miller, Richard Pillmore, Joyce Talal and Jim Zeigler drove me over villainous roads. Gayle and Gwen Waldrop took me to Gresham before it vanished; Florence Green accompanied me on my trip to Holy Cross City and waited patiently at the foot of the mountain while I plodded to the timberline camp; Mary Lou Cox and Leslie Merrill led the way to Lamartine; Mrs. Albert Colville, Mr. and Mrs. Carrol Wetherill and their daughter Carol Ann made my trip to Beartown and Carson possible; and Frank Geck and Ed and June West assisted with the Leadville Opera House record.

Ira Current, Walter Johnson and Floyd Walters photographed my sketches; Victor and Frances Dorrell proof-read the manuscript. Frances Shea, Virginia Holbert, Mary Lou Lyda, Ethel F. McCarthy, Margery Bedinger and

Ina T. Aulls, all librarians, ferreted out obscure information for me. Joseph Ewan, Aileen Fisher, Maim Gale and Olive Rabe "discovered" places for me and took me to them; George Harris, Pierce Clark (deceased), and C. W. Hansen drove me in a car, a truck and a jeep respectively, to places that defied even a "Ford 6."

Floy Campbell (deceased), Kady Faulkner, Olga Ross Hannon (deceased), Ann Jones, Eleanor Lindstrom, Clara Straight, Ruth Zeigler Talovich, and Ethel and Jean Zeigler were my painting companions on more than one trip. Mina Burney, Hannah Praxl of Gunnison; Margaret Shaffer of Idaho Springs; Mrs. Raymond Johnson of Ward; Rudy and Dorothy Pozzatti of Silverton; Don and Bess Ripley of Victor; and Louisa Ward Arps arranged interviews and took me on personally conducted tours of the places they knew.

Mrs. John R. Barry, Mrs. Elias Cohn, Alfred Freedheim and Charles H. Hill of Denver; Mrs. Mason of Lyons; Mr. Deering of Gunnison; Miss Emerson, Mr. and Mrs. Noah Mayer, Mr. Handy and Mr. Marshall of Crestone; Mr. Mosher and Dan Slane of Saguache; Mr. and Mrs. Seeton of Tin Cup; Eino Pekkarine and Mr. Snodgrass (deceased) of Telluride; Eutana Wolcott Davlin of Creede; Corder Smith of Fort Morgan; George Bauchmann (deceased), Mr. Cochran, Frank Pangborn and C. R. Ewing of Del Norte; Mary Pharnes of Grant; Ruth Hall of Alma; Everett Bair of Fairplay; Mrs. Miner of Breckenridge; Henry Forsyth (deceased) of Howardsville; Mr. Rathburn of Eureka, and N. C. Maxwell of Silverton were good enough to give me interviews.

I wish to acknowledge the gracious permission given by Mrs. Mary Lyons Cairns to make use of material from her book, *Grand Lake: The Pioneers;* by Mr. Donald C. Kemp and John R. Langley to use information from their book, *Happy Valley, A Promoter's Paradise;* by Mr. Roscoe Fleming and *Rocky Mountain Life* to quote from Mr. Fleming's article, "Colorado's Verbal Volcano"; and by Mr. Lafayette Hanchett to use excerpts from his book *The Old Sheriff and Other True Tales.*

Victoria Seigfried Barker, Rebecca Smith Lee, Elizabeth Mowrey and Helen E. Sibell ventured willingly with me into the unknown parts of the state, and Peg Mabee saved me from a broken leg on Smith Hill. None of my friends gave me more assistance than Mrs. Clara G. Norton of Leadville, and none accompanied me on more hair-raising and exhausting trips than Elliot and Elizabeth Evans, Eugene and Charlotte Irey, and Francis Wolle. Without his encouragement, inspiration and complete understanding this project would not have reached fruition.

In a sense this book belongs to all these people.

MURIEL SIBELL WOLLE
March 4, 1949

On more recent trips (1949-1973), my drivers were Russell Olin, Clare Small (deceased), Mary Lou Stephenson, Jeffrey Quiggle, Dr. and Mrs. George Nahrgang, Joel Baker, all of Boulder; Theora Hoppe of Lawson; Gordon Tripp of Bailey; the Rev. and Mrs. Edward A. Rouffy of Salida; Richard Wagner of Telluride; and Fern Schertfeger and Dennis Smith of Denver.

MURIEL SIBELL WOLLE
March 4, 1974

CONTENTS

ILLUSTRATIONS

CHAPTER ONE

Gold in the Hills

I AM not a historian nor a writer but an artist gone slightly berserk. Twenty two years ago I started sketching the old Colorado mining towns as a hobby and today, whenever I hear of one that I have missed, I prick up my ears and am off to find it like a hound on a scent. I know of two hundred and sixty-seven ghost or semi-ghost mining towns of the state, all of which were established between 1859 and the early nineteen hundreds by prospectors whose eyes were so intent upon the streambeds and mountainsides up which they toiled that they seemed unaware of the almost insuperable hardships which they were forced to endure. The country was wild and none but Indians, fur trappers and animals had ever explored it. A great wall of mountains both challenged them and hampered their advance.

Colorado is unique in its share of the Rocky Mountains. To the north and south of the state the Continental Divide rises as a single range which when crossed puts the mountains behind one. In this state however, the mountains do not comprise one great range, but extend west across three or four hundred miles from the place where the first foothills slope sharply from the Great Plains. After winding through the foothills, you reach a towering divide, climb to the top and then see beyond range upon range extending to the west as far as the eye can see. Down you go on the far side of this first barrier merely to climb to another, and then to another and so on. This great pile-up of mountain ranges contains fifty-two peaks which reach an altitude of over 14,000 feet and hundreds which rise to over 12,000 and 13,000 feet. In such an area of rugged mountains intersected by valleys, open parks, deep gorges and narrow canyons, driving even now over highways is somewhat difficult.

How the prospectors ever managed to find ways through the intricacies of this forbidding country to where the pockets of gold lay, continues to excite the imagination. Even when these men reached a vein or pocket of gold, you still wonder how they maintained the supply lines for food, clothing and tools. Their courage and endurance appalls you, not only when you drive over a main highway and see mine shaft houses perched on top of inaccessible crags but even more so when you force a car over an old abandoned road, up grades that would now be considered intolerable, or reach a place where the road disappears, forcing you to leave the car and go on into these mountain fastnesses on foot. I am no pioneer, but every old mine road and abandoned trail not only invites me but commands me to follow it, not for the gold that lies at its end but that I may see the traces left by the

(1)

men whose quest was gold and whose findings were often both bitter and bright.

It is this picture and the story of the indomitable perseverance of such men which has led me away from the highways and deep into the mountains, even when the going got really tough.

At first I recorded only the most famous towns, such as Central City and Leadville, but when I learned of others, some completely abandoned years ago, I was anxious to visit them too. To locate them was often hard enough, but to reach them in almost inaccessible parts of the Rocky Mountains resulted many times in an exciting trip or an arduous climb. The more places I heard of, the more I realized what a huge task I had undertaken by my self-appointed job as pictorial recorder of the mining camps of the state. And now, at the end of the year, 1948, I have visited and made lithographic crayon drawings of two hundred and forty of these camps, and this book is their story and an account of my adventures in finding them.

Classification of Towns

The towns may be grouped in certain categories: First, mining towns that are still alive, like Aspen and Fairplay, which started as mining camps but depend for most of their present existence on other industries. They have a permanent population and contain some of the original buildings.

Second, towns which are partly ghost—such as Breckenridge and Telluride—where many of the former buildings both commercial and private still stand but are unoccupied, although a portion of the town is inhabited and is carrying on a normal life, the chief industry still being mining.

Third, mining towns which are true ghosts, completely deserted, although their buildings still line the streets. Leavick, near Fairplay, and Bachelor, near Creede, are of this type.

Fourth, mining towns which have disappeared and whose sites only remain. Stunner, Irwin and Hamilton are in this class.

Colorado Mining Eras

Ten years after the California gold rush the slogan was "Pike's Peak or Bust," and prospectors began stirring up the streambeds and tapping the rocks on the eastern side of the Continental Divide. The initial gold strikes were made in 1858 and 1859 by Jackson, Gregory and Russell, and thereafter mining in this state had booms at approximately ten-year periods from the sixties through the early nineteen hundreds. Of parallel interest is the fact that metals were sought and mined in the following sequence: first gold, then silver, lead, zinc, concentrates, and now fluorspar.

Gold was the only metal sought in the sixties; gold was still sought but silver was found in the seventies; most of the camps of the eighties and nineties boomed on silver and would have continued to do so had not silver been demonetized in 1893. The silver crash nearly finished mining in Colorado; but fortunately the Cripple Creek gold rush almost coincided with the silver crash, and through its great mines the complete collapse of mining was averted.

Camps cannot always be classified according to the metal that was first mined in them, for often they grew up around a single mine or group of mines, all producing one metal, perhaps gold. The camp flourished until

(2)

GOLDEN AGE MINE NEAR JIMTOWN

↓ EMPTY CABIN, LEAVICK

the ore played out. Then the miners left and the camp became dormant or deserted. Later on other prospectors came and found traces of another metal, perhaps silver, and another boom was on until the silver crash of 1893. Again the camp slept until some other mineral was found in its mines or until it became a summer resort or a stock-raising center. During the years its population fluctuated with the booms, until today it may be a "dark town" as a present resident of Silver Plume told me only last summer, because its houses are owned by summer tourists who spend but a brief season of the year in them and then board them up during the other nine months.

Mining methods were also responsible for the varying durations of the camps. The rockers and Long Toms of the '59ers caught most of the free gold but let much of the less precious metals escape down the streams. Prospectors in California Gulch in the sixties cursed the heavy black sand that clogged their sluice boxes, only to learn too late that it was lead carbonate rich in silver which they had been washing away.

The early sixties were rich years for the placer miners. These men followed up the streams in search of color and, when they found it, staked off claims and began to pan the streambed and banks. Other miners left the streams to scramble up the mountainsides looking for float or exposed ore. This ore was also profitable, but by 1862 or '63 most of the easily obtained gold in the stream beds or at the grass roots had been found and shipped out by pack train.

Lode mining followed, the miners sinking shafts and tunnelling into the mountainsides to get at the veins. This ore when found was not pure but was combined with quartz and other minerals, and to extract the gold from it posed a problem. At first stamp mills were built to crush the ore and thus free the precious metal from the worthless rock.

The deeper the mines were developed the more varied and refractory the ore became, and other methods of extraction were needed. Smelters and chlorination, lixiviation, and reduction works were erected, each one equipped to cope by chemical processes with the complex ore bodies. In recent years improved methods of milling have enabled companies to recover valuable minerals both by re-working the old mine dumps and by producing concentrates of low grade ores. It is therefore evident that many a camp was deserted long before its paying ores were exhausted, simply because limited methods of milling failed to extract all the values obtainable.

Architecture   Architecturally all camps followed the same pattern. First tents and then log cabins with square-hewn timbers housed the avid prospectors and merchants whose sole interest was to strike it rich as quickly as possible. As soon as a sawmill was packed in, frame structures of dressed lumber were built, including many with imposing false fronts. These fronts hid the one-story stores behind them and helped the miners to believe in the enterprise and elegance of their pioneer surroundings, even though they wallowed knee deep in mud every time they walked up the street and entered one of the pretentious "emporiums."

If the camp continued to flourish and promised permanence, brick and stone buildings were erected, and it is these that one sees today—the court-

CABIN ON THE CASEY. CENTRAL CITY

◄FALSE FRONT, SILVER PLUME

house at Fairplay, the jail at Silver Plume, and the brick schoolhouses at Central City, Georgetown, Leadville, Lake City and Telluride.

Tents and log cabins are all much alike, and it was not until the miners and merchants began to build permanent homes and stores in the mountains that an architectural style was apparent. Just as they named their mines for their native states or cities, they built in a style reminiscent of their recent homes in so far as they could duplicate them with the limited materials at their disposal.

Since the towns were built during Victorian times the architecture follows Victorian tendencies with Greek Revival and Gothic thrown in. Black Hawk and Central City are rich in elaborately carved bargeboards and gabled windows. Georgetown is New England transplanted, especially its carved wooden posts and picket fences. Wood was also used for sidewalks, which were laid as soon as a camp had enough streets and buildings to warrant them, and many of them have lasted through the years—notably in parts of St. Elmo, Nevadaville, Tin Cup, Lake City, Silverton and Kokomo. When I first visited Robinson, its wooden walks were careening drunkenly into a marsh, and even now Black Hawk has a plank sidewalk laid over a flume. Pitkin's main street is flanked with boardwalks; and when I inquired as to what was left of Bachelor (near Creede), I learned that it could be located by its rotting wooden sidewalks bordering the gully which was once the chief thoroughfare.

The cemeteries, overgrown with grass or shadowed by pines, are another link in the story of the ghost towns. The first grave markers were of wood, with names and dates painted on them. Winds and snows have weathered the thin boards to a nondescript brown; but now, the letters and dates stand out in relief, for the paint has protected the wood. By the seventies marble stones were used, and upon seeing several of these in the windswept cemetery at Caribou I began to wonder if all the mountain burying grounds had similar stones and inscriptions. A study of thirty cemeteries followed, and the photographic record of their stones shows an amazing similarity of design. Furthermore, the inscriptions chiselled on their surfaces are not regional but reflect the culture and taste of the pioneers and the eastern cities from which they came. Even these stones show the ravages of time, and more than once I have had to kneel in the long grass in front of one in order to feel out the letters.

Fire was a constant menace to the tinder-dry wooden towns, and almost all of them were swept at least once by a disastrous blaze; therefore their present appearance is quite unlike that of their early glory. Cripple Creek and Victor, Creede and Rosita were all nearly razed by fire. Gold Hill early in its history had a severe fire during which the inhabitants took to the mine tunnels for safety until the danger had passed. Caribou was reduced to ashes on more than one occasion, so that now scarcely any traces of the town remain.

My Hobby   In 1926 when I came to Colorado from the east I had never heard of a ghost town, but on one of my first mountain drives I was shown Central City and was told something of its history. I had always been interested in archi-

(6)

tecture, and the skeletal shell of the once booming town fascinated me. I liked the Victorian houses, set tidily along the streets; the few active stores flanked by many empty ones; the rusty mills, and the rows of deserted buildings perched high above Eureka Gulch. Central City was not entirely deserted —in fact it never has been—but so little of its former glory remained that the footsteps of those living in it echoed loudly on the board sidewalks, and at night only an occasional window showed a lighted interior. The place was full of echoes, and memories, and history, and I felt strangely stirred by it. Here was a piece of the old west, a tangible witness to Colorado's pioneering achievement. It was disappearing fast; it was important that it be preserved; it challenged me. Someone should record it before it decayed or was restored to twentieth century needs. The place itself seemed to cry out for a pictorial rendering, and I determined then and there to try my hand at it and to return in September to sketch the streets and individual buildings. After that I decided to return again and again until I had Central City on paper.

Of course, before I'd done much painting I became interested in the history of the place; and after talking to the old miners who looked over my shoulder as I worked, I realized that I must do historical research as well.

At first my efforts were limited to Central City, since I did not know of other towns of similar character; but as I learned more of Colorado and heard about Leadville, Ward, Gold Hill and other places, my vacations began to be hunting trips, and each September I added more sketches to the pile of the year before. Mining records introduced me to areas and towns of which I had never heard; and to each of these I went, either by auto or, as they became more remote, and as roads disappeared, on foot or on horseback.

In making this pictorial record I have taken no liberties with the composition of the subjects sketched. Buildings are grouped as they actually appear; mountains are rendered as rocky or timbered, snow-capped or barren, just as I found them. Consequently the graphic record is an authentic one, but in order that the resulting sketch might be as artistic as possible, I walked around each subject seeking the best possible angle for pictorial delineation. Often the trip to an inaccessible spot meant leaving the car on a shelf road and hiking miles to timberline up an abandoned wagon track, even at times walking precariously over the rotting logs of an old corduroy roadbed. *My Method*

Rather than take photographs of each place, I chose to make drawings and paintings, for through them I hoped to catch the mood and quality of the town portrayed and to see it, in the mind's eye, at the height of its development. Finally, after visiting it, I again looked up historical and anecdotal information, using as sources old newspapers, diaries, manuscripts, scrapbooks, photographs, and maps which I found in library collections. The most exciting map was a large one that was pasted up on the third floor hall of the Healy House, the historical museum in Leadville. On it were not only the names of places but also the mountains and the valleys, all drawn with imagination, the peaks very white and the valleys very green, covered with a network of streams and old trails. By studying it one could see how railroads and toll roads had had to twist their way between peaks and up gulches.

(7)

From it alone I obtained a better picture of the state than from any other single source.

This record of the mining towns could not have been made without the help of countless numbers of people, some of whom are unaware that they have helped. Filling station agents and postmasters and storekeepers have told me about road conditions and have directed me to obscure trails and to landmarks that were not clearly indicated on a map. Miners and mine engineers and truck drivers have answered my questions and identified my sketches. County clerks and librarians, newspaper editors and housewives have written replies to my questions concerning some detail that I had overlooked or could not clarify from my notes.

Everyone has been helpful and many have put themselves out to find an answer for me, coming to the hotel or tourist camp where I was staying to deliver the information in person or mailing it to my home. More than once men or women have put their own articles at my disposal that I might cull historical data from them; one woman loaned me her mother's diary. A librarian permitted me to work overtime so that I might complete certain notes, locking me into the chill building which had to be closed at a certain hour. Another librarian allowed me to take a bound volume of old newspapers to the hotel for the night, that I might work all evening; several people in Denver have invited me to visit them that they might show me photographs of the early days or talk to me about the places in which they grew up.

In 1881 George A. Crofutt wrote a book called *Crofutt's Grip-sack Guide of Colorado, A Complete Encyclopedia of the State*. It was illustrated and it described "What Is Worth Seeing, Where To See It, Where To Go, How To Go, Where To Stop, and What It Costs." Crofutt's descriptions of each of the mining camps have been of invaluable help to me, and as I have sketched the many towns and have delved into the history of each I have felt very close to Mr. Crofutt. Since I have visited most of the places that he knew and since I have described them as they are today, I sometimes amuse myself by thinking that I have written a twentieth century edition of the "Grip-sack." I could even use a portion of the preface to describe my aims:

> The GRIP-SACK is not written in the interest of any corporation—railway, land, or mining company—but is wholly independent, without fear, favor, or hope of reward, further than the merits of the book will justify. We have given a hasty review of the State at large; made 'Tours' over all the railways; described 527 cities, towns, stations, mining camps, etc., and how to reach them. . . . The above, together with . . . nearly one hundred illustrations . . . is the only apology for writing this book. . . .

The material in this book is grouped by areas. A map precedes each chapter and indicates the relative location of each place mentioned therein. By comparing the map with any road map of Colorado, existing places can be checked and roads or trails which lead fairly close to the other places can be traced.

The illustrations picture the towns as I saw them, but because over a quarter of the buildings shown in the sketches have disappeared since I drew them, I am thankful that I was able to be on the spot and preserve them before they vanished. Half the fun of this hobby, however, has been the adventurous trips connected with the finding of each place, and it is these together with bits of the picturesque history of the early days that I share with you in the following pages.

CHAPTER TWO

Central City Starts a Hobby

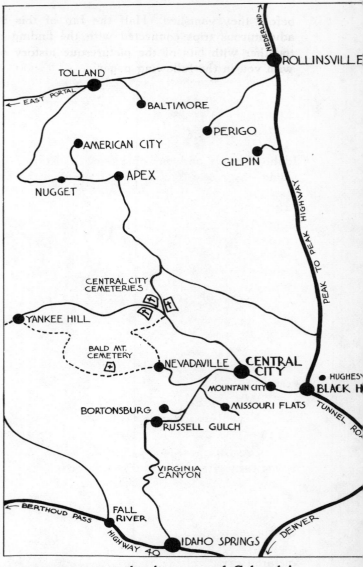

Central City

WHEN the sightseeing bus climbed the long, steep mile from Black Hawk to Central City in the midst of the Colorado Rockies, I sat up a little straighter and could hardly believe my eyes. Wooden sidewalks! Gingerbread frets under eaves; houses tier on tier and mine dumps, with rusty shaft houses everywhere.

"What you see here," said the man in the next seat to me, "is what's left of the old West. You won't see it much longer for it is disappearing fast."

Craning my neck and looking from side to side I watched the old houses slip by together with the gaping mine tunnels, and the monument commemorating the discovery of Colorado's gold on this spot. Still the car climbed toward more mines. Ahead, to the left, was an empty fire house with its bell, standing beside a gulch down which gray tailings poured, proof that the mines in the distance were working. On the right were streets, one above another built on terraces cut from the hillside and on one stood the native stone high school from which, I was told, were graduated the first trained teachers of the state.

Crowning the hill was another school building, this one surmounted with a cross. "That," said my neighbor, "was St. Aloysius' Academy, and just below it, on Eureka Street, is one of the most famous hostelries in the west —the Teller House. And beyond it is the Opera House, and beyond it Gilpin County Courthouse, and farther up the streets, the Brewery, and at the top of the hill the cemeteries." My head reeled.

Buildings everywhere, many of them deserted and definitely built many years ago. Few people were in sight when we stopped for soda-pop and a quick walk along the main street, and our footsteps echoed as we climbed the wooden steps to the Masonic Lodge, one of the sights of the city. This was Central City, once the biggest place in Jefferson Territory, and in the sixties surpassing even Denver in size. And here *I* was, fresh from the east and surrounded by a culture which flowered in the seventies and eighties and slowly faded in the nineties.

We stayed all too short a time in Central City and were hurried on toward Idaho Springs and our objective, St. Mary's Glacier, where there would be skiing—a great attraction to easteners on the Fourth of July! We climbed the long, curving hill that led out of Central to Russell Gulch and Idaho Springs, and before we reached the top of the grade I glanced back for a last look at Central City, cupped in a hollow of the mountains and emanating such a strong flavor of the past. The rest of the day I do not remember. The skiing and the snowballing are hazy recollections, for my whole attention was centered on Central City and my mind was made up then and there to know more of its history and to return to its picturesque streets and sketch its tumbling buildings and gaping mines.

A year passed before I could carry out my decision, a year spent in New York. But now New York had lost its fascination; more and more I longed for the mountains and the West. And I well remember the day that I walked into the president's office at the Art School where I was teaching and tendered my resignation.

"What's this?" said that gentleman, "Are you going to be married?"

"No," I replied with a wicked gleam in my eye, for I knew how he loved the city, "I'm tired of New York and I want to go west to live."

So, a few months later, having sought positions from Montana to Arizona, I was fortunate enough to find an opening in the Art Department at the University of Colorado and I knew that my Central City dream was beginning to materialize.

During the summer of 1926, while teaching at the University, I asked questions about Colorado's past, its mining booms and its ghost towns, but my real interest in the history began when I returned to Central City to start my pictorial record of the place. As soon as school closed at the end of August, ignorant of the lack of regular transportation in the west to many mountain points at any time, I made preparations to spend the vacation in Central City, forty miles from Boulder, and when I was ready to start, there was no way to go. The sightseeing companies had left until the following season; the daily stage up the canyon went only halfway—and twenty miles is a long hike at seven thousand feet elevation. In desperation I called the local taxi company and presented my problem to them. They seemed a little stunned at the request but did some quick calculating and announced that the trip would cost $15.00. Knowing that the canyon stage to Nederland, twenty miles away, cost considerably less I decided to take it and hunt the rest of my transportation there.

Armed with sketching materials, I set out on Labor Day on what seemed an innocent excursion. I reached Nederland by noon. Surely someone would

(11)

be willing to drive me to Central City for a modest sum, and I began inquiring at the garages and hotels; but seemingly no one was interested in a trip to Central. Finally one man agreed to drive me over. "And how much will the trip cost?" I asked. "Fifteen dollars," was his prompt answer. At this point the hotel proprietor came to my aid by assuring me that if I spent the night in his hotel I might be able to get a ride over the next day with the Boulder bread man who served the mountain towns once a week and who sometimes took passengers. Such an arrangement seemed worth trying, and much more economical; so I settled down to stay in Nederland, a small mining town, which by the twenties had become a summer resort. All afternoon I tramped the streets, sketching the false-fronted stores, the log cabins, and the big tungsten mill on the creek. To the west was the Continental Divide and up the winding road to the south lay Central City, twenty miles away. From time to time during the afternoon great roars and cheers came from the Baseball Park where a game was in progress, and upon inquiry I learned that the Nederland team was playing the Black Hawk Club. That was the last straw, for I knew that Black Hawk was one mile from Central City and here in front of me were nine men who in a few hours would be going to within one mile of my destination while I sat in Nederland waiting for the bread man. But I was from the east, and one doesn't just offer oneself to a ball team and beg transportation. Yet, the more I mulled it over in my mind the more foolish it seemed to spend the night in Nederland with Central so accessible. I entered a restaurant for an early supper, perhaps because, parked in front of it, was a car with a Black Hawk license! At one table sat a ballplayer with his wife and family, and as I ate I gathered courage. Just as they were leaving I told them my plight and said that since I saw they were from Black Hawk maybe they would know someway that I might get to Central. This thin disguise worked, and while I ran for my suitcase they filled the tank of the touring car with gasoline and in less than five minutes I was on my way to the Teller House.

It was a ride I shall never forget. The road in those days was steeper than the new highway and was not surfaced. The car pulled slowly but steadily up the long grades while the driver told me of seeing some autos which couldn't make them and had to back up the worst hills. All the while I sat in the backseat between two small boys, with a gaily flowered coverlet tucked under our chins to shut out the cold wind of a September evening.

I watched the sunset colors fade, as we drove between stands of lodgepole pines and passed occasional ranch houses. Just before dark we dropped down into Black Hawk with its mills and smelters and its homes perched crazily on the mountainsides. With true western hospitality my "benefactors" drove up to Central and deposited me in front of the Teller House, refusing to take any remuneration for the trip. I thanked them profusely and was so confused at my temerity in thumbing a ride that even their names have escaped me, and to this day I regret that I do not know to whom I am indebted for starting me on my ghost town hobby.

The Teller House was big and substantial and a little gloomy. The dining room was empty by the time I arrived save for Mr. Teller, who invited me to join him at the long table in the farthest corner. There over crackers, cheese

CENTRAL CITY
PANORAMA

NEWSPAPER
OFFICE,
CENTRAL
CITY

and milk he told me something of the hotel's history. It was built in 1872 and at one time was the most famous caravansary west of the Mississippi. He showed me a newspaper clipping describing the New Year's Evening dinner of Dec. 31, 1872 which read:

GRAND DINNER AT TELLER HOUSE TOMORROW

The most elaborate bill of fare we venture to say that has been provided by any hotel west of the Mississippi River for a public dinner will be served by the Teller House tomorrow, New Year's Evening at half past eight o'clock. Every description of wild and domestic meats to be found have been gathered. There are fishes, beef, veal, mutton, pork, oysters in every style, turkey, maillard duck, mountain grouse, prairie chicken, wild turkey, antelope, venison, bufflalo, Rocky Mountain black bear, with entrees, vegetables, relishes, side dishes, pastries, puddings, ice-cream, jellies, and dessert, to be ornamented also with elegant pyramids of cakes and other elaborate designs in confectionery. It is intended to be the great dinner of the Territory—incomparably greater than has ever before been witnessed in the west . . . The price is fixed at $5.00 per head or $10.00 per couple. It is expected that a large number of ladies and gentlemen will be present.

Another clipping from the *Central City Register* of June 25, 1872, described the grand opening of the building.

"Four years ago," it began, "the *Register* began the agitation of the hotel subject and its editors resolved that it should never cease until a new hotel went up or the paper went down. . . . This resulted in a proposition from Henry M. Teller to build a $60,000 structure . . . if the citizens would subscribe $10,000 cash, toward purchasing the ground. Three gentlemen canvassed the city and in about three days raised the money. . . . The furniture cost $20,000 . . . the Senior partner and his estimable lady supervising arrangement throughout the building. . . . The Parlors are perfect marvels of elegance . . . all sleeping rooms to the number of ninety are tastefully fitted with all essential conveniences. . . . The majority are without transoms. . . . Guests may therefore lie down to peaceful slumbers undisturbed by apprehensions of getting their heads blown off or valuables lifted by burglars."

For four days I explored Central City, returning to the hotel only for meals and to sleep. There was so much to see and sketch that the days were all too short. At noon time if I were halfway down the gulch I had only to put my painting paraphernalia in a deserted cabin and climb up the hill to the hotel for lunch knowing that they would be safe during my absence. Children and passers-by stared curiously as I worked and made comments about the pictures. One lady admired a watercolor of Eureka Street showing several residences including her own. When her husband returned from work she brought him to see the picture and he, seeing her interest offered to buy it for her. "No," said she emphatically, "I don't want it unless she will paint it again and make our house look bigger."

One morning I was sitting in an alley making a watercolor of some buildings and a crazy flight of wooden stairs to the next street level when a girl of about ten stopped to look over my shoulder, and as we talked she found that I was an art teacher. Later she returned with several little friends and standing just within earshot said of my work, "It's pretty good for her being just a teacher and not an artist."

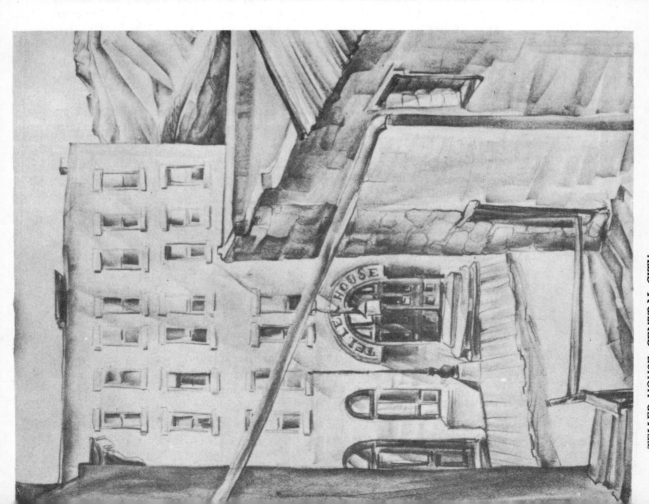

TELLER HOUSE LOBBY, 1931

TELLER HOUSE, CENTRAL CITY

Each day was a new experience, and my enthusiasm to capture the town on paper was greater than my resistance to the cold September winds which swept down the empty streets and up my arms. As a greenhorn I had not realized how much warm clothing I should have brought for these mountain altitudes. I had planned to spend two weeks in the town but at the end of five days I had caught cold in one shoulder and could neither sketch nor move about with any comfort. The Teller House was cold, and dank too in those days, and hot water could be gotten only at intervals, brought in a pitcher by a solicitous but elderly bellhop. Plainly it was time for me to return to Boulder. But how was I to get there? Inquiry after inquiry convinced me that no one ever went to Boulder, and again I was marooned forty miles from my destination. Then someone remembered the Boulder bread man who was due the following day. Maybe he would take me. I mentally resolved that he jolly well would, and an hour before he was due I was sitting in front of the store where he made his deliveries, my suitcase beside me. He was not glad to see me and when I told him of my plight he did not say that he would take me; so desperately, I insisted, "But I won't take up very much room," and began to move my luggage toward the automobile. I remember no more except that in a few minutes I was riding beside him with my feet braced against the dashboard as we bounded down the canyon toward Boulder. The truck was short on springs and air-cushions but speedy, and by the time I was unloaded in front of the apartment house in Boulder I felt as if I'd had a thorough osteopathic treatment. Out came the suitcase from the bread wagon, and slowly but gratefully I limped into the house, my first adventure with Central City over.

Thereafter I returned to Central as often as I could persuade a friend to drive me, each time sketching more of the picturesque buildings, crooked steep streets and empty shaft houses of the mines. People were cooperative, especially the manager of the Chain-O-Mines hotel, where I stayed one night. The next morning in roving about the hotel, looking for "compositions" out of the various windows I stumbled upon a small back porch completely hung with washing. Peering through the sheets and towels I discovered an excellent view of Gregory Gulch and Black Hawk. "Is this what you want?" said the proprietress, who had followed me in my wanderings about the building. "It certainly would make a good water-color," I hinted; whereupon the lady swept two sheets from the line, leaving me an unobstructed view, and for the rest of the morning I sat, draped in flapping wash while Black Hawk and the gulch grew stroke by stroke on my stretched paper.

Each time I returned to the city I missed something—a building was gone or a shaft house blown down, and worse still, an occasional house was restored past all semblance of its former architecture. So my trips to Central City and other places became more frequent and I scrambled more frantically over the noisy wooden sidewalks and up the crumbling dumps in search of vistas which were changing too quickly, or I made portraits of houses whose past was being gradually lost.

Black Hawk   I wandered down the mile-long hill to Black Hawk, walking part of the way on the wooden sidewalk that covers the big rock flume. There was much to sketch, and as in Central City everything clung to the sides of the hills.

(16)

I looked into the mouth of the Bobtail Tunnel, the first to be driven in the district, and I read the marker at the site of the Gregory Diggings from which the first gold was taken. Except that there was no noise, I could have described the town in the words used by Crofutt in his *Grip-Sack Guide*:

> The buildings, mills, churches, stores and residences are sandwiched in between the gulches, ravines, mines, rocks and projecting mountain crags in the most irregular manner. . . . Quartz mills are numerous in and around Black Hawk; the rattling of their descending stamps, night and day, speaks in thunder tones of the great wealth of this mountain country, one of the great treasure-chambers of the American Continent.

At the foot of the hill was the railroad trestle which crossed the main street just above the roofs of the stores. The road, the Colorado Central, was extended up North Clear Creek from Idaho Springs and reached Black Hawk in 1872. The railroad station was a large stone ore mill which stood beside the stream. It had never been used by the company which built it; so when the railroad grade was surveyed and the mill was found to stand directly in its path, the engineers instead of destroying it cut an opening in either end of the building large enough to permit the train to run through it. In 1936 it was washed away in a cloudburst which raged down Clear Creek and swept everything before it.

I was sketching the trestle when one of the merchants came over to watch me work. He pointed out the dim scar along the mountainside which marked the right of way and told me how the road had had to loop back down Clear Creek for two miles before it could gain sufficient elevation to continue to Central, one mile away. Years later I recalled the storekeeper's remarks when I found Fossett's *Colorado, Its Gold and Silver Mines*, an account of the author's ride from Black Hawk to Central.

> At one place streets are crossed above the level of the housetops, and at another, circling the mountain sides for two miles the train makes its appearance hugging the mountain side hundreds of feet above, and almost directly over the town. One can almost look down into the fiery chimneys of the great smelters, while streets rise above, and seemingly bottomless shafts and excavations yawn beneath in this thrilling ride among the gold mines.

Black Hawk and Central City were rivals from the start. When the people of Black Hawk learned that Central was planning to incorporate they hurriedly obtained the services of Hal Sayre, who had made the original survey map of that city, and had him make a survey of their town. By their efforts they were the first to present a petition requesting incorporation.

Black Hawk, whose population reached 2000 in the sixties, is said to have laid out the first cemetery in the state. It was located on Dory Hill two miles from the town and contains some of the most interesting markers that I have found. Dory Hill was covered with timber in 1859, when a site was set aside for the burying-ground, but the hillside was cleared of its trees by the woodchoppers to provide fuel for the mills and timbers for the mines.

As early as 1863 Black Hawk held dances which attracted the miners of the entire district.

Go to Colonel Selak's ball this evening and rap your heels together. There will be fun till you can't resist—*Black Hawk Mining Journal*, Dec. 9, 1863

Those who preferred less active entertainments could attend one or more of a series of lectures on edifying themes.

Judge Armour's Lecture at Lawrence Hall.

It was profuse in eloquence, in pathos, in high and noble thoughts. Three or four word pictures were introduced which were as fine as the tomes of the classics, ancient or modern afford. The Judge has one merit. He speaks from the heart; is original. He is not ashamed of being a *man.* —*Black Hawk Mining Journal*, Dec. 22, 1863.

During the seventies a Skating Rink was opened at Black Hawk which provided entertainment "at once healthful and innocent." When it was razed in 1878 and "its lumber put to another use," Central built a rink to take its place.

In 1926 a number of mills stood along North Clear Creek canyon, both above and below the city. One had been run by water power, and its huge wheel stood nearly as high as the building which housed it. I planned to return to Black Hawk later on and sketch all these old mine and mill properties but I had no car and the Boulder bread man was not handy. I kept putting off the trip, and discovered too late that a new highway had been built into Black Hawk and that the mills which stood in its path had been destroyed. From this I learned my lesson—never to put off sketching anything of historic value.

A little beyond the lower end of the town was the site of Professor Nathaniel P. Hill's smelter, built in 1867 and called the Boston and Colorado Smelting Works. Prior to its construction all ore which could not be handled in the stamp mills was sent to Swansea, Wales, where the gold, silver and copper were separated. To eliminate the expense of shipping ore such a distance, a group of capitalists invited Hill, who was a professor of chemistry at Brown University, to visit Black Hawk and see what could be done. When he arrived in the middle sixties he found the camp almost deserted, for the easily treated surface gold was exhausted and the deeper ores were too complex to respond to stamping. Hill tested the ores and then built his furnace. His smelter was such a success that new life and impetus was given to mining throughout the district. In 1872 he removed his plant to Argo, near Denver, where he ran it with equal success for many years.

One day while exploring the upper levels of Black Hawk I passed the schoolhouse and climbed up the adjoining terrace to a white frame church. When I looked through the half-open door I discovered that the building contained nothing but two basket-ball rings. The church was built in 1863 by the Presbyterians but in recent years it has been used as the gymnasium for the grade school. "Would you like to go into the school?" asked the lady who had told me about the church. "It's closed, of course, during vacation, but I know the teacher who has the key." Later that day I met the teacher and walked with her back to the schoolhouse. The interior looked like all other schoolhouses, but in the hall in a glass case was an exhibit that interested

BLACK HAWK STREETS   ↓ OLD HOTEL, BLACK HAWK (GONE)

me. It consisted of examples of student work in English, Arithmetic and Art, each dated 1904. As I looked at it curiously my teacher-friend explained: "This is the exhibit that was sent by J. H. Matthews, the principal of the school, to the St. Louis Exposition. Come into the eighth grade room and see the award it received." There on the wall hung a framed certificate which said:

United States of America.

Universal Exposition, Saint Louis MDCCCCIV

Commemorating the Acquisition

of the Louisiana Territory.

The International Jury of Awards

has Conferred a Bronze Medal

upon the Board of Education

Black Hawk, Colorado

Elementary Schools.

From the school we walked down the steep flight of wooden stairs to the level of the highway, and my escort showed me several old frame houses still adorned with bargeboards so delicately carved that they hung like lace frills from the eaves. Just before she left me, she asked the proprietor of one of the stores to show me a photograph taken after the big flood which washed away the street on which we were walking. It was after that cloudburst that the citizens raised $32,000 and built the rock flume under the sidewalk. I thanked the teacher for her help and trudged back to Central City, determined to return to Black Hawk for more sketches.

Central City continued

In 1932, Mrs. Ida Kruse McFarlane gave the Central City Opera House, which her father had owned, to Denver University, and they commenced to clean and restore it for a sensational theatrical revival of *Camille*, with Lillian Gish in the leading role, set for July of that year. Central City buzzed with activity. Old stores were opened and the dust and plaster of years swept out. Antique "Shoppes" appeared, and as the opening date drew near, small restaurants, a Tin Type Gallery and gambling rooms were installed for the two-weeks' season. I, too, got the fever and hired a store in which my sketches of the old towns were displayed. The store was musty and its floor sagged a bit, the plaster hung in precarious festoons from the water-stained ceiling, but the walls took thumbtacks and the windows could be used to display pictures of Central City and its environs, and people thronged in. Some were merely curious; some were really interested and a few were indignant that I should record only the old, dilapidated portion of the present town. One man stood in front of a drawing of a private house and shook his fist at it, saying to anyone who would listen, "That's the house I live in but there's not one thing about it that I recognize." Another gentleman brought his wife to the exhibition and showed her a sketch which I had made of their home. He was pleased with it and suggested buying it. "Humph," snapped his wife, "I wouldn't have it in the house. There's a paling out of that fence she drew and we've had the fence mended."

OLD POST OFFICE, CENTRAL CITY

CENTRAL CITY   ✦BLACK HAWK

Each day during the two weeks of the theatrical festival I followed a definite pattern, devoting the mornings to hiking and sketching. On these jaunts I followed old narrow gauge mine railroad beds to rusty ore houses and gaping mine shafts, or I pushed tall grass aside from the graves in Central City's five cemeteries and read the inscriptions on the stones. One fact troubled me—so many children had died in 1879. Upon investigation I discovered that all the mountain towns had been ravaged by an epidemic of diptheria in that year. One family stone revealed that a mother and two children died within a week.

By noon I was back at the store as people were beginning to drive into town and the shops were open for tourist trade. By matinee time the streets were seething with visitors until the bell of the head usher called them into the Opera House. An hour or two of quiet followed and then the crowds came again and continued until after the evening performance. About nine P. M. I locked the store and clutching my money bag, went hurriedly up Eureka Street past the Opera House, the City Hall, the County Courthouse and the darkened residences until, with a sigh of relief, I came to my rented room.

It was also in 1932 that my curiosity about the history of the city was aroused. That summer the Teller House had been cleaned and opened for business in a big way and in the lobby, as an item of interest, was an old hotel register of 1882 which, when I looked through it gave me ideas. In it were written the names of the theatrical troupes which played in the Opera House next door, and I realized that if all the old registers could be located and read a complete list of performances and performers would be available. Of course only a few of the books could be found, but fortunately across the street w s the newspaper office of the *Central City Register-Call*, upon whose editor I promptly called.

The newspaper office was housed in a three-story structure approached by steep and musty stairs. Mr. G. M. Laird, the veteran editor, after listening to my request for permission to peruse the old papers put his entire file from 1862 on at my disposal. In this I was peculiarly fortunate, for I later learned that few towns had a complete newspaper record, due to frequent fires which consumed both towns and papers. Cleaning off sufficient space on a large cluttered table, Mr. Laird pointed to the huge pile of bound copies of the paper and left me to dig in.

For the next few weeks I spent every available minute scanning the dusty, brittle sheets, squinting at the faded print and grinning at the often pompous phraseology, but I never dared really laugh at what I read, for there, not ten feet away, sat the man who had written the notices that I found so engaging and so valuable. Occasionally he would lean over my shoulder, look at my hastily scrawled notes and say, with a dry chuckle, "Bet you can't read 'em when you get home."

No day was long enough for my work, and I arrived as early as the office opened each morning, munched a sandwich at noon while I skimmed more columns of small print, and stayed as late as the editor and his sprightly seventy year old assistant remained. This assistant was Mr. Marble, the linotype setter, and when he saw how reluctant I was to leave at the end of each day he called me aside and told me that although the front door was not unlocked until nine each morning the back door, over the alley, was never locked and I could come as early and stay as late as I wished. Both Mr. Laird and Mr. Marble loved every inch of the office in which they had worked so long. They showed me the composing stones that had been brought across the plains by oxteam and used ever since, and they pulled open drawers where fonts of wooden type of all sizes lay in orderly compartments and showed me handbills and theatre posters printed from them.

The office was cluttered with all sorts of oddments, but the strangest item was an empty washbasket which was kept behind the door. Less than a week after my arrival I learned its use. By 1932 the *Register-Call* was a weekly paper serving all of Gilpin County and vicinity, and although most of each edition was distributed in the city, a number of issues were neatly wrapped ready to mail to Apex, Russell Gulch and Black Hawk. On Friday the paper was printed and the issue prepared for distribution. On Saturday morning all those which were to be mailed were piled in the washbasket, which the two men then carried several blocks to the postoffice. Returning with the empty basket between them, they deposited it behind the door ready for the next issue.

At first I read only the theatrical notes in the papers and the various recreational activities of the pioneer community, such as the Tissue Paper Social and the Milkmaid's Contest, but before long I was deep in Colorado history some of which was made in 1859 half a mile from where I sat. In that year eager prospectors crossed the plains from the east to Auraria, the predecessor of Denver, and finding but little gold there, pushed doggedly up the streams into the "Shining Mountains" to find the precious metal which must be somewhere. On May 6, 1859, John Gregory struck gold in the gulch which now bears his name, but for ten days he was prevented by a heavy storm from further testing his discovery. From May 16 to 23 he "worked five hands on the claim and with a sluice took out $972. Soon afterwards he sold the claim . . . for $21,000 and commenced prospecting for other parties at $200 per day." This proved so profitable that the following fall Gregory left for home with $30,000 in gold dust.

"By the first of June, 1859, Gregory Gulch was literally crowded with human beings." And by midsummer 1869 it was estimated that "not less than 15,000 people . . . were located within sight of the spot where now stands one of the most substantial and enterprising towns in the Territory."

At first the prospectors panned the gold or used sluices, rockers or Long Toms, but when the surface ore had been exhausted, the rocky hillsides remained and more drastic methods of extracting the gold became necessary. Much of the machinery brought to the mountains by oxteam across the plains was useless and soon discarded but some of it was utilized, and before long many stamp mills were built in which the precious rock was crushed. The thud of the falling stamps was so insistent that visitors to the camp were aware of the "noise of the stamps, which could be heard four miles outside of town."

Such a tremendous stampede to the district in 1859 caused the laying out of townsites and almost simultaneously four emerged—Mountain City, Black Hawk, Central City and Nevadaville! Mountain City was the first, growing up

Mountain City

(23)

around the Gregory Diggings and consisting of tents and log cabins along the stream whose gold-bearing sands were being so assiduously examined. Some prospectors scrambled up the steep hillsides and pitched their tents high above the stream while searching for the source of the gold and pitting the ground with prospect holes, many of which with development became paying mines.

One of the earliest bars was in existence in 1860 at Mountain City and was run by Jack Keeler. "The beverage stood on a shelf behind the bar in a coarse ugly black bottle and as glasses hadn't made their appearance . . . was taken from a battered tin cup." Credit began on the day of the opening. Some of the entries were:

Buckskin Bill dr. to 1 tin cup whiskey .25

Howling Jack dr. to 25 lbs. flour 5.00

Blatherskite Sam dr. to bacon, flour and coffee 10.00

Damphool dr. to sundries 20.00

Damphool came in to settle his account and wanted to see the ledger. Keeler didn't want him to see his name so the matter was finally adjusted by a discount and Damphool was mellowed by a cup of whiskey.

Mountain City boasted of a theatre, held in a two-story log building, and of the first religious services held in the mountains. Even during the first year of the camp such meetings were popular. The "gold hunter laid aside his pick and shovel on Saturday night and on Sunday morning put on his best 'boiled shirt' of woolen stuff, combed his hair . . . concealed his revolver and knives and went to hear the Bible read . . . and best of all the music that lifted him out of his pioneering condition."

As the gulches and hills overflowed with miners, Mountain City could not hold them all and Black Hawk, Central City and Nevadaville were laid out within a two mile radius. All four towns clung to steep hillsides and were built in terraces, street above street and mine above mine, (although Central City claimed to have been laid out on the only land level enough to permit the building of a city!)

Black Hawk and Central grew up side by side, and the two communities were largely interdependent. Most of the smelters and mills during the peak of the mining era were located in Black Hawk, to which the railroad was extended in 1872, thus facilitating the shipment of ore from the region. On the other hand most of the dramatic entertainment centered in Central as the long list of theatres—the People's, National, Montana, Belvidere and Opera House testified.

Central City cont'd.
In 1877, when *The Bohemian Girl* was given in the Belvidere Theatre, its inadequacy for such a performance was realized; consequently an opera house was talked about and built with amazing dispatch, opening on March 4, 1878. Both the musical and dramatic organizations of Central clamored for the honor of opening it with the result that two formal openings were held, the music group appearing first.

During the seventies and eighties the Opera House drew to its stage the finest talent the country afforded, Emma Abbott, Madame Janauschek and Joe

CENTRAL CITY OPERA HOUSE

OPERA HOUSE AUDITORIUM

TELLER HOUSE BAR

TELLER HOUSE PATIO, 1931

Jefferson giving spirited performances to appreciative audiences. In the nineties travelling companies made one night stands in Central, presenting minstrel shows and vaudeville acts. In one of these a female contortionist was the leading attraction. The following day the newspaper account was lavish in its praise of the lady's performance. Adjective after adjective described her suppleness and skill. Finally, in a burst of journalistic eulogy the editor wrote: "In fact, she was like a boned chicken."

Occasional boxing matches were featured in the theatre; but by the late nineties and early nineteen-hundreds the house was dark except for infrequent movies and school commencement programs.

Then in 1932 the heirs of Peter McFarlane gave the building to Denver University and its restoration began. During that summer I spent as much time as possible in Central, collecting data about the town for a booklet which I intended to write. Since the Teller House was across the street from the newspaper office I found it most convenient to stay there, sometimes occupying the small room where President Grant stayed and sometimes rattling around in one of the huge front bedrooms with its stiffly starched, dingy lace curtains and china wash bowl and pitcher.

One hot Sunday, as I was working in my room with my door open, I heard a group of tourists approaching and the manager's voice describing historic anecdotes and facts to the gullible visitors. The group stopped near my door and the leader said distinctly, gesturing as he spoke: "This is General Grant's room; this" (pointing to me), "is an artist from Boulder, and this is the Ladies Rest Room." Later that day, tired of showing visitors through the hotel, he placed a board across the foot of the main staircase on which he had scrawled, "NO ONE ALOUD UPSTAIRS."

The Teller House itself is interesting. Built in 1871 at a cost of $60,000, the four-story structure was opened on June 25, 1872, and was for several years "the largest and finest hotel in Colorado."

> Having announced the opening for Monday noon the twenty-fourth, Bush and Co. (the proprietors) sent out invitations to nearly a hundred citizens of Central and vicinity. Most of them came with their ladies. After dinner the party assembled in the spacious parlors where a few brief speeches were made, garnished with exquisite music by Prof. Barnum's orchestra.

On April 29, 1873, General Grant, President of the United States, and his party visited Central for a few hours. To quote again from the paper:

> The sidewalk, immediately fronting the entrance to the Teller House, was paved with silver bricks to the value of twelve or thirteen thousand dollars, sent over from the Caribou mine. . . . The president was quite incredulous when told the slabs were genuine silver but had finally to accept the truth. . . . They were shown to superb rooms on the parlor floor. The dust brushed away, Mayor Mullen with the city council appeared and were presented to General Grant to whom they extended the hospitality of the city. . . . After dinner a short reception took place in the parlor when the President and Mrs. Grant bade the callers a polite goodbye, entered their carriages and proceeded over the hills to Idaho (Springs). . . . Arrived at the Divide some one asked Jim Allen, one of the very best of Colorado's reinsmen, how far it was to the foot of the hill on the other side. 'About four miles', was the reply. 'How long does it take

to go down?' About seventeen minutes generally', says Jim. 'Well, we don't want to run any risks, you see, driver, and if it should take a little longer than seventeen minutes we shouldn't care.' 'H--l', says Jim, 'Don't you suppose I think as much of my neck as you do of yours?

When fire destroyed the city in 1874, the Teller House was one of six buildings which resisted the flames, with the aid of wet blankets which were hung at every window. The fire started in the house of a Chinaman where incense was being burned on live coals to exorcise an evil spirit. By some means these embers broke out and set fire to the frame structure; the flames spread and got beyond control and, since there was no system of waterworks, raged unimpéded, although aid was sought from the valley towns of Denver and Golden. The "train that brought the fire Company up from Golden made such speed that one man was shaken off and the train went one mile up the heavy grade before it could be stopped and backed down for the lost fireman." Everyone fought the fire, but by night the entire population was huddled on the mountain sides surveying the utter ruin of the city. Central City was immediately rebuilt with stone and brick and most of the buildings standing today date from that year.

On the opening night of *Camille*, July 1932, the Teller House came into its own once more. The bar, with its classic murals (discovered in the cleaning up process under ten layers of wall paper) was open for business and the lobby, with its exhibit of mineral specimens and its gold-scales, was full of people. The parlors upstairs were converted into gambling rooms where Faro, Chuck-a-Luck, Monte and Roulette attracted crowds of gaily dressed customers. Everyone was in costume, dressed in the styles of 1878, (the year that the Opera House opened)—the ladies laced into basques and bustles and the gentlemen suffocating in tight waistcoats and high collars.

Old-fashioned coaches and rigs kept delivering Denver socialites and celebrities of the press and theatre at the door of the hotel or in front of the Opera House, and as more and more guests assembled, Eureka Street became thronged with the gala crowd, slowly congregating around the theatre. The moment one stepped into the Opera House, one felt that he was living in 1878, for everyone was wearing clothes of that year, and when the curtain rose the effect was tremendous, for the actors' costumes and the setting of the play were of the same period. The house was crowded, its seats, which were stout hickory chairs, being set so closely together that all but those holding aisle seats were compelled to stand on their chairs to permit late comers to enter each row; and ladies and gentlemen were popping up and down throughout the evening as others squeezed past them during the intermissions. The orchestra was excellent; Robert Edmond Jones, the producer, had outdone himself in planning the decor for the performance and the production was such a feast of color, rhythm, and music that by the end of the first act my companion and I were aesthetically drunk.

It was full moon that night and between the acts everyone trooped down the steep street to the Teller House Bar or smoked a cigarette, leaning against the old Assay Office, or had his picture taken in the Tin Type parlor, or visited the Central City Art Emporium where paintings by Coloradans were displayed.

(27)

At the close of the performance, when Robert Edmond Jones took his curtain call, he confided to the audience that he had been given a slender volume written by a former native of Central City entitled "Echoes from Arcadia," which contained many nostalgic and historical passages about the city's heyday. He perused the book with great interest and he was pleased to say to his friends in Colorado that as the years passed, he would always remember that he had spent a few brief weeks in "Arcadia."

The rest of the night was a whirl of dancing and dining in the "grand ballroom" of the Teller House and in its red-walled dining room. Every summer thereafter until 1942, when the war curtailed all activities, the Central City Association planned a two or three weeks festival, assembling notable producers, actors and opera stars who performed in the historic Opera House. Under Robert Edmond Jones' artistic touch the *Merry Widow, Othello*, a revue—*Central City Nights—Ruy Blas* and *Orfeo and Eurydice* were given. Since the war more operas have been performed, including such little known gems as Mozart's *Abduction from the Seraglio* and Beethoven's *Fidelio*, for both of which Donald Oenslager planned notable settings. During this period the restaurants and pool rooms flourish, the antique shops and art emporiums attract their curious customers, and even those churches which have been closed all year hold special Sunday services. Most of this summer activity is carried on by outsiders, and the residents of the city pursue their daily routines relatively untouched and a little exasperated by all the fanfare and commercialism that exists during the theatre season.

Both Opera House and Teller House are closed now all year long except for the summer festival period, so on more recent jaunts to Central City I have stayed in private homes. In one house I was given my choice of two rooms, one upstairs and hot and the other downstairs and much cooler but hazardous, for directly over the bed a large swag of wallpaper and plaster hung poised for instant descent and each night, upon retiring, I looked at it with considerable interest and some apprehension. Another time I was told of a comfortable room for rent and found the landlady who was to show it to me working in a nearby store. She took me to the house, apologizing that we had to enter by the back door, explaining that the "front porch fell off last winter in a snow storm," which was indeed true as the ravaged facade of the residence revealed. The room which she showed me looked clean and comfortable and I told her I would take it for a week and asked her how much it would be. "Five dollars," she replied and then added, "or less if you like," and I've been trying to figure that one out ever since.

People were always friendly and helpful and from each one I learned something either of western hospitality or of historic importance. There was Grandma Stevens, who spoke to me one hot afternoon when I was sketching in Black Hawk. She pointed to her house on the topmost terrace of the town and invited me to go home with her and she'd give me a drink of cold well water. Together we climbed the steep wooden stairs from the road to the upper street, and while I got my breath she darted into the cool interior of her home and returned with the water. "Grandma" was full of stories, and while I sat rocking on her porch and enjoying the splendid view of Black Hawk

EXTERIOR OF CHURCH, 1931

INTERIOR NEVADAVILLE EPISCOPAL CHURCH

and its mines below me, she told me how she came to Black Hawk as a bride, when most of the population was Cornish—the Cousin Jacks and Cousin Jennies—as she called them; and as she talked she helped me to see vividly the wrestling matches, the rock-drilling contests and the great song fests in which the Cornish miners and their families excelled. She brought from the house treasures of earlier years; a patch work quilt that she had made; old photographs of the town, and a huge Willow Ware platter that she bought from another pioneer woman and carried across the hills in her arms, wrapped securely in a bed quilt. She spoke of the mines and of the bob-tailed ox for which the famous Bobtail mine was named and she sniffed scornfully about an old maid who used to live in town who was too proper to speak of the mine as anything but the "Robert Appendage."

Nevadaville   One day I started for Nevadaville, a mile above Central City. It was not like Central City but was a real ghost town, with scarcely any population left. The road to it climbed steadily from the site of the old Baseball Park to the Chain-O-Mines mill and settling pond, past the deserted stone brewery and the Masonic cemetery. On one side the gulch cut a gash through crumbling rock and sandy banks, and on the other side the hill rose steeply to the distant terraced streets of the town. Many of the houses were gone but their fenced yards and stone terraces marked their location. The roadbed was rough, the sun was hot and the 8000 foot altitude made me pant, but Nevadaville lay just around the corner and I plodded on. The main street was more imposing in the nineteen thirties than it is today when so many of its buildings have been razed. The town had two-story brick stores lining the right hand side of the street while on the left stood the diminutive City Hall with its bell, and the post office. Upon investigation, the City Hall, which was little larger than a garage, was found to house the Fire Department, and its basement contained a one-room jail. Next to it stood the Bald Mountain post office, its windows boarded up as were most windows in town. When the people of Nevadaville petitioned Washington for a post office the name Nevadaville was refused and Bald Mountain on which the town is located was substituted. Therefore, Bald Mountain it became, although the people persisted in calling it Nevadaville. Opposite it stands the Masonic Hall of the Rising Sun Tribe to which annual pilgrimages are still made.

At the far end of the main street, crowning the hill, stood the Episcopal church. Its weathered door was ajar, and although I was accustomed to old buildings, the wreckage inside appalled me. The floor was buckled and broken, velvet kneeling cushions were scattered about, hymn books with torn pages, mouldy and watersoaked were strewn at random, and everything was so musty and dank and utterly neglected that it was difficult to picture this church as it once must have been during its years of service in a live community.

A year later I returned to Nevadaville and found that the steeple of the church had blown down in a heavy wind storm and lay rotting into the ground. A few years passed and the entire church was gone, only a slight depression in the ground indicating its location.

The frame schoolhouse also disappeared, but luckily on my first visit

(30)

CENTRAL CITY RAILROAD STATION
(BURIED IN CHAIN-O-MINES TAILINGS POND)

NEVADAVILLE STORE

GRAVE AT MISSOURI FLATS

to the town I had sketched not only its exterior but its empty rooms where desks, books, maps, a clock, and a tattered flag were strewn about.

In its day Nevadaville had a brilliant existence. As early as 1863 it had its halls and its entertainments.

> Rev. Mr. King delivered the second of a course of lectures in Nevada Hall last evening. His subject was—'The Age and the Woman.' The hall was crowded with an intelligent audience and after the lectures a silver Hunting case watch and Thirty dollars were presented to him by the citizens.

Surprise parties were another popular from of amusement. One was "in compliment to Mr. Harry Armfield, very quietly gotten up by Misses Nellie and Rosa Tucker. The young man was sort of nonplussed over the affair but recovering his composure the surprisers were soon at home."

> The fair at Armory Hall closed Saturday evening with a large attendance. . . . The closing scenes in the contests for the diamond ring were very animating and when Miss Kate Reilly of Nevada was declared winner of the ring with 1876 votes the applause of the Nevada contingent . . . was deafening. Mr. James Cody won the fancy crazy quilt and immediately, with his usual gallantry, turned it over to Miss Maggie McGinnis according to contract.

Lack of sufficient water limited the town's development during the sixties. It is even whispered that a rival company diverted its proposed water supply to nearby Central City. At any rate Nevadaville died a slow death and today only its skeleton remains.

Missouri Flats and Lake Gulch

By 1935, having heard of other mining camps close to Central City, I persuaded Boyd, who knew that territory well, to drive me to them. Just as we reached the top of the long hill that leads out of Central City and took a last glance at its terraced streets, Boyd turned the car into a side road saying, "I'm going to show you two relics of the past—a grave and a schoolhouse. Straight ahead is the site of Missouri Flats but all you'll see of it today is a little marble tombstone which marks a child's grave. When all these hilltops and gulches were infested with prospectors in the early sixties, there was a town here which was a close rival of Central City, Black Hawk, Mountain City and Russell Gulch. In fact it was expected to outlast the others, and there was talk of moving the Central City express office and post office here, as many believed it was the only town in the county that would amount to anything."

He stopped the car beside the tiny plot with its iron fence and marble stone on which was cut the inscription:

CLARA A.

DAU. OF F. S. & D. F. DULANEY

DIED JULY 5, 1865

AGED 1 YR. 12 DS.

And a bunch of fresh wildflowers lay on the tiny mound! We searched the meadow for other markers or signs of Missouri Flats' existence but could find nothing. Here on top of this windswept hill, within sight of the highway, this tiny grave served as the sole monument not only to the child buried beneath it but to the camp that did not survive.

The Lake Gulch road was steep and not much travelled, but partway down it stood the brick schoolhouse to which the miners' children had tramped each day when Lake Gulch was a camp much like Missouri Flats. It had been remodeled into a private home; and not wishing to intrude upon the present owners, we merely took a look at it and drove away.

"The road between Central City and Russell Gulch is made of gold," announced Boyd as we turned onto the highway again. "Many of the old mine dumps have been shovelled into highway trucks and hauled here to surface this four-mile stretch. There is always some ore left in the dumps, so it's true that we are riding on gold." Before I could comment, he pointed to a hill to the right and said, "There's where Bortonsburg was. If we had time we could climb up there and find some of the old foundations. It wasn't a big place and it didn't last any longer than the other little camps, but you'll find it shown on early maps of Gilpin County." By this time we were nearing Russell Gulch, which lay in a hollow below us. The town lies scattered over many acres, and beyond it are the mine dumps and the shaft houses. The old road ran through the main street, but the new highway is built higher on the hill, skirting the two-story brick schoolhouse and the frame church with its colored glass windows.

William Green Russell, for whom the town is named, came to the mountains in 1859 at the same time as John Gregory, and while the latter explored the area where Central City and Black Hawk now are, Russell and his followers pushed farther south until they turned up color in a gulch about four miles away. This was not the first gold that Russell found, for he and a group of prospectors had mined first in Georgia and then in California, and in 1858 had even found a little gold in the streambed of Dry Creek near the present site of Denver. Feeling sure that the source of the gold was high in the hills he started for the mountains and in June, 1859, locating an abundance of free gold in this gulch, set to work.

As soon as news of the gold field became known there was a stampede to the diggings, and all through the summer men sloshed up and down the stream, taking out quantities of flakes and nuggets. By the end of September over eight hundred were at work in the Gulch and were producing an average weekly amount of $35,000. That fall, before cold weather drove them back to the valley, a meeting was held at which mining laws were drawn up for the newly created Russell District. This district adjoined the Gregory District on the southwest and embraced Lake, Willis, Elkhorn, Illinois, Leavenworth, Saw Pit, Graham and Davenport Gulches and Missouri Flats. The laws were concise and covered all anticipated situations including the following:

Sec. 67 Discovery Claims.
    Females have the same right as males. Youths under the age of ten shall not be allowed to hold claims.

Sec. 73. Witnesses are entitled to receive one and a half dollars at the time they are summoned if they demand it; and the same sum for each day's attendance (at the trial), after the first.

An indignation meeting was held in Nov., 1859, to contest the right of Denver merchants to fix the value of gold dust at $15-17 an ounce instead of $16-18. The miners declared that they would support mountain dealers rather than those of Denver as long as the former would take gold in payment at the original value. In their anger they pledged themselves to provide teams and men to the freighters so that the supplies could be brought direct from the "states" if necessary and thus boycott the Denver scalpers, and to make their position clear they requested that this ultimatum be published in the newly created *Rocky Mountain News.*

By 1860 the gulch had a population of 2500, and the town of Russell Gulch was built with sturdy log cabins and frame dwellings and the usual number of stores, saloons, and boardinghouses. Festivities centered in Federal Hall, where as early as 1862 Cotillion Parties were the thing, with McDuffie's band providing the music. But no entertainment surpassed that given on the Fourth of July, 1859, less than a month after the camp was established, when the entire population quit digging to celebrate. Wearing their best clothes, the miners began the day by firing a salute from their revolvers. This was followed by one extra shot for Pike's Peak, another for Green Russell and a third for John Gregory. After this outburst, they listened to an oration delivered by one of their number and they watched the hoisting of a homemade flag that did credit to their ingenuity. When plans for the day were being discussed it was found that there was no flag nearer than Fort Laramie, two hundred miles to the north, whereupon the patriotic miners contributed blue overalls, a "biled" shirt and red flannel drawers, and from these a flag was made. A banquet followed the oration and was served in style with printed menus which included: "Bean Soup; Brook trout, a la catch them first; Antelope, larded pioneer style; Biscuit, handmade, full weight, a la yellow; Beans, mountain style warranted boiled forty-eight hours a la soda; Dried apples; Coffee in tin cups, to be washed clean for the occasion." The program of the day continued with a yarn-spinning session, at the close of which the men marched over to Gregory to see what the "boys" there were doing.

At the end of two or three years of intensive digging, the rich, gold-bearing soil of the gulch was so nearly exhausted that placer mining was abandoned and was supplanted by lode mining. Some mining has been carried on at Russell ever since, although the town's population was gradually decreased from 400 in 1881 to a mere handful today. Flurries of excitement have resulted from occasional sensational strikes such as the finding of uranium deposits in 1920, but most of the time the town is pretty quiet. During prohibition Russell had a new boom—the selling of bootleg whiskey; and its mines were used as hideouts for the hunted criminals of Denver's underworld. Old mine tunnels were used for this purpose, and more than once strange men appeared at the local store, put money on the counter and, demanding supplies and food, slipped away unquestioned.

Apex   "What other places are there near Central City?" I asked as we drove to the brink of Virginia Canyon and looked across the valley to the immense expanse of Mt. Evans, miles away.

"Up above Central is Apex, and near Rollinsville are Perigo and Balti-

(34)

MAIN STREET,
APEX

STAGE OF
BALTIMORE
OPERA HOUSE

more, and there used to be a little place named Gilpin, and near Black Hawk was a still smaller camp called Hughesville."

"Can we get to them today?" I asked eagerly.

"Of course," replied Boyd. "They're not far away," and turning the Ford, we retraced our steps to Central, and climbed the long hill up Eureka Street past the Teller House and the County Courthouse, past the tidy frame houses with their terraced front yards and picket fences, and past the water-works, to the cemeteries. There the road forked, and taking the right hand branch we started to Apex. We rolled across the tops of the hills all the way, climbing steadily through aspen groves and across open stretches until we drove up the main street, between false-fronted stores and a few log and frame houses. Bits of wooden sidewalks led from one store to the next; the Palace Saloon was open for business, and the Miners' Hall, although closed, was fully furnished. Looking through the screened, dusty window I could see rows of chairs and a stove against one wall. A short flight of steps led from the auditorium to the stage which was built across one end of the building and on which, framed by scenic wings, depicting panelled walls and leafy groves, was a square piano covered with an old piece of drapery. Peering through my cupped hands, I memorized what I saw and then rapidly sketched it. While I worked, a young girl looking over my shoulder told me that the stage curtain was painted in 1899 by a man named Coltrin.

"Haven't I seen you in Central?" she queried. "I was a waitress over there and I'm sure I've seen you on the street making pictures."

"If you live here perhaps you can tell me something about Apex," I suggested. "I don't know much about it," she replied, "and most of the people here now didn't live here in 1896 when it was the center of the Pine Creek Mining District. It had several hotels and restaurants then as well as general stores and a school. There were a lot of mines around here, but the Mackey was the biggest. It was discovered in the seventies by Dick Mackey but it changed hands many times until a man named Mountz got a lease to work it. That's all I know."

"I know the rest of that story," Boyd interrupted. "As soon as Mountz obtained a lease on the mine, he and another man formed a company of which the latter was to be the treasurer. They found good pay ore, and when they had taken out over $30,000 the treasurer absconded with the money leaving Mountz with only $400. He attempted to continue work on the mine alone, driving a cross-cut tunnel which he hoped would cut the main vein within a distance of ninety feet. Using his meagre funds carefully, he proceeded to tunnel until ninety feet had been dug. There was still no sign of the vein, and he hacked away for another twenty feet with no success. By the time his last dollar was sunk in the mine he was so discouraged that as a vent for his feelings he put all his remaining dynamite into the end of the tunnel, came out of the mine, lighted the fuse and walked away. Next day he rose later than usual and rather indifferently wandered back to see the result of the explosion. The entire breast of the tunnel was filled with rock, which upon examination proved to be high grade ore. The blast had penetrated the vein.

"Rushing back to his cabin he telephoned to Denver for one thousand ore sacks saying excitedly to the astonished dealer, 'I haven't a dollar but I've struck it rich. Send the sacks up on the first train.' A second telephone call was to a Central City livery stable ordering two four-horse teams and ore wagons to be sent up to the mine. When the ore was sacked it was hauled to the Black Hawk Sampling Works where it assayed $1800 to the ton; but the sampler, fearing some mistake in his calculations, ran the sample again and obtained the same result. The mine continued to produce in such quantities that a mill was built to handle the ore and it has continued to be a good producer."

As we left Apex we looked back down the long street at the end of which, in the blue distance rose Mt. Evans, looming high and white above all the surrounding peaks. "Where do we go next?" I inquired.

"We climb a little higher and take the turn-off to American City, where there was once a little mining," answered Boyd.

"I've been there already," I replied, "and except for a cabin called the St. Elmo Hotel, a log block-house and a shattered mill there's little to see."

"All right," said Boyd, "We'll keep on and drop down the other side of the hill to Tolland. Then taking the road that leads to Rollinsville I'll show you a place you don't know."

A mile or two east of Tolland we turned off the highway and drove *Baltimore* through the trees over a slight hill to a deserted camp. Looking around I recognized some familiar buildings and glancing at Boyd I said with a grin, "Why I've been here too but never in summer. Last year I heard of a place called Baltimore where there was an Opera House with scenery, and a bar with bottles still standing on it. With a skeptical acquaintance who didn't believe there was such a place, I followed directions and landed here. We couldn't drive in as we did today because of snowdrifts, but we left the car on the highway and ploughed through the snow to this little, protected meadow.

"Just as we left the car and were starting to explore the place an old man came out of a cabin and walked over to us. He was the caretaker and he showed us about with pride. 'Yep,' he said, 'we had our Opera House— on a small scale of course, but you should have seen the shows—they were great.' Pushing open the creaking door, he ushered us into the two-storied frame building with the bell on top. At the end of the big room was a shallow stage on which was a motley collection of furniture and stage props, but the most amazing feature was the painted canvas back-drop of a castle, which was nailed to the back wall. We followed the old man up a steep flight of stairs leading from the auditorium to the loft above. This space, obviously remodeled since its operatic days, was divided into several small cubicles, the partitions of which were made from old scenery cut up and nailed together to form walls and cupboards.

"Next our guide led us across the meadow to a small cabin which he called the Baltimore Club. This was the saloon of the camp, and brushing away the drifted snow from the porch he unlocked the door and waved us in. Here was the famous bar I'd heard of, made of mahogany and backed with a mirror which now reflected the heaped up debris with which the room was

(37)

piled. There were bottles on the bar but they were empty, and after I picked my way between old chairs and a billiard table and made a sketch of the interior, we thanked the caretaker and left. That's all I know about Baltimore," I concluded.

On this summer afternoon in 1935 as Boyd and I left the little hidden camp we talked of Rollinsville which lay ahead and of Perigo, Gold Dirt and Gilpin—camps which had lain quiet for some time, and I saw no more of Baltimore for eight years. In 1943 I revisited it only to find it transformed into a summer resort. The Opera House no longer flaunted its bell or its name, and crisp white curtains hung at its windows, and all the cabins were occupied by tourists. Even its bar had been moved over to Central City.

Rollinsville and Perigo

Rollinsville, which today is a shipping point on the railroad, and whose main street is by-passed by the new Peak to Peak highway, was one of the early camps of the region. It was founded by John Q. Rollins and was unique among mining camps in that saloons, gambling houses and dancehalls were prohibited within its limits. To handle ore from the nearby mines Rollins built a six-stamp quartz mill in 1861 and soon had to enlarge it to sixteen stamps. He also constructed the first wagon road over the Continental Divide into Middle Park, and so sure was he of the permanence of his camp that he boasted that it would be located on any road that should ever enter Middle Park. His prophecy came true with the building of the Moffat Road from Denver, through Rollinsville and over the pass at Corona to the Western Slope.

Close to Rollinsville is Gambell Gulch, a scene of mining in 1859. It was winter when A. D. Gambell wandered into the region, and in spite of snow and frozen ground thawed enough dirt over a fire to pan out eight dollars worth of dust. Later in the season he built a sluice and washed out ninety dollars worth in coarse flakes, and with these he went to Denver to get supplies, paying for them with the gold he had panned. Starting back to the hills that night, he slept near the site of Golden, and next morning found to his surprise that he had been followed by a group of determined men, who gave him the choice of leading them to his strike or of being hanged then and there. He sensibly agreed to humor them. This was the beginning of the Independent District, which comprised this area and included the camps of Perigo and Gold Dirt, both of which were located on Gambell Gulch.

Gold Dirt

"The Perigo mine was a great mine," Boyd commented. "I've heard my father tell about it. It was producing in the eighties and has since been worked profitably. Last year I drove up there and found a new mill working a force of men. The old post office is still standing, but most of the other cabins have disappeared or have been taken away. Gold Dirt was one mile from Perigo, and I've read that over two millions was taken from it in its boom days. The only other camps near here are Gilpin, nearly all summer cabins now with very little mining going on, and Hughesville which is just a memory. I've found a place called Nugget, west of American City, on an old map but I've never been able to locate it exactly. We've done about all we can today, so let's go home," said Boyd, and turning toward Boulder we left the little Kingdom of Gilpin and its adjacent camps.

A botanist friend of mine asked if I had ever been to Yankee Hill, four miles above Central City. He described the large ore mill and trestle to the mine, which were still standing, and when I questioned him about the road there he assured me that it could be driven to within a mile of the mill, and that from there on it was "just a little stroll up a pleasant valley filled with wildflowers." So, with an adventurous companion I started off.

Reaching Central City, we got a good running start up Eureka Street's steep hill past the Hendrie and Bolthoff Foundry, the first in the state, up beyond the waterworks and the picnic grove below the stone brewery, and up to the flat meadow where the cemeteries lie and where the road branches in three directions—to Apex on the right, to Bald Mountain and Nevadaville on the left via a road no car should be coaxed over, and to Yankee Hill ahead. The first three miles were about what I expected—rough, steep, rocky and narrow but navigable, although at one point a mountain stream made a bog of the road and we had to build a detour across a marshy meadow, where we left the car and started our "little stroll."

In the distance stood the mill, and guiding by it we started up what had been described as a "pleasant valley." Perhaps because we were not botanists, used to scrambling over terrain in search of plants, it proved a stiff climb up an abandoned road, which by now was rutted and washed and full of loose gravel and boulders. Furthermore the "valley" was a hill, up which the road, now merely a trail, wound. Finally we reached the mill and looked about. Where were the cabins, the grass-grown streets and the false-fronted stores that I thought were part of every mining camp? Perhaps we hadn't reached our destination and should hike the additional quarter-mile to the top of the hill. Neither of us was especially enthusiastic about going further, but I had a feeling that if nothing more than this was left of Yankee Hill I wouldn't be returning to it again and I'd better do a thorough "prospecting" job on this trip. So, urging my companion on, I took a deep breath and started the climb. On top we found a government marker verifying our location and many prospect holes dotting the top and sides of the hill. The view to the east was superb, for we were so high that we looked out to the front range of the Rockies, silhouetted against the line of the Great Plains, which stretched in an unbroken horizon in the distance.

But even here there were no streets and only an occasional battered log cabin beside an abandoned mine shaft. I was frankly disappointed; but I'd come to sketch the place, so, before we started back to the car, I rather half-heartedly drew the mill with its curving trestle and ore cars and the pine-clad hill with its scattered cabins. Our descent was as tricky as our ascent, for gopher holes lay in wait for our toes and hummocks of grass made slow going. Yet from Yankee Hill I learned a lot about the ghost mining-camps of Colorado. Every camp was the result of a spectacular "strike" made by some prospector, and his good fortune brought others stampeding to the same location. At first a city of tents appeared followed by log cabins. Many of the mining camps never developed beyond this stage, and Yankee Hill was one of them. On my trips around the state I soon became able to "spot" how old

(39)

a town was and for how long it had boomed by the type of its buildings and by the materials from which they were constructed.

By 1933 I had sufficient notes from the old newspapers and enough of my sketches of Central to enable me to publish the book on which I had been working. I called it *Ghost Cities of Colorado. A Pictorial Record of Central City, Black Hawk and Nevadaville.* The book was received with reservations, especially by some of the people of Central, who were distressed that I had illustrated it with only the old and dilapidated buildings and had made walls lean crazily where to their accustomed eyes they still appeared straight. The title, too, was unfortunate, for as Mr. Laird, the Central City editor wrote:

> . . . we hardly approve of the title of the book . . . in which Central City and Black Hawk are mentioned among the number. They are far from being "Ghost Cities" as the young lady author well knows through her many visits here.

Because of this I hastily revised my plan to do a whole series of books using the ghost town title. Years later, when the entire edition of fifteen hundred copies was sold out, a Central City woman asked me if I were ever going to "do" Central again and added, "If you do, make us look nice," completely unaware that my whole thesis was to preserve the past rather than record the present.

The more I learned about Central City and its environs the more I wanted to remain in it for further study of its history; but by 1933 I had heard of other towns in the state which I longed to visit. So reluctantly I left Central City to push farther into Colorado and record other mining camps whose history was equally colorful.

CHAPTER THREE

Leadville

The Cloud City of the Rockies

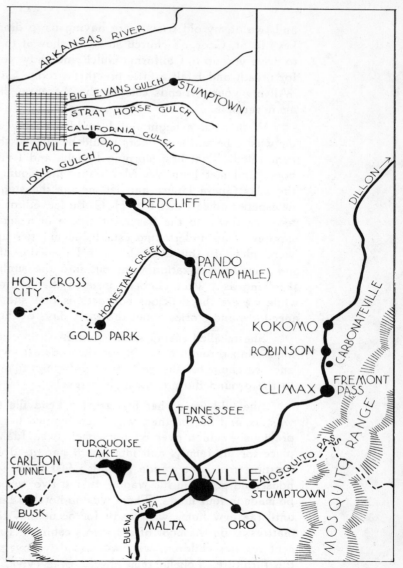

"CENTRAL CITY is all right, but wait till you see Leadville; there's a mining town for you," said my friends, and so on my next vacation, instead of returning to Central I set out across the mountains for Leadville. All that I knew about the city was that it was located in the Arkansas Valley near the foot of Colorado's two highest fourteen-thousand foot peaks, Mt. Elbert and Mt. Massive; that it had a smelter and that it was "the highest incorporated city in the world," having an altitude of 10,200 feet.

I knew no one there, but through another friend I was given a written introduction to a Leadville pioneer, Mrs. H. H. Norton, who had lived in Leadville since she was a small child. Learning of my plan to sketch the city she invited me to be her guest and set a date for my arrival.

The Denver and Rio Grande train reaches Leadville at 5 A.M. but it was two hours late the morning that I stepped down from the platform into the arms of a taxi driver who had been sent by Mrs. Norton to greet me. My first reaction to the place was that it was bigger and livelier than I had expected, but all general impressions were cut short when we stopped in front of an attractive, white house and a gray-haired lady in a red smock threw open the door and figuratively gave me the keys of the city.

"Come in, my dear," she said, leading me into a sunny dining room where breakfast was waiting us, "I have so many things to talk to you about, and I've arranged with the newspaper editor for you to use the files of the paper, and two of my old friends are having us to dinner this week, and I have the keys to St. George's church so I can show it to you, and a Judge has offered to drive you up to California Gulch and show you the old mines." She paused for breath and I felt a little breathless too. "Call me Lobelia," she continued. "All my young friends call me that because, like the flower of that name, I am never blue."

With such a beginning I could see how delightful the research before me was to be and how doors would be opened that otherwise I could not have penetrated. That first morning Lobelia and I visited the Lake County Courthouse and met John W. McMahon, the County Clerk, who agreed to open the Elks Opera House and let me see the stage and the clubrooms. At the newspaper office I met Mr. H. C. Butler, editor of the *Herald-Democrat*, who took me down to the basement where in a small, stone room (formerly the morgue of an undertaking establishment) tier upon tier of bound newspapers were piled. In this dimly lit room I read day after day, until my eyes ached, and then for relaxation went out into the sunlight and tramped the streets, sketching as I went. Lobelia insisted that I come "home" for all meals, and while we ate the delicious concoctions that she "threw together" she told me anecdotes and stories about the early days of the mining city.

She recalled seeing small children sitting in the gutters early each morning sifting through their fingers the sawdust sweepings from the saloon floors and searching for the gold dust and coins that might have slipped unnoticed to the ground during the night's revels.

She told me of her first trip to Leadville to join her parents, when she was six and her brother, who accompanied her, was sixteen. Her father had previously ridden over on horseback from Idaho Springs in 1878 to make a place for his family, and later, both parents drove over the range to the new location in a light wagon behind a fast team, while a freighter brought their household goods in his wagon, taking two weeks to the trip which today can be made in four hours. There was no hotel in Leadville when they arrived, and until the new home was ready for occupancy they were glad to spread their mattresses on the floor of a friend's cabin. As soon as practicable the mother sent for her children, who were to drive over in a wagon with the rest of the furniture. Lobelia remembered every vivid detail of the journey, for the trip was made in March when the roads were muddy, and late one night the loaded wagon stuck to the hubs. The pole, used as a fulcrum, not being heavy enough to lift the wheel free, her brother made her add her weight by sitting on it. Every time the wagon moved she fell off into the mud. While crossing South Park they were caught in a blizzard, and her brother gave the horses their heads, knowing they would keep to the road even though the drifting snow made it invisible to human eyes. About dark, when they were nearly frozen with cold and the snow was still swirling about them, the horses floundered through a ranchhouse gate, and the next thing she remembers is a woman giving her an apple and saying in amazement, "Why, it's a little girl." Next day the storm ceased, and before they had gone very far some freighters caught up with them. The rest of the trip was not so hazardous, for their wagon and those of the freighters kept together, climbing

(42)

A. Y. AND
MINNIE
MINE,
LEADVILLE

OLD
CABIN,
ORO

slowly to the top of Mosquito Pass, 13,188 feet above sea level, and then setting the brakes hard for the steep descent on the far side. When they were still several miles from Leadville they heard a wagon approaching at a fast pace and at first they feared "foot pads," but as it drew nearer and they recognized their father, who had come anxiously looking for them, all the suspense and weariness of the trip disappeared, and they drove on to their new home in the booming mining camp. Going to the window she pointed out a faint line, zig-zagging up one of the knife-like peaks in the distance, and identified it as Mosquito Pass, now no more than a rocky trail.

The man who panned the first gold in California Gulch was Abe Lee. "When the history of Lake County and California Gulch is finally written there should be no mistake as to who actually made the first gold discovery," says a clipping from the scrapbook of the Society of Leadville Pioneers. "The first party was under his leadership, and although they worked up the gulch they found very little and blinded by snow, were about ready to quit when Lee said We'll try another pan,' and that was it." Ever since that day in 1860 when he yelled, "Boys, I've got all California here in this pan" the fabulous mineral wealth of "California Gulch" and its surrounding hills has been constantly ripped from the now barren slopes of the region. Even before his discovery there had been rumors of gold in the Arkansas River and a few hardy prospectors began to thread their way across the mountains, examining the dirt for color: Among the first of these were Stevens and W. P. Jones and their respective parties. Later Jones wrote his "Reminiscences" which describe the grilling trip over the range.

> . . . In March we made a party of four, E. Johnson, Old Man Boon, Sailor Jones and myself. One had a little money, one had provisions, one had a pack mule and one was a great hunter and trapper and it was his business to keep us in fresh meat. With a pair of ponies and a light wagon and provisions for a couple of months we started out.
>
> As we were crossing South Park our little old wagon broke down so we made a cart of it and pushed it ahead. . . . Then we were caught in a blizzard which delayed us a week . . ." so that the "Stevens party had gotten ahead and gone up California Gulch. . . . We had agreed if any party found good pay dirt they were to build a big bonfire and discharge four shots.
>
> One evening I was up on the hills gathering wood when I heard four shots ring out clear and loud. There was no one around to hear. I just lifted my hat and gave three cheers, for our own party was not so fortunate. . . . I climbed with the others to the top of the hill and saw the campfire. We followed that light all night long, tramping through the snow. . . . It was the first pay dirt in the gulch. Ours was the first party to join theirs—in a few days there were others." (From the "Reminiscences of W. P. Jones" in the Historical Archives of the Society of Leadville Pioneers.)

Eager prospectors, hearing the good news, were not concerned as to who located the first color but lost no time in arriving at the gulch and establishing their claims, working feverishly and panning from $10 to $100 a day.

From the first there was a scarcity of water; so it had to be used over and over again in its descent down the gulch; therefore those whose claims were down at the mouth of the gulch literally worked in liquid mud. The miners also complained of the heavy black sand that clogged the riffles of their sluice-boxes, making it almost impossible to separate the gold from the gravel.

By the summer of 1860, 5,000 miners had arrived, and to accommodate their needs the town of Oro sprang up—a long single street along the stream, lined with frame houses, saloons, tents and wagons. It was here that H. A. W. Tabor had a store long before he became a notable figure in the state, and that Mrs. Tabor ministered to the needs of the miners by cooking for them and nursing them when they were ill. The spring of 1861 found 10,000 miners in Oro, yet by the end of the year the gulch was worked out and the place almost deserted. When the last of the population left, the log gambling hall was torn down, and $2,000 worth of gold was panned out of the dirt floor where the gamblers had dropped their "dust." Then the gulch lay quiet until the late seventies when another boom, madder than the first, began.

Oro

In 1874 W. H. Stevens of Detroit, in company with A. B. Wood, came to the diggings and began the construction of a twelve-mile ditch for the California Gulch placer claim which they had purchased. Having a knowledge of mining they soon suspected that the heavy black sand was rich in carbonate of lead carrying silver, but they kept their secret to themselves until they were sure of it and had obtained eight other claims which looked promising. No one paid much attention to them, for gold, not lead, was in everyone's mind; but when Wood sold his interests for $40,000 to Levi Leiter of Chicago, mining began to pick up and a silver rush began.

The first discovery of importance was made in 1878 by George Fryer and his partner on what is now known as Fryer Hill. The next bonanza was the Little Pittsburgh, from which Tabor made his fortune. Before long, so many rich mines had been developed that a smelter was needed which was soon unable to handle all the ore that was brought in. As more paying mines were discovered, other smelters and reduction works were constructed to serve the "Carbonate Camp" which was daily expanding at a tremendous rate.

Leadville cont'd.

The first arrivals found plenty of company but few accommodations. A huge tent was hastily constructed in the fall of 1878 to accommodate political meetings and later provided with three tiers of bunks with calico curtains, in which 1000 men could sleep—and thus yield the owner a thousand dollars a night. "The lower beds were reserved for Governors of States and Mayors of cities but no one of less political standing was considered."

Aside from its vast wealth, which at first was only guessed at, it was the incredible speed with which Leadville became a city that surprised the world. At first any sort of shelter was sufficient for the prospector—tents, lean-to's and dug-outs in the mountainside; but within a year streets lined with frame buildings appeared, and by February 1879, the "Town Board petitioned the Governor to issue a proclamation declaring Leadville a city of the first class." While the petition was pending and before the town was laid out, several log cabins were erected, which were later found to have been built right in the middle of the main thoroughfare. By May the population was 1500, but by the end of the year it was 18,000, and people were forced to walk down the middle of the street for speed and safety. The choice of a name for the city was decided by a committee, which weighed the merits of Boughtown, Carbonate, Cerrusite, Harrison, Cloud City, Meyer and Leadville. When the latter was selected it was sent to the proper authorities, along with the request for H. A. W. Tabor's appointment as Postmaster.

During the year 1879 Leadville made rapid strides in the number and character of its buildings. In January Harrison Avenue, which was to be the main artery, was a "waste of sagebrush," yet before the end of the year it had "four blocks of business houses, the Clarendon Hotel and the Opera House." *The Tourist Guide to Colorado and Leadville* written by Cass Carpenter describes the growth of the city by stating that

at this writing, May 1, 1879, Leadville has . . . 19 hotels, 41 lodging houses, 82 drinking saloons, 38 restaurants, 13 wholesale liquor houses, 10 lumber yards, 7 smelting and reduction works, 2 sampling works for testing ores, 12 blacksmith shops, 6 livery stables, 6 jewelry stores, 3 undertakers and 21 gambling houses where all sorts of games are played as openly as the Sunday School sermon is conducted." And it adds that "the social condition of the city improves every day . . . many ladies of culture and refinement having come in recently to make their home here.

Rents were high, water was still scarce and sold for fifty cents a barrel, and hay, equally scarce, brought from $60 to $120 a ton. Lumber was also scarce and building materials high, so that, although at least twenty-five sawmills were located on the road to the camp, individuals whose orders were being filled had to go several miles down the road to meet their own loads of lumber and ride in on the wagons, armed with guns, to prevent the planks from being appropriated by unscrupulous men who were also awaiting shipments.

One young man upon reaching the camp, early in '79, found lodging at the Grand Hotel, but at dinner when a man at the next table was shot, he thought it safer to withdraw to his room and go to bed. He immediately became aware, however, that the man in the next room, whom he could see through the cracks in the partition, was suffering from a bad case of delirium tremens. The fact that the two dollars in his purse was the last of his money was all that kept this new arrival to the carbonate city from immediately returning east.

Nearly everyone wore a revolver and at night, if a man was compelled to walk along unlighted streets, the weapon was carried cocked in his hand ready for instant use, for "crimes of all sorts were so common that they ceased to be a matter of comment." The newspaper reported such a quantity of murders that "a man for breakfast" was expected in each day's news, and the heading "Breakfast Bullets" appeared in nearly every issue.

After Lobelia had introduced me to Leadville I started to explore the city systematically. Along Harrison Avenue were several buildings of interest, the Courthouse, the Vendome Hotel, the Opera House and Pap Wyman's saloon. I visited the Courthouse first. The two-story brick building with its cupola, supporting Blind Justice with her scales, stood opposite East Fifth Street, up which were located so many of the mines. The graceful, curving staircase which led to the second story was divided near the top. Where it divided was a large sign which read, "SPITTING ON THE FLOOR WILL

(46)

BE REGARDED CONTEMPT OF COURT," and directly below the sign, on the wedge-shaped step that broke the main flight into two parts, was a shiny brass cuspidor.

I found Mr. McMahon, the County Clerk, in his office ready to show me the sights. Opening a closet he displayed with undisguised pride his collection of trophies—several guns, a bullet-pierced coat and finally his most prized possession, the contracted noose with which one of Leadville's 'bad men' had been hanged. He handled it lovingly and described the incident with relish and graphic detail. Feeling a little ill (no doubt the altitude was affecting me), I murmured something about seeing the courtroom and he obligingly unlocked it and stood by while I made a sketch. The judge's desk was on a dais, flanked by two large light globes, and backed by an American flag. The room was heated by a large pot-bellied stove whose stovepipe was cockily tipped to one side. Next day I returned to the courthouse to make further sketches and Mr. McMahon was waiting for me. "You know," he began, "I didn't like that drawing you made yesterday. You made that stovepipe crooked and I didn't like that. So this morning I went in there and I looked at the thing and be-danged if it isn't crooked."

Pap Wyman's saloon and gambling house on the corner of Harrison Avenue and State Street was my next objective, for it had been a famous gathering place in its day and had many unique features. On the face of a huge clock, painted in black letters were the words "Don't swear," and below the clock chained to the desk was an open Bible. By the time I reached Leadville "Pap" was gone and the building itself was rather dilapidated and sway-backed, but there were lace curtains and geraniums at the windows of the "Montview House," as it was now called, and its huge flagpole swayed drunkenly out over the street.

On the other side of Harrison Avenue was State Street, the colorful and infamous Red Light district. Back of it, in early days, were Tiger Alley, Still Born Alley and Coon Row, all of which had a "fearful reputation for thievery and robbery." Many a victim was a drunken miner who was unfortunate enough to stumble into this unsavory and lonely neighborhood, where he was given whiskey mixed with snuff and then, while deathly sick from it, was robbed.

Nearly a hundred licensed saloons and a dozen gambling houses were in full blast night and day—"the largest in the state, situated on Chestnut Street averaging profits of $32,000 a month." The Leadville *Herald-Democrat* of January 1, 1891, paints a picture of New Year's Day in 1879:

> At no hour of the day could pedestrians make haste in going up or down the street upon the narrow walks . . . because of the mass of humanity pressing to and fro.
>
> . . . On all sides was a conglomerate mass of diversified humanity—men of education and culture, graduates of Harvard and Yale and Princeton, mingling with ignorant and uncouth Bull-whackers; men of great wealth mixing with adventurers of every degree without a sou in their pockets with which to pay for their night's lodging at the big corral down the street; men of refinement jostling against cheap variety actors and scarcely less masculine actresses, dancehall herders and others with callings less genteel; representatives of the better element in all the callings of life—hopelessly

STATE STREET
RED LIGHTS,
LEADVILLE

MONTVIEW HOUSE
LEADVILLE (RAZED)

entangled in throngs of gamblers, burro-steerers, thugs, bullies, drunkards, escaped convicts, dead beats and the 'scum of the earth' generally.

The buzz of conversation . . . was almost deafening and kept up all through the night, for because of the scarcity of sleeping accommodations many . . . were waiting for more fortunate and earlier comers to vacate beds at various lodgings, and thus afford them an opportunity of snatching a few winks of sleep in the early morning hours . . . waiters were busy all night . . . for the throng was ever present. . . . Meantime bartenders, nearly fainting with exhaustion, strove hard to satisfy the thirst of the multitude which eddied back and forth between the curbstone and the bar. . . . You could get a poor meal for $1.00 and possibly bad whiskey for 25 cents a swallow. Everyone kept open house but no silk hats were visible, no 'boiled shirts,' no four-horse sleighs, no calling cards.

The most fashionable restaurant of the early days was the Tontine. Here it became the custom for those who sold a mine to invite their friends to a blow-out where "champagne flowed like water."

Broken Nose Scotty was imprisoned for drunkenness in '79 and while in jail was called upon by a stranger who asked what he would take for a claim he held. The deal was made for $30,000, whereupon the stranger said, "Come to the lawyer's and make out the papers and the money is yours." Scotty, his fine paid, and having received the $30,000, returned to the jail, paid the fines of all who were "incarcerated," took them to town, bought them complete new outfits from shoes to hats, and then took them to the Tontine restaurant where he ordered the best meal the house could set up; and before midnight every one was back in jail for disturbing the peace.

On State Street were located many famous Sporting Houses, one of which was the Red Light Hall, whose sign was a beacon to guide

the seeker after the 'elephant' . . . to one of the most respectably kept and managed houses in the metropolis. . . . The decorum of the place is remarkable—to be sure it is a sporting house in all that the term implies. . . . The girls are rounder, rosier and more beautiful than elsewhere and will take you through the mazy waltz in refreshing movements that will make you feel that you don't care a cent whether school keeps or not, so the girls are all there.

Other resorts were the Pioneer, the Bucket of Blood, and the Carbonate Concert Hall which recommended:

Wine, Women and Song.

These three are supposed to make life palatial and while nothing of an improper character is permitted we can furnish all three any night.

The Pioneer is still in existence, and years after my first visit to Leadville, although I had sketched State Street with its "cribs" as well as the exterior of the saloon, I felt that any pictorial record of the city was incomplete without a more intimate view of the famous cafe. Corder, a young lawyer friend, made this possible. First we drove to the Crystal Palace Hotel on Chestnut Street, which was seemingly all shut up except the cafe, run by Johnny Bernat. The windows were dusty and shrouded with faded cretonne curtains just high enough to keep one from looking in. Inside was a long, narrow room, bare save for the bar and a few tables and chairs, and dominated by a huge Wurlitzer automatic player at the far end of the room. Choosing a table at the back, we waited for Johnny to take our order. He was a typical German bar-tender spare, tall, with handlebar moustache, hair parted in the middle and combed sleekly up in two points off his forehead, steel-rimmed spectacles and a beaming, anxious smile. He wiped his hand on his apron before greeting us while Corder explained why I was there. Johnny was delighted and said of course I might sketch his Wurlitzer. He had ordered it from Germany in the eighties where it had been especially made for him. It was almost as wide as the room and was all mirrors and stained glass doors. In the middle stood a bronze figure of a girl holding aloft a bunch of glass grapes which were lighted from within by electricity. Corder put a nickel in the slot and the music began. The din was outrageous. Cymbals clashed, drums boomed, a fiddle squeaked and a calliope blared. Whenever he was disengaged Johnny would come to our table to peer over my shoulder and see how the sketch was coming along. When it was finished he looked at it closely and said, "Will you make another one?" "That means he wants one for himself," I thought as I started to dupilcate the first drawing; but I was wrong, for as soon as I agreed to do a second one he ran nimbly up to the bronze lady and clutching her in his arms staggered across the room and deposited her upon the floor. Returning to the instrument he began to remove all the doors, revealing the intricate "innards" of cymbals, pipes, and strings. He then stepped back, beamed upon me again and indicated that perhaps I would draw the interior for him too. Groaning inwardly I started the second picture, for the amount of detail was terrific and I knew he would accept nothing but a realistic sketch of its myriad parts. When I finally offered it to him however, he declined it, saying that he knew I'd like to have a record of the insides and darting to the bar, returned with a glass of Schnapps. With profuse thanks for his hospitality we left and started for our real objective.

This was State Street's Pioneer Bar, known for years as the toughest spot in town. It was early when we entered and few customers were about, so I was able to get a good look around by the time that Corder found the proprietor, a tight-lipped, cold man, and introduced him. "Sure, you can sketch," he said, and walked off to more profitable trade. The room was long and narrow and rather dark, with a blood curdling number of bullet holes spattered about the walls. Except for the huge and beautifully carved mahogany bar, with its fine mirrors, it was a bare and ugly place. At the bar sat a girl of about eighteen, dressed in blue jeans and shirt. She was one of the girls of the block and was quite as drunk as the three men who were kidding her and buying her drinks. The Hostess, a fine looking, rather flashily dressed woman in her early forties, joined our party and visited with us while I finished my drawing. Gambling was going on in the back room and I started toward it with the intention of sketching, but Corder looked in and stopped me, saying that it might not be safe as several games were in progress and the men might not understand my wanting their pictures.

On every trip to Leadville, sooner or later I gravitate to the mines. The hills to the east of town are studded with crumbling dumps and empty shaft houses, and each one has its story. Up at the top of Jonny Hill is the mine which made John Campion a multimillionaire. Like many another mine it was found by chance, when an Englishman with pick and shovel stopped to ask a geologist where to dig and the geologist, busy and disinterested, answered, "Underneath that tree." The Englishman dug and struck the Little Jonny which became one of the richest mines in Leadville.

Off of Harrison Avenue, any street to the east takes you past busy stores, churches and residences, but as you climb higher, the houses block by block become less pretentious, and at last the streets become mere roads between dumps of crushed ore. In some cases the ore heaps spill over between the grey unpainted houses; in others, rows of modest frame dwellings are overshadowed by great masses of discarded rock, topped by dingy shaft houses. The road up Big Evans Gulch leads to Stumptown; in California Gulch is the site of Oro, the first settlement in the district; and east Fifth Street becomes lost in the road up Jonny Hill. Jo Roche introduced me to Jonny Hill, guiding my Ford roadster the four miles up the steep, rough road flanked by mines and their russet, green, ochre and blue-grey dumps, past the Little Jonny property to the top of Breece Hill and the Ibex shaft. The view from there was tremendous. To the west and south rose Mt. Massive and Mt. Elbert, with the Collegiate peaks, Mounts Princeton, Harvard and Yale, visible in the distance; but it was the view to the east that stopped me, for straight ahead, beyond the many mines that studded the hills below us, were the bare, grey, thirteen thousand foot knife-blades of the Mosquito Range. No wonder both Weston and Mosquito passes over those mountains were so treacherous and difficult to maintain, even without the added hazards of rock and snowslides and of "road agents" lying in wait for the slow climbing stagecoach or the freighter's wagon! Jo pointed out the location of many of the big producers, the Chrysolite, the Little Pittsburgh, the A. Y. and Minnie, the Penrose, the Garbut, the Resurrection, the Wolf Tone and the Matchless. He showed me Fryer Hill where the first discoveries were made, and Carbonate, Yankee and Iron Hills where other important mines were found. He identified the gulches up which miners had prospected so persistently, Big Evans, Stray Horse, Iowa and Big Union. Upon our return to town he invited me to dinner at his home, promising that his father, who was a miner, would talk to me about his experiences.

As I sat in Joe's parlor handling specimens of ore, his father identified them and told me about the mines from which they came. That same week Lobelia and I were invited to dinner at Ex-Governor Jesse McDonald's where we dined off silver plate and, both during the meal and afterwards over coffee, listened to story after story of his experiences as a young lawyer in the rip-roaring camp. He reached Leadville in 1878, having borrowed $52 with which to buy his ticket, and made the last two days of the journey by stage from Canon City. Arriving in the new camp he had but two dollars left with which to find lodging, and he billeted in a hotel room with four or five other men, all as eager as he for work in the growing metropolis. Later he had an office in Robinson, in the Ten Mile District, when that camp was booming and once, while straightening out some tangled mining claims, he was shot at, but the bullets went wild. On another occasion he made a trip into Leadville, eighteen

PIONEER
SALOON,
LEADVILLE

CRYSTAL
PALACE
HOTEL,
CHESTNUT ST.,
LEADVILLE

miles away, that he never forgot. Riding into town when the courthouse was being built, he saw two hanged men dangling from its rafters with placards on their backs, which listed thirty other persons who were advised to get out of town and get out quick. One name was that of the City Marshal!

One of the first buildings that I was shown in the city was St. George's Episcopal Church. It is a well proportioned, frame structure with wooden buttressed walls and stained glass windows and when Mrs. Norton turned the key in its front door and led me in, I was glad I knew something of its history. The evening before this visit to the church she had read me her account of its founding from which I quote:

> It was a warm summer day in 1878 when across a pass, high in the mountains came a weary man astride as weary a mule. . . . Halting the mule . . . he looked down on a cluster of cabins and two-story frame buildings that huddled together below him. Talking half to himself he murmured: 'It doesn't look like much down there, but I believe there is work to do,' and rode wearily on. . . . In California Gulch he found the man whom he was seeking and that evening gathered around the supper table, the family and their guest made plans for the first service . . . and the following Sunday service was held in the only available place—an upstairs room over a saloon, where there were cracks in the floor an inch wide that gaped down on the crowd drinking at the bar and gambling over the green tables below.
>
> The chips clinked, the Faro dealer shouted, the men shuffled about and the bartender served the drinks. Suddenly over this conglomeration of noise rose the strains of 'Onward Christian Soldiers' . . . sung by some lusty young voices and led by a sweet well-trained alto. It overrode all other sounds—the men below had stopped to listen. Some of them stole upstairs and shyly peeped in, even slipped inside and all was still. Business was suspended in at least one saloon that morning for an hour or more. . . . The young clergyman went through the sermon amid quiet and respectful attention. . . . He rode away in a day or so on his rested and revived mule but the seed had been sown, and not on barren ground, for from it sprang St. George's church. It is still standing on the corner of 4th and Pine Streets—a beautiful example of architecture with fine windows. The young clergyman who was responsible for its beginning was Arthur Lake.
>
> Until a church could be built services were held in a room in the new courthouse but soon that space proved too small, when the congregation met in the newly completed Tabor Opera House. H. A. W. Tabor loaned money for St. George's and was generous enough to forgive us half the money we owed when the debt was cleared.

Churches and Sunday schools appeared almost as early in the history of the Carbonate Camp as the variety theatres and gambling halls. In 1860 Father Macheboeuf crossed the mountains to California Gulch to celebrate mass and for many years he paid annual visits to the camp. Even before the silver boom Father Robinson, who was stationed at Fairplay, came regularly to Oro to hold services, and later in 1878 it was he who came to Leadville and, finding a sufficient group of followers, established the first place of worship. The following year other denominations founded churches and held regular services. Even the non-religious element was impressed; for when a church bell rang for the first time, a miner far up one of the gulches stopped his work in surprise and listened. Then turning to his companion he said, "I'll be damned if Jesus Christ hasn't come to Leadville too." The parson ringing that bell was the Rev. T. A. Uzzell, the "Fighting Parson" as he was later called. He secured the use of a log hut and "went around among miners, saloon-

ST. GEORGE'S EPISCOPAL CHURCH, LEADVILLE

TIGER ALLEY, LEADVILLE (GONE)

keepers, gamblers and merchants . . . inviting them to come to the log hut and hear him preach." In a very short time funds were raised for a church building, but until it was completed meetings were held in saloons, barns or private homes. One day while passing the lot on which the church was to be built the parson noticed several strange men unloading lumber upon it and realized that they were going to "jump the property." "Seeing that they were not disposed to listen to his words of protest he stripped off his coat and made a determined assault upon the invaders." Later he told a friend, "I made up my mind if the Lord wanted me to recover that lot He would give me strength to lick those fellows . . . and He did."

Parson Uzzell never hesitated to go among the gamblers and less reputable members of the community and was respected wherever he went. Once when a notorious character was murdered, Uzzell was asked to preach the funeral sermon, and every gambler, saloon man and prostitute turned out. After the sermon the man who had asked Uzzell to officiate said to him, "You gave us hell, but I guess we deserved it. Here's fifty dollars." On another occasion a rumor got around that Uzzell was to visit a certain variety show and the participants were warned to "Keep sober, look your best and don't swear." The proprietor did not know Uzzell, so when a reporter dressed for the part appeared, he was shown every attention. An hour later Uzzell arrived to find the place back to normal and everything wide open.

The first time I walked down Harrison Avenue I noticed a large, cream-colored building which was distinctly bigger than any of its neighbors, and upon reaching it I read, painted across its facade in large letters, Elks Opera House; yet looking at the cast iron doorstep I saw the words Tabor Opera House. Knowing that there must be a story behind this I hurried home to ask Lobelia. From her I learned that Horace A. W. Tabor was made Mayor of Leadville in 1878, the same year that his Little Pittsburgh mine began to pour money into his pockets in increasing amounts. He was inordinately proud of the fledgling city of which he was a part and as fortune continued to favor him he put lavish amounts of cash into civic projects which reflected glory both upon him and upon his city. What better memorial could he erect for the people of Leadville than an opera house to which all the best theatrical talent would come and whose performances he too could enjoy? While he was doing this he might just as well build a first class hotel; so the two structures, the Opera House and the Clarendon Hotel emerged side by side on the main thoroughfare.

Next morning I stopped by the courthouse to see if I could persuade Mr. McMahon, who had the keys to the theatre, to accompany me there and show me around. He was most agreeable and when we arrived insisted that I first look at all the framed photos of actors and actresses which lined the hallway and lobby. Next he took me up to the second floor where he showed me the Elks Club Rooms and finally the theatre. The auditorium was a little musty from having been closed for some time, but it was large enough to seat four hundred people on its main floor and another four hundred in the graceful, curved balcony. The last row of orchestra seats were of cast iron with red plush upholstery—the sole survivors of its 1879 grandeur.

I did not see any of the scenery that day, but the following Christmas, —seven of us from the University of Colorado drove to Leadville, especially to make a study of the Opera House. I wrote beforehand to my friends, requesting permission to invade the theatre for a few days while we carried on our research, and as usual the permission was not only granted but everything was arranged for our convenience. Mr. Jolly, who had been scene-shifter during the palmy days of the house, agreed to leave his store long enough to assist us in locating and setting up the canvas flats and drops with which the theatre was equipped. Mr. McMahon arranged with the janitor to prod the furnace a bit so as to remove the December chill from the auditorium, and Max Vawter of the *Herald-Democrat* came down to meet us and get a story for the paper. Our group from Boulder included the technical director of the University Theatre, his wife, two students from the stage crew, a photographer, a professor of art and myself.

The morning after our arrival we met at the Opera House, ready for action. Each had his own special work assigned and together we made an excellent team. The director and his two helpers set up the flats, Mr. Jolly let in the drops, the photographer clicked his cameras, the professor took measurements which the director's wife tabulated, and I sketched each set and made color notes which were later developed into large watercolor paintings. Meanwhile Mrs. Norton and one of her friends sat in the empty auditorium enjoying the excitement and exclaiming over each set, most of which they had not seen since the Opera House closed.

As each set of flats was dragged out Mr. Jolly regaled us with stories about some particular show for which it was used. We found the prison set painted on the reverse side of the Baronial hall. The "wood wings" had for a backdrop a leafy vista ending in a mountain torrent. The street scene "curtain" featured not only the Leadville courthouse but behind it, like ghostly blue shadows, were painted skyscrapers which the artist no doubt envisioned as part of Leadville's future skyline. One series of flats was all marble columns and red plush draperies; and another was a kitchen with an alcove painted in violent perspective right on the wall, furniture and all; but the set which was Mr. Jolly's favorite was the "Light Fancy" as he called it. Its walls were a tender apple green shading to deeper tones near the base and each flat was panelled with festoons of roses in natural and unnatural colors. This set he always used for High School Commencement exercises or for any performance using the stage, and few people in Leadville today have seen any other.

Most of the scenery we found was built for the present stage, but a few scattered pieces were of smaller size and of a definitely earlier school of scene-painting. Mr. Jolly explained to us that when Tabor built the place its stage was smaller than the present one, and that when the Elks bought the opera house in 1903 it was extensively remodeled and enlarged. He pointed with considerable pride to the original roll curtain, which he had been commissioned to take to Denver and install there in the Tabor Theatre for the world premiere of "Silver Dollar," the movie which depicts the life of Tabor.

We expected to spend three or four days setting up the old scenery, but the crew worked with such enthusiasm and dispatch that they were finished in a day and a half and ready to return to Boulder and a less frigid climate than Leadville's 10,000 feet of altitude provided. It was dark when we left and as we drove down the long hill that passes the Arkansas Valley Smelter, we saw one of Leadville's most colorful sights. For years the smelter has remained the big industry of the city, and around it in Stringtown cluster the miserable shanties and cabins of its foreign workers, the Czechs, Slovaks and Bohemians. Each morning the people of Leadville look down the valley to the big smelter stack and if it is belching thick yellow smoke they are content, for only infrequently, when it ceases operations, is Leadville in a precarious condition and its working population financially embarrassed. Jo took me through the plant one day, beginning at the storage bins where ore waiting to be treated is kept, and ending at the Bag House, where the smoke is screened to recover valuable metallic particles which might otherwise be lost. Just as we reached the huge black hulk of the slag pile, which almost clogs the highway at one point, right beside us, like a bursting rocket, great red fingers of molten metal hissed down its sides sending waves of heat toward us and as quickly cooling to a charred grey mass.

The streets of the city never ceased to fascinate me, for buildings representative of all its periods survive. About a mile up California Gulch is one skeleton cabin—all that is left of once-flourishing Oro City. Next oldest perhaps, is the Dexter Cabin, built in 1878 of sturdy square-hewn logs. When the Leadville Historical Society decided to purchase it for a museum it belonged to a woman, formerly better known in less respectable neighborhoods. She readily agreed to sell the cabin to the society, especially when she learned the purpose to which it was to be put, for as she said, "I've always been very civic-minded." A picket fence surrounds its pocket-handerchief lawn and its gate squeaks when you enter, but inside are pioneer treasures worth seeing, such as the check paid to Lobelia's father for having been a witness at Leadville's one legal hanging. She was a child when this happened but she told me she remembered that when her father reached home that noontime he could not eat and lay all afternoon in a darkened room recovering from the spectacle. He never cashed that check and years later she gave it to the Historical Society.

On the wall of the cabin is the architect's watercolor sketch for the Ice Palace, "The Cloud City's Great Crystal Castle," which opened January 1, 1896. To be sure the palace had been officially opened on December 27 "by the people who built it" for as the newspaper of that date stated, "Leadville will go it alone at the start and wear the 'wire edge' off"; but the world was not permitted to see the marvel until the first, when the "Dodge City Cowboy Band, the Mayor, the Ladies Carnival clubs and the Miners Union 2000 strong," marched up to the portal where the dazzling nineteen foot figure of Leadville, carved from ice, pointed "with outstretched right arm . . . to the rich mineral hills from which Leadville's wealth is taken." Built in "Norman Style, nearly half a mile long and three hundred and twenty feet wide," with walls eight feet thick, it covered five acres, the walls and towers alone containing five thousand tons of ice.

The palace itself was a gigantic undertaking, and despite an unusually mild winter which threatened to melt the structure, it drew large crowds until it

(58)

PRESBYTERIAN CHURCH, LEADVILLE (GONE)

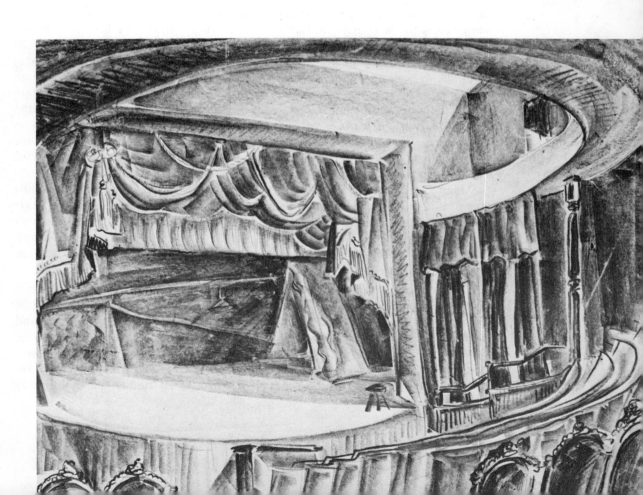

was officially closed with the city's annual May Day Festival. Special trains brought Toboggan Clubs from distant cities to enjoy it, and for their pleasure a breath-taking toboggan run was built from Harrison to Leiter Avenues, a distance of several blocks. The interior of the palace was also full of surprises.

Entering the north gateway the visitor passed up a broad stairway and found himself in a fine ice rink 80 feet by 190 feet. To the left was a grand ballroom and at the right, the rink auxiliary ballroom and dining room.

Each ballroom had an adjoining parlor and "both ball and banqueting rooms were heated by eight large hard coal base burners." Exhibits of all sorts were frozen into the icy walls, while the ice pillars which supported the roof "glistened and glowed with colored lights of eery description . . . enrapturing the senses." All in all "the frozen fastness of the stream gleamed in a translucent glow. There was a warmth and kindly color in cubes of ice that thrilled the soul like a rainbow's hues on a spring morning." There was also "warmth and kindly color" in the tea that was served in the restaurant. No intoxicants were allowed to be sold in the building, but somehow the "tea" had a peculiar flavor not found at tea parties. Fifty cents admission permitted people to skate to the music of a "band equal to the best in the state and to waltz to the same fine music," and when they left they agreed that it was very cheap entertainment for the money.

No matter where you stand in Leadville or in what direction you look there is evidence of great mining activity in the region. To the north lies the road to Climax where vast stores of molybdenum are found, and to the west rises the smoke from the smelter. Still farther west is Malta, where the first smelter was located and the charcoal burners created fuel for the furnaces and threatened the region with forest fires. To the south lies Iowa Gulch and washed-out placer diggings, as well as the roads over which early pioneers found their way into the region. But it is the view from Capitol Hill that is the richest of all. Here to the right lies California Gulch, scene of the earliest diggings, and to the left of the gulch is a series of hills that have yielded such rich returns to so many men. The hills are riddled with mines whose dumps stand grey and gaunt against the green pines and patches of aspen. The view from Capitol Hill reveals even more than this. Straight ahead is Harrison Avenue with its hotels and banks, the Elks Opera House and the Lake County Courthouse, while beyond this the city rises to the hills until it is lost among the mines, where shaft houses and the homes of miners are side by side. Above the city, the hills to their very crests are full of mines whose dumps stand out so aggressively, and beyond these nearby hills stands the bare, challenging Mosquito Range, grim and uncompromising.

There are no large or palatial homes in the city. Street after street is lined with frame houses of Victorian extraction, some large and some small, behind whose lace-curtained parlor windows grow geraniums, fuchsias, and other house plants in riotous profusion. Almost every house has its iron or picket fence and its tiny front yard in which mountain wildflowers and tame varieties grow side by side. There are very few trees left and those that remain are hardy pines, for most of the first growth of timber which formerly covered the hills was cut years ago to provide lumber for building purposes and for the mines.

Except for Harrison Avenue, the business street, and the highway which leads in and out of town, no street is paved. Some of the side streets, up near the mines, still have wooden sidewalks and other streets have virtual flumes for gutters with narrow boards bridging the ditch in front of every house. Different sections of the city have picturesque names—Chicken Hill near California Gulch, Bucktown, Stringtown and Jacktown near the smelter, Finntown on the lower part of Jonny Hill, Stumptown up Big Evans Gulch, Shanty Town in Ten Mile Gulch, Tin Town in Poverty Flats and Hangtown.

In my wanderings I found several old landmarks such as Turnverein Hall, the Tabor house and the Vivian house. The latter I would have passed without a second glance had it not been pointed out and its story told me. Perhaps I should have known that Charles Algernon Sidney Vivian was the founder of the Jolly Corks, but I did not. Perhaps I should have known what the Jolly Corks were. Even Vivian had no inkling that the society which he organized in New York in 1868, would become an organization of over one hundred thousand in twenty-five years. Born in England, the son of a clergyman, he came to New York in 1867, became a variety actor and ballad singer and then toured the country with various troupes. In New York he gathered around him twelve congenial men and organized the Jolly Corks, patterned after the "Buffaloes," a social order in England to which Vivian belonged. When a committee was chosen to select a name for the permanent organization, they were impressed by a fine elk head on the wall of Barnum's old museum and looked up the history of the animal. Finding that it was "fleet of foot, timorous of doing wrong, avoiding all combat save in defense of its young, the helpless and weak" it was adopted, and the Benevolent Protective Order of Elks was born.

Vivian came to Leadville in 1879 with Jack Langrishe and his company and appeared at the Tabor Opera House, the Grand Central and Wood's Theatres, but his stay in the city was cut short by his death the following year. The simple frame building on East 2nd Street, its windows boarded up and its whole appearance suggesting loneliness, is a historic and touching spot to Leadville's Lodge No. 236, B. P. O. E., for in a room in this house Vivian died on March 20, 1880. At his funeral there was a long procession of carriages preceded by an escort of twenty men on horseback. "There was a band too, which on the way to Evergreen Cemetery played the 'Dead March' from Saul but on the way back when Harrison Avenue was reached, struck up 'Ten Thousand Miles Away,' Vivian's favorite song, which he had sung to thousands before the footlights." His body remained in Leadville until 1889 when it was removed to the Elks plot of the Boston Lodge.

Not far from the Opera House is the Tabor house, a modest two-story frame building with a bay window. It was boarded up the last time I saw it, yet at one time it was the comfortable Leadville home of Horace A. W. Tabor and his wife Augusta. They came to California Gulch in the sixties and opened a grocery store and post office, first at Oro and later in Leadville. Mrs. Tabor was one of the first women to reach the gulch and immediately endeared herself to the miners by her "infinite kindness of heart and her acts of benevolence

(61)

which were legion." Tabor was a colorful character and many stories are told about him, such as the one concerning a customer who purchased two needles for which she was charged forty cents. The lady objected to the exorbitant price, whereupon Tabor replied smoothly, "But Madame, consider the freight."

He and Augusta worked hard during several lean years, until Tabor grubstaked two prospectors, August Rische and George T. Hook, to the extent of $64.75. This investment paid for itself many times over, for as a result of their efforts the Little Pittsburgh mine was discovered which ultimately paid Tabor $1,300,000. His luck at mining was so phenomenal that he was said to have the "Midas touch." The Chrysolite mine was "salted" when he bought it. After he discovered this, instead of giving it up as a bad deal he hired men to develop it further, struck rich silver ore and turned the mine into a bonanza. He bought the Matchless mine for $117,000 and for a time received monthly returns from it of $100,000; his other mines paid well, and he became the richest man in Colorado.

In 1873 he was elected Lieutenant Governor of the state, and when Senator Henry M. Teller became a member of President Arthur's cabinet, Tabor filled his unexpired term of thirty days as Senator from Colorado. As his fortunes grew his tastes increased also, but his lavish mode of living did not appeal to Augusta, whose New England background was satisfied with simpler things. The two began to drift apart, especially after Elizabeth McCourt, known as Baby Doe, appeared and caught Tabor's roving eye. They were divorced, and while Tabor was United States Senator, he married Baby Doe. For a few brief years they lived in splendid style, with a suite at the Clarendon Hotel and one at the Vendome, as well as a mansion in Denver. The silver crash of 1893 was the death blow not only to Tabor but to the silver mining world and from it Tabor never wholly recovered. His fortunes gone, he and Baby Doe lived in extreme poverty in Denver until, just before his death, he was made Postmaster of that city. As he lay dying in 1899, attended by the faithful Baby Doe he gave a command, —"Hold on to the Matchless"—which she heeded the rest of her life.

For years before her death in 1935, she lived by choice in the shaft house of the mine, in utter squalor, believing in its future and guarding it as she had promised to do. Long after its levels were filled with water and its machinery rusted, she stayed on, meeting all intruders with suspicion and a cocked rifle, and accepting charity from no one. Provisions and clothing sent to her shack by sympathetic persons were returned untouched to the stores from which they came, for she insisted that she needed nothing. In summer and winter, in good weather or bad she tramped the long mile to town to get occasional necessities. After a heavy snow storm which made the road almost impassable, a few people who had become accustomed to her habits missed her usual visit and went to the Matchless to see if she was ill. There was no answer to their knock and entering, they found her dead upon the floor.

I was in Leadville shortly after her death and a friend drove me up to her shack at the mine. Never have I seen such utter dessication. As soon as the news of her death was known, curiosity seekers from all over rushed to the spot and began hunting through the shabby cabin for money which they be-

GARBUT
MINE,
LEADVILLE

SCHOOL HOUSE
AT LITTLE
JONNY MINE,
LEADVILLE (GONE)

lieved must be secreted in the walls or under the floor. When I saw the place I was horrified, for it was literally torn to shreds and the floor was littered two inches deep with tattered paper and plaster flakes.

John Morrissey was one of Leadville's wealthy but illiterate miners and to him are attributed many stories connected with the camp. Morrissey couldn't tell time, yet when his mines made him a rich man, he dressed the part and one of his first purchases was a diamond-studded watch. Realizing that he couldn't read its face and anxious not to disclose his ignorance, when asked the time he would hand the watch to his inquirer with the remark, "See for yourself, then you'll know I'm not lyin' to yez." Mathematics were beyond him also. One day, feeling in an expansive mood, he went to one of his mines armed with a bottle of whiskey, and shouting down the shaft inquired. "How many be yez down there?" "Three" was the prompt response, whereupon John called down to the underground voices. "Well, half of yez come up and have a drink." When he was asked if he would provide the funds necessary for a chandelier for one of Leadville's churches he was perfectly agreeable but expressed a doubt as to its success, for "he was damned if he knew who'd play on the thing." One day his judgment was sought on a weighty issue. Twin Lakes, a resort about seventeen miles from Leadville, was being developed. A hotel had been built along the shore of the larger lake and arbors and pavilions erected in the groves of trees along its margin. The promoters of the development wanting to add a final, unique touch of beauty and individuality to the place agreed to purchase some gondolas for the use of the guests. Unable to decide on the number, however, they asked Morrissey to settle the question for them. "That's easy," said he. "Just get two and let them breed."

During World War II Leadville enjoyed a boom, when Camp Hale was built a few miles beyond Tennessee Pass. This camp, which was established for the training of Mountain Ski Troops, employed hundreds of men during its construction period and accommodated a large number of troops after its completion. During this time Leadville overflowed with people who occupied every available hotel, house, cabin and trailer. Even State Street was cleaned up and its "houses" rented as apartments.

Leadville is a city of contrasts both in its present appearance and in its history. Harrison Avenue is the lively thoroughfare of today but Chestnut Street, the main street of the eighties, is a little shabby. The Opera House is just as imposing in appearance as it was in 1879 when it was known to be the "best one night stand in the country," but for entertainment today, there are the Liberty Bell Movie Theatre and the bars. Within a mile of each other are Poverty Flats and Capitol Hill; today the streets are treeless, yet once there were so many trees that the camp was to have been called Boughtown. The population grew from a mere handful to as high as 60,000, and then dropped again to a meagre 4,500. The booms of 1859 and 1891 were based on gold. that of 1878 on silver, that of 1901 chiefly on lead and zinc, and that of 1942 on the nearness of the United States Army. The mines and industries brought fortunes to persons as diverse as John Campion, H. A. W. Tabor, and John Morrissey; but at the same time thousands of prospectors and business men lost every cent they had in following false leads or putting money into worthless

MOSQUITO
PASS FROM
JONNY HILL

SCHOOL HOUSE,
ROBINSON (GONE)

shafts. Between these booms came years of hard times to Leadville with mines shut down, whole streets of houses empty, many stores closed and real estate well-night worthless. Always, however, through ups and downs, a solid nucleus of loyal citizens stayed on, continuing their businesses and bringing up their families, regarding this city, high in the Rockies, as their permanent home. Leadville today with its mines, its historical landmarks, its spirit and its setting is not the Leadville of '79, but the city is unique and indomitable, man-made and successful, a city of paradoxes and superlatives, the great "Carbonate Camp" in the shadow of Mount Massive.

Robinson

Ex-Governor McDonald had, as I have mentioned, told me interesting stories about Camp Robinson. It was therefore with considerable anticipation that I accepted an invitation to visit the place with a mining engineer and his family. As we drove the eighteen miles to the camp, over Fremont Pass, my companions told me that Robinson was one of the important towns of the Ten Mile District and had sprung up in 1880 when the mines began to produce.

There was some placer mining in the region beginning in 1860, and from McNulty Gulch alone $300,000 was obtained; but by 1862 the gulch was worked out, the miners trickled away and for nearly twenty years the region was deserted. Then in 1878 George B. Robinson, a Leadville merchant, outfitted two men whom he sent to prospect in the Ten Mile District with the understanding that he be entitled to half their findings. By the following June they had located ten mines, which became known as the Robinson Group and which George Robinson hastened to acquire. Backed by New York capitalists, he organized a company with a capital stock of $10,000,000 and sold shares. Other prospectors located the Wheel of Fortune, White Quail, Rattler and Oriental mines, and in spite of deep snow sunk shafts and dug tunnels. These mines produced such promising ore that the 1500 inhabitants of the district believed their camp might rival Leadville which also was in its infancy.

A stampede to the diggings began, and even with the snow ten feet deep, the town of Carbonateville was laid out in December 1878. It was followed early in 1879 by Kokomo, which from the first challenged Carbonateville for supremacy. In the spring of 1880 Ten Mile City or Robinson's Camp materialized, becoming from the first the rival of Kokomo, two miles away. George Robinson took great pride in his town and was largely responsible for its growth and development. With his own capital he built a smelter and a hotel and he watched with interest as streets were built up with miner's homes, a Catholic church, a bank, a newspaper and telegraph office, and stores of all kinds.

Then in November 1880 two unexpected events brought the new camp to the attention of the whole state. In the election Robinson was chosen Lieutenant Governor of Colorado, but before the end of the month he was dead. The tragedy was the result of a dispute over the ownership of his Smuggler mine. When the situation grew tense Robinson decided to go over and investigate matters. There were rumors that an armed posse of one hundred men were planning to attack and capture the mine during the night, and to forestall this Robinson stationed guards with rifles about his property with orders to fire on anyone not authorized to approach. On the evening of November 27, "hearing that a guard whom he had stationed at the mouth of the tunnel was not in his place, he went down to see if it was true." Approaching the barricaded door at the mouth of the tunnel without revealing his identity he was immediately challenged by the guard. Replying that it was "All right," he turned to leave when a bullet struck him in the side. Mortally wounded, he was carried to his hotel where he lingered until morning. Although his sudden death was a severe blow to the town, it continued to grow during the eighties, "having a resident population of seven or eight hundred and a prospecting element of three hundred or more."

In 1880 the Rio Grande railroad extended its track to Robinson and Kokomo, under the most adverse circumstances, since "much of the grading and most of the track laying was done under a heavy fall of snow"; but on New Year's day, 1881, the first train puffed into Robinson and thereafter trains ran "with gratifying regularity." All through the eighties the town flourished, but by 1890 the high grade ores were nearly exhausted, and since then mining in the region has been spasmodic. McNulty Gulch produced some gold in 1920 and Kokomo's mines continued active, but the Wheel of Fortune's huge mill stood idle and Ten Mile Creek began to suck Robinson's wooden sidewalks into the swamp meadowland.

As we neared Robinson I looked in vain for the masses of buildings I had hoped to see, but very few remained standing. The road into town led through a swamp which was sucking at foundations and half submerging the swollen and warped wooden sidewalks. Before I had time to explore the place a sudden mountain shower sent us scurrying for shelter into the school-house, whose floor was buckled and broken and from whose water-stained walls the paper hung in shreds and festoons. While the rain swept by in windblown sheets and dripped through the soggy roof, we set out the picnic lunch on the rows of school desks, and squeezing into the small seats, enjoyed our meal.

Across the street stood the Catholic church, a good-sized structure but doomed; for the only family living in the town was stripping it board by board for lumber and firewood. Except for the rain, the place was dead quiet, and it was hard to picture it as ever having been a threat to Leadville's supremacy or even to nearby Kokomo's status. The shower passed as suddenly as it appeared and I slipped outside and began to explore the dripping town. Only one of its several streets remained and on it the houses were few and far between, with piles of lumber or stone foundations marking where others had stood. Close to the hillside rose a solitary smelter stack and out on the flat, near the marsh, stood a second stack as well as some ruined sheds and machinery from the furnaces. I could have stayed all afternoon in this place so full of ghosts, but my host was starting the car, and while I was whisked back to Leadville I determined to return to Robinson at the first opportunity. It was several years before I could do so and by then I was driving my own car, which was used to stopping at unlikely places while I explored crumbling buildings and rusty shafthouses. To my amazement Robinson was gone. Where were the false-fronted stores and the crazy, crooked sidewalks? Had I passed the spot or was it farther on? Finally, close to the hill I saw the smelter stack and not far away the second one, and I knew that I stood on the site of Robinson although the swamp and the huge settling ponds of the Climax Molybdenum Company were claiming it inch by inch. Looking about me I was thankful for that former trip on which I made sketches, for now I was too late to add to my pictorial record of the town.

Climax

On that first trip to Robinson we passed, at the top of Fremont Pass, the company town of Climax and even then I noticed its big settling pond, which covered several acres. Now it reached at least a mile down the valley, and the surrounding land was cleared and prepared to receive more of the waste silt as soon as increased production of the plant demanded it. I knew very little about Climax, except in 1932, in driving home from Leadville over the old road which climbed the mountain at a higher level than the present paved highway, suddenly, right in front of us stood a mountain, inside out, gashed to its core and composed of colored metallic earths in rust colors, ochres and greys, at whose base stood a few mine buildings. As I had no idea what molybdenum was I began to ask questions and learned that certain deposits, at first mistaken for galena, were found on that mountain and were identified in 1900 by the Colorado School of Mines as molybdenum. Little was known about the metal and its uses at that time, and the lode, named the Climax, was not explored or developed until 1911. There was little market for the metal until 1914, when its value as an alloy for toughening steel was realized and the systematic development of the property commenced. By 1917 about 200 people lived near the mine at the top of the pass, 11,320 feet above sea level, and since then a large and completely modern company town has been constructed on the spot.

From this mine eighty-five per cent of the world's molybdenum is procured and its concentrates are shipped all over the world. As the mine and its tremendous plant grew, first one settling pond and then another was constructed to hold the tailings from the mill, for by law this waste material cannot be turned into mountain streams. Today these ponds extend miles beyond the main property, and as they fill they are gradually burying everything in their path. Robinson is waiting, although the wet, clawing fingers of the pond and its pulverized waste have not as yet covered its site. I have heard that Kokomo too is doomed and that the Climax Company has bought the town and will raze it and use its land for further expansion whenever that becomes necessary.

Kokomo and Carbon-ateville

In December 1878, with the snow ten feet deep, the town of Carbonateville (between Robinson and Climax) was laid out—the first settlement in the Ten Mile District. The houses, although "rudely and uncomfortably constructed . . . overflowed with lodgers," while those who could find no other shelter shivered in "fragile and windworn tents." As more prospectors flocked in more claims were located, extending from Carbonateville for several miles down Ten Mile Creek on both sides of the stream, and new townsites sprang up.

Kokomo, the next town to appear, was founded in 1878, at an elevation of 10,618 feet, by a group from Indiana who named it for the city in their home state. It was platted in 1879 and from the first it challenged Carbonateville for supremacy. This new town, with Recen which adjoined it, drained the population from Carbonateville, whose boom was of short duration. By 1880 a Summit County newspaper stated that "Carbonateville has passed from

(68)

a place of unusual prominence to a staid and quiet little town with a population of one hundred and sixty-seven, a post office, several stores, a good hotel and saloons." A year later it was a true ghost town and today only its site remains.

Kokomo is not a "ghost town," although it might be hard today to find the "two excellent hotels, the Summit House and the Western, a new church, a bank, and the *Summit County Times*, published at a higher altitude than any other paper in the world." It flourished in 1880, but an eastern magazine-writer took exception to its claim by saying:

> Then we passed the Ten Mile mining district and in due time came to Kokomo, a mining camp supposed to be 'Booming' but giving no marked evidence of the process; surely it is one of the queerest and quaintest places that was ever seen. One very narrow street is carved out of the side of a steep hill and below it are numbers of skeleton houses—mere wooden frames, the very morbid anatomy of architecture."— Vacation Aspects of Colorado, A. Haynes, Jr., *Harper's Magazine*, March, 1880.

That same year, the local paper, with true civic pride, spoke of its "handsome streets and a number of pleasant residences" and of "four sawmills, running night and day at full blast with people standing around awaiting their turn to get lumber at $50 per thousand."

Many lots were jumped in the new town where lumber was scarce and men were unscrupulous. It was rumored that a house which had just been completed would be jumped, and its owners "whispered that they would take forcible possession of their property." Before they had time to do so two men

> and gentlemen in their employ, all armed to the teeth, rode in town at breakneck speed and reaching the building, demolished the door and took possession. Five hundred citizens joined them and tore the building in fragments and scattered it upon the streets. Public sentiment is so strong against jumpers that hanging is openly discussed. —Leadville *Weekly Democrat*, May 22, 1880.

Rich placer gravels had been found near the location of Kokomo in the early sixties, but active mining did not begin until silver bearing ores were found at the time of the Leadville boom.

The discovery of the White Quail mine on Elk Mountain was the first strike of importance and one of the earliest in the district. The Aftermath group of mines, which included the Climax claim, were also valuable properties, their immense bodies of ore "running well in both silver and gold and sufficiently high in lead to rank as fine smelting ore."

Two smelters, the White Quail and the Greer, were built to handle the local ores which were hauled to the plants from the Wheel of Fortune on Sheep Mountain, the Grand Union on the main range, the Reconstruction on Copper Mountain, as well as from the Snowbank group, the Michigan mine, and the Wilfley mine—all good producers. In 1881, just at the peak of Kokomo's boom when its population reached 10,000, the town burned. After the fire, a large portion of the "floating and prospecting element" left, looking for "new fields of adventure." Kokomo rebuilt at once and the railroad facilitated the shipment of ore, but its heyday was past, and slowly, bit by bit, the town slipped downhill until only a few of its mines were worked and its population was numbered in the hundreds.

In 1934 I spent some time in Kokomo, sketching the Masonic Hall and the tiny Community church, the tall, thin, two-story school which looked all the taller perched on the hillside, and the snowsheds that covered the railroad tracks at the edge of town. One day as I worked, I watched two men who were busily painting the front of a store building. Naturally we began to talk, and they told me with pride about A. R. Wilfley, whose mine was less than a mile from where we stood and who invented an ore separating process while working his property. His invention, the Wilfley Table, was put into successful operation in 1895 and it is still used for certain types of milling.

One of them told me the grim story of the Dead Man Claim: "It was winter. Scotty had died and the boys wanting to give him a good burial, hired a man for $20 to dig a grave through ten feet of snow and six feet of hard ground. Meantime Scotty was stuffed in a snowbank. Nothing was heard of the gravedigger, and when the men went out to look they found a note pinned to a tree—'Struck it rich at 4 feet below grass roots. Gone to town to record location. Will be up to plant old pard in the morning!' "

When I packed up my paints and was about to leave they called after me, "Kokomo's coming back. There'll be another boom here. You wait and see." And sure enough, in recent years Kokomo has roused itself to some extent. Several of its mines are again producing steadily and a government housing unit has been constructed within the city limits. Kokomo is safe until such time as the Climax Molybdenum Company's settling pond flows over its streets and buries it under tons of silt.

CHAPTER FOUR

Dredge County

(For map see inside of front cover)

Breckenridge LATE one afternoon my companion and I drove toward Breckenridge along the Blue River. On either side of the highway were swampy meadows and beyond them low pine-studded hills, while to the west the peaks of the Ten Mile range were sharp silhouettes against the sunset light. Suddenly the landscape changed and we found our view to the west cut off by great mounds of clean washed rocks and pebbles, fifteen to twenty feet in height, which stretched before us as far as we could see. What were they, where did they come from and why were they deposited in such orderly fashion along the narrow stream of the Blue River? The further we drove the more mystified we became until, driving into the town of Breckenridge, we found, just behind the false fronted stores of the main street, floating in a sluggish pool, a gold dredge, surrounded on two sides by more piles of stones, washed so clean of soil that not even weeds would grow between them. Having never seen any dredging before we were curious about the whole process and, leaving our car, scrambled down the bank to get as close to the "boat" as possible. Apparently it was not in use, for its machinery was a little rusty and the canvas which covered the long stacker, up which the discarded rock and gravel were carried, was frayed and torn. Behind it, for miles, were the mounds of waste rock beside which we had driven and which it had deposited in its wake. In front of it was the rest of Breckenridge and the gold-bearing gravel of the Blue River, ready to be gouged and sucked up by the hungry buckets and fed to the dredge which would separate the precious gold grains from the mud, ooze and rock of the streambed. As we looked about we saw that the entire country around Breckenridge was piled with gravel dumps where other dredges had torn up the earth and extracted gold from the meadowland.

That evening, sitting comfortably in the Victorian parlor of the Brown Hotel, we listened to an old-timer who, between puffs on a potent pipe, spoke of the early days of the town which he knew so well. The discovery of gold in the mountains in 1859 was the spark which set hundreds of adventurous men scrambling over uncharted mountain peaks and scrutinizing the wet gravel of countless streambeds in their eager, mad search for the shining flakes. During the summer of 1859 at least two groups crossed the Continental Divide and worked their way down the rivers later known as the Swan and the Blue, until near the present site of Breckenridge they began to wash color from the sand. One man, roping pieces of saddle blanket around his feet, waded into the water and dug up pay dirt worth ten dollars the first day.

Some prospected in the vicinity, at Gold Run, Delaware Flats, or in the Corkscrew district, while others worked up the nearby gulches which they

BRECKENRIDGE FALSE FRONTS   ↓ MAIN STREET AND DREDGE DUMPS

named Georgia, French, Nigger, Gibson, Galena, American and Humbug. Within one year these camps had a total population of eight thousand, while the tents and cabins which clustered about the blockhouse fort on the Blue was called Fort Meribeh. This fort was built by the miners, as protection against the Ute Indians who roamed the territory and resented the presence of these white men who dug up the earth and frightened away the game. As the camp of Fort Meribeh grew, the need for a post office and for government mail service was realized. In the hope of procuring this, the camp was formed into a town and named for John C. Breckinridge, Vice President of the United States. As a result the post office was obtained, and everyone was satisfied until a year or two later when the sympathies of J. C. Breckinridge were found to be for the Confederate cause. In indignation the "Union" population substituted an "e" for the "i" in the name, and as Breckenridge the the town has been known ever since.

By 1863 most of the rich gravels were washed clean and the miners drifted away, some to prospect in new areas and others to fight in the Civil War. From then until 1879 there was little activity in the district, for placer mining had played out and no one as yet knew the possibilities of quartz mining. Not until Leadville and Aspen beckoned to the mining world in 1879 and 1880 did prospectors return to the lonely camps of the sixties and feverishly comb the hillsides, where the mineral pockets and faults which fed the streambeds must be located. This led to an era of quartz mining, during which Breckenridge had its second and biggest boom.

Our storyteller was full of anecdotes which he recounted to us, shaking with laughter and sucking on his pipe. One was of the miner who while having his hair cut was asked by the barber if he were a sign painter. "No," he replied in some indignation. "Well then," said the barber, "how did you get all this gold leaf in your hair?" Leaping up the man dashed off to his place in the hills and began to pan gravel in the rushing mountain stream behind his cabin. Next day he was in town again recording a placer claim on his land.

Judge Silverthorn came to Breckenridge in 1859 and was made judge of the Miners' Court, for in those days each mining district wrote its own laws and administered them. On one occasion the court determined the manner by which a duel should be fought between two miners who had come to blows over a girl. It ruled that the two should stand back to back and at a signal, walk fifteen paces, whirl about, and approach each other shooting until one was killed or the weapons were empty. All of Breckenridge turned out for this event and waited the outcome with unfeigned enjoyment. The two men met, were placed back to back and were ordered to march. Each made his fifteen paces and then, instead of turning, continued walking faster and faster until both were out of sight, and Breckenridge saw no more of them.

Shortly after his arrival Judge Silverthorn brought his wife to the camp, where she endeared herself to the miners by caring for them when they were sick and by preparing tasty meals which relieved the monotony of their sowbelly dinners. As the winters in the mountains were too severe and uncomfortable for the lady, each fall she departed for Denver, returning in the spring. When the "boys" heard that she was on her way back they put on their snowshoes and, trudging to the top of the Divide in the deep snow, met her and drew her to town on a sled. In 1863 the Silverthorns opened a hotel, the Silverthorn House, which is still on the main street, although it has been closed a number of years. Curious to see it, I peered through its grimy, patched windows the next morning and wished that I could get inside; but it was securely padlocked.

There were other stories too—about the woman who papered her house with newspapers, placed so that they could be read, and often when the mails were delayed she and the miners who stopped at the cabin read and reread the news for want of fresher headlines; and the one about the man who floored his cabin with worn-out sluice boxes, whose knotty boards were so uneven that he covered them with several inches of sawdust from the nearby mill, while his wife sewed together burlap sacks to serve as a covering which could be nailed down over the sawdust cushion.

Breckenridge has wide streets and a number of buildings that date back to the eighties. The present firehouse is a modern structure; but back in the thirties when I first saw the town, the fire appartus was kept in a two-story building whose upper story housed the city hall. Its lower floor, with its hook and ladder, hand-drawn hose carts, buckets, ladders, fire hooks and axes fascinated me, and while I sketched the gaily painted carts an old lady touched my sleeve and said softly, "You don't know the names of those carts but I do. One is the Blue River and the other is the Independence." And smiling reminiscently she walked away. Beside the firehouse stood a tall wooden tower with a crooked stovepipe protruding from its side about half way up. This tower was where the hose was hung to dry after it had been in use. The new firehouse, lacking a tower, is not nearly so picturesque.

The whole day was spent wandering up one street and down another, sketching buildings, churches, the main street with its backdrop of dredge dumps, and the dredge itself. On a side street was a large store window containing all manner of stuffed animals. Bighorn sheep, deer, antelope, wolves, an eagle and small furry creatures filled the entire space. The store was closed and the window panes were dusty, but the display was excellent and worthy of a museum. While I was wondering about it a passerby said, "That collection was assembled by Edwin Carter, one of the oldest settlers who mined during the sixties up and down these gulches. Later on he hunted big game and to preserve it he became a taxidermist. By 1870 he had as fine a collection of mounted specimens of animals and birds native to Colorado as you'd want to see. At first he sold specimens to eastern museums, but by 1874 he decided to keep his collection intact and from then on refused to sell. He called his collection the Carter Museum, and this is some of it in the windows."

False-fronted buildings are common to all midwest and western towns of a certain era, but in Breckenridge the ingenuity and flair with which Victorian carpenters varied the false front beggars description. Usually a one-story structure is hidden behind a facade which rises straight up above the ridgepole and then is neatly cut off and topped with the simplest of cornices; but not so in Breckenridge. To be sure, some of the stores followed the traditional pattern, but in certain ones, the builder let his imagination go and added ornate cornices which rose high above the modest first story. One in particular was a two-story facade, shaped as if to meet a ridgepole which did not exist, and to further deceive and impress the passerby its second-story blank wall was ornamented with two fake windows, complete with slat shutters. A peep around the edge of this imposing breastwork revealed the usual long, narrow one-story shed. Next to it the Arlington Hotel, with its colonaded porch and second-story balustrade, boasted a kind of ornate cornice of unusually inventive cut with curves, corbels and castellated trim. A glance down the main street showed it lined with two and three-story structures, but a walk up the alley behind these edifices revealed their modest proportions.

No railroad runs to Breckenridge today but its right of way can be traced, not only through the town but up the hillside to the east, past Windy Point and on toward the Divide. The road, the South Park, was built from Como on the other side of the range, over Boreas Pass, and down into the valley of the Blue, reaching the isolated mountain town in 1881. Boreas Pass was well named, for even seasoned train crews dreaded its howling winds, intense cold, and drifted snowbanks which so often impeded their progress.

Prior to the arrival of the railroad, all transportation and freighting was over the passes—Georgia, Breckenridge, and Hoosier—and it must have been rugged going during much of the year. In winter—and snow lies early and lasts late on the high peaks—freighters and the intrepid mail carrier would arrange their trips so that they might reach the snow during the night and travel over it while it was crusted. One terrific story is told of cattle being moved across the range too late in the season, of their being caught in a snowstorm, and of how the men driving them went ahead and broke trail for the bewildered beasts, many of whom perished in the cold.

No matter where I started my day's work, the dredge and its endless gray hummocks of washed stones drew me to the banks of the Blue. It was placer mining that brought the first miners and settlers to Breckenridge, for the ground was so rich that a man could make wages panning the dirt in the gutter. And had there been an abundance of waterpower, hydraulic mining would no doubt have been introduced when the placers were exhausted, but the Blue and its tributaries could provide neither enough water nor sufficient pressure to wash down the banks of the streams in whose beds the golden particles had lain. For years the placer claims remained untouched while prospectors carried on lode mining in the hills; and it was not until 1907 that Ben Stanley Revett introduced boat-mining by means of dredges and built the first two hulls, one of which floats in its pond behind Breckenridge's main thoroughfare. Each dredge by means of its metal fingers and complicated machinery was able to dig up, wash and screen huge amounts of gold-bearing gravel and thus clean up placer deposits which had been abandoned as "worked out."

Smaller dredges were built to operate in the nearby gulches, eating their way up the streams and leaving behind the useless mountains of neatly stacked stones. The earth was rich, the boats recovered the elusive gold and Breckenridge boomed for the third time. The Tonopah Shops were built at one

OLD FIREHOUSE,
BRECKENRIDGE (GONE)

TIGER ON THE SWAN RIVER

TONOPAH SHOPS, BRECKENRIDGE, WHERE DREDGE
MACHINERY WAS MADE AND REPAIRED (GONE)

end of town to equip and repair the machinery, and years after the dredges squatted idly in the mud, the large red buildings stood empty beside the highway. In the scrap metal drive during World War II they disappeared, and another landmark is gone.

Lincoln City   "Go up French Gulch if you want to see dredging," said the garage man as he filled the tank of the car. "Four miles up you'll find what is left of Lincoln City and you'll see Farncomb Hill where the 'Wire Patch' was." Never having heard of the Wire Patch or of Farncomb Hill I was eager to explore new territory and, taking two companions, started up the road which cut through pine woods at the edge of town and brought us with startling suddenness to the brink of the gravel-filled waste of French Gulch. Piles of rock were everywhere as far as one could see, and as the road skirted the gulch for some distance we were more and more amazed at the immensity of the dredging operations that had produced this devastation. The gulch was wide, and to cross it the road had to dip and twist in and out around the mounds which in some places were higher than the car, so that it was like riding through a narrow canyon whose walls were almost close enough to touch. One empty house stands stranded in the middle of the gulch, and by scrambling over loose stones we reached it and explored its interior. No furniture was left in it, but wallpaper of the nineties or early nineteen hundreds hung in limp shreds from the walls, and the floor buckled and sagged under our feet.

Once out of the bed of French Gulch, we rolled along past the Wellington mine with its colony of idle sheds, past the Country Boy and the Minnie, until we saw a few scattered cabins and some half-overgrown foundations and knew that Lincoln City must be close by. Parking the car, I started up the road toward the cabins. The first two were deserted but a line of wash waved from the third, and approaching it I heard voices. Climbing the steep bank onto the porch, I knocked at the door. Two men answered the knock, and to my question as to how close Lincoln City was they replied, "You're in it."

While one of the men began to talk about the early days of the camp, the other went into the cabin and returned with a small glass full of gold dust and a pill box containing a gold nugget wrapped in paper. Both specimens were from Farncomb Hill, and stepping to the edge of the porch he pointed to a nearby, yellowish hillside full of dumps and said, "That's it." The men seemed glad to have a visitor and broke in on each other to tell additional facts about the place. From them I learned that Lincoln City grew up in the sixties, shortly after Breckenridge, and that it had had a fluctuating population of from three hundred to fifteen hundred. It had reached its peak during the eighties, when good dirt was found in the bed rock of French Gulch and paying lode operations were developed on Farncomb, Mineral, Nigger and Humbug hills.

Harry Farncomb came to Breckenridge as a young man and engaged in placer mining in French Gulch near the base of the hill which he later acquired. The deposits of gold in the streambed were so rich at this point that he decided to search for their source, which he believed was somewhere

(78)

FARNCOMB
HILL

LINCOLN
CITY

above the workings. He bought a few acres of the land and kept adding to it until he owned a considerable portion of the hillside. This he then developed, finding crystallized gold, which looked like matted, tangled wire, in such quantities that he became one of the wealthiest men in Breckenridge. Not until he deposited a sack of the gold in a Denver bank was there any trouble; but immediately thereafter, a conspiracy was formed to wrest the property from him by force, and what followed became known as the "Ten Years' War." The fight broke a bank, provoked a battle on the property which lasted for seven hours and involved forty men, caused a legal war in which some of Colorado's ablest lawyers participated, and caused the death of three men. Finally the property was bought by neutral "parties," and the struggle for possession ended. Walking back to the car I saw more foundations, one of which was probably that of the Lincoln City Smelting Works, and I tried unsuccessfully to find the location of the original city which had been a mile distant from its later site.

Next morning, just before leaving Breckenridge I took a last look at the exterior of the Silverthorn Hotel. While I was peeping in the windows a car drove up, a man jumped out and coming up to me said, "Do you want to see the inside of the hotel?" Producing a key he unlocked the door and ushered me into a low-ceilinged room full of furniture, boxes and odds and ends, all thickly coated with dust. "Didn't I meet you yesterday up at Lincoln City?" he continued, and to be sure, he was one of the men from the cabin. It was so dark in the building that I followed close behind him as he endeavored to show the rest of the hotel, pushing boxes and chairs about and lifting aside musty draperies which covered the doors to the ballroom, sleeping rooms and the store. He produced a candle, lighted it, and pressed it into my hand, while he fumbled with locks which his key would not open. The candle flickered and dripped in the dead air, revealing only more discarded furniture and packing cases. When we were outside again I sighed with relief that the place hadn't gone up in flames while we were exploring it with our feeble light.

Swan City

The night before, I learned that extensive placer and dredge mining had been carried on along the Swan River, not far from where we were; so at a fork in the road we began to follow the Swan, passing the level swamplands where Delaware Flats was situated and along the willow-edged marshy meadows to the site of Swan City. Not a vestige of it remained. We drove on several miles to Tiger, a deserted company town where no one lived but the watchman, who appeared from nowhere the minute the car came to a stop.

Tiger

Tiger is a much more recent town than any other in the region and is therefore very well preserved. Its big bunkhouse, general store and employees' cabins are in good repair and could be used at a moment's notice. I knew little about the place except that the property, which includes the old IXL and Cashier lodes, was now known as the Royal Tiger Mines and that as late as 1930 much money had been spent to develop it and to build the mill and town, but with meager returns.

By the side of the road was an iron ball about the size of a cannon ball. "That," said the watchman, "is one of the balls from the Ball Mill in which the ore was crushed. There was a hopper full of those balls and they ground the ore to powder. If you can lift that ball you can have it," he added slyly; and as he spoke I saw in my mind's eye that black ball resting beside the hearth at home and causing much comment. It was heavy, and it took both hands, but as I eased it off the ground the old watchman nodded to himself and opened the car door so that I might deposit the prize gently on the floor. After this he became more talkative and told how, when the mill was running, it was necessary to use sleds half the year to haul the concentrates to the railroad. He spoke of the gulch mining that had been done above Tiger at Swandyke, and of the frame of the dredge that was still resting in the river bed. He mentioned Swanville and the early prospectors who had done placer digging at Georgia Gulch, when the Swan with its tributary gulches was the most prolific of all the gold producing districts of the section. He described Parkville on the South Swan, which had bristled with life and activity during the boom of the sixties and had had its own theatre, and when we left he called after us, "Those were great days, and I saw some of them myself; but it's all past now, and there aren't many today who come to Tiger on the Swan."

Hoosier Pass lies to the south of Breckenridge, and on many a trip over the pass I had looked at Mt. Lincoln and at the distant mill at its foot, which marks the site of Montgomery; but not until 1947 did I leave the highway and explore the forgotten town. Walter Johnson was my companion on this trip, and as the car climbed the divide we talked about Montgomery, the little camp that once polled the most votes in the mining district. At the top we stopped to enjoy the view. To the right was a bowl of snowclad peaks with Mt. Lincoln and Mt. Bross the closest, and Sheep and Horseshoe Mountains farther away. Beyond were the high mountain meadows of South Park, and on the horizon the faint, silhouetted peaks on the far side of the open basin. Close by, at the end of a narrowing valley, lay the site of Montgomery, one of the oldest camps in the state, which flourished in 1861 and by 1870 was but a husk of itself.

Montgomery

There is a new road leading to Montgomery along the valley floor and up to the new Magnolia Mill above the waterfall, but from the top of Hoosier Pass the old highway winds down the mountain; and it was this road that we took. It is not kept up, and in places it was so washed and rocky and full of gullies that I began to wonder if the Ford could straddle the ruts and ride over the washed-out cuts. We got down somehow, drove till the road at the foot of the mountain turned to eroded sand, parked the car and began to hunt for the old town. Up the hill above the waterfall and the Magnolia Mill we discovered, among the trees and half-hidden by bushes, a number of cabin frames and hollows in the ground, the latter marking the location of other cabins whose timbers had long since rotted into the earth. Above the mill the road flattened out, and we entered another valley, blanketed with alpine flowers, growing flat to the ground or hidden in rock crevices, and dotted with small clear lakes which reflected the great peaks with their snowy crowns. High on the mountainside were old shaft houses and mine tunnels, one of which, called Robber's Roost, was reached by a crazy ladder of over two hundred rungs which was hung perpendicularly against the cliff face and was the only means of access to the mouth of the mine.

Retracing our steps down the mountain and looking out over the marshy flat at its base, we saw only the ruins of a stamp mill and a row of three or four skeleton cabins to suggest that at one time Montgomery had three streets, a two-story hotel and the largest theatre in the region. This theatre became the dancehall whenever a ball was given, and the dancers came from miles around, the girls in wagons with their party clothes in bundles on their laps, and the men riding horseback behind the wagons. The camp grew rapidly until the middle sixties; but by then the readily worked ore had been exhausted and only hard rock confronted the miners, so that one by one they abandoned their claims and slipped away. During the seventies the camp slept; but in 1881, when silver was discovered on Mt. Lincoln and on Mt. Bross and the towns of Alma and Quartzville sprang up, mining was resumed at Montgomery, even though many of its more substantial houses were torn down and rebuilt at the two new camps. Another revival of mining at Montgomery commenced in 1898 and continued with increased acitvity into the early nineteen hundreds. Every house in town was occupied, and there was even talk of building an electric road to the mines, but the boom was shortlived and the road was never built.

Quartzville   On our way back to the car I noticed a half-obliterated trail which started at Montgomery and disappeared from sight high on Mt. Bross. "That must be one of the trails to Quartzville," I told Walter. "I want to go to Quartzville, but it's a four-mile hike to timberline by the regular trail from Dudleyville, and maybe this is a shorter way to go. Let's see if we can find out." There was no one to ask, however, so we started to drive down the valley toward Fairplay. Before we had gone three miles I noticed a group of men building a sluice along the stream and driving as near them as possible I asked them about the trail we had seen.

"Sure, that's the old mule trail to Quartzville," said the boss of the group. "But don't take it. It's full of rock slides and I doubt if you could get across them in some places." Thanking him for the information, we were about to leave, when he called us back. "If you two want to go to Quartzville why don't you go from here? It's only a mile and a half this way. There's no trail and it's straight up the mountain. Gets pretty steep in spots, but you can't lose your way and it's a lot shorter. You just go up through this patch of timber and keep the stream on your left. After you are out of the timber you climb straight up until you come to the power line. Follow it to the left a quarter of a mile till it turns to the right and goes up to the Russia and Moose mines. Keep straight ahead and you'll see Quartzville in the hollow below you. It's just below timberline."

Walter and I looked at each other. We hadn't planned to go to Quartzville that day, it was nearly noon, and we'd already hiked three miles around Montgomery. Besides, we had no lunch with us and we had no certainty that we could get to Quartzville on account of snowdrifts, for this was June and snow lies at the high altitudes until July. "What do you think?" I asked dubiously. "I'm game if you are," he replied; whereupon our miner started

(82)

OLD SMELTER, DUDLEYVILLE

to stride ahead of us, calling over his shoulder, "I'll take you up into the timber and start you right and you can go on from there. If you aren't back by sundown, we'll look for you."

We started for Quartzville. The man was right—there was no trail and we had to push aside branches and work our way between them or pick spots for our feet among rocks and roots. At one point the stream was at our side and the ground was slippery, not only from pine needles but from spray. Before long we were out of the trees and could see our way ahead all the way to timberline. The terrain on this part of the climb was steep and rough. Dead stumps were everywhere, for it had originally been a forest which the prospectors cut down to provide timber for their mine buildings and tunnels, for their cabins and for fuel. Long matted grass, flattened by the winter's snow, hid rocks and chipmunk holes from sight ; so hiking was a slow process, as each step had to be tested.

The higher we climbed the more breathless we got, for we had started from the valley at ten thousand feet elevation, and according to the maps Quartzville was eleven thousand five hundred feet. It was necessary to stop and breathe every fifty or hundred feet, balancing ourselves on the slanting earth which rose at about a forty degree angle. Far away, at what appeared to be the top of the mountain, was the power line, and toward it we labored step by step. Each time we stopped to rest, not sitting but standing in good mountain climbing fashion so as not to waste any energy in getting up again, the view around us was stupendous. On every side were high peaks, and in the distance the flat endless meadows of South Park seemed to merge with the cloud strata. By the time our hearts stopped pumping so wildly and our breathing became normal again, we would stride on for another lap of the climb. Each spurt brought us nearer to the power line, and never had telephone and light poles looked so good before. Long before we reached them we had to detour around great snowbanks. Except for the sound of the wind the silence was overpowering; yet to be so high and so alone was an exhilarating experience.

The nearer we got to timberline the more animals we saw—fat marmots, who whistled at us peremptorily or sidled away through the tundra, and jack rabbits which were startled from hiding and crossed the snowbanks with great leaps. When we reached the power line we felt as if our goal was near, but there was still more climbing to be done. Some stunted bushes and ground-pine grew at this altitude, and a mere trail below the poles was cut through this growth. Following this we continued climbing until suddenly we looked down into a hollow, and there was Quartzville.

It lay in a cup of the mountains in the last stand of timber, and above it was the rocky summit of Mt. Bross covered with immense snow fields. At first we saw no buildings at all, but as we scrutinized the land below us we spotted first one and then another dilapidated cabin half hidden in the trees or sagging into the boggy meadow. Half sliding down the hill into the town site we examined its few rotting cabins and its corduroy bridge over a stream. Crossing the bridge we found two large log-house frames, in front of which were deep ruts through the marsh, all that was left of a street. The other cabins were scattered over such a wide area that it was impossible to locate where streets or roads had once been. Both of us made sketches and ate the last crumbs of some crackers I had fortunately put in my pocket that morning, and scooped up handfuls of clean snow to quench our thirst.

When we were ready to leave a question arose—which way should we go back? The way we had come meant climbing up to the power line again, while right before us was a well-defined road which we believed to be the other trail of which we had heard. We decided upon the untried road, and for the first mile our progress was easy and pleasant, and as we walked I told Walter the little that I knew about Quartzville—how it was built in the seventies and flourished until the early eighties, when it had a bank and a population of nearly 2,000. All of its five promising mines were silver bearing ore except the Democrat, in which some free gold was found. The Hoil group of mines was worked perhaps longer than the others, and when it closed down many of the cabins were removed to other locations.

The road now cut through a meadow in which stood two cabins and as suddenly ended. We scouted about and could find no trace of it, but soon we discovered a foot trail leading in the right direction. The next half mile was easy; then again our trail disappeared. Crossing a log footbridge over a rushing stream we picked up the trail and went merrily along until it ended in a thicket of bushes and trees on the brink of the same little stream. This we jumped, only to find we were on an island with the main stream still in front of us. It wasn't very big but it was too wide to jump, and it was so deep and tumbling so fast that it could not be waded.

Tired as we were, the thought of retracing our steps seemed impossible— there must be a way to get across. I noticed some branches and roots which extended out over the stream and almost formed a natural bridge across it, but whether they would bear our weight remained to be seen. Telling Walter to fish me out if I catapulted into the rushing water I stepped gingerly onto the mat of branches. They held. I knelt upon them and began to crawl out over them, waiting for them to break under me. They still held. Inch by inch I crawled further over the dashing water until I could step to the opposite bank and climb it. Walter threw the camera and sketch pad over to me and crawled over too. We had scarcely gone any distance before we discovered our lost road, and the rest of the trip was simple and without adventure. When we reached the car, I sank wearily into the driver's seat and started the motor, while Walter hunted up the man who had put us on the trail and told him we were safely back.

Though we were worn out from our scramble to timberline and back, we were also elated by our accomplishment, especially as just the day before a friend had pointed out to us the real four-mile trail through the "quakers" and had warned us against trying it because of the deep drifts which would still be lying in the pine and aspen groves. "Come back next month and try it," he suggested. "By July you can make it easy." We looked at the thin slit through the aspen grove that marked the road he had pointed out, but it no longer held any interest for us. By the time we reached Dudleyville, we had revived sufficiently to detour to its old smelter and to climb down through the empty

Dudleyville

(85)

building, which once handled the ores from the Moose. Russia and Dolly Varden mines, located high on Mt. Bross, even above Quartzville. It was mid-afternoon when we drove down Alma's main street, ravenously hungry and looking for a place to eat. While we sipped hot soup and nibbled an ice cream cone, we agreed that the day had been a little wearing but a huge success.

Fairplay

In June 1942 I collected two adventurous friends to accompany me on a three weeks' trip to as many remote camps as I could reach. Jim Zeigler, a student, was the chauffeur, and knowing that he had driven coal trucks in Denver I felt confident that he could handle the coupe on any type of mountain road. Not until we were well on the trip did I ask him about his mountain driving experience, only to learn that he'd never done any! But by the time he was home again he was a graduate in mountain grades and hair-pin turns. Victoria had never explored the lesser known parts of the state and welcomed the opportunity to go along. She became the historian of the trip, reading pertinent facts from guidebooks as we approached each objective, talking to all the oldtimers whom we encountered, and jotting down her findings for my use, so that my entire time might be spent in sketching. One of our first objectives was Fairplay, in the middle of South Park, not because it was a ghost town but because it was one of the oldest of the mining centers and was full of history.

In 1859 when "Pike's Peak or Bust" was the slogan which brought thousands of men to the west, to tear at the earth along the eastern rim of the Rocky Mountains, some who had not succeeded in finding gold drifted more deeply into the hills and made their way across the broad expenses of South Park to the banks of a creek in which they found the colors they had been seeking. Here they made a camp, calling it Tarryall, and so jealous were they of their location that they ran off all newcomers who tried to join them. In indignation, these late arrivals dubbed the flourishing camp Graball and pushing on found gold in the deep gravel bars of the South Platte River. A mining district was established, a town of log cabins was hastily constructed, and mining laws were drawn up. Only a name was lacking. Jim Reynolds, a prospector who later became the leader of a notorious band of highwaymen, made himself boss of the camp and demanded "fairplay" for everyone. When a committee met to choose a name for the newly platted town, "Fairplay" was suggested and unanimously accepted. The town grew steadily, having the usual number of hotels and dance halls, and twelve bawdy houses; and even after the placer mining played out and prospectors commenced to mine the surrounding hills and mountains of the Park Range, Fairplay remained the trading center of the region.

Years later dredge mining began and is still being carried on by the largest gold dredge in the state, which is scooping up acre after acre of land along the bed of the Platte. As long as the dredge operates Fairplay prospers, for it is the main industry directly connected with the place. Its shrieking and clanging machinery can be heard in town even though the dredge is situated about two miles away. If the night shift is working, the lights of the great hull twinkle in the dark like a miniature city, while its groaning and squeaking

(86)

FAIRPLAY COMMUNITY CHURCH

FAIRPLAY COURTHOUSE

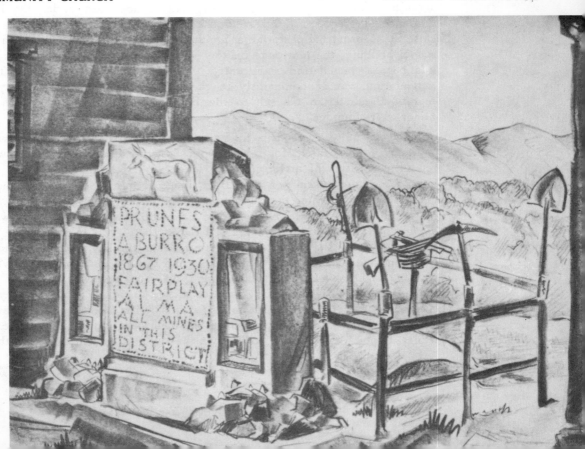

PRUNES' GRAVE, FAIRPLAY

bucket chain sucks the dripping gold-bearing mud into the belly of the boat.

Whether one approaches South Park from Colorado Springs or from Denver the first view of the vast mountain meadowland is breath-taking. Seventy-five miles long and twenty wide, it lies so far below the highway that grazing cattle look like dots and the town of Jefferson at the foot of Kenosha Pass seems no larger than an average ranch. On all sides of this mountain valley, which is ten thousand feet in elevation, are mountains—blue silhouettes in the distance and rocky peaks close by, where they form the western barrier beyond which lie the Arkansas Valley and the valley of the Blue. The Park is especially lovely in late spring when the wild iris is in bloom and the meadows are blue with its blossoms. The highway stretches ahead like a ribbon toward Fairplay, but low hills hide the town from view until one is almost in its streets. The road from the north cuts through a grove of trees and suddenly, spread out on the flat at the foot of the hill, reveals Fairplay.

Three buildings dominate the town, the Fairplay Hotel (a modern structure), the stone Courthouse, and the Community Church. The church stands by itself, surrounded by a cast iron fence, a gleaming white bit of American Gothic transplanted to the Rockies. It was erected in 1874, two years after Dr. Sheldon Jackson, a Presbyterian pastor, reached Fairplay and organized a church, which ever since has served not only the town but the surrounding ranch and mountain territory. Two sounds belong to Fairplay, the screech of the dredge and the peal of the church bell which has cut the still air since it was hung in its white cupola in 1875. For years it was the only bell in town and was used as a school bell and as a fire alarm, as well as for Sunday services. For the past ten years the church has been under the inspired guidance of the Rev. J. N. Hillhouse whose comfortable log manse stands close by. During his pastorate a Youth Center has been established in an old school building, the mortgage on the Manse has been lifted, and the church has been renamed and redecorated. In 1945 the congregation, after due deliberation, voted unanimously to change the name of the Fairplay Community Presbyterian Church to the Sheldon Jackson Memorial Chapel in honor of its founder.

On virtually every trip to Fairplay I make at least one drawing or painting of the church, for it is the most picturesque building in town and represents a style of architecture no longer found in the mountains. Never having seen the interior, on this trip I hoped to meet the Rev. Hillhouse and get permission to enter the building; but the Manse was closed, and he and his family were away. The following day, while talking to a lady who has always lived in Fairplay, I expressed regret that I couldn't enter the church and asked her if she could tell me if anyone had the key to the building. "It's with someone here in town," she replied; and turning to a young girl who was working in her kitchen she said, "Anne, do you know where it is?" "Yes," replied the girl, "I have it in my sweater pocket, or rather, I have the key to the Manse. The key to the church hangs just inside the front door on a nail. Just go in and get it." So, feeling a little like a burglar and decidedly like an intruder, I entered the Manse, took down the key and, hastening across the road to the church, made my sketch. The interior was a little disappointing for it was not so picturesquely Gothic as the exterior, but its sturdy pews and well-worn carpet showed signs of constant use. An open hymn book stood on the piano, fresh curtains hung at the tall windows, and by the side of a comfortably large stove was a well-filled coal and wood box. The building had such a pleasant and friendly atmosphere that I did not wonder that it was the social center for South Park.

The two-story, sandstone courthouse, built in 1874, is the oldest in Colorado and has played its part in the history of Park County. In it all the women and children were placed for safety during the Indian scare of 1879, when a drunken fool, who had shot holes in his hat, rode a lathered horse into town and announced breathlessly that Indians were burning Breckenridge and scalping everyone there and that the band was headed for Fairplay. Immediately the town was in a panic, the men drilling and gathering what ammunition they could find, while scouts rode off toward the doomed camp to reconnoitre. Not an Indian could be found in the entire county, and when the scouts returned with this information, the man whose drunken imagination invented the story hid in an attic until the people's anger cooled and he could get away.

It was the janitor of the courthouse who told me about the lynching that occurred there in 1880. I had wanted to sketch the courtroom, but it was locked and no one seemed to know the whereabouts of the key. Finally, with the help of the magistrate, I located the janitor who had the key, and together we climbed the handsome, curved, white staircase to the historic courtroom. It was a big room with many windows and big comfortable chairs, and while I drew, the janitor tipped back in one of them and told me this story.

There was a good deal of lawlessness and not enough swift justice in Fairplay in the late seventies, when the town had a population of over a thousand persons and was still growing; so when a brutal murderer was tried and given a life sentence instead of the death penalty which he deserved, the citizens were aroused and took the law into their own hands. Late that night a band of Vigilantes marched to the sheriff's house and demanded the keys to the jail, which he refused to surrender. Taking him with them, they surrounded the jail, broke down the door, locked the sheriff in a cell, and took possession of the prisoner. Next morning his limp body dangled from the second story window of the courthouse, almost blocking the doorway when Judge Bowen, who had sentenced him, entered the building. Reaching the courtroom the Judge was startled to see a noosed rope thrown across his bench and another lying on the table marked "for the District Attorney." Both of these gentlemen lost no time in hiring a rig and driving to the Red Hill station of the railroad, where they waited apprehensively for the first train to Denver.

"That year 1880 was surely a bad one," continued the janitor. "Not only was Hoover, the murderer, lynched as I just told you, but there was another lynching too. A drunk named Sam Porter announced that he would kill the first man he met. Shortly afterwards John Carmody came around a corner and was instantly shot by Porter. In less than half an hour a group of men nailed a stout beam to the outside wall of the jail and threw a noosed rope over it. Just before the noose was tightened Porter was asked if he had anything to say, to which he instantly replied, 'Yes, pull.' "

I was still sketching, so the janitor commenced a third tale. "Fairplay had its jail breaks and perhaps the strangest one was due to a violin. The jail used to be in this building and we had a couple of pretty tough characters in the cooler when it happened, as well as a young chap who was something of a musician. He had a fiddle and used to play hours at a time to amuse himself. This tough guy was planning to light out and had a file with which to cut the cell bars, but he knew the noise of his filing would be a give-away; so he persuaded the boy to fiddle, and while he played, the man sawed. Finally he cut through the bars and made his getaway. The kid with the fiddle lit out with him but instead of escaping ran to the sheriff and reported the escape. Funny things happen in a jail."

On the main street is the grave of Prunes, a burro. The first time I visited the grave it was late summer, and tall grass and wildflowers almost hid the low mounds which mark the location of the bones of the animal and the ashes of the man who requested to be buried beside his partner. Fastened to the iron fence surrounding the plot were the pick, shovel and other tools which Rupert Sherwood, the old prospector, used during fifty years of mining in the vicinity. At the front of the plot was a monument, and a more unique memorial was never seen. A large stone or concrete block was surmounted by a bronze plaque on which in bas-relief was a portrait of the faithful Prunes, while beneath was an inscription which read: "Prunes, A Burro. 1867-1930. Fairplay, Alma, All Mines in This District." This inscription was made of colored marbles, pressed into the concrete face of the slab, but their novelty had tempted too many souvenir hunters, for nearly half of them had been pried out. At the sides, glass-fronted cases contained newspaper clippings and photographs of Prunes and his master and the entire monument was set with specimens of ore from all the mines in which the burro had worked.

Prunes had many owners and packed in many trains to and from the mines of Alma, Fairplay, Buckskin, Mosquito, Quartzville and Montgomery. He was known to have wandered alone down trails on errands and to have waited patiently in front of a store until the written order tied to his bridle was read and a load of provisions was packed on his back. His last owner was Rupert M. Sherwood, who came to the mountains in 1877 and prospected, trapped and mined all over the area until his death in 1930. When the burro grew too old to work he was allowed to wander about the alleys of Alma and Fairplay appearing at back doors and accepting any food given to him, for by now his sight was so dim that he could not forage for himself. Finally he died, and his many friends decided to mark his grave in some suitable way. A year later, when the old prospector, Rupe Sherwood, lay dying he made a request that he be placed in the same grave with his old pal, and his wishes were carried out by the citizens of Fairplay.

Mosquito→ Not far from the foot of Hoosier Pass is Alma, which is as brisk a place as Fairplay, and close to Alma are some forgotten camps that I wanted to see. One of these was Mosquito, or Musquito as it was originally written, which

(90)

was settled in June 1861, much as Montgomery had been, by prospectors who were attracted by the placer gold found in the creek bed. Almost immediately a meeting was held to organize a mining district and to choose a proper name for it. Of the several that were proposed none met with the general approval, and the meeting broke up before one had been selected. When the book in which the minutes of the meeting were recorded was opened at the next gathering of the miners, it was found that a large mosquito lay crushed between the pages, and by unanimous vote the district became known as Mosquito. By 1882 two hundred and fifty men were working in the gulch or climbing up the perpendicular cliffs to tunnels high above the streambed, and a small town called Mosquito grew up around the stage station and saloon.

Long before a toll road was begun over Mosquito Pass, the London and other paying mines were discovered and developed. The London mine is still one of the largest in the county, and on our ride up Mosquito Gulch we saw its gleaming group of buildings close to timberline long before we reached the junction of the road, one fork of which leads to the mine. The other fork leads over old Mosquito Pass to Leadville, cutting the distance to the carbonate camp in half. Even when stagecoaches began to make regular runs between Alma and Leadville in the eighties, and freighters' wagons lined the pass, it was a difficult road to travel. The upper portion was a toll road and was fairly well maintained, but the stretch below the toll station on the Alma side was poorly graded and rough. A good part of the year the top of the pass lay covered with snow, for its summit was 13,280 feet, and travel was treacherous. During the winter only hardy mail-carriers and other determined men crossed the range on snowshoes or glided down the steep slopes on skiis, always alert for sudden snow slides which could bury a man in an instant under tons of packed snow. At other seasons footpads lay in wait for the slow-moving stagecoach, ready to rob its "box" of gold dust and securities. A Fairplay doctor made more than one trip across the pass to treat patients at Oro and on one such mission encountered six mountain lions on the trail. He was unarmed, and only his lusty yelling turned the beasts back into the timber. Another time he was called to Leadville and upon his arrival found that he must amputate a patient's arm. Not having his surgical kit with him he was forced to borrow dental tools and a meat saw and with these improvised instruments he performed a successful operation.

There was little to see at Mosquito except scenery, for its buildings are gone and its mines deserted. The giant windmill, with its sixty-foot arms, which was built at the London mine to furnish power for the compressor and drills is gone, blown down in a storm. Only the trail over Mosquito Pass remains, and although it has been closed for years, it can still be seen zigzagging up the mountainside over bare rock, until it is lost between the shoulders of two peaks.

Buckskin Joe   On the way to Buckskin Joe I told my companions the story of Silver Heels. She was one of the dancehall girls, and everyone agrees about her extraordinary beauty; though some say she lived in Fairplay and some in Buckskin Joe. A new face could always arouse excitement among the women-hungry men of the camps, and from the day that she stepped daintily from the stagecoach which brought her to the mountains, she became the idol of all the miners and the envy of the other camp women whose charms were not so great. No one remembers her real name, for the whiskered miners called her Silver Heels and fought for a chance to dance with her. Late in 1861 sickness swept the camp, and almost overnight most of the miners were desperately ill. This was not the usual pneumonia which took its annual toll in all the camps, but smallpox, which left its victims pitted and scarred. Each day the living carried the dead to the little hillside cemetery and buried them under the aspens. Business was suspended and the dancehalls were deserted. Everyone who was not stricken helped as much as possible; but the danger was great, nurses were scarce, and only two or three responded to a frantic telegram which was sent to Denver imploring help. During these days of horror, Silver Heels went from cabin to cabin, caring for the sick and dying men and easing their last moments. Finally, she too was stricken and through her long and serious illness was tenderly cared for by the surviving citizens. Gradually the epidemic passed, and the remaining miners resumed their digging. Newcomers arriving in camp were told of the heroism of the girl who willingly risked her life and looks to nurse the stricken men and was eventually stricken herself. In gratitude the miners made up a purse of $5,000 and took it to her cabin, but there was no response to their knocking, and in bewilderment they left. A search for the girl proved fruitless; and no trace of her was ever found. One version of the story mentions that years later a heavily veiled woman was seen weeping over the graves in the little hillside cemetery but that she slipped away before she could be overtaken. Perhaps it was Silver Heels whose beauty had been sacrificed during the plague and who thereafter shunned contact with her former admirers. In any event, the purse was returned to its donors and the people of Fairplay and Buckskin Joe, not to be thwarted in their gesture of gratitude, named a mountain in her honor. Mt. Silverheels rises behind Fairplay, a majestic monument to the mysterious girl whose silver slippers intoxicated a camp and whose unselfish nursing saved so many lives.

There is so little left of Buckskin Joe that on my first trip to this ghost town I was distinctly disappointed. Where was the long gulch street with its cabins and its saloons in which two thousand men had gambled? Glancing around, I saw little to indicate what Buckskin must have looked like in 1861, when the Phillips Lode was discovered and the lonely gulch became a milling camp practically overnight.

"What brought us here?" asked Jim, expertly maneuvering the car around a deep rut in the road, "There's no town for you to sketch."

"I see two buildings, and we're driving on the main street, and we passed the cemetery as we came in, and, look, across the gulch is a big log cabin. Let's go over and see what it was."

While I sketched the meagre remains of the once flourishing camp I told Victoria and Jim something of its history: "Prospectors swarmed all over this country in 1860, pushing up gulches beyond Tarryall and Fairplay, and wherever they found gold in the stream a camp grew up. Joseph Higgenbottom, known as 'Buckskin Joe' because of the leather clothes he wore, made a placer strike in 1860 at this place, and naturally, as soon as the news got out,

other prospectors poured in. Among the first to come were Griff Harris, J. P. Stancell, M. Phillips and N. J. Bond. They and others organized a mining district and at the same time christened their sprouting camp Buckskin Joe. Late in 1861 the Phillips Lode was struck, and Buckckin was on the map. Hoards of disappointed prospectors from California Gulch poured over the range to the new diggings at the rate of seventy-five to a hundred and twenty-five a day, and the little camp became a booming town. The district was re-organized by the miners and new laws were drawn up. Even the name of the town was changed to Laurette in honor of the only two women residents, Mrs. Laura Dodge and her sister Mrs. Jeannette Dodge.

"The Phillips, the most fabulous lode in the county, consisted of a vein of quartz twenty-five to sixty feet wide, and its ore was free milling. During 1861 and 1862 it was worked to its utmost production, and from its open pit over $500,000 was taken during that period. Phillips sold his share in the mine soon after its discovery, but Stancell, Harris and the others who developed it found such rich deposits almost at the grass roots that they were said to have taken pay dirt out by the bushel. At first the gold was gathered in sluices and in arastras built along the stream, and as one old-timer put it, "The gold came in at every turn of the wheel.' "

"What on earth is an arastra?" interrupted Jim at this point.

"It's a primitive method of crushing ore," I replied. "In fact, it's such an early method that one or two old Spanish arastras that antedate any known mining here can be seen further up this gulch. A hollow stone basin is prepared in such a way that water can flow in and out of it. In this hollow a heavy stone is fastened to a windlass and a wheel, and depending upon the size of the arastra, a man or a mule walks round and round, turning the wheel and dragging the stone, which by its sheer weight grinds the ore which is fed into the basin, while the water washes away the pulverized and worthless rock and sand, leaving the heavy gold particles on the bottom.

"Before long nine stamp mills were erected and they pounded away at the rich soil which was dug from the open pit. The vein quartz ran well under the stamps, until a depth of thirty or more feet was reached. At this depth the easily milled, oxidized ore changed to sulphides which could not be broken down by the stamps, and so much gold was lost by this process of extraction that mining almost ceased. Almost overnight the town folded up. Cabins were torn down, the stamp mills were removed, the miners left, and by 1864 Buckskin, which had once surpassed both Mosquito and Montgomery in size, was deserted.

"Buckskin had the first courthouse in the district. It was Buckskin Joe's log cabin, and the sheriff of the town held an election in it in 1864. A year or so later it was moved to Fairplay, where it served as a courthouse until the present one was built. It is a private home today, standing in the middle of a block of houses across the street from the stone courthouse which took its place.

"That cabin over there with the big window was H. A. W. Tabor's grocery store. He worked a claim here and his wife, Augusta, kept boarders;

and the two-story log house across the creek was one of the dancehalls—perhaps the one where Silver Heels performed.

"In its boom days the town had its own newspaper, stage office, theatres and saloons, billiard halls, a post office, a dancing school, and all the necessary stores, as well as a Grand Hotel and the Bank of Stancell, Bond and Harris. Stancell, who was one of the early owners of the Phillips mine, became the richest man in the camp less than a year after he left Oro, where he had been a door-keeper in one of the theatres. Even when mining ceased at Buckskin, his faith in the Phillips Lode was unshaken, and he stayed on, working the mine for years, although he was practically the only resident who remained. That's all I know about the early days except the stories about Father Dyer, a Methodist preacher who came to Colorado in 1861 and made his headquarters here. He preached in all the mountain camps, crossing the range on foot to Oro and Breckenridge, summer and winter. At Mosquito he preached by the side of a campfire before any houses were built there. One Sunday he walked the eight miles from Buckskin to Montgomery, intending to preach to the miners there. When he arrived there was only one man in camp as all the rest were out staking claims, so he climbed on up to Quartzville where he preached to a group of thirty men. At Buckskin an old gambling hall was his meeting place, and he had keen competition from the variety theaters, dancing school, saloons and gaming houses. During the week, when he wasn't preaching he carried the mail between Buckskin and Oro, with a thirty-pound pack on his back each trip. During the winter he made the trip on what he called snowshoes, which were really Norwegian skiis; and more than once he narrowly escaped losing his life in blizzards and snowslides. He wrote an account of his experiences and called it 'The Snowshoe Itinerant,' and to anyone who knows this territory it is thrilling reading."

"Let's drive up the road a few miles and see if we can find those Spanish arastras," said Jim, starting the engine, and off we went up Buckskin Gulch toward the Paris mine. We found one well-worn arastra, hollowed out of some big stones along the stream, and got out of the car to investigate it. The canyon narrowed as we drove deeper into it, and there were old shaft houses perched on ledges at the very top of the cliff walls, like bird nests tucked into inaccessible crannies.

As we drove back through Buckskin Joe and on toward the highway, I caught a glimpse of the cemetery on top of a low hill. Scrambling up to it, we wandered through an aspen grove, examining the graves. Some of them were nearly eighty years old and were marked by weathered, wooden head-boards. At least half of them were surrounded by wooden or iron fences, while in some plots small evergreens or aspen saplings had seeded themselves. It was cool in the cemetery and through the fringe of trees the distant peaks were silhouetted against a blue sky. From the hilltop we could see the site of Buckskin Joe and I wished, as I so often do, that I could have seen the town when mining was at its peak, or even in 1879, when a mild boom brought prospectors back to the surrounding territory. This time their discoveries were not along the gulch but at timberline, and at night their campfires dotted the hills; but the boom was shortlived, and by 1881 Buckskin was a ghost camp once more, just as it is today.

Before we left the Fairplay area we asked if there were any ghost towns we had missed. "Well, there's Horseshoe and Leavick, and of course, up Tarryall Creek there was Hamilton, but it's all gone now; and in the nineties there was a little flurry of mining over at Puma City; and the other side of Kenosha Pass is Hall Valley. That's about all," said our informant.

Next day we started for the first two places, taking the first dirt road beyond the Platte and following its rocky and rutted surface for twelve or fourteen miles. At first we crossed meadowland, where the road was lost in marshy mud and herds of mountain cattle grazed on the lush, wild hay. Then it wound through groves of aspen and pine, where spring torrents had completely cut away the surface, leaving exposed boulders and rocks which had to be straddled or driven around, with the car tipped at precarious angles. Climbing steadily all the time, we reached the top of a particularly steep hill only to have the road pitch sharply down the other side and deposit us in what must once have been Horseshoe. A spur of the Colorado and Southern railroad once ran through here to Leavick, and between the two remaining cabins was the track, overgrown with weeds and strewn with ties. There was little left of Horseshoe other than the two cabins; but between 1879 and 1890 it had been a mining and lumbering center with a population of 300. At one time it had two hotels, a smelter, a sawmill and two stores, each of which did a $5,000 a month business, but as we could find no traces of them, after a very short stop we continued up the road.

Beyond Horseshoe the auto road and the railroad bed are one, and in the next three miles we passed several loading platforms and a watertank. The view was unbelievably beautiful, for it was so early in June that the winter's snow lay deep on every peak and, straight ahead, Horseshoe Mountain was easily identified by its curved, rocky cirque, rimmed with snow. Just when we were commenting upon the good roadbed and the easy grades, our progress was stopped by a broken bridge and a large snowbank which completely covered the road. There was no way to drive around it, so, leaving the car, we clambered over the bridge timbers and ploughed into the snowbank up to our hips. Beyond it the road was dry, but the grade was steeper and the going much rougher, so that after about a mile's climb at over eleven thousand feet elevation we were all tired. Jim strode ahead and after a few minutes called out, "Here it is," and disappeared over the crown of the hill. With added zest, Vic and I climbed the last fifty feet that hid the town from view and saw Leavick, a true ghost town at snowline, with cabins, mills and an aerial tram disappearing over the mountain. Behind the town was Horseshoe Mountain, with Mt. Sherman on the right and the bare, pointed peak of Sheep Mountain on the left.

The snow lay all around us, in great patches and drifts, some of which choked the doorways of the cabins or partly hid the rusted machinery in the mill. High above, hung the buckets on the aerial tram, whose towers led up above timberline on Sherman Mountain, to the Hilltop mine. There was much to sketch, and I darted from one end of town to the other trying to record it

HORSESHOE   ↓ ROAD TO LEAVICK

all. One of the cabins was bigger than the rest, and Jim waded across the marsh to it and found on the wall inside a scribbled inscription which identified it as the Baker Boarding House.

"You should have seen it," said Jim, "The note was written in pencil and said that a woman had been there a year ago to revisit the place and that she had lived in that house years ago when it was a boardinghouse; and at the end she wrote, 'We loved every old building. Happy children were we.'"

In Fairplay I found an old miner who knew the history of Leavick. "The tramway you saw led to the Hilltop mine," he began. "The mine was located in 1882, but most of its development was later on, in the nineties and nineteen hundreds. The main workings were at 13,150 feet, and there was a bunkhouse there where the men lived, but it's gone now, crushed in by snow. The tram which ran from the mine to the mill in Leavick was two and a half miles long and its buckets are still full of ore. When silver crashed in '93 and word reached the mine, the **men just quit, and left everything as it stood. Queer thing about that mine," he continued.** "It's just a big ice cake and needs **no timbering because the ground is frozen all the time and nothing ever drops from the stopes or from the tunnel walls. The shaft was covered with ice the entire year, so they had to cut the ice away to let the cage pass through. Even the mine boilers used snow water."**

"It was named for Felix Leavick, a mining man who came to Colorado in the early days and prospected in almost every mining district in the state. He helped develop the Hilltop—in fact he always believed in it even when he sold his share in it to new owners. After the crash in '93 there was no more use mining silver, but zinc was needed and the Hilltop has plenty of it. In 1901 they hauled new machinery up to the mine and installed electricity throughout it. The mine has been worked on and off until about 1930, and the railroad, which was built in time for the 1901 boom, brought the high-grade zinc carbonate ore down. Of course during the winter months it had to stop running because of snow.

"As I said, Leavick had a boom in 1901. All the mines on Sheep Mountain were working then and a force of men were cutting wood up there for a paper company. There was also a group cutting railroad ties in the vicinity. Quite a few families lived in Leavick, and there was a school and a Sunday school. That summer a barber moved his chair from Horseshoe up to Leavick and barbered and gave baths until late fall. There was also a dentist in town. They were a husky bunch of men up there and athletics were very popular. They had a baseball team, and I remember jumping contests in which Swedes from Horseshoe used to compete. I went to a dance there in the old boardinghouse, given by the young people of the town in honor of the woodmen, just before they left for the season, but there's good ore up on top right now and someday I'm going back to gopher around a bit."

Como Having visited so many of the old camps in the South Park area, it seemed foolish to ignore Tarryall Creek where all the excitement started, even if little trace of the early diggings remained. A few miles northeast of Fairplay and a mile off the highway is Como, and since the only way to reach Tarryall Creek by car today is through the town, we stopped there first. Few

LEAVICK AND HILLTOP MINE

AERIAL TRAM, LEAVICK

people live in Como now, for it was always a coal and railroad town, and when the trains stopped running through South Park, Como almost died. Yet in July 1879 it was a typical end-of-the-track camp. It was built entirely of tents, for everyone thought that as soon as the railroad pushed on toward Leadville, the town would move with it. Workmen, freighters, miners and trainmen milled around its muddy streets or packed its variety shows every evening. One tremendous canvas pavilion had a solid board dancing-floor, a good band, a twenty-five-foot bar, a lunch counter and gambling rooms, all of which were crowded night after night.

Incoming freight trains brought twenty carloads of merchandise and supplies a day and left with ten or more loads of ore and bullion and a few cars of coal. With the Leadville excitement at its peak and men rushing to the carbonate camp, the road brought swarms of travelers to the tent city, where they were transferred to stagecoaches and conveyed over Mosquito Pass to the new mining center. For its length, it was carrying more freight and passengers than any road west of the Mississippi. By the time the Colorado Midland was completed to Leadville and the South Park's spur ran over the range to Breckenridge, Como was a lively place. Daily passenger trains pulled into its station; four-engine freights chuffed by on their way west; and the night-freight's whistle was a familiar sound. Not only was Como a division point for the railroads, but their shops and roundhouses were located there, as well as the coal mines which fed their engines.

Years before the town was laid out the coal bank was discovered on the homestead of George W. Lechner and was subsequently sold to the railroad. Italians who were brought in to work the mine named the place Como, after the Italian lake, although no similarity to it exists in the nearby pond in which white-faced cattle drink. Labor trouble flared up in 1879 between the Italians and some Chinese who were imported from Fairplay to work in the mine, and in the battle which followed the contractor who hired them was attacked by thirty men and badly injured. He and the Chinamen returned to Fairplay, leaving the Italians triumphant. Later on some Chinese were again brought in and were allowed to work in peace. In 1911 the shops and roundhouses were closed and people began to board up their houses and move away, but the exodus was gradual. In the 1930's when I first saw Como there were many families living there, but in 1947 I missed most of the landmarks that I had sketched on previous visits.

Tarryall and Hamilton

I was not sure which road led to Tarryall Creek, so when Victoria, Jim and I drove into Como in 1942, we stopped at the general store to ask directions.

"Hamilton and Tarryall?" repeated the storekeeper incredulously, pushing his glasses up on his forehead, "You won't find anything left of them. They were located a couple of miles up the stream but they disappeared years ago, and all traces of them are lost now since the dredge started working up Tarryall way. You can drive past where they were and continue several miles up the creek, as far as the Fortune Placers and a little beyond. They took a lot of gold out of there in the sixties and the gravel is still worth working."

Not far from the edge of town the results of recent dredging **began** to appear, and before long our road was lost under piles of rock. Car tracks climbed over the lower mounds of gravel and stone, and for about three quarters of a mile we followed them across the debris. We passed an occasional cabin or prospect hole, and washed gravel-banks which were the remains of earlier mining. About four miles from Como we arrived at the Fortune cabins. There were quite a few good-sized buildings to be seen, and some machinery and rusty boilers, while across the stream the land was gouged out and piled up from hydraulic operations of considerable extent, which began in 1912 and continued for several seasons thereafter.

Ever since I first learned of the railroad which used to run from Como to Breckenridge I have dreamed of following it over the range, of riding horseback up the deserted roadbed to Boreas Pass and down the other side to the valley of the Blue. I noticed the railroad grade as we left Como and followed its course among the trees as far as I could see it, until it was lost in heavy timber. Now, as I walked up the road I began recalling stories of trips across the pass in the dead of winter and of the woman who carried her baby in her arms all the way, while she walked on the crusted snow. I was so immersed in these reminiscences that when I looked up and saw a foot trail leading off to the right of the road, marked "Breckenridge," it was all I could do to keep from following it.

"What about this place on the map marked Tarryall?" asked Jim, "It's miles out in the park from where we are."

"That is Puma City," I replied, "It's very new compared to these places. *Puma City* for it didn't exist until the nineties and its boom was very short-lived. I talked to one man last summer who got in on the boom and has lived there ever since. He said it was a promotion scheme and that little ore was ever found there or in the vicinity. It's good ranch country, and the place, which is now called Tarryall, is a summer resort with lots of good fishing."

On the return trip we stopped at the approximate site of Hamilton and Tarryall City, two miles from the mouth of the creek. The two camps were close together; in fact, one description of Hamilton states that in 1860 it was known as Tarryall Diggings. At any rate, both attracted hordes of prospectors, who feverishly panned the stream and obtained about a pound of gold a day. The claims at Tarryall were one hundred and fifty feet each along the stream, and it was this fact that so exasperated the latecomers to the diggings, who felt that the claims should be limited to one hundred feet per man. In disgust they left and called the place Graball. When rich fissure veins were discovered at Fairplay and Alma the population drifted away, until in a few years only a handful of dilapidated cabins marked the site of the once prosperous settlement, and now even they have disappeared.

Each time I drove past the site of Webster on the highway to Kenosha *Hall Valley* Pass, I looked longingly up the dirt road which led toward some snowy peaks. Somewhere up that road were Hall Valley and Handcart Gulch, and the latter name alone made me want to explore the territory. I knew that in 1866 three men left Georgetown, and climbing over the range, prospected the far side and eventually found some claims that looked likely. These they sold to Col. J. W. Hall, who became interested in the district and its further discoveries. The Whale mine at the head of Hall Valley was located in 1869, at an altitude of 12,530 feet, and from the first was a bonanza. Hall built one of the first smelters in the state to treat the ore from this mine, which was silver-bearing barite and extremely difficult to smelt. By 1873 Hall Valley, or Hallville as it was sometimes called, was a booming camp with a population of 300 and a railroad which ran to the smelter, in which ore from the Whale, Cashier and Ypsilanti mines was treated. About this time an English company took over the Whale property and ran the mine on such a lavish scale that, in spite of its steady output, the profits were eaten up and the company went broke. The mine and mill were forced to shut down, the camp was deserted, and the Whale lay idle until 1883, when it was reopened and operated for several years, but never again on such a grand scale. Adjoining Hall Valley is Handcart Gulch, so named because the first prospectors pulled their outfits up its steep sides in handcarts. It is now full of the prospect holes they dug and of the one or two mines they started; but as they were unable to find gold in paying quantities they soon abandoned the place. Later, silver and some nuggets of native copper were washed from its streambed.

One weekend in 1947, Walter and I started for Hall Valley, but before reaching the turnoff we stopped at Grant to visit the postmistress, whom I had been told knew more about that region than anyone living. She knew we were coming and, inviting us into her living room, told us stories of Hall Valley that made us itch to get started on the road.

"You can't get lost," she assured Walter and me, "There's just one road up the valley until you come to the fork that goes to the sawmill. Crowe's place is up Handcart Gulch to the right, so keep to the left and you'll be all right. There's a cabin at Hall Valley and the ruins of the smelter. You may have to walk the last part of the way but keep going till you see the iron spring. The turnoff to Hall Valley is just beyond it. I know that country well," she continued, "for I've hiked and ridden over it all my life and I wish you had time to go to the top of Handcart Gulch or to climb Teller Peak. There's an old trail across the range to Montezuma that used to be travelled on foot or horseback, and more than once I've climbed to the top of it and looked down on the Montezuma side.

"Hall Valley was a pretty wild place in the seventies and there was lots of trouble up there. In fact at Fairplay they used to expect at least one case from Hallville to be brought up for trial at every court session. Two men were strung up on trees one night close to the town; and another man who terrorized the camp was finally arrested and taken to Fairplay, but he made his escape and came right back again. There's said to be treasure buried somewhere up Handcart, although some say it was found years ago by a sheriff. But plenty of people still go up there and look for it. Why, during the war, you'd be surprised how many soldiers came here on their furloughs and went digging."

"You say two men were lynched up where we're going?" asked Walter. "What had they done?"

"They tried to run the camp by bullying everyone," replied Miss Pharnes, "and they threatened to shoot anyone who disagreed with their methods.

(102)

The miners naturally resented such high-handed doings, and ganging up on them, succeeded in arresting them. They were told to leave camp peaceably; but they refused to do so and, becoming abusive, threatened to shoot Col. Hall on sight. That night they were taken from the jail where they had been placed, and next morning their bodies were found swinging from trees a little way down the gulch. The camp was much more quiet for a while after that."

"Tell us about the buried treasure," teased Walter.

"The stories vary about it," she continued. "Some say it was $50,000 and some $100,000. Some believe it is buried up Geneva Gulch, and others are equally sure it lies in Handcart Gulch; but all agree that it was loot accumulated by the notorious Reynolds Gang who terrorized South Park and held up stagecoaches and lone riders for their gold. All sorts of clues have been found which should reveal the location of the cache, even to the dagger-marked tree near which it is believed to be hidden. There's one man who lives up the gulch who has found lots of clues but even he can't locate the exact spot."

"What are we waiting for?" asked Walter impatiently. "Let's get going!"

A few minutes later we left the highway and began our five-mile drive up the valley. The road was good and we followed a stream which our map showed us was the North Fork of the South Platte. After about three miles, we came out into an open meadow, at the far end of which was the sharp and snowy peak we had been watching as we drove. It was miles away but it looked near enough to climb, silhouetted against the intense blue Colorado sky. In this meadow the road forked, but after much doubt we decided to keep straight ahead. Another mile brought us to a boggy stretch where we left the car and proceeded on foot. We'd hardly gone any distance before we saw an old man, leaning on a stick, coming toward us. So few people go into that country today that I hoped he wouldn't resent our presence and that maybe he could tell us where we were and what we should look for. He came on slowly and barely acknowledged our greeting. Telling him that we were looking for the remains of Hallville, we asked him how far we were from it. He became interested at once and began to point out landmarks and to reminisce about the camp which he obviously had known.

"There were lots of people here, hotels and saloons and everything. Even a smelter. You can see the ruins of it along the gulch. Hallville was right here but the buildings are all gone. The hotel used to stand over there, and this was a store here. . . ." His voice trailed off in memories, and turning away from us he continued down the valley. We looked about us with added interest and began to see signs of the camp which at first we had missed. A broken flight of steps lay half-hidden by a wild rosebush, some jumbled lumber indicated all that was left of a cabin, and a board fence that leaned crazily toward the road probably once stood in front of a home or a hotel.

The gulch narrowed as we approached a stream whose bed was red with rust, and we recalled Miss Pharnes' instructions—"Look for the iron spring and just beyond it is the turnoff to Hall Valley." Picking our way over the wet rocks to the far side, we came to a second fork in the road. This was clearly marked—Handcart Gulch to the right and Hall Valley to the left. Following the proper trail we dropped into a hollow filled with aspens and saw through their branches the Shaylor cabin—the one remaining building for which we were looking. Near it were sheds and a stone cellar dug into the rock. The rotting frame of an old ore wagon lay at our feet as we scrambled down the bank past the cabin toward the stream. It was rough going, for the bank was steep and we had to push our way between bushes and under-brush and clamber over rocks; but soon we saw below us, the foundations of the Hall Valley smelter and a dilapidated boiler. Nothing else remained ex-cept a great mass of splintered wood, heaped among the stones like a giant pile of jackstraws. By now it was late afternoon, and the sun cast long shadows through the aspens. Perhaps it was the hour and perhaps it was the stories of Hall Valley and its desperadoes that made me willing to leave the site of a camp which is so rich in memories and so completely desolate today.

CHAPTER FIVE

Georgetown and Its Neighbors

(For map see inside of back cover)

IN 1925 I took the Georgetown Loop Excursion trip to the mountains west of Denver. The famous "Loop" was known even in the east, and before reaching Denver I had determined to do two bits of sight-seeing—one, to climb the dome of the Capitol and the other, to take the narrow gauge road to the old silver camp of Georgetown. I had climbed the dome of the State Capitol and gazed at the solid barrier of mountain peaks which constitute the Continental Divide, and now I was on the train about to explore one of the canyons which led up toward their summits.

When the conductor discovered that he had a tenderfoot aboard he refused to let me miss any of the interesting sights along the way. As the little train puffed along Clear Creek, its track high above the stream or almost in the water, he pointed out Floyd Hill down which the pioneers had to snub their wagons and he indicated the canyon up which the Black Hawk branch of the railroad was laid. At Idaho Springs he showed me the smoke screen that was placed over the engine's stack to prevent stray sparks from igniting the timber and causing forest fires and he told about the hot springs which gave the town its name. As we pulled out, he insisted that I look at certain gravel banks which marked the sites of the Jackson Diggings and of Spanish Bar, where the first gold around Idaho was panned. Although all of these things were interesting, it was Georgetown that I was anticipating. I had planned to leave the train there and to spend the hour or two before the return trip was made in wandering about the place and making thumbnail sketches of its streets. How it happened I'll never know—perhaps the scenery was too engrossing—but I completely missed the Georgetown station, and before I knew it, the train was climbing along the edge of a mountain and I was looking down upon the town where I had expected to remain. Climbing all the time, the train swept up the valley, around the curves and over the bridges of the famous "Loop" and stopped at Silver Plume, another mining camp. The excursion crowd was deposited at a pavilion at the upper end of town, close to the mines, and there I stayed until time to return to Denver, looking hungrily at the distant, snowy peaks and longing to get closer to them. On the way back my conductor gave me specimens of ore, and had I known then that the next twenty years would be spent learning all I could about the mountains and the mines, I would have listened more closely to his stories. Years later, when I visited Georgetown, I found it quite as delightful as I had expected it to be and, as with Central city, I returned to it again and again.

The drive from Denver into the mountains is over wooded hills with the snow-covered barricade of the Continental Divide always ahead. There is no indication of mining activity in the area until one reaches Idaho Springs, where the first gold found in Clear Creek was panned by George A. Jackson in January, 1859. Like Green Russell and Gregory, Jackson was looking for gold. Setting out with only his two dogs, he worked his way up Clear Creek as far as the mouth of what was later called Chicago Creek, near the site of some hot springs. The vapor from these springs could be seen for miles in the cold frosty air, and clustered around them were hundreds of mountain sheep drinking or grazing. With his hunting knife he scratched enough frozen soil from the streambed to pan out nine dollars worth of gold. Duly recording his findings in his diary and marking the location of the gold-bearing gravel, he returned to Denver to wait for spring. Then, accompanied by a party of men from Chicago, he returned to the mountains and showed his companions where he had found the golden flakes. By May, 1859, Jackson Bar was crowded with men placering the streambed and taking out as much as $1900 in a single week. A town was laid out at this spot and was known

Idaho Springs

as Sacramento City, Idaho City, Idaho and finally as Idaho Springs. By 1862 its forty houses and its hotel, the Beebee House, formed the nucleus of a settlement which today boasts a population of twelve thousand.

Long before placer mining was abandoned along Clear Creek, quartz veins were located on the steep hillsides and mine after mine was developed. During the seventies the medicinal value of the hot springs was realized, the waters were bottled and shipped all over the country, and Idaho Springs became, in addition to a mining center, a health resort. The narrow gauge reached Idaho in the seventies, bringing tourists to the mountain towns all summer long and greatly facilitating the shipment of ore from the mines of the region. In 1892 two drainage and transportation tunnels were constructed, which also simplified the shipping of ore from the mines. The Newhouse Tunnel, now called the Argo, was built at a cost of $10,000,000 and was the longest tunnel of its kind in the world. It was cut five miles through the mountains from Idaho Springs to Central City, thus providing a commercial tunnel through which ore from the mines which it tapped could be trammed to the railroad.

The road to Georgetown goes through Idaho Springs and passes close to the sites of mining camps which have long since disappeared or which today look to summer tourists for their sustenance. Each of these places has its colorful history, and on every trip to Georgetown I visited at least one of them and learned what I could of its past. Just beyond Idaho Springs is the site of Fall River, and short detours from the highway at this point lead to Alice or to Freeland and Lamartine. Next beyond Fall River the main road passes through Dumont, Downieville and Lawson, finally reaching the fork whose left-hand branch leads straight to Georgetown, once the most flourishing silver camp in the state.

Alice and Fall River

I heard about Alice and Freeland from a mining man in Idaho Springs, and when I was ready to visit the two communities, he suggested that his daughter accompany us and point out all the landmarks. Leaving Idaho Springs, we drove about two miles to the Fall River road. In 1942 two mills marked the site of Fall River, one of them set high above the road and the

(106)

ARGO TUNNEL, IDAHO SPRING

other standing among some big trees at the river's edge. Both are gone now as well as all traces of the gold camp of the sixties which was located at this spot. In those days there were hundreds of claims extending up the stream for miles, embracing the Iowa, Lower Fall River, Lincoln, Cumberland and Upper Fall River Mining Districts, where tent cities sprang up overnight and as rapidly disappeared.

At Fall River we turned up the canyon road and followed it for miles. Higher and higher we climbed until we reached a side road, barred by a gate, beyond which lay Alice. The property was not being worked, and had we not had a guide with us, we might not have seen all the mine buildings nor fully understood what we saw.

"We know this property well," she began. "It was first worked in 1881 as a placer deposit, with hydraulic giants which cut out an area of five or six acres. A good deal of gold was found in this way, about $50,000 in all. Later a stamp mill was erected here and it ran successfully for several years until the free-milling ores were replaced by pyritic ores, which could not be handled by the stamps. Then operations ceased and the property lay idle for years. Come over here, and I'll show you the great pit or glory hole, one hundred feet across and fifty feet deep. The tunnel that you see extends from it to the mill, to which the ore was trammed for processing. The Alice mine closed down in 1899, although there is still an immense body of low grade lead and silver ore here which carries some gold in it. Over there in the trees is the schoolhouse. The last school teacher never got paid, for the mine closed down before payday.

"The road beyond here goes to Yankee Hill, but it has high centers and is so rough and rocky that only a specially geared car can make it. It used to be the regular road from Central City to Georgetown, when this entire gulch was full of camps. Silver City was near here, and there were one or two little diggings between here and the mouth of the river. St. Mary's Glacier, the source of Fall River, is near here too and so is Silver Lake, but if we're going to Freeland today, we'd better get started."

Freeland   The view on the way back was magnificent, for as we dropped down Fall River we faced the Clear Creek valley, beyond which rose Mt. Evans. As soon as we reached Clear Creek again we crossed the highway and, taking another dirt road, cut a sharp corner around a mine building and started to climb the long four mile hill to Freeland. The road went nearly straight up the whole distance, twisting along a ledge at the bottom of which ran Trail Run. There were mine dumps, shaft houses and cabins all along the way, proving that at one time Trail Creek had been an active mining district. Nearing Freeland, we passed more cabins and the stone foundations of deserted mills and furnaces.

"What can you tell about the place?" I asked.

"It was a pleasant, quiet and peaceful camp," she replied. "In 1881 it had a population of about 400 people, mostly men, and it had at least two stores and a saloon, and later a public school. I've heard my father say there were about eighty homes here, neat frame houses. There was no church, but occasional religious services were held in the homes. The community depended upon the Freeland, the Lone Tree and other mines for its prosperity. Where the Freeland vein crosses the road the group of mills and houses was called Bonito. In 1884 the Bullion Smelter was built to treat the ore from the Freeland mine, employing about twenty-five men and smelting about 6000 tons of ore."

All the time she was talking we were driving higher up the mountain on the one long gulch street. Occasionally we passed houses from which children waved or we caught a glimpse of women who paused long enough in their work to glance curiously at the car as it passed, but most of the cabins were deserted and were as dilapidated as the old, weathered mills, surrounded by their piles of useless machinery. In the distance a group of shiny, new buildings caught my eye. "What's that?" I asked.

"That's the new Lamartine Tunnel property," she replied. "There was another camp on top of this mountain in the eighties, built around the Lamartine mine, and recently a new outfit has put up this mill and is working it successfully."

It was several years later that I reached Lamartine and before attempting to find it I made inquiries of several people, none of whose answers coincided.

"Sure, there was a mining camp up on top called Lamartine," said an old man in Georgetown. "There may be a cabin or two left standing but nothing more."

"There's nothing left of it," said another. "You wouldn't even find the site."

"The best way to reach it is up Ute Creek and then hike along it till you reach the place," said a third.

"Go to Freeland and turn off to the left," wrote someone who had been there. "You can drive to within two miles of it but there are so many mine roads which turn off into the timber that you'll probably get lost." After such conflicting statements I decided to take Mary Lou Cox, a member of the Colorado Mountain Club, with me as a guide—a young woman who had been to Lamartine seven times and had led Mountain Club hikes to the deserted camp. She met Les Merrill and me in Denver and drove with us to Idaho Springs. From there we took the old road to the foot of Trail Run. I had forgotten how steep the four-mile hill was until the car began to protest and to refuse to make it in second, and long before we reached Freeland I was pushing the gas pedal clear to the floor. As we passed through Freeland I was startled at the almost complete desertion of the place and by the deterioration and dilapidation which had taken place in only five years. At the edge of the town we took a road to the left and climbed another hill, twisting through timber until we reached a group of deserted mine buildings. Here we parked the car and taking our lunches, cameras and sketching paraphernalia, hiked up the mine road to a point where it split in five directions. This was where we needed our guide. Without hesitation she chose the least travelled trail and led the way over loose stones and runnelled grooves where water had gouged away the roadbed. The sky had looked threatening all day and now a gentle mist-like rain began to fall. As it was difficult to keep cameras and pads dry we were relieved after fifteen minutes to have the rain stop as suddenly as it had begun. By now we were getting pretty high and I was forced to stop frequently and breathe. There was no sign of mine or town—in fact the road looked the same no matter how far we climbed. Aside from ground pine and some Indian paintbrush, the most colorful growth along the trail were large, cream-colored toadstools with brilliant red and yellow markings.

"The mine's around the next corner or the next beyond that, I'm never sure myself," said Mary Lou, striding along with the easy gait of the seasoned hiker. "We come to the mine first. It's on the edge of an open meadow which we have to cross. The town is built in the timber over the crest of the mountain and down the far side."

Rounding a corner we entered a wide, rolling meadow on top of the mountain and there, to the right, was a shaft house and some sheds and the big dumps of the Lamartine mine. Leaving the others to explore the mine property, I started across the meadow toward a patch of aspens in which roof tops were visible. There were quite a few houses left in the town—one-story cabins and some two-story buildings, many of them hidden in the trees or beside a little stream which cut its way down the gulch. All were weathered and lacked windows and doors but an amazing number of them were still roofed. Since the camp had been built along the side of the mountain, the houses were arranged like steps down the steep hillside, each one having its own terrace. Below us were more cabins, one here and one there, at least twenty in all, not counting foundations and terraced plots where houses had stood. What must have been a road or street was now a mere foot trail, overgrown with bushes and seedlings. Wherever the trees were thinned out, the twisting ribbon of the Mt. Evans highway could be seen far below, and the roar of the creek beside it came faintly up to us. There were many sketches to make, and to get the best composition for each it was necessary to climb up and down the gulch which was as steep as a flight of stairs.

"Do you know anything about the mine?" asked Les as we ate our lunch beside the stream.

"I ran across its story in a book by Hanchett. Four prospectors from Idaho Springs named Cooper, Chavanne, Medill and Bougher formed a partnership and working their way up Trail Run to its source found some float near the top of the mountain and a large fissure vein containing gold ore, which they immediately staked out as a claim and called the Lamartine. Soon afterwards Bougher died, leaving his widow with a lap full of mining claims. Her brother-in-law, Peter Himrod, bought a quarter interest in the Lamartine claim from her for $250, not because he was interested in mining but because she needed the money. Sometime later he visited the Lamartine mine, getting Cooper, one of the other partners, from Idaho Springs to take him to it. Thereafter he visited the property regularly and in time began to believe in it.

"In 1872 Congress passed the 'Chaffee Act' by which every owner had to perform $100 worth of work annually on each claim or forfeit it. When Himrod next visited the mine, Cooper offered to sell him his share for $25, and Himrod accepted. The road up Trail Run at that time was a toll road, and strangely enough Chavanne, the third partner, was the tollgate keeper. When Himrod returned from his trip to the mine and stopped at the gate, Chavanne offered his claim to the eastener but Himrod was not interested in purchasing it. Chavanne insisted that he buy it and to get rid of the man Himrod gave him $5 for it. He now owned three-quarters of the mine for which he had paid a total of $280. The fourth partner, Medill, could not be traced and was declared legally 'out' of the property.

"Himrod now patented his claim but did not visit it again until 1887, when he found a man named Comer sinking a shaft on it, unaware that the land was patented. Himrod gave him a contract to continue digging and the real development of the mine began. From that time on Himrod put capital into the Lamartine, much to the disgust of his wife and son who had no faith in mining. On Himrod's next trip to Colorado, he was taken ill and died. His son then came west to settle with Comer and to ask him what he thought of the mine. Good silver ore had been found and the prospects looked so promising that the son began to put money into the mine. After another seventeen feet of development still better ore was uncovered, but young Himrod had had enough and refused to invest any further. The mine was sold, and the new owners sank a shaft which immediately struck rich ore, bringing them a profit of $5,000 on a $360 investment within sixteen months. The Lamartine produced several millions of dollars in gold, silver and lead before 1905 when it was taken over by lessees. The town was built in the late eighties and flourished through the nineties."

"That accounts for the date I found on the wall of one of the houses," broke in Les. "The walls were covered with newspapers and the one I read had a headline: 'The Invasion of Cuba Put Off One Week,' and it was dated May 8, 1898."

We took a last look around and climbed back to the saddle of the mountain, passing the mine and hiking down the road to the car. On the way back toward Freeland a streak of tan crossed the road and disappeared into the heavy timber. It was an unusually large coyote and it was the only animal that we saw on the trip. Late that afternoon I put a red dot on my map of Ghost Towns, indicating that Lamartine was now a "mission accomplished."

Between Idaho Springs and Georgetown the hills are covered with pros- *Dumont or* pect holes, mine dumps and shaft houses, while along the streams are the *Mill City* crumbling ruins of mills and occasional new structures where some enterprising lessee is reworking an old property. Whenever I drove through Dumont on my way to Georgetown I noticed an old log building on whose side was painted "Mill City House, 1868," and one day, my curiosity getting the better of me, I stopped to learn something of its history. The man at whose cabin I knocked got a key to the old hotel and began to talk about the log building before we reached its massive door. It was an old stage station built when the only road along Clear Creek was a toll road. A fire consumed its bar and ruined part of the building and its porch has disappeared, but inside are a few relics of its prime. My guide assured me that it once housed the first saloon west of Denver and that the Singer sewing machine, which he pointed out in a dusty corner, was the first one in the Territory. There was also a billiard table which came from Oswego, New York, and a square piano which was brought across the plains by ox cart to Central City and later to Idaho Springs, Fall River and Freeland, eventually finding its way to this mountain hotel. Sitting at the dusty instrument he played a few bars upon it and then undraping a small organ in another part of the room he performed upon it. Old dusty account books dated 1873 lay on the piano, and dog-eared liquor accounts listed sales of whiskey and brandy at fifty cents a glass, or the equivalent in gold dust. The walls of the room were still covered with hand-blocked paper brought from Nauvoo, Illinois, in 1877 by the owner of the hotel, Mrs. Sarah Green, who fearing that she would be unable to get a selection of patterns in the region brought twenty-seven varieties with her. The upper story of the house was once used as an Opera House, and perhaps it was there or perhaps it was in this parlor that General Grant was entertained when he visited the hotel on his trip to Idaho Springs.

While we stood in the half-light of the cluttered room I asked when Mill City was founded and learned that a townsite was laid out in 1859 by some Californians who pitched their tents at this spot. A log settlement grew up as mines were discovered, and to handle their ores several stamp mills and smelting furnaces were erected. By 1878 there was one store, one billiard room and bar, one boardinghouse, and the Mill City House which catered to most of the trade.

"When was the name of the town changed to Dumont?" I inquired, fingering some old photographs of miners and pack trains lined up in front of the building.

"That was in 1880, when it was named for John M. Dumont, the owner of the big mines—the Whale, the Freeland, the Lincoln and several others. He undertook to revive the place and its mines, and since there was another place called Mill City, the town was renamed in his honor. There were

Silver Creek

mines at Silver Creek too," he added, locking the door of the building. "You can see their dumps high on the mountainside from here. There's only a trail up there now and there are no buildings left, but there used to be a school, a hotel and several cabins. Last time I was there all I could find of the camp were some broken pine coffins strewed around where an undertaker's cabin used to be. It's a five mile hike from here. Want to go?"

Refusing his offer with thanks, we drove on past the roadhouse at Downieville and as we neared the little town of Lawson noticed, high to the left, a group of mine dumps that were no doubt at Silver Creek.

Lawson

Lawson has a diminutive postoffice, a bevy of cabins along the highway and a store or two. Back in 1872 there was nothing at this point but a new inn, the Six Mile House, so called because it was six miles from Georgetown, built by Alexander Lawson who had just eloped with the daughter of the proprietor of the roadhouse at Downieville. Besides running his inn, Lawson freighted between Central City, Black Hawk, Leadville and Georgetown and owned a stage-coach line between Georgetown and Silver Plume. In 1876 when mines were discovered in the vicinity and prospectors poured in, a town grew up around the inn and was named for the enterprising proprietor.

MAXWELL HOUSE, GEORGETOWN

ALPINE STREET, GEORGETOWN

In the eighties, the mines on Red Elephant Mountain, one mile to the north, and at Silver Creek two miles away were being worked, and their development brought prosperity to Lawson, increasing its population to 500. Reduction works were established, four stores, a school and a postoffice were opened and the town continued to boom through the nineties as long as its mines produced. By the time they began to close down one by one, Lawson had become a resort, and today its small permanent population is augmented each year by summer residents who occupy its neat, attractive cabins.

Just beyond Lawson the highway forks, the right hand road leading to Empire and Berthoud Pass and the left hand to Georgetown and Loveland Pass. Until a few years ago several old mills were to be seen on this five-mile stretch, but one by one they have tumbled down or been moved away, so that today only foundations or an overhead tram cable mark their location.

Georgetown   Straight ahead, at what appears to be the head of the valley lies Georgetown, locked in on three sides by steep mountains and nearly hidden by the trees which line its streets. It is unique among Colorado mining towns, for from the first it was a city of homes, to which the miners brought their families and where they tried to reproduce as closely as possible the culture and architecture to which they were accustomed in the east. Touches of New England and the Middle West survive chiefly in the architecture, but this nostalgic clinging to the past can also be seen in the hitching posts and carriage blocks which stand in front of a few of the larger residences, and even in the little park which resembles so slightly the village greens by which it was inspired. An air of neatness, charm, comfort and well-being pervades the place, giving it a character all its own—dignified, genteel and wholly Victorian. There are more trees along its streets than in any other mountain town—not pines or willows, which grew along the stream, but good shade trees, planted years ago by forward-looking citizens who intended to make this mountain valley their home and who took pride in developing it.

Picket fences surround many of its homes and protect well-kept gardens where tame and wild flowers grow side by side. Every house has flowers, either in its garden or in a window, framed by starched lace curtains or by heavy draperies. Very few shades are drawn at night and the soft glow from shaded lights shines through windows along the dark, quiet streets. The architecture is also Victorian and embraces all the fussy variants that the term implies and that man could create from combinations of wood and iron. Wrought iron fences enclose a few properties, where trees and vines half hide a mansard roof or a carved barge board from view. Georgetown "pink," a soft muted tone, with which many of the houses are painted, is best seen in the Maxwell House, whose dormered cupola and cocoa-colored trimmings dominate a hill at the upper end of town. On Alpine Street and on Taos Street are false-fronted stores and more than one structure whose facade is embellished with Corinthian pilasters and columns upon which rest the carved corbels of the overhanging cornices. The houses themselves are sturdy and well proportioned, but upon their exteriors unrestrained imagination was lavished, resulting in textured orgies of diapered shingles, jig-saw swags, intricate cupolas and wrought iron lace balustrades. Even the park, which occupies a city block, is surrounded by a cast iron fence with ornamental archways at each corner entrance. Inside its gates blue spruce trees shade the long grass, the clumps of columbine and the tiny pond in which mountain trout swim. It is a peaceful little town where footsteps sound loudly on the stone pavements at night and no one hurries. For years I have spent whole days or weekends in its quiet atmosphere, captivated by its charm and eagerly unraveling its history.

George and David Griffith were Kentucky farmers who joined the gold rush to Denver in 1858 and spent the winter in that raw-boned settlement. Hearing of Gregory's discovery in 1859 they hastened to his diggings but found that all the good claims had been staked out. Drifting over to Russell Gulch, George began to prospect and gradually worked his way down Virginia Canyon to a new camp called Sacramento. Here, too, the best claims were taken, forcing him to continue his prospecting further up Clear Creek. He passed one group of men who were washing gold in Mill Creek and, travelling nine miles further into country which had not been penetrated, he reached a flat where his progress was halted by dense masses of willows and lodge pole pines and by beaver dams which were gradually making a lake of the creek along which he was travelling. To get around the ponds he climbed the side of a hill and, stopping to rest and to look about him, caught sight of some rock, which upon investigation proved to be auriferous, and the Griffith lode was discovered! Staking a claim, he returned to the Gregory Diggings to tell his brother the news. The two young men and three others returned immediately to the claim and worked all summer, taking out $500 in gold from the rock crevice he had discovered. By common consent they called their camp "George's Town" and left it reluctantly during the winter months. By the spring of 1860 they were back again, with another Griffith brother and his wife Elizabeth, and with their father. For him they staked out the entire valley as a homestead ranch and built a cabin in the middle of it. They also brought with them a crude stamp mill which they had built during their winter at Gregory, and with this they crushed their ore until better machinery was available.

George's Town attracted other adventurers until the valley was alive with miners, who in June 1860 called a meeting and drew up the laws of the Griffith Mining District. Scattering over the hillsides and up the creek and its forks, the prospectors searched for such gold as Griffith had uncovered in his mine but they found very little. In 1861 Lee R. Seaton, a gold miner at Fall River, found gold that was almost white and that brought but eight dollars an ounce at the few banks which would buy it. From assays he learned that the ore was chiefly silver, but no one cared about silver during a gold rush.

Other miners in the Griffith district met with similar disappointments until 1864, when James Huff, Robert Steele and Robert Layton set out to prospect McClellan Mountain near the camp. The men separated into two groups and agreed to meet at the summit. When Huff joined the others he exhibited a piece of quartz which contained appreciable amounts of silver. Excitedly, he showed them the ledge where he got it and staked a claim which he named the August Belmont lode. When it was learned that fifty pounds of quartz assayed one thousand ounces of silver to the ton a new rush was on, and in less than a month two thousand men were searching for blossom rock on the mountain and staking off hundreds of claims. At the same time a prospector named Coley discovered a silver lode about fifteen miles from Georgetown. His discovery and that of the Belmont Lode started a general stampede from the gold camps, which were beginning to play out, to the new silver district.

Early in 1864 Georgetown had but four cabins and its hills were thickly forested. By fall, the hills were stripped of their timber to provide rows of cabins for the growing camp and supports for the mine tunnels which were being bored into the mountains. By 1866 there were really two camps half a mile apart, separated by a beaver dam. The original camp, Georgetown, was located on the flat beside the creek, but as more men arrived, buildings were constructed at the base of Leavenworth Mountain, and this "suburb," which grew with amazing rapidity, was called Elizabethtown after Griffith's sister. When the place was granted a post office in the fall of 1866, a public meeting was held and both camps agreed to combine under the name of Georgetown. The next year the citizens petitioned the territorial legislature to grant the town a charter, and that accomplished, they clamored so aggressively for the county seat to be moved from Idaho Springs, a small hamlet, to the growing metropolis at the foot of Leavenworth Mountain, that the legislature was forced to call a special election in 1868, and Georgetown won by a large majority.

The silver craze was well started by 1867 and Georgetown was its center. The discovery of the Anglo-Saxon lode, whose ore assayed $23,000 a ton, brought still more men to the mountain town, which by now was known as the "Silver Queen of the Rockies." Concord coaches from Denver arrived at least once a day laden with adventurous men, bent upon wresting a fortune from the earth or from their comrades. The streets were crowded with freighters' wagons bringing in supplies and with jack trains packing them to the miners in the Argentine district west of town. Clark & Co. of Central City established a branch of their bank in Georgetown and rented an office in it to Wells Fargo Express Co. Money was spent freely—two bits being the smallest coin in use. Saloons, restaurants and hotels cared for the milling crowds, but none surpassed the Barton House, which opened its doors in 1867 and was said to be "second to none in the Territory."

Georgetown's churches, of which there are still three, stand quietly today, waiting for the congregations which once filled their pews Sunday after Sunday; but the history of the early churches which I was seeking I found in yellowed newspapers and diaries. Methodism came to the mountains in 1865 when a circuit was organized at Empire. Deacon Smith held occasional services at Georgetown, calling his congregation together by blowing lustily on a four-foot horn that could be heard for miles. The first church to be built in the town promptly blew down in the "Big Wind of '67." This was Grace Episcopal Church, which was immediately rebuilt and is still standing on Taos Street. Beside it stands a sturdy belfry built of heavy timbers, anchored to rock foundations, and supporting the church bell which no longer rings on Sunday mornings.

Visitors to town are always interested in the Hotel de Paris, the *Courier* office and the firehouse of the Alpine Hose No. 2. This two-story, false-fronted white building, with its tall tower, houses one of the five fire companies of Georgetown which flourished in the seventies and eighties. In its dark interior fire fighting apparatus of an earlier era is neatly arranged, as well as the more modern equipment kept for use today. The Alpine Hose was not the first company organized in the seventies, but its building, the headquarters of the present Georgetown Volunteer Fire Department, is the most imposing. Three of the city's companies—the Star Hook and Ladder Co. No. 1, the Hope Hose Co. No. 1, and the Alpine Hose Co. No. 1, (the ancestor of No. 2)—were organized in 1874, and the Old Missouri Hose Co., whose firehouse stands half hidden by big trees opposite the park, was established later. The Georgetown Fire and Hose Co. was the first to be organized, in 1870, and its firehouse on Alpine St., across from the Hotel de Paris, is used today for the City Hall. The sagging balcony has been removed, and the building has recently received a startlingly white coat of paint, but the carved insignia with the crossed ladders and fire hook is still in place just below the tiny belfry.

Although the first fire bell was bought in 1873, it was not until 1880 that William A. Hammill, wealthy mining man, offered to present a bell to the Alpine Hose Company if the town would provide a suitable tower for it. The tower was built and the twelve hundred pound bell installed in its belfry where it has rung out alarms and the nightly curfew ever since. The Alpine Hose Company won first prize in the State Fireman's Tournament in 1877 and again in 1879, receiving, for its successful performance in running seven hundred feet with a hose cart carrying two hundred and fifty feet of hose in twenty-nine and three-quarters seconds, a silver tea set and a brass cannon. When the State Tournament was held in Georgetown in 1886, great preparations were made for the event and for the entertainment of the thousand delegates who attended. Fourteen bands provided music for the parade and torchlight procession which opened the three day program. Tests of skill between rival teams were performed before huge audiences, and the festivities concluded with a special concert and a grand ball given at the Opera House.

"I've read about the McClellan Opera House. Where did it stand?" I asked an old man one morning as I sat in the doorway of a store making a watercolor of Alpine St. He sat down on the doorstep beside me and told me that McClellan Hall was built in 1867 but that the Opera House wasn't built until 1869. It was two stories high and stood on Taos Street, on the vacant lot next to the Hotel de Paris. It burned to the ground in 1892 in spite of fourteen fire companies trying to save it. In the eighties all the first class actors and actresses who came to Denver played on its stage and scarcely a night went by without some entertainment in its auditorium. Road companies traveled by stagecoach in those days and played in all the mining camps, usually coming here from Central City or Idaho Springs.

Georgetown had two opera houses, the McClellan and the three-story brick building on the corner of Alpine and Taos streets, known as the Cushman Block. The theatre, which was on its top floor, was used from 1876 to 1882, when Madame Janauschek gave a performance to such a packed house, that it strained the beams supporting the auditorium, and the place was condemned as unsafe and closed. Later it was used as a lodge room. For other entertainment the men had their lodges and the ladies their Shakespeare Society as well as concerts and balls, toboggan parties and church sociables.

I learned from the old man that General Grant made three visits to Georgetown and only one to Central City! During his first visit, in 1868, he stayed at the Barton House and gave his speech from its front balcony. In 1873 he returned, arriving a day before schedule, to the discomfort of the town which wasn't quite ready to receive him. But when he came in 1875 four fire companies and the Emerald Rifles Drill Team escorted him through town and three Governors and two Mayors headed the reception committee.

Although the Georgetown Loop was a thing of the past I was eager to learn its history and again I questioned the old man.

"When the big mines were producing we needed a railroad to haul the ore to the smelters," he began. "Georgetown mines produced $200,000,000 in gold, silver, copper and lead during the thirty-three years that the camp boomed and if the Sherman Act hadn't been repealed in 1893 this town would be booming yet. With the big mines closed down, people began to leave and the population dropped to a few hundred, just the same as it is today. But, as I was saying, about the railroad, it took six years to get her built and by then the mines at Silver Plume and above Graymount were sending rich stuff down the canyon by wagon; so they had to build the road on up the gulch to serve those mines. The Plume is only two miles away but it's a thousand feet higher and to build a railroad up there was a real engineering job. It took four miles of track to do it and five years to build it. The Loop was in the canyon between the two towns with each trestle built at a higher level— the highest one being three hundred feet above the bed of Clear Creek. The road reached the Plume in 1882, and the next year they built it as far as Graymount and Bakerville. It was built to haul ore but it hauled twenty thousand passengers each summer on its famous excursion trip. Postcards showing the Loop were mailed all over the country. They even tried to photograph the thing from a balloon, but a current of cold air hit the bag and it burst, and they never tried that notion again. The Loop was abandoned in the nineteen-thirties and its tracks were torn up, but you can see the trestles and the roadbed from the new highway. It was a pretty piece of engineering," he concluded, getting stiffly to his feet and walking away.

"Have you visited the County Courthouse?" asked the editor of the *Courier* the day that I stopped in his office to see his mineral collection. "The jury room has rocking chairs in it. Incredulously I hurried to the white frame building and, entering the Clerk's office, asked his permission to visit the courtrooms and the jury room, all of which were on the second floor. The courtrooms had the usual appointments, and after a hasty glance at each I walked along the hall to the jury room. It was bare and drab except for one round table and twelve identical rocking chairs, which shone under coats of fresh varnish. Each was of ample size and—I could hardly believe my eyes —had its headrest and curved arms elaborately painted with scrolls and festoons of flowers. Would that I could have seen a miners' jury rocking in

HOTEL DE PARIS. GEORGETOWN

SILVER PLUME CHURCH

JURY ROOM, CLEAR CREEK
COUNTY COURT HOUSE

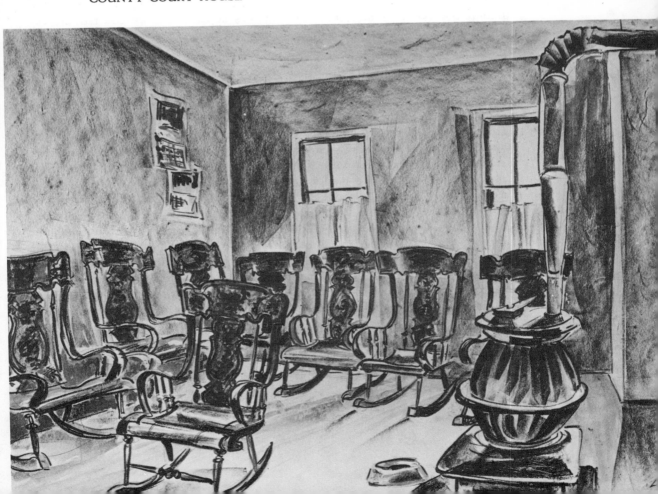

those gaudy and comfortable chairs as they deliberated some intricate mine litigation or other weighty matter.

Near the head of Argent Street stands one of Georgetown's mansions—the Hammill House, built in 1880 by W. A. Hammill, who made much of his money in the Pelican-Dives mine at Silver Plume. The large frame house is set back from the street and is surrounded by a low stone wall. Flower beds surround the house, and in the center of the lawn is a cast iron fountain, ornamented with calla lilies and ram's heads. At its base are eight flower urns placed about an empty pool which once caught water from the basins above. I knew the exterior of the house well but not its interior, although its grandeur had been described by one of Georgetown's residents. "It was quite the show place of the town," she said. "The parlor has the most beautiful imported wallpaper, and there's a Roger's Group on one of the tables and the mantle-pieces are Italian marble." Hoping to gain admittance so as to see these treasures I rang the old-fashioned spring bell, but there was no answer to its peal. Later on I obtained the key to the house and one morning a friend and I went there to sketch. Although it was mid-summer the interior was cold and clammy and, wrapped in sweaters, we each made a painting of the parlor with its crystal chandelier, its shuttered windows which extended from the floor to the ceiling, and its red plush armchairs. We explored the upper floors and peeped into the big bedrooms, each with its fireplace. Though the glass-roofed conservatory contained nothing but an empty plant stand and fountain, we tried to imagine how the room must have looked when it was filled with flowering plants and trailing vines. The walnut sideboard in the dining room with its handsome carving was superb, and we coveted the cut glass castors and decanters which stood upon it.

Back of the house were two stone buildings, the mine office and the stable, both built of native granite, and since one of our keys fitted the former, we explored it too. Very little light filtered through the slatted blinds of the office but even in the half light we could see the massive, curved, wooden counter which swept from the door across the room to the foot of a graceful, spiral staircase. Behind it were bookcases and a large wall safe, while strewn about the room were law books, old newspapers and pieces of furniture. Everything was covered with a gray film of dust and with chunks of fallen plaster. Just behind the mansion was an out-house, whose white clapboard sides, carved and cupolaed roof and walnut appointments were in perfect keeping with the lavish architecture of the house. Since then the Hammill House has been opened as the Alpine Lodge, and many people have fingered the imported flock paper in the parlor or have used the long, narrow tin bath-tub, which in itself is almost a museum piece of Americana. The Hammill House is the symbol of an era and every time I see it or other houses like it, I marvel at the vision of the pioneers who in so few years transplanted so much of the culture and comfort they had known back east to the western frontier.

No trip to Georgetown is complete without a visit to the famous Hotel de Paris. Its tan facade and red-trimmed windows hide an interior such as the west had not seen before 1875 when Louis Dupuy opened its doors to a curious public. Perhaps the paint was a little fresher then and the velvet draperies at the windows were less faded, but the figure of Justice on the roof, the gilded deer on the retaining wall and the lion couchant over the gateway have not changed with the years. Most people see only the dining room with its walnut and beechwood floor and wainscoting, its diamond dust mirrors, its photographs by Jackson of Green Lake and Gray's Peak and its cabinet filled with Haviland china. Or they finger the silver castors on each table and look idly at the name of Louis Dupuy, painted over the dining room door. Louis' name also appears behind the desk, on the carved board from which hang keys to the rooms above. In the center of the dining room is a fountain, whose cast iron cherub is perpetually clinging to the back of a gilded duck from whose bill a slender stream of water was intended to spout but into which were stuck a French and an American flag the first time I saw it. The hotel has attracted me like a magnet ever since 1930 when I spent my first weekend in its hospitable atmosphere and learned its picturesque history.

When Louis Dupuy reached Georgetown in 1869 or 1870 he had no thought of building a hotel. In fact, for the moment he was prospecting, and had he not been injured while saving a friend's life in a mine explosion, he might not have stayed in the vicinity at all. Even after his recovery he was not strong enough to return to mining; so being something of a gourmet and versed in the art of cookery, he found employment in Delmonico's Bakery and Restaurant on Alpine Street, and later became the sole owner of the business. He gradually enlarged and improved the property, purchasing more ground and adding to the original building. Sending abroad for the finest engravings, statuary, and furnishings (all of which had to be brought to Georgetown by freighters' wagons), and stocking his kitchen with most exotic delicacies, he became host to the most discriminating patronage in the west. In 1882 he added wine cellars and vaults to the building, for although the hotel had no bar, wines and liquors were served in the dining room. In 1892 he again added to the structure, which by now housed his library of three thousand volumes. Dupuy was a mystery to the town, for he sought few friends, avoided women and found in a French cabinet maker, Monsieur Galet and his wife, his closest companions. They were older than he, and when Galet died, Dupuy offered his widow a home in the hotel, giving her a monthly allowance of twenty dollars. Mme. Galet's affection for Louis was touching and when he died of pneumonia in 1900 her grief was pitiful. He left everything to her, and in gratitude she tried to keep the hotel open by renting rooms and closing the dining room, but she spoke no English and the task was too hard for her. In 1901 she died and was buried, at her request, in the Georgetown cemetery beside Dupuy, where a stone to the memory of them both still stands. Perhaps no finer tribute could have been paid the Frenchman than that which appeared in the Georgetown *Courier:* "Louis Dupuy—an eccentric, a philosopher and a student, who brought refinement to the granite slopes of Colorado."

Fortunately the hotel remains both outside and inside very much as Dupuy left it, for Mrs. McAdams, the present proprietress, has with unerring judgment preserved the place so that the spirit of Louis still pervades the entire building. The fine etchings, engravings and photographs which he selected hang on all the walls. There are mirrors everywhere—at the ends of dark passageways and over the stairwell. The parlors, with their thick carpets, open fireplaces, massive furniture and handsome chandeliers, complete with colored glass globes, reflect the taste and comfort with which Louis furnished the hostelry and in which he took such pride. Only once was I permitted to see his famous library, and on that occasion Mrs. McAdams pointed with pride and a little awe to the shelves filled with French and English classics. She opened large, handsomely bound volumes that lay on the center table that I might see their excellent illustrations and fine typography and, lest I disarrange anything in this sanctum, she courteously but firmly led me from the room and locked the door behind her.

Whenever I stayed at the hotel, I painted from the roof of the side porch, for from this vantage point all of Georgetown was visible. The Alpine House No. 2, the Maxwell House, the Cushman Block, the City Hall, the Episcopal Church, the old railroad grade to Devil's Gate and the switchbacks on the road to Green Lake—all presented compositions for my brush. Mrs. McAdams' dogs joined me at such times, lying close to my paint box or thumping cheerful tails on the balustraded roof. These dogs were strays who had found a home with the friendly proprietress, and whose presence were as much a part of the atmosphere of the hotel as the gilded deer on top of the wall. Mrs. McAdams presides over the hotel with calm detachment and stately poise, unhurried, unruffled and courteously diffident to all but her friends. Like Louis Dupuy she spends hours, when the hotel is quiet, in the library reading the books which he selected with such discrimination.

Georgetown is the center from which I have made many trips to the mountain towns, and the Hotel de Paris is the center of Georgetown. Whenever I stayed at the hotel I always planned an early morning departure so as to complete the day's objective before afternoon mountain showers put an end to outdoor sketching. One morning a friend and I entered the dining room a little after seven. We were not too early, for through the glass door we could see Mrs. McAdams moving about the kitchen. She took our order, and we waited for breakfast. Five minutes, ten minutes went by and still no food. Impatient to get started and thinking we might help the lady, we entered the kitchen and offered to carry our food to the table. "That isn't necessary," said Mrs. McAdams, placidly, "I'm in no hurry"; and baffled, we returned emptyhanded to the dining room, envying the poise of our hostess.

Waldorf   Very early one Sunday morning Charlotte, Gene and I left Georgetown and started for Waldorf, taking the road up the mountain to Green Lake. We'd been told about the road—that it was narrow and had few turnouts, that one was liable to meet cars full of fishermen at every turn, and that beyond the lake it was unbelievably steep. As we drove the switchbacks which zigzag up the mountain, Georgetown lay spread out like a toy village below, and far beyond its well-shaded streets and neat houses stretched the narrow, steepsided valley that leads to Clear Creek. The little town grew smaller and smaller the higher the road climbed, until a turn hid it completely, and we cut back into a basin in which lay Green and Clear Lakes. The road turned right at a fork where a dingy sign pointed upwards to Waldorf, five miles. It was little travelled, its ascent was swift and steep, and the going was decidedly rougher, with the road just wide enough for one car. We climbed steadily between bushes and low trees with no sign of habitation except two bevies of cabins and mine buildings, all deserted and partly dismantled. Still the road led upwards, even past timberline and entered high, rolling meadows and marshes. Through them Leavenworth Creek cut its way, looping and twisting below us, while ahead were great barren peaks in whose broken contours lay banks of last winter's snow.

The road wound on over the tundra until it brought us to a cluster of buildings along a street, at the end of which was a mine tunnel. This was Waldorf, which according to a sign on the biggest false-fronted building is 11,666 feet above sea level. A railroad, the Argentine Central, ran up here when the mine was working, and its ties and roadbed could be seen half submerged in the swampy grass below the mill. A number of houses stood along the one street or perched above or below it on the mountainside. One we recognized as the assay office by its array of cupels and cast iron moulds in which the ore was roasted and tested.

According to mining reports there were about eighty veins in the main group of claims belonging to the Waldorf Mining and Milling Company, but only nine were worked extensively. These mines produced over $4,000,000; but much ore lay untouched underground. Consequently the Wilcox Tunnel was driven through McClellan Mountain in 1903 to cut many of the known veins in the district including all the mines belonging to the Waldorf Company. This made more than four miles of underground workings in this mountain. Most of the ore was silver, but some gold was found in the Independence, Bullion and Mendham Mines. The Stevens, which was one of the big producers in the early days, was tapped by the tunnel and its ore brought out here at Waldorf. Back in 1868, shortly after the mine was discovered, its owners hired two men to take out ore at thirty dollars a ton. As the men had no means of hauling the ore from the mine to the trail which they had cut through the trees, they filled rawhide sacks with the ore and rolled them down to the trail. For those that did not burst they received full pay; but so many of them broke open on the rocks that the system proved unprofitable.

Our exploration of the town was interrupted by Gene, who called to us excitedly, "See what's coming up the trail." Just below us, on what used to be the wagon road over Argentine Pass, was a prospector and his pack train, consisting of his horse and three burros loaded with equipment, each with a tinkling bell attached to its harness. We watched the procession pick its way up the trail until it was out of sight and, having seen it disappear over the top of the pass, we found it hard to realize that this was 1942 and not 1872, when solitary miners and their jacks were everyday sights in these mountains, and Argentine Pass was the main road into the Snake River country.

Having been told that the Santiago Mine, two miles above Waldorf, was being worked and that we could drive to it, we once more urged the Ford up cruel grades until it reached the dump and loading platform of the mine. There was just room to turn the car around by backing it to the end of the dump, below which the slope fell sharply away for some hundreds of feet.

(123)

Just as we had maneuvered into a position on the ledge road where we thought it safe to park, an empty ore truck droned up to the platform and came to a grinding stop.

"How did you get up here?" asked the driver. "Not in that car? Very few can make this grade." We chatted with him as he pointed out other mines nearby and identified the peaks, which were so close yet towered so far above us. "Be sure and visit the Santiago Mill," he called after us, as we started back toward Waldorf. "Take the first turn to the right and you'll see it."

Following his suggestion we detoured a quarter of a mile to the mine proper. Here, at a 12,000-foot elevation, we found the main workings and a general air of activity. Cars were parked alongside of the mine office, and electric lights burned in all the sheds and lighted the mine tunnel from whose opening men emerged at frequent intervals, pushing ore cars out to the dump. The whole setting was so picturesque that I decided to make a watercolor. Sitting on the edge of a dump, I blocked in the composition, which included the track over which the ore cars were being run. Before I had been long at work, a trammer noticed what was going on and obligingly posed on each of his trips to the dump, that I might incorporate him in the picture.

In talking to some of the men we learned that though the Santiago was an old mine which, with the Commonwealth and Centennial veins, had been worked in the seventies and eighties, the bulk of production had been since nineteen hundred.

"This is great country," commented the timekeeper, coming to the door of his office to visit with us. "Just last week two Public Service company linemen came up here to repair some wires. One of them was new to the job and had never seen such high country before. 'What do you think of it?' I asked him. The lineman looked about him in all directions, took a deep breath and said with awe in his voice, 'Ain't she big?'" We felt much the same as we looked around from the Santiago Mine, taking in the stupendous views of the towering peaks and ranges even though we ourselves were standing at a 12,000-foot elevation.

The men at the mine seemed pleased that we had come up there and showed us all through the gold mill. It was running at full capacity and the interior was noisy, dusty, wet and alive. This made it exciting in a way quite different from the many empty and deserted mills through which I had so frequently prowled. Although I cannot describe the intricate process by which the ore is reduced to a dark, grayish sand called "concentrate," I looked at it respectfully as it lay in its hopper waiting to be loaded in trucks for the haul to Idaho Springs, and from there to the smelter.

We hated to leave Santiago and the feeling that we were on top of the world, and by the time we reached Waldorf, I was so obsessed with an idea that I couldn't repress it. "I've got to climb Argentine Pass!" I blurted out to my astonished companions. "I'll never be any closer to the top of it than I am now, so this is the time. Do you want to wait for me or come along?"

"We'll come along," they responded, and in less than five minutes the

WALDORF,
ELEV. 11,666 FT.

ARGENTINE
PASS

three of us had started up the long, snakelike trail toward the top of the pass over McClellan Mountain.

"If we got to the top what would we see on the other side?" asked Charlotte, as we took off our shoes and socks to wade across a clear stream which crossed the trail just beyond Waldorf.

"We should be able to look down to the site of Argentine and Decatur and see the Pennsylvania mine which is still working, and we'd probably see where Chihuahua and Peru were situated," I replied. "The whole area was called the Argentine District, and this road connected the camps on both sides of this mountain and linked Georgetown with Montezuma and Sts. John."

The higher we climbed, the less we talked and the oftener we stopped to admire the scenery and to conceal the fact that we were getting short-winded. This was to be neither the first nor the last time in my hunt for ghost towns in the rugged Colorado Rockies that I let my enthusiasm outstrip my physical endurance. I am short and decidedly plump, and sometimes my heart, wind, legs and even my nerves play me false.

Looking back frequently while we stopped for breath, we saw, far below us, Waldorf, with its long, covered mine tunnel and weathered buildings, and the winding bed of the railroad clearly distinguishable as it twisted through the tundra.

"Maybe we'll see the prospector and his pack train," suggested Gene by way of encouragement as we struggled up the rocky path.

As the trail rose before us I began to set goals for myself and to wonder how much farther I really wanted to go. Surely at the next curve we could see the top. But the trail wound on and up to another curve, and our grim plodding continued. After five or six such experiences my enthusiasm began to wane. The sun beat upon us, and the more I thought of pushing another mile at least to the top the more foolish it seemed. What was to be gained by looking into the next valley except personal satisfaction? The towns on the far side could be reached by auto road and I could then look up at Argentine Pass and see its summit from the western side. We were now over 12,600 feet, the trail was rough and every step was an effort. I decided therefore to go on to the next switchback and, if the top was still far away, to give up the idea entirely. Hopefully I approached the curve and, rounding it, looked for the desired top of the 13,286-foot pass. Instead, only an endless set of switchbacks led up across a rocky waste. "Don't be an idiot," I said to myself and started back to Waldorf.

The drive down to the junction with the Green Lake road was an adventure in itself, for its pitch was so steep—twenty-five percent grade our mining friend at Santiago had told us—that the whole of the Rocky Mountains seemed to be rising up in front of us. Tired as we were we detoured to the lakes, finding Green a quiet, rock-rimmed body of water and Clear a larger, longer lake in the hollow of a narrow mountain valley. Though they were beautiful they looked so tame and peaceful after our morning's adventures that we left them almost immediately and came down the rest of the descent into Georgetown, worn out, elated, disappointed, and dreadfully hungry all at the same time.

One day while I was sketching in Silver Plume a crowd of curious children stood nearby watching the picture grow. The scene of the street contained a church; so turning to one of the children I asked, "What church is that?" "I don't know," he replied; "it doesn't go any more." Much of Silver Plume doesn't "go anymore," and many of its buildings have disappeared within the last fifteen years; yet it is not a ghost town. In summer its frame houses are full of life but each fall the visitors close up their vacation homes and depart, leaving a small permanent population to carry on through the long winter months.

It was not until 1870 that a town was built in this picturesque valley between the steep mountainsides. At first its tents and cabins were located high on the slopes, but gradually, as the valley was cleared of trees and its swampy land was drained, homes were built on the flat and the townsite began to take shape.

The Pelican mine had been discovered two years earlier by Owen Feenan, who was working at the time in another mine and kept his discovery to himself. Becoming dangerously ill and believing that he was going to die, he confided to two friends the location of his mine. For more than a year he hovered between life and death and when he finally recovered, it was only to learn that the mine had been opened in the spring of 1871 and that he had been completely left out of the transaction. From the first the mine was a good producer employing large numbers of men, many of whom lived at the Pelican House. Its beds were never empty, for no sooner had one shift of men left for the mine than the second shift entered and flopped down upon the well-warmed bunks. The men were paid on Saturday nights, and each week when they reached the Pelican House to settle their board bills they found a crowd of children waiting for them, confident that the miners would toss small change their way in order to see them scramble for it.

By 1875 the population of the mountain town, 9,040 feet above sea level, was 2,000 and two churches, a school, a postoffice, a theatre and several general stores and saloons served the growing community. Brownsville, which was always regarded as a suburb to Silver Plume, had, besides its homes and business houses which catered to the miners' needs, an Odd Fellows Hall where a portion of the population found entertainment. Brownsville's history was cut short by a mudslide, and the town was never rebuilt. Graymount and Bakerville, however, which lay several miles farther on still exist, although many years have passed since an omnibus line ran at regular intervals between them and the Plume.

The richest and most famous of the mines were close to the town and were reached by narrow roads which can still be seen, crisscrossing the mountainsides or zigzagging to almost inaccessible tunnel openings. The lodes carried silver, lead, zinc, copper and gold and were located on all the surrounding mountains. The best producers were the Pelican-Dives, Payrock, Corry City, Dunderburg, Burleigh, Seven-Thirty, Terrible, Mendota, Baker and Stevens, and the ore from them was carried by jack trains to the Plume, from which a regular express service hauled it to Georgetown. These properties produced millions and as long as they prospered the town flourished too.

(127)

The Seven-Thirty mine was discovered in the late sixties by Clifford Griffin, a young Englishman who was one of the first miners to come to the Plume. Little was known about him, except that his fiancee had been found dead in his room on the eve of their wedding, and that he came to the Rocky Mountains and became a miner in order to forget the past. The mine was rich in both silver and gold and the deeper it was developed the richer the ore became; so before long, the young Englishman was the wealthiest mine owner in the camp. But nothing erased from his mind the memory of his fiancee's death, and he withdrew more and more from the other miners and their families. He built a cabin high on Columbia Mountain, near his mine, and in front of it he hewed a grave out of the solid rock. His sole companion was his violin, and after his day's work he would stand in front of his cabin and play until dark. At the first notes of the music, the miners would step out of their cabins to listen, looking up at the solitary musician on the rock. Some times they would call to him and request some special selection, and at the end of his recital their applause would roll through the gulch. One summer evening in 1887 he played especially well, and his admirers commented upon his remarkable performance. As they watched him they saw him walk toward the grave, and no sooner had the playing ceased than a shot rang out. Rushing up the mountain they found his body, as they feared, lying face down in the grave he had prepared, a bullet through his heart. In his cabin was a note requesting that he be buried in the stone tomb, and the miners not only followed his wishes but erected a granite shaft over it with the inscription:

CLIFFORD GRIFFIN
SON OF ALFRED GRIFFIN ESQ. OF
BRAND HALL, SHROPSHIRE, ENGLAND
BORN JULY 2, 1847
DIED JUNE 10, 1887
AND IN CONSIDERATION OF HIS OWN REQUEST BURIED HERE

When the railroad reached Georgetown in 1877 the shipment of ore from Silver Plume's mines was greatly facilitated, and when in 1882 the famous Georgetown Loop was completed, not only to Silver Plume but as far as Graymount where the Baker and Stevens mines were located, the Plume reached its peak. The Loop trip became known all over the country, ranking with Niagara Falls and Yellowstone Park as a "must" on vacations. All summer long trains brought as many as twenty-five or thirty carloads of passengers a day to the Plume. Tourists filled the streets, blocking all vehicular traffic and filling the eating places to capacity. Many brought their lunches and picnicked in the grove at the far end of town or along Clear Creek. The La Veta Hotel and the Windsor Hotel vied with each other to provide tempting dinners which were ready upon the arrival of the excursion trains.

Everything was very prosperous and very gay until November 1884, when fire consumed the business portion of the town and destroyed over fifty buildings. The fire started in a saloon in the middle of the night and made terrific headway before it was discovered. The Silver Plume Hook and Ladder Company did its best, but its efforts were fruitless. As the newspaper stated: "Everyone realized the town's helplessness in battling such a monster without waterworks, fire engine or hose company." A messenger was sent to Georgetown to secure aid, and before long the Star Hook and Ladder Company's truck with its four horses dashed up the hill to the rescue. "In the meantime the destroyer was marching west on Main St. devouring in its path the buildings on either side of the street," and citizens battled the "fiery serpent which hissed defiance" at them in spite of all they could do. From time to time other fires took their toll of buildings and possessions, with the result that gaping holes or empty lots, overgrown with weeds which half cover crumbling foundations, are the only evidence today that buildings once stood on these sites.

Anyone in Silver Plume can tell you the story of the Pelican and Dives mines whose eight-foot silver vein was the richest in the region and whose huge dumps loom high behind the town, and they can describe the feud over the underground property which resulted in litigation, graft and murder. The two mine shafts were not only on the same mountain but were so close together that it was believed that both were tapping the same vein. Experts hired at $100 a day, showed that this was true—the original vein, although diverted in one spot by a mass of rock, was being worked by both mines. Both companies eyed the ore which the other extracted, believing it to be stolen. Lawsuits were brought against the property endeavoring to settle once and for all on which property the vein apexed. At one time, twenty-three suits were on file before Judge Belford contesting "prior rights to the vein." Court scenes during the hearings were so heated that the judge was forced to keep a brace of pistols on his desk. Feeling ran so high that all of Clear Creek county was involved and took sides on the issue. Hundreds of thousands of dollars in fees were paid to mining experts and to lawyers, and still the struggle continued.

On one occasion the Pelican mine got a writ of attachment for all Dives ore. To spike the decision, $65,000 was shipped from the Dives mine on Sunday before the sheriff could serve the papers. Jacob Snider, one of the owners of the Pelican mine, believed that J. H. McMurdy, resident manager of the Dives, was stealing his ore. Investigating underground, he heard the pickaxes of the miners in the rival mine coming closer and closer to his wall of rock. Another night word was sent to Denver for six coffins for men who had been killed in the mine. These were delivered and were lowerd down the shaft. All six were later drawn up with their heavy loads and hauled away. It was discovered later that the boxes contained stolen high-grade ore and not bodies; but by this time the ore was far away at the smelter. Both companies placed armed guards about their property, and a virtual state of siege existed.

One morning in 1875 Snider left the mine and on horseback, started for Georgetown. He had almost reached the city when he saw Jack Bishop, a mercenary from the Dives mine, waiting beside the road ahead of him. Sensing danger, he dashed into Georgetown with Bishop close behind him. Seeing the open door of a livery stable, he made for it, but just at the doorway Bishop overtook him and struck him to the ground with the butt of his pistol.

He then shot the wounded man in the head and rode off. As no attempt was made to seize him until an hour later, he succeeded in making his escape. Shortly after this incident McMurdy died, and W. A. Hammill of Georgetown bought the Dives mine at a sheriff's sale for $50,000. In 1880 he sold the combined Pelican-Dives properties for $5,000,000 and became Georgetown's wealthiest citizen.

One by one the Plume's landmarks are disappearing. La Veta Hotel is gone, the City Hotel next to St. Patrick's church has been razed, two houses have lost their ornate Victorian porches, and the wooden bandstand beside Clear Creek sags more and more each year. But the city hall, the fire house, the tiny stone jail and the large brick school house, as well as a row of false-fronted stores remain. The Windsor Hotel with its Victorian parlor and clean lace curtains is open for business, and a few stores serve the three hundred residents of the town, whose main street the new highway neglects. Few people turn off the main road to wander along the winding streets and to admire the columbine and larkspur growing in gardens which surround the neatly painted houses with their picket fences, and few visitors know that the stone for the Denver Capitol was cut from the granite quarry just beyond the edge of the little mountain city.

Montezuma
and
Sts. John

"I've been reading about the discovery of silver in this part of Colorado, and most authorities agree that it was first smelted in 1864 near where we're going today," I told Rebecca and Norman as we left Silver Plume behind us and passed the crumbling two-story log house that marks the site of Graymount. "The narrow gauge ran as far as Graymount and Bakerville, and it was here that tourists obtained saddle horses for the popular trip to the summit of Gray's peak to see the sun rise."

Bakerville, beyond Graymount, was formerly a busy mining camp when the Stevens mine was flourishing, but now it is only a summer resort and fisherman's retreat.

"Where are we going?" asked Norman as we climbed over Loveland Pass and looked back at Clear Creek and the sliver of road that had been our highway, and now lay so far below us.

"We leave this highway at the foot of the pass and follow the Snake River as far as Montezuma. It isn't a ghost town, but Sts. John, which is two miles further on, is; and it's our real objective today. I went to Montezuma once before," I admitted; "but I hadn't heard about Sts. John then and I knew nothing of the silver mining history of this area, so this return trip is a necessity."

Summer cabins built among the pines line the six miles between the highway and the town, and from many of them people waved at us as we drove by. Montezuma is completely hidden from view by a low hill around which the road sweeps to enter one end of the long main street. Wide and unpaved, it is lined with frame houses, placed far back from the roadway. What wooden sidewalks existed have disappeared, except for occasional splintered boards half overgrown with weeds and grass. Driving the length of the street, we stopped in front of the large, frame hotel and entered its one-room post office.

(130)

SILVER PLUME (by permission of the Ford Motor Co.)

From the postmistress I learned that it was possible to drive to Sts. John, which was located at an elevation of 10,800 feet, and that the one remaining family there had moved to Montezuma the day before; therefore we need have no fear of meeting anyone on the narrow road. She pointed across the river and said: "Take that road behind the houses till you get to Sts. John," and, waving goodbye, she left us.

The road was narrow and steep and its surface was a mass of loose rock. The switchbacks were short and sharp, and on one of them even my Ford coupe had to back up before completing the turn. By driving in low gear and by dodging the biggest boulders, we reached the top of the hill and drove on through more gentle terrain, past an old mine and watermill, until we saw some buildings through the trees and entered what remained of the town. Close by the road stood a brick stack and the ruined walls of a smelter, while straight ahead was a whole group of buildings and an enormous mill. To our surprise, a large, red truck was backed up to the house from which the people were moving, and a man and some boys were busily loading it with furniture. Sending up a little prayer of thanks that we hadn't met the truck on the road, I began to talk to the man and learned that Sts. John had been a camp in the late sixties and had boomed in the seventies and eighties.

"You should have seen it then. Part of the town was above the mill and part of it was down here. There were lots of houses then, but some have been torn down, and once a snowslide wiped out a whole end of town. You can see where the slide ran," said he, pointing to the opposite mountainside. "It was always a one mine camp, depending chiefly upon the Sts. John property which was located on top of Glacier Mountain. That's the assay office over there, and next to it is the guest house where mine visitors were entertained. The big three-story building was the boardinghouse, and you saw the smelter when you drove into town," he concluded, and turned back to his loading.

Rebecca and I explored the assay office with its furnace and clay cupels, and in the scattered debris we found a record book of the mine whose last entry had been made in 1914. The boardinghouse was a wooden shell with every window a gaping hole and the doors wide open. Cautiously testing the staircase, I went up and peered out of the second-story window at the mountainside, which was a mass of dumps and tunnel openings, with foot trails leading from level to level and a few buildings fastened against the steep slopes. The huge mill was a skeleton structure through whose blackened beams and girders the cracked, gray mud of a settling pond could be seen.

I finished my sketches and we drove back to Montezuma. There I found an old man sitting on the steps of the hotel and from him I learned the history of Sts. John.

The first man to smelt silver ore and locate a silverbearing lode in the region was John Coley. In 1861 some gulch miners from the Blue River were hunting deer and ran out of ammunition. Finding some ore that they thought was lead, they used it to make bullets, and continued their hunting. Three years later, in 1864, one of them saw some silver ore in Nevada which closely resembled that from which they had made their ammunition, and writing to John Coley, who was living in Empire, Colorado, this man urged him to go over and locate the lead vein. Coley made the tough trip and found the heavy galena ore. He built a crude forge, and later a furnace against a ledge of rock, in which he roasted samples of ore and reduced them to bullion. The remains of his old furnace are still there about a half mile from the tunnel of the Sts. John mine. He was clever, and when he needed a draft in his furnace to carry off the smoke and sulphur fumes, he built a smokestack by placing in position a hollow log and covering it with rocks and clay. He then burned out the log on the inside and had left a perfect stone flue. Roasting his ore in this furnace, he took the buttons of silver across Argentine Pass to Georgetown; but the ore was too low grade to be worth much, and no one paid any attention to him. Besides, the boom in Clear Creek was at its peak, and an eccentric fellow whose mine was across the range was not worth listening to.

By 1865, however, the Comstock lode of the Sts. John mine had been discovered, and a small town at the foot of Glacier Mountain sprang up, while prospectors combed the hillsides for other paying veins. In 1866 the Boston Silver Mining Association was organized, and by 1872 a concentration mill was finished; but only a few tons of ore were treated, for the barite it contained could not be smelted by this process. In 1878 the mine was taken over by the Boston Mining Company, and its development from then on was chiefly made by Boston capitalists.

From another resident we learned that the hotel with the post office was originally called the Summit House and that the two-story white structure across the street, with the ornate porch, was built in 1879 and called the Rocky Mountain House. The rest of the town consists of log cabins and frame houses scattered over a wide area. I found several examples of an architectural style which is common in these smaller towns—the log cabin with a bay window, invariably hung with lace curtains and serving as a conservatory to several geraniums, which grow to immense heights and whose gay blooms add a colorful note to the drab exterior.

At the lower end of town lived a delightful old lady to whom I had been directed. She ushered me into her cosy parlor and offered me a rocking chair. Taking one herself, she asked in a sprightly voice what I wanted to know about Sts. John.

"I knew the place well," she began, "for I lived there for a number of years. Its boom was in the seventies, when it had a population of about 200. The town was founded in 1867 and was originally called Coleyville after John Coley, who discovered silver there, but the name was changed the same year to Sts. John. People call it St. Johns today, but it was named by a group of men, many of whom were Masons, and they called it Sts. John.

"There used to be many more buildings above the mill, and a few below on the willow flats. They had a library too in the little building that is now the assay office. I know, for I was the librarian," she said proudly. "The log schoolhouse was at the top of the switchbacks you drove this morning and it served both towns. Sometimes the teacher lived in Montezuma and sometimes in Sts. John. There was a post office up there, but the mail was carried up from Montezuma by saddle. There was a store and a sawmill too, as well as a smelting furnace in 1881, when only about fifty people lived there. The ore was lead and silver you know, and the stamp mill which ran for a time made its own silver bars. The Boston Silver Mining Company owned the property and developed it. The mine was worked until a few years ago. There was a still smaller place above Sts. John called Preston's but it was just a mine, never a big camp.

"Father Dyer used to cross Webster Pass between Collier and Teller mountains on his trips to Fairplay and Breckenridge and on one of them he discovered a mine at the top of the mountain. A good deal of ore was shipped from it by ox team to the railroad and then on the rails to the east, where it was taken by water to Swansea, Wales, for treatment. There are still lots of ox shoes found on the mine trails; but there's no mining at Sts. John nowdays," she concluded, smiling a little sadly. Rummaging in a chest of drawers she produced a photograph album and showed me pictures of the mine buildings at Sts. John and of groups of miners who worked there. With the graciousness that I have encountered so often on these trips she gave me, when I left, a photograph of the mine and she urged me to come back again for another visit.

Before we left Montezuma I looked at the high mountains which hem in this little town and noticed several mines and shaft houses above timberline, with slender thread-like trails winding down the steep sides of Glacier and Teller mountains, and I envied my friend from Grant who had often ridden to the top of Webster Pass and looked down at Montezuma far below.

"What do you know about Montezuma?" asked Norman when we left the town behind and were driving back to the highway.

"It is said to be the oldest town on the Snake River," I replied, "and for a long time it had the only smelter that handled custom ores of the neighborhood. The first silver discovery here, according to one authority, was made by Henry M. Teller, but how that checks with the discoverey made by Coley I don't know. Communication with the outside world was via Argentine Pass or over the road to Breckenridge. In 1868 Governor Evans made a tour of the region, coming from Central City and Georgetown and crossing Argentine Pass to visit Peru and Montezuma. By 1871 Montezuma had a summer population of 200, a steam sawmill, a hotel and a post office. By the eighties there was a good wagon road over Handcart Pass to Webster, eighteen miles away. By 1881 the population was nearly 800, and besides stores there were a smelting furnace and concentration works to handle the gray copper and galena ore which was hauled from the mines high above the town. The Montezuma Silver Mining Company alone worked eleven lodes on Glacier and Teller mountains.

"As with all other silver towns, Montezuma went through a dreadful decline in 1893, but it never was entirely deserted, and a little mining is still done on the surrounding mountains. Chihuahua, Argentine and Decatur are only three or four miles from Montezuma, on another road, and some day I'm going to visit them, too."

Chihuahua   A year later I drove up the Snake River again toward Montezuma but, before reaching the town, turned the car onto a side road, which led to the Pennsylvania mine, four miles ahead. The road was unbelievably rough, and I rode the humps and hollows as best I could. Somewhere along this road was the site of Chihuahua, the little camp that was destroyed by the forest fire of 1889 which had also threatened Montezuma. Fifty houses in the camp were burned and the wagon road between it and Montezuma was almost ruined by the burning logs which fell across it. Chihuahua was incorporated in 1880, had a population of 200 and boomed for several years. There were stores, a sawmill, a reduction works and two hotels, the Chihuahua and the Snively. The chief mine was the Peruvian. That name gave me a clue or rather a sense of complete confusion. On an old map I had seen Montezuma, Chihuahua, Argentine and Peru indicated by dots as towns or camps. Yet I had been told that there never was a town called Peru. Perhaps the buildings around this Peruvian mine constituted "Peru!"

Similar confusions in sites and names and the renaming of towns were a constant source of interest and despair to me in my research and my explorations. Any group of prospectors who found a good sized pay-streak of ore called their cluster of tents and cabins a camp or town, and gave it a name. A year, or ten years, later their town might have died or it might have reached proportions that necessitated incorporation. When incorporated, it might retain its original name or select a new one. On this trip I was determined to find out just where Argentine and Peru stood; but making sure of the site of Argentine was further complicated by a statement in the *Daily Mining Record* of 1903 which read: "Up at Argentine (Rathbone), the Rothschild Co. is pushing ahead on a 3000-foot crosscut tunnel." According to this, Argentine was also known as Rathbone; yet I already knew that a place called Decatur, close to the site of Argentine, had been called Rathbone in the middle eighties. To untangle such conflicts and discrepancies in the names, dates and sites has been one of my purposes in pushing up so many forgotten roads, in asking so many questions of so many people, and in poking among so many trash piles and foundations. My hope of establishing accurate information about nebulous campsites has in some cases succeeded; in other cases I am still searching for an answer. Driving about a mile along the road toward the Pennsylvania mine, we passed a few rotting cabin frames, and so far as I can find out, that was the site of Chihuahua.

The location of Argentine was equally elusive. I had asked any number of people about a place called Argentine and as usual had received conflicting answers. One said there had never been a place of that name—just a mining district. Another assured me that it was beyond Decatur, at the foot of Argentine Pass, and a third was positive that it had been swept away in a snowslide. I was therefore anxious to get first-hand information, by going to the presumable site of the town and seeing what I could find out about it.

Argentine and Decatur

Just before Ethel Zeigler and I reached the Pennsylvania mine with its many buildings and its big and busy mill, we saw, across the stream from our road, some empty houses and the foundations of some that had vanished. Maybe that was Argentine! Parking the car in the shadow of the Pennsylvania mill, we started to explore the property. Before we'd gone fifty feet, a cook stepped out on the porch of a two-story bunk house, and hope-

(135)

fully I shouted to him, "Are we on the site of old Argentine?" "Blessed if I know," he shouted back. "There's no one around but me, and the next shift won't be in for hours."

In the distance, the old Argentine Pass road cut a diagonal up the mountainside and I recalled the day that I'd started to climb to its summit from the Waldorf side with the hope of looking down into this very valley. We sketched for a while until we saw some men leaving the mine office, whereupon I hurried after them and repeated my question as to the whereabouts of old Argentine. The foreman was extremely helpful and, looking up some records, explained that the buildings about half a mile away across the stream were those of Decatur. Argentine had been further down the road and Chihuahua was about three miles back. The Pennsylvania mine, which was an old property, discovered by J. M. Hall in 1879, was developed in the eighties, and had produced a total of over $2,000,000. He showed us around, and as we were inspecting the mess hall the cook stuck his head in the door and said: "Say, Boss, IS this place called Argentine?" A long table in the center of the room was set for lunch, and the foreman invited us to stay and eat with the men but my urge to get to Decatur made me refuse the invitation and keep on going. Returning to the fork in the road, past the site of Argentine and its snowslide, I crossed Chihuahua Creek and trudged half a mile to the houses the foreman had pointed out. There was no doubt but that this was all that was left of Decatur and that Argentine had been located almost opposite it.

"There's quite a story about Decatur," I said to Ethel as we drove home. "The town was named for a pioneer prospector of the Georgetown region, who in 1868 established a mining camp on this site. In 1880 the place, which was by then well established, was named for him, although the name was later changed to Rathbone. It was a small camp with a population of only 100 and with one hotel, the Sautell House. The Pennsylvania, Delaware, Peruvian, Queen of the West, Revenue Tariff and other mines were located here and their ores assayed from $20 to $2000 a ton.

"Stephen Decatur was a colorful character and was surrounded with mystery. He came to Colorado in 1859, fought Indians, mined successfully, and was once a member of the territorial legislature. In 1876 he was sent as a commissioner from Colorado to the Centennial Exposition in Philadelphia. Decatur was believed to be the brother of Governor Bross of Illinois; and when the governor, who had lost a brother in 1854, heard that there was a man in the Colorado mining camps who looked like him and who called himself Stephen Decatur, he became curious and came out to see for himself. Reaching Colorado, the Governor soon located 'Commodore Decatur' as he was called, and welcomed him as his lost brother. Decatur refused to acknowledge any relationship, and even though the governor was sure that this man was his brother he could never prove it, for the Commodore was completely non-committal about the whole matter.

"There's a story about the Peru claim, too," I continued. "The men who owned it didn't know much about mining but they wanted a tunnel driven one hundred feet into their prospect hole before winter and they hired

MINE DUMPS,
SAINTS
JOHN

RUINED MILL,
SAINTS
JOHN

Gassy Thompson to dig and timber it for them. He agreed to do this and they left, promising to return in the spring, inspect his work and pay him. Gassy had a load of timbers brought in, got a helper and began digging, taking out a little dirt and timbering the mouth of the shallow tunnel. Then as winter snows began to collect on the mountainside, Gassy had an original idea which, if carried out, would save him and his partner lots of work. Instead of pushing the tunnel through hard quartz rock he suggested building the tunnel backwards, through the ever-increasing snow drifts. Beginning at the face, he timbered outwards for one hundred feet and when the job was completed, he and his helper spent a cosy winter in the mine bunk house. As successive snows fell, the timbering of the false tunnel became completely buried until only its new face was visible. By April, although the snow still lay deep on the slopes, the directors of the Peru claim snowshoed in to see how the work was progressing, to accept the tunnel, and to pay Gassy for his labor. They inspected his work and said it was a fine job. They slapped Gassy on the back, congratulated him on his arduous digging and paying him in full, they snowshoed to warmer temperatures. It had been a severe winter, and the deep snow did not melt from shaded slopes until July. Then, as the snow fell away from the new timbers, the astonished owners saw the bare framework of the useless tunnel and a search for Gassy was made; but he was far away probably prospecting for more suckers."

Empire   On our way home from one trip over the range, we passed through Georgetown and as we left the little city and started toward Denver, I pointed to a steep and narrow road which swept up the mountainside to our left and disappeared at the saddle. "Want to go to Empire as the old-timers did over Union Pass?" I asked Elizabeth and Elliot, who were my companions on this jaunt.

"Is it really used nowadays?" asked Elizabeth, looking apprehensively at the narrow shelf which rose so abruptly from the valley floor.

"Of course," I replied, turning off the highway to approach the steep grade. "I enquired about it in Georgetown and was told that it is constantly used as a shortcut to Empire."

"It's a shortcut to somewhere," murmured one of my companions, as we climbed the ledge road and looked straight down on the highway we had left and at the Georgetown cemeteries across the creek. We climbed fast and reached the saddle in less than five minutes. Crossing it, we entered a new valley and rolled down a less harrowing hill to the town.

"Of course Empire isn't a ghost town and isn't really much of a mining town any more," I explained as we drove toward the highway which cuts the town in half; "but it was the mining craze that caused two prospectors to come over the hills from Central City in August, 1860, prospecting as they went. They found a little gold on Eureka Mountain, and as the news spread, men flocked in so fast that by September the Empire and Keystone lodes had been discovered and prospect holes covered Columbia, Lincoln, Douglass, and Breckenridge mountains.

"A number of prospectors from Idaho Springs joined the restless assemblage of miners and helped organize the Union Mining District. As more miners arrived from Gilpin County, log cabins began to replace the tents. The second cabin erected was used as a courthouse, sheriff's office, recorder's office and town hall. The little camp was called Valley City but the name was soon changed to Empire, the nickname of the state from which its founders came. As mining increased, the town grew, boasting in 1862 a hotel and blacksmith shop, as well as a combined grocery and post office, and two or three cabins.

"There was considerable bar mining on the creek and a number of arastras and stamp mills ground the auriferous quartz which was washed from the gravels. By 1864 the miners, who were getting down to the pyrites, which required different treatment from the placer gold, began to explore the adjacent hills for lode mines or drifted to new mining districts where silver was beginning to attract attention.

"Empire by 1866 had two intersecting streets, one of which climbed a mile and a half up the hill to North Empire, where the Empire mine and several small mills formed the nucleus of a little camp on Lyons Creek. Empire's only water supply was a well one hundred feet deep, which stood in the middle of town and to which everyone went with jugs and pails to obtain water. The town began to decline in 1866 both because of the scarcity of water for mining needs, and because the new camp of Georgetown was attracting a large proportion of the population. By 1881, although hydraulic mining was being carried on and certain lode mines were productive, the population dwindled to two hundred. The town was incorporated in 1882, although but thirty-nine miners quit work to vote for the measure.

"I've read some letters and diaries of pioneers who went to Empire in the sixties, and their accounts of living conditions and the cost of food sound strangely familiar today. One woman recalls her first Christmas dinner there in 1862. A head of cabbage, which cost $5.00, was the special treat, for fresh vegetables were almost unknown during those first years when all supplies were freighted in from Denver behind several spans of mules. In bad weather wagons couldn't get through without men getting out and shovelling every drift which blocked the road. There's one story of a freighter who, in loosing the traces of a mule which was hopelessly stuck in a drift, received a kick from the sharp hooves and had his cheek laid open. As it was intensely cold weather, the man put a cud of chewing tobacco on the wound, covered it with a cabbage leaf, and bound this poultice about his face with a bandanna. This protected him from the cold until he could reach home and get proper care.

"The trip to and from Denver was long and arduous, especially crossing Floyd Hill. Oxen and horses couldn't pull that hill without the help of men, who tied ropes to the wagons and wound these around stumps or trees. They would then laboriously pull the wagon foot by foot up the steep grade or on the down grade gradually pay out the rope to check its speed.

"Provisions were expensive. Butter was $3.00 a pound, eggs $3.00 a dozen, sugar fifty to seventy cents a pound, and flour $18.00 a hundred. The greatest expense of all was feed for mules and stock, for during the long winters when the snow was deep, animals could not dig their way through

(139)

the snow to the frozen grass. During one severe winter hay was $200 a ton. Native hay was cut by hand, was cured and was fed to the horses. Finally the wild hay meadows of Middle Park were discovered, and hay was cut there and brought by muleback over the narrow Indian trail which is now Berthoud Pass.

"Ute Indians used this trail when they went to Denver to trade, and whenever they passed through they stopped at the mining camp. They were friendly enough, but their visits were a drain on the settlers, as they always expected food and got it. One woman recalls that one day, just as her mother put the noonday meal on the table and was about to call the men from the mill, a band of Utes rode into the yard and the chiefs entered her house. Filing by the laden table, they helped themselves to all the hot, tempting food, scooping it up in their hands as they went by. Outside, the braves and squaws waited their turn. Since the table was now devoid of food the braves cleaned the closets of provisions, and when the squaws came in there was nothing left but some sacks of feed corn. Each squaw took a handful of the kernels in the corner of her shawl and followed the menfolk, who by now were off to Denver. When the mill men arrived for their dinner they found their food gone, so, going to the cabin door, one of them shot a mountain sheep which was grazing on the hill and dressed it, and after some hours they ate wild sheep meat."

"How discouraging," commented Elizabeth. "How could the people stand it?"

"Oh, they had their compensations," I replied. "I've read about their coasting parties down the mile-long run from North Empire, on sleds whose runners were made from ox-bows. And I recall reading how proud one woman was of her cabin, because its roof beams were whitewashed and the walls were covered with wallpaper pasted upon cotton cloth. The houses in both Upper and Lower Empire were lighted with sperm candles those first years, and if the head of the house was a good hunter, deer, mountain sheep and bear furnished good, substantial food.

"Empire today is so modern with its cafes and hot dog stands, that there's little of the old left to see; so let's drive up the hill to North Empire."

"Up the hill" was the right phrase, for the street which bisects the highway rises almost perpendicularly up the mountain. On its slope I could picture the mile-long toboggan run, which on cold, moonlight nights must have provided thrilling adventures to the coasters. Not far up the hill we passed a large, empty house over whose door was a sign, "Bachelor's Roost," once probably a mine boardinghouse. The road wound and climbed higher past deserted mines and rusty shaft houses until at the top of the hill it reached a mill with its sheds and offices. Across a gully stood a boardinghouse in good condition, boarded up and with its windows unbroken, probably built in the late nineties. I made some sketches of it and of the mine before we drove slowly back to Empire. Far below us and across the valley was Union Pass and the twisting ribbon of Mad Creek, and beyond rose the snowy peaks back of Georgetown. As we dropped down the last steep mile I recalled an item from a pioneer's letter which described a mine accident in Upper Town and how the men carried the casket down this hill over the deep snow to the quiet cemetery.

"Don't you know any blood and thunder stories about Empire?" asked Elliot, as we neared the junction of Highway 40 and took a last look at Georgetown at the end of the shadowed valley.

"I know two. One dates back to 1860," I began. "A man named Lindstrom built a sawmill on Mad Creek with a thirty-foot overshot water-wheel. The framework of the mill was held together with wooden pins but the gudgeons needed for the wheel could not be made of wood. Machinery ordered from St. Joseph, Mo., would take some time to reach the mountain camp. In the meantime a set of suitable gudgeons were offered to Lindstrom by a stranger for sixty dollars, and were bought and paid for. Soon after the wheel was completed another man arrived at the mill who claimed that the gudgeons were his and had been stolen and sold to Lindstrom. The seller of the disputed property was arrested and tried by the first miners' court in the district, which found him guilty and sentenced him to be hanged. Lindstrom, protested this decision, saying he wanted no man's life on his conscience, and offered to pay for the gudgeons again and thereby reimburse the lawful owner. Thereupon the court ordered as a substitute sentence, forty lashes with a cat-o-nine tails to be administered to the thief, and in addition demanded that the right side of his head and the left side of his beard and moustache be shaved. The sentence was vigorously carried out and the wounds washed with salt water to prevent infection, whereupon a barber shaved the right side of his head. The court then agreed to rescind the rest of its sentence and the beard and moustache were left intact. The culprit was ridden out of town on a rail and warned never to return; and six months later word came that he had been hanged for horse-stealing."

"That's some story," commented Elliot. "Is the other one as good?"

"Not quite, although it deals with a murderer and with the Lindstrom family," I replied. "The same family that built the sawmill built a brewery which stood where Glenn Arbor Lodge is today. You remember I told you about the murder of Jacob Snider in connection with the Pelican-Dives feud? The murderer, Jack Bishop, rode through Georgetown after the killing, over Union Pass, and dashed up to the Lindstrom brewery where his friend Harry Carns lived. Telling Carns that a posse was after him, he begged to be hidden until they went by, whereupon Carns led him into the dark cellar and pushed him behind some large brewing vats. Carns then took Bishop's horse and hid it in the willows beyond Mad Creek and returned to the brewery before the sheriff and his hard-riding deputies pulled up in front of the building.

" 'Have you seen Bishop?' called the sheriff to Harry, who by this time was sitting lazily in front of the brewery.

" 'Sure,' replied Harry.

" 'Where was he?' asked the sheriff impatiently.

" 'Hiding behind old man Lindstrom's beer kegs. Go in and look for him,' answered Carns, chewing a straw.

(141)

"The sheriff dismounted, entered the brewery and glanced quickly around the dark inner room, not believing Carns but taking no chances. 'Come on, boys, let's go,' he shouted gulping a glass of beer which Carns gave him, and galloped off, followed by his posse of armed men.

"That night Carns led Bishop to the willow grove, where he had previously taken food and blankets and had tethered Bishop's horse. The fugitive hid in the willows nearly a week while the sheriff continued to search for him. Then, taking his horse, he worked his way out of the dangerous territory. Months later an envelope containing paper money but no writing was received by Mrs. Lindstrom. She had always believed that the cooked food which Carns had requested from her on the night of the murder had been meant for Bishop, and now she was positive that this money came from him in payment and in thanks for it."

We drove in silence for awhile, thinking about Empire and its colorful history, which so few people today realize as they speed through the quiet town on their way to Grand Lake or to Winter Park.

CHAPTER SIX

The Arkansas Valley and Monarch Pass

(For map see inside of front cover)

THE Hotel Princeton in Buena Vista had seen better days. Its furniture was shabby, its lace curtains were gray with dirt and it smelt musty, but I chose it rather than any other hotel in town because, built in 1889, it was a relic of the early days. The three-story building looked just as dingy and unkempt the next morning when I sketched it, before starting an extensive ghost-hunting trip in the Arkansas Valley. I put the sketch away and completely forgot it for a few years, until news of a fire which had razed the building made me glad that I had recorded it.

Buena Vista today is the quietest of valley towns through which the motorist speeds, with scarcely a glance at its shaded side streets, its county courthouse and, on the edge of town, the grim, stone buildings of the State Reformatory, but during its first years of existence it was the most lawless community in the west.

Prior to 1879, when W. M. Kasson acquired land for a townsite, it was ranch country across which few people travelled except occasional prospectors, panning the banks of the Arkansas and its tributaries, or bands of Ute Indians bound on hunting or trading expeditions. With the simultaneous building of the railroad to this spot and the silver booms in Leadville and Aspen, everything was changed, and a tent city sprang up almost overnight along the banks of the river. Like all camps which burgeoned at the end of the track, it attracted gamblers, bunko men and desperadoes, as well as prospectors, freighters and merchants whose stocks filled every available shelter. Huge tents and canvas-topped buildings were transformed into freight houses to hold the ever-increasing volume of supplies which arrived by train and awaited transportation to the mines. This was the transfer point at which all supplies were re-loaded either in freighters' wagons or on jacks or mules, ready for the slow journey over the mountains to the distant mining centers. The depot platform sagged under the weight of tons of bullion, hauled in from the mines and stacked ready for shipment east. Four-horse stagecoaches stood beside the freighters' outfits waiting to load passengers for Leadville, Alpine, Pitkin, Gunnison and Aspen.

There were dozens of saloons—one called the Mule Skinner's Retreat— and scores of gambling houses lining the wooden sidewalks of the lusty new camp. So many gamblers, and others of the "sporting element" with assumed aliases, received their mail under several names that a special mailbox was provided for them and "the postmistress gave out their mail through a broken pane in the front window" of the office. The government of the town was in the hands of gamblers and saloon men. Shooting affairs were common and offenders went unpunished. Men were killed every day, and the killer simply went before the judge, pleaded guilty, and paid a ten dollar fine. When the railroad was pushed further west toward Leadville, the sporting element moved with it to the next track-end, and Buena Vista became the quiet, law-abiding town that it is today.

Harvard City   Prospectors found traces of gold in the sixties and seventies on placer claims below the site of Buena Vista and along Cottonwood Creek, where, at the forks of the South and Middle Cottonwood, a town called Harvard City was laid out. Not only mining but the newly-built toll road over Cottonwood Pass drew men to this little city. Here freighters repacked their loads for the difficult climb over the range or joined the miners in the dancehall or saloon before starting the long trek to Aspen. Once during 1879, a freighter was compelled to build a ninety-foot tunnel through the snow, large enough to enable him to take his trains and wagon through, and then as if that were not enough, he had to let the wagon down the mountain seven hundred feet by hand to the valley floor below.

As lode mines were discovered and developed in 1874, the town grew, and its population rose until Harvard City was made an election precinct. Had a new trail to Aspen over Independence Pass not been opened in 1881, Harvard City might have continued to expand for many years; but with the abandonment of Cottonwood Pass by the freighters in 1882 and with more lucrative mining areas beckoning across the range, the camp died and today it is just a memory.

"There were several early camps west of here," I told Dan Macky when we left Buena Vista and headed toward Leadville.

Granite   Prospectors washed the river bed and banks of the Arkansas for a mile or two below the present town of Granite in 1860 and 1861 and found the gravel bars rich in gold. Kelley's Bar, four miles below Granite, was worked prior to the discoveries in California Gulch as well as for several years thereafter. Georgia Bar, two miles below Granite, proved good placer ground from which several thousand dollars were taken out during the first season.

A mining camp grew up along Cache Creek in 1860, about two miles from its mouth, when gold was discovered in its bed. By 1863 over 300 men were placering along the stream, using sluices or Long Toms to wash the gold from the gravel. Cache Creek was then declared an election precinct and the first post office in Lake County was located in one of its cabins. In 1870 lode mines were discovered in the hills at the mouth of Cache Creek where a townsite called Granite was platted out.

The Yankee Blade was the best mine, producing $60,000 in gold, and the Belle of Granite a lesser amount; but it was placer mining that proved most profitable and was carried on continuously from 1860 to 1889, when ground sluicing by individuals gave way to hydraulic mining. That, too, was discontinued in 1911, and little mining is done in this area today. From

HOTEL PRINCETON,
BUENA VISTA (BURNED)

CARVED BARGE BOARDS
ON CABINS AT TURRET

ST. ELMO AS SEEN
FROM THE RAILROAD GRADE

the highway just below town, an old dredge can be seen submerged in the river.

Dayton

Leaving Granite, we turned toward Independence Pass, enjoying the superb scenery afforded by the Twin Lakes, in whose surface were reflected two fourteen-thousand foot peaks—Elbert and La Plata. The town of Twin Lakes consists of a combined store and filling station, a hotel, a schoolhouse and a cluster of cottages and cabins set back from the lake shore. Behind it towers Mt. Elbert, Colorado's highest peak, on whose sides were the mines which drew the early prospectors to this vicinity.

A small mining camp named Dayton was built at approximately this spot in the sixties and later became the second county seat of Lake County. The county seat had first been at Oro, but in the election of 1866 its removal to Dayton was voted. Two years later Granite had so outstripped Dayton in population that the county seat was moved there. In 1879 the townsite of Twin Lakes was laid out, and no more is heard about Dayton. Farther up the road toward Independence Pass there was a two-story stage station at the site of Everett, near where the road forked to the Red Mountain Mining District. Last year when I passed the spot the building lay flat on the ground. "Let's drive back to where Clear Creek crosses the road," I said to Dan. "That's the site of Georgia Bar, and from there the road follows the creek to Vicksburg and Winfield."

Vicksburg and Winfield

The road up Clear Creek was narrow, as all side roads are, and the further we drove the narrower it became, causing us to drive slowly, especially after nearly colliding with a car from whose windows fishing poles extended in all directions. No sign was left of Beaver City, nor of Silverdale nor Rockdale—three of the five camps that were located along this gulch in 1880 and 1881, but after a drive of several miles we reached Vicksburg and three miles farther on came to Winfield. The afternooon sun turned the aspen grove in which Vicksburg is built, to shimmering gold, and the trees under which we drove along its main street to a flaming arch. Its cabins were sturdily built and were in good repair, for both Vicksburg and Winfield are now summer resorts. Both towns reached their peaks in the early eighties, when each had a population of 250, and when nearly two hundred mine locations were staked or worked along the gulch and on the hillsides. Winfield's cabins are widely separated, and no trees line the rocky ruts which define its main thoroughfare. A false-fronted building, once a store, is flanked by a dozen log cabins along the one street, at the far end of which stands a small and decrepit shack bearing a sign, "Meals at All Hours." Aside from some horses which were grazing between the cabins and one group of fishermen who were packing their car preparatory to leaving for another week, we saw no signs of life. Returning via the one rutty road and trying in vain to identify the site of Rockdale, which an old map had shown as being between Winfield and Vicksburg, we reached the highway just at dusk and drove back to Buena Vista for the night.

Chalk Creek

Fishermen and the Fourth of July are natural affinities, and had we remembered this, Elizabeth, Elliot and I would not have had such difficulty finding a place to stay overnight on our first trip up Chalk Creek. The road to it leaves the highway at Nathrop, close to the first grist mill built in the Arkansas Valley in 1868, and cuts across the plain toward the canyon, formed by the steep sides of Mt. Antero and Mt. Princeton, at whose foot are the Chalk Cliffs. Mt. Princeton is a perfect mountain, symmetrical and majestic, its three peaks rising in cones far above the valley floor and its' upper third stretching way above timberline. High on its rocky, southern peak a zigzag thread of trail leads to the Hortense Mine, 12,000 feet above sea level. Discovered in 1871 by Captain Merriam, it is said to be the first silver producing mine in the district. The mine proved to be a bonanza, and the Captain and his company were soon jacking to Buena Vista two tons of ore a day which netted them $100 a ton. Transportation from the mine was a major problem, for the trail was narrow and never in too good condition. Stories are told of unfortunate jacks who, when loaded with ore, fell off the trail, and lay where they landed until some man could reach them and help them back to the narrow ledge. When Eugene Teats became manager of the Hortense, he built the five-mile-long road which looks like a tiny ribbon above timberline on Mt. Princeton. When it was finished, ox teams drawing wagons replaced the pack trains. At the foot of the mountain was a group of hot springs near which were built two hotels, some cabins and a group of mine buildings. A post office called Hortense was opened at this place in 1879.

Hortense

Our road up Chalk Creek led straight toward the mountain until it reached the crest of a little hill, beyond which was our first surprise. There just ahead of us stood a four-story frame, green and tan hotel, such as might have graced an eastern Spa, with a backdrop of the snow-capped Rocky Mountains! This was the famous Antero Hotel whose history is as fantastic as its architecture! Two of its four stories were enclosed with wide verandas, its upper tier of windows perforated the mansard roof, while at each corner a tower, surmounted by a dome, broke the otherwise rectangular plan of the building. No two towers were alike, for each was ornamented with a different shaped cupola—an especially flamboyant creation topped with a flagpole capping the largest one.

Mt. Princeton Hot Springs

The hotel's history is clouded by conflicting dates and by numerous transferals of property from one unsuccessful owner to another. So far as I have been able to unscramble the details, ground was broken for it in 1877, and its walls were completed in 1891! In 1917 it was finally finished, furnished, and open for business. The next year the small rock hotel and bath house, at the foot of the hill by the Heywood Hot Springs, were built, primarily to serve winter guests and aching miners who reveled in the hot water. These hot springs were a drawing card for the hotel, which for some time thereafter ran successfully, clearing about $12,000 a year. In 1925 a new company owned the hotel and further improved it, adding a tennis court and a golf course. This latter was the cause of new litigation, for a grazing permit had been taken out on the course thereby restricting its use. When a guest threatened to sue the hotel because he was unable to play golf on account of the cattle grazing on it, there was the dickens to pay.

Between 1925 and 1929 the hotel was so successfully operated that the

Baker Hotels of Dallas and Fort Worth were negotiating to buy the four-story curiosity. Then the stock market crashed, the hotel was closed, and for thirteen years only a caretaker lived in its draughty rooms and listened to the eery, inexplicable noises that all empty buildings develop. An occasional weekend dance was held in its huge, empty hulk until, in 1945, it was converted into a private school and as such it is still run by its newest enthusiastic owners.

On the summer afternoon in 1941 when we first met this relic, we had to stop and see what its interior was like. There had been signs along the road for miles which further intrigued us:

> "Come Join the Fun at Mt. Princeton Hot Springs. Old Time Party-Square Dance. Sat. 9-1 A. M. Come and Have Fun Without Your Bottle."

We regretted that this was not Saturday.

The hotel door was closed but not locked, and after opening it, we called out to whoever might be within. There was no answer, but one room near the door was certainly being lived in, for it was completely furnished and its bed was made up with fresh linen. Walking warily into the dark, empty ballroom from whose ceiling hung crepe paper streamers and immense paper butterflies, we tried to imagine what a dance here would be like. Elliot, always more curious about the insides of old buildings than I am, had vanished to the top story and was exploring the upper corridors and forgotten bedrooms. Having had enough of the place, I opened the door and went outside. In less than a minute Elliot appeared breathless, having taken the stairs two at a bound.

"What's the matter?" Elizabeth asked, amazed at his appearance.

"What did you do?" he asked. "I was on the fourth floor, looking into the rooms and finding lots of old furniture and china wash bowls and pitchers and expecting to see a skeleton in one of the beds for the place was so spooky, when suddenly, a gust of wind blew down the corridor and all the dusty curtains at the open windows blew outside with a whishing sound, and dry wallpaper rattled, and doors creaked, and I came downstairs."

"That must have been when I opened the door to go outside and the draft up the stairwell set everything, including you, in motion," I replied, picturing his sudden departure from the building.

By now it was late afternoon and we were anxious to find a place in which to spend the night. All the cabin camps and fishing resorts at the lower end of Chalk Creek were full, and not wishing to return to Buena Vista, we started up the road toward St. Elmo, hoping to find accommodations there or at Alpine.

The present auto road up the valley, which crosses the creek just below the Chalk Cliffs, is the bed of the abandoned Denver, South Park and Pacific Railroad. It is easy to drive for the grade is gradual, but it provides plenty of thrills for those who traverse it. As it climbs steadily up the canyon, the creek bed appears farther and farther below, until at a point where it crawls around a sheerfaced cliff, high above the valley floor, the drop is several hundred feet. Most of the way, however, it curves between walls of rocks or evergreens or winds through an avenue of aspens which arch overhead. Above the cascades, the stream again runs beside the road, while above on either side of the valley steep cliffs rise sharply, shutting out the sun or casting long shadows on the opposite canyon walls.

We had been told that there might be a cabin near Alpine and as we approached the little auto camp we looked hopefully at the new cabins set in the pines. The woman at the filling-station and store was agreeable but dubious, for she had but one cabin left and it had but one bed! As we looked tired and discouraged, she said, "If you really want to stay here I guess we can fix you up. If the two ladies will take the cabin I'll put a cot in the loft over the tank by the gas station for the gentleman." Elliot was game, and after a sketchy supper hastily cooked on the cabin's one burner, we were all ready to turn in. Elizabeth and I slept soundly and were up early in the morning ready for St. Elmo. Elliot joined us at the store where we had been promised breakfast. A look of grim endurance flashed across his face as he said: "I had quite a night. When I climbed to the loft that our host calls a room I found it full of mattresses and cots which had been stored there for the winter. One cot was made up, ready for me and I started to go to bed. It was dark and the light from the filling station tower just outside my window attracted quantities of millers which had been wintering in my 'apartment.' They flew in clouds about my head, trying to find their way out to the light. When I finally got rid of them, the light on the tower shone directly on my cot, so to get any sleep at all, I had to hang my sweater over the one window and the rest of the night was quiet but a little too stuffy for comfort."

"Where are you off to today?" asked the owner of the cabin camp as she piled pancakes on our plates.

"We're going to St. Elmo, at the end of the road," I replied, looking at the map which lay beside my plate.

"That isn't the end of the road," she said, "There are two ghost towns beyond St. Elmo and you can drive all the way to them. I know, because my husband worked on that road. It's pretty too—goes through the Quakies most of the way."

So, once again, luck was with me and we were off not only to St. Elmo, but to Romley and Hancock which lay beyond. Before we left Alpine we questioned our hostess about the early days of that little camp.

"Alpine didn't last long," she said as she stacked the dishes. "Riggins built the first house here in 1877 and it was he and Col. Chapman that really started the place. Chapman was the first mayor too. Alpine was incorporated in 1879 by a town company which was bonded to last for twenty years but by 1882 there wasn't any town to worry about. It boomed in 1879 and 1880, but as soon as St. Elmo was laid out, the people just moved upstream to the new camp. The 1880 census said there were 503 people here but we know better. There were at least a thousand and some say five thousand. They tell me that Alpine had lots of stores and two hotels, the Badger and the Arcade, *Alpine*

(149)

and wooden sidewalks and a two-story dancehall and twenty-three saloons. It had a newspaper too, *The True Fissure*, which was published until January, 1880 when its editor left for St. Elmo and began to publish a paper there. Chapman built the smelter here but he didn't have the proper flux for it, so it was overhauled and remodeled for a sampling and concentration works. In 1883 it employed forty men and could work thirty tons of ore in twenty-four hours. It's in ruins now but you can still see one of its stacks.

"Ore from the Tilden Mine used to be packed here by burros and then loaded on wagons and hauled to Pueblo, taking eight days for the trip. Ore from the Mary Murphy up at Romley used to be hauled here too, until the tram was installed from the mine to Murphy's Switch. Alpine had three banks but no school until 1881 when George Knox opened one. The town was so rough and wild that he wouldn't bring his wife and seven daughters here until things quieted down some. There wasn't any church either, but one of the ladies opened a Sunday School. When she asked one of the kids what Christ was doing on the Mount, he said, 'Guess He was prospecting.'

"Until a few years ago there were a few buildings in the old town which was below us here in the valley, but they've either blown down or been moved away. Some of these cabins came from there. Alpine's a nice place to live in. The peaks are so high here that they protect us and keep it from getting as cold in winter as it does in some places."

St. Elmo

We thanked her for her information and especially for word of the two ghost towns and, leaving Alpine, we started up the railroad grade for St. Elmo.

The approach to the town dips down from the grade and leads directly to the main street, which even today is bordered by wooden sidewalks. St. Elmo is alive in the summer with tourists and fishermen, but its buildings date from the eighties when the town reached its peak.

The general store and post office, toward which everyone gravitates, is run by Mr. Stark, whose cabins had been advertised all along the road. He was a talkative gentleman who had lived in St. Elmo all his life and knew everyone. Each visitor who entered his store was greeted by name and warned to "watch out for the street cars." This harmless but persistent joke he repeated three years later when I again visited him. Mr. Stark was most gracious and insisted upon bringing me an armchair to use while I sketched. As I worked, he told me much about St. Elmo's past. His mother knew even more than he about the place, but she was ill and could not be questioned. He brought out old photographs, showing the huge snowbanks which bury the road and the town in winter and he told how, when he was a boy, he rode a burro to Romley and carried the mail to the Mary Murphy mine.

From him I learned that the town was originally called Forest City, and that it was located at the junction of five gulches—Grizzly, Poplar, Pomeroy and the North and South Forks of Chalk Creek. It was also at the foot of four mineral mountains—Chrysolite, Murphy, Lehigh and Barren. In 1879 the townsite was covered with a dense growth of spruce and pine trees. hence its name; but in the fall of 1880 when the town was incorporated, the

(150)

RESTAURANT,
WINFIELD

OLD STAGE
STATION,
EVERETT
(COLLAPSED)

Post Office Department objected to the name because California had a Forest City and a committee of three selected St. Elmo instead.

Toll roads to the Gunnison and Aspen districts started from the upper end of town and wound over the Divide to the distant mining camps. These roads brought business to St. Elmo before the railroad reached the little city. Freighters' wagons passed constantly along its main street, the oxen and mules churning the mud into a poultice or raising clouds of dust as they trudged slowly through the town, loaded on the outgoing trip across the range with supplies and returning with even heavier loads of ore. Prospectors crossed the Divide on foot, carrying packs, blankets, tents and cooking utensils or driving loaded jacks ahead of them. The trails were choked with traffic —impatient men pushed their outfits as fast as they could travel over the passes, and discouraged miners stumbled back to town to drown their disappointment in whiskey.

The town grew rapidly, its population being estimated at between 1500 and 2000 during the boom years. There were five hotels, all one-story log buildings except one, the Briscoe Block, which was the only two-story building in town. One old timer recalled stopping at a new log hotel which was still under construction, and upon asking for a private room was amazed to see the landlord draw a chalk mark around a bed and designate it as his "suite."

The first issue of the town's newspaper, which appeared in August, 1880, was called the *St. Elmo Rustler*, but subsequent issues appeared as the *St. Elmo Mountaineer*. Excerpts from its July 11, 1885 issue mention the Mary Murphy Silver Cornet Band which furnished music for the Fouth of July celebration and "did just splendid." Sports on the Fourth included a "Scrub horse race, a striking match race, a slow jack race and five rounds at the soft glove."

At first there was no church in the town, and services were held in a store or cabin whenever Father Dyer or Bishop Macheboeuf visited the isolated camp. On one occasion the Bishop held his service in a bunk house, to which a high-backed rocker had been brought to be used as a Bishop's Chair. After the schoolhouse was built in 1882 the church services were held in it.

The mines made the town, and although many of them never produced valuable ore, others were paying properties. The Mary Murphy was the biggest, but its history is centered around Romley, four miles beyond St. Elmo. The Brittenstein group of mines in Grizzly Gulch "promised well"; the Iron Chest shipped in 1882, but out of the fifty properties that were reported as thriving in 1883, only a couple were working as late as 1897.

In 1881 Alpine and then St. Elmo were railheads of the Denver, South Park and Pacific Railroad which was built up Chalk Creek from the Arkansas Valley. The D. S. P. & P. was out to win the race to Leadville against the Denver and Rio Grande which was building up the Arkansas to the same goal. Both roads reached a point south of Buena Vista at the same time; but because its materials were delayed, the D. S. P. & P. had to watch the D. & R. G. forge ahead up the Arkansas Valley to Leadville before it even reached Buena

Vista. The South Park never did reach Leadville but it did build south of Buena Vista from Nathrop up Chalk Creek, with Gunnison as its goal. The D. & R. G. was also aiming at Gunnison, and another railroad race began. The D. & R. G. started from Salida and built through Poncha Springs and over Marshall Pass, reaching Gunnison in 1881. The South Park reached that city in September 1882 by tunneling through the Divide at Altman Pass above St. Elmo. The completion of the road did not, however, end its problems, for the expense of maintenance through this mountain country was a constant drain upon the company. In 1889 it was sold to the Denver, Leadville and Gunnison Railway Company, which also lost money on it. Ten years later it was sold to the Colorado and Southern Railroad, but its heyday had passed. In 1910 the last train ran through the Alpine Tunnel above Hancock, and in 1926 the last train ran down the length of Chalk Creek. With this trip the C. & S. abandoned the road and began tearing up the tracks.

During the years that the road ran, St. Elmo and the other towns along Chalk Creek were on the most travelled road to the silver fields. In 1881 hordes of prospectors rode the rails to the end of the track and then started the tedious trek over the range on foot, horseback, driving pack-trains or, later, riding in stagecoaches. There were several roads to choose from. The Maysville and Chalk Creek Toll Road crossed to the next valley and skirted Mt. Shavano. The Altman Pass road led to Pitkin and Gunnison. The Chalk Creek and Elk Mountain Toll Road crossed two ranges, over Tin Cup Pass and over Taylor Pass to Ashcroft and Aspen. Rival claims were made as to whether Tin Cup Pass out of St. Elmo or Cottonwood Pass out of Buena Vista was the best route to Aspen, but with the opening of Independence Pass the rivals were outrivalled.

Before the railroad succeeded in tunneling the range, daily stagecoaches left the Pacific House in St. Elmo for Aspen. The trip was difficult, and all too often passengers had to walk part of the distance or help push the stage out of the mud or drifted snow. For years the mail was carried over the range to Tin Cup, a horse-drawn toboggan making the hazardous trip in winter. But Gunnison was the goal toward which the railroad was pushing, and mile by mile it fought its rocky way toward Altman Pass, under which the Alpine Tunnel was built at a cost of $120,000. The tunnel, which was the first to be bored through the Continental Divide, was completed in April 1881. It was 1845 feet long, 12 feet wide and 17 feet high and was lined with California redwood. To insure better drainage it was sloped up from both ends to the center where it reached its highest point at 11,608 feet.

Even when St. Elmo was no longer at the end of the track it continued to be the largest town on Chalk Creek, and to it the miners and freighters and the laborers from the railroad gravitated on Saturday nights to spend their pay and to whoop it up in the saloons and dance halls.

Fire swept through the town in 1890, destroying two business blocks and leaving only a line of fire hydrants standing bleakly along the streets. The postmaster-and-storekeeper was the hero of the day for, to save the mail from the flames, he suffered a scorched ear and the complete loss of his stock of liquor and cigars.

(153)

While in St. Elmo, I wandered up and down its streets and especially along one until it became a mere trail. Wondering where it led, I walked a little further along it, until right in front of me was a marker—"Tin Cup Pass," and the same longing to follow it to its destination swept over me as had tempted me at Como, when I yearned to cross Boreas Pass to Breckenridge. On the edge of town I stopped to sketch a false-fronted saloon and even crawled through its open window and picked my way over the glass strewn floor, to see if there was anything of interest inside. Only shredded wallpaper clung to the interior and disappointed, I crawled out again. The following year when I revisited St. Elmo the saloon was gone.

"Before we leave here we must visit the old cemetery," I told my companions. "It's a mile away, but I think we can drive to it." We found it in a dense grove of trees and, to see its graves and the many rotting wooden headboards which marked them, we waded knee-deep in grass and wild flowers. Some of the graves were fenced in like those in the Buckskin Joe Cemetery, and on others the markers were weathered beyond legibility. The wooded valley road was so picturesque that we continued on it another mile to Iron City, where we found the remains of an old smelter, built in 1880. Upon our return to St. Elmo, we set out for Romley.

Romley   Climbing back to the railroad grade we looked down on St. Elmo with its neat streets spread out below. The road swept around blind corners high above the valley and whisked us between rows of aspens, until we saw mine buildings and red frame houses to the right and left of the highway and knew that we were approaching Romley. A tiny structure beside the road bore a sign "Romley" and proved to be the railroad depot. Up the bank to the left of the road was the two-story mine office and boarding house, in which Elliot found buried in a litter of paper on the floor a telegram dated 1911, sent from Boulder to the Mine Superintendent, and saying that E. H. Crabtree was coming up the next day by train. Fifty or more feet below the road, on a flat meadow, was a group of mine buildings, all painted red with white window trim and in pretty good condition. The biggest had a sign over the door "Post office," and stepping gingerly inside I examined the dusty pigeonholes where letters had once lain.

This whole community grew up around the Mary Murphy mine, the big bonanza of Chalk Creek. Whether the Mary Murphy was discovered in 1870, in 1875, or in 1879 seems to be a matter of uncertainty. Different authorities give the three dates with equal assurance. Both John Royal and Dr. A. E. Wright are given sole credit for its discovery, as is also a nameless Irish prospector who fell ill and was sent to a Denver hospital in the early seventies for treatment. While there he was cared for by a nurse named Mary Murphy, and when he recovered and returned to the mountains, he discovered a lode which looked promising. In gratitude to the nurse he named it the Mary Murphy.

Royal and Wright developed the mine and finally sold it for $75,000. The new owners immediately started the Kansas City Smelter in Alpine to handle the ore, but the smelter was not a success and they were glad to sell out in 1880 to a St. Louis company which offered to buy the mine for $80,000.

By 1881 the mine became the largest producer of the district, yielding 75 to 100 tons a day—the best ore assaying $125 per ton in gold and silver.

By 1883 ore was being shipped by rail from Murphy's Switch (it wasn't called Romley until 1897), at the foot of Pomeroy Mountain. A tramway, which was 4996 feet long and carried 96 buckets, each with a 200 pound capacity, ran from the No. 4 level of the mine to the switch. The mine office and boardinghouse at the station had a capacity of forty men, while the boardinghouse at timberline accommodated sixty more.

In 1909 the mine was sold to a rich English syndicate which spent $800,000 in improving it. Further improvements boosted production until in 1915-1916 two hundred and fifty men were working steadily in the mine and in the mill, and quantities of gold, silver, lead, iron and zinc ores were shipped regularly to the smelters. From 1917 on the output decreased, and the mine was run sporadically by lessees until it finally closed down. With the Mary Murphy dormant there was no longer any need for the railroad to haul its ore, so in 1926 the tracks were torn up. Any shipments from the mine today are made by truck down the old railroad grade.

While we were looking around Romley a car drove up and parked beside ours. "This is the place," an excited voice said, as a woman got out and began to hurry down the trail toward the lower buildings. "I used to live here when it was a lively place. Just look at the post office, it's just about caved in. Come on down the road," she called to her party, "and I'll show you the schoolhouse where I went as a child. The teacherage is next to it. There were lots of people here then—about eleven hundred at one time. Their cabins are all over the mountain up to timberline. There are miles of tunnels in the mountains leading to the different levels and crosscuts. They say the mine only produced $14,000,000 but that isn't right—it produced $60,000,000."

Following the lady and her party down the hill, I peeped into the tiny teacherage half hidden by towering pine trees and sketched the equally small schoolhouse with its half-dozen desks and scattered furniture.

Hancock

Back at the road I called to Elliot and Elizabeth, who were still investigating the mine office, and we started toward Hancock. The track on which we were driving was cut through a wooded slope where aspens and pines met overhead. At intervals we could look through the leafy curtain at the snow-clad peaks which seemed so close, yet lay miles away, and after a short drive we reached Hancock, or rather what is left of it, set in a mountain meadow through which the creek runs. Our road crossed a bridge with dressed stone abutments, beyond which loomed a red watertank. There were a few widely scattered cabins in various stages of dilapidation but nothing else, and the road from the watertank on was so full of ruts and quagmires that we willingly agreed to go no further. It was very still, except for the sound of the running water and the wind whistling through the trees, and as I looked about I tried to picture Hancock as it must have been in 1881 when it was a thriving railhead with five stores, one hotel, two sawmills, plenty of saloons and a population of two hundred.

It was located in 1880 by prospectors on the Hancock Placer Claim, and although the Hancock Town Company, which was formed in 1881, platted the site and sold lots, it was never incorporated. Both the mining excitement, which lasted two or three years, and the building of the Alpine Tunnel, two miles further on, kept it booming until shortly after the completion of this first bore through the Rocky Mountains. During these construction days three hundred laborers worked to push the railroad through the Divide and if possible to win the race to Gunnison against the D. & R. G. One prospector has left a written account of a trip over the divide during this construction period, in which he describes getting a horse at Forest City (St. Elmo) and riding it as far as the tunnel. There he found a small log camp, which was by now half buried in snow. Dismounting, and tying the reins according to directions, he started the horse back to Forest City alone. Scrambling as best he could up the remainder of the slippery trail, over snow ten feet deep in which he often sank to his waist, he crossed the pass and began the long, treacherous descent on the Gunnison side.

Although the tunnel was not completed until November 1881, passenger trains ran as far as Hancock earlier in the year, and freighters transferred their stocks from the cars to wagons at this point. With the completion of the road its real troubles began. Rock slides buried the track and caused damage to the rolling stock. But snow was its worst enemy, and even seasoned railroad men dreaded the hazardous winter months when slides were a constant menace. One especially disastrous slide buried thirteen men, women and children under thirty feet of snow. Another one swept the substantial snowsheds between Hancock and the tunnel down the mountainside, leaving them splintered like a pile of jackstraws.

W. C. Rupley, chief train dispatcher for the C. & S. from 1900 to 1909, knew all the headaches that the road produced. He wrote me reminiscences of his railroading days which are full of drama. On one occasion "one hundred and ten men were digging snow between Hancock and the tunnel to keep the line open. Mrs. Stark, (the mother of the storekeeper in St. Elmo) alone fed all of them for twelve days straight during which time she hardly closed her eyes. She had to stay up all night baking bread. The men filed in in groups, eating off the dishes their predecessors had eaten off of, without them being washed. She had two or three little children besides."

"Between the tunnel and Hancock was the worst snow blockade I have ever heard of," he continues.

"I have photos of box cars in the deep snow cuts, a man standing on top reaching up as high as he could with a shovel extended above him and unable to reach the top. It wasn't railroading in the Winter, it was just fighting snow. We would couple four engines together at the tunnel mouth, two on one end headed down grade and two on the other end headed the opposite way so that when they got through (if they did) they could again back up through the snow that rolled back in. Once in a while these engines were crowded off by the snow on the high side and they rolled down the mountain. It was not unusual for engines starting from the tunnel at high speed, to tunnel through entirely under the snow for a long distance like a mole, and if they stopped, the fireman had to get busy quickly to open a vent over the smoke stack so the fumes would not back into the cab and suffocate them. All windows were boarded up. Slides on two occasions came down from the hill and carried cars right out of the middle of the train down the hill."

TRAM FROM MARY MURPHY MINE, ROMLEY 1950

E. Wilbur, roadmaster of the South Park Railroad, once took a flatcar to the top of the pass behind a passenger train, and when he was ready to return, rode the car down the hill, using a brake club to control it. Mark Twain, who was visiting in the vicinity, heard of this trip and decided to do it too, that he might enjoy the scenery more than he would from a car window. The trip down was wilder and faster than he had anticipated, and when it was over, he insisted that Wilbur must have tied a rope around an Irishman and thrown him off as a brake!

As we started back down the long grade to the Arkansas Valley we noticed the mines around Hancock. The Stonewall was the biggest producer, discovered in 1879 and worked until 1915. The Allie Bell and the Flora Bell had loading bins beside the track and trestles extending over it to their dumps. As we neared Romley we talked of the Pat and Mary Murphy veins—parallel seams upon one lode, both of which were six feet wide. Nearing St. Elmo we wondered just where the Iron Chest, the Pioneer and the Tressie C. had been located. Below St. Elmo the canyon narrows and deepens so that the tops of the silver-gray crags seem almost overhead. Sweeping out over space around the rocky cliff below Alpine was just as thrilling on the down grade as it was on the up, and the Chalk Cliffs were even more impressive seen in the late afternoon light, when the shadows model their ashy whiteness into fantastic domes and minarets. We did not stop at the big hotel but drove directly down Gas Creek to the main highway, and on to Salida for the night.

Turret   I knew nothing about Turret except that its name suggested that it was high on a mountain and its designation on a road map indicated that it was an obsolete place. Hoping that it might have been a mining town, one summer afternoon Dan and I set out to see. The first few miles out of Salida were well graded and easy to drive, but the last four were a challenge to both driver and car. Over these miles the trail, for it was hardly a road, scrambled over mountain meadows, up sharp grades and around rocky cliffs, until it finally passed a boarded up schoolhouse and then dropped suddenly into the middle of the empty camp. One dome-like knob of rocks rises above the rest of the mountain and at the foot of this the town is built. Most of the buildings are lined up along one street, from the Sample Room, with its false front and hanging sign at one end, to the two-story hotel with its balcony and wall-papered interior at the other. Several of the log cabins were ornamented with carved barge boards—an architectural feature I have not found in any other camp.

While I stood sketching one of them, a piping voice behind me said: "Don't you want to see the schoolhouse?" Startled to find that the empty town was not deserted after all, I turned to find a small boy watching me. "I live here with grandma," he announced proudly, "and I play in all these buildings. That's the post office up on top of the hill, and there's books in the schoolhouse. The door is locked but I can get in. I just take the nails out of the hinges." Following him into the two-room school, I looked at the bookcases which lined its walls and at the few tattered books, maps and papers that strewed the floor. In the inner room was a rusty bedstead on which, no doubt, the teacher had slept. "We live here all summer," my small guide chirped. "Just grandma and the rest of her family and me. We work the mine a little too. That's grandma calling. I've got to go," he added, scampering between the buildings and across the creek to a larger house which we had not noticed before.

From "grandma" we learned that the town was platted in 1897, that it reached its peak in 1899 when it had a population of over 500, and that its boom was shortlived. Some say that the Vivandiere was the first mine discovered in the district in 1896 and some say it was the Gold Bug, but the former became a producer, whereas the Bug vein pinched out almost at once. The Independence was the biggest mine, shipping ore to the smelter at Pueblo in 1899 and being worked fitfully until as late as 1916. In this year the Turret Copper Mining and Reduction Company shipped from it one hundred tons per month of good grade copper and gold ore.

The camp was well established by 1898, when a county election was held, at which 200 votes were cast. No city election was necessary as there were no officials except a marshal. During Turret's boom year of 1899, a bi-weekly stage ran between it and Salida, and the new camp, which by now had added a post office, a butcher shop and a saloon to its other buildings, produced a newspaper called the *Gold Belt*. The whole town turned out for the Fourth of July celebration in 1900 when United States Senator William Mason of Illinois gave an address; but before the end of the year the mines began to peter out, many of them never having shipped any ore at all, and one by one the people drifted away, some to nearby Whitehorn and Calumet, where mining was still active.

In 1896 cattle ranged over Cameron Mountain on which Whitehorn is situated and tie-choppers cut timber. The following year one of the choppers, Derius Patro found some float on the mountain and had it assayed. His discovery led to the staking of the Independence, Cameron, Golden Eagle and other properties by prospectors, and to the laying out of a little camp in June 1897, only four miles from Turret.

It was called Whitehorn in honor of Arthur L. Whitehorn, an assayer and civil engineer who was always ready to grubstake a prospector, to assay his float, or to survey his claim, and take a chance on being paid. By the end of 1897 the *Whitehorn News* was being published and early in 1898 two mines were shipping to the smelter, while six others hauled their ore to the Whitehorn mill.

The camp was a flourishing place in 1900, when new stores and residences were added, sidewalks were laid and streets graded. Fire almost destroyed the town in 1902, for since there was no fire-fighting equipment other than a bucket brigade which was hastily formed by the miners, twenty buildings were lost. From the ashes rose a new town with a "cafe and one or more saloons, a schoolhouse, a livery barn, meat market, stores, two brothels and several dozen frame residences." A stage-coach line operated between it and Salida, carrying passengers, freight and mail. A post office was maintained at Whitehorn until 1918, although by then mining had almost ceased and cattle were again grazing on the mountain.

In 1942 I inquired about the camp and was assured that none of it re-

Whitehorn and Calumet

mained except a few rotting wooden sidewalks. In 1946 Cecil R. Miller of Cincinnati bought the townsite of 332 acres at a delinquent tax sale for $1550, and Whitehorn is now private property.

The Calumet iron mine was opened in 1898 by the Colorado Fuel and Iron Company. A camp of the same name, which lasted but a few years, was built near the mine, and a spur of the D. & R. G. railroad was built to it to haul away the ore. As this camp and railroad were but four miles from Whitehorn and only a little further from Turret, ore from both camps was hauled in wagons to the railhead for transportation to the smelter.

Poncha
Springs

Never having been into the Gunnison country which lay over the range from Salida, and having read of its colorful mining history and of the many camps once located in its territory, I laid out an elaborate itinerary which would include as many as could be reached. In my innocent enthusiasm, I felt sure that a single trip to each would suffice; but some were too inaccessible to be reached at once, others were gone, and a few were much too full of material to be exhausted in one trip. Therefore the Gunnison country was visited again and again, over a period of several years, first with one companion and then with another.

The approach to Monarch Pass from Salida is full of ghost towns, or at least of towns whose existence is due to a mining boom in 1880, which brought prospectors tumbling into the region. Poncha Springs was laid out in 1874 before the boom, by James True, who came to the valley, bought the McPherson claim and laid out a town in which he opened a general store. In fact Poncha was a well-established town before Cleora or Salida, which were railroad towns further down the valley, were even thought of. Both the mining boom and the arrival of the railroad in 1880 gave the town a spurt of activity. Several hotels were built, including the Jackson, which is still in use, and the Poncha Springs. It is high on the mountainside, close to the ninety-nine springs for which the town is named. These were well known to the Indians, and soon after white men filtered into the region they too recognized their medicinal value and built the hotel and bathhouses close to them. The hotel, which was run by a retired Memphis steamboat captain, became the headquarters for the railroad and stagecoach men during the year that the town swarmed with all the elements that a track-end town invites. After the rails were extended along Silver Creek toward Marshall Pass, and the stage road was built as far as Maysville, the "disturbing elements," which the local newspaper deplored, moved on to the new locations and Poncha resumed its normal and much quieter existence.

The substantial element endeavored to make it a dry town as well as a law-abiding one. The *Chaffee County Times* of January 1, 1881, states that:

> "The prohibition tendency of the principal owners of town property has caused them to insert a clause in all deeds, prohibiting the sale of intoxicating liquor on any lots belonging to them and the consequence is a small proportion of saloons to other classes of business. We believe there are only two or three in town. How many grocers and drug stores have private barrels on tap cannot be definitely stated."

The most unexpected feature of the town was the public library, "a neat, cozy building, containing over 1600 standard volumes, and a large number of choice novels, including liberal selections from Harper's half-hour series." The library was the gift of Mrs. Magruder who "in a spirit of enlightened liberality selected and donated it from her private means. . . This will be a great boon for the army of strangers, young men and others, who in coming to this mountain town will be provided with a profitable place to spend their evenings instead of frequenting saloons and dancehouses," continues the paper in a burst of optimism.

Fire destroyed most of the town in 1882 and from this catastrophe it never recovered. Today its remaining buildings are scattered through a grove of trees, with great gaps between them where no doubt former structures once stood. The Elgin Smelter down by the river is gone, the picturesque church burned about twelve years ago, and only the two-story brick schoolhouse and the Jackson Hotel stand out like sentinels.

On August 4, 1879, the town of Maysville was only eight days old. It *Maysville* was full of life, with lots being sold to the miners who came swarming in and tents being erected along its non-existent streets. The townsite, which was known as the Feather Ranch, had been taken up some years prior to the discovery of minerals on the property by Amasa Feathers and used by him for a stock ranch. The new camp was called Maysville in honor of the town in Kentucky from which came Gen. William Marshall, the discoverer of Marshall Pass. In 1879 it was platted and began immediately the steady growth that made it by 1882 the largest town in the county. At first it had "two lawyers, two assayers, two surveyors and no physician," but as it was "not afflicted with booms" it continued to grow until it had "two smelters, several hotels, numerous stores and saloons and all other branches of trade as well as good fishing for tourists." Its two newspapers were eagerly read by the population of one thousand and by the miners in the entire district. The *South Arkansas Miner* was a seven column folio, and its rival the *Maysville Chronicle* claimed the "largest circulation of any paper in the county," which was no wonder as it carried "items of home interest and the more important State and foreign news."

The toll road to Monarch Pass was built in 1879 and was completed across the divide to Whitepine in 1880. There was a toll gate at Maysville and another on the western slope at Black Sage. In 1880 a toll road was also built from Maysville up the North Fork of the Arkansas to the mining camp of Shavano, ten miles away. The toll roads and the mining insured Maysville's existence, and for years it was a busy and flourishing place. When the mining ceased in 1893 it began to decline, until by 1895 only a handful of buildings remained.

A comfortable yellow house and some cabins stand by the side of the highway at Maysville today, and on one trip Jane Miller and I spent the night there, preparatory to exploring the old camp of Shavano the next morning. We talked to the lady who ran the place and learned from her the way to Shavano, the probable difficulties we would encounter on the road, and various shreds of information about Maysville itself. She showed us an old photo of the two trees from which two murderers were hanged, and she pointed out the large, substantial schoolhouse on the flat below the railroad. Every now and then a whistling and chugging ore train from the Monarch Mine further up the pass, would rattle by, but outside of its cheerful tooting there was no sound save the swish of cars rushing by on the highway, unaware that they were passing the former toll entrance of the Gunnison country and were whizzing through a town whose population had once reached a thousand.

Shavano   Jane and I rose early the morning of our trip to Shavano. Every time I had passed Maysville for the past five years I had inquired the whereabouts of the deserted town and how it could be reached. First one drove four miles to the county bridge. From there on, one was on his own, climbing the remaining five, six, seven or eight miles (informants were vague as to the exact number), until one reached the place. Some said to park the car at the bridge and hike the rest of the way. Some suggested horses and some said that cars *had* made it but that the road had a high center, that beaver ponds had destroyed parts of it, that the grade was fantastic, and finally, that it was impossible except on foot. Others warned us that there were no turnouts on the road and that if we *did* try to drive it, we would probably meet fishermen coming down from a lake and *then* what would we do?

Fascinated by this diversified information, we started off at six in the morning so as to avoid traffic problems, trusting that all fishermen were still in bed. The first four miles were easy and pleasant, following the North Fork of the Arkansas among groves of trees through whose branches the morning light slanted. Our first quandary arose when we reached the bridge. There were two of them, with roads leading beyond and out of sight. We chose the newer "county bridge" and decided to drive as far as the road permitted. It was rough, of course, and narrow and decidedly steep, but our Ford took it in stride. At one point a gate barred the way and a little higher up beaver ponds were flooding it. Since it led through trees all the way, we had no opportunity to look about us and check our location or elevation. Five miles, six miles, until at last we came to a few empty cabins which we decided to examine on the way back. Was this group of log cabins Shavano or was the camp closer to the top of the mountain? Not being sure that these few isolated ruins comprised the camp and not daring to lose our speed on the upgrade, we drove on. Seven miles. Now we were in the open and could see the peaks around us. The road got steeper still, and with some difficulty we maneuvered several sharp switchbacks and pulled over sudden rises until we reached timberline.

A sharp curve brought us to an abrupt stop as the road ended in two ruts in a swampy meadow, and with careful picking of firm ground we turned the car around and headed it down hill again. As soon as it stopped, water began to stream from the radiator and in horror we watched it flow onto the ground. Had a rock punctured it, and could we get eleven miles back to Maysville with no water? Well, we'd come up here to see Shavano and since we could drive no further we'd better hike to the top of the hill ahead and look into a basin in which Shavano might be hiding. Far across the mountain top was a mine, whose buildings and dump were the only signs of man's construction. We looked into the hollow basin. There were no buildings or mines in sight, and turning, we retraced our steps to the car. It was very high country and

(162)

the rocky peaks around us looked close in the sharp morning light. As the car had now stopped boiling and leaking, we started down the road.

Reaching the cabins, we stopped to study them. There were quite a number dotted through the trees and beside the road, and there were clearings in the timber where other roads had been hacked out to form crude streets which joined others farther back in the trees. One of the cabins had shelves along one side, suggesting that it had been a store or saloon. Down by the creek stood the forlorn skeleton of a mill. As soon as our tour of inspection was over we again started down the road, anxious to get off it before anyone decided to come up. On the last steep hill above the county bridge, where the road was narrowest and was cut along the face of a cliff, we met a carload of fishermen. Both drivers got out and sized up the situation and then, while we climbed the side of the bank until our fenders scraped it and the chassis was perched at a drunken angle, the other car crept by, its outside wheels sinking into the soft shoulders of the shelf road and its fenders rubbing ours. We were back at our cabin in Maysville by nine o'clock, in a ravenous state and full of questions as to what we had seen.

Finding a native who knew the country and questioning him, we learned that a camp called Clifton sprang up in 1879 and was platted in 1880. It was later named Shavano, after the mountain on which it was situated, which in turn was named for the War Chief of the Uncompahgre Utes. The little camp, which was at 11,000 feet elevation, lasted only about three years and by 1882 was a ghost town. As with all new camps the promoters believed in its future, and early in 1880 the toll road was built from Maysville to this mining center. Hack fare from Maysville was seventy-five cents. "Outside of one murder and hanging, there were no outstanding events in Shavano," our informant told us. "Lots were given away, as well as water and firewood, to anyone who would agree to grade one-half the width of his own street to the extent of his twenty-five foot frontage. The town was built entirely of logs; and at least ten cabins are still standing. The general store on the main street was the one with the long shelves in its interior. Down across the creek was the three-story mill. It's been razed for its lumber but its machinery is still there. Cyclone Creek provided water for the town."

"We drove miles beyond the cabins. In fact we were up on top and saw a mine and its buildings across the rocky flat. What were they?"

"You saw the Billings Tunnel. Its portal was built of cut stone, laid by a mastercraftsman. The wagon road you were on once led to within four hundred feet of the mine. Too bad the mine wasn't profitable and had to be abandoned after all that preparation.

"A rich silver strike was made up in this general vicinity on New Year's Day, 1904, by Judge J. H. Akin of Shavano and E. W. Carpenter of Salida. They set out on snowshoes and climbed this snowy range until they saw some rich float. Digging through three feet of snow and driving stakes, they located the Netsie Castley claim. From a four-foot vein they hacked out a piece of ore weighing 200 pounds and broke off a specimen to be assayed. It contained 119 ounces of silver, 89% lead and $3.50 in gold to the ton. The claim was near the crest of the Divide, about equidistant from the Madonna mine at Monarch and the Mary Murphy at Romley. It adjoins the Michigan group of claims near the Billings tunnel. Which way are you heading now?''

"We're off to the Gunnison country," we replied, thanking the old man and starting up the highway to Monarch Pass.

It is hard nowadays to picture the region as it was in the eighties when Maysville was so alive and when Arbourville, Garfield and Monarch were rivals of each other. In 1880, when Arbourville was less than a year old, it was a prosperous town, doing considerable business with the surrounding camps and handling their ore in its smelter. A letter written early in August, 1879, mentions "a large encampment of men four miles above Maysville, cutting and hauling timber for houses. . . cutting and thinning out cottonwoods and . . . a surveyor laying off the tract into town lots." The land was laid off July 31, by Arbour and three other men, all from Silver Cliff, and one hundred of its lots were taken up the first day. "About fifty people were preparing to build and some of the cabins were already three or four logs high." The town company offered five acres to the first smelter brought in, and $1,000 to the company when it was ready to treat ore. The most colorful item about Arbourville today is the old prospector, F. E. Gimlett, the Hermit-of-Arbor-Villa, who has built himself a retreat in an aspen grove where he relives the past and reminisces about the country and its mining history, both of which he knows completely.

Arbourville

Garfield, just beyond Arbourville, was once called Junction City. It is easy to locate, for the Highway Department's orange buildings stand at one end of town. Most of its old buildings have disappeared, but the ruins of a mill are about to topple into the South Arkansas River, and its schoolhouse has a unique feature—a snow tunnel from the lower road to the schoolyard, through which children reach the building during the winter's deep snows and drifts.

Garfield

Junction City was laid out during the last half of 1880 and by 1881 had a population of 500. It was so named because it was situated at the junction of two wagon roads—one over Monarch Pass to the southwest and the other over Alpine Pass to the northwest. The rich mines on the Middle Fork of the Arkansas and on Taylor Gulch supported the town, brought business to its Cummings House and to its many stores, mills and shops. The Black Tiger claim high above the town was a producer, as was the Columbus mine located at the head of Kangaroo Gulch. A stamp mill on the banks of the creek treated the ore which was carried by a wire tramway from the Columbus mine.

Like so many other places Junction City had its big fire, which nearly razed the town. It occurred on election night, 1882, when most of the young men were miles away in Salida, attending a celebration of the Knights of Pythias. The town was rebuilt and continued to be the busy camp of the district. In 1883 the United States Postal Department changed its name to Garfield in memory of the President who had been assassinated the year before. In 1885 both the Tiger and Columbus mines were producing, and the town prospered. There is so little left of Garfield today that the average tourist whisks by it without a glance and is on his way to Monarch, the next place on the Pass.

(165)

In 1878 a prospector, traveling by horse and wagon, was told by twc men named Boone to try the Monarch district. They directed him to it and even gr● staked him. The prospector was N. C. Creede, who in the nineties started the stampede to Willow Creek but who was unknown when in 1878 he discovered the Monarch and Little Charm mines. Soon afterwards the Madonna deposit and one or two others were discovered, whereupon prospectors hurried in and pitched their tents. Camp Monarch, also known as Chaffee City, was located May 15, 1879, by J. G. Evans, Boone and Miller, and in a short time its population, including miners on the surrounding mountains, was 3000. One hundred and twenty-five houses were built, three stores, three saloons, three hotels and three assay offices. A building for a Mining Exchange was erected, in which specimens of ore from the principal mining claims in the region were exhibited.

Although the Monarch mine was discovered in 1878 it was not developed until the following year, when an eastern company invested capital in it and uncovered quantities of good ore. The Madonna, Silent Friend and Eclipse lodes were also developed, and their ore was hauled in wagons one hundred miles to Canon City. When the railroad reached Maysville in 1881, the hauling problem was reduced, and when in 1883 Anton Eilers bought the Madonna mine and secured an extension of the railroad to it, the district really began to boom.

By 1884 a town had grown up in the narrow gulch at the foot of the mountain and its name had been changed from Chaffee City to Monarch. The Madonna mine shipped thirty carloads of ore per day and employed three hundred men. When in the early part of 1893 the government stopped purchasing silver, the crash came. The Madonna, Eclipse and Silent Friend closed down, and the miners began to drift away. Even the railroad stopped running, the last train pulling out with most of the remaining residents of the doomed town. What few were left tore down first one building and then another for fuel, so that board by board the Miner's Exchange, the Palace of Pleasure, the Eureka Dance Hall and the Welcome Hotel disappeared. Soon, only the bars and their fixtures were left, exposed to the elements, as were the stocks of merchandise piled on the open shelves of empty stores. Next a snowslide obliterated part of the mile-long townsite, and still more recently the new highway buried another portion of once prosperous Chaffee City, leaving but a few buildings and the schoolhouse standing on its one curving street.

Between 1893 and 1906 very little mining was done, but even during the time Monarch did not become completely deserted, for the Colorado Fuel and Iron Company operated limestone quarries there and still does. The whole side of the mountain is terraced with tracks leading to tunnel openings from which the limestone and zinc carbonate ores are loaded onto the ore trains, whose tiny but powerful locomotives chuff down the grade to Salida. One evening, while driving over the pass, suddenly, out of the dark, appeared a blaze of lights—the tier upon tier of illuminated terraces of the Monarch mine, punctuated with puffs of smoke and steam from shunting engines pulling rattling ore cars in long queues from level to level.

I have never been able to find the site of Hartville, which was said to be one and a half miles below Monarch and which contained a saloon, blacksmith shop, restaurant and a few cabins. It is not only a ghost town but a ghost site.

Beyond Monarch Pass lies the Gunnison country with its many mining towns whose very names intrigued me—Iris, Chance, Tin Cup and Gothic. I could hardly wait to reach them. My next objective was, therefore, the region beyond the range; and having once discovered it, I visited it again and again.

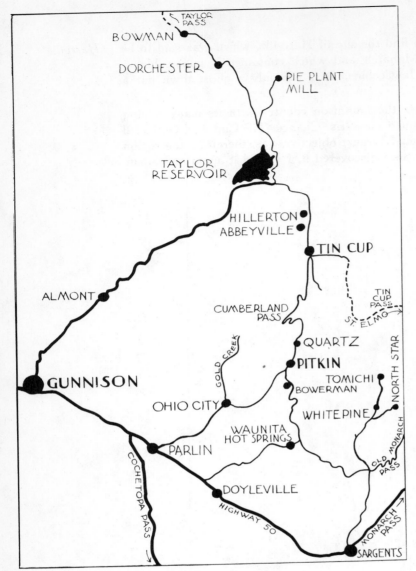

CHAPTER SEVEN

West of the Divide

THE old road over Monarch Pass leaves the new highway near the summit and cuts through the trees across the mountain top, snaking its way down the other side to the sage-covered flat. At the bottom the road to the right, which skirts the meadow, is the fork which leads to Whitepine; and one summer afternoon in 1941 Dick and I took this turn and maneuvered the car up the long four-mile hill to the little mountain town. What would be there—an empty husk or a live camp? I had no idea, for to me Whitepine was only a dot on the map and I knew nothing of its history. The road wound through trees all the way, and we stopped only once, when we discovered the shady cemetery with its weathered headboards and fenced-in graves. As we neared the "city limits" there were glimpses of old dumps high on the hillsides and cuts through the trees that had once been mine roads. Passing a few cabins set far back in the pines, we turned a corner and there was Whitepine! Its long straight street led up the hill and was bordered with log cabins and frame houses. There was no one in sight as we drove up in front of the town well, in the very center of the place, but before we had time to peer into its cool depths a woman came over to us.

"Whom did you want to see?" she began. "The men are all up at the mines and the superintendent's gone to Gunnison."

"We want to know about Whitepine and if there are any other mining towns near here," I replied.

"I've only been here a year so I don't know much, but they tell me that two miles farther up this road was Tomichi Camp; but it's gone now, not even any buildings left. What weren't smashed in the snowslide have been moved down here. There's a lake up there where the men go to fish. North Star is up Galena Gulch. It has buildings but no people. Go back the way you came till you come to a side road marked 'Galena Gulch.' Take it for two miles and you'll be there."

Before following her directions we continued our tour of the "business section." The Grand Hotel was dingy and empty; the Tivoli Theatre, next to it, stood wide open. Within its shadowy interior was a square piano half buried in debris and fallen plaster. Part of the old scenery lay rolled up at the back of the hall or hung precariously above the tiny stage. The one-story City Hall sagged to one side and its small room was strewn with furniture, including the mayor's desk which rested on two legs. Further down the street a two-story boardinghouse was falling to pieces, each window a staring black hole and its door hanging askew on its hinges. Across from the Grand Hotel were two or three store buildings and some sheds. The rest of the town was made up of dwellings.

"Since there's no one else to question here, and as there's nothing left of Tomichi, let's go to North Star," I suggested, putting my sketch pad back in the car.

We left Whitepine and drove slowly down the hill looking for Galena Gulch. A battered sign pointed to an opening in the trees and we turned off into the clearing. There wasn't much of a road, in fact the trail which stretched ahead made the Whitepine road look like a highway; but we took it, crossing a log bridge and clambering over the debris of a deserted mill and its dump before striking the winding gulch road, which cut through an aspen grove and was edged with a facing of rocks about three feet high. It was just wide enough for one car, it was quite steep and its walls gave one the feeling of driving in a ditch. Overhead the aspens met, and for more than a mile we drove through a leafy tunnel until it opened onto a meadow surrounded with buildings. This was North Star.

Aside from about ten cabins in the trees and a flagpole which stood in the middle of the meadow the chief buildings standing were the office of the Morning Star mine and, across the green from it, the false-fronted white boardinghouse and a two-story cabin of hand-hewn square logs. The mine office was open, and in it we found old reports, the usual debris and a pile of schoolbooks dated about 1914. The boardinghouse, with its wooden sidewalk, was locked but by peering through the dusty windows we could see that it was still furnished. There was no sign of life in the camp, and after a few minutes of exploration we returned to the Whitepine road and drove on to Gunnison. A couple of years later, while doing some research in the library at Western State College in Gunnison, I discovered many bound copies of the *White Pine Cone*. From them I learned North Star's history.

The camp, first known as Lake's Camp, sprang up in 1878-79, its mines producing large quantities of rich galena ore. The North Star lode was located in June '79 and was the first to produce paying quantities of ore, which was hauled to Salida and then shipped to the smelter at Canon City. The camp's development and history are similar to those of Whitepine and Tomichi. During the eighties it boomed and in 1893 it was abandoned, but its mines were not worked out and by 1901 the camp was in full swing again. During that year the North Star Mining Company worked three eight hour shifts in its new tunnel and teams hauled the ore to the Tomichi Valley smelter.

The property of the May-Mazeppa mine of Whitepine included the town of North Star and a hay ranch on which were built stables, wagon sheds, bunk houses and repair shops for the mine.

Despite the camp's proximity to Whitepine it had a life of its own.

Once when two men wanted to go to Whitepine they hitched a horse to a forked log and made a rapid trip down the gulch road, one man holding the other on while the second "pushed on the lines and urged the horse out of the way of the improvised sled." The Soup Bone Musical Club seems to have been a popular organization, providing music for both North Star and Whitepine. The *Cone* often mentions it and comments upon the abundance of talent to be found in Galena Gulch. One Sunday evening the group rendered "McGinnis' Raffle," "Ever of Thee," "McCarty's Mare" and "Gwine to Git Home", accompanied by a bell harp and a guitar. The club must have been hardy, for "the storm may roar and snort but Galena Gulch will have music when the last willow has dropped and the last soup bone has boiled away into the dim vista of the unknown."

After reading the *White Pine Cone*, I longed to go back to North Star and hunt for the mines which had made the camp. I now knew that the false-fronted white building with the furniture in it was the Leadville House and that the log cabin next to it was probably the "new post office" which was opened in 1901. In 1945 I visited North Star again, driving first to Whitepine to inquire about the condition of the trough-like road to the deserted camp. It was Sunday morning and the town was alive with people working in their tiny gardens, tinkering with their cars or just sitting in the sun. "Sure you can drive up there," said a man to whom we talked. (All miners say "Sure you can drive up there," no matter what you ask them.) "The boys drive their cars up every day. Just go back of these mine buildings and you'll soon strike the old road to the camp. Watch out for loose rocks and high centers, but you won't have any trouble."

It was very rough as well as narrow, and the car jumped from rock to rock like a mountain goat. A few minutes later we reached the meadow with its flagpole and were greeted with loud brays from a burro which was watching us from a corral. More doors were sagging open than in 1941 and we could now enter the boardinghouse and inspect its dusty interior. The big front room contained a stove, a rocking chair and an old bedstead, and the newspapers strewn around the floor dated from the nineteen twenties. Next door in the log post office was an old coffee mill and more old newspapers and magazines.

Back in Whitepine we asked two old cronies, who were sitting on the steps of what had been the Grand Hotel, if they could tell us about the

OHIO
CITY

WHITEPINE

camps in the district, and for the next two hours we listened to their stories and anecdotes of the Tomichi District. Before we left one of them invited me to his cabin that I might look through some faded copies of the *White Pine Cone*, dated 1885.

There were rumors of gold in this region as early as the 1860's and there is a tale of two men who located some pay dirt, built a flume and washed out a pound of gold per man per day. Snow drove them away from their diggings for the winter, and while working their way out they either became snow-blind or were killed by Indians. At any rate their story became a legend and hundreds of prospectors tried to find "Snow Blind Gulch," the source of their gold. Years later in Snow Blind Gulch on Tomichi Creek, some traces of Long Tom sluices and the remains of an old whipsaw were found in the bushes along the stream, lending credence to the story.

Prospectors poured into the area in 1878, finding their best prospects along Galena Gulch and in Snow Blind Canyon, five miles below the source of Tomichi Creek. They reached the head of the stream and found rich gold and silver ore just as the threat of a Ute outbreak sent them all scurrying out of the district. When the Indian scare was over they returned and set up their tents and cabins, only to be driven out a second time by the winter's snows. Returning in the spring of 1879 they continued to prospect and built three camps, Tomichi, Whitepine and North Star, all of which were within a mile radius of each other and some of whose mine properties overlapped.

Tomichi   By 1880 Tomichi, which was at first called Argenta, was bigger than Whitepine and had a population of 1500. By 1882 it had a bank, an assay office, a smelter and a newspaper, the *Tomichi Herald*. The smelter burned in 1883, and the bank and assay office were moved to another camp. On Feb. 14, 1885, the *Herald* was half the regular size and was printed on wrapping paper. The editor explained that storms had delayed the arrival of supplies to the camp, including paper for the press, and concluded: "So our readers must be content with a half-size Valentine."

There were a number of good mining properties—the Eureka, which produced from 1882-1895, the Lewiston, the Sleeping Pet, Brittle Silver, Little Carrie and the Magna Charta Tunnel, which became the great mine of the camp. It was located on Granite Mountain, but its tunnel reached for more than a mile until it was under both Whitepine and North Star. The town boomed until the silver crash of '93, which came just as the biggest mining company was tunneling to reach a rich silver vein. By 1894 there was not a soul left in camp. A few old-timers straggled back in 1896 and began to rework their properties about the same time that the Magna Charta Company resumed work on the tunnel. Just as things were getting on a sound basis again a snowslide in 1899 wiped out the city, killing five or six people and destroying the machinery and buildings of the tunnel. That was the end of Tomichi, and today "not a stick or stone remains of the once booming town."

Whitepine   Probably the first prospectors who came across the range from Chaffee City in the fall of 1878 were the Boone brothers. Others followed, and by

1879 Whitepine was a lively camp surrounded by mines rich in lead and silver. Native, glance and wire silver were found in the mines on Granite Mountain; Contact Mountain was a mass of magnetic iron pyrites carrying silver; and the eastern part of the district was a lime belt. Many lodes were discovered and developed, among them Morning Star, Evening Star, May-Mazeppa, Black Warrior, Copper Bottom and Copper Queen.

The name Whitepine seems to have been chosen because of the "dense growth of pines reaching down and verging upon the principal street and even clustering about the doorways of the cabins."

In the 1880 election the ballot boxes were made at the "Pine" and the first voting was done there during the morning when the "boys" from Lake's Camp (later called North Star) were notified to come down and vote. At noon the boxes were "loaded on a couple of burros and with the judges in the lead" were started up the trail to Tomichi. "Any prospector met along the road could cast his ballot as the burros were halted for that purpose. Arriving at Tomichi, the population of the camp was accommodated and the returns duly certified and sent to Gunnison, the new county seat."

The *White Pine Journal* appeared in 1881, but the camp's real paper was the *White Pine Cone* edited by George S. Irwin from 1883 to 1893. The *Cone* was a mining paper, carrying news of the nearby camps and famous for its spicy editorials and witty local columns. These appeared under the heading "Little Cones" and "Cone Chronicles" and contained such gems as:

> The boys all washed their feet in the Hot Springs Sunday. There will be no fish in Hot Springs Creek this summer.
>
> At a party last evening Milton Spencer introduced a new game entitled "Komical Komplications" which caused a great deal of amusement. The usual cribbage and whist contests were held and a superb lunch added to the evening's enjoyment.
>
> We will present a copy of the *Cone* for one year to the first couple that marries in the gulch between the first and last day of Feb. proximo. Marriage comes high but we must have one occasionally.
>
> Two weddings, (this week) so two subscriptions to the *Cone* were given.
>
> Crawling the range is the way they put it when a man walks out of the gulch.
>
> The Soup Bone Musical Club met for practice last Sunday evening in North Star.
>
> The Soup Bone Club might wander down this way sometime and give us a little music. There's a stray gazoo in the gulch and we'll have it on hand to turn loose in the audience if there is any interruption of the concert.
>
> White Pine suffered an agonizing famine this week. For two whole days there was not a drop of whiskey in town. Nothing but a liberal supply of peach brandy and bottled beer prevented a panic.

Toward the end of 1892 when mining began to taper off the *Cone* was hard pressed to collect its bills. The last issue of the paper was printed on Dec. 20, 1892, and contained the following statement: "Something over $1,000 is due the *Cone*. We need half of it. Please pay what you can on account."

The road between Sargent's and Tomichi was the only artery which connected the three camps with the outside world and during the winter months "parties of snowhaulers" were kept busy opening the road for travel. Ore from the mines was taken the twelve miles to the railroad by wagon in the summer but during the winter months it was hauled on ox-drawn sleds. On April 24, 1885, the *Cone* announced that

The first wagon over the road between Sargent's and White Pine since last fall was the stage last Friday. It was quite a treat to our people to once more see a wheeled vehicle. The stage will hereafter make regular daily trips.

In 1889 the stage was held up. The *Cone* of February 15, 1889, describes the incident as follows:

BOLD HOLD UP
THRILLING EXPERIENCE OF PASSENGERS ON THE SARGENT TOMICHI STAGE LINE

Ingold Peterson drove merrily day by day through the dark canon without thought of disaster. . . . But the events of last Monday are calculated to cause the traveler of the near future to traverse the canon with fear and trembling. Weird shadows will flit across his path.

Last Monday, clouds obscured the sun and a snow fall darkened the heavens. A feeling of depression came over the passengers. On the stage were Joe Domandel, Miss Lily Dinkins of Sargent and an alleged drummer. . . . He frequently glanced at the mail bags and nervously watched on either side of the road when once the canon was entered.

About midway between Cosden and White Pine as the driver hurried the team around a curve, there suddenly came into view a dark grim sentinel who stood silently by the roadside. Not a word was said but his actions were ominous and the passengers shuddered as the stage drew near.

With dilated nostrils and trembling limbs, but obedient to the lash and rein, the horses sprang forward in the face of a broadside well delivered.

A few sharp screams, muttered curses and stifling gasps, and the danger is past. But the holdup has done his work. Peterson and Carr are badly hurt . . . but the faithful horses bring the load to White Pine . . . a crowd gathered as the stage approached; . . . but no one remained long—the smelibility was offended and the victims of the tragedy were left to their fate.

The holdup escaped and the drummer left. Peterson is recovering.

A later issue of the paper explained that the drummer was suspected of being an accomplice in the holdup and that the driver whose "smelibility" offended the citizens, was drunk.

Supplies were brought to town in freighters' wagons and on one occasion fifty pounds of giant powder fell from the top of the wagon and struck the ground with such force that the box broke open and threw sawdust and powder all over the street. There were 600 pounds of powder on the wagon and men watching the vehicle lumber by scattered in all directions. By some miracle the powder did not explode.

Whitepine's markets supplied the town with staples and luxuries. Venison was sold in season as well as "all kinds of fresh meats and game, fresh oysters and sweet butter." With the opening of a second market "beefsteak dropped two cents a pound."

Preaching at the schoolhouse on Sunday was a "new departure" for the camp in 1885. Professor Turner's talks were reported as being "both interesting and instructive. The professor is a very pleasant speaker and says nothing to mar the feeling of anyone, either saint or sinner."

The social life of the Pine centered around afternoon parties given by the ladies, picnics to the Hot Springs, and "hops" given by various organizations. The Tomichi Post No. 29 of the G. A. R. had a Grand Hop followed by a supper consisting of baked beans, beef, hardtack, bacon and applesauce. The Miners Union also gave a Hop at which "all the talent which swings the hammer and pounds the steel was in attendance with wives, sisters and sweethearts."

When in 1889 funds were needed for a new schoolhouse the money was raised largely by the generous subscriptions of the unmarried men. A drama, "Out In the Streets," was given at the building after its completion, by local talent, and the entertainment closed with a farce "The Lick Skillet Wedding," for which two handsome sets were painted.

Fourth of July, 1885, was a gala day for the gulch and included a "picnic for the world at large." The festivities opened with a firing of a thirteen-gun salute, followed by the gathering of the entire camp at the speaker's platform to hear the Declaration of Independence read. The afternoon was given over to contests—foot races, sack races and a "striking match contest between miners," in which the contestant who drove the deepest hole in fifteen minutes "wet or dry, straight down in granite" won a nickelplated striking hammer. In the evening there was square dancing and a display of fireworks, culminating in the sending up of a "large illuminated balloon."

As in all the silver camps, mining boomed during the eighties and until the silver crash of '93, when even the best properties in Whitepine, such as the May-Mazeppa, were forced to close down. The people left, and by 1894 the Pine was deserted. The recovery period was slow, but before 1900 some hardy miners were back again and old mines were re-opened. In 1901 the Tomichi Valley Smelter, located three miles below Whitepine, was blown in and proceeded to treat 1,000 tons of ore a month, supplied from the North Star, Eureka, and other mines. During that year the camp payroll averaged $10,000 a month. The year 1901 was a successful one for the silver camp, for in the words of the newspaper:

"When the 1901 leaf is torn from the calendar one of the most prosperous years ever enjoyed upon the zone of the White Pine mining district will be rounded out and the year 1902 will be ushered in full of promise and assurance for both the mining and smelting industries."

Mining has been fitful at Whitepine during the twentieth century. At times the Pine has been nearly deserted, only to "come back" again when some old property has been reworked or when several lodes have been consolidated and developed by a new company with new and improved machinery. In 1938 the town was almost dead; by 1941 it was returning to life, and in 1945 there was considerable activity about the place. During 1947 the Callahan Zinc-Lead Company began steady operations at the North Star and associated

(175)

claims and erected twelve new buildings in Whitepine as well as snowsheds over the entire trackage outside the mine. Their mill is operating twenty-four hours a day processing sixty to seventy tons of lead-zinc ores from the North Star, Erie, May-Mazeppa and Akron Tunnel. So, the camp is now enjoying a mild boom.

Waunita Hot Springs

It was late one afternoon when Gene and I turned off the main highway at the foot of Monarch Pass and started across the sage-brush hills toward Pitkin. As we had never been there but had only heard of the place, we felt the expectant thrill of adventurers as every mile of the dirt road disclosed new country, mellowed by the sunset light. The road meandered across the sage flats or climbed low hills through pines and aspens, whose slender trunks cast barred shadows in front of us. About halfway to Pitkin we passed Waunita Hot Springs, a once popular resort built around soda and sulphur pools. In 1880 a mere trail led to the springs, but by 1885 they had become a regular picnic spot to which groups of young people drove to spend the afternoon "swinging and picking flowers, mosquitoes and ticks." By 1889 a two-story log hotel had been built as well as a swimming pool and bathhouses. When the post office was discontinued in 1904, there were only fifty patrons at Waunita, and for a few years thereafter the place led a quiet existence. But by 1916 its radium hot springs, its new hotel and "numerous daintily furnished cottages and well equipped sanitarium" brought patrons to dabble in the waters, attracted by the advertisement which promised that:

> Drinking the waters at the hot fountain, bathing in the large and excellently appointed swimming pool . . . inhaling the gases and steam rising from the impregnated waters . . ." and having "packings of the radium mud are some of the means and methods of transforming the sick and the invalid to health and restored vigor.

After this flush of prosperity the resort again fell into neglect, except for its swimming pool which still attracts bathers.

Bowerman

"Bowerman must have been somewhere near here," I remarked after the springs were a few miles behind us. "It was a little camp that mushroomed overnight in 1903 because a woman talked too much. Her husband had found gold on a mountain top and brought it to the cabin in sacks. The ore was pretty and she carried some of the nuggets around with her. One day while shopping in the Waunita store, she casually showed them to the storekeeper and to others and, when asked where they came from, said that her husband dug them out of a mountain not far from the Springs. Next morning there were twenty-five men staking claims all over "his" mountain, and in a few days more than six hundred prospectors were tapping and digging its slopes. J. S. Bowerman, the husband, and a man named Dunn were the original discoverers of this phenomenal gold deposit, and the new camp grew up on the site of their cabin in the Box Canyon District, three miles south of Pitkin. In 1904 another strike was made in the district near the Camp Bird mine on Copper Mountain, and more prospectors flocked in.

"This Gunnison country is full of camps, most of which date from 1879 or '80 and few of which have weathered the fluctuating booms and depressions that bet all mining camps. Pitkin and Tin Cup have survived and to a lesser

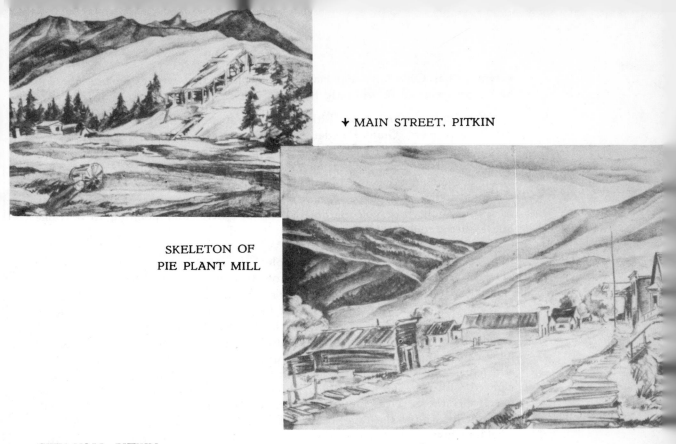

↓ MAIN STREET, PITKIN

SKELETON OF
PIE PLANT MILL

CITY HALL, PITKIN

extent so has Ohio City, but many of the places that we are looking for will be almost deserted or will only be sites."

Pitkin At a safe distance from Pitkin we passed the small stone Powder House where the miners' Giant Powder was kept and just at dusk we drove up the long main street looking for a cabin camp. There wasn't any, and the hotel looked deserted. Stopping at the filling-station-postoffice-store, we inquired about accommodations for the night. "Don't know where you'll stay," said the man at the gas pump. "There's no cabin camp, and the hotel is closed. My wife might take you in though. Go ask her," and pointing to a frame house surrounded by tall pine trees, he waved us toward it. His wife met us at the door with her hat and coat on. We explained our plight and she agreed to "put us up." "But I don't feed people," she added edging toward the door. "I'm on my way over to Ohio City now to buy a loaf of bread. The bread man passed us up today and tomorrow's a holiday." She looked us over, came to some conclusion and taking off her hat started toward the kitchen, saying over her shoulder, "I can't let you starve. I've no bread but would biscuits do?" In less than half an hour we were sitting family style, around her big round table consuming home-cured ham and gravy, fried potatoes, homemade pickles and jellies and a heaping plate of delicious biscuits. While we ate our hostess chatted with us. She had lived in Pitkin since she was a girl and had raised her family there. Now they were married, and she had some time to herself. During the winter she taught Adult Education classes in several of the surrounding towns, driving over the mountains at night to her work and thinking nothing of it. She was collecting antiques and pioneer relics as well as data and stories of the early days from the people of the region.

She showed us a Sandwich glass vase that she had rescued from a neighbor who was about to discard it, and she told us about the time that a landslide on the Pitkin side of the Alpine Tunnel detained the train to Gunnison. The passengers were impatient to continue their journey, by handcar if necessary, but there was none to be had. However a push car was found and boards placed on it so that it would hold the ten adventurous passengers, who then induced the engineer to pull them to the tunnel at the top of the pass. From there they assured him they could make the sixty miles down grade to Gunnison unaided. The trip down was thrilling, and when the slide area was reached workmen carried their car over it. Once more aboard, and rolling toward Pitkin, their speed increased until they were traveling at the rate of a mile a minute. As they flew by one little community after another they were hailed by the people living along the right of way and all in all enjoyed their hair-raising trip immensely. At Parlin they left their impromptu "train" and took the Rio Grande the rest of the way to Gunnison.

"When was Pitkin built?" asked Gene later that evening as we returned from a walk along the dark main street where only an occasional glow of lamplight filtered through curtained windows. "Some say that prospectors, who were placering in every gulch in the vicinity in 1878 made a camp which was called Quartz, along the creek of the same name, and others say that it was not until early in 1879. At any rate, a camp called Quartz or Quartzville was laid out by April 1879, and the name was changed to Pitkin in honor of Gov. Frederick W. Pitkin by late summer of the same year.

"Mr. M. A. Deering of Gunnison told me about the first rich strike. Silver was found by accident by two old prospectors. They had worked constantly for nearly two years and found nothing. By the second summer they were completely disgruntled and while eating lunch one day, sitting on a slab of rock, one of them said: 'Ain't anything in this country. Worked it for two years without a strike.' As he spoke he struck the rock with his hammer. 'Think I'll pack up and pull out,' he continued, banging the rock once more. With the second blow a chunk broke off and dropped, but not to the ground, for it was held suspended by wires to the large rock mass. Both prospectors leaped to their feet to investigate this phenomenon and discovered that wire silver was holding the severed fragment securely to the rocky ledge. All plans to leave the region were cancelled that instant. The two men staked off a claim and had their ore assayed. It ran eighty percent solid silver. That was the beginning of the Fairview mine which produced steadily until 1893."

The Red Jacket, the Iron Cap, the Silver Islet, the Silver Age and the Silent Friend mines were also located, and ore from them was shipped to Leadville on burros. About thirty men stayed in the region all winter in spite of the severe cold and waited eagerly for spring, when teams could begin bringing in goods from Alamosa over Cochetopa Pass. By the first of April freighters' wagons began to flounder in through the deep snow drifts that still obstructed the trail. Even before their arrival impatient prospectors had snow-shoed in, ready to stake claims as soon as the snow melted. A few log cabins roofed with poles and earth were built, and with the arrival of more miners and supplies the camp began to boom. By fall a town was laid out, ditches were dug and a few sidewalks laid.

Ingham in his *Digging Gold Among the Rockies* describes the early days of Pitkin. One lodginghouse was a large tent with a dirt floor covered with several inches of sawdust. It was furnished with a stove and with boxes and trunks in lieu of chairs. Two tiers of bunks were arranged in rows at the sides of the room, each bunk filled with loose hay. A thin gray blanket was provided for bedding but each customer was forced to use his own coat as a pillow. For all this comfort a charge of fifty cents per night was made. Saloons and stores were open all Sunday, freighting went on as usual, and "reports of giant powder were frequent."

By the middle of May fifteen hotels, restaurants and lodginghouses and saloons had been built to accommodate the 1050 people within the city. Another thousand were camped on the hills near their claims. Prospectors were flocking in at the rate of seventy-five a day; some merchants were carrying stocks of goods valued at from $3,000 to $10,000; mail arrived daily from Alpine, carried on horseback across the range, and a daily stage ran to and from Gunnison. Pitkin's boom was on, and for the next few years the little city outstripped its mining neighbors.

Early in 1880 the people began to agitate for a newspaper, for as one of them wrote: "Pitkin has 3 women, 7 children, 180 dogs, 1 cat, 2 burros and 3 fiddlers and they are not happy. They want a . . . newspaper." By July the *Pitkin Independent* was established, and later the *Pitkin Mining News* also served the lively camp. The *Independent* carried columns of local interest under such headings as "Pitkin Pellets" and "Mining Matters," and on July 12, 1882, when the first passenger train on the Denver and South Park railroad arrived in town through the newly opened Alpine Tunnel, the paper immediately referred to the nearby boom towns of Tin Cup and Gothic as "temporary camps" because they had no rail facilities to move their ore. The coming of the railroad opened the entire territory, for heretofore the only entrance to the region had been by means of mountain passes which were closed by snow eight months in the year. Now it was hoped trains would run even during the winter. The road's constant struggle with snowslides has been mentioned in the preceding chapter, but even so it served the Gunnison area for years. After the road had crossed the pass it was easily extended to Ohio City and from there to Parlin, where it joined the D. & R. G. on its way to Gunnison.

Like all mining towns Pitkin had its rougher element, and especially during the building of the Alpine Tunnel this group was reinforced on Saturday nights by a tough gang of laborers who came down from the Tunnel to "whoop it up" in the saloons. At such times the "respectable" citizens would lock their doors and go to bed, leaving the town to the boisterous crowd.

By 1891 Pitkin had many stores, a bank, two churches and the Colorado State Fish Hatchery, situated one half mile below town. The mines were producing, the Islet turning out silver bricks weighing 774 ounces and the "Little Tycoon" striking a new rich vein which brought more miners spilling into the district. Mining was suspended in 1893 when silver was demonetized, but some persistent miners remained and worked their properties, looking for other valuable metals. Between 1893 and 1895 mining was in better condition than formerly because "the formations in which ore was found were better understood" and because the work was being done by more experienced men. During this period the Fairview, Nest Egg, Tycoon and Little Roy were further developed.

In 1901 the new City Hall was built, in 1904 a contract was let for a new Odd Fellows Hall and that same year a telephone switchboard was installed in town. The gold strike at Bowerman in 1903 aroused new interest in the district, and as late as 1916 men were searching the granite formations for gold deposits. But by 1925 Pitkin was undergoing a depression. Many people had moved away and only two or three stores and one hotel served the entire community. Little mining was being done but a new industry, the cutting of timber for railroad ties and mine props, was keeping the city alive.

We spent part of the next morning exploring, walking almost the entire length of the town on wooden sidewalks and locating the old railroad grade and the depot, now a private home. Main street with its tall flagpole, the long empty blocks lined with foundations, the false-fronted assay office and the Community church were all sketched. Then, thanking our hostess for our comfortable lodgings we were off.

Tin Cup The road to Tin Cup twists and climbs for miles to the top of Cumberland Pass. A little way beyond Pitkin is the site of Quartz, where today only foundations and rotting logs mark the cabin sites built in 1879 and 1880 when rich carbonates were found in the vicinity. The railroad ran through here in the eighties and at this place the D. & S. P. trains put on two engines to "go over the hill" to Hancock. Oldtimers remember when an engine crew tried to force a passage through the Alpine Tunnel which was blocked with snow. Driving the engine through water on the track caused a hot box, and three men were killed by the steam.

Our road cut its way high up in the mountainside, until looking back we could see for miles down the narrow valley, while ahead of us were timberline and rocky peaks. Before we left the timber we passed a group of log cabins and a long curving trestle leading to a mill. This was the Bon Ton property where gold, silver, copper, lead and zinc had been mined. Switchbacks soon took us above the mine and we could look down through the treetops to the buildings tucked away in the timber. At the summit of the pass we stopped to enjoy the view. Snowclad peaks rimmed the horizon and pine-covered mountains lay folded in ridges below us as far as we could see. Over the crest of the pass was the weathered shaft house of the Blistered Horn mine, battered by years of wind and snow. A shelf road drops down into Tin Cup past the ruins of the West Gold Hill mill, near the foot of the grade. Tin Cup is spread over a wide meadow, the road bisecting the main street, at the corner of which stands the Community Hall, the largest building in town, built in 1906, partly to save the rent paid for the use of a meeting room in Neiderhut's store.

Next to it stood the firehouse with its hand-drawn apparatus and up the street stood the shell of a two-story, false-fronted store. Scrambling across the fragments of wooden sidewalk in front of it and climbing over the broken doorstep, I looked around the interior which was littered with broken furniture, a brass bed, old newspapers and rolls of wallpaper. Dirt and plaster coated the creaking floor so completely that it was necessary to test each step to find out whether the boards would hold or crack beneath us. Was this Neiderhut's store in which the town meetings had once been held? There was no one to ask, and when next I visited Tin Cup the store had burned down.

There were cabins in all directions, some built of logs with "bay windows" and ornamental eaves, and others of more recent construction. The fireplugs, installed in 1891 when water was piped into the town, stood at intervals along the streets, each one rusty and surrounded by a flourishing tuft of grass. Looking around the quiet town it was hard to believe that it had been a thriving camp until 1893 and that in 1890, a year before a telegraph office was installed, the newspaper had printed news of a small boom with the headlines:

> The Tin Cup Strike is All Right
> It Is the Best Showing I Ever Saw
> It Is the Biggest Thing On Earth.

Tin Cup is the same age as Pitkin and Whitepine but its early history is involved with that of Hillerton and Abbeyville, two small camps just north of it, and it is unique in having been incorporated twice, first in 1880 as Virginia

City and again in 1882 as Tin Cup. In the summer of 1860 Ben and Charles Gray and Jim Taylor came over Red Mountain Pass from Granite and prospected the country which later became dotted with the mining camps of Tin Cup, Hillerton, Abbeyville, Bowman and Dorchester. They camped on a creek and one morning couldn't find their horses. Taylor went to look for them and in the next gulch found a small, dry wash where the sand looked promising. He took a sample of it back to camp in a tin cup and when he panned it found that it was gold! The rest of the summer the three men worked near their claim, but eventually cold weather forced them out for the winter. In the spring of 1861, when they were ready to return to their diggings, knowing that they were being watched and would be followed by other prospecting parties, they made a roundabout trip by way of what is now Salida and Cochetopa Pass. At the same time another party consisting of Fred and Carl Siegel and Fred Lottis were prospecting in the same region, crossing the headwaters of Gold Creek and discovering Union Park, where their placer diggings are still visible. Some accounts say that Taylor and his party gave the name Tin Cup to the gulch; others assert that Fred Lottis was the man who used a tin cup to wash the first gold flakes from the stream, and because of this named the region the Tin Cup District. At any rate, some placering was carried on in the vicinity until 1878 when, with the discovery of the Gold Cup mine, a stampede to the region began and the camps of Virginia City and Hillerton were laid out.

Hillerton   Hillerton rose out of the sage brush in 1879, one month later than Virginia City, and was situated two miles north of it in a little park on Willow Creek. At its peak it had several stores, one bank, one hotel—the New England House where according to a traveler's report "you pay the highest prices for the most ordinary spread"—several sawmills, some "comfortable private residences," and a newspaper, the *Hillerton Occident* published by Henry Olney. Olney visited the district in 1879 after the discovery of the Gold Cup mine and, believing that the camp would grow, decided to "bring in a newspaper." This he accomplished with difficulty, upsetting the press in the Taylor River and finally installing it in an unfinished shack. The first issue appeared on June 23, 1879, and was enthusiastically received by the miners. Olney printed the paper until October of the same year, when he decided to move his press to Virginia City and start a paper there. Although there were many lode mines in the vicinity of Hillerton, such as the Adeline, Little Earl and What Is It, few of them were developed, and one reason that the town was shortlived was that since the bigger mines were closer to Virginia City the population drifted gradually that way.

Abbeyville   Abbeyville, one mile north of Virginia City in the same park as Hillerton, grew up around a smelter which was built in 1881 by C. F. Abbey to handle ore from the Jimmy Mack and other mines in Virginia City. As soon as it was completed the remaining citizens of Hillerton moved out "bag and baggage and cabin logs" to the new town. In 1884 Abbeyville itself collapsed and its cabins were dismantled and moved into Virginia City which by then was called Tin Cup.

Tin Cup Cont'd   Virginia City was laid out in May, 1879, a month before Hillerton, by a party of men from the Black Hills. There was great rivalry between the

(182)

two camps during the first year. Each had a population of 1500 and the 1880 census estimated the total population of Virginia City and its surrounding territory as 4000. The camp was incorporated in August 1880 and was soon the leading mining town in the county. Thousands of miners and gamblers gathered there, the latter running the place to suit themselves. By 1882 its population had risen to 6000; it contained a dozen stores and shops, as well as several hotels and twenty saloons, of which Frenchy's Place was the most notorious. It was a wild town in wild country and grizzlies and mountain lions were often seen close to camp.

In 1880 the rough element elected a mayor, a council, and a marshall who was told that the first man he attempted to arrest would be his last, and that he was to see nothing and know nothing. They pointed out that he was selected to give the camp an appearance of being orderly so that tenderfeet could be lured to it and then fleeced. The next marshall showed his authority by periodically rounding up a group of drunken miners and gamblers, disarming them and herding them to the calaboose, where he would release them. In 1882 Harry Rivers became marshall. By this time dancehalls and gambling houses were running day and night and some effort to control the disorderly classes was attempted. Jack Ward, one of the region's dangerous characters, would come to Tin Cup to pick a fight with the miners. During one pitched battle over a hundred shots were fired, and to put an end to such brawls Rivers and Ward "exchanged shots," after which the marshall arrested him, locked him up and fined him. Ward reformed after this experience, and two years later was occupying a pulpit in Glenwood Springs, where he warned gamblers of hell fire and colored his remarks by personal experiences!

Charles La Tourette, the saloon keeper, was the toughest man in the camp. One night Rivers was called upon to arrest him, and in the ensuing quarrel guns were drawn and shots fired. Rivers finally got possession of La Tourette's gun and the two men started arm in arm for the jail. After going a block or so La Tourette pulled a gun from his other pocket and shot Rivers. Tin Cup's next marshall went insane, and his successor was killed. With so much lawlessness in camp it was thought wise to set aside land for a burying ground. Cemetery Hill is south of town and contains four separate knolls designated as the Community, Jewish, Catholic and Boot Divisions. This last was for those who "died gloriously or otherwise in the thick of smoke from guns."

Even in 1881 most of the buildings in the camp were tents or wooden foundation frames roofed with canvas, for there was no time to waste in building homes while mining was booming and each day's work might uncover a bonanza. Whenever a freighter arrived with his wagon heaped with supplies it was surrounded by a clamoring, pushing throng of men who bought its contents on the spot before it could be unloaded. One freighter, bringing in 3500 pounds of flour in his six-mule wagon, sold every hundred-pound sack for $14.00 the minute he drew up in front of Frenchy's Place. In 1881, before Hillerton "evaporated," Olney moved his press to Virginia City and started the *Tin Cup Record*, using a picture of a tin cup in place of the words for a caption in the first issue. Other papers appeared in the little camp, the *Tin*

Cup Banner in 1882, the *Tin Cup Miner* in 1884 and the *Tin Cup Times* in 1890.

The discovery of the Gold Cup mine in 1878 started the stampede of prospectors into the district. It and the Jimmy Mack became the biggest properties of the camp. Both were located on Gold Hill three miles east of Tin Cup and both were steady producers of gold and silver. Ore from the Gold Cup ran as high as 191 ounces in silver and 7 ounces in gold to the ton, while its total output exceeded $2,000,000.

During 1879 and 1880 ore was packed out by burros twelve miles over the range to St. Elmo, where it was loaded on wagons or sleighs and hauled to Alpine, the railhead of the Denver and South Park road; from there it was shipped by rail to the smelters of the Arkansas Valley. By 1881 the railroad was extended as far as St. Elmo and a toll road was built between it and Tin Cup over which six-horse teams dragged ore wagons at $3.50 a load. After the railroad reached Quartz and Pitkin in 1882 ore was taken to Quartz, ten miles away, by wagon in summer and by sled in winter. As soon as the railroad was built to Almont on the Taylor River, thirty miles from Tin Cup, there was agitation to extend it to the mining camp, for by 1883 the Tin Cup mines had produced a million dollars worth of ore; but despite pressure by Tin Cup and Gunnison business men, the road was never built. And by 1883 it had also been proven that the ore of the Jimmy Mack mine was too difficult for the Abbeyville smelter to handle, and the plant closed down.

By 1884 mining was beginning to wane and the population of Tin Cup dropped to 400, but as long as the Gold Cup produced, the camp was not dead. Even during the panic of 1893 the mine was worked, as well as in 1896 when Robert Clark obtained a lease on the property. Three weeks after he took over it was still so early in the season that he and three other men improvised a toboggan with which to get down and up the ice-coated incline of the mine tunnel. One morning they started down as usual, but three hundred feet below the surface the toboggan caught on some caved-in rock. Three of the men jumped to safety and signaled the engineers to stop the hoist; but Clark stayed on the sled and succeeded in working it loose. Fifty feet of slack cable connected it with the hoist, and as the toboggan gathered speed Clark was unable to leap off. When the slack was taken up the sled stopped suddenly, throwing Clark headlong down the tunnel to his death.

By 1900 Tin Cup was virtually a ghost town, but in 1903 a second boom brought 2000 miners scurrying back to the camp. This time big stock companies invested capital in the mines and began to develop them. During the boom the Brunswick Milling and Mining Company extended the Blistered Horn Tunnel 1600 feet under Gold Hill to reach the Jimmy Mack vein, and the Tin Cup mine, an extension of the Gold Cup, was further explored.

During this revival there were two rival stores in Tin Cup, one run by Gallager and the other by Neiderhut. The two establishments stood opposite each other on Washington Avenue and each carried stocks of goods greater than any found in the county today. Neiderhut kept an iron box containing thousands of dollars of gold in cash in his cellar, for during the winter his store served both as a distribution center for goods and as a bank for the hardy miners who "dug themselves in" for the long cold months. It was at this time that the Community Hall was built and that a "well equipped school-house and one of the finest Masonic buildings in the mountains" were boasted of in the *Gunnison News.*

The last great placer project was carried on near the site of Hillerton by the Columbine Gold Dredging Company between 1908 and 1912, but the project was a financial loss. By 1910 much of the mining in the vicinity had ceased, and by 1912 the town was almost deserted again. The final blow came when the Gold Cup closed down in 1917. Thereafter the town was only a summer resort with a population of seventy-five or a hundred and with no one about in the winter but a watchman. By 1933 it had no post office, no school and no voting precinct, and except for sporadic leasing of old properties it comes to life only during the summer months when fishermen fill its cabins and tourists ask the way to the cemetery that they may see the old graves in the Boot Division.

Before leaving Tin Cup I visited the Gold Cup mine. Following the road that turns off the highway at the south edge of town, we drove toward the property. After two miles of dodging ruts and rocks the road became hope-lessly washed and we decided to go no further by car. Leaving my friends, I started on alone, until after a mile's hiking I saw the mine and its buildings ahead. White-faced cattle grazed below the mine and as I hurried along they watched me with curiosity and suspicion. After completing a couple of sketches I started back, but before I could leave the meadow the cattle bunched up and came toward me. Not wanting to be crowded by them, I picked up a stick and waved it, at the same time yelling as loudly as possible. These tac-tics worked and the whole herd hightailed it ahead of me down the gulch. Every little while they would wheel about and stand staring at me until I brandished the stick again and yelled, when away they would go bawling and crashing through the brush. Long before I reached the car my friends were aware of my approach, for down the road came the whole herd on the run.

Leaving the Gold Cup road we drove again through Tin Cup and continued north toward Taylor Park and the Reservoir. Driving through the sagebrush sites of Abbeyville and Hillerton we looked for signs of the towns, for I had been told that two dilapidated cabins were still standing and that halfway between the townsites, "in the middle of sagebrush waves," stood the wreckage of a gold dredge that had operated until 1915 when all dredging operations ceased. But we saw nothing.

Pie Plant
Mill
"Our next objectives are Bowman, Dorchester and the Pie Plant Mill," I announced as we neared the Taylor Reservoir and took the road to the right that skirts the lake. "The old stage road to Bowman, from Tin Cup, went by the Pie Plant Mill, and the National Forest map of today shows a passable road leading from the Pie Plant Cow Camp to the mill." We found the Cow Camp and left a fair dirt road for a rough untravelled trail. A few miles' drive through woods brought us to a clearing where a group of mouldering log cabins marked what had once been a small but well laid out camp along a stream. Across the stream was the bleached skeleton of a mill

(186)

and higher up the mountain was the mine. The property produced lead and silver, and from the looks of the buildings it must have been deserted for some years before our visit.

"Now let's go up to Dorchester which is about six miles farther, and Bowman which is ten," I said as we retraced the road to the Cow Camp. Bowman is the oldest town in Taylor Park with the exception of Tin Cup and was started about the same time. It was not only a mining camp but also the shipping point for Aspen, as all provisions for that camp were taken in at first over Taylor's Pass, which lies just beyond. In 1881 it had a population of one hundred, two general stores, a log hotel, a stage depot, barns, cabins for freighters, and a smelting works which handled the ore from the mines in the vicinity.

"A pioneer woman's description of Bowman written in 1884 describes the settlement. Her father filed on the 160 acres of land that comprised the township. He ran a grocery and miners' supply store, and he built cabins and enough stables to accommodate 150 horses; for two stages a day, between St. Elmo and Aspen, stopped at his station and changed horses. During bad weather passengers and travellers often were forced to stay over until the storm abated. On one occasion the stage and all its passengers were marooned for three weeks. Food was plentiful and the guests entertained themselves with music from the square piano, which her father had freighted in over the rocky roads.

"Dorchester was not founded until 1900 when the Italian Mountain District gold mines were opened up. A dozen or more small properties were developed and many prospectors worked in the vicinity. The strike brought new life to Taylor Park and people poured in every day from Tin Cup and Aspen. The town was built on the Bachlor Ranch in the midst of the surrounding mines. Southwest of it was Italian Mountain where the Bull Domingo mine was located, to the north was the Enterprise, to the south the Star, to the east the Pie Plant and to the southeast the Forest Hill. Later on during the first World War, lead and zinc were found in the Doctor and in the Star mines, and thirty four-horse teams hauled the ore to Almont; but after the war the mines closed down.

"All the traffic between Aspen and Tin Cup passed through the camp of Dorchester, and teamster Frost, who made regular trips, became famous for his successful crossings of Taylor Pass. But once in July even he was stalled in an immense drift on the summit. In fact, both mining and freighting were usually retarded until late summer because of the heavy snows, and even then, with four-horse teams, it often took three weeks to make the round trip to Aspen.

"In spite of deep snow some of the mines were worked through the winter. One miner wrote that 'Mail is rare but there are comforts in camp and amusement like snowshoeing whiles away spare hours.' The Italian Mountain Snowshoe Club made the most of 'the beautiful', as the snow was called, although snowslides were frequent and their imminence made the sport hazardous.

"The miners in the Star mine bunkhouse counted fourteen slides on the day the news arrived that 'the management contemplated stopping work for a few days, and immediately fifteen pairs of snowshoes were made in a single day by twenty men who concluded to spend the time in Aspen.' A couple of toboggans were also constructed on which to haul provisions, and with these the men set out. Leaving the mine in the morning, they reached Bowman that evening completely worn out, for the soft, fresh snow was very deep. They then had to wait for Frost and his team to take them over the pass."

Our road became rougher and rougher, but since it was passable we went on. On the site of Dorchester we found an overnight cabin installed by the Forest Service and one of the old, original cabins with its overhanging ridge pole and sod roof. "And this," I said pointing to the surrounding meadowland, "is what a mining expert from Boston, who was staying at the Dorchester Hotel in 1901, said was the 'coming mining camp of the new century'!"

Beyond Dorchester the road almost disappeared, but with careful driving we avoided the worst rocks and hollows and finally drove triumphantly up the main street of Bowman. There wasn't much to see, but I poked among some foundations and found what appeared to have been a stone mill or smelter and an old flume. One two-story building was standing, and beyond Bowman the mountains made a solid barrier over which the stream of traffic used to wind via Taylor Pass.

We drove back along the Taylor and East Rivers to Gunnison and as we passed the Taylor Reservoir and crossed Lottis Creek we remembered that it was Jim Taylor and Fred Lottis who had opened up this region so many years before and whose names stand as a memorial to their pioneer discoveries.

Ohio City The first time I went to Ohio City I was disappointed. There were a couple of stores and quite a few houses and cabins but no signs of the mining that had been responsible for the town. It was Sunday afternoon, the stores were closed and everyone seemed to be away, so after a cursory glance around I left. Shortly afterwards I learned that the mines were up Gold Creek; so on my next trip to Gunnison I made a side trip to Ohio City, determined to find the Raymond, the Carter and the Gold Links, all of which had been active properties in their day. The drive from Parlin to Ohio City is through ranch country, but I was so impatient to reach Gold Creek that I hardly noticed the scenery we passed. Ohio City was more deserted than ever; only one store was stocked with supplies and it was locked, and fewer houses seemed inhabited than on my former visit. Just as I was turning away from the store, a young woman came across the road with the key and let us in. Between sips of soda pop we asked her questions about the mines.

"You can drive up Gold Creek as far as the Gold Links," she told us. "The Sandy Hook mine is beyond the Links, but they dismantled its mill and installed it at the Roosevelt mine near Pitkin." We soon left, and as we drove up the creek road I told Ann Jones and Peg Mabee about Ohio City.

"It is one of the oldest camps in the county. Although placer gold was found in German Flats and Ohio Creek in the sixties, it was not until the silver rush of 1879 brought many men to the region that a town was laid out. It was founded in 1880 and was called Eagle City, but as it was situated at the mouth of Ohio Creek the name was later changed to Ohio City. Later still in the nineties, when gold was found in paying quantities, the name of the creek was changed to Gold Creek.

"During the eighties the town was active, especially after Chicago capitalists invested heavily in lots and erected a large hotel and several substantial buildings. With the collapse of silver in 1893 most of the mines shut down, but in 1896 gold was discovered and the camp came back as the booming center of a rich gold district. At first lumber was brought in from Pitkin and was very expensive, but when a sawmill was set up only two miles away building picked up."

Of course we were looking for mines and mills, and the Carter was the first we came to on Gold Creek. Its buildings were in excellent condition and its mill perforated with more windows than I had ever seen in one structure. The next morning we talked to a mining man in Pitkin and learned the history of the mines on Gold Creek.

The Carter Group we learned consisted of seventy-nine patented claims in the Gold Brick district and was developed (as were most of the mines on the creek), by a tunnel which was a mile and a half long. Carter spent $250,000.-000 developing the property, blocking out ore enough to run a twenty-stamp mill for twenty years. The mine was excellently managed, shipping a gold brick worth $3000 every two weeks and paying for itself by the ore which was cut out of the tunnel while it was being developed. In fact during all this period of expansion the company never ran behind a single day in meeting its payroll and other bills.

A mile beyond the Carter was the Raymond mine, whose red buildings reflected in a little lake made a perfect picture. The Raymond was the pioneer mine of the section and up until the death of its manager in 1916 was one of the most active in the district, having produced over $7,000,000.

Less than a mile further was the Gold Links property on which stood the biggest mill in the gulch. Our first glimpse of it was through a screen of aspens and we lost no time in crossing the creek on a shaky bridge and driving close to the golden skeleton. The Gold Links Mining Company held more property than any other in the district, 6000 acres of mineral land; and as we explored the forty-stamp mill and its surrounding buildings where two hundred men had worked we were impressed by the large scale on which it must have operated. There were a big two-story boardinghouse and several other frame cabins, besides the usual shops and machine sheds. The mine tunnel, which ran from the creek for 4000 feet and extended under German Flats, cut many veins. From it nearly a million dollars was taken in gold and silver ore. For years the mill has stood abandoned, and some day it will be dismantled and another landmark of mining days will disappear.

Retracing our way to Ohio City I thought about the days when a daily stage ran from there to the mines and when the McKinney Hotel catered to the mining men who thronged to the district. I remembered reading how in the early days forest fires threatened the lives of hundreds of prospectors along the creek and I told my companions the story of the freighter who dug a grave for his mule on the road to Pitkin and placed a stake over the grave on which he scrawled:

> "Death went prospecting
> And he was no fool
> Here he struck faithful Pete
> The emigrant mule."

Having seen no place to spend the night in Ohio City we decided to visit Pitkin again. Surely by 1945 they would have a cabin camp! An eight-mile drive brought us to its main street, and we drove slowly up and down looking for lodgings. There was nothing, and the house where I had stayed in 1941 was closed. When we asked the storekeeper where to go he only shook his head, but one of his customers said: "Why don't you stay in our house? There's just me and my husband and we'll be out all evening. There's plenty of room and you can cook your supper on the range. The fire's all laid. You have a dog with you? That's all right, I like dogs." And as we gasped with amazement and relief, she jumped into her car and drove off, with our Ford in hot pursuit. In less than fifteen minutes two of us were preparing supper in her immaculate kitchen while the third made up the beds.

Pitkin's streets are dark and the irrigation ditch which flows by the side of the main thoroughfare is wide enough to be bridged in front of each house, but before we turned in that evening we walked along the street, sniffing the pungent scent of the pines, listening to the gurgle of the ditch and watching the moon whiten the pineclad slopes until it sank behind the black mountain wall across the narrow valley. In the morning our generous hostess had waiting for us a country breakfast of bacon, eggs and sausage, griddle cakes, coffee and jam. From this we reluctantly tore ourselves to drive "over the mountain" to Waunita and then home.

CHAPTER EIGHT

The Gunnison Country

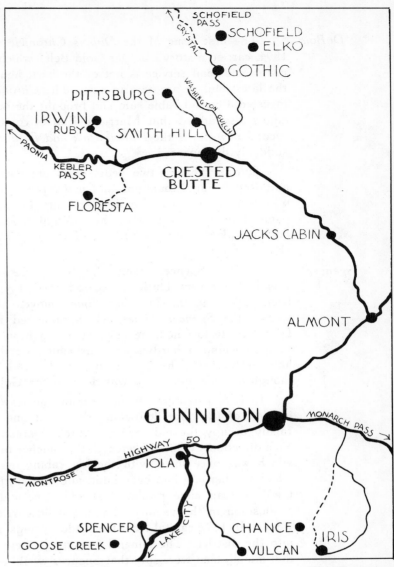

The Gunnison Gold Belt

I'D heard of the Gunnison Gold Belt — forty square miles which included the mining districts of Cochetopa, Gold Basin, Beaver, Powderhorn, Willow Creek, Goose Creek, Camp Creek and Cebolla, where in the middle nineties a gold strike, which promised to duplicate that at Cripple Creek, caused thousands of men to hurry to the sage-covered hills to search for outcroppings of gold. It was believed to be a continuation of the great San Juan belt, extending across the county and over the Continental Divide to Leadville. The fact that the same character of ore was found in it as in the Golden Fleece mine at Lake City and in the Little Jonny at Leadville was taken as evidence that the mineral belt was a continuous one. The whole region, from Mineral Hill near Iris on the east to Vulcan on the west, justified exploration, for somewhere in the Belt there was believed to be a Mother Lode for which prospectors searched from Cochetopa to Cebolla creeks.

Between 1893 and 1895 a group of promising camps were located on the Gold Belt which ran northeast and southwest through the mountains of this part of the state. The Goose Creek district, which was organized in the fall of 1893 just after gold was discovered in the region, lay at the west end of the belt. A new gold camp called Goose Creek appeared, which in less than a year had a population of 1,000. The camps of DuBois, Spencer, Tolifaro or Tolliver, and Cebolla Springs also sprang up and all could be reached by stage from Iola, after rail passage over Marshall Pass. In fact Iola became the shipping point for the entire western part of the district.

DuBois   The first issue of the *Dubois Chronicle* which was published April 14, 1894, carried a story of "Our Gold Belt" which stated that "We have no telegraph and mail service is not of the best, hence outside news may not be of the latest but we are here to stay. The *Chronicle* is not on wheels. We have invested a considerable sum and brought the outfit in at heavy expense." The editor also added that Marriage Blanks could be procured at his office. A second newspaper the *Dubois Pick and Drill* appeared briefly in 1894 and as suddenly disappeared.

During the first two years good ore was found on Gold Hill, Tolifaro and Republican Mountains and many properties were developed, but capital was lacking to push the developments to big-scale production. Ten companies mined at the base of the mountains, and later in 1894 the first car of ore, all taken from the surface of the Carpenter Group on Gold Hill, was shipped to Denver.

Spencer   In 1894 Spencer, named for S. P. Spencer, county clerk and recorder, was laid out near DuBois. By fall of that year C. A. Frederick, who had been publishing the *Tin Cup Times*, moved his outfit to the new camp and started the *Spencer Times*, which appeared for four years. Business men from Creede lost no time in establishing branches of their stores in the new camp, opening a hardware, a furnishing goods store, a saloon, and an ore hauling service. The Iron Cap and the Old Lot were the chief mines, although considerable work was done in the Golden Etta and the Head Light.

In 1946 I detoured to Spencer on the way to Lake City and found nothing left of the once flourishing camp but one log cabin. A rancher and his family occupy the old townsite—their nearest neighbors nine miles away in each direction. While I sketched, the rancher talked. He pointed out the gulch which was once lined with the log cabins that comprised the camp and on which the big mill had been built, and he described the prosperous days when the Iron Cap mine produced steadily and paid better than any other gold proposition in the vicinity, shipping a little brick of gold every two or three weeks. In 1897 capital from Colorado Springs and Cripple Creek really rolled into the district. The mineral formations were so similar to those at Cripple that mining men were sure that Spencer would equal it; but the veins that were found pinched out the deeper they were cut. Spencer was developed between 1894 and 1897, but by 1898 it was almost dead as a gold camp. In 1900 it was booming again, this time as a copper camp, with 500 people milling around and working the Copper King lode, which adjoined the Iron Cap on the north. The rancher to whom I was talking worked as a foreman for the Copper King over twenty-five years ago, until the mine closed down due to too much litigation, too little capital and poor management. He liked the country and decided to stay on and try ranching. Evenings after work he and his son gopher around a little in the old shafts and set some ore. I looked at the one log cabin and a schoolhouse, and recalled a copy of the *Spencer Times* printed in 1894 which said that "another winter will not have passed before this gold camp will be employing thousands of men and its output reckoned in the millions." There used to be some mining a few miles away at Powderhorn too—big iron deposits, but today it's all ranch country.

(192)

One weekend I took two friends to Gunnison and, after asking questions of mining men and perusing faded copies of newspapers, was ready to hunt for Iris and Chance, two of the camps in the eastern end of the Belt. Elliot, Elizabeth and I left the city early one morning and after five miles on the main highway turned south on a narrow dirt road which wandered across marshy meadows until it started its gradual climb into the sagebrush hills.

Both camps were laid out in 1894, and Iris was the larger of the two, being close to the Mineral Hill group of mines. The Lucky Strike and the Only Chance were the chief mines at Chance.

The first issue of the *Cochetopa Gold Belt,* Aug. 23, 1895, described the "lively camps" where free gold in float formation was found as well as rich veins four to five feet wide.

> In each there are stores, hotels, saloons, blacksmith shops, livery and feed stables, surveyors, assayers and mining engineers. New buildings are constantly erected and additions to the population are being made daily. It is connected with Gunnison by telephone and tri-weekly mail services from the same point.
>
> Probably 1000 men are now prospecting and working in this district. The veins are large and outcrop frequently. They pan well and the camp is at this time a great free milling proposition. Three mines have steam plants, there are 2 stamp mills and there is an abundance of water the year around.
>
> This camp is but a year old but it is a very healthy youngster. The camp is going forward with lusty strides. There are many promising claims and syndicates from abroad have representatives in camp watching its progress.

By 1896 over $100,000 had been invested in mining property and so many new houses had been built that the camp was said to resemble Cripple Creek in 1891 at the beginning of its boom. Like all the camps in the Gold Belt more capital was needed to develop the properties that had been opened. The *Saguache Crescent* of 1897 in speaking of Iris and Chance said that "Times are hard. The wave of prosperity not yet having arrived in this camp of the hills, but people always seem to have a little money with which to pay the fiddler and the social dance at the hotel last week was well attended." A couple who planned to live in Iris had some difficulty in finding a minister to marry them. There was none in Iris; those in Gunnison could not be found; a local magistrate would not do; so the Chaplain of the Denver and Rio Grande railroad who was at Pueblo was telegraphed for and upon his arrival the knot was tied.

By the end of 1899 the camp was still waiting for capital and all but one property was idle. In 1900 and 1901 there was a spurt of activity caused by some free gold strikes, but within a few years the mines became idle, and today both camps are deserted.

About halfway to Iris we met a Geological Survey truck driven by a sun-burned chap who pulled off the road to let our car pass. Always curious to get information about roads and places we began a conversation and found that the road ahead was in good shape.

"Why do you want to go to Iris anyway?" asked the driver of the truck. "There's nothing there, only a bunch of empty cabins. The survey gang is running a line across that section and I drove them to Iris this morning. I'm on my way to Chance now to pick them up later in the day. There used to be a road between the two camps which are just a mile apart, but now it's all broken down. The best way to get to Chance is to go the way I'm going, but there are so many side roads between here and the turnoff that I don't know how to tell you which one to take. Tell you what I'll do. I've got to change a tire on this truck and that will take about an hour. I'll park the truck at the fork that leads to Chance and when you come back I'll still be there and you can follow me in."

That was fair enough, and thanking him we drove on toward Iris. A curve in the road brought us to the deserted camp. There were about a dozen one-story cabins and a few mine shafts visible on the low hills beyond the town. One mine had an empty shaft house, but I had no idea which mine it was. Grazing cattle wandered over the sage brush flats or plodded through the marshy grass beside the stream. Earlier in the season the meadow would have been blue with wild iris. Some of the cabins had remnants of furniture in them, but most were empty or littered with debris. We did not stay long but retraced our steps to the fork where we would find the survey man and go with him to the mines of Chance. His truck was gone. Just as we were debating which side road to try I noticed three sticks propped beside the road in such a way as to point toward a fork to the left and realized that our friend had built this marker for our use. Before long we caught up with his truck and passed him and in a few more miles we began to pass mines and to see mine buildings dotting the hills. Chance was more scattered than Iris but its mines were equally dead. After exploring the region we started back toward Gunnison.

Although Chance was smaller than Iris it produced more ore. A. E. Reynolds and his outfit bought two claims in camp and built a $50,000 mill, but in spite of their preparations they never took out more than $20,000 or $30,000. The veins were wide at the surface but tapered off underground and, partly for this reason, the property was all worked out in one year. Anne Ellis, who wrote "Plain Anne Ellis" and "Sunshine Preferred," went to Chance as a bride. She describes a trip to Gunnison in an ore wagon, when she had thirty dollars to spend for household equipment and for clothes for a new baby. She bought things for the baby first, and then she bought a mirror and lace curtains for the cabin. That left three dollars, which she spent for house plants!

Vulcan   Vulcan is only 12 miles from the highway; so with plans to run out there and back in an hour or so and go on to Montrose for lunch, early one morning three of us turned up the road between the sagebrush hills. The country was lonely and the road soggy from last night's rain. Passing through a thicket of willows we startled a covey of quail from bushes and watched their whirring flight across the sage. There was nothing to see but sage and an occasional empty cabin or ranch house or corral. After four miles the road forked and we were uncertain which way to go, for our map showed no side road. The better road turned left and disappeared around a hill, the other led through a ford where the water was fairly deep and

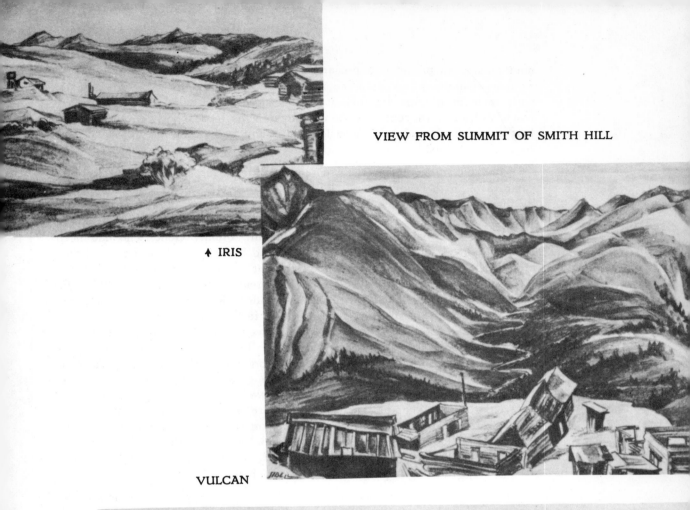

VIEW FROM SUMMIT OF SMITH HILL

↑ IRIS

VULCAN

mud and rocks provided a precarious bed for the car. It might not be the right road anyway but, as it led in the direction in which we wanted to go, with some misgivings we took it. After eight more miles we would either reach Vulcan or we could retrace our steps to the ford and try the other fork. Just as we had made this decision we found a sign beside our road half covered with bushes, but it was distinctly marked "Vulcan 8 miles."

The next four miles were without incident, just a steady and gentle climb through the sage-covered hills. Then the road ahead was gouged out by the heavy rains which had swollen the creek and cut away the bank and the road with it. We could not drive ahead, there were still four miles to go, and I hated to abandon our trip at this point. Finally Gene, who had been scouting ahead, announced that a truck had driven through the sagebrush around the washout and that he thought our car could make it too. While we walked behind, he drove off over the greasewood and sage stubble, the stiff bushes scratching and rubbing the sides the entire way as the car bounced over the rough ground. Two miles farther on the road became such a mass of deep ruts and high centers that we dared not drive it for fear of slipping off the crown and breaking an axle. This time we did a bit of road-building, cutting down the high center and filling the deepest ruts with stones and the dirt we had shovelled. With great care Gene crawled across the improved road, and in two more miles we reached Vulcan—a completely deserted group of cabins, sheds and a store or two, scattered over rolling meadowland. At the far end of the street on the crest of a hill was a mine with its buildings and big dump, while halfway down the hillside was the stone foundation of a smelter or large mill, its rock walls stained a bright orange from the iron-impregnated water which flowed over it.

Most of the cabins stood open and had served as shelters for cattle. In a few, broken bits of furniture or crude benches and shelves strewed the floor, but in one we found stacks of books, some watersoaked and some in good condition; and leaving my two friends sitting on the floor eagerly looking them over, I climbed up to the mine and poked about the deserted office. On the way back to the car I found the schoolhouse and a cabin whose stove was propped crazily aslant on the porch. Collecting my two literary companions I started back toward Iola, and although the twelve miles had to be driven slowly and carefully even the ford posed no problem now. When we reached the highway Gene looked at his watch. It was noon! The entire morning had been spent driving twenty-four miles and spending half an hour in a ghost camp. It was not until years later that I learned Vulcan's history.

The discovery of the Vulcan and Mammoth Chimney mines late in 1895 in the Gunnison Gold Belt brought prospectors to the region, and with the development of the mines a town called Camp Creek was laid out. This was the best of all the camps, for more mineral was found in its vicinity than in any of the other camps which were located on the same strip of mineral land. The Vulcan mine was a "sulphur proposition mixed with gold." It worked two hundred men and for a time sent two cars of ore a week to the smelter, but the sulphur in the mine was in loose formation and sluffed in,

(196)

making the timbering of the tunnels and shafts difficult. The Mammoth Chimney was 400 feet west of the Vulcan, and the St. Patrick was near by.

By 1897 Camp Creek had a population of 500 and its name had been changed to Vulcan. The owners of the Vulcan mine refused fabulous offers for their property, regarding it only as a "prospect" and believing so firmly in its future that they would not sell at any price. Rumors that English and French capitalists were seeking investments in the area aroused a good deal of interest, and had plenty of such capital been put into the district it might have become really prosperous.

By 1897 the camp was booming and was publishing its own paper, the *Vulcan Enterprise*. By 1900 the *Vulcan Times*, the "representative paper of the Southern Gunnison Gold Belt" appeared, and by 1901 so many people had crowded into the little town that there was not a vacant house to be had. Dances were held and a five-months school was conducted in an old store building. The Good Hope and the Vulcan mines were continuous shippers as long as the camp flourished, producing in the early days $400,000 in gold and silver. After a few years the mines closed down and the camp became deserted, only to be rejuvenated when the Vulcan Mines and Smelter Company consolidated the Good Hope, Mammoth Chimney and Vulcan group and unwatered all the properties through the first-named mine. As mining was resumed, valuable copper deposits were found, and a matte smelter with a capacity of 40 tons was built to smelt the immense sulphide and quartz dumps.

A few years later Vulcan was quiet again. Yet it was always wild and lonely country; in fact, a stage driver stopped his stage on one trip to shoot a large wildcat, lurking beside the road.

Having explored the old mining camps south of Gunnison I next planned visits to those northwest of the city. My first objective was Gothic, a ghost town in the mountains beyond Crested Butte, 30 miles from Gunnison. Gene and I drove along the Taylor River to Almont, where the highway to Crested Butte joins the Taylor River road. For miles we crossed ranch country with wide meadows, green with alfalfa or wild hay, where herds of Herefords grazed. The valley produces the best hay crop per acre in the region, and everywhere we looked, a green sea of grass covered the valley floor and pushed its way up the lower slopes of the mountains.

Jack's Cabin was along this road, and having read about the tiny community which is hardly discernible today save for one old building and the cemetery, I watched closely until we saw the sign over the gate to the overgrown, neglected burying ground. Between 1880 and 1890 a road ran through the middle of the valley, and at an intersection a lane led over the hill to the Taylor River. At this intersection was the cabin of Jack Howe. His place became known as Howville and later as Jack's Cabin. The crossroads consisted of two hotels, two groceries, two saloons, two restaurants and one post office, all contained in two buildings—thus Jack's Cabin and its contents comprised half the place. Freighters, taking in supplies to Crested Butte and Gothic and bringing back ore, would stop here overnight on their trips to and from Gunnison. Hunters and fishermen also started from this point, and in

Jack's Cabin

(197)

time a few more cabins were built, and a schoolhouse, which is now over sixty years old, was established for the ranch children of the vicinity.

Crested Butte   Beyond Jack's Cabin the road leads to a barricade of peaks, one of which is the Crested Butte, at whose foot is the town which bears its name. Crested Butte is located at the junction of Slate and Coal creeks, and was laid out in the spring of 1879, shortly after vast coal fields were discovered close by and when a mining boom in the vicinity brought men to the region. Both anthracite and bituminous coal were found in the mines, the former being the only such deposit located west of the Pennsylvania coal fields. The town, which was founded by Howard F. Smith who brought in the first sawmill to be operated in the Elk Mountains, grew rapidly, although its coal beds did not attract roving prospectors as much as did the gold and silver strikes in the surrounding hills. Early in 1880, however, there were 50 houses and tents and a population of 250, as well as a newspaper, the *Crested Butte Republican.*

Coal mining and stock raising became the chief industries. Three anthracite and three bituminous mines close to town and a coke furnace with 150 ovens provided employment for most of the population. There was little mining at the Butte other than coal, except for placers which were worked on Slate and Coal creeks. By 1881 the town was incorporated, the railroad had been extended from Gunnison to the city, and Sanderson's Stage Line stopped overnight at the Butte before leaving early in the morning for the new camps of Ruby, Irwin and Gothic. Between 1879 and 1881 mining camps sprang up all through the Elk Mountains, with Crystal, Aspen and Ashcroft over the range and Gothic, Ruby, Irwin and Pittsburgh only a few miles from the coal town. These mining camps produced gold, silver, iron, lead and copper, and through the fame of many mines—the Painter Boy and the Silver Jewel mines in Washington Gulch, six miles from the Butte; the Augusta at Pittsburgh; the Sylvanite at Gothic, and the Forest Queen at Irwin—thousands of men scurried through the town and into the hills beyond.

The booming camps of Aspen and Ashcroft across the Elk Mountains were in desperate need of a road to Crested Butte, for their freight was shipped by rail to the Butte, the nearest rail connection to the camps, and from there had to be packed in. A road between the places would enable teams to haul freight over the range. In 1882 a group of men from Ashcroft and Aspen met with men from the Butte to discuss the feasibility of such a road. The best they could do was plan and construct a difficult road over Pearl Pass, which was used as the main artery between the camps for a number of years.

The Butte's best years were 1882 and 1883, for by then the railroad was in use, the Anthracite Coal Breaker was built, and the C. F. & I. mine was opened and employed a force of 200 to 300 men. During these years it was a common sight to see 200 burros standing in the streets waiting to be loaded with supplies for the camps. The Crested Butte House shared patronage with Mrs. Sanger's and the Forest Queen Hotels until the Elk Mountain Hotel was finished. In February 1882 that hotel, advertised in the paper as the "finest in the land," held its formal opening and was "ready to entertain 150 guests with a grand ball and supper. Such a dinner," continued the paper, "we believe was never before given in Colorado west of the range. On the bill of fare were no less than 86 different articles, any one of which could be had in call."

Through the long winter months snow falls almost constantly, until by spring ten to twenty feet lie on the ground in protected places. Since many houses have outside toilets and the depth of the snow covers the average out-house, the ingenious residents of the Butte have solved this problem by building two-story "Johnnies," the upper level for winter use.

Crested Butte is still a coal town, its streets gray with coal dust and its houses sombre in color, yet behind many windows blossoming plants flaunt splashes of color or lace curtains shut out the drab view of other sombre homes. There are few trees and the grayness is relieved only by pocket-sized gardens overflowing with delphinium and other native plants. The city is surrounded by mountains, but none towers so close nor rises so majestically as the great butte whose crested summit looms 3300 feet above the level of the city streets.

Before starting for Gothic we drove up one street and down another, passing the C. F. & I. company store, the movie, the tiny post office and the white steepled Catholic Church. The City Hall with its hand-drawn hose carts, the three-story frame hotel opposite, and the schoolhouse date from earlier days. Just beyond the two-story stone schoolhouse with its cupola and bell the road to Gothic branches away from town, passes the cemetery, and climbs out of the valley, to twist around hillsides until, at a sharp curve it becomes a ledge, clinging to the side of the cliff. Far below is the valley, where a stream loops its way across the wide green meadows and where cattle and ranch houses look like small toys. Above are the peaks and before us the narrow road cuts along the mountainside toward a flat meadow in the shadow of Gothic Mountain.

Here we found a few widely scattered cabins. Was this Gothic? It hardly seemed big enough for a town, and that we might be sure we drove on for another mile or so to a fork in the road beyond which travel by car was impossible.

"Where is Gothic?" I asked some picnickers who were camped near the fork.

"It's back about two miles. You drove through it," they replied, surprised at my ignorance.

"Most of the buildings are gone," said one man of the group. "When the Rocky Mountain Biological Laboratory established their camp at Gothic they tore down the hotel and many of the cabins, or they remodeled them for their use. Each summer they hold a six-weeks school there for field work in botany, zoology and related sciences."

Thanking him, we turned back toward the town and as we drove I told Gene what I knew about the place.

Silver and lead ores were discovered in the Elk Mountains in the late seventies, and when the assay reports became known a stampede began. All through the summer of 1879 long immigrant trains toiled over the range from the eastern slope, and the camps of Irwin, Gothic, Pitkin, Hillerton and Virginia City were founded. As soon as the news of the strike at Gothic reached Hillerton and Virginia City, forty miles away, those camps became temporarily deserted as miners rushed over to the newest diggings.

The camp of Gothic was laid out at the junction of Copper Creek and East River, but the Sylvanite mine which drew men to the region was four miles away at the head of Copper Creek. James Jennings discovered the Sylvanite in 1879, finding in it rich deposits of native silver in wire form. Some of the ore was so interlaced with wire that it clung together even when broken off. The ore, which was in pockets, was so rich that much of it ran over $15,000 per ton. The mine was worked until 1885 when no more ore pockets could be found.

When we reached the top of a little hill above Gothic and looked down over the green meadow where the town had once stood we were disappointed. So few buildings remained that it was impossible to picture what the town had been like, but the surrounding mountains were so high and the profile of the Crested Butte eight miles away was so majestic that I made a sketch anyway. As we started toward the townsite and drove past a log cabin with a bay window an old man standing in the doorway waved to us.

"He's old enough to have been in Gothic during its boom," said Gene. "Let's talk to him."

The old-timer came over to the car and rested his arm on the door. He explained that he had a mine nearby and that he always came up during the summer to work it a little.

"I used to live in Gothic," he began. "I was just a boy then, but I've heard my father tell of his first trip here before there were any roads. He was with a train of freight wagons, each drawn by an eight-mule team. The freighters had to pick their way through the brush and bottom lands so as to avoid the rocky canyons. A train of freight wagons looked just like a snake winding over the hills. Once it took nine days to travel the twenty-two miles from Jack's Cabin to Gothic through four to nine feet of snow.

"Old McKee told me about coming to Gothic with his parents before there was any town of Crested Butte. The road followed the East River all the way and it was packed with freighters, prospectors with rolls of blankets on their backs and pack trains, all traveling in one continuous cloud of dust.

"By 1881 they'd built roads to the camp, the one up Copper Creek from the Butte going on to Aspen. Passengers and mail service went over this road, by stage in summer and by bobsled in winter. The sleds would leave the Butte at eight in the morning and if snowslides didn't turn them over they'd arrive in Aspen about four o'clock. Ore was shipped out and supplies were shipped in by this method. The roads were always in use and you were never out of sight or smell of a dead mule.

"My father told me that Gothic, which was started in June 1879, had a hundred tents and cabins in it when it was less than a week old. They were pretty rough affairs, for the miners were too busy to spend time building.

"The town grew up along both sides of one long street, but cabins and

(200)

tents were sprawled all over the flat and even up the hills and gulches. There were plenty of saloons, gambling places and two dancehalls. In one, the girls wore skirts up to their knees. Some dames!

"When the sawmill was set up board shacks were built, and before long there were three streets built solid with business houses and stores. Every evening a big bonfire was built on Main Street, and the crowds would gather round to smoke and swap stories. Sometimes there would be a footrace with plenty of money changing hands in the betting. On Sundays horseraces were run on the road at the edge of town, and at night a four-piece orchestra played for the dances. The miners were a tough lot, but stealing was unheard of. Half the town carried guns, but only two murders were committed during the boom. One was on Main Street, when an unarmed man was shot down in a quarrel over a lot.

"Until we had a post office, one of the men in camp would be sent out every few days for mail and when he got back he'd stand on a box on Main Street and call out the name on each letter, pitching the envelope to the man who answered his shout.

"Gothic grew fast, for it was the supply depot for the other small camps around here. Big stocks of goods were freighted in, and the gambling halls and saloons were well stocked. Three sawmills were kept busy cutting lumber, a smelting works was in operation, and a log schoolhouse large enough to care for the twenty-five or thirty pupils was running. The *Elk Mountain Bonanza* was the first newspaper. Then there was the *Gothic Miner*, and finally the *Gothic Silver Record*. The two original hotels were called the 'Olds' and the 'Bums,' but my father preferred the hotel of Uncle Charlie Howe and Mother Howe because of the good table they set. The Howes were from Vermont, and their place was the cleanest in town.

"By 1881 there were a thousand people here, everyone engaged in mining or storekeeping. The miners used to say that there were none here for their health, although it was a healthy place, and a poor place for doctors. As the town grew more buildings were put up including the two-story hotel which stood right over there, and before long Gothic was bigger than Irwin, across the mountains. At one time it had a population of 8,000.

"You should have seen the issue of the *Gothic Miner* on September 24, 1881, which told of President Garfield's death. There were heavy black borders between each column of print, and on the front page was a request that the people of the county wear the usual badge of mourning for thirty days.

"Did you ever hear how Gothic's mayor was chosen? Both Lew Wait and G. H. Judd were interested in the job and to see who would get the office they threw dice and Wait won. By October 1885 Wait, who edited the *Gothic Silver Record*, printed a squib in his paper: 'We have lived on Copper Creek soup, Gothic scenery and the promise of business subscriptions for three years and we have no idea of being starved out for the next century.'

"Getting the mail in here was a problem before roads were built. The mail carrier could carry only one hundred pounds at a time, and more than once he left piles of mail marked for Gothic at the Butte while he brought in drygoods and liquor.

"The first winter was a lulu, and twenty-six families were marooned in camp with the snow six feet deep on the level. Their only contact with the outside world was through letters and packages which were carried on the back of a powerful man who never failed to mush over the trail, even with the heaviest packs. My father remembers how he once carried a five-gallon can of coal oil and a fifty-pound sack of flour besides the regular mail. One miner ordered a pair of hip boots and was pretty mad when they were brought in one at a time. I've talked to a woman who lived in Gothic that first winter and heard her stories of how her father sometimes carried the daily mail on snowshoes eight miles over the East River Divide to the Butte, or over Gothic Pass to Crystal, another boom camp which sprang up at the same time. Once he floundered over the hardest trail of all, Pearl Pass, from Crested Butte to Ashcroft.

"Snowslides took many lives around here. The weight of the snow on these steep slopes caused it to run often. So many miners were lost in slides that women used to tell their fathers, husbands and brothers goodbye when they left for the mines each day, fearing that they might never see them again. I remember watching slides here. There would be a loud roar as the huge mass of snow broke loose and slid down Gothic Mountain, across the river from the town. It kept everybody pretty much worried. Everybody in town wore snowshoes a good part of the year."

"Can you tell me about the time that General Grant visited Gothic?" I asked eagerly, when he paused for breath.

"Of course I can," said the old man. "In July 1880, when General Grant returned from his trip around the world, he wanted to see some live Rocky Mountain mining camps. Gothic and Irwin were booming then, so naturally he headed this way. There was no railroad, and he had to drive from Salida in a Barlow-Sanderson Stage, with his son, Fred Grant, Governor Pitkin, and Ex-Governor Routt, and several other state officials. At Gunnison the party got a mule team and drove to the Butte, and from there to Gothic where we met them with guns popping. When they left here they went to Irwin where they stayed two days and then drove back by way of Castleton. The General drove most of the way. He never allowed anyone but himself to hold the reins if he could help it—he even hated to ride in a stage unless he could drive. We put on a good show for him and sent him off to Irwin with a good taste of a boom town in his mouth.

"Did you ever hear of Gatwood H. Judd, the man who stayed in Gothic after all the others left? He lived in the camp the best part of fifty years. He came in like any other prospector during the boom and made his home here. When the town folded up, he still believed in its future and stayed on. As he got older he used to winter in Gunnison but as soon as the snows melted he was back in his cabin where he soon became known as the 'man who stayed.' The Fox Film Company came up here and made a two-reel picture about him in 1928 and he was written up in feature articles. When tourists and stockmen and students at the laboratory began to come to Gothic they always visited him at his cabin and got him to reminisce about the old days. He kept a scrap book of clippings and his cabin was a regular pioneer museum. He

(202)

even made you register when you went to see him. When he died his body was cremated and his ashes scattered in the streets of the town which he knew so well. During the years when the camps around here were empty towns he was called the mayor or ruler of three cities, Gothic, Pittsburgh and Irwin."

Elko and Schofield
"If you want to see some pretty country you ought to get horses and ride up Rock Creek to the sites of Elko and Schofield. The two camps were at the head of the creek near the Crystal River. Elko was at the base of Galena Mountain, and Schofield was on the edge of a little park. Elko never amounted to anything. It was five miles from Gothic and consisted of two cabins and 'great expectations.' Schofield, which was between Elko and Crystal City was surveyed and platted in August 1879 by a company composed of several mining men including B. F. Schofield. It was never a camp of much importance, having but one hotel run by a woman from Peoria, Illinois, and a smelting works which was built in 1880 before paying ore had been found. It was an inaccessible camp too, the snow lying forty feet deep for eight months of the year and the snowslides running two hundred feet deep.

"Funny thing, in 1872, seven years earlier, a bunch of prospectors from San Juan had gophered around in the same place. They found some silver-bearing ore around the head of Rock Creek, just beyond the summit of the divide. The next spring a small party was organized for the purpose of investigating the prospects, and later that summer a larger company of thirty members was formed to develop these discoveries. This company assembled eight wagons and a string of pack animals, all loaded with provisions and mining equipment, and started from Denver for the mountains. Fearing trouble with the Utes they took a roundabout course through South Park and over Poncha and Cochetopa passes. The Indians objected to their entry into the territory, but Chief Ouray quieted them, and the group proceeded to the site of Gunnison. From there they worked their way to the head of Rock Creek, where they camped for two months about five miles inside the Indian Reservation. Here they set up a small smelting furnace where they tested all the ores found. Returning to Denver they raised sufficient capital to enable them to begin systematic mining at the head of the creek. The panic in the fall of 1873 put a stop to their plans, and no other mining was done there until 1879 when Schofield was laid out and the Rock Creek mines were discovered all over again."

Having obtained this fund of information about Gothic and its neighbors, we started back toward the Butte. The pyramided cones of Gothic Mountain were in shadow, but in our mind's eye we could see the sheets of snow rushing down the steep slopes and piling up in a solid mound beside the stream at the base of the cliffs.

"Before we go back let's see if we can get to Pittsburgh." I said as we neared a fork in the road where a sign indicated that it was seven miles away. "I don't know a thing about it except that there was a mining camp there at the same time that Gothic and Irwin were booming. Maybe we will pass a ranch house where we can ask some questions."

Turning at the fork we followed the narrow lonely road for nearly four miles, passing no ranch house and seeing no sign of life. About half way we passed a hidden lake at the bottom of a bowl of low hills. Beyond, the road wound for another two miles, until we reached a coal breaker beside which stood a partly dismantled house in which some people were living.

"What is left of Pittsburgh, and can we drive to it?" I asked the woman who looked out of the door as we approached.

"There's nothing there but one cabin in which they sometimes keep salt for stock," she replied. "The road's bad too. Beavers have dammed the stream and you can't get through."

Taking her word for it we gave up the Pittsburgh trip and returned to Gunnison for the night.

Five years later I took Ann and Peg with me to the Gunnison country, that we might go to Floresta, another ghost camp that I had heard of in the vicinity of Crested Butte. It was September, the weather was perfect, the aspens were turning the hillsides to molten gold and we felt equal to anything. In Crested Butte I inquired of the postmaster the way to Floresta, and just as I was leaving he called after me, "Have you ever been to Smith Hill? It's three miles in along the Pittsburgh road and there are some old cabins up on top. It's only a half mile hike up the mountain. You'll know when you get there by the coal breaker and the coal dumps. Just go straight up the hill and you'll find the empty cabins."

"A half mile hike won't take long," said Peg. "Let's do Smith Hill this morning and Floresta this afternoon." A few minutes later we rolled out of Crested Butte and climbed the reddish clay road which leads to Pittsburgh, Washington Gulch and Gothic. The road was familiar for I'd been over it in 1940 when I was looking for Pittsburgh, but today it was more picturesque, for the aspen colored the higher hillsides and the sun made even the lonely lake less haunting. High on the hill we could see the silhouettes of cabins and we kept them in sight as we drove. Three miles brought us to the coal breaker and to the dilapidated house where I'd once inquired the way to Pittsburgh. Now it was empty, and parking our car near it we started to climb up the old road back of the breaker that the postmaster had mentioned as going halfway up the hill. We were very gay and we laughed as we recalled the night before in a Gunnison hotel where, not knowing whether they allowed pets or not, I had smuggled my dog Chipper in and out under my coat, not realizing that his white tail hung well below its hem!

The postmaster suggested that when we reached the end of the road that led up the face of the hill, we continue "right up by the tram;" but when we had climbed the gritty trail to its end and saw the tram high overhead and a soft cinder dump underneath it we knew that such a procedure was impossible.

Our only other alternative was to cross a shale slope about one hundred and fifty feet wide and about two hundred feet above the ground, which slanted at such a steep angle that to walk on it almost defied gravity. We reasoned, however, that one hundred and fifty feet weren't much and started to pick our way over it to some timber beyond, through which we could climb the rest of the way. Peg, an accomplished mountain climber, went first, rubbing footholds in the shifting shale for herself and for our feet as well. We followed her cautiously, I second and Ann last. I had my sketch pad and bag and my dog on a leash. Each step had to be tested to see if the shale would hold, while the steepness of the slope made it psychologically better to look up than down. About three-quarters of the way across I lost my footing and started to slide. Instinctively throwing myself on my back and digging my heels into the slope I was able to stop skidding toward the road far below. In my mind's eye I could see myself either scooting to the bottom of the dump and arriving there with broken arms or legs or spending the rest of my life stretched out on Smith Hill like a spread eagle. In a moment Peg was leaning over me and helping me to rise shakily to my feet. Chipper meanwhile had stood stock still like a cowpony. There was still the rest of the slide to be crossed and it was shorter to go ahead than to go back, so still trembling, the three of us crept inch by inch over the shifting footing and into the scrub timber. Even here the slope was so steep that we had to pull ourselves from bush to bush and from tree to tree. Leaving Chipper with Peg in a clearing I went on alone, wondering why I drove myself into such predicaments. Just as I was completely exhausted and was deciding that this was the most stupid thing I'd ever done, I scrambled up another few feet and came upon the cabins on a flat, near the top of the hill.

There were about fifteen of them, all roofless and in sad states of disrepair. Over the edge of the hill were the remains of some machinery, which probably had been used in operating the tram to the breaker. The view was tremendous—in one direction mountains, to the east Crested Butte, in front a deep valley through which a stream and road cut a looping pattern, and far below, beside the stream, the breaker and the tracks of the railroad spur which once conveyed the coal to the Butte.

The coal land was located in 1876 by some of the earliest prospectors to the region and was later developed by H. F. Smith. The place was sometimes called Anthracite and sometimes Smith Hill, since the property was known as the Smith Hill Anthracite mine. There was never a real town here —just a few miners' cabins and the mine equipment. In the eighties the mine employed over 200 men and shipped 10 to 20 cars of coal a day over the spur of the D. and R. G. road which ran as far as the breaker. The railroad ran only from July first to January first; the rest of the year snow lay as deep as fifteen feet and prevented rail shipments. Because of its high carbon content the coal was excellent for coking purposes and was used for smelting.

Making a few sketches of the cabins atop the hill I scrambled back to my friends. Working our way through the timber we found a little trail which took us back to the road a short distance below the place where the car was parked. On our way toward the Butte we discussed plans for the rest of the day. The Smith Hill adventure had dampened our ardor for exploring, and now no one seemed enthusiastic about the Floresta trip. It was two years before I returned to the region and reached the abandoned coal camp.

Floresta   "It's a three-mile hike to Floresta along the old railroad grade," said the storekeeper in Crested Butte when I next stopped to inquire my way. "You can't get there yet anyway," he added. "The drifts will be too high. Better wait until July."

So. later in the summer Jane and I drove through Crested Butte and on toward Kebler Pass. The highway runs high above a mountain stream, and for part of the distance the old road bed of the railroad parallels the dirt road. "Drive ten miles west of the Butte and turn south on the road to the sawmill. Maybe you can drive to it, but from there on you'll have to follow the 'grade,'" the man in the store had said. Watching the mileage carefully we drove ten miles and, just before the turnoff to the ghost town of Irwin, found a left-hand fork and saw the sawmill dump in the distance. The sawdust pile shone yellow in the afternoon sun, and leaving the highway we started along the narrow road toward it. The ground was so marshy that we had to park the car almost immediately in the sagebrush and strike off on foot on the two muddy tracks which constituted the road. Near the sawmill was a tent in which a family was living, and as we approached it a woman came out to hang washing on a wire stretched between two trees. "Which is the path to Floresta?" we called, and she pointed to a road that led through the trees instead of to the railroad grade, which swung off in the underbrush and disappeared. The road was easy to follow except where rivulets cut across it or where swamp grass grew completely over it, swallowing it up. Picking our way across a swampy stretch, we discovered the road again and plodded on. Two miles—two and a half miles—higher and higher we climbed until at last we came to a level stretch beside a small lake where a few cabin frames and an old ore wagon stood, overgrown with bushes and vines. Surely Floresta must be near! But the road led on between tall pine trees which arched overhead. Suddenly through a break in the trees we caught a glimpse of Floresta, far below us. The road dropped sharply down to the gray waste of the townsite and as we descended we looked at the camp from above. There at the end of the little valley, surrounded by mountains whose bare sides were studded with a few hardy evergreens, stood the huge gray tipple pile, and on the flat below were the grimy remains of ruined cabins.

At first the camp was called Ruby-Anthracite, but when the railroad was completed, the name was changed to that of the mine from which the coal was obtained.

The Colorado Fuel and Iron Company operated the Floresta mine on an extensive scale in the early nineties, building the railroad in from Crested Butte and encouraging the development of the camp, which soon contained one and two-story business houses along its main street and workmens' cabins up and down the gulch. The camp became the shipping point for the coal and metal mines of the vicinity and was active until 1936, when the mine was abandoned.

It was a lonely place, and after making a few sketches we started back to the car. The return hike was all down hill, and we strode along past the lake, across the boggy ground and down to the sawmill. Just beyond it were a man and his dog sitting under a large tree. "Where've you been?" he asked as we came up to him. "Didn't know there were any folks around here. Have you been fishing?" And before we could answer he went on: "I've been setting traps up the gulch all afternoon. Been to Floresta, eh? How did you go? Up the old wagon road? It's a good thing you didn't try the railroad grade, cause it's all washed out in spots and the trestles are gone. Five miles, too, that way. You'd have had to crawl down from the grade to cross the stream. Hard going! But the road you took was all right. I used to haul freight in here 40 years ago when the mine was running. Part of the year we used to drive in over snowpacked roads. Did you notice the trees all along the road with scars as high as twenty-five feet up on their trunks? The snow used to pack deep in this country and the road was a little higher after each storm. It was barely wide enough for one team anyway, and everytime the horses' singletrees rubbed the trunks they made a new set of scars. In the summer it looked funny to see those rubbed scars twenty-five feet up in the air, but in the winter the road was that high up. You can see those scars yet. A lot of the trees around here had their tops cut off twenty-five feet high too. When we cut wood in winter we cut it at the snow line and by spring when the snow melted, there stood the trees with their tops gone.

"I was here when the railroad was built to the mine. When the beams for the great trestle were being raised, there was an accident and a little boy was killed, and when the trestle was being dismantled a workman was killed, so a death marked the beginning and the end of Floresta. Speaking of death, there's a grave along the road in the pines—a young girl's grave. Folks from Irwin used to come down this way to bury their dead. It was too rocky up there for a cemetery."

Thanking the man for his stories we started on toward the car. Gratefully tumbling into the seat we rested our tired feet and drove toward hot baths and civilization.

Pittsburgh   Having made two unsuccessful attempts to get to Pittsburgh, I decided to try it a third time; so one spring morning Francis and I passed the Crested Butte cemetery, with its terraced graves surrounded with iron fences and ornamental chains and posts, and twisted up through a valley toward the mountains. I knew the road as far as Smith Hill but, beyond, the valley narrows and the Slate River beside the road is rocky and clear. About half a mile this side of Pittsburgh beavers had effectively dammed the creek and flooded the road making progress precarious. Francis was all for driving through the flood but I, who am always too cautious, preferred to leave the car on dry ground and wade through the edge of the water to the other side, hiking the rest of the way. Beyond the beaver pond the road led through a meadow, and there to my chagrin stood a car which had driven through the water, beside which sat an old man.

"Wife's gone fishing," he remarked as we came up to him. "You going fishing?"

When we told him no, that we were only interested in finding the site of Pittsburgh, he became interested at once and started to reminisce.

"The Augusta mine up Poverty Gulch made Pittsburgh," he began. "See that black spot way up above timberline in that snowbank? That's the Augusta. Durndest place for a mine you ever saw. Couldn't get in or out all winter and the summers were short. The only way to get to the mine

(208)

was by foot or on horseback, and the trail was so steep that it was a stiff pull to get a horse up there. All supplies had to be packed in by burro and all the ore had to be sacked and packed out. In the fall all the necessary supplies for a crew of ten to fifteen men would be packed in; for the crew stayed at the mine all winter without coming out. Once a week some fool miner would slide down to Pittsburgh on snowshoes at the risk of his life to get the mail. Sometimes he didn't make it.

"It was snow more than anything else that crippled the development of this mine. One summer the owners built an overhead cable tramway from the mine to the valley, but before it was finished and put into operation the following spring snowslides wrecked it. A few years ago they built a mill at Pittsburgh so as to treat the low grade ores, but it failed through bad management and because you couldn't get ore from the mine to the mill during the winter months.

"The Augusta was in the limelight during the eighties when Gillette was Superintendent. The mine was a true fissure, ten to thirty feet wide, carrying gold, silver and lead ore. It was the strongest lead in the county and could be traced for miles.

"Col. Stanford, brother of the California senator, got an option on the mine in 1886 and sailed for London to raise some capital. Before subscribing, the London investors sent an Englishman over to look over the property and make a report. He arrived in the middle of winter when the snow was deepest and when it was worth your life to get to the mine. But he'd come to see the mine, so he got two guides to go with him and set out on snowshoes. They were gone four days. It's a wonder the three of them got back alive.

"In 1901 there was a little mining in the gulch when the Black Queen and the Augusta were operated by the Standard Mining Investment Company. During the winter of 1904 a force of men worked at the Augusta. In February nine of them started for the Butte on snowshoes. There were two feet of fresh snow and the mine superintendent wanted the men to wait until he had set off several sticks of powder to see if the snow was in condition to run. The men wanted to be off and set out at once, but they'd only gone a little way when a huge slide caught them and killed six of them. The other three laid down on their snowshoes and rode to the bottom of the mountain on the crest of the slide. The rescue party risked their lives, too, in getting the bodies—the snow was that treacherous.

"There hasn't been much done at the mine for forty years. A few lessees work it every summer but they don't make much, for the ore has to be hand sorted, sacked and packed out on burros just as in the old days. The mine was worth $300,000 fifty years ago and it's worth more now. Some of its ore assayed $10,000 a ton.

"Pittsburgh was right here, but it never amounted to much. If the Augusta mine had panned out better it would have been a real town. Charlie Robinson and his brother had an assay shop over there, and the post office and grocery store stood under those trees. The camp never had more than 300

(209)

people in it. See that trail up on the far mountain? That led over to Crystal, but the slides wrecked it and it was never kept up.

"Did you ever hear the story of Yank Baxter and his mine? Yank was a character. He'd ridden express in the sixties, fought Indians and killed buffalo. He had a mine in Poverty Gulch called the Excelsior. One day while he was sitting on the dump George Hold climbed up to the mine and asked him what he wanted for it. 'Thirty-five thousand dollars.' 'It's a deal,' said Holt starting to count out the cash. Yank jumped up all excited and shouted, 'Hold on! If you have thirty-five thousand on you stick it in the corner of your eye and get the hell off this hill.' Holt 'got' and ten years later Yank died without a cent in Salida, and was buried by the county. That's mining for you."

Irwin

"Have you been to Irwin?" asked the mine inspector whom I met at Ouray on one of my trips. "It was a big camp with lots of buildings and you should see it. The boom started in the winter when there was plenty of snow on the ground, and trees for cabins were cut off at the snow line. In the spring when the snow melted, the stumps were found to be ten feet high!"

The thought of ten-foot stumps intrigued me, as well as the idea of cabins gently sinking ten feet down to earth during the spring thaws. So I went to Irwin. Leaving the Kebler Pass highway ten miles west of Crested Butte, I turned onto the dirt road that led to the ghost town. This last stretch of road was rough and washed out, and when I had driven a mile and should have been at the site of the town there were no signs of the place. The road was by now a streambed, so, stopping the car, I started to explore on foot. Suddenly, in front of me, on either side of the gully, at regular intervals, I saw water hydrants, rusty and overgrown with weeds, but still erect. So this was Irwin and the gully was the main street! Where were all the buildings that my mining friend had mentioned? Completely disgusted I drove away.

Several years later I was in Gunnison and in a store window saw an old photograph of a booming mining camp, with several streets, hundreds of buildings, and a white church with a steeple. The town lay in a sloping valley surrounded by timbered hills, beyond which rose a rim of snowy peaks. Entering the store I asked the name of the town and was told that it was Irwin. The town in the photograph was so large that I was anxious to visit it again, to look for vestiges other than the hydrants; consequently in June 1946, I drove again over the rough rocky road. Since it was early in the summer, snow lay in drifts under the trees and little rivulets of snow-water cut across the grass and joined the stream which flooded parts of the meadow where the town had once stood. Masses of yellow dogtooth violets were everywhere, whole patches of them blooming only a few feet away from the snowbanks. My companion and I crossed the marsh and got on the road up to the lake, which used to be the main street. Walking along it, we passed the tall, slender waterplugs, which were installed in 1882 when the water from Lake Brennard above the town was piped to Irwin and the water-system was installed. On either side of the gully-like road were the remains of frame buildings, which by now were nothing but flattened piles of lumber. A large pile of boards had been a store; a small pile, a cabin. Partway to the lake we met a truck full of people who stopped to talk to us. One of them, an old lady who had once lived in Irwin, was the leader of the group. She pointed out this or that mass of lumber and identified it as a certain store or a former friend's cabin.

"See what we found?" she said with pride, showing us some square, hand-made nails. "They were in that store building. My uncle built it and he had to make the nails himself. Everything had to be freighted in, and that first year it was hard to wait for things when you needed them, so you often made your own or did without. We're going down to Pine Ridge to the cemetery," she continued. "It was too rocky up here to dig a grave, so we put the cemetery just about where the road goes up to Floresta. There are lots of graves among the trees but only one marker is left. It's a granite stone and it says:

MARY BRAMBAUGH
DAUGHTER OF FOSTER K. BRAMBAUGH
DIED JULY 31, 1882   AGE 17 YRS.

"J. E. Phillips who was editor here helped lay out the cemetery. The first man buried in it died with his boots on. He was killed by exploding dynamite with which he was killing fish. Some of the miners made a coffin but there was no parson here. Phillips had a Prayer Book and he agreed to read the burial service. Many of those buried in the cemetery were killed in snow-slides. We always expected a lot of deaths from slides in the spring. In 1891 a slide ran at the Bullion King and four people were killed. I remember that they took one body all the way to Crested Butte on a sled made of snow-shoes and drawn by nine men.

"Phillip's Prayer Book saved the day more than once. In 1880 when the camp was just beginning to boom, Bishop Spaulding came up here to hold an evening service in a tent. The boys put fresh sawdust on the dirt floor, ar-ranged candles around a make-shift altar, fixed up a box for a pulpit, and bor-rowed the Prayer Book. The tent was next to a gambling hall, and you could hear the clink of the chips and the shouts of the dancehall caller as he sang out 'Honors to your partners, allemande left, ladies and gents waltz up to the bar.' The Bishop asked if business couldn't be suspended for an hour and was told, 'No!' However, the manager of the hall yelled out, 'You fellows, plug up the kitty and give the Bishop the benefit of the next play.' After that the Bishop decided that this was no time to start a church here but that Irwin offered a fertile field for missionary work," she concluded with a twinkle in her eye.

"We did have churches though, a Methodist, an Episcopal and a Pres-byterian; although in the third you could always see through the holes in the roof which were caused by the weight of sliding snow. Be sure to go up to the Forest Queen before you leave and look down over the town." Her eyes looked far off, and as she drove away with her family we knew she was re-calling incidents when Irwin was the biggest camp in the district.

Up near the lake we got into snow drifts four feet deep which lay at

(211)

the edge of the timber, and we looked through the door of the roofless log schoolhouse which the old lady had pointed out and within which pine trees thirty feet tall were growing. The lake was frozen and snow lay all along its shore. On its far side rose three snowy peaks, Ruby, Owen and Purple, at the base of which were situated the Ruby Chief and Ruby King mines.

Climbing the trail to the Forest Queen property and noting the old, rusty machinery as well as more modern equipment, we looked down on the meadow and on beyond to the backdrop of mountains. And as we looked Irwin came to life, for not only was the location of the streets visible when seen from this height but the piles of flattened boards now lay in rows, indicating where each house had stood. Irwin of the water hydrants became Irwin, the town of 5000 population, and except for the emptiness and silence of the place we might have expected to see people in the streets and hear the reverberation of exploding giant powder in the hills. Days later I pieced together Irwin's history from data culled from early issues of the Gunnison *News-Champion* and obtained through talks with mining men there and in Crested Butte.

Irwin's rise and fall covered a period of less than five years, but within that span, its life was typical of Colorado's boom mining-towns, all of which were optimistically believed to be embryo camps from which great cities would spring. Its history, therefore, reveals the verve, hopes, ambitions, excesses and accomplishments of the men and women who believed in it and in its future, and who succeeded in building a town and a culture greater than its economic resources could support.

In 1879 when a man named Fisher drove an ox-team up the valley no town existed and no one knew that rich ore deposits lay in the immediate vicinity. A few days later Fisher located two claims, the Forest Queen and the Ruby Chief.

About the same time, Dick Irwin and other men who had made a strike in the vicinity packed several tons of ruby silver on burros and sent it to Alamosa, which was the nearest rail point. From there it was shipped to Denver to be smelted. Then winter set in and the prospect holes were abandoned; but in Denver word got about that rich ore had been found in the Elk Mountains, and by spring the news had spread from the Atlantic to the Pacific. Ore had also been found in the Sylvanite mine near Gothic and in the Augusta in Poverty Gulch; so as soon as weather permitted, prospectors from all over the country began stampeding to the new silver belt.

The Ruby Mining District was organized in July 1879, and the town was laid out and surveyed at about the same time. Two or three mines containing rich ruby silver had been discovered earlier in the summer and others were located before fall. In spite of unusually cold weather, fifty people decided to stay all winter in the camp. Fifty feet of snow fell during the winter, completely burying the log cabins of the miners, who were forced to shovel tunnels from their front doors to the surface. Early in the spring a party of prospectors, travelling on snowshoes, mushed in, and although they felt sure that they were near the camp they saw no cabins. Finally they spied a man standing by a hole in the snow where smoke was issuing from a chim-

ney. One of the party asked him where the camp was. "It's right here. You're in it," he replied. "Where's the post office?" inquired the stranger, "Right in the next hole, sir," was the answer.

Another group of prospectors, impatient to reach the camp early in the spring before the best locations were taken, hurried in as early as they could travel, only to find all the bare ground already staked. The snow lay too deep for prospecting, so in disgust they started back across the range. They were well stocked with grub and supplies and had even strapped a sheet iron stove on one of the burros. Whenever the beast came to a tree he tried to rub the stove off his back. On the way out, at the bridge over the East River near Jack's Cabin, they decided to abandon the stove. Setting it on the bridge they attached a note to it, stating that it belonged to the first man who wanted it.

More and more mines, containing appreciable amounts of silver-bearing ore carrying brittle wire, ruby horn, and native silver with arsenical iron, were discovered. The Ruby Chief and the Ruby King were located across Lake Brennard and the Bullion King, Monte Carlo, Lead Chief and Last Chance were developed near the camp; but from the first the Forest Queen was the great mine. From the day in 1879 when Dick Irwin and others packed out samples of ore from it and the Forest King and sent them to Denver to be assayed the fame of the mine spread, and its ruby-silver ore, some of which was worth $3000 a ton, attracted thousands to the area. Even between 1884 and 1890 when there was virtually no mining being done in the district, the Forest Queen and the Bullion King were steady producers. As late as 1891 the Queen employed a force of thirty men, and in 1900 it was unwatered and was worked again. Then for years it lay idle, until in 1932 it was assessed at $1,000 and advertised for tax sale. The buyer paid $40.45, although its owner once refused $1,000,000 for it.

Certain of the silver strikes were made on Indian land, and Irwin itself was laid out within the boundaries of the Ute Reservation. At one time it was estimated that there were 1500 prospectors on the reservation, and, fearing that the Utes would resent this encroachment, the miners organized a company of Minute Men who were ready for any emergency. Capt. Curtis, the United States interpreter for the Utes, stayed in the camp all through 1880 to see that no skirmishes occurred. The Indians were peaceful, however, and no trouble developed.

Since the town was on the reservation, its plat could not be recorded in Colorado nor could the sale of its lots be registered; therefore, when Gunnison County demanded that it pay taxes, it at first refused to do so, for it was technically not in the county.

By the spring of 1880 tons of goods had been dumped by freighters at the foot of the long grade below Irwin, waiting for the snow to melt. Much of this freight consisted of perishable food, and the business firms which had ordered the produce, hired packers to move the stock in on their backs at ten cents a pound. These men started at three o'clock in the morning while the snow was crusted, carrying one or two hundred pounds apiece and making ten or twenty dollars a trip. In this way a ten-gallon keg of liquor was brought in as well as pitchers and some glasses. The liquor was delivered to a saloon—an unfinished cabin with a dirt floor and no doors or windows. The packers spread their blankets on the floor and played cards for drinks. One man, expecting to be served a glass of water as a chaser, asked the proprietor where the water was. "It's in the whiskey, you fool," shouted the barkeeper who, as each gallon of liquor was drunk from the keg, promptly filled it with a gallon of water, dipped from the creek which ran by his door.

There were really two townsites, Ruby and Irwin, and several names by which the camp was known. Three placer claims were taken up by three companies, each of which laid out a town. Haverly, Silver Gate and Ruby City were all one, while Irwin was a separate place a quarter of a mile away. Ruby City was platted by a man from Leadville who commenced selling lots and promised to build a six-story hotel, a wholesale grocery store, an office building and a theater in the center of his town. After selling a number of lots and pocketing the money, he vanished. Haverly seems to have been the last name of Ruby Camp and was, according to an old settler, separated from Irwin "by a villainous bit of road." Irwin, which was also known as Ruby Camp because of the ruby silver found there, was platted in 1879 and was named for Dick Irwin, one of the original discoverers of ore in the region.

Another old timer explained the confusion of names by saying, "the oldest part of the camp was called Irwin. Then a new town called Ruby was built a quarter of a mile to the south and the rivalry between the two places began. Some of the old maps show Ruby Camp and some Irwin, but by the end of the first year it was all one place anyway."

At first it was a city of tents and its main street was full of rocks and stumps, but after three sawmills were brought in it began to build up. In no time there was a population of 1200, living in tents and cabins, while seventy-five business houses and a host of unfinished buildings were being hurried to completion. Moreover the surrounding hills and woods were thick with more tents and cabins.

At first there were no dairies nearer than Crested Butte, and the milkman who delivered milk and butter to the residents of Irwin hit upon a novel way to serve his mountain customers. By leaving the cream on the milk he found that the ten-mile drive over the rough road produced a lump of butter in each milk can. He was therefore able to provide fresh milk and butter to his patrons with little effort.

In January 1880, J. E. Phillips and J. L. Lacey were working as journeymen printers in Rosita, Colorado, when, hearing of the Irwin boom, they conceived the idea of starting a paper in the new camp. On March first Phillips shipped a handpress from Rosita to Alamosa, the nearest rail point to the camp, and then forwarded it by freight from there. Phillips also ordered type and a complete printing outfit from Chicago, and on March fifteenth he left Rosita and drove overland to Irwin by way of Mosca and Cochetopa Passes. As the snow still lay deep in Irwin, he was forced to remain in Gunnison from April first to May first, when Lacey arrived with the freight. Ox-teams then hauled everything up to the snow-line, three miles from Irwin, taking six days to cover the forty miles. Here the handpress and everything else were dumped out to wait their turn to be packed into the camp. The ground was piled high with large stocks of goods of all sorts, and the packers, sorting out the supplies, carried some in and left the rest to be freighted in later on "Jerusalem Ponies," as the burros were called.

Crofutt, who according to J. E. Phillips was publicity man for the Union Pacific railroad, and who reached Irwin in September 1880 continues the story as follows:

> The citizens of Irwin . . . are self-reliant, honest and industrious. As an instance of what can be done, when prospects of wealth are bright, is the case of the *Elk Mountain Pilot*, the pioneer newspaper of the Elk Mountain country. The proprietor purchased his press, type, galleys, cases and ink, hired his type-setters, and reached the snow-line on Cottonwood Pass, to the east of the mountains, to find the roads impassable, the snow deep, and not even a trail visible. The land of promise was beyond this snow-barrier . . . with hungry multitudes waiting for the newspaper; the mighty lever that moves the world.
>
> A meeting was called by the snowbound, and a committee of the whole resolved to cross the "range," and immediately set about making snow-shoes. When each was provided with shoes, the printing material was distributed among the persons, when with type in pockets, parts of handpress under each arm, "cases" and paper strapped on their backs, the journey across the great mountain range commenced. The ascent was made, many times at an angle of forty-five degrees, and the descent commenced, the typos gliding, gracefully down on their snowshoes, over an unknown depth of snow, in a style peculiarly western, evincing pluck, energy and perseverance, American in the extreme. The material reached Irwin safely and the first number of the *Pilot* was issued June 17, 1880.

When the editors reached the camp they could get no lumber, and for weeks they lived in a log hut without windows, doors or floor and with only a tar-paper roof. In this shack the *Pilot* was printed until an office could be built; the first copy from the press selling for $55, and the first six copies bringing a total of $158.

By 1881 the main street extended for a mile up and down the gulch and was lined solidly with one and two-story buildings and with tents. Two other streets paralleled it, and beyond them more cabins and tents perched on the slopes at the edge of town. Several hotels, a theatre, a bank, six saw-mills, a host of general stores, a stamp mill and a large sampling works catered to the needs of the community. Twenty-three saloons, "some fitted with mirrors and the best mahogany furniture money could buy" and equipped with every gambling device imaginable, attracted the jostling, seething mass of people who surged along the streets, pushing their way between freighters wagons and pack trains and listening to the bands in front of the theatre. During the summer three livery stables ran daily stages between Irwin and Gunnison, some via Jack's Cabin and others by way of Ohio Creek and the Western Toll Road. Now and then there was a shooting affair, and two marshalls were needed to keep law and order—in fact, as a mining man said to me, "Irwin had everything a modern city of 3000 to 5000 people needed and all in the space of six months."

Everybody had money and everybody, it seemed, wanted to come to Irwin. Phillips, the editor, received a letter from a man who planned to bring his family to the camp and who wanted to know about church and school facilities. Irwin had neither. Phillips therefore assembled a group of men and held a meeting, at which, with the aid of prayer, it was agreed to make an effort to start a church. He then replied by saying that "At the prayer meeting the night before it was decided to build a new church and as to schools, it was summer vacation and schools would start in the fall." He didn't mention the twenty-three saloons!

The years 1882 and 1883 marked the peak of the camp. Iron street signs and the water hydrants were installed and mining boomed, but by the end of 1883 the mines were less productive, and by the spring of 1884 "Irwin was getting down to a whisper." Years after the town was deserted, curious visitors roamed through the old bank building and investigated the four-cell jail, whose walls were made by two-by-sixes spiked together. Old timers would return to wander along the desolate streets recalling how, when the snow was deeper than usual, they skiied off the cabin roofs and retelling the story of the family who, when the snow was five feet deep, moved into a house and three weeks later discovered that it was surrounded by a picket fence.

In its day Irwin was visited by all kinds of people, including Wild Bill Hickok, Bill Nuttall of vaudeville fame, Theodore Roosevelt, Governor Routt and General Grant. Grant's visit caused the greatest excitement, the town being all agog as to how to entertain its distinguished guest. Every man who had a horse galloped half a mile down the road to meet the party, followed by a spring wagon drawn by two little mules, in which had been loaded a kettle and a base drum, in lieu of a band. The spokesman of the day, spying the party in the distance, dashed ahead, waved his hat and shouted, "Welcome to our City" and then, whirling on his horse, led the procession back to town, followed by the visitors and the whooping, shooting cavalcade of miners. At the Ruby Chief, some fine specimens of brittle silver were laid out for the guests' inspection and a trip through the mine was arranged. Later, Grant was entertained at the exclusive Irwin Club, the only place outside of a saloon where members could meet their friends or discuss business.

The club had a membership of 100 and ladies were welcome only on specified nights. The ladies were always suspicious of the club, for it was rumored that gambling and drinking went on behind its doors. To dissipate this rumor, the members gave a ball which was a great success. A second ball was therefore planned, but just as the grand march was about to begin, the ladies excused themselves, the men began to squirm, and the dancehall was deserted. The mortified club members soon found out that someone had sprinkled cow itch on the floor and had successfully broken up the ball.

By the end of 1883 the camp was dwindling and only five members of the club were left. An auction of the club's possessions was held and Phillips was delegated to collect the money from the sale, pay the bills and if any proceeds remained, give an oyster supper to the surviving members. Nine dollars were left but he was never able to get any two members together for a feast.

CHAPTER NINE

The Aspen Country

Crystal FOR years I'd wanted to get to Crystal but it was inaccessible, and each time I was near it something prevented my going the rest of the way. The road beyond Gothic turns into a trail bearing a marker "Crystal Pass nine miles," and I had inquired hopefully in Crested Butte about getting horses and riding over it, only to be told that the trail was in poor condition and that rock slides in a couple of places made it almost impassable. "You'd better go in from the other side," suggested one old-timer. "You can drive as far as Marble and from there it's only eight miles. If you can't get horses, you can get some miner to take you in when he goes up to his mine."

So, in 1942 I started from the opposite side of the range, following the Crystal River from Carbondale to Marble, along a winding road which skirts the stream the entire way. A spur of the D. & R. G. Railroad parallels the auto road, its track often close to the water, and at first I was perplexed at seeing great slabs of pure white stone scattered along its embankment or serving as breakwaters or abutments along the bank. This was the marble from the quarry, dumped beside the tracks or used so prodigally to reinforce the right of way! The further we drove the higher we climbed, with the tow-

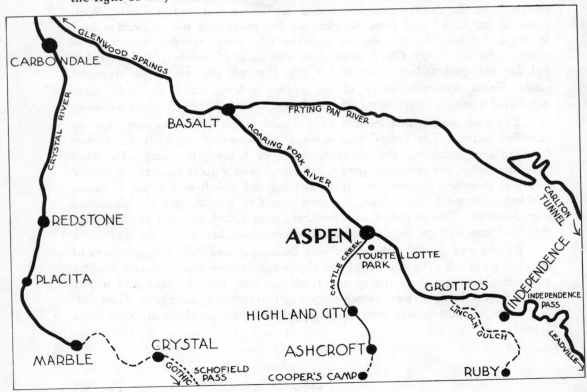

ering peaks always ahead, until rounding a corner we entered the town of Marble and drove past a row of empty frame houses.

The town is built in a grove of trees whose branches temper the light and shade the frame buildings which line its streets. In the midst of this green shade the marble, which is used for sidewalks, foundations, and even for entire buildings, looks startlingly white and austere. At the post office we stopped to inquire the way to Crystal.

"There's one family living there this summer," said the postmistress. "They come down about once a week in their car. You can make it up there, only look out for ore trucks coming down. There aren't any turnouts on the road. If you hear a truck coming, try and find a place wide enough for it to squeeze past you and wait for it to go by." As we left the post office a woman followed me and touched my sleeve, "Don't go to Crystal," she said. "It's an awful scary road. It goes straight up the mountain on the very edge. I vow I'll never do it again." Since opinions seemed to differ, we trudged up the hill to see an old miner who used to live at Crystal and who went up there frequently to see to his mine. Both he and his wife were at home and, although he was cordial enough, he flatly refused to drive us up to the camp. When I asked him about the road and said I'd heard it was awful he bridled up at once. "What's the matter with the road?" he roared, "It's in the best condition it's ever been in!"

Before I could answer, his wife came into the room with a framed photograph of Crystal as it had looked in its prime. "At least you can see from this what it was like," she said as she dusted the glass with the corner of her apron. "There are still a dozen or more cabins there. There's a professor of geology up there this summer with a group of students but nobody else goes up except miners."

All the time that we'd been talking peals of thunder were coming nearer and nearer and, as we left the house with its marble fence, the heavens opened, putting an end to any trip to Crystal that day. Since there seemed to be no place to spend the night in Marble we drove back down the canyon as fast as possible, for the thirty miles of dirt road was rapidly becoming muddy and slippery.

In 1946 I again tried to reach Crystal. This time I wrote to the postmaster at Carbondale and inquired how I might get there. He replied that the mail carrier went to Marble three times a week, that he took the mail for Crystal, and that he carried passengers. Inferring that he drove to Crystal when there was mail, I joyfully engaged a seat on the "stage" for a certain morning in August, arriving in Carbondale the night before so as to be ready for the early trip. I looked up the mail carrier that evening only to find that he never went beyond Marble. So I was foiled again. In the fall of 1947 I tried once more. In Carbondale my husband and I heard of a Mr. George Harris who lived in Marble and who drove up to Crystal every day. Perhaps we could get him to take us with him! The next morning we telephoned from Carbondale to the schoolteacher in Marble (for hers was the only phone there), asking if Mr. Harris was about.

"He's around," she replied. "But he's getting ready to leave."

"For goodness sake stop him and tell him we want to go to Crystal with him and that we'll be in Marble just as soon as we can drive up from Carbondale," we urged, hanging up the receiver and dashing up the Crystal River highway as fast as its curves and roadbed would allow.

Mt. Sopris loomed ahead of us and we watched its striking silhouette change in contour as we drew nearer to its slopes and then passed beyond it. Before long we began to see the chalk-white chunks of marble strewn along the railroad embankment and the blood-red cliffs from which Redstone gets its name. We whizzed through this deserted coal town with its modern Inn, and we bounced past the coal mine at Placita, and came to a sliding stop in Marble in front of the only house in which we saw signs of life. The miner was still there but he was impatient to get on the road. To our dismay he announced that he wasn't going to Crystal that day but was off to Carbondale to buy groceries. Was Crystal to elude us again?

At this point my husband took things in hand. He tried to persuade Mr. Harris to drive us to Crystal first and to go to Carbondale later, but the old miner was a bit crusty and stuck to his plan.

"What do you want to go to Crystal for?" he asked suspiciously. "You goin' fishin'?" We assured him that we were not fishermen.

"Look here," said Francis, "my wife's a crazy artist who likes to make sketches of old towns and she wants to go to Crystal to make some pictures of it. She won't want to stay there more than an hour and a half. Will you take us there for ten dollars?"

"Did you say ten dollars just to drive you eight miles? I sure will. I need dynamite for my mine and I need groceries. Put it there, sir, and we'll get going."

Mr. Harris' car was old and somewhat battered, and the back seat had been removed so as to make room for tools and supplies to be hauled to the mine. While Francis rode beside the old miner, I sat on the floor of the car surrounded by wrenches, chains, wire and tin cans and watched the tree tops go by. First we crossed a narrow new bridge which spans the creek down which tons of mud poured in 1941, when a cloudburst inundated Marble and the resulting mudslide wiped out part of the town. Once across the bridge we drove over the gray, muddy silt which covered everything, until leaving the town behind we began to climb the long, gruelling three-mile hill that I had heard so much about. It took a seasoned driver to guide a car up its steep rocky surface. There were no turnouts, but fortunately we met no traffic. After a long grinding pull the road leveled off, only to plunge down a rocky ledge to the Crystal River far below. The scenery was incredibly beautiful, wild and lonely. Sharp peaks rose about us, their timbered slopes gouged by rock and snow slides, while far below was the clear tumbling river. Toward the bottom of the mountain we began to pass deserted mines and the foundations of old mills.

At an opening in the trees Mr. Harris stopped and pointed to the Sheep Mountain Tunnel mill, the most picturesque I had ever seen. It was rustic and it clung to a cliff beside a waterfall. With its background of peaks it looked like a stage set for some Wagnerian opera.

CRYSTAL

↓ SHEEP MT. TUNNEL MILL, CRYSTAL

A little further on we crossed the stream on a bridge which had a gate at one end. This was kept closed so that cattle could not wander outside of the "city limits." Closing the gate behind us while the car straddled the stream, we drove up a short hill and directly onto the main street of Crystal. I had expected a few tumble-down log cabins but instead I found a dozen houses, some of them two-story and most of them in good condition. Several families were living in Crystal, and while I walked to the far end of the street, past the last house, and began to work my way back sketching each group of buildings, Mr. Harris chatted with his friends. An old photograph in the State Historical Society's library, taken from the top of the pass looking down into the town, showed a pack train snaking down the slopes and picking its way along this one long street which was lined with houses on both sides.

One look around convinced me that Crystal is the most beautifully situated of all the old mining camps. It is high and it is set on a lush mountain meadow through which runs the river. On every side rise high peaks—Mineral Point, Crystal Mountain, Bear Mountain, Sheep Mountain, and Treasury Peak, their summits well above timber line and their sides covered with aspens and pines. Suddenly an explosion reverberated through the hills and a column of smoke wavered in the thin air halfway up the nearest mountain, and slowly faded away. On the way up Harris had said that he'd show us where his mine was and that his partner was going to blast at ten-thirty. Sure enough, he had.

By the time I had made half a dozen sketches it was time to leave, but before we climbed back into the rattling vehicle, Mr. Harris pointed out the old printing office where the *Crystal River Current* had been published as early as 1880 and he showed me the "Crystal Club," which is now someone's home.

As nearly as he could remember, the silver boom was in the middle eighties, although the first prospectors in the Rock Creek district as it was then called, had gone in about 1864. Rock Creek was now called the Crystal River. Although Crystal and Marble were the chief towns of the mining district, their development had been greatly hampered, he believed, by lack of proper transportation facilities.

In the eighties a good wagon road connected Crested Butte, seventeen miles away, with Crystal, although dangerous rock slide areas had to be crossed in the summer and the road became impassable in winter except on snowshoes. A friend of his had a close shave on that road—he'd been crossing it on horseback when a rock slide started, and his horse jumped just in time to avoid being carried down the mountain. The trail, a very high one, was narrow but beautiful.

In the early days the camp was called Crystal City and consisted of a cluster of miners' cabins, a post office, hotel and store owned by Al and Fred Johnson. The brothers were ambitious and thought the place needed a newspaper; so they packed in a press and a man named Tom O'Brien to run it. Shortly afterwards the *Crystal River Current* appeared and was published regularly by Al Johnson until 1892. Fred Johnson carried the mail on snowshoes in winter from the Butte to Crystal, often making the round trip in one day. Al ran the store, post office and hotel, and when not too busy he would slip over to Crested Butte with his jack train and bring in a new stock of goods.

The camp was often snowbound, making "snowshoe express the only means of getting anything into this neck of the woods," wrote the editor of the *Current* in December, 1886; and the *Denver Post* on Feb. 11, 1899, printed the following letter from the town:

> Crystal is snowbound. The stage road between the city and Marble, six miles below, is under ten to fifty feet of snow and the mail carrier has only been able to come through once in the past week and then on snowshoes. Supplies will be exhausted in a short time and unless the road can be opened, several of the mines will probably be forced to close down and the miners go out on snowshoes.
>
> As soon as the storm ceases and weather settles, a force of fifty men will begin work to open the road for a train of pack horses to bring in supplies and it is believed that by tunneling through the snow at points most exposed to avalanches it will be possible to open a terminal station.
>
> The past week witnessed the worst storm ever experienced in the Elk Mts. district but . . . no lives have been lost . . . the people know too well the severity of storms to take any chances.

We re-crossed the bridge, closed the gate and started back toward Marble, Mr. Harris talking all the way about mining and pointing out the Black Queen, the Lead King, the Black Eagle and others as we went. All of these produced fortunes in gold, silver and lead before the end of the eighties.

The Black Queen was shipping ore in 1890, packing it on 150 jacks and sending it over the pass to Crested Butte. Silver ore from the Black Queen was shown at the Chicago World's Fair in 1893. The Sheep Mountain Tunnel and the Lead King were good producers, the latter shipping ore until 1913. Crystal City itself, however, along with the other silver camps faded out with the demonetization of silver in 1893. Of recent years, the old Harrison and Farley claims, the Carbonate mine, the High Tide and other groups are being worked by Wm. H. Knapp of Marble, and Harris himself continues to mine in the district. Honking his horn almost constantly, he drove the tortuous ledge road out of the canyon, explaining that, "there was getting to be too much traffic around. Why, last week he met a truck and he had to back a mile before he could find a place where it could pass him. Too many fishermen were coming into the valley, too. He didn't like it. Used to be you never saw a soul in the hills."

On the way back we realized how steep the grade had been and as we groaned down the last hill in low, Harris pointed out the location of the marble quarries and the site of the old smelter on the flats at the edge of Marble.

Marble

"Ever hear about the first piano in Marble?" he asked, as we crawled over the silt-packed road. "Back in 1889 a piano was a curiosity here. The proprietor of one of the hotels gave one to his wife as a wedding present and to get it here, it had to be packed on jacks over the range. By the time it was set up in the hotel parlor it was all out of tune. When you started to play on it, it sounded like a crash of thunder mixed with falling bricks, tin pans and horns. No one could stand to hear the thing. A cook for a camping party came into the hotel one day and after he had heard the noise he said to the hotel-keeper's wife, 'Ma'am, if I had a monkey wrench I believe I could tune that thing so people could sleep around here, and I'll do it free.'"

In Marble, we could see the extent of the damage done by the mudslide. A strip of town several blocks wide was simply washed away, leaving nothing but heavy grey mud and silt several feet deep over everything. Looking at the dreary mess that had once been the business section, I tried to recall how it had looked on my first visit.

"Where are the marble stores and the band stand that I saw in 1942?" I asked.

"We had another mudslide," said Mr. Harris laconically, "and it took out the rest of the town that stood in its way. I figure it out this way. The mountains are pretty high around here and sometimes the clouds can't get over them. When two clouds meet, the water has to go somewhere and it comes down Carbon Creek and washes away everything in its path. The heavy rain loosens the coal shale and mud along the sides of the creek above here and it comes down, too, like a lava flow."

The first mudslide struck the city in August, 1941, and washed away many houses and some stores. The business section was beyond Carbon Creek, which on its rampage tore out a bridge or cut a new channel for itself across the main street, I never knew which. Even in 1942, a year after the flood, the water rushed across the street and pedestrians picked their way cautiously over the boiling torrent on planks lodged between boulders or placed on hummocks of dry land. One board had to be taken up by each person, laid ahead of him and used as a bridge across a narrow offshoot of the main stream. The next person who returned moved the board ahead of him and returned it to its original position. We teetered across these planks when we were looking for the miner who had once lived in Crystal and who thought the road there was in such fine shape!

Beyond the stream had stood what was left of the stores. Some were completely demolished, some were torn open, and of those that were made completely of dressed marble, only the walls remained. The fire bell on its tall steel tower and the hexagonal wooden band-stand had withstood the first flood but were surrounded by rocks and splintered timbers in the midst of the new streambed. Houses broken in half or sagging, as if some giant had stepped on them, leaned drunkenly over the brink of the water or were filled with mud and debris. Now, in 1947, the entire main street near the creek was gone; even the marble buildings had vanished, the bandstand was a pile of splintered lumber, and only the tall steel tower with the bell had stood the shock of the second disaster.

A mere handful of people live in Marble today, for the marble quarries closed down in November, 1941; but even with "quarry workmen and their families leaving the desolate town, the residents who remained did not think of the place as a 'ghost town.' They had seen floods strike before and they had seen fires. . . . They had even seen the mill and quarry close down only to reopen again." But as a last blow, during World War II the railroad was torn up and sold for scrap and more families moved away.

Mining, not marble, attracted three or four prospectors from Schofield, across the range, into the Crystal River valley in the late seventies, and shortly after the discovery of the mines others came in and laid out the camps of Crystal City and Yule Creek, later called Marble City. While Crystal had a population of 500 as early as 1880, Marble grew more slowly.

A few mines, which produced gold, silver and lead, were worked before the close of the eighties, and the Hoffman brothers built and operated a small smelter on the flats near the town in 1890. Coke was hauled by mule team from Crested Butte, over the mountains and down Crystal canyon to the smelter. The Lead King mine was the most consistent producer of the region and, long before the railroad was built to Marble, its ore was hauled by team to Carbondale for shipment.

George Yule, a Colorado pioneer for whom Yule Creek is named, was the first to discover the marble deposits high above the town. The beds are immense, as White House Mountain, a fourteen-thousand-foot peak, is composed of an almost solid mass of statuary marble. The first quarries were opened by the Kelly brothers in 1890, the marble being "wagon hauled" to Carbondale and the railroad. A second and third quarry were opened during the decade by A. J. Mitchell and Billy Fine and by J. C. Osgood of the Colorado Fuel and Iron Company. In 1901 the new Hoffman smelter, which employed twenty men and "produced a No. 1 Matt," was blown in and was said to be a "complete success besides being an ornament to the town."

The *Marble Times* was published from 1892 until the early 1900's, although evidently under different editors, one of whom was Sylvia Smith, a former editor of the Crested Butte *Weekly Citizen*. Miss Smith moved to Marble in 1906 bringing her printing press with her and started to print a newspaper. She was an outspoken woman and she attacked the Yule Marble Company and its policies in vituperative articles. When a snowslide wrecked part of the marble mill she "exulted over the catastrophe." This was too much for the townspeople, whose livelihood depended upon the operation of the marble industry. Deciding that she had gone too far, a committee "waited on the militant lady and told her she would have to leave town," and to be sure that she did, they escorted her to the train.

When the quarries were productive the town flourished. When the plant shut down, or was sold at a sheriff's sale, or was temporarily dismantled, the population dwindled. In 1910 fifteen hundred people lived in the town, yet in 1914 the population shrank to four. By 1916 it was a bustling place again with a population of 1000, all supported directly or indirectly by the marble business.

The same year a force of 500 to 1000 men were working at the Colorado Yule Marble quarry and the last of the big shipments started east— stone for the Lincoln Memorial worth $1,070,000. Besides the Lincoln Memorial, the Tomb of the Unknown Soldier in Arlington, the Customs House, the Colorado National Bank, and the Colorado State Museum, in Denver, as well as certain buildings in New York and San Francisco are made of marble from these quarries. The block of marble for the Tomb of the Unknown Soldier weighed fifty-five tons and took a year to remove from the quarry. "The plant consisted of finishing mills, an electric power plant, cable and electric tram and a hundred cottages."

In 1926 fire destroyed the mill and damaged the town. At the time of the fire the mill was the largest single marble finishing plant in the world. Jacob F. Smith then bought the property and operated it until 1939. A company-owned railroad connected it with the D. & R. G. at Carbondale, and on it were carried the huge blocks cut at the mill.

The flood of August 1941 was not the principal reason for the quarry's shutting down. The increasing use of marble substitutes and marble veneers, instead of blocks, caused the business to shrink to a non-paying size.

After we had got back to Mr. Harris' home and had thanked him for taking us to Crystal, we started to look around and see how much of the town had escaped the mudslide. Many of the company houses are still standing and rows of foundations and piles of lumber showed where others once stood. One is now the school, and peering through its big window I could see five desks of assorted kinds and sizes, a teacher's desk, a blackboard, a stove and a few textbooks. Near the schoolhouse was a frame church with a tall, slender tower surmounted with a cross. On the way to the marble-sheds we passed the site of a house within whose white marble foundation grew weeds, bushes and young trees.

The huge marble cutting-shed looked like a ruined Mayan temple, with its square columns and thick white walls. All the metal piers, trusses and window frames had been removed at the same time that the steel rails had been pried from the railroad ties and sold for scrap during World War II. Inside this great, roofless shed stood great blocks of marble waiting to be cut and shipped. The smaller company buildings were also made of marble, the bank of the stream was faced with it, and even the circular foundation for the locomotive turntable was of the same dead white stone. To walk around the deserted plant was like exploring some forgotten civilization—there were no people and no sounds—just marble and vegetation which was gradually overgrowing this man-made temple.

Before leaving I went in search of the old smelter site. Finding a foot-bridge over the Crystal River, I followed a trail through the bushes to a meadow, at the edge of which stood the rusted machinery of the old smelter. While sketching its remains, I heard voices and the sound of hooves. Out of the brush came two men on horseback, leading three pack horses and a protesting nanny-goat. They climbed to the old quarry trail and disappeared over the mountain.

As we drove down the one long street which leads out of town and saw the railroad cut and the roadbed stripped of its rails I remembered a sentence from a pamphlet published by the *Colorado Western Slope Congress* which read:

> . . . with the advent of the railroad a new era will begin. When the locomotive whistles its "open sesame" to these rugged mountains, the cliffs of the rock will open and the hidden treasures be revealed.

Redstone   We did not hurry back to Carbondale, for the scenery along the Crystal River was stunning and we had not had time to enjoy it in the morning. At

ASSAY OFFICE, RUBY

CHURCH AT MARBLE

↓ FOUNDATIONS AT MARBLE

Placita we passed the abandoned coal mine which was forced to shut down when the railroad was scrapped. We glanced at the McClure Pass road which switchbacks up the side of the mountain and provides a shortcut to the Gunnison country, and we tried to see the million-dollar mansion at Redstone, built and furnished in 1900 for the Osgoods, owners of the C. F. & I. town, but it is so surrounded by trees and shrubs that it is invisible from the highway. Redstone, a model company town which lies at the foot of rocky cliffs whose brilliant color gave it its name, is almost deserted today. The workmens' houses are attractive in architecture and are set back from the winding road, in a grove of aspens. They have lain empty ever since the coal town closed down, except for occasional tenants. The Clubhouse, intended for the workmen, with its Swiss-German architecture and its clock-tower, has only recently been opened as the Redstone Inn; its furniture and massive woodwork date from 1900, the year it was opened with a Grand Ball.

Ashcroft   The twelve mile drive up Castle Creek to Ashcroft from Aspen, follows a green valley, sometimes high above the water and sometimes in the midst of aspen groves. Close to Aspen is the old Newman property, where until recently a skeleton mill clung to the steep bank on the far side of Castle Creek, while just below the highway other mine buildings stood in various stages of decay. Since the revival of Aspen as a ski resort, the large "mansion" on the property has been converted into the Four Seasons Club, and more people frequent the place than in the best days of the boom. A few miles farther, is the Bavarian Lodge built in 1936, opposite which the road cuts through the old site of Highland, Ashcroft's predecessor.

Ashcroft, which once rivaled Aspen, now consists of the little group of weathered buildings at the foot of the Elk mountains. It has stood lonely and unspoiled for years, the grass growing high in the main street and the deer flies feasting gluttonously on any chance visitor who dares invade its quiet. Store after store lines the principal street, each in a different state of disintegration. The roof of one is caved in; the false front of another is stripped of its cornice and presents a bare upthrust palisade of boards; a third has shuttered windows, through whose cracks the interior with its counters and shelves can be seen; and a fourth has succumbed to wind and snow, and lies a pile of jumbled lumber. Other empty houses stand back from the main group, dotted over the meadow which once teemed with life. Castle Creek tumbles noisily along one side of town and aspen groves creep close to outpost cabins. The jagged peaks of the Elk mountains tower beyond, their perpetual snow comb indicating their lofty elevation.

Highland   During the summer of 1879, when prospectors were searching most of the Colorado mountains for gold or silver, T. E. Ashcraft and his party worked their way over the Elk mountains and, having made some good strikes, laid out the townsite of Highland where Conundrum Gulch joins Castle Creek. He and his friends expected to spend the winter in the new camp and had it not been for the restlessness of the Ute Indians in the region would have done so. But since the Meeker Massacre had just occurred in September, and since Highland and all the Elk mountain country was in Ute Territory, and since Indians didn't like miners anyway because they dug up the earth and disturbed the earth gods, it seemed a good time to go to Leadville until things quieted down.

Two of the party decided to stay in spite of the Indian scare and dug in where the two forks of Castle Creek meet, calling their location Castle Forks. In the spring of 1880 a townsite was laid out on this spot on a placer claim, which was known also as Chloride. As soon as the deep snows began to melt that spring, the passes swarmed with prospectors, many of them heading for Highland, which in no time became a three-street town with thirty cabins, three stores housed in tents, and mail delivery three times a week. Everything was "supervised by the President of the Town Company of Highland, T. E. Ashcraft." Although Highland flourished during 1880, it died as quickly as it rose and one cabin today marks its site, opposite the Bavarian Lodge halfway between Ashcroft and Aspen. In the spring of the same year, 1880, the rival town of Castle Forks began to build up and this before long became known as Ashcroft. Jack Leahy, who died in 1939, was the last resident of the town. He and two others first came to the Elk mountains in 1878 hunting for silver, and they returned again in 1879. By the spring of 1880 they had filed claims on the Columbia group of mines on Brilliant Hill, and for many years he, at least, continued to mine in the hills above the town.

During 1880-1881 Ashcroft was a "thriving camp when Aspen was a dusty, sleepy little hamlet." The first school was opened in October 1881 with the desks made of wooden slabs and the seats, from old boxes. A telegraph line to Crested Butte was completed in November, "subscription rates being one pole." Ashcroft continued to boom during the summer of 1882, having two main streets, Castle and Main, on both of which were stores, saloons and hotels. There was even a jail. The Farrell, the Riverside and the Fifth Avenue Hotels, catered to the miners, but today only a husk of a two-story building, on whose bleached facade are the faded letters, "Hotel . . . View," indicates where any hotel stood.

Ashcroft cont'd.

At first Ashcroft could be reached only over Taylor Pass, where it was necessary to lower wagons piece by piece over a forty-foot drop near the top. Independence Pass was no better; the first wagon spent a month getting over it. By 1882 three stage lines ran regularly between Ashcroft and Crested Butte—two over Taylor Pass and the third over the new Pearl Pass road which shortened the distance to the railroad by fifty miles. Miners' trails led in all directions over the mountains; up Richmond Hill near the site of Highland, up past Cooper's Camp, and up Conundrum Gulch where a lonely grave bears the inscription: "Here lies Dick Reynolds. Died Only God Knows How."

In 1883, when Aspen became a real town—Ashcroft began to fade, and a number of its buildings were "taken down the curving twelve mile road" to the newer place. Then when the D. & R. G. reached Aspen in 1887, making it unnecessary to haul ore over Pearl Pass any more, Ashcroft lost more of its trade and population, even though some optimists believed that Aspen and Ashcroft would be eventually linked by rail.

That there was life in the town is shown by the "Ashcroft Anglings" in the *Aspen Evening Chronicle* of 1888, which reported that "the camp presents considerable animation. The reports of giant and chimes of the hammer and drill are heard on all sides." Miners even kept boxes of powder in their homes and heated sticks of it in their stoves to dry them out, preparatory to blasting, to the dismay of their wives.

The Fourth of July, 1888, was celebrated by all.

> The day was ushered in amid the roar of giant powder that continued until nightfall, at which time ladies and gentlemen of the locality repaired to the City Hall, that had been appropriately festooned, and to the melody of rich music, discoursed by the Thistle String Band, began to trip the light fantastic that was continued until early morn.

> Joe Vannah observed the national festival by pulling the plug from two lusty kegs of Zang around which his friends collected. A case of three star brandy was added to this and the walls of his hospitable cabin were lashed with eloquence that would have done credit to the swell clubs of the east.

The mines produced silver and lead, but with depth the ores became more complex and a quantity of zinc was found intermingled with the other metals. In the eighties, no one knew what to do with zinc ore or how to handle it. When a shipment of ore was sent from the Tam O'Shanter mine to the smelter at Pueblo and assayed twenty percent zinc, the smelter dumped the whole lot into the Arkansas River. Some mining continued to be done in the nineties, although the silver crash of 1893 put a temporary stop to production.

The Tam O'Shanter property above Ashcroft (13,572 feet elevation), was one of the best producers of "white metal" operating in the eighties. Joel W. Smith and H. A. W. Tabor of Leadville were the original owners of the property which included the Montezuma claim.

In spite of Tabor's phenomenal luck with mining investments, the Ashcroft mines were one of his bad business deals, for he put more money into the Tam O'Shanter and Montezuma mines than he got out. There were years when they produced fabulous amounts of pay ore—in 1892, $20,000 a month—but there were other years when the property was run at a loss. At the peak of their productiveness Tabor leased the Aspen smelter to handle his ore; he built a house in Ashcroft which rumor says was papered with gold-encrusted panels; and he declared a twenty-four hour holiday at the mine with all the drinks on him whenever Baby Doe came to town. In all he spent $12,000,000 in thirteen years. In 1895 pack trains were still hauling ore from the Montezuma but its best days seemed over. In 1906 the property was sold to a New York syndicate.

Cooper's Camp
Two miles above Ashcroft extensive iron mines were once worked. The mines were discovered in 1880, but they attracted little attention until a smelter was built at Aspen and a flux was needed for the ores of the region. In the spring of 1886 the property was purchased by the Colorado Coal and Fuel Company for $35,000, and thousands of tons of iron were sent to the smelter fourteen miles below. As soon as two railroads reached Aspen, however, it was found cheaper to ship ore to more distant smelters, and the demand for the iron from Cooper's Camp ceased.

On my last visit to Ashcroft I tried to find the site of the camp. The road beyond Ashcroft is good for a mile and is a mere trail the rest of the way. At the edge of a grove of aspens and further among the trees were the frames of a few log cabins and the stone foundations of one or two other buildings.

ASPEN STORES

ASHCROFT STORES

We continued up the trail for a mile or so but saw no other buildings. Perhaps what we found was Cooper's Camp. Perhaps not.

Aspen   Aspen, like Georgetown, is a city of homes surrounded by mines. Lying in a valley at the foot of Aspen and Smuggler mountains, its wide streets are lined with frame and brick houses, surrounded by flower gardens and shaded by big trees. In summer the sweet peas grow to prodigious sizes and every yard has at least one clump of them, covering a fence or trellis with a riot of color. When I first saw it, Aspen was a quiet place with a small but permanent population engaged in local business and occupying a portion of its Victorian homes. The High School looked like a large, private home; the Opera House, although empty since its fire, accommodated on the street floor, the Public Library and a grocery store and the Jerome was a comfortable old-fashioned hotel. Almost every building, both public and private, was built in the eighties or early nineties and whether occupied or vacant offered picturesque and historic material to be recorded.

One morning I was out as usual, standing in the street sketching away, when a car driven by an old man drew up and the driver said: "Want to see an old house? If you do, come down to my place and my wife and I will show you through." Since I seldom have an opportunity to inspect the interiors of the buildings I sketch, I hurried after him. The house was a particularly ornate residence with an octagonal tower, balcony, and leaded glass transoms in several of its windows. It had little furniture, for the present owners used it rather as a storehouse than a home. Now that they were about to leave on a two-weeks' fishing trip they stopped by to get some things they needed.

The inside was not as imposing as the exterior, and I was a little disappointed until we went upstairs and entered an octagonal room with a leaded glass door opening on to the little balcony. Here was material for a sketch! Turning to my host I inquired how soon he and his wife were leaving for their trip.

"Right away," he replied, "Why do you want to know?"

"If you weren't leaving immediately, I'd like to make a sketch of this fascinating room."

He stepped back and looked me up and down before answering. "Well," he said, "I don't know who you are but be sure to shut the front door tight when you leave." Last year when I returned to Aspen for another visit, the house was burned!

It was in the eighties and nineties that Aspen boomed, being called the "City of the Sulphurets" and the "Richest Five Acres on Earth;" but in 1879 there was no city at all.

In the summer of that year a few prospectors from Leadville struggled across the Continental Divide by way of Twin Lakes and Independence trail, and working their way down the western slope, made camp at a spot which they called Ute Spring. These men, most of whom had been grub-staked by Leadville capital, had been unable to make their pile in Leadville and were on the lookout for new and profitable territory. At almost the same time a group of men from Crested Butte entered the region; and both groups made locations upon Aspen, West Aspen, and Smuggler mountains and staked off claims which later were developed as the Durant, Spar, Smuggler and other famous mines. Just as the miners prepared to dig in for the winter, word of a Ute Indian uprising drove all but thirteen of them back over the range until the spring of 1880, when they were on the road again, climbing slowly over almost impassable snowy trails.

One of the first to enter the region was Henry Tourtelotte, who came to Denver in 1878 and to Leadville in 1879. He prospected on Weston Pass, in Big Evans Gulch and on Mosquito mountain with no success. Disgusted, he outfitted himself with mining equipment and with one "jack" started for the western slope, following wagon roads and trails until he had passed Twin Lakes and had worked his way to the top of Independence Pass. There all trails seemed to end, and for "four days and nights he stumbled over underbrush and waded through Frying Pan creek until he found the Roaring Fork and the mesa on which is the city of Aspen." The country was wild and full of game, and after resting a few days, he started up Castle Creek. Branching off from its banks he climbed a mountain and found on top a natural park in which he spied outcroppings of ore. Continuing to prospect in the vicinity he located many mines including the Castle lode. The mountain park which he discovered became known as Tourtelotte Park.

The prospectors who had pitched their tents at Ute Spring expected to develop the land around their camp as a ranch, but in the spring of 1880, when so many men poured into the region, D. M. Hyman, B. Clark Wheeler and other newcomers secured the meadows for a townsite, and the plat of Aspen was laid out. At almost the same time, real estate speculators laid out Roaring Fork City on land between Maroon and Castle Creeks. One cabin —the only building ever constructed there—was built on the newly platted townsite and lots were advertised and sold, especially in Leadville; but the town company collapsed and the one cabin was moved to Aspen.

As prospectors poured in, the new trail from Twin Lakes was used more and more. Men arrived with hands or feet frozen and wholly blinded by the glare of the sun on the snow. Those who attempted the trip in the spring generally left Twin Lakes in the morning and reached the foot of the pass by dark, continuing over the range through the night while the snow was frozen and provided safer footing. By the time the first crude wagon road was built across Independence Pass in 1881 the camp was beginning to boom.

Prospectors were attracted by immense quantities of float found in the debris on the sides of Aspen and Smuggler mountains, and they began to explore the area for lode mines. Aspen itself was "located on a great lode" or "contact vein, the ore lying on magnesium or dolomite lime, and overlaid with pure carbonate of lime and shale." Many mines were located between 1880 and 1884, some of which became world famous. By the fall of 1883, as the mines began to show their greatness, the camp began to grow rapidly, eclipsing Ashcroft which had rivalled it in size for two years.

In 1883 a large body of ore was uncovered in the Spar mine, and soon afterwards the Washington, Vallejo, and Emma proved "bonanzas." "A single chamber in the Emma, no larger than an ordinary sleeping apartment, netted the owners a half-million dollars." By December 1884 the Aspen and Smuggler mines were extensively developed, and mining on a big scale began. One of the most unique and beautiful sights remembered by all "old-timers" was the lines of twinkling lights winding down the mountains at night as hundreds of miners tramped wearily home along the narrow twisting trails lighting their steps by their own lanterns and lamps.

The Durant, one of the oldest locations of the camp, was staked in 1879. A year or two later D. H. Hyman of Cincinnati purchased it and adjoining claims and developed it until it paid at the rate of $150,000 per month. The original claim ran into the territory of the Aspen mine and other properties, and a famous litigation case followed which cost $400,000 and ended in compromise.

The Aspen mine was also one of the earliest mines developed and soon ranked second as a payer of dividends. Its ore was carried down the mountain by an electric tramway (the first ever built for mining purposes), constructed and owned by the Hon. Jerome B. Wheeler, whose capital later built a smelter, a hotel and an opera house for the city. Such tramways were a great help in bringing the ores from the mines near timber line to the mills at the base of the mountains. Some were electrically run, and others worked on the principle that full buckets dropping by their own weight would carry the empty ones back to the mine on the endless belt, for, as the miner said, "We lave it to the impudence of gravity."

The Mollie Gibson, located in 1880, became the most talked-of mine in the camp. Ore taken "twenty-eight feet below the surface assayed 3300 ounces of silver to the ton." Its claim ran alongside of and was said to overlap that of the Lone Pine, and disputes over the boundaries caused litigation which lasted two years and ended, as usual, in a compromise. The two properties were consolidated under the name the Mollie Gibson and were worked successfully for years, shipping high grade silver ores, "which ran as high as $4,896 per ton in carload lots." By 1887 a mill, equipped to treat 50 tons per day, was built to handle concentrates of the ore. Year by year the mine produced more and more silver, one piece of ore weighing 1700 pounds and bringing over $3,000.

Aspen had more than its share of great mines—mines which created millionaires such as Hyman and Wheeler. Not only the Mollie Gibson and the Durant but the Midnight, Newman, Aspen and Smuggler produced fabulous amounts of high grade ore which netted millions for the stockholders.

Nuggets of incredible size were found first in one mine and then in another. In 1883 the largest body of ore in the world was struck in the Compromise mine—"140 feet between walls at the only point where it has been cross-cut." In 1894 a nugget taken from the Smuggler weighed 2060 pounds and was 93% pure silver. More high grade ores were mined than in any other camp in the world, but all ores had to be shipped out for treatment until a smelter was built. J. B. Wheeler completed the first smelter at the mouth of Castle Creek in 1884, but this did not begin to supply the need of the booming camp, nor was it so efficient as the well-established smelters at Leadville and Pueblo. When it was rumored, therefore, in 1885, that Wheeler, who was one of the stockholders of the Colorado Midland Railroad, had persuaded the company to extend the line to Aspen, mining began to mark time, for the cost of transporting ore from the mines to the distant smelters by pack train and wagon was exorbitant. The camp remained in a partially dormant state until 1887, when a railroad became a fact. Then the old mines began to ship heavily, and new developments started up. A spur of the D. & R. G. from Glenwood Springs reached the city in November 1887, followed the next year by the Colorado Midland.

As soon as the D. & R. G. narrow gauge branch was completed to Aspen, a celebration was held, with fireworks and bonfires on all the peaks surrounding the city.

In 1888 the Colorado Midland reached the city with a standard broad gauge track. While the D. & R. G. had only to build a spur up the valley from Glenwood Springs, the Midland had to extend its track from Leadville, tunnel through 14,418 foot Mt. Massive, and build down the length of the Frying Pan canyon to Basalt and then up the valley to Aspen. The Hagerman Tunnel was an engineering triumph, and that the road was completed only one year after the D. & R. G. seems amazing.

When both roads entered Aspen trouble developed. The Rio Grande obtained a fragmentary franchise to reach the mouths of the mines on the south side of town; but the Midland had already been granted the right to lay its tracks to the mines—both permits having been given apparently without the city having figured out that each road would have to use or cross Ute Avenue. The Aspen paper of September 19, 20 and 21, 1888, gives a play by play account as follows:

BABY AND BROAD GAUGE RAILROADS AT WAR.
CONFLICT BETWEEN RIVAL ROADS.

. . . The Rio Grande was reaching Ute Ave. when the Midland exposed its *coup d'etat* and laid its iron along the thoroughfare at a point where the Rio Grande was to intersect it. . . . The Rio Grande riveted its rails and crossing the avenue, left one detachment to construct the approaches. . . .

In the mellow light of a full moon a posse of armed men with the barrels of Winchesters glistening beneath the laughing face of the moon could be seen, with orders to shoot if it became necessary to resist the Midland tracklayers. . . .

Hundreds of spectators who expected bloodshed lined the avenue. Timid mothers . . . gathering under the stubborn roof of a log dwelling and waiting patiently for the roar of rifles, barred doors.

All the while

the Midland tracklayers were doggedly stretching out the steel ribbons. . . . Any attempt to proceed as far as the rails of the rival would elicit fatal resistance. The bystanders who blackened the thoroughfares at this time, stood waiting for the exciting collision, and increased as each bar of iron was spiked. The tracklayers were approaching the danger point. The spectators crowded forward, leaving only the aisle between them for the spikers. The clear ring of the massive hammer was piercing the chilling atmosphere with its rhyming notes, while confronting them were the dozen or more guards with their fingers on the treacherous trigger of the Winchester . . . but a few feet more . . . the leaders of the Rio Grande guard admonished them that a fatal penalty awaited the first man who attempted to put his brogan upon the forbidden ground and the grim furrows of resolute determination that were revealed by the moonlight made the blood of the bystanders run cold. The tracklayers had now butted up against their limit; the spectators surged back as the guards deliberately lifted their weapons, the sanguinary shriek of the rifle was imminent, when Mayor Webber pushed forward through the crowd and ordered both sides to suspend operations and retire from the scene until nine o'clock the next morning. This forced an armistice.

TUSSLE FOR THE TRACK.
RIO GRANDE STANDS PAT.
HOLDS THE CROSSING OVER UTE AVENUE.

Next morning, ". . . at the disputed crossing, over which the combative baby road had extended its track, a dozen or more dagos were filling in the approaches that traffic might not be impeded, while from the massive rails of the broad gauge, the spikers were laying an arm of steel toward the Rust Sampler. Keeping in these directions, there was no possibility of the forces again colliding. . . ." A meeting of the city council was held and "an order was issued instructing the D. & R. G. to retrace its steps to its own grounds within twelve hours from the time of the order, which was nine o'clock at night." That evening the crowd collected again. The time limit expired and "yet the Rio Grande stood pat." They even ran a car of rails, called by the newspaper a "train of iron," onto the crossing. At this point "an Alderman appeared and summoned a representative of the Rio Grande to an interview" whereupon . . . "the engineer poked up his fire . . . the car load of rails began to retrograde and . . . the thoroughfare, save where the broken link in the Midland track was open," was cleared. "About midnight the graders on the Midland departed for Glenwood Springs." Municipal authorities then asked that "the whole question be taken up for reconsideration and the case decided upon its merit."

Though some of the details above seem contradictory, the result was that the Midland used Ute Avenue and that the Rio Grande circled the town to get to the south side. Both roads successfully handled shipments of ore and both built stations—on opposite sides of town.

The 80's and early 90's were Aspen's best years. In 1884 Aspen produced $3,500,000. By 1888 the output reached over $7,000,000 and by 1889 it was nearly $10,000,000. So many profitable mines were being worked that over 200 Jacks were plying between the mines and the city, over trails inaccessible to wheeled vehicles. As one newspaper man put it, "The donkey, like the Chinaman (who by the way is not tolerated here in Aspen), always defies competition."

The year 1888 found Aspen a well-established city, secure, modern and proud of its achievements. After eight years it had a population of 8,000, 3 daily papers, electric street lights (the first town in Colorado to have them), a telephone exchange, waterworks, two railroads and "all modern conveniences."

By 1889 the county court house was built, free mail delivery was established, a city jail was under consideration (the county jail was unhandy since none of the city officers had a key to it), and 33 lawyers had hung out their shingles. "Luckily those who first made money out of the mines, became thoroughly attached to the beautiful location and salubrious climate and instead of going away to enjoy their prosperity, they remained and built handsome and artistic residences. . . . Now no town of its size in the state can boast of a finer class of inhabitants or better society."

Living was lavish—restaurants offered the most exotic delicacies that could be shipped in from either coast, and both men and women sent to New York and Paris for their wardrobes. D. H. Hyman, owner of the Durant mine, celebrated his silver anniversary by having many sacks of "high grade"

BARBER SHOP
(NOW OFFICE OF
JEROME HOTEL)
ASPEN

MILL STREET,
ASPEN

from the mine sent east and made up into a silver table service. As soon as the new opera house was completed, all the best theatrical companies on the Silver Circuit played in it, en route to Salt Lake City.

That year two impressive structures, costing $1,000,000 each, were built on the main thoroughfares—the Hotel Jerome and the Wheeler Grand Opera House. Jerome B. Wheeler backed both buildings. Attracted to Aspen first by its mines, he invested heavily in them, completed the smelter on the bank of Castle Creek, bought several coal mines, established and edited the *Aspen Daily Times*, urged the building of the Colorado Midland to the camp and finally financed the hotel and the opera house.

The hotel, three stories high and built of stone from the Frying Pan canyon, boasted that "nothing was wasted in external touches or architectural extravagance . . ." Its hundred "choice rooms, single and en suite, with electric bells in each room, its well fitted bathrooms and first class barbershop, its billiard and bar room are models of costly elegance, and its office and dining hall capacious and handsomely arranged. . . . Connected with the hotel is a large green house in which are raised the vegetables and various products practicable for use on the tables of the hotel."

On November 28 the hotel opened with a grand ball

rivalling in luxurious splendor some of the festivals of the capital of ancient Rome . Beautiful women flitted like birds of paradise in their glorious plumage, under the mellowed and softened lights in the mazes of the dance. Slippered feet and forms clad in shimmering silk floated like the billows of the ocean in rapturous motion . . . the endless tints of fashion's toilette appeared beneath the volume of light that burst from bulbs and arcs . . .

The banquet was served in the Ladies' Ordinary and embraced every gustatory luxury which eastern and southern markets could furnish and was prepared under the sole supervision of the Jerome *chef*, Mons. Fronesca, who has but recently arrived from Paris.

The Opera House opened with a performance of the *King's Fool*, including a cast of eighty artists and promising "Bewilderingly Beautiful Marches, Dazzling Electrical Effects and Enchanting Music." There were twelve complete sets of scenery and a handsome drop curtain representing "Brooklyn Bridge viewed from the New York side of the East River," painted by Charles Graham, an artist from *Harper's Weekly*, "while from the ceiling will depend a veritable firmament of electric bulbs."

The Proscenium boxes are elegantly upholstered in brilliant colors of plush, set off with brass trimmings, the whole surrounded by handsome curtains and the ornamental woodwork finished in dark colors and gold. The lower portion of the walls are papered and the upper part is frescoed. . . . In the matter of dressing rooms, the accommodations of the theatre is singularly replete, there being no less than twelve in all. . . .

Stage scenery and stage properties are modern and nothing is wanted in completeness, even the various many-colored trees and plants of the tropics being included in the selection. The stage scenery is all "boxed-in" and no entrances need be made from the flies. . . .

The theatre was on the top floor of a three-story building, the banking house of J. B. Wheeler & Company and stores occupying the lower floors.

Fire gutted the auditorium in 1912. I was told the day I climbed the steep stairs and peered into the charred interior. The entire stage with its flanking proscenium boxes was gone as well as most of the seats on the main floor but the graceful, curved balcony remained. In 1947 the Opera House was restored sufficiently to permit it to be used, a new stage, masking-screens and wooden benches transforming its bare interior into a summer theatre. Modern players and dancers perform where once such performances as *The Three Musketeers, The Sign of the Cross, Faust,* and *The Taming of the Shrew* were given and where the Elk's Benefit Minstrels produced *It Is To Laugh,* advertised as "A Regular Blizzard of Fun."

Even before the opening of the Opera House, there were variety theatres in the city, the Rink Opera House giving in a single week, *Shavogne or the Bould Boy of '98, Father and Son, Pygmalion and Galatea, Fanchon the Cricket,* and *The Two Orphans.* Not all plays brought to the city were well done or well received:

> The dramatic atrocity with which an effort was made to impress upon the amusement seekers of Aspen the magic of Haggard's Graphic deliniation made its escape via the Midland on Sunday and it is to be inflicted on the unfortunate people of Pueblo tonight. As a failure the company are a histrionic climax and the remainder of the circuit is entitled to heart felt sympathy.

Besides going to the theatre Aspen amused itself in other ways:

> Foreman Talbot of the Mollie Gibson was agreeably surprised by the presence at the property of a number of young ladies who demanded a lesson on the underground operations of a mine and who made the drifts chime with merry laughter.

Then, too, there was always the Bathing Train. Glenwood, with its famous swimming pool and hot springs was only a few miles away and the railroad ran an excursion trip which left Aspen at six p. m. and returned at ten, "Fare round trip including bath, $2.00."

Aspen's several papers covered the news both vividly and picturesquely as a few headlines and items from the *Evening Chronicle* of 1888 show:

THE JAWS OF GRIM GIANT
SHOCKING FATE OF A PROSPECTOR IN FRYING PAN GULCH

> . . . Prospector almost devoured by a blast of giant. The blast didn't go off so he hit it with his pick . . . His partner keenly realized the absolute frailty of physical manhood and with tears blinding his eyes at the awful spectacle, he appealed to his neighbors. The miner was then taken in a blanket stretcher to a freight train which landed in Aspen at 3 A.M.

DROWNED IN ROARING FORK

> not for some minutes was it definitely ascertained whose child it was that had vanished like a bauble on the ruffled bosom of the stream, so that the spectacle that was hastily sketched by the hand of doubt was of unique pathos.

AN UNGOVERNABLE ANIMAL CREATES A STAMPEDE
AND DEMOLISHES THE LUCKLESS DRIVER.
A LIVELY RUNAWAY.

> . . . the collision of the two delivery wagons was very violent and in the shock, young Everett, driver of the runaway conveyance, was thrown several feet in the air, descending with almost fatal effect.

"BLADES AND BULLETS" was the headline of an article describing a street fight; "HORROR HAUNTED HILLS" told of a mine accident; and "A DUEL AT DUSK. A SAVAGE ENCOUNTER BETWEEN A DESERTED HUSBAND AND THE DASHING PARAMOUR," needs no explanation.

Crime in Aspen seems to have centered at Aspen Junction and along Durant Ave., for, as the paper says:

> Aspen Junction is where a number of saloons raise their gables to mark the progress of civilization, and the gilded flies are cast alluringly before the unwary stranger. . . It was here that a man was fleeced of his money by a woman known throughout the district as the Oregon Shortline.
>
> The Grand Jury has subpoenas for as many as twenty-four women of the town who have come before them and explained their manner of conducting business in the city of Sulphurets. . . . The nymphs put on their best clothes and endeavored to make as much capital as they could out of the event, parading into the courtroom four abreast, swishing their skirts and tossing their heads in the most approved fashion.

The reason for indicting these women was to try to get them to move from Durant Ave., so that the property there would be more valuable for business and residence purposes.

Aspen had religion and culture from the start, the first Sunday School and the first Literary Society having been established by Mrs. Gillespie shortly after her arrival in the camp, while she and her husband were living in a large canvas tent. (Years later they built the elaborate frame house with the octagonal tower and leaded glass windows which I had been shown through.) Aspen's churches represented the leading denominations, and added to the city's life by their socials, entertainments and benefits. Its lodges and societies included the Masons, Odd Fellows, Knights of Pythias, Good Templars and Caledonian Club.

Fire, the threat of all camps, was guarded against in Aspen by six companies. A series of pistol shots served as a fire alarm, until a fire bell was installed in the rustic pavilion which is still standing in the middle of the square.

On the Fourth of July, 1888, the Aspen Hose No. 1 held its Fifth Annual Ball at the Rink Opera House, "rendering the event one of *eclat* and happy abandon . . . till an early hour when the guests returned crowned with enjoyment." That afternoon people had hurried to the new Race Track (which was opened by members of the Jockey Club), crowding the new grandstand. It was

> while the entries in the pony race were being jogged by their mountmen and the pool crier was rising with the band for the attention of the crowd, that the boards and pillars of the stand began to tremble (amid) a surging fusion of cries from women and children. . . . A lady fainted and found that a limb had been broken between the ankle and knee joint. . . . The grandstand is to be reconstructed on a more secure principle.

By evening most of the visitors returned to Glenwood Springs by the excursion train whose "coaches, elaborately festooned, were almost obscured by the symbols of American freedom."

(240)

Christmas Eves were equally enjoyable, with "jostling throngs on Cooper and Hyman Avenues" and long lines of people at the post office waiting for mail or presents. Long before closing time the meat markets were sold out of "suckling pigs, opossums, wild turkeys and ducks." High Mass was celebrated at St. Stephens's, after which "the wedding march from Lohengrin was given with electric force."

In 1892 and the beginning of 1893 Aspen was the greatest silver camp in the world. The population, which in 1880 had been 35, was now 11,000. Two railroads vied with each other to handle the freight and passenger service of the city, ten passenger trains arriving and departing daily. There were streetcars, both horse and electric, as well as 6 newspapers, 10 churches and 3 banking houses. According to *Leslie's Illustrated Newspaper*, Aspen's

> . . . fortunate miners and business men have their own princely homes which adorn her beautiful thoroughfares and make her a marvel to strangers coming into the heart of the Rocky Mountains. The climate is good, clear and dry in winter with a bracing tenacity conducive to good health and longevity . . . there is a street railway . . . and all other concomitants of an advanced civilization. (February 22, 1890)

Aspen became the "leading commercial center between Salt Lake and Denver," and for two decades its mines produced silver, lead and other metals, reaching an annual average output of $6,000,000. Surely Aspen was secure. And then in 1893 the bottom dropped out; and like all the silver camps, Aspen was stunned and temporarily ruined. Gradually the city came back, partly because the mine owners of the district "took a stand which kept the industry from striking bottom" by agreeing to pay the miners $2.50 a day. In this way the miners were not thrown out of work. Old properties were tunneled and profitable ore bodies, at new depths, uncovered in many of the mines. The Free Silver shaft, constructed in 1896, to cut rich ore at great depth in the Smuggler and Mollie Gibson, was successful. The Cowenhoven tunnel, over two miles in length, was strictly a "revenue project," through which ore from the Bushwhacker, Park-Regent, and other mines was hauled. By 1897, 2000 miners were steadily employed, and all the big mines except the Argentum, Juniata and Smuggler were being worked, in whole or in part, by lessees. According to one writer:

> The history of undaunted courage contending for years against the stern forces of nature and wresting vast treasure of silver after many days, from the clenched fist of granite fingers . . . continued.

The Smuggler and the Free Silver shafts were flooded in 1910. Deep workings and underground water, coupled with inadequate pumping facilities, caused the water to rise until certain levels were submerged and production was curtailed. When pumping in these areas was stopped water poured in and covered the pumps.

Elias Cohn, general manager of the Smuggler and Aspen mines had theories about unwatering these mines and believed, that if deep sea divers could reach the submerged pumps and start them, the mines could be drained. Unless this was done the mines would have to shut down. At first his idea was scoffed at, but finally the company agreed and sent for two divers from New York, who were paid $100 a day from the time they left until their return.

They arrived in December and spent two weeks sizing up the situation. Aspen was tense. There was no Christmas spirit. If this scheme didn't work, it would mean the death of Aspen. People greeted each other with the words, "Merry Christmas! What's the depth of the water?" On the twenty-fourth the divers descended through sixty feet of water to reach the pumps and before noon reached the bottom, started the pumps, and immediately the water level began to lower. A sleigh, sent down from the mine entrance for Mr. Cohn, took him to the main office, where his health was drunk in iced champagne. The city was jubilant, and the divers left on the afternoon train.

Aspen had a very merry Christmas, but two days later the pumps became clogged with debris and stopped again. The divers were wired for, and returning once more, set the pumps in motion. A diving suit was purchased by the mine, and the professional divers trained certain miners how to use it in case of future emergencies. Finally a new pump was installed and the danger was past.

During World War I and up to the 1920's mining fell off, and the city became quiet as more and more people moved away and fewer mines operated. In December, 1926, the editor of the *Aspen Daily Times* wrote: "Until Dear Old Aspen shows some dependable sign of 'coming back' and our millionaire mine owners show some disposition to help the town that made them rich, we bid you farewell."

As years passed Aspen became a tourist center in the summer—its fishing streams, its incomparable scenery and its many trails and excellent climate attracting nature lovers; but it was a quiet shell of the city it had been, and one train a day arrived where ten had once come chuffing in.

Then the mountainsides began to attract skiers, and weekend enthusiasts skimmed over the snowy slopes and stamped through the lobby of the Jerome Hotel. Next came the war, and the Tenth Ski Division, stationed at Camp Hale, came over on weekends to glide down Aspen Mountain. In 1945, Walter Paepcke, Chicago business man, dreamed a dream, and the metamorphosis of Aspen began. His plan was to make the city a year round playground, and to do this he began to restore the empty business blocks and private homes. He redecorated the Jerome Hotel, and in January, 1947, he reopened Aspen as a new pleasure resort. If Aspen's past was built on silver its future was to be built on tourists.

The episode of the divers is typical of the undying spirit of Aspen, which in its newest phase again leads an era, this time of sports.

Ruby   On every trip over Independence Pass I looked longingly up Lincoln Gulch, for somewhere on that narrow, rocky road was Ruby, a small mining camp. Once, I even crossed the rickety wooden bridge and drove a few hundred feet along the road, just to convince myself that it was as bad as it looked! Now, in the fall of 1947 I was off to Ruby in a jeep—my first ride in one.

Bracing my feet against the sides of the vehicle, I watched the scenery

RUBY INDEPENDENCE

fly past as our driver, whom we had hired to take us to Ruby in this contraption, skimmed up Independence Pass to the turnoff at the Grottos and then slowed down to a respectable speed of five miles an hour as we began the ten-mile ascent back into Lincoln Gulch.

For miles the road wound through a forest, at times within sight and sound of a rushing stream and again passing between huge rocks or thickets of wild raspberries. This old mine road is rarely traveled and is not kept up, so in certain parts all of its surface was washed off, leaving ledges of rock-like steps, to be mounted by the four-geared wonder in which we were riding. After about six miles, we left the timber and entered a high valley through which ran a large irrigation ditch. The water filled a small reservoir, from which it was carried by flume to the valley ranches miles away. Crossing the breast of the dam, we came to a house where the gatekeeper of the reservoir lives. While he talked with us, his wife canned peaches, whose fragrance made us so hungry that I thought woefully of the small lunch we had packed.

Leaving the reservoir, we climbed four more miles up the long, green valley, on either side of which rose rocky slopes whose tops were above timber line. Beyond these slopes were the peaks, ragged and snowcapped. Just about a mile from Ruby, cabins appeared, tucked in the trees or built beside the trail, and as we drove closer to our destination, the cabins became more numerous. At last we passed a dilapidated mill, a big stable and half a dozen sturdy log buildings set up and down the hillside. I was out of the jeep almost before it stopped and on my way up the hill to the mill, pad and pencil ready for sketching. Passing a cabin with a tall brick chimney, I pushed open its door and found I was in the assay office, complete with furnace, cupels and all other equipment needed to test ore. While I sketched Mr. Hansen, our driver, pointed out the trail to Petroleum Lake and told us what he knew about the Ruby mine. It had been a silver property producing ruby silver, and was worked around 1900. The very size of its mill and boarding house and the number of surrounding buildings showed that it was considered the most promising property in the Lincoln Gulch district; but like so many mines, its development was retarded by its inaccessibility to a railroad or smelter and by its difficult road. The county built the one we had come over about 1916 but didn't attempt to keep it up. Back in 1889 the Galena Belle, near Ruby, was producing, and a few miners stayed at the property until late in the fall.

"I thought you might want to see this," said Mr. Hansen handing me an old newspaper clipping dated November 2, 1889, which read:

AWFUL EXPERIENCE OF JAMES HACKET WHILE ON HIS WAY TO LINCOLN

. . . James Hacket while on the road to Lincoln Gulch with a large cargo of provisions for the Galena Belle mine at Lincoln was caught in a blizzard. The sky was threatening but he kept on. Snow began to fall, faster and faster. Night fell. Hacket soon wandered from the trail and abandoning his journey, resigned himself to a night with the hissing blizzard. . . . Fighting the shafts of frost that ate their way into his fast freezing limbs, he kept up a rotary motion, until benumbed by the dancing blasts, he sank on the cold pillow of snow. Arousing himself again from the fatal drowsiness that was gradually overcoming his senses, he resumed his movement which was kept up until morning. The trail was then recovered and pushing on he arrived half living, half dead at the Galena Belle cabin. His feet and ears were badly frozen.

Our return trip took nearly as long as the trip in, for the road was so full of ruts and stones that even the jeep had to take it carefully. Half way to the timber a mountain shower drenched us, and even with the water running in streams from our hat brims and dripping off our elbows we were glad to be in an open jeep rather than in one with a top, for the scenery was too gorgeous to peer at through a windshield. Long before we reached the Grottos and climbed back to the main highway the sun was out and we were dry again.

It is much more thrilling to approach this ghost town from the top of Independence Pass than from the Aspen side, for just as you begin to round the upper curves of the ledge road, west of the summit of the 12,095-foot pass you see far below, a little group of weathered cabins.

"That's Independence," said Boyd, who was driving. "It once had a population of 2000, and now look at it."

We drove carefully down the mountain road until the cabins lay in a meadow just below the highway, and pulling off the road, we stopped to examine them. Rows of empty log house-frames, a few with battered-in roofs or tipsy gables, lined what had once been streets. Grass grew as high in the road ruts as on the more level ground. Some of the cabins were quite large and had obviously been stores or hotels and others were tiny. An old boiler and some mine machinery lay neglected, not far from the center of town, and a few prospect holes showed on the sides of the hills.

Independence was a gold camp of 1879, which went by many names, such as Chipeta, Mammoth City, Mount Hope, Farwell and Sparkill, until Dick Irwin and the miners named it Independence after the Independence lode which had been struck on the Fourth of July. The Independence became the leading mine, and its "brest of pay ore" continued fairly uniform for some years. The Farwell group of mines produced too, and although after a few years the camp was nearly deserted, some mining continued until 1900. A slight revival was experienced in 1907 and 1908, when stagecoaches drawn by six horses drew up in front of the one eating place and unloaded prospectors, eager to hunt for new lodes. A few years later only two or three buildings were occupied (and they were saloons), and when they closed only one man was left. He lived the year round in his cabin and "held all the town offices," telling strangers who drifted in about the early days when Concord coaches dashed by en route to Aspen bringing with them a "singing tide of gold suckers." "Who knows?" he would say. "Independence may equal Leadville yet."

The drive over Independence Pass is exciting even today, over the present road, and I never drive it without thinking of the little old lady who told me about going to Aspen as a bride and of how she was driven there over the old road in a sleigh in the dead of winter!

CHAPTER TEN

Off the Beaten Track

DURING World War II, I heard about Holy Cross City. It was inaccessibly tucked away at an elevation of 11,-335 feet and was at the end of an abandoned wagon road. Furthermore, it was within the limits of the army reservation where Camp Hale was being built for the training of Ski Troops. Had word not reached me that it was being considered part of a bombing range, I might have been content to wait for the end of the war and then ferret it out, but fearing that it might become a target, I determined to get to it first. That meant "crashing" the army post by requesting permission from the Major to be allowed to hike up to

Gold Park
Holy Cross
City

the ghost town. In answer to letters I received courteous but evasive refusals, based on the supposition that it would not be safe or wise to explore the spot while so much construction was going on and while the roads were torn up.

Then in 1942, while on a "ghost hunting" trip with Jim and Victoria, I drove through Red Cliff which is near the deserted camp, and learning from the postmaster that it had been deserted "for a generation," I asked him how it could be reached.

"It can't," he replied flatly with a nostalgic sigh. "I own all the land at Gold Park, which is four miles below Holy Cross City, and even I can't get in; but I'll show you pictures of Gold Park if you're interested." Producing some snapshots from his wallet, he pointed out the cabins and the big Community House, which was still standing.

When we left him we were the more determined to see both Gold Park and Holy Cross City, and driving up to the government gate at the edge of the camp we began negotiations. Of course we were refused admittance, but I was permitted to phone to the Major, who was understanding and said we might drive as far as Gold Park but that we must be outside the gate before dark.

"I know Holy Cross City," he added. "I flew over it in a bomber last week."

"Were there any buildings standing?" I interrupted breathlessly.

"I don't know. We were going at three hundred miles an hour," he replied. "We're making an artillery range out of all this you know."

In no time Jim had the car on the Homestake Creek road headed for Gold Park. There were no cabins along the way, only flocks of sheep; and after ten miles of nuzzling through them, we reached the end of the road.

Gold Park consisted of eight or ten cabins and the two-story Community House—the cabins dotted over a meadow and the large building in the edge of the timber. A trail at the end of the auto road was marked by several signs which read, "Fancy Pass 6 miles; Hunky Dory Lake 4 miles; Holy Cross City 4 miles." I looked longingly up the steep trail, which disappeared in a grove of aspen. There wasn't time to take it and get back to the gate before dark, but someday I'd go up it.

Both Gold Park and Holy Cross City sprang up at about the same time as the Leadville excitement, but their boom was brief. Prospectors had neglected this part of the country until an old Frenchman, who had been living at the foot of the mountain for several years, babbled about the gold float that lay thick around his cabin. Then the rush was on. During the spring of 1880 prospectors explored the slopes of Homestake Mountain and French Peak, staking off claims and finding an abundance of float, which promised rich gold deposits nearby. Homestake Creek was also found to be rich in placer gold, and before long it too was staked off for nearly its entire length. During the summer, claims were located on the mountainsides, but before they could be developed winter set in and the holes were abandoned till spring. The New Year's edition of the *Summit County Times* of 1881 carried an article about the district which brought scores more of optimistic miners scurrying to the mountains.

As a result of these reports the camp of Gold Park grew during 1881 until it had a population of 400, a postmaster, a notary, a shoemaker, a general store, two hotels—the Gold Park and the Homestake—a lumber and transfer company, several saloons, and a forty-stamp mill, run by the Gold Park Mining and Milling Company. As soon as the D. & R. G. road was completed to Red Cliff, a daily stage and mail service was established, and mail was carried to Holy Cross City also.

During 1882 mining continued, the Gold Park Mining Company holding many claims and operating two mills, one at Holy Cross City and the other at Gold Park. These two were connected by an iron flume two and a half miles long, which carried ore from the mines and mill at the upper city to the mill at Gold Park. But by 1883 the quality and quantity of ore found at both camps was not sufficient to warrant further investments, and property after property was deserted. Even the mills closed down. By the end of 1883 only one elderly couple remained in Gold Park, while H. W. Roby, the resident manager of the Mining Company, and his family were the only inhabitants left in Holy Cross City.

The latter was never as large as Gold Park, but it had its mill, boarding-house, general store, post office and bunch of cabins as well as a justice of the peace and an assayer. Gold was found in "twelve foot crevices with eighteen inch veins, some of it assaying as high as thirty ounces in gold near the surface." Millions of dollars were spent in the Holy Cross district, both at Holy Cross City, at Missouri Camp, six miles away, and at Camp Fancy on Fancy Creek. By 1883 a number of bodies of ore had been developed, but the "actual yield had been almost nothing," and one by one the Belle of the West, the Backus, the Tip Top and the Hunkidori mines were forgotten.

As the summer progressed the memory of the trail to Holy Cross City haunted me. I *had* to climb it and see what was left of the old camp before it was too late. The Major at Camp Hale and I exchanged more notes, but he still refused me permission to enter the camp. When the summer was nearly over I grew desperate. Perhaps if I could see the Major I could talk my way in. It was at least worth a try.

Taking a friend with me, I again reached the gate on a Saturday afternoon, just as the work crews were quitting and cars were tearing madly in every direction. Telling the guard that I wanted to see the Major I waited for a pass of admittance. Instead of issuing one he shook his head and said, "You can't see him. He's in conference with some brass hats from Washington. Has been all day."

"What are the chances of seeing him tomorrow?"

"None, he goes fishing."

"What's the chance of seeing him tonight?"

"Pretty slim. He may be in conference until ten P. M. Your only hope would be to see him between conferences."

"Let me go to his office and I'll wait."

"You can't take this woman in with you," said the guard eying my friend suspiciously. So Florence was left at the gatehouse with other marooned visitors, and I drove through, angling my way between trucks and cars which were so enveloped in clouds of dust that they were almost upon me before I could see them. At headquarters the only available parking space was in front of a NO PARKING sign, but by then nothing bothered me and I drew up in front of it. The barracks-like administration building seemed empty at first, but I discovered a secretary and asked for the Major. He was still in conference, but I was ushered into the presence of a Captain, to whom I told my story and presented my credentials. He read them slowly, while I waited in an agony of suspense. Looking up with a smile he said, "I don't see why you shouldn't go up there. If I weren't so busy I'd go with you." As the Captain started to write out a pass for me, I remembered Florence back at

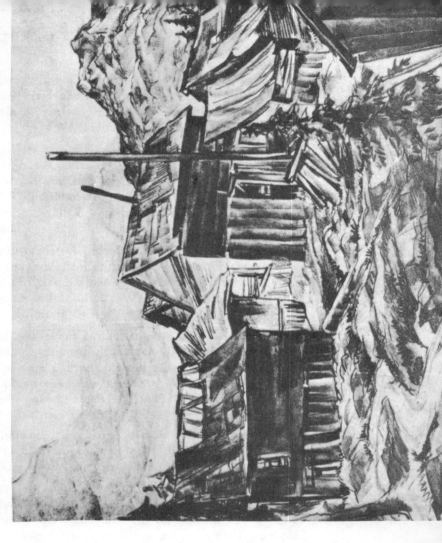

DUTCH TOWN

MILL, HOLY CROSS CITY

GOLD PARK

the gate. "I'm not alone. There a young woman and her little daughter with me. They'll have to come too," I said confidently, although my knees shook for fear he wouldn't let them. He reached for a second piece of paper. "What are their names?" he asked patiently.

Back at the gate I waved the passes at Florence and we started back to Leadville for the night. Next morning we drove along Homestake Creek to Gold Park where I left the car with my two companions. Not until my return did either of us realize how foolhardy it was for me to hike alone to timberline, leaving a woman who couldn't drive a car alone in a completely empty town with a two-year old child, ten miles from the highway.

At ten-fifteen I set off for Holy Cross City, carrying a pad and pencil and a bag of lunch. I was scared, for I'd never hiked alone to a strange place and I'd heard too much about the dangers of climbing alone in the mountains for fear of turning an ankle or falling. But since it was a case of going alone or not going at all, I was willing to try it.

The trail was easy to follow, for it was the old wagon road, but it was steep and rough, with a surface of small rocks and stones which slipped underfoot. For the first mile it switchbacked up the side of the mountain through young aspens, whose branches were not dense enough to shut out the sun. Far below was Gold Park, its cabins looking like toys and the car like a mere blue spot.

I had started hiking at about ten thousand feet elevation, and the heat, the steep grade and the altitude slowed me down and made me stop frequently. While I waited for my heart to quiet down I talked to myself saying:

"You are a complete ninny. Why aren't you satisfied to stay home and not get into places like this? It's no fun climbing up here, and no one is making you do it." At the same time the other half of me egged me on by saying: "Go on, go on, you'll never get a chance like this again. You're a fool but go on. Nothing will happen to you."

It got so hot and the trail was so steep that it was necessary to stop and rest every fifty feet. I'd look ahead and think, "I'll try and make it to the next patch of shade before I stop to breathe again," and as I spoke I'd gasp on. I looked for animals, but except for marmots which whistled at me and chipmunks which scurried over rocks, I saw no signs of life. It was a strange sensation, to be all alone in such big country, surrounded by nothing but rocks, trees, clouds, wind—the only person in the midst of a vast, pulsing silence.

Finally, the road cut through a stand of tall timber. It was less steep here, and the pine needles were easy to walk on and smelled fragrant. Through a break in the trees I saw the summit of the mountain miles away, and on its very top hung two or three shaft houses. They gave me both hope and despair; hope that I was going in the right direction, and despair because they looked so far away.

As I got nearer to the camp I began to wonder what I'd find there. A friend who had made this trip had written about it, saying:

I've been to Holy Cross City. It is a good four mile hike up a pleasant valley. (Where was the Valley?) The camp is arranged differently from most. First you come to the mill. Above that is the two-story boarding house and above that, in the last patch of timber, are the cabins where the miners lived. Above the cabins, above timberline, on the mountain tops are the mines and shaft houses.

I trudged on. The grove of trees was behind me now and the country more open, with great slabs of grey rock everywhere and small, stunted timberline evergreens growing out of crevices between the rocks. A gushing stream cascaded down between the rocks, and lying on the bank I drank from it. At a fork in the road there was a government marker. I was almost afraid to look at it, for if it said: "Holy Cross City 2 miles" I knew I couldn't make it. The marker read: "Hunky Dory Lake 1 mile, Holy Cross City 1 mile," and turning to the left I plodded on. "If I count my steps it will keep me from thinking about how tired I am," I thought, beginning to count up to 5280.

The view on all sides was breathtaking, for I was so high that range after range of mountains rose on all sides. The air was now crisp and cool and the ledge road, almost level. "One thousand twenty-nine, one thousand thirty," I counted on. After about three thousand I turned a corner and saw a cabin with a washbasin sitting on a shelf outside it. Further down the road was the mill. "Holy Cross City at last," I thought and hurried ahead.

If I hadn't been used to camps at timberline I would have turned and fled when I reached the mill, for the wind was blowing and everything rustled and sighed and rattled and whined and fluttered. The road ran right beside the mill, so close that I could look into its dark interior. I never go into mills or old buildings unless I'm certain that the floors will hold me, and I certainly had no intention of entering any of these skeletons and perhaps vanishing down some shaft. Knowing the camp had been deserted for a generation, I wasn't trusting any rotten timbers, so walking rapidly past the mill I turned the corner. There stood the boardinghouse, sadly dilapidated, and with a jaunty "Johnny" askew at one side, propped up with a tree trunk. Climbing up past the boardinghouse I came to the handful of cabins, half hidden in the last patch of timber. Beyond them were the bare, rocky peaks with the shaft houses of the mines clinging to them like woodpeckers against a tree.

Having made sketches of the various buildings, I started back, swinging down the trail until I reached the last mile. There the grade was stiff, and the gravel loose, causing me to slide at each step, and by then I knew that I had blisters on both heels. For the first time I was glad to be alone so that I could limp all I wanted to! The last stretch seemed the longest, but at quarter of two I reached the car, took off my boots and lay down in the shade too tired to talk. Later that afternoon we drove through Red Cliff, over Vail Pass and home, exhausted but exultant.

Nowadays the tourist looks down on Red Cliff from a new concrete bridge, whose graceful span arches the Eagle River, but years ago the road from Tennessee Pass ran along the bottom of the canyon, crossing both the railroad and the river, and after passing through the length of the town.

Red Cliff

(251)

climbed a narrow shelf road onto Battle Mountain. Red Cliff is not a ghost town, but it was mining that caused it to spring up at the junction of Turkey Creek and the Eagle River, back in 1879 when miners from Leadville came pushing into the region in search of more silver ore.

The first discoveries were on Battle Mountain and on Horn Silver Mountain, where before the end of the season claim stakes bristled all over the steep slopes. A cabin was built on the site of Red Cliff, stocked with provisions and liquors, and the miners' tents were pitched nearby.

In September, 1879, when news of the Meeker Massacre reached the miners, a log fort was hastily built for protection and a scouting party was sent out, but no Indians were found. Until a sawmill was set up on Turkey Creek, the camp consisted of tents and ten or fifteen log cabins. When the first log was sawn on March 17, 1880, it was "bound to the back of a burro, decorated with evergreens in honor of St. Patrick's Day, and was followed to town by a very respectable procession." All the participants became drunk before the day was over, even the burro.

Wm. B. Thom, editor of the first newspaper, the *Eagle Valley Shaft*, later called the *Red Cliff Comet*, told many stories of the early days of the camp.

The first grave was dug for a man attacked by a bear. The first funeral was held in 1880. A man was crushed by a falling tree, and the camp decided to give him the best funeral possible. There was no lumber to be had, but a coffin was made from some packing cases and an old wagon box. There was no minister, but a lawyer agreed to deliver a suitable oration, followed by a prayer spoken feelingly by a Confederate soldier. "At the appointed hour every man in camp reverently appeared in his best clothes" and attended the service. The body was then placed in the new cemetery and the miners went back to work. A few weeks later two prospectors from Astor Flats got in a quarrel and killed each other. Their friends brought the bodies to Red Cliff and asked for a similar burial, but the miners refused to desecrate their new cemetery with the bodies of murderers, and the friends of the deceased "finally buried them with their boots on, beside the original Battle Mountain road."

An inmate of a dancehall, who was called Big Hat, becoming "maudlin, cast herself in Turkey Creek to end it all," but perhaps because of her befogged condition, she chose a spot where the water was only four inches deep. In spite of her efforts to drown, she was rescued by the miners.

By the fall of 1881, when the railroad reached Red Cliff, the little settlement had three business houses and five hotels, of which the Star, with its imported chef, was considered the best. A brass band was organized and was in great demand for dances, which were held in a hall over the store. On one occasion a concert of classical music was received with stony silence. The pianist was furious and struck up "Chippy Get Your Hair Cut," a popular tune of the day which was received with cheers. "She Stoops to Conquer" was presented by home talent, and the Vincent Dramatic Company played one week for several summers at the Red Cliff Opera House, their repertoire including "Josh Whitcomb" and "Hazel Kirke."

In 1884 Red Cliff was snowbound, traffic to Leadville being cut off for

FULFORD

↓ HOTEL AND STORE, FULFORD

several weeks. During this time the newsprint at the *Shaft* office was used up; but rather than miss an issue of the paper, it was printed on wallpaper, the copy of April 5 using a dotted background covered with sprays of ivy. A headline read: "Still More Snow. . . . A More Perfect and Complete April **Fool** Could Not Be Imagined."

Gilman   North of Red Cliff the highway climbs twelve hundred feet up Battle Mountain, so named because in 1849 it served as the battleground for two war parties of Ute and Arapahoe Indians. At the top of the mountain is Gilman, a company town whose houses are perched along the steep sides of the cliffs. Far below, beside the river, is the mill, past which run the D. & R. G. main line tracks, twisting through the narrow canyon of the Eagle River. Between the mill and the town is an interminable flight of steps zigzagging up the sheer face of the mountain, on which the miners used to climb to and from their work.

Gilman was founded in 1886 and was named for Henry M. Gilman, a mining man who represented eastern capital in the district. The original camp "grew from the overflow of silver seekers from Leadville," the nearest town, and at first was called Clinton, Battle Mountain, and Rock Creek. These early prospectors swarmed over the mountain in 1879, staking claims and digging shafts in more than one hundred prospect holes. Most of the mines worked in the early days produced silver, except the Ground Hog which contained gold in nugget form.

Halfway between Red Cliff and Gilman was Bell's Camp, an early mining and logging camp (also called Cleveland), and on the north side of the mountain was Astor City. It contained lots of tents and "wickiups" and two cabins, one of which was a store and the other, beside the road at the foot of the long hill, a saloon called Saint's Rest.

James A. Burnell, one of the founders of the *Leadville Chronicle*, sold his interest in the paper in 1879 and went to Red Cliff. He purchased several undeveloped mining claims, among them the Iron Mask, situated high on Battle Mountain near what is now Gilman.

This mine, Gilman's most valuable property, was responsible for much of the town's growth, the population reaching three hundred in 1899. That year half of the town was destroyed by a fire which razed the Iron Mask Hotel, the schoolhouse, several stores and residences, and the Bell mine's shaft house and machinery. During its best years the town had a newspaper, the *Gilman Enterprise*, and a dramatic club which provided entertainment for the community.

In 1890 it produced a State Legislator, Obediah M. Warner who, although not looked upon as a suitable candidate, was nominated and elected. Not long afterwards, being accused of "obtaining $500 under false pretenses," the sheriff of Eagle County went to Denver to bring the Hon. Mr. Warner back to the county seat for trial. That evening the two left by train for Red Cliff and since the sheriff had known Warner for a long time, he did not handcuff him. The two men lay down in opposite berths but Warner only pretended to be asleep, and after awhile rose, dressed, and went out on the platform. "At last a halt was made at a lonely switch. He stepped off . . . and next thing he knew the train was a mile and a quarter away. . . ." When the sheriff awoke "the pathetic lines, 'Empty is the Cradle, Baby's gone' came to his mind with startling force." It was later believed that by this ruse Warner not only evaded the law but gladly got away from his wife.

No one told me that to reach Fulford it was necessary to go through private land, open three gates between pastures and climb a ledge road, so the first time I drove up Brush Creek looking for it I landed in an abandoned CCC camp, beyond which the road was flooded by beaver dams.

The next time, I inquired at Brush Creek Lodge, a resort that advertised chicken dinners, and learned from the proprietress that the road to Fulford crossed her land and that the camp was three miles further on, up the mountain. Three miles didn't sound like much of a drive, but what a three miles it was! First the road crossed some fenced pastures, and after leaving them it zigzagged up the side of a mountain through underbrush and timber—a road so narrow that the leaves and branches brushed the sides of the car. Fortunately, my car was short enough to turn without having to back up on the sharp corners, but each switchback had a little turnout and bruised shrubbery, where cars had pressed into the bank. Coming out on a small clearing, we went through another gate and then stopped to let the engine cool and to ask further directions from a Basque sheepherder who was grazing his flock in the meadow. The next mile was across a level, marshy meadow, at the end of which was an insecure-looking log bridge across a roaring stream. Beyond was the camp, with roof tops hidden among the trees and bushes, and one long, meandering, grass-grown street. The houses on either side of it were in good condition, amazingly so for a deserted town, and I began to wonder how long the camp had been empty. The two largest buildings were an old hotel and a false-fronted store with a wooden sidewalk in front of it. Beyond the town rose the rugged top of New York Mountain toward which the road wound, disappearing among the trees. At the door of the hotel stood a woman, who with her mother, were the only occupants of the town. The mother was ninety-one; this was her old home and she liked to spend her summers in it; the two women had no car, but early each year friends drove them to Fulford, left them at the old hotel, and came after them at the end of the summer. While Elizabeth and Elliot talked to the younger woman I began to explore the buildings.

The store was boarded up, but by looking through the cracks between the boards I could see packages and cartons on the shelves. One corner of it had been the post office, and on top of the cubbyholes was a large stuffed eagle. Elliot, who had driven my car for me, asked if we could open the store but, although the lady had the key, she said "No." Instead, she gave him a crowbar and a hammer, so that by prying off a big board across one window, I could sketch through the glass. After I had made a drawing of the cluttered interior, he replaced the board and nailed it tight.

We trudged up the stony road to find the group of cabins in the upper end of town, passing an old mill and a spring on the way. There were not as many cabins above as in the Lower Town and they were not as big. One of them, which I learned later was an assay office, had a ridgepole at least

(255)

three feet in diameter. By looking through the crack in the door of another cabin we could see a pool table and a square piano.

After having made a complete tour of Fulford, we went back to the car, thinking of the chicken dinner we'd ordered served at the lodge below. Although we approached the rickety bridge carefully, we slid neatly off it into the streambed, with our front wheels rammed against a log and resting deep in mud. For an hour we tried every way to extricate ourselves. Finally, at the risk of ruining the pan under the car we tried backing up. That did it, but before we could cross the stream we had to rebuild the bridge, log by log. When we did reach Brush Creek Lodge how good that chicken tasted!

Several years after visiting Fulford, I received three letters from strangers who knew of my interest in the ghost mining-towns of the state; all of them had lived in Fulford and offered to give me information about the place. One lady wrote that she still spent part of every summer there and invited me to be her guest, promising to show me around that country. From Charles H. Hill I learned about "The Wheel," a huge arastra built in 1893 or 1894, not far from Fulford. It was on the Fool's Peak trail up Brush Creek, two or three miles from Yeoman Park. Near it were the remains of a cabin in which he and a friend spent a few days in 1928. His description read:

> The Wheel is the remains of a cabin and an old water powered gold processing mill. The wheel is about 20 feet in diameter by about 4 feet in width and was still resting on its enormous wooden bearings at that time. It could easily be turned by walking on the inside (like a squirrel in a cage) even though it did squeak and groan as tho it were being tortured.

But it was the third person, Mrs. John R. Barry, who gave me the most. Her father went to Fulford in 1890 just as the camp was starting and lived in a tent until he could build a house. The hotel which I had seen was built by her parents, and was named for them, the Lamming Hotel. Her mother ran it for twenty years, and she was the old lady whose other daughter had talked to us in 1942. The interior of the hotel was papered with rotogravure pages from the *Denver Post*, and the hotel became known for this unique decorating feature. Later I called on Mrs. Barry in Denver.

"Both Upper Town and Lower Town were built at the same time," she explained. "Upper Town was smaller but it had a log hotel, also built by my father, some boarding houses, saloons, a livery barn, a store and an assay office. The post office was originally in Upper Town but it was moved below later on. The cabin in which you saw the pool table was a saloon. There was no real cemetery, only a few graves in the meadow beyond the bridge in the Lower Town.

"Beyond Fulford in a little park below New York Mountain is another settlement called New York Cabins, which still has a few crumbling ruins. Above them was a boarding house and a mine, and farther still was the Polar Star property and its buildings. One mine was so inaccessible that its entrance could be reached only by climbing up a cable. East of Upper Town is Adelaide Park where a few old cabins are still standing."

Pulling out a photograph album, she showed me pictures of Fulford's schoolhouse in Lower Town, of the hotel half-buried in snow, of the cabins on New York Mountain and, best of all, of the huge arastra known as "The Wheel."

If ever a place had a tragic background it was Camp Fulford. The town was originally called Nolan's Creek Camp after an early prospector, who with another man discovered some rich mines in the vicinity in 1887. While making camp one night, Nolan crossed Brush Creek on a log, carrying his gun straight up. Then the trigger caught and the gun went off, cutting out his tongue. There was no one around to give him proper medical care, and he bled to death. The creek was then re-named Nolan's Creek and his name and the date of his death were blazed on an aspen tree.

The hills and mines around the camp are graves as well as storehouses of treasure, much of which has never come to light. Its early history is grim and consists of a succession of rich strikes, snowslides, deaths and lost mines. The *Denver Republican* of May 8, 1892, refers to the "evil genius about the place" and hints at the "Spirits of men who lie buried" at the base of grim old Slate Mountain, and it tells the first of the strange stories which are linked with the camp.

In the late summer of 1849 "Buck" Rogers organized a party of thirty men "at Bloomington and other Illinois towns" for the purpose of seeking a fortune in the California placer gold fields. They pushed on, and "when one hundred and seventy miles, or eight days' journey" beyond Pike's Peak, they again found "color" in the stream. Six of the men decided to remain and prospect, and in time were rewarded by finding rich nuggets of gold near the surface in paying quantities. After six weeks of digging they were in high grade ore, and "as fast as the ore was taken out it was stored in a drift until such time as it could be transported to market." They extracted gold which they estimated as worth between $60,000 and $100,000.

As their provisions ran low, and an early snow further isolated them, one of their number, Buck Rogers, was chosen to make the hundred and fifty mile trip to the nearest camp for supplies. He was given $500 in dust and nuggets. For seven days he battled blizzards, ultimately reaching the camp, where further storms delayed him two weeks more. During this time he drank up all the gold with which he was to have bought provisions and became a loafer around the saloons. But after six weeks had elapsed, he became worried and, fearing some disaster had befallen his companions, started back in search of them. Within five days he reached the creek. At first he doubted his eyes. During his absence, a terrific snowslide had crashed down the mountain, taking with it not only trees and rocks but also the cabin and the men. Worse still, the slide carried with it the whole surface of the mountain, leaving exposed a "smooth, polished stratum of solid slate." All that remained of the mountain was a huge mound. Its base, many acres in circumference, completely filled the gulch and buried the drift where the gold was stored. Horrified, Rogers went for help, but after many days of fruitless digging by the rescuers, the five miners were left in their "rocky and snowbound tomb." Rogers never recovered from this tragedy. He wandered from camp to camp, a broken man. In 1881 as he lay dying he told the preceding tale.

The second tale begins with Arthur H. Fulford for whom Camp Fulford was named, a member of a pioneer family who owned a ranch on Brush Creek during the eighties. After serving as Town Marshal at Red Cliff, he ran the Halfway House, a stage stop located on the Fulford ranch between Eagle and the gold camp. In 1891 he met a prospector claiming to have in his possession a notebook belonging to Rogers and containing a description of the location of the tomb of those who died in the 1849 snowslide.

This man had secretly searched for the place for several years and had finally arrived at Slate Mountain, where he found the bare face of rock and the mound of earth at the base. His digging resulted in the location of an abandoned tunnel in which he found "fragments of tools and parts of human bones," and the piled-up treasure of nuggets stored nearly fifty years before. These he quickly covered and then began looking for a partner who would help him get out the cache.

Fulford was skeptical until he saw the man's samples of ore. Two weeks later the man was killed in a drunken brawl in a Red Cliff saloon. Though still skeptical, Fulford searched for the man's cabin and in it found descriptive notes of the location. With these Fulford went to Aspen to consult a mining speculator and ex-prospector whom he hoped could help him to locate the drift. Outfitting for a long trip, he started back in September for Brush Creek. Presumably he got there and returned to the vicinity of the hidden gold, for months later a party of men reported having seen him in the gulches of Brush Creek. Fearful snowstorms cover the mountains in mid-winter, and during one of them word was received that Fulford had been caught in a slide on New York Mountain. Mrs. Barry told me that this happened on New Year's day in 1892, while he was on his way to jump some claims on which he knew assessment work had not been done the preceding year. Although she was only a small child at the time, she remembers his stopping at her mother's hotel in Fulford for food. That was his last meal. Whether Fulford had found the hidden treasure or was still searching for it is unknown, but with his death all clues to the location of the gold were lost again. Fifty men searched two weeks for his body, but it was never found.

Another interesting story of the region is told by Burt Pottinger in the *Denver Republican* of 1890. In 1886 two men stopped at the Fulford ranch, at the mouth of Brush Creek, secured horses and rode up the creek. They were gone several days; then returned and went away. A second and a third time they returned, procured horses and disappeared up Brush Creek, only to reappear after a few days at the Halfway House from which they rented their horses. On the last visit they told Mr. Fulford that they were searching for a lost mine and related to him the following incredible tale.

One night in 1881 an Irishman showed a Denver bartender gold nuggets and dust, which he asked the bartender to exchange for currency. The two men became friends, and later the Irishman confided to his Denver friend that he had killed his mining partner and that the body lay near the head of Brush Creek. He and his partner had quarrelled over dividing their rich strike and he had been forced to kill him in self-defense. He then gave a

CARBONATE

HAHN'S
PEAK

description of how to reach the mine, in which he said there was at least a million in gold to be found. The bartender never saw him again.

Before the bartender could use the information he became ill, and in order to compensate the doctor who tended him, told him the story of the lost mine and gave him a paper with a description of the route to it. The doctor tried in vain to locate the mine, and then showed the paper throughout the neighborhood, so that by 1890 nearly "every family along the Eagle River had a copy of it:"

> Take the D. & R. G. to Tennessee Pass; from there take wagon road and trail along Eagle River to mouth of Brush Creek. Follow up Creek 5 miles to the forks, then take east branch about 5 miles until you come to a shift of rocks, coming almost at the water's edge; from there you find on the right a dry gulch running north. Follow up the gulch until you come to 4 large trees standing close together, with the bark all taken off, about two feet around them. Turn due east and go directly up the hill until you strike a small hole dug in the ground and keep directly on until you come to another one and so on until you have reached the third one. This line is also marked by blazed trees on both sides. Here turn due north and about two hundred feet from the last blazed tree you will see three tall trees standing in a triangle. These trees have their tops broken off about thirty feet up. This is about 300 feet from timberline, and the vein runs about north and south from the place described. On the top of the hill you can see the Mt. of the Holy Cross and west, the Taylor River Range.

The descriptions were explicit and everything was found as described except the vein.

In 1892 the district attracted attention as a producer of gold ores; and over five hundred claims were staked. "Everything pans out gold, copper is plentiful and here and there are strong indications of silver and lead. The mining interests of Brush Creek alone are promising enough to warrant the belief that a fair-sized town will be someday built here," prophesied the optimistic miners.

By 1896 there was ore enough in sight in the Polar Star and the Cave mine to run a process plant for five years, and by 1901 and 1902 a twenty-five stamp amalgamating and concentrating mill was handling ores from the Mendota, Kittie B., New York, Adelaide and Layton.

The silver bcom came to Brush Creek in 1912 and 1913 and lasted up to 1918. During this boom the old log hotel in Upper Town was razed, and its logs were bought and used to timber the Lady Belle mine.

Fulford is quiet now, its streets overgrown and its cabins surrounded by willows. It is a peaceful place and a provocative place, tenanted in summer by one or two former residents, who return to relive the past and to ride the old trails up New York and Porphyry Mountains, or it is visited by restless men who stalk the hillsides, still looking for the gold hidden in its lost mines.

Carbonate   Somewhere up on the Flat Tops was Carbonate, a completely deserted camp that I learned about from deer hunters who had run across it one fall. Like so many others it grew out of the discovery of ore by two Leadville prospectors, who in 1878 crossed the Ute reservation and found on the surface of the ground evidence of carbonate deposits. In 1879 other parties explored the place, and since the land was part of the Ute Indian reservation, the

(260)

miners, fearing that Indians would find them on forbidden territory, built a block house, which they called Fort Defiance, a few miles from their diggings.

There was much prospecting in the spring of 1880, for George R. Ryan had sunk a shaft one hundred feet and in it had found large quantities of ore containing lead and silver. The report of his strike was greatly exaggerated but, as a result of it, hundreds of men flocked in from their winter headquarters at Dotsero, beside the Colorado River, where they were waiting for the snow to melt at the higher altitudes. During that spring and summer two thousand men visited the site, digging pit holes and taking out samples of ore to be assayed, but they discovered only low grade ore, too poor to warrant further development.

Up to the spring of 1883 not a house was built at the campsite. That year the Carbonate Town Company was formed, filing on 640 acres of land and surveying and platting 160 of them for a townsite. As soon as Garfield County was organized Carbonate Camp, or Carbonate City as it was called, became the county-seat, remaining so for four months, when the records were moved to the new seat at Glenwood Springs.

A few lots were sold; fifteen log houses, a store and a post office were built, and wagon roads were constructed up to the high park on top of the Flat Tops where the embryo town lay. But the rich strikes that were promised did not materialize, and by fall it was evident that the camp would not "develop into another Aspen." Low grade ores together with the difficulty of transporting them to the valley curtailed its development and by the end of 1883 it was a ghost town.

James L. Riland has left an account dated May 31, 1883, of life in the camp, in which he mentions bad weather and much snow and says that he dug the full length of his shopel and blade to make space in which to spread his blankets. He continues:

> a building for the printing outfit will be small as logs have to be moved from one eighth to one quarter of a mile and only small ones can be handled while the snow is hard in the mornings. . . . Sawmills will be here as soon as possible but being heavy must come near the last.
>
> The bridge over the Grand (Colorado), is not yet completed and the road up the mountains is only commenced. There are about a hundred men in the camp, a fine group, for it takes both nerve, muscle and money to get here. It has cost us $200 to get into the camp. . . . The miners met and signed articles for a union or league; mining claims to be 300 feet by 1500 feet. . . . We paid (to have our supplies brought in) five cents a pound from Red Cliff to Dotsero and from there to snowline six or seven cents per pound. From Coffee Pot Springs in via hand sled and man power, rates have been ten to fifteen cents per pound.

In 1884 E. E. Winslow procured a government contract to furnish daily mail service to Carbonate, Glenwood Springs and Carbondale. The trip to Carbonate added forty miles of poor and difficult road to the daily circuit and to Winslow's surprise, when he reached the remote camp, there was but one inhabitant there, an old miner who still believed in the place. When Winslow asked him how much he would take to move out, the old miner thought a while and then replied that he'd go for a hundred dollars. **Winslow** gladly paid over the money, the miner packed up his things and left, and with his departure Carbonate died.

In the fall of 1947 Francis and I set out to get to Carbonate, armed with maps, descriptions of the road given us by hunting friends, and the name of a guide who could take us in if we needed him. We stopped at Gypsum where Pierce Clark, the guide, lived, only to find that he worked for the county and was running a grader up near Eagle. We returned to Eagle and inquired as to his whereabouts at the county garage. "He's up Brush Creek five or six miles. You can't miss him," we were told, and sure enough, we found him and asked if he'd take us to Carbonate. It was a little hard to make the arrangements, for he was high up on his grader and we were below in the road, shouting over the noise of his machine, but it was finally settled that we were to be at Dotsero at six-thirty Sunday morning and he would be there with his pick-up truck. Since we were spending the weekend at Glenwood Springs, we had to rise at four A. M. so as to be at the rendezvous on time. Clark was there, and leaving our car beside the road, we climbed into his truck.

About a mile in from the highway we started up a twelve-mile climb to the summit of the Flat Tops. The road was a new one, built by the government to enable paper companies to remove diseased timber before it became worthless and before the beetles which had ruined it attacked more trees. Over three billion feet of this timber stands in the White River National Forest, killed by a plague of spruce bark beetles which have attacked all but the newest growth. Clark told us about the withered forests and the need for the road, part of which he had built, as we slowly climbed the steep shelf around the edge of the mountain. As we got higher, we could see for miles in every direction, as range after range of mountains melted into blue haze, with Mt. Sopris to the south and the gaunt Flat Tops to the north. We passed Coffee Pot Spring, which I had read about in Riland's report. We saw deer and quail as we neared the end of the new highway after miles of steady pulling. From there on no road existed, only six miles of wheeltracks twisting across the high meadow country. Over this we averaged five miles an hour, driving in low gear and dodging high centers, deep ruts and mud holes all the way.

Now that we were on top we could see the blasted forests in the distance— great trees completely brown, acre after acre of them, a truly terrible sight; for no remedy has been found for exterminating the beetle, and the Forest Service is afraid that other sections may be affected if this area is not removed quickly.

The truck rolled slowly down to Broken Rib Creek, crossed it, and pulled sharply up the opposite bank. It climbed slowly over rocky meadows where there was nothing to watch but the two faintly discernible tracks, indicating the way we should go. We passed a sheep-herder and his outfit and listened to the endless bleating of the lambs he was driving off the range at the end of the season to ship to market. All this time Clark was talking constantly, describing the country and pointing out spots where a certain buck had been shot or a certain campsite made. Finally he pointed out Carbonate ridge about a mile away, thickly timbered and faced with flat rocks. Leaving the wheeltracks, he drove across the broken land, maneuvering the truck around rocks and swampy spots until a two-foot wall of stone made further going impossible.

It was still about a quarter of a mile to the ridge, through sagebrush and low bushes or over slabs of grey rock. Close to it were the broken-down frames of several cabins and a marker stating that this was the site of Carbonate, the first county seat of Garfield County. "Some old timers say there was once three thousand here, and there used to be a lot more cabins," said Clark, "but most of them have been tore down."

Seeing more cabins among the trees, we climbed the ridge to examine them. One was larger than the rest and inside its rotting walls was a mine shaft, with a ladder sticking out of the black hole. Was this the Ryan shaft? None of us knew. Although there were few remnants of the camp left, I sketched what I found. Carbonate was different from any other place, for although other camps were just as high, the terrain here was relatively flat and the distant peaks were flat too. We were over 11,000 feet, and the air was thin and sharp.

The trip back was slow too, for the truck had to pick its way across the broken land with great care. But we let Mr. Clark do the driving, while we gazed at the complete semi-circle of jagged peaks blue-gray in the distance, and then down upon the gypsum hills and the ribbon of the Colorado River in its narrow valley. Far below, the enclosing mountains stretched out like a great topographical map printed in an almost unbelievable variety of colors— the pinks, lavendars, oranges, reds, browns, grays and greens of Colorado's rock formations. Back at Dotsero we thanked Clark for getting us to this inaccessible spot, the only mining camp in the Flat Top country, so lonely and yet so exciting.

Driving east from Eagle, we turned north at Wolcott and crossed miles of lonely wild country, past State Bridge, Yampa and Oak Creek, until we reached Steamboat Springs. North of the Springs half way to the Wyoming boundary is Hahn's Peak, a ranch town now, but originally the center of a mining district. Its wide grass-edged roads serve as streets, and its houses are widely scattered, low and rambling. Back of the town stretch long "ricks" of boulders, left by hydraulic operations and by ground sluicing. Most of the old buildings are gone (including the old courthouse), as they were sold for lumber to the ranchers or were swept by fire, so that today, except for some mounds of gravel, there is no sign of the mining boom which caused two camps to be built close to the gravel bars near Whisky Gap.

Hahn's Peak

Joseph Hahn, working his way west from Empire through wild, uncharted country, found traces of gold at the base of the peak, in Willow Creek, in the late autumn of 1862. Continuing his prospecting, he returned to the eastern side of the divide before snow covered the ground and during the winter of 1863 he told Wm. A. Doyle and Capt. George Way of his discovery. The three men agreed to organize a company; but it was the

(263)

spring of 1865 before they and their party of adventurers worked their way over the range and resumed prospecting around the high peak which Hahn had first seen. On this trip the mountain was named, Doyle climbing to its summit and placing there, in a can with a screw top, a written account of the journey, including dates and the statement: "This is Hahn's Peak by his friend and comrade Wm. A. Doyle, Aug. 27, 1865." By fall the men had "found gold on every side of the peak but not in sufficient quantities to pay to work with the pan."

Another version of the discovery of gold at the peak states that Capt. Way left Empire in 1864 and crossing the range found gold at the base of the peak. He returned to Empire and stayed with Lindstrom at his sawmill, where he met Joseph Hahn whom he told of his discovery.

The following spring Hahn, Way and Doyle worked their way through the rugged country to the gold field, and again in 1866 they made the trip, leading a company of fifty men into the unexplored region. Although it was June, the snow was six to eight feet deep and the men had to shovel a trail for their sleds and pack animals. By August, 1866, the party camped near Hahn's Peak, where some prospected while others built houses. Six gulches were named for the discoverers and the countries from which they came: Hahn's Gulch, German Gulch, Doyle's Gulch, Nova Scotia Gulch, Way's Gulch and Virginia Gulch. A mining district was organized with Hahn elected president. The rest of the summer of 1866 the men washed out considerable gold and staked many claims, but before snow closed the passes for the winter, all but Hahn, Doyle and Way left for the Eastern Slope, expecting to return the next season to their properties. The three who remained planned to spend the winter getting ready for work on their rich gravel bars the following spring.

On October 2 Capt. Way left camp to go out for supplies, promising to return by the middle of the month. While he was gone Hahn and Doyle whipsawed 4000 feet of lumber and put up a snug cabin. Way never returned, and the two men faced the winter without adequate provisions. As the cold increased, the wild game left for warmer regions and the snow from successive storms piled up until it lay twelve feet deep on the level. Rabbits were the only game left and they were not plentiful. By spring, facing starvation, Hahn and Doyle prepared to work their way out in search of food; and on April 22, 1867, they started on snowshoes for Empire, across the Divide, although the snow was soft, and travelling extremely difficult. A week later they had only reached the banks of the Muddy in Middle Park, and completely exhausted they stopped to rest. When they were ready to continue their gruelling journey, Hahn was too weak to walk and after a delirious night, in which Doyle made him as comfortable as possible, he died.

Some men who were wintering in the park saw something floundering through the snow and discovered that it was Doyle, snowblind and almost dead from fatigue and exposure. Taking him back to their cabin, they cared for him until he was able to travel again. Hahn's body lay unburied until November, when Lindstrom of Empire, who had originally grubstaked him, sent a man to bury the skeleton. The grave, which was said to be not far from the town of Kremmling, or between the Big Muddy and Alkalai Slough, was marked by a pile of rocks and a broken snowshoe placed as a headstone.

According to Henderson's *Mining in Colorado*, paying quantities of gold were first discovered in the camp by Sam Conger, during the summer of 1869, and as a result of the discovery, two large companies were formed to work the bars—the Hahn's Peak Co. and the Purdy Mining Co., both of which operated on a big scale. The Purdy Mining Co. succeeded in interesting J. W. Farwell of Chicago, "who spent $60,000 in constructing a twenty-seven mile ditch from the Elk River, at a time when all work had to be done with pick and shovel." He also superintended the work, spending several summers in the camp.

The mining district was divided into two camps. Farwell's property was in Way's Gulch, and his camp was called International Camp or National City, but the miners called it Bug Town because all the "big bugs" lived there. The other camp, which ultimately became the town of Hahn's Peak, was called Poverty Bar. During 1873 Hahn's Peak was a placer camp, with gold worth $15 an ounce attracting many to the bars. Nuggets worth $50 were taken from the gravel, and lead in silver was found northwest of the peak at the grass roots. But even when the ore was washed out, it had to be hauled 110 miles through the mountains to the railroad, and after transportation costs were paid, the profit per ton was small.

Aside from Nugget Gulch and parts of Way's Gulch, the placers were not extraordinarily rich; yet hydraulic work proved satisfactory and was carried on for some time, with one year's washing at Poverty Bar producing more than $100,000. The season was short, only six to eight weeks, for the gravel beds could be worked only when the spring floods furnished sufficient water to run the one hydraulic giant.

After ten years, Farwell's operations at String Ridge proved "disappointing," and he sold out in 1879, taking $32,000 for what had cost him $150,000. Being a deeply religious man he had allowed no saloons in his camp and permitted no work on Sundays. Instead, he brought in ministers to talk to the "boys" whenever possible. Poverty Bar had no such restrictions—its saloons ran wide open and poker games were going at all times with the sky the limit.

For thirty years Hahn's Peak was the seat of Routt County, yet four times, over a period of twenty years, the people tried to move it to a more accessible location. Routt County was created in 1877 and the county seat was temporarily located at Hayden. But in both 1878 and 1879 the camp near Hahn's Peak won the election over Hayden. The county records, however, were not moved until the spring of 1879, when a bill of $37 was presented for moving them from Hayden to the new location. Actually the records were bundled into bags and packed in on a burro to National City. That year, when Farwell's development at String Ridge folded up, the records and the post office (which had been established in 1877) were moved to Poverty Bar, which had always officially been known as Hahn's Peak.

Within ten years the camp began to dwindle, and as the county became filled with ranchers who lived miles from the Peak, the question of relocation was re-opened. In 1883 and again in 1887 the people of the county demanded a change, but not until 1912 was the issue settled, with Steamboat Springs winning the tussle.

Columbine and Royal Flush

Four miles north of Hahn's Peak is Columbine, a new town in 1897 which, according to Calhoun's *Colorado's Gold Fields*, with its "score of houses and cabins may round into a city someday." It was no city in 1942, when we stopped at the one store to inquire the way to the Royal Flush mine. The proprietress, who is the only inhabitant during the winter, pointed out the road and told us it was two miles to the property, on the west slope of Hahn's Peak.

Before we had gone a quarter of a mile, the road was covered by a mountain stream too deep to ford or drive through. Parking the car, taking off our shoes and stockings and rolling up our trousers, we waded into the cold water up to our knees and crossed the slippery, oozy mud bottom without mishap. Hahn's Peak was always ahead of us, its fire lookout station silhouetted against the sky. At the mine were a number of cabins, an office and a dilapidated mill. Just when the Royal Flush mine was discovered I do not know. The first date that I have been able to trace is 1904, when the mine was "re-opened and working." In 1916 it was working, but no ore was shipped; in 1918 the mill was overhauled. The last mine report, made in 1935, mentioned a fifty-ton flotation mill but added "not producing." After we had explored the place and even ventured into the entrance of the tunnel, I made a few sketches and then swung down the trail, forded the stream and returned to the car.

Lulu

"Have you ever been to Lulu?" wrote a man from Chicago. "I hear that it was deserted so fast that the clothes were left hanging in the closets and the dishes standing on the table. Is this true?"

Not having been there I could not answer his questions, but a few weeks after receiving the letter I made a trip to Lulu. Stopping at a Dude Ranch not far from Grand Lake, I hired horses and with several companions started up the valley of the Colorado River toward the forsaken camp.

First we rode across swampy land, fording the twisting North Fork of the Colorado several times before reaching the flat where Shipler's cabin stood and where the Shipler mine shaft and dump perched on the side of a low mountain. In the timber was the old stage road, which once led over Thunder Pass. The trees were huge and so dense that most of the sunlight was shut out and we rode through a green gloom. Festoons of dry moss, a rank parasite, hung from denuded branches or wrapped itself around tender, young growth. There was little underbrush; but farther on, away from the big trees, the road cut through aspens, elderberry bushes and masses of wild flowers. After about three miles a trail switchbacked steeply down the mountainside, at whose base ran the same twisting river and where, on a meadow, lay Lulu City.

The camp, which had an elevation of 9400 feet, was founded in 1879 by

LULU CITY IN DISTANCE

TELLER CITY

Benjamin Franklin Burnett and was named for his daughter, although another source states that Capt. Yankee founded the settlement. At any rate, Lulu's name was also given to a mountain and a pass (also called Thunder Pass), and to the settlement which sprang up overnight and melted away almost as fast. Its real boom lasted one year, but some mining was done in the vicinity through 1883.

Like all the camps it was platted and its townsite was laid out on an ambitious scale, with one hundred blocks divided into nineteen streets and four avenues, named Mountain, Trout, Riverside and Ward. There was a large hotel, saloons, stores and homes, all built of logs and each with its stone fireplace. Dances were held in the dining room of the big hotel, to which the population of 500, who were scattered up and down the gulches, swarmed on Saturday nights.

An abundance of low grade silver ore, most of which wasn't valuable enough to ship, was found, but in spite of persistent prospecting very little gold was uncovered. Many claims were staked out—the Ptarmigan, Garden City, Eureka and Silver Heels, and the Hidden Treasure and Wolverine in Bowen Gulch southwest of Lulu and northwest of Gaskill, another camp a few miles away. By July, 1883, Lulu promised to be the liveliest camp in the vicinity. A few placer properties were worked in the fine sand of the stream, but as only low grade ore continued to be found, the mines were abandoned one by one and the disappointed miners drifted away. Mary Lyons Cairns, in her book *Grand Lake, The Pioneers*, tells of one discouraged prospector who prophesied that "Someday you'll see nothing but a foot-trail along this street. Raspberry bushes and spruce trees will be growing through the roof of the hotel yonder." When Lulu was abandoned its post office remained, and mail was delivered long after everybody had gone. In January, 1886, the post office was discontinued.

Today its once sturdy cabins form log fences, enclosing wild raspberry, gooseberry and currant bushes. Spruce and pine trees grow inside the walls, and all vestiges of the roofs have disappeared. South of the town, an old wooden bear trap still stands; its door ready to drop behind anything rash enough to enter the enclosure.

Gaskill

When we left Lulu, our guide told us about Dutchtown and Gaskill, two other ghost towns in the vicinity. Gaskill, also known as Auburn, was settled in 1880, along the North Fork of the Colorado River, eight miles northwest of Grand Lake. It was named for Capt. L. D. C. Gaskill, manager of the Wolverine mine, and was a silver camp. Some old timers tell of a camp called Wolverine, but seem uncertain of its location. Was it at the Wolverine mine?

Gaskill flourished during the middle eighties, its main street being lined with stores, restaurants, a good-sized hotel, the Rogerson House, saloons and cabins. The Grand Lake lode was worked in 1883 and was predicted to be "one of the richest silver mines in the state." By 1884 the Grand Lake Mining and Milling Co. of Chicago built a mill at Gaskill, of which today only the ore dump remains. No elections were held at either Gaskill or Lulu in 1883, yet in 1884 "Gaskill looks for lively times this year" wrote the

Grand Lake Prospector in its column, "Gaskill Glints." Mail routes were established between the camp and Grand Lake, and even over the range to Teller City; and as usual in this country, the mail had to be carried in on snowshoes several months of the year. Stage routes connected it with Georgetown, sixty-five miles away, and with Hot Sulphur Springs. By 1885 the town was on the wane. Gradually, the people left, the buildings fell to pieces, and for years no one disturbed the sleeping camp. Occasionally hunters or adventurous tourists stumbled upon it and found the old blacksmith shop and the cobblestone wall of an old wine cellar of a saloon. Just as I was about to investigate it in 1947, I learned that the remaining shells of buildings had been burned and that Gaskill was no longer even a ghost.

Next morning we again took horses for the day and started switchbacking up the trail back of the camp toward the Grand Ditch, which runs along the face of the Never Summer Range. It was built to carry water from the western to the eastern slope for irrigation purposes, and the water flows into the Poudre River.

Dutchtown

Ten of us made the trip up Red Mountain past Hell's Hip Pocket, a deep and rocky pit, until the steep and rocky trail brought us to the edge of the ditch and our horses clambered up on the road which skirts it. To our left was the irrigation trough, several feet wide and ten or more feet below the roadway, and above us were the ragged barren peaks of the range. To our right was a sheer drop of hundreds of feet down the mountainside up which we had just scrambled, and beyond was a view of the whole valley, rimmed on three sides with mountains. After riding along the ditch for nearly three miles, we came to a trail that led further up the mountain, but to reach it we had to ford the ditch and climb up its far side to the narrow footpath through a rocky meadow. This was Hitchen's Gulch, and by following it we reached Hitchen's Camp, established in the nineties, with its mine, shaft house and buildings, all deserted but in good repair.

The trail ahead led up through timber and across boggy meadows edged with flowers. After a mile's climb we reached Dutchtown, consisting of five or six cabins spotted through the pines around a dried mud-hollow that had once been a shallow lake. Dutchtown was built in the last stand of trees below timberline, and through the fringe of tall pines we could see huge chunks of rock and tundra slopes, leading toward the top of the mountain. Leaving our horses in the meadow, we began to explore the place. We found crumbling logs that had once been cabins, now half covered with young trees or bushes, and we saw a roofless cabin with gaping doorway and stone fireplace. Some of the party searched for the trees "girdled by axes for fire wood," indicating that the miners had planned to stay in the camp long enough to need a supply of fuel. Others hunted for the corral fence which had stood outside the saloon and to which patient horses and burros stood hitched while their masters celebrated a strike or swapped yarns inside.

Had it not been for a dunken brawl in Lulu there would have been no Dutchtown. Two intoxicated German miners returned there one Saturday night and proceeded to shoot up the town, whereupon they were promptly run out by the citizens. Prospecting higher on the mountain they struck ore at this place, and a tiny camp, named Dutchtown in their honor, sprang up, only to flicker out in two years.

The trail back seemed steeper than the ascent, and the bowl of mountains ahead seemed to change constantly. Just before leaving the road beside the ditch to drop down the mountainside again, I looked far below and saw black dots in a meadow on the valley floor. They were the cabins in Lulu. Far away at the head of the valley was Lulu Pass and across it lay Teller City, another ghost camp of the same era, which was to be my next objective.

Teller City   The little hotel at Rand was full, but the proprietor Mr. Leatherman, gave us lodging in a log cabin with a sod roof behind the main building, so that we could get an early start for Teller City in the morning. For several years I had been in communication with him and had learned that the road up Jack Creek was rough, that it could be driven but that only some broken down cabins were left at the camp. Even a pile of boards is enough for me; so after a huge country breakfast we were off for what was once the principal town of North Park.

The drive to Teller City became increasingly difficult and toward the last we were travelling about five miles an hour so as to avoid deep ruts, high centers and loose rocks. We drove through timber most of the way, and by the time we reached the camp the trees were close around us. There were nearly three hundred ruined cabins, on both sides of the "street" and many more back in the trees, some large and some small, some blackened by fire and others bleached by sun and weather. I wandered from one pile of logs and boards to another, but could find few traces of the identity of any building.

Most of the streets are partly overgrown with trees; a forge is all that identifies the blacksmith shop; and a few unmarked graves lie in the cemetery nearby. Rusty machinery is piled on the ore dumps—machinery which was brought in by freighters who sometimes "made 1000 feet a day" over bad places in the road. In the hollow by the creek stands the ruined mill.

The camp was established in 1879, when reports of rich silver deposits in the southeastern corner of North Park brought people flocking into the wooded area at the foot of the divide. A post office, named for Senator Henry M. Teller, was established at the silver camp, and passengers and mail were carried in by coach from Laramie in 1880, fare $11.00. The camp reached its peak in 1882, when its population reached 1300, and by 1883 it was almost dead. The townsite was 18 acres, with numbered and lettered streets, C street being the main thoroughfare. The cabins in Teller do not have fireplaces because they were equipped with stoves which were freighted in. Further up the valley, nearer the mines, the cabins had fireplaces "built of porphyry."

As the camp grew, various business houses were opened, a newspaper was published, a smelting works and two steam sawmills were established and ore was shipped. The Yates House was the big, two-story hotel with more than forty rooms and a piano; other large buildings were the mine office of the North Park Mining Company, and the office of the Endomile mine. There was a blacksmith shop, an assay office, two doctor's offices and "three to twenty saloons."

↓ OLD SMELTER, PEARL

SIDEWALKS, PEARL

Mrs. Cairns, in *Grand Lake, The Pioneers,* describes a famous race run during the summer of 1883. About once a month the miners from Teller, Gaskill and Lulu went down to Grand Lake to celebrate. A man named Sharp, who was working at the Wolverine, beat all the other miners at foot-racing and was looked upon as a champion. His fellow-workers bragged about him when they went to Grand Lake, until a man there said he had a man named Montgomery who could beat Sharp. Immediately bets, starting at $100, were placed, the bets totalling $4000. Sharp trained at Gaskill and Montgomery at Grand Lake, but the race was run on C Street in Teller City. Montgomery won by seven feet, and Sharp," who had a good part of the stakes in his possession, kept on running to the end of the street and then out in the timber where a saddled horse awaited him and rode away." He was never heard of again. With him went one of the girls from Teller's red light district. When the men at the Wolverine paid their bets they were all stony broke.

The Endomile mine three miles above the town was one of the best properties, producing both gold and silver "in almost inexhaustible quantities." All that was needed was "the means to reduce the ore to bullion," but capital was lacking and the mine was forced to close down. The last shift lasted seventy-two hours, as the men bailed water by hand after the pump broke down, and came up to the surface only to eat. According to one old timer, the last time he came up he fell asleep at the entrance with a cold biscuit in his hand.

The story of the Twin Shafts as told by Mrs. Cairns is illuminating. A contract was given by an eastern company to two men to sink a hundred-foot shaft in their mine to determine the quality of ore at that depth. The men dug a shaft fifty feet deep and struck water. Finding it hard to keep ahead of the water with their crude windlass and buckets, they abandoned one shaft, and moving sixty feet away, sank another fifty-foot shaft in the same vein of ore. When they had finished they signed a statement that they had done one hundred feet of work and sent it to the company. As soon as they were paid they "skipped out," and today the two shafts and two piles of earth and rocks mark the site of the swindle.

The mining boom at Teller City, Lulu and Gaskill petered out at about the same time in all three places, although a little placer mining was done in the vicinity for several years after the camps were gone. Although town lots were sold to the amount of $750 in January, 1883, the town was already beginning to fold up. "Teller was a lively place while it lasted," but when the end came the camp was deserted so fast that the people left everything standing as it was, "even to dirty dishes on the table."

Pearl   Before leaving Rand, I suggested that we drive to Pearl, close to the Wyoming state line. Pearl had been a mining town, and although I knew nothing of its history except that it, like Lulu, had been named for another daughter of Benjamin Franklin Burnett, I wanted to sketch what was left of it. At Cowdrey, which had been the supply station for Pearl in the days when everything was brought in by freight or stage, we left the highway and started off across rolling ranch country toward the mountains. The dirt road was narrow, and during the twenty-mile drive we passed but one car.

(272)

Winding up and down and around sagebrush covered hills, we eventually climbed a wooded hill on whose side was an abandoned smelter, which we stopped to investigate.

The valley below the far side of the hill was fertile and dotted with distant ranch houses. Where was Pearl? This was the second time I had come here, and I saw no more now than I had seen five years before. Driving to the nearest house, I asked where the site of Pearl was. "This is Pearl," said the woman who came to the door. "There aren't many buildings left. This house was on one side of town. That barn over there was one of the old buildings and there are a few over across the meadow." Realizing that all the remaining landmarks had been re-modeled into ranch buildings, I started on a tour of the meadow and located the old barn, but little else. There *were* three or four buildings about a quarter of a mile away, but they were modern houses, not at all what I was looking for; but so that I might be sure, I walked over toward them. Two of the four were old and weathered, but the remaining two white ones were obviously occupied. Just as I was turning away disappointed, I saw, half hidden in the sage brush which covered the meadow, a long line of broken, weathered, wooden sidewalk, which ran in front of all four houses and beyond them, and I suddenly realized that I was standing on the main street of Pearl!

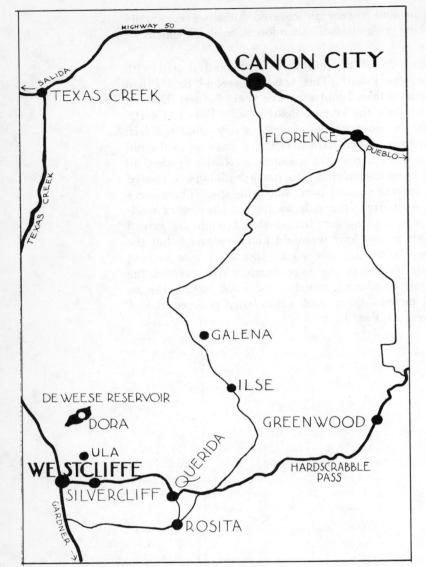

(The map shows: HIGHWAY 50, CANON CITY, SALIDA, TEXAS CREEK, FLORENCE, PUEBLO→, TEXAS CREEK, GALENA, ILSE, DE WEESE RESERVOIR, GREENWOOD, DORA, QUERIDA, HARDSCRABBLE PASS, ULA, WESTCLIFFE, SILVERCLIFF, GARDNER→, ROSITA)

CHAPTER ELEVEN

The Wet Mountain Valley

THE car pulled steadily to the top of Hardscrabble Pass and cut across meadows and between stands of timber. "There used to be a little mining in what was called Hardscrabble Park," I said to Victoria and Jim. "The real mining district, however, is over this ridge in the Wet Mountain Valley. At first lone ranchers staked off homesteads near the sites of Ula and Dora, but it was Carl Wulsten and his German colony that first settled this fertile valley between two watersheds — the Wet Mountain and the Sangre de Cristo.

Wulsten was the founder and leader of the colony. In 1869 he came to Colorado from Chicago to select a location for the group, and chose a site in the Wet Mountain Valley as offering excellent agricultural and industrial prospects. In February, 1870, three hundred Germans led by Wulsten left Chicago for their new home in the Rockies, traveling by rail and ox teams and arriving five weeks later in the valley. They immediately laid out the townsite of Colfax, named in honor of the Vice-President of the United States, and proceeded to develop their ranches. By the end of the summer the colony (which was 15 miles southwest of Westcliffe) was in trouble. Funds were believed to have been mismanaged, and an early frost ruined their crops. Denver business men sent some provisions to the valley but not enough for the entire population, and the disgusted colonists began to leave. In December a barrel of powder exploded in the general store, de-

(274)

molishing it and leaving the people without provisions of any kind. Again food was sent in, on which the dwindling group managed to survive until spring. Having had enough of the experiment, each man then struck out for himself; and in no time Colfax was forgotten.

On the crest of a hill we got our first glimpse of the great valley, with a towering wall of snowtopped peaks, the Sangre de Cristo range, just beyond. The peaks were silhouetted in the afternoon light, and since this was early June, the snow lay not only on their summits but far down their slopes, forming a band of solid white the length of the range.

"We'll have time to visit Rosita this afternoon," I told Jim as we left *Rosita* the highway and started over rolling hills, at the bottom of which the sleepy little town was tucked away. A few ruined stone buildings and some frame dwellings and cabins made up the town, while many foundations and vacant lots indicated where houses had once stood. Driving toward the end of the main street, past the town well, I noticed a large, two-story frame residence with shingled roof and with an "air" about it, although the building was in a sad state of decay. Through one of its windows we could see the sky through the broken, rotten roof, yet the front portion of the house seemed to be inhabited. Opposite it was an old log cabin with a board sidewalk in front of it, in whose doorway stood an elderly man to whom we turned for information. "Carl Wulsten lived here until his death in 1915," he began. "I've heard him tell about the first time he rode down here in 1868 and of how he found an Indian family at the spring, chanting over the body of a young brave which lay at their feet. The old Indian explained that he had caught a bear, but that when it turned on him his son had come to his rescue and had been disembowelled by one stroke of its paw. His own arm had been broken in the struggle. Wulsten made a splint out of aspen boughs and bound up the Indian's arm. He then buried the son. The spot where all this happened was fifty feet east of the portico of the Episcopal church which was built here." While we were listening other people gathered around and contributed to the conversation, so that before long, I learned the history of Rosita.

"Daniel Baker picked up some bright galena outcroppings near where the Senator mine now is, while he was herding cattle back in 1870," volunteered one man. "He dug up some likely specimens and put them on the window ledge of his cabin. Dick Irwin (for whom the camp of Irwin in Gunnison county was named) passed through the valley in June 1870 and picked up some float too. That December, when the snow was a foot deep, he and Jasper Brown came back here and got Baker to show him where his ore sample came from. For two weeks the men camped at the spring, prospecting these hills and locating several lodes near here, and a couple of copper and gold bearing veins east of here; but the ore didn't assay high enough to warrant further development then, and they finally left.

"Other prospectors came nosing around these hills, tapping the rocks and picking up float, until in 1872 the Hardscrabble Mining District was organized. This camp didn't start till April 1873. That summer the town grew, but the first winter was dull. No ore was shipped and no mines were sold. There were some tents and cabins and a mine boardinghouse by then, but the one store closed down."

"That must have been the time," I interrupted, "referred to by Baskin in his *History of the Arkansas Valley*, when he says:

> . . . many who had fared sumptuously on canned goods and sugar-cured hams were compelled by the exigencies of the situation and the yearnings of their bowels, to strike out with the rifle in hand and scour the hills for the festive rabbit, the melancholy grouse, or perchance the substantial black-tail deer.

"Do you know why it's called Rosita?" broke in a young woman who had been listening. "Dick Irwin named it 'Little Rose' because he found so many wild roses here. There's also a legend that it was named by a Frenchman whose Spanish sweetheart died and who wandered aimlessly north from Mexico City until he reached this place. He found it so beautiful that he stayed here and named it for his lost fiancee."

"Rubbish," said the old man in the doorway. "Who cares how it was named? It was the mines that made the camp. Robinson and Irwin and Pringle discovered some of the first lodes here. There's Pringle Hill over there and Robinson Hill up here, with Hungry Gulch in between. Robinson knew the region, for he'd driven cattle through the valley, and later he furnished Rosita and Silver Cliff with beef. Once when he was driving a thousand head of stock he slept with a bag of seventy-five silver dollars under his saddle. In the morning the bag was gone and he accused the men with him of taking it. After a search they found it hidden under a rotten log, where it had been dragged by a packrat. When the Humboldt and Pocahontas were located in 1874, that's when Rosita boomed. The Pocahontas employed 90 men, and it and the Humboldt together produced over $300,000 in 1875. Ever hear of the Pocahontas War? Didn't think so," and settling himself in an ancient rocking chair he told the following story:

In 1872 a German named Frederic discovered an extension of what was then known as the Virginia lode. He sank a shaft for a few feet but found nothing worth while, whereupon he stopped digging, and the hole, which he called the Humboldt, lay idle. Frederic was hard up and since he was a skilled basket-maker he decided to weave potato baskets and sell them to the ranchers in the valley. Having no way to get the willow branches to his workshop he hired a young German, Paul Goerke, to haul them with his ox-team. Goerke demanded twenty dollars for the job, but Frederic had no money. Instead he proposed a trade. Goerke was to give him a sack of flour instead of a freight bill and Frederic was to deed him the prospect hole "Humboldt." By this transaction Goerke became the owner of what proved to be a valuable mine. At the time he had no money to put into the development of his prospect, so he simply left it alone. Shortly afterwards George O. Bannon came to Rosita to work for the Transylvania Tunnel Co. The tunnel site was on the western slope of Lucille Hill, one of several coneshaped porphyry hills which surround the town. Bannon had to cross Goerke's ground four times a day and, like most miners, he was in the habit of looking for float ore. One day he found a piece of rich chloride of silver and, digging into the surface

(276)

ROSITA RESIDENCE

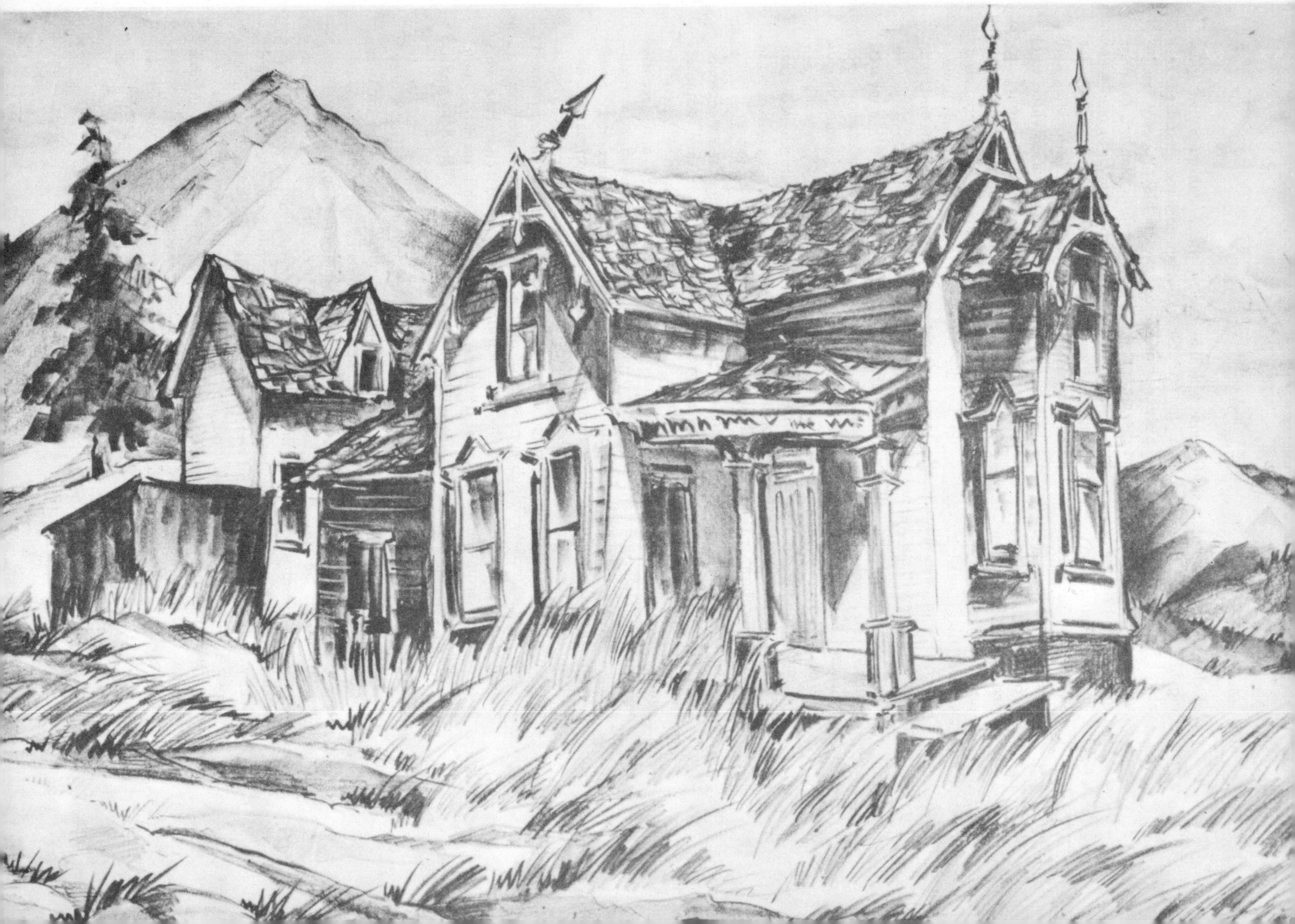

of the hill, uncovered a silver vein which he called the Pocahontas. In staking his claim he discovered that he and Goerke claimed three hundred feet of the same ground! Bannon needed money to develop his property; so he sold one-third of his interest in the mine to L. W. Patterson, who had assayed some of his ore, for $75 in "grub." Then the trouble began, for both men were working their respective claims, and they overlapped! Armed men were placed on the two properties, and night after night they sat guarding the disputed holes from which such rich ore was being taken. The camp was divided into two factions, one siding with Goerke and one with Bannon. Everyone carried guns. Finally the dispute was referred to a miner's court of arbitration and was settled without bloodshed. Later the Pocahontas changed hands several times until it was bought by the Messrs. Herr (as they are always called), who also bought the third interest owned by Patterson and who worked the mine successfully until 1875.

One morning a well-dressed stranger, called Colonel Boyd, appeared in town. He smoked good cigars, drank good whiskey and wore a conspicuous, thousand dollar watch chain. Ten weeks later another stranger, named Stewart, arrived from Denver where he had been a bank director. The two men had much in common and decided to open a bank. They even purchased some gold claims in the Pocahontas mine. Everything went on as usual, but the "hyenas of capital without capital were silently and steadily at work."

Having been unsuccessful at the local election in getting their henchmen placed in office, and envying Herr his prosperous mine, they bribed Topping, the superintendent of the Pocahontas, to turn it over to them. When the news leaked out the town was aghast. The "Messrs. Herr" had recently visited their mine, paid the men and departed for Denver, leaving the property in the trusted hands of Topping. Boyd and Stewart immediately fortified the recently acquired mine and paid guards to patrol its approaches day and night. Little work was done in Rosita during the next few days, but a good deal of drinking and talking went on, and finally the citizens organized a Committee of Safety which consisted of over a hundred men. In the meantime a gang of ruffians led by "Major" Graham, a notorious character who had escaped from the Territorial Penitentiary and who had recently come to Rosita to run a restaurant and gambling hall, was hired by Boyd to guard the property.

As soon as Topping turned the mine over to the "jumpers," Mr. Posey, attorney for the rightful owners, sent a mounted messenger to the nearest telegraph station and wired them of what had happened. An injunction was obtained from the Chief Justice of the Territory and served upon Boyd and Stewart by the Sheriff. By its terms the two men were forced to stop working the mine, and triumphantly the "Messrs. Herr" returned to re-obtain possession of their property. But again they found the mine guarded by armed men, who threatened them and ordered them off the land. A warrant was then drawn up against the guards and was delivered by the town constable, accompanied by an armed posse who marched with him up the hill to enforce the law. The guards yielded and were tried before a justice's court, where they received light fines, which were paid by Stewart's bank, and were then discharged. An hour later the residents of Rosita heard loud cheering at the mine and discovered that the guards had taken possession again.

The following day was one of terror, Stewart and his gang threatening to kill everyone who opposed them. Boyd was also abusive, knocking down a man on the street, drawing a pistol, and threatening to kill him if he uttered a syllable. The day was ominously quiet. No one worked, the streets were empty, and even the saloons were ordered closed. The Committee met that night, and when the gathering broke up about midnight and the members started home, the town seemed deserted except for the Town Marshall who was talking with a small group of men in the Plaza. Shortly afterwards, a volley of rifle shots accompanied by yells startled the citizens, as Graham's voice was heard shouting: "Down with every one of the cursed Vigilantes. Shoot them down, boys!" Then began a pitched battle between the ruffians and the aroused citizens which lasted till dawn. As day broke and the streets filled with armed men, it was found that the hoodlums had been forced to retreat to the mine and that the Committee of Safety held the approaches to the town.

Graham and his gang had now gone too far, and the people were determined that this should be the last day of the "reign of outlawry." Suddenly, another distant volley of shots was heard, and the armed citizens rushed up Tyndal Street toward the mine, meeting Graham and his rowdies coming down. In the fighting which followed Graham was shot dead. With the loss of their leader the gang broke and fled but were pursued "on foot and on horseback" until most of them were captured. Topping, however, escaped; but Boyd and others were caught, and "in good order and with military precision the committee marched to town with their prisoners and lodged Boyd in the town lock up." Stewart had left two nights before the attack, taking all the bank's money with him. At first there was talk of hanging Boyd, but he was finally released upon his promise never to enter Colorado again. Stewart was caught and brought back days later for trial. When the safe in his bank was opened it was found to contain eighty cents in currency and $15,000 in bonds on a Kansas railroad which had never been built. Graham's body was tossed into a prospect hole; and the owners Herr, with a deep sigh of relief, took possession of their mine again. "Since that day," remarked the old man in the rocking chair, "Rosita has been one of the most orderly and peaceable towns in Colorado.

"There was a brewery here in 1874—one of the largest in the state—and a cheese factory too, the first of its kind in the Territory, turning out 250 pounds of cheese a day until the milk became contaminated with the wild garlic which grew in the valley at that time. That put an end to the factory.

"The business section of town was up and down Tyndal Street. All the buildings were frame, and when we had our fire in 1881 four blocks burned to the ground. We had no fire department and the only water came from the town spring. After the fire we spread the business district over a wider area and built of brick and stone as much as possible.

"We had two hotels here, the Snowy Range and the Windsor House, two reduction works and a smelter. Until the Masonic Lodge was built in 1879, meetings were held in the Odd Fellows Hall. The first Masonic jewels were made of tin but they were soon replaced with more valuable metals. I wasn't a Mason, but I belonged to the Knights of Pythias who also had a chapter here. We had dances and concerts, horseraces, dog fights and fist fights. We had churches, too, four of them—Methodist, Presbyterian, Catholic and Episcopal. The Methodists had a sweet-toned bell, the Episcopalians were proud of their organ, the Catholics of their chapel, and the Presbyterians were in good running order until a few years ago; but they're all gone now.

"Rosita had a newspaper, the *Rosita Index*, which was neutral in politics at first and then went Democratic. Later it was called the *Sierra Journal*. There were 2000 people here between 1875 and 1877. Those were our peak years. By the end of 1877 times were getting dull, but when the Bassick mine was discovered only two miles away, this place picked up for awhile. A good many of the men who worked at the Bassick lived here. In 1878, when the mines at Silver Cliff were discovered, most of the population rushed to the new camp and many of them moved their houses with them. Then we lost the county seat to Silver Cliff, and we had our fire and after that Rosita sort of slipped into a decline. By 1882 business was at a standstill. There's been a little mining here on and off and a few people have stayed on, but the good days are gone. Why, in 1887, when they gave a ball for the benefit of the Rosita Fire Department, all they netted was $23.50."

"Tell them about the lynching," prompted a small boy who had pushed his way into the group.

"Well, the Odd Fellows had a dancehall above a saloon. The Floor Committee for the dances wore big badges so they could be easily recognized. At one of their 'hops' two drunks came upstairs and began to raise Cain, so the committee threw them downstairs. After a while the "bouncers" got dry and went down to the bar. The two drunks saw them, fired, and killed them. Next morning, printed invitations were issued in Rosita and Silver Cliff for a Necktie Party to be held at midnight in Rosita. I was a kid then, living in Silver Cliff, and of course I wanted to go; but all of us kids were sent to bed. We had agreed to sneak out and meet at the schoolhouse and then hike seven miles through the sagebrush to Rosita, so as not to be seen. We reached there just before midnight. There was no one in sight. Suddenly 200 men appeared out of the brush. They rammed in the door of the jail with a steel bar, took the two men, tied their hands and feet, and strung them up, one at each end of the jail. Then we boys hoofed it back home across the fields getting back just at dawn. Our parents didn't know anything about our little trip until a year later."

"While you are here you should visit the cemetery," said another old man. "Commodore Stephen Decatur is buried there."

"I know about him," I interrupted. "I've been to Decatur and I've heard some of the stories about him."

"He was one of the Commissioners for the State at the Centennial Exposition in Philadelphia, you know. The state appropriation was exhausted about six weeks before the end of the Fair, but Decatur would not close up the Colorado exhibit and stayed till the end. The State never reimbursed him and he went broke. He came to Silver Cliff hoping to recoup his fortunes but met with an accident and lived in Rosita for several years 'on the town.' He lived about a quarter of a mile from our house, and many a time I carried a piece of pie or cake or something of that kind to the old man from my mother, and we were not the only ones who did the same. I often called on him, for he liked to talk to me about history. Several years ago I read in an eastern newspaper that his burial place was unknown. I can testify as to that because I helped to dig his grave and helped cover him up. He is buried in the Rosita cemetery. It must have been in the summer of 1887. He had a great funeral considering the population. He was very much esteemed."

Following directions, we drove up a hill at the edge of town and on to the cemetery. Deep grass and summer wildflowers covered the ground and obscured many of the graves, whose inscriptions we read from the weathered, marble stones. As in all the old mountain cemeteries, there were many children's graves.

VERA GRACE
born June 24, 1881
died Aug. 30, 1881
Weep not Papa and Mama for me
For I am waiting in heaven for thee.

LITTLE DICK
Earth has one poor spirit less
Heaven one inmate more.

We lay thee in the silent tomb
Sweet blossom of a day,
We just began to view thy bloom,
When thou art called away.

God blesses in an early death
And takes the infant to Himself,
She like a rose, bloomed a few days
But now lies silent in the grave.

A few of the newer stones were of granite, but the majority were of marble, which had acquired that warm, creamy whiteness that only age and exposure produces. Some of the plots were so overgrown that it was necessary to kneel in front of the stone and push aside the grasses and weeds in order to read the inscription. As the carved letters were frequently worn smooth or had broken off through years of exposure, we had to run our fingers over each letter and feel what it must have been, for even in strong sunlight it was impossible to decipher.

Above the inscriptions and dates were carvings, often of great beauty, representing all the typical symbols found on such memorials—doves and lambs, clasped hands, urns and floral garlands. Among the elaborate inscriptions, admonitions and promises of eternity, one simple stone stood out:

ELIZABETH DEBORAH
The beloved Wife of
THO. DOWNER
born
Sept. 15, 1844
died
Aug. 16, 1888

I AM READY

We never did find Decatur's grave. Perhaps we missed it, or perhaps it is unmarked. At any rate, as the sun sank behind the Sangre de Cristo Range, we left the quiet grove and drove on down the valley road to West-cliffe, the county seat of Custer county.

Westcliffe   The county-seat has moved about considerably since it was established at Ula, the oldest town in the valley, three miles northwest of Silver Cliff. But Ula, which had three mines and a population of 100, was forgotten as soon as Rosita grew to importance, and the county seat was transferred to the newer camp. In 1881 Silver Cliff was the big city, and at a county election it won the prize from Rosita, only to lose it after a few years to West-cliffe, where it still remains. Rosita was never reconciled to its loss and when-ever the bell in the new courthouse rang, to the people of Rosita it said, "Stole, stole," while the clock said, "Take me back, take me back."

We drove up and down the wide streets of Westcliffe, impressed by its tidy gardens and comfortable homes. Having found hotel accommodations next to the false-fronted fire house, we set out to find dinner. At Min's Cafe I questioned the proprietress and waitress about Silver Cliff and Westcliffe and learned that Silver Cliff was the older of the two. When the mines at the Cliff were producing and there was ore to be shipped, a branch of the D. & R. G. was built to within a mile and a half of the city and a new town, Westcliffe, sprang up at the end of the rails. The road was completed in May 1881, and for two days afterward everyone celebrated. Visitors came from all over the state! Trips were arranged through the most important mines and reduction works, a dinner and speeches were given on Game Ridge at Rosita, and a Grand Ball was held at Robert's Hall in Silver Cliff.

Westcliffe was first known as Clifton but it was renamed by Dr. W. A. Bell for his birthplace, Westcliff-on-the-sea in England. Bell came to the val-ley with General Palmer in 1870, when the latter was searching for a south-ern route for the D. & R. G. Railroad, and became so fond of the country that he took up a large tract of land here and started ranching. The city was incorporated in 1897, and is now the biggest place in the valley.

The old Beckwith place, up the valley toward Hillside, used to be a show place. Its log house, built in 1869 and since then re-modeled, was the largest in the valley. Beckwith built big feeding troughs and cattle sheds, and he im-

WESTCLIFFE

QUERIDA
AND THE
BASSICK
MINE

ported fancy, registered animals and turned them out on the open range with all the other stock. In two years his cattle looked like deer from running the range, and they didn't hold up as well as the scrub animals. He was elected Republican Representative to the State Senate in 1886. After his death the place changed hands several times, and the last time I saw it, the fountain in front of the house was choked with weeds.

"Are there any other old mining towns near here?" I inquired of the waitress.

"There's Querida and there's Ilse. At Galena there's only one house left, and Yorkville, Ula and Dora are all gone.

Ula and Dora "Ula was settled in 1870, becoming the first real settlement in the Wet Mountain Valley and the headquarters for all the valley trade. Although it was to have been called Ure in honor of the Ute Indian Chief, in sending in the request for the post office to Washington, the name was spelled Ula instead of Ure as intended. Because it was settled by English colonists, it was also spoken of as Briton's Paradise.

"Dora was six miles northeast of Silver Cliff. In June 1879 there were only a few tents and shanties there, but after the Chambers concentrator was built a small village grew up around the smelter. The town was in existence in 1892, but the Grape Creek or DeWeese Reservoir covers its site today."

Querida Next morning we got an early start and drove through Silver Cliff to Querida, a few miles beyond. Very little of the town is left, but the ruins, foundations and machinery of tremendous mine buildings stand on either side of the highway.

"All this was the Bassick mine," I told Victoria and Jim as we started to explore the ruined millsite and eroded settling-pond. "It was the biggest property around here.

"The original discoverer was John True, who, with another man, was sent out from Pueblo by Capt. Baxter to prospect for minerals in the early seventies. They found a location and sunk a shallow hole, from which they dug agatized quartz but no valuable ore. They thereupon abandoned the prospect and left. Later on the Centennial Mining Company, which owned a claim on the hill above this hole, cut a tunnel into the mountain and employed a small force of men to develop it. Edmund C. Bassick, who lived in Rosita and who had been unsuccessfully prospecting the region for years, worked for this company and in going to and from the mine noticed a spot on Tyndal Mountain which was covered with float. Some say that Bassick remembered hearing stories about True, who had sunk his hole at approximately this spot, and therefore determined to try and re-locate it; others say that one night he went home over the hill instead of around it and found the spot by accident; and a third version states that in going over the hill he got some sand in his shoe and sat down to take it out. He jumped up suddenly for he had sat upon an ant hill! Starting on again, he decided to return to the spot and demolish the ant hill with his pick. A few inches from the surface he struck rock. He tried another angle and struck more rock. Take any version of the story you want; but at any rate, he found a sample of ore which

(284)

assayed 109 ounces of silver to the ton, and after a little more prospecting, on January 4, 1877, he re-located the original hole and began to develop it, striking rich ore at once. In fact, the first carload of ore shipped netted him $10,000.

"While working his shaft he found traces of free gold, although at the smelter he was assured that there was no gold in his ore. As this made him suspicious, he sacked some ore and sent it to the Black Hawk smelter where his ore was unknown. Their analysis showed 150 ounces of silver and eleven dollars in gold to the ton!

"The mine was so rich that it was easy to raise capital for its development. Ore worth $500,000 in gold and silver was taken out in the first year and a half. Bassick sold the mine to eastern capitalists in 1879, receiving half a million dollars in cash and a one-tenth interest in the stock of the new company. After selling the mine, Bassick went east and invested his fortune in Bridgeport, Connecticut, his birthplace, where he purchased the home of P. T. Barnum.

"I have a letter from a man who knew Bassick, John H. Barker, who once lived in Rosita:

"Old Man Bassick was a pioneer," he writes. "He made a fortune in California in '49 and lost it and another in Ballarat, Australia, about ten years later and ran through that. When he found the Bassick he was too poor to pay for the assay and cut and split a load of wood to pay for it. But after that he could not spend the money as fast as it came from the mine. He sold it for $300,000 and one million in stock and returned to his home town of Bridgeport, Conn."

"The new owners of the mine changed the name of the town from Bassickville to Querida; although it is also said that David Livingstone, a nephew of the great Livingstone, came to Rosita from Scotland, and was one of the hardy prospectors who spent the first two dreary winters in the embryo camp. He left in 1875 and returned in 1878 with his wife, settling close to the Bassick mine in the new town, which he re-named Querida.

"The new company was only interested in promoting the mine. Anything which would affect the price of the stock was of interest to them. At one time there were rumors that the mine was about to be jumped by a gang and a dynamite bomb exploded in the office yard. The whole thing was a publicity trick to affect the price of stock.

"This company, which was a 'get rich quick' outfit, sank a three-compartment shaft some distance from the original hoist, with the hope of cutting the ore at a low level by means of a tunnel. The whole proposition was expensive and futile, and the stockholders began to grumble. From then on the property became involved in almost interminable litigation, resulting in the mine being shut down by court order in 1884, after which it lay idle for seven years. During this period it filled with water. It was far from worked out, for even at a depth of 1400 feet, the ore body showed no evidence of giving out, and it was estimated that $1,000,000 worth of ore was blocked out before the shut-down. Some of the ore was found in pockets, the best of which ran $50,000 to the ton. The mine was always a mineralogical curiosity, the ore appearing in shell-like coatings on boulders of various sizes. All the best ore lay in a giant chimney, which was said to have been the chute of an extinct geyser, lying in a porphyry belt.

"In 1903 the Melrose Gold Mining Company acquired the property and, after demolishing the old buildings, erected a huge cyanide reduction plant and an electric light plant on the old foundations. In 1904 a large body of ore was found which produced $2,000,000 in gold from a deposit near the surface. Ore was shipped from the mine from time to time until 1915. In 1923 the dump was treated by cyanidation. In 1926, after a second period of idleness, another company, with a ten year lease, opened the mine and began hauling concentrates in trucks to Westcliffe for shipment by rail to the smelter.

"As soon as the Bassick mine was discovered, a small settlement, which contained a sawmill, a drug store, a three-story hotel and a smelting works sprang up around the mine, until by 1882 it was a flourishing town with a population of a thousand and not an empty house in the place. It prospered until 1884 when the mine was shut down and 400 men were thrown out of work. By 1895 less than a dozen families were left in the camp. The closing of the Bassick mine was the final blow to both Querida and Rosita, as there was no other industry in either town to support a population."

We climbed to the top of the big dump, to the site of the mine, and looked down over the waste that had once been the town. Less than a dozen buildings dotted the meadow—a false-fronted store veneered with black tar-paper, a mine shed, the schoolhouse and one frame house were the best preserved of those in sight. Below us lay huge wheels and drums, belts and hoppers—the rusty and bleached remnants of the great mill that had once stood at the foot of the hill. The stream cut its way through the oxide-stained sediment of the settling pond, and the wind whistled through the rigging of a windlass beside us on the crest of the dump.

Galena and Ilse

"Even though there won't be much to see, let's go on to Galena and Ilse while we are so close to them," I urged as we left Querida.

Leaving the highway, we drove through rolling ranch country until, across a creek to the right, we saw a large two-story house which we believed to be the lone building which marks the site of Camp Galena, which started up at about the same time as Silver Cliff. By 1880 it had several stores and a post office, as well as an assay office and a hotel. Two or three hundred people lived there and in the immediate vicinity, and they worked at the Star Mine, the best property in the camp, and at the Slip Up. Galena was on the stage road between Canon City and Rosita, and the stage station was near the hotel. The old post-office-and-saloon is still back of it, now used as a chicken house. Yorkville was two miles down the road, but nothing is left of it.

Taking the other fork of the road back to the highway, we passed through Ilse, a small place with one store, a boardinghouse and hotel and a few houses. In 1878 an eccentric Dutchman located a prospect which contained rich silver ore. No other good mines were found in the area, and even his vein finally played out. Like all prospectors he had faith in the mine and continued digging, looking for the mother lode, but he couldn't find it. He even went into debt in trying to develop the property, and when he could extend his credit no further he skipped out and left his creditors holding the bag. Years afterwards there was a silver boom up in Idaho at a town named De Lamar, which was the name of the man who had left Ilse. The Idaho strike made him a millionaire, and he began tracing his Ilse creditors and repaying all his debts, five-fold they say.

The mine at Ilse was named from the enormous deposit of crystallized lead which it contained. As one miner said, it was a "terrible big deposit," and the mine was therefore named the Terrible. It was worked from 1878 to 1888, and intermittently after that. In 1887 a fire, which started in the second-story of the post office, destroyed most of the town. In 1903 a new 300-ton mill was built at the mine. At first about thirty men were employed and later the force was increased to nearly a hundred. The Grant Smelter of Denver finally bought the mine to get control of the ore.

"Silver Cliff, the infant of Sept. 1878; the mushroom of 1879 and the *Silver Cliff* giant of 1880, that jumped from nothing to *third* rank in the list of Colorado cities, in population and in wealth, is a monument to the progress of 'Young America,' " wrote Crofutt in his *Gripsack Guide* in 1881. The town took its name from the argentiferous cliff thirty feet high which stood on the prairie near the old road across the valley, and the blackstained face of which attracted many passing prospectors.

The first discovery of silver was made in July, 1877, by R. J. Edwards of Rosita, who "paused on the edge of the cliff whose iron-stained face now confronts the city, and out of idle curiosity broke a piece of surface rock from the frowning black wall," carried it to an assayer to have it tested, and found that it ran twenty-four ounces per ton in silver. He tried to keep his discovery a secret, but the button of silver had been seen and was believed to run high in gold; so immediately the entire populations of Rosita and Bassickville stampeded to the new Eldorado and staked off all the land around the Cliff. When the tests for gold were made, the results were so disappointing that the locations were abandoned and the miners returned home. The next spring Edwards and some men were prospecting in the Greenhorn range but were finding very little ore. Finally Edwards said to the others, "Why work so hard to dig ore that isn't worth much when I know where there is some on top of the ground, at a cliff not far from here?" He led the men to the Cliff, where they staked off a claim and took new specimens of the dark, greasy looking mineral to Rosita to be assayed. These ran 740 ounces in silver per ton, and the men realized that they had a mine. They named their claim the Racine Boy in honor of Edwards, who came from that Wisconsin city, and as soon as news of the strike became known, the boom was on. Claims were staked all over the Cliff once more and over the surrounding ground too, much of which was later covered by the city. People swarmed in, prices went up, a few were successful in locating good mines and many were disappointed.

Almost pure horn silver was found all over the ground no deeper than the grass roots, and the frenzied miners worked every inch of their claims with such thoroughness that before long all the surface silver was picked

(287)

up and the diggings were exhausted. Some of the prospectors left, others ran up debts they couldn't meet, the newspapers of the state ran down the new camp until many believed that the ore had played out, and times were dull until the summer of 1879. At that time James Craig, of St. Joseph, Missouri, brought an expert with him to examine the mining properties. A few hours after his arrival, he bonded the Racine Boy and adjacent properties and left. Later, he was swindled out of his property; but he re-purchased it for a still larger figure, and this action of his put such confidence into the camp that a third boom commenced. In the meantime some men had sunk shafts and had uncovered rich pockets of ore, but most of the veins were small and soon petered out. Even so, two and a half millions were gouged out of the ground, and such mines as the Racine Boy and the Bull-Domingo continued to produce for years. Mine jumping was frequent, and often, when guards were placed on the disputed properties each night, their blazing bonfires could be seen for miles. By 1881 many mines were producing and new strikes were reported every day.

The Bull-Domingo, which was one of the most important mines of the area, had a stormy history. The Johnny Bull mining claim had been located in 1868 by Hunter and Martin. They dug a ten-foot hole and staked the ground but, becoming discouraged, left before they discovered anything. In 1878 Daniel L. Rarick of Leadville was grubstaked to prospect at the Cliff, and while looking around near the Johnny Bull, he "stepped on loose rock and fell forward. To prevent slipping further he stuck his pick into the ground above him and as he pulled it out, discovered small pieces of galena sticking to it. He returned and dug seven feet in solid galena ore." He then erected a discovery stake, called the claim the Domingo, and returned to Silver Cliff to tell his good news.

When Hunter and Martin heard of this, they tried to resurvey their claim so as to include this rich pocket of ore and they started court action against Rarick and his employer. They remained in possession of the property and worked their findings for some time, until the Domingo owners obtained an injunction which prohibited both parties from working the disputed territory. The case was in and out of court, first one side winning and then the other.

Once when the Judge of the District Court of Custer County was on a fishing trip, the attorneys for the Johnny Bull claimants went after him and found him on the banks of a trout stream. After "liberal applications of whisky and flattery . . . they prevailed on him to sign a document which he later found to be a revocation of his former decree annulling and reversing all former rulings" and ordering that the Domingo "parties" be ousted from the property. Armed with this order, the attorneys hurried to the Cliff and gave it to a deputy sheriff to serve on the holders of the Domingo mine. They, recognizing its illegality, refused to vacate the property, and fortified it instead.

That night, while most of the Domingo men were underground, 75 men from the Johnny Bull surrounded the Domingo mine, took possession at the surface, barricaded the mouth of the tunnel and closed the tops of the

SILVER CLIFF

↓ CUSTER COUNTY COURT HOUSE (OBSOLETE)

shafts. This imprisoned 25 men underground. During the night the intruders tossed balls of burning waste, saturated with ammonia, arsenic, sulphur, brimstone and "other hellish compounds" down the shafts, forcing the trapped men to come up and surrender to escape suffocation. After this the Johnny Bull claimants held the property until, in 1879, both sides agreed to sell the mines to a New York Company for $325,000. That December the Bull-Domingo Consolidated Mining Company was organized with a capital stock of $10,000,000, and for several years thereafter the mine continued to be the big producer of the camp.

In September, 1878, Mr. Bailey, who had bonded the Racine Boy, was visiting Rosita and asked Ed Austin, who was conducting a saloon and lunch house, why he did not open a similar place in the Cliff. Austin replied that he did not think it would pay. Bailey then took from his pocket a large piece of horn silver and said, "Where you can dig stuff like this out of the ground, there is sure to be a town, and you can bet your lunch house will succeed." Austin, acting on this suggestion, pulled down a small, vacant house that he owned, moved it to the Cliff, and at an outlay of about $200 opened the first business house in that city—the Silver Cliff Lunch House, which "consisted of a rude bar and a cold lunch, cooked in Rosita and brought over on horseback every morning. The bartender slept on two planks laid on the joist above the bar." Business grew so rapidly that the proprietor opened a new place, the Horn Silver Saloon, on December 4—the first in the city to contain a mirror and billiard tables. But before the Horn Silver Saloon could be built the town had to be surveyed and platted, for until streets were laid out no one knew where to build permanent structures.

Louis Slavich opened a saloon at about the same time and in ten weeks cleared $2000. His house had no sash in the windows and his counter was a rough pine plank. He washed his glasses but once a day, setting them out clean in the morning and allowing them to remain on the counter. Customers drank from the handiest glass. Water was scarce, and business too good to lose time washing them.

Unlike many mining camps Silver Cliff had no Indian troubles, but the "78ers remember the hurrah element which existed during the fall and winter when the gambling group predominated, the lowest of the demi-monde wielded their sceptre and road agents went flying through town." In fact, for the next couple of years it was known as the most exciting place to live west of the Mississippi.

The population fluctuated between 6,000 and 10,000 persons, the city contained nearly ten miles of streets, and citizens planted evergreens and flowers around their homes so that the sagebrush waste began to "blossom as the rose."

The *Silver Cliff Miner* of Jan. 7, 1880, gives a glowing resume of the city's development under the heading: "An Historical Descriptive Epitomo."

No town in the country with the exception of Leadville has grown with such astonishing speed as the gushing, energetic little city of Silver Cliff . . . 29 Fire plugs have been placed through out the city and mains laid. At present water carts haul the water from the springs a few miles away and deliver it through town—40 cents a barrel being asked. The Police department consists of but five men . . . but they are handsomely uniformed and are represented as being energetic and thoroughly capable.

Principal arrests are of vagrants, and for drunkenness and disorder and prisoners number sufficient to form a very efficient chain gang who contribute by their labor on the streets, very materially to the prosperity and appearance of the city.

In the way of stores and business houses, saloons of course lead, there being 25; groceries follow with 20, blacksmith 10, drygoods 8, clothing 7, meat markets 6, bakeries 6, barber shops 5, hairdressers 4, harness 4 and some 30 other places.

The Mint Saloon and Billiard Hall, Cheap Charley's Clothing store, the Elk Horn Corrall, the Colorado House and the American House lined the main street. The first drug store was conducted in a tent on Mill Street, opening with $100 worth of goods. In less than a year the proprietor was able to erect a building and carry over $2000 in stock. There were 2 banks, 3 excellent hotels and "seven inferior ones," and 6 restaurants. The Western Hotel was the first public boardinghouse and was soon followed by the Cliff House.

A. Arbour came to the Cliff in September, 1878, from Alamosa and built a dance house which opened before Christmas, offering the first dramatic entertainment in the city. At that time it was a resort for the entire community. "There were no churches, no reading rooms and no pretty and interesting young ladies to entertain the boys so they were either forced to wrap themselves in their blankets and lie down in a pile of straw to keep warm or go to the dance house." By 1880, however, the Gem Novelty Theatre and three other halls were opened affording amusement for the people and supplying accommodations for such combinations of performers or lecturers as wandered into the city."

The Variety Shows advertised with a nightly parade at six o'clock. A brass band led the march, boys were hired to carry banners, and the performers and dance house girls, driven in buckboards, smiled and waved at prospective patrons. The Silver Palace Saloon and Club, run by Ike Morris and Charles Kamerick, enlivened the evenings with music and with "the presence of Jennie Creek and Belle McLain, the first two girls of the town. . . . The place was literally packed every night, so much so that Morris often feared that the thin walls would be pushed out."

When the miners began sending for their families and respectable women began to arrive with every coach, "Society" at the Cliff was born. Balls, concerts, parties and lectures abounded.

With family life established, churches and schools were needed. The Rev. Teitsworth of Rosita preached the first sermon in the streets of Silver Cliff. Later, the Rev. Drummond ministered each week to both Silver Cliff and Rosita, walking the seven miles between services until his health failed. The Episcopalians were the first group to organize, although the Presbyterians held the first church service. In time the Roman Catholics, Methodists, and Baptists were represented, as well as a Union Sabbath School organization.

The ladies of St. Luke's Episcopal church were much given to social and charitable activities. A Fourth of July Lunch and Ice-cream Table and an Oyster Supper provided the first payment on an organ. A fair which netted

(291)

the ladies $390, offered prizes which consisted of a gold-headed cane and an "elegant celluloid toilet set."

The first church bell was presented by Mr. Bailey of the Racine Boy to St. Luke's "in accordance with a promise he made to present such a token to the first house of worship erected at the cliff."

W. H. F. Wonderly issued "a six column weekly paper," the *Silver Cliff Weekly Prospector*, whose "tone was always spicy and refined," as the following headline shows:

"Suicide. Mrs. Lora Barton Snaps the Subtle Thread with the Six-Shooter." The article described how the lady put her house in order and then, "dressed in her bedclothing, she lay down on the bed and deliberately pulled the trigger."

Four papers in all were published at the Cliff, the *Prospector*, the *Republican*, the *Miner*, and the *Gazette*; and by 1880 the *Prospector* had become the leading paper of southern Colorado.

Civic pride produced bursts of oratory in the daily press, such as the following extract which prophesied the city's coming importance as a summer resort:

> From this spot there is no grander view in Colorado as far as the eye can reach, the jagged peaks of the Sangre de Cristo and Spanish range of mountains—grand monuments of antiquity, that for ages have kept silent watch over the fertile valley that spreads out in emerald beauty from their base, like the cloak from the shoulders of a dismantled warrior. . . . Lakes above the city, whose shimmering waters the sunbeams kiss and kiss again without warming into emotion their icy bosom. When the broad verandaed hotels with all the conveniences of luxuriant eastern palaces rise up from their water's edge, and pleasure boats on their quiet bosom float, will the pleasure loving monied kings of the east swelter in the putrid summer atmosphere when such places are easy of access? We will leave Time to answer our questions.

The Grape Creek extension of the D. & R. G. railroad pushed from Canon City toward Silver Cliff in 1880. "Following their usual piratical custom," writes an old-timer, "instead of bringing the road to the Cliff they started a new town one mile to the west, so as to make money selling town lots. The road reached Westcliffe in May, 1881, and we listened eagerly for the sound of the first train, whose shrill whistle was re-echoed by our grand old mountains." Since the terminus of the road was one mile away passengers were forced to travel between the two towns by Concord coach.

For over a year Silver Cliff had wanted the county seat, and as soon as Westcliffe was founded, there was talk of moving the courthouse from Rosita to a more central location. In the next election Silver Cliff, with Westcliffe's support, won and prepared to move the courthouse to its new location. Rosita refused to give it up; so a committee of vigilantes marched to Rosita, took the records and brought them to the Cliff. Later they were properly deposited in the new courthouse, which was built, in appreciation of Westcliffe's aid, halfway between the two towns. This courthouse is still standing, although it was a weathered skeleton the last time I saw it. As Westcliffe grew and Silver Cliff declined, the county seat was moved again, and today it is Westcliffe that holds the coveted "plum."

Fire was always a threat in mining camps where so much of the construction was of wood; and Silver Cliff had two disastrous blazes, one in 1880 which nearly razed the town, and another in 1882 which consumed one business block. The city had a well organized fire department, the only one in Custer County. It was made up of volunteers and was composed of the G. B. McAulay Hose, the H. M. Zeigler Hose, the W. J. Robinson Hooks No. 1 and Hooks No. 2. Of these the McAulay Hose Company was the most famous, winning first prize at more than one state tournament. In August 1882 Silver Cliff was host to the State Fireman's Tournament and made great preparations for the event. The grandstand was nearly a block long, and McAulay, as a special feature, bought a small sized hose cart to be drawn by boys who weighed less than 100 pounds. This proved to be a very popular innovation but was banned by the judges from the official race.

Excitement ran high as the nine competing teams from other cities paraded and practiced. The McAulay's were defenders of the Prize Belt they had won the preceding year at Colorado Springs. The great day arrived and the races were on: hose teams and hook and ladder companies displayed perfect timing and team work as they made the prescribed tests. The McAulay's won, and the citizens subscribed $200 with which to purchase medals commemorating the wonderful record of 34¼ seconds in a wet hose test, which the team maintained for the second consecutive year. A banquet was also tendered them at the Powell House, at which "the tables were spread with relish and vim and the supply was sadly weakened till bodily contentment prevailed."

In 1882 a two-story Fireman's Hall was built to serve as a headquarters for meetings and to supply a "pleasant place for the reception of brother firemen who frequently visit the city." Three bedrooms were provided, so that in the event of a fire "members from each company could be at the carts almost as soon as the alarm was given." Until a few years ago a large wooden sign in the shape of a fireman grasping a hose ornamented the facade of the building.

Another source of local pride was the water works. After much discussion and many committee meetings, Silver Cliff voted in 1880 a bond issue to be used in building the works, and the city council bought Trapper Smith's Springs to provide the water. The firm of Russell and Alexander, who had built similar plants in Colorado Springs and Leadville, was selected for the enterprise. The original contract was $70,300. Extras were $2900 and the cost of the Springs $1500, making the total expenses $74,700. When tested the water works was considered completely satisfactory, for it could throw a perpendicular stream 150 feet high, and the springs which supplied it were believed good for an indefinite period of time.

By 1882 the mining boom was over and many mines had closed down. People began to drift away and payments on the bonds lagged. In 1883 James W. Callaway, who operated a store at the Bull-Domingo mine, traded his house in Silver Cliff for a saddle pony, so greatly had property values fallen. By 1885 the city defaulted on its bonds and a new city council refinanced them at $40,000. To meet the payments taxes were increased; but to avoid paying the higher rate, those who could, put their houses and shops on rollers and moved them one mile west to Westcliffe. At first only four of five stores were so moved, but soon most of the town was rolled away and the bonds were again defaulted.

It was the silver crash of 1893 which finished the Cliff, as it did all other silver camps, and the population dropped lower and lower—576 in 1900; 250 in 1910, until today only 50 to 75 persons live in the once famous city. Its ten miles of streets are hard to find, although a few can be located by their rows of fire plugs; but most of the townsite has returned to sagebrush. Yet in 1880 an enthusiastic editor wrote:

"The National Capitol will doubtless remain at Washington for some time, but look out Denver, the State Capitol is coming to Silver Cliff. Two years from now the Governor's inaugural address will be delivered to the solons convened at Silver Cliff.

"Silver Cliff is a bustling, energetic, progressive little municipality. If its past is a criterion of its future it is destined to take a permanent rank among the magic cities of the Centennial state, among whom it is even now making itself felt, and pushing its claim to recognition to the front."

CHAPTER XII

The San Luis Valley

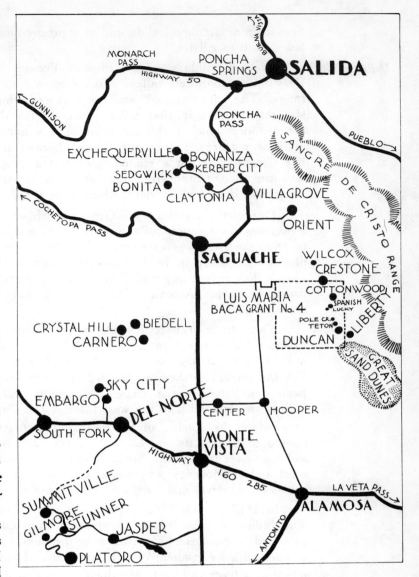

Cleora

ALL the time we were in the Wet Mountain Valley I kept looking at the Sangre de Cristo range, partly because of its stately beauty and partly because I was anxious to get into the next valley and see it from the other side. There were old mining camps there, too, and since there was no way to cross the range except by pack train, we returned to Westcliffe and followed Texas Creek back to the highway which leads to Salida.

Just this side of Salida is a cemetery. It is all that is left of Cleora; and as I passed its untended graves I recalled what the old man in Silver Cliff had told me about the D. & R. G.'s habit of laying out new towns at railheads so as to sell lots.

In 1878 when the Atchison, Topeka and Santa Fe was planning to build a road through the canyon of the Arkansas, they secured the necessary ground and laid out a town which they named Cleora, about a mile below the mouth of the South Arkansas river. The town grew rapidly all through 1879 and was the supply point for the mining camps along the Arkansas and for those of the Tomichi district.

When the D. & R. G. instead of the Santa Fe obtained the right of way along the Arkansas river to Leadville, Cleora was "denied any assistance," and a new town about two miles away was laid out by the officers of the road, to which the residents of Cleora moved, bag and baggage. The new town was called Salida and is a prosperous city today, whereas Cleora has ceased to exist.

Villa Grove

Leaving Salida we drove through Poncha Springs and on over Poncha Pass into the San Luis valley, whose eastern boundary is the Sangre de Cristo range. The valley is vast, and the highway which runs the length of it lies straight ahead, mile after mile. After lengthy driving I saw a few trees in the distance which I thought must be a windbreak next to a ranch house, until, as we drew nearer, my "ranch" became the town of Villa Grove. It, like Cleora, was not a mining town but a supply point, established in the seventies for the ranchers in the valley and for the mining camps of Bonanza, Claytonia, Bonita and Orient, which were tucked away in the foothills.

During the eighties Villa Grove, which was then entirely surrounded by trees, was the terminus of the narrow gauge railroad from Poncha Pass; but in 1890 the road was extended down the valley as far as Alamosa. An old photograph, taken in 1891, shows the town with a few more buildings in it than it has today, and many false-fronted stores which lined both sides of the main street. A sign in front of one store read: "Fresh eggs, rubber boots, corsets."

There have been settlements in the valley since 1859, when a group of Spanish-Americans from Santa Fe built a settlement called Lucero Plaza near the present town of Monte Vista. The ranchers stopped in the valley, but the miners pushed on toward the San Juan country, where gold had been discovered in the sixties. Gradually toll roads were built into the valley, and beyond it to the west through the Cochetopa hills.

Before the coming of the railroad, a stage line was established from Pueblo to Lake City via La Veta Pass, Del Norte and Antelope Springs, and then over the divide. Stage stations were located every twelve to sixteen miles and the journey was made in large Concord coaches, drawn by four horses on the level and by six in the mountains.

In 1877 the D. & R. G. built its track from Walsenburg to La Veta. The following year it was constructed over La Veta Pass, and was then extended to Alamosa. The road over the pass was considered an engineering wonder with its gradient of two hundred and eleven feet to the mile and its muleshoe curves, on each of which, it was said, the conductor could hand the engineer a light for his pipe! In 1881 it was extended to Del Norte and South Fork as well as to Antonito and Durango through Cumbres Pass.

Orient

"There's little left of Villa Grove, so let's drive over to Orient," I said to my friends. "If you look closely at the base of the mountains to the east you can see the road which leads to it and the terraces of the mine. I've found one reference that mentions the discovery of free gold six miles northeast of Villa Grove and close to the old camp of Oriental; so I suppose Orient and Oriental were the same place."

Orient is an iron camp. When the steel mill was built at Pueblo, iron ore was obtained from Leadville; but when the Colorado Coal and Iron Co., the predecessor of the C. F. & I., developed this mine, the railroad spur was built here to transport the ore. This iron mine was operated on a large scale,

(296)

employing one hundred men and shipping one to two hundred tons of ore per day to the smelters in Pueblo and Durango.

The mine was still operating in 1924, and perhaps later; but in 1939 when I first visited it, the buildings were closed and the company houses were empty.

The road to Orient cuts across the valley to the base of the mountains and then winds up past the Valley View hot springs and along the edge of a hill to the camp. Row after row of tiny homes line the lower slopes of the mountain, while behind them are the big dumps and the sheds belonging to the company. The view from the camp is breathtaking, for the valley is so wide that the low, rolling hills on its western rim are blue with haze and the ranches on the valley floor look like green dots on an immense checkerboard.

As there were several camps in the area that I needed to look up before I visited them, we drove on to Saguache, to the County courthouse. Saguache appears to be a sleepy little town, with wide streets lined with huge cottonwoods and with homes surrounded by well-tended gardens, but its community center is most active, and its stores and hotels serve the northern end of the whole valley.

The County Clerk and I scrutinized the wall map of Saguache County, searching for the locations of Bonita, Claytonia and other old camps.

The Kerber Creek Camps

"If you go to Bonanza you'll pass Claytonia and Sedgwick and you'll be a mile from Exchequerville. They all started at the same time," he told me.

The road to Bonanza follows Kerber Creek up a narrow valley between sage-covered hills, through groves of cotton-woods, and passes an occasional ranch house or a deserted cabin, until, swinging around a sharp corner it skirts the foundations of an old mill and enters the long street which bisects the town. There was smoke coming out of the chimney of a cabin and I knocked at the door.

The woman who opened it invited me inside. She was putting lunch on the table while her husband was "washing up" back of the cabin, but she urged me to sit down. When I asked her about Bonanza she said, "I can't tell you any of the history, but you go across the street to the red house and John can."

Knocking on another door I was again ushered in and seated in the parlor. The young woman who greeted me called to her husband and told him what I wanted to know, whereupon "John" came into the parlor and said emphatically, "Dad's the man who can tell you. Do you remember passing a sawmill on the way up here? That's Dad's place. He lives in the old ranch house next to it and runs the mill. I'll call him up and see if he'll be there and will talk to you." Going to a wall phone he rang a number and began talking to his mother. Apparently "Dad" was busy at the mill and wasn't to be disturbed, but "John" persisted, saying, "But she won't take more than ten minutes, and it's the only way she can find the history, for Dad knows it all. You tell him she'll be along in half an hour," and smiling broadly, he hung up.

"I know a little of the history of the Kerber Creek mines," I told Jim and Vic as we started back toward the sawmill. "Just as we leave town we pass the old smelter site, and a mile below here, where the road makes a big bend, are the sites of Sedgwick and Kerber City. There used to be a brewery about half a mile up Brewery Creek, but you can't see it from the road."

Sedgwick and Kerber City

Bonanza and its satellite camps date from 1880, for after the Leadville excitement in 1879 prospectors swarmed in and discovered gold and silver veins up Kerber Creek. There were really four towns—Sedgwick, Kerber City directly across the stream from it, Bonanza City one mile above, and Exchequerville two miles beyond Bonanza. Sedgwick, the lower town, which was the first to be built, was laid out in July, and had a population of 650 by the end of the year. Besides stores, saloons and assay offices, it had a large billiard hall and bowling alley, two hotels, several sawmills and two dancehalls where, according to the paper, "the giddy mazes of the dance can be enjoyed with giddier girls from Silver Cliff and adjoining towns. . . . One round in the dance with your fair partner costs $1, fifty cents in excess of charges in other towns but the freights, you know, are high in this country."

Exchequerville

The Exchequer was the first mine discovered in the district and the Bonanza was the second. Around the Exchequer a small town grew up, but when a prospector uncovered a rich vein and shouted, "Boys, she's a bonanza!" the last and biggest of the settlements was christened. Bonanza

Bonanza

City, which was closer to the chief mines, soon became the rival of Sedgwick, outstripping it in size and popularity. As Bonanza City grew it became the center of the district and in time absorbed the populations of the other towns. So promising was the outlook that by January, 1881, Bonanza was spoken of as the "New Leadville."

Anne Ellis, the author, lived in Bonanza during the boom and writes vividly of the rivalry between the towns. The road between Bonanza and Sedgwick was a "rare specimen of engineering skill," the skill consisting of the road's having been left "in such a condition that a vehicle could get over it without upsetting." She recalls how on the Fourth of July the miners always left their diggings and came in to one of the camps to celebrate. The Bonanza bunch usually got liquored up early in the day and, led by the editor of the *Bonanza News,* marched down to Sedgwick to clean up on the boys there.

By the rule of the camp a man was allowed ten days in which to commence work after sticking his location stake into his property. At the end of that time if no development had been done, others could work the claim.

Many lodes were discovered, the Rawley being the best prospect. It was always a good producer, selling in 1881 for $100,000 and continuing to ship lead and silver throughout the eighties. The Bonanza mine continued to produce until 1898, and the Empress Josephine in Copper gulch, from which a total of $7,000,000 was extracted, also shipped ore for a long time. It was reopened in 1947 after having been shut down for nearly forty years.

The Wheel of Fortune and the Defiance lodes on Mineral hill were also good properties but, as so often occurred, their claims overlapped. Both owners re-surveyed their properties preliminary to receiving patents, and lawyers began "buckling on their armor and rejoicing in the prospect of a legal fight."

Although a great deal of ore was found, much of it was low grade, and the cost of mining, freighting, shipping and smelting it was too great to keep the camp going. In the hope of reducing this expense, a smelter was erected in 1881 but it was not equipped to handle the low-grade ores and lay idle for years. The price of silver also declined, and as mining ceased toward the end of 1882, the population of 1300 began to drift away, and the boom was over. At this crucial moment Mark Biedell, experienced mining man of the valley, moved in, took a lease on the Michigan lode, built a mill and began experimenting with various processes of concentrating the low-grade ores. In 1899 he sold his mill but continued his experiments in dry concentration.

By 1896 less than 100 people were left in town, but in 1900 there was a revival in mining and the town began to come alive again. Two concentration mills were erected and run successfully, and the Bonanza, Exchequer and Eagle mines were again active. A little mining is still done around Bonanza but very few people live there.

"Here's the sawmill," said Jim. "Now let's find 'Dad.' "

We walked over piles of clean, pungent sawdust to the mill, where several men were busily guiding logs through the whirling saws, whose snarling whine made it hard to carry on conversation. Making my way over boards and moving belts to the side of an older man, who was engaged in feeding lumber, I shouted into his ear and finally got his attention. Beckoning me to follow him, he left the mill and found a quieter spot in which to talk.

"Didn't I see the foundations of a smelter a little way back up the road and across the stream?" I began.

"Yes, that was the Parkville smelter which blew in in 1897. The quaking asps along the creek made excellent charcoal for it, and two pits were kept burning all the time. Bonita was over the hill from Bonanza and was always reached by a trail. It was a little silver camp and is all gone now. There was some mining at Ford Creek, too, six miles southwest of Bonanza. You'll pass Claytonia on the way back to Villa Grove. It's all gone except two cabins. It petered out fast. Go to the house and ask my wife to show you the old newspaper dated 1881 that mentions Claytonia."

Claytonia

Thanking him, I hurried to the big ranch house and requested the newspaper, from whose faded columns I copied the following:

> Between Sedgwick and Villa Grove, on what is known as the Clayton ranch, a contact has been found between lime and porphyry . . . similar to the Leadville formations. Another year will show a large and populous city resounding with the noise and clatter of mills and workshops where a few months ago, the deer and coyote roamed unmolested. Even now the weird sweet note of our mountain canary is an earnest of what is to come. O thou fair, bright one, soon will thy melodious voice be hushed in solemn awe at the shrill notes of the steam engine.

It was late afternoon when we drove once more through Villa Grove and Saguache on our way to Crestone. Jim drove the car straight toward the mountains, heading toward a mass of trees right against the foothills. Somewhere in that green grove stood Crestone, pressed against the foot of the range below the jagged Crestone Needle. Just before reaching the town we noticed a huge ranch on our right, with an imposing gate and wrought iron sign which read: "LUIS MARIA BACA GRANT No. 4," and not realizing that more ghost towns lay on that ranch, we went innocently on.

A drive through the shady streets of Crestone brought us to the heart of town, where two general stores face each other across a broad avenue.

Crestone is the only surviving town in a mineral belt twenty-five miles long which extends along the lower slopes of the Sangre de Cristo range and which first attracted prospectors in 1879. A second boom occurred in 1890, when free-milling gold was found in gash veins which promised well but pinched out the deeper they were worked. During this boom the major portion of the town was built, and a mail and passenger express and freight line ran between it and the new town of Moffat. Shortly afterwards a number of miners from Rio Grande county began prospecting in the Crestone area, reopening the old Cleveland mine and laying out a new camp called Wilcox, two miles to the north.

"You could hear shots of giant powder in the mountains almost continually, and at night there were camp fires scattered all over the hills. This camp was prosperous then," said an old man who was sunning himself on a bench in front of one of the stores. "In 1899 Crestone was on the eve of its third boom and the following year, when its population reached 2000, it was incorporated. Real estate boomed, a hotel was built, the railroad was finished as far as the town, and miners were making strikes everywhere. Then in 1901 came the big strike at the Independent; but as soon as that was over Crestone slumped into the quiet little town that you see today."

"Can you tell me anything about the big ranch that we passed on the way here, the Baca Grant No. 4," I asked.

The old man shifted his position and his eyes looked far away. "It's a long story, but I know it," he said rather bitterly.

"In 1823 King Ferdinand 7th of Spain rewarded one of his subjects with the title of Don Luis Maria Cabeza de Vaca and granted him a huge tract of land in the new world. The original grant included the present site of Las Vegas, New Mexico. The ownership of the property was disputed, but Mexico recognized the rights of the Vaca family and gave it authority to select four new ranch sites totalling 400,000 acres in return for giving up its claim to the Las Vegas property. The family then selected the four tracts, one of which was located in what is now Saguache county, and is the 100,000-acre Grant No. 4.

"When, at the close of the Mexican War, the United States came into possession by treaty of Spanish and Mexican land grants, this grant was found to be the principal one in this state. The grant is twelve miles square with 14,000-foot Crestone peak as its northeast corner and the summit of the range its eastern boundary. Six streams have their source on the land.

(300)

CRESTONE

↓ ORIENT

It was located by the Surveyor General of Colorado in the name of the heirs of Luis Maria Baca, by authority of an act of Congress, June 21, 1860.

"When gold was found on the slopes of the range within the grant, trouble began. As gold, silver, copper, lead and iron ores were found in paying quantities, the camps of Cottonwood, Spanish, Duncan, Pole Creek and Lucky sprang up. Just as the mines were beginning to pay and the camps to flourish, the owners of the grant threw us miners out and took over the mines themselves. All our work was for nothing, and we had to sit by and see strangers run the mills and the mines that we had started. We never got over it."

"I've heard of Liberty," I broke in to change the subject. "Where was it?"

"Just outside the grant," said the old man with a gleam in his eye. "When the miners were ordered out of Duncan they established Liberty, just outside the grant fence. If you're looking for ghost towns you should see Liberty and Duncan. You can't drive to them, but maybe you can get permission at the ranch house to cross the property on horseback."

Liberty   It was the following summer before I was able to return to Crestone and the Baca grant. Before I made the trip I wrote to Mr. Collins, the president and manager of the San Luis Valley Land and Cattle Co., asking permission to cross his Hereford ranch in search of the old camps. His reply was prompt, courteous and business-like. He granted the permission but said that it was no place for a lady to drive a car alone; furthermore it was too far to hike. He therefore suggested that he secure a guide for me and provide horses for the trip.

Setting a date and taking Ethel with me, I started for the Baca grant early one July morning, wondering what was in store for us. As we drove toward the old adobe ranch house which is now used as the office, I looked around for the horses. There were none in sight. Entering the office, I asked Mr. Collins where my guide was.

"He's outside waiting for you," he replied, pointing to a lanky cowboy leaning against the corral fence. "This is a much bigger undertaking than you realize. At this season the sand is hard on the horses' feet and they have to go slowly. You couldn't get back till ten-thirty tonight. Even so, Jim, your guide, doesn't want to take his horses down there. He's seen horses just lie down and scream with pain and refuse to get up because the sand burns their feet. But he thinks he can get you there in his car, and there will be room for your friend to go, too."

So it was settled, and we were introduced to Jim and his car, an ancient Chevrolet with an eleven-inch clearance underneath. We piled in and, with a grinding of gears, were off. As I sat in the middle and as the seat was low and the windshield high, I saw nothing but the sky all the way to Liberty. The back of the car was filled with bits of corrugated iron, tin cans for water, baling wire and other necessary odds and ends. The mileage gauge didn't work, but the needle swung drunkenly back and forth; the gearshift trembled as if with palsy; everything rattled and shook. But the car ran.

Occasionally we passed sleek cattle (or so I was told, for I could not see them). Jim handled the car as he would a horse—swerving out of the road to find smoother going, carving out a new track across an arroyo, and even leaving the road entirely and ploughing through deep grass. We passed big wooden watertanks where the stock drank; we went through gates between enormous pastures; and once we met a man driving a team of mules hitched to a light wagon. Occasionally I caught a glimpse of the mountains to our left and could see that we were getting closer to them, and after a while Jim pointed out the masses of white sand at their base—the great sand dunes of the San Luis valley.

When we turned east and drew nearer and nearer to the dunes our progress was slower. The land sloped upward in low, rolling ridges, and as the ground became more sandy we ran into bits of quicksand. Jim knew where most of these were and would quickly turn off the road and drive through the tough, resilient Buffalo grass until the treacherous place was passed. The day got hotter and hotter. The hills became steeper and the sand deeper. The engine boiled and the car stopped. Jim got out and filled the radiator from a gallon can which had been making an infernal rattle in the back of the car. Taking some baling wire from his cache behind the seat, he opened up the sides of the radiator and wired them together. Now I couldn't even see the sky! After the engine cooled off we started again. Halfway up the next little hill the engine died. We rolled back down and tried it again, getting perhaps twenty feet further before the engine again sputtered and died. We rolled down again and made another run for it, getting a little closer to the top before the engine quit. "This is the way a road is made," commented Jim dryly. The fourth time we *just* got over the hump and rolled easily down the other side. On the next hill the same thing happened again.

"Do you think you can get us there?" I asked.

"Sure," drawled Jim; "if I don't we'll have to walk, and cowboys don't like that."

"Why was this place called Liberty?" I asked, wanting to get his version of the naming.

"Duncan was an older camp than Liberty and it was inside the fence. After the Baca grant was turned into a Hereford ranch we naturally didn't want miners on the property so we told them to get off. They left Duncan taking some of their cabins with them and went just about three hundred yards outside the fence at the edge of the grant and established Liberty."

We reached the barbed wire at the southern edge of the grant and Jim unlocked the gate. We walked through it and started up the sandy trail. The sand was deep and heavy and so hot that even with shoes it was painful to walk on.

"This isn't a good time of year to come here," said Jim. "In winter the sand is a perfect surface for horseback trips. You could make it in half a day."

Ahead in a clump of trees, toward whose shade we hurried, were the buildings of Liberty. Hung on the outside of a good-sized cabin was a collection of skulls and bones from horses, steers and sheep. Beyond was a little clearing in the trees, on one side of which was a small, false-fronted cabin which was once the post office and in which, Jim told us, a harmless lunatic had lived until recently. "He must have been mad," said Jim laconically. "I came down here once and stopped to see him. I opened the door of the cabin and found him there dead drunk and a dead skunk in with him. He'd been there a week."

Across from the cabin ran Short creek, narrow but clear, and in the midst of the tangle of bushes and trees which bordered it stood a large wooden waterwheel with a small cabin nearby. Jim and I started up the creek on a narrow foot trail which was so overgrown that we had to push through the bushes that blocked the path. Every now and then we found an abandoned object half-ridden in the tangled vines, such as an old saddle with all of its leather rotted away and only its wooden frame left. Further along was a wagon, so nearly covered with underbrush that we almost passed without seeing it. In another spot only fenceposts marked the site of a home and its garden. A few houses were still standing but their doors and windows were gone and their roofs sagged. On the porch of one was a wicker rocker and in the front room of another was an old iron bedstead. Jim pointed to where the schoolhouse had stood; but it, like many cabins, had been moved to Crestone after the mining ceased. Between 1908 and 1910 there were but three pupils, all from one family.

Some prospecting was done along the creek in the eighties, and mining was active again for ten or fifteen years after the miners were thrown out of Duncan in 1900 and moved to Short Creek, or Liberty. Too much money was put into promotion schemes and stock sales, but even so enough gold and silver were found for a five-stamp mill to be installed by the Blanca Mutual Mining and Milling Co. in 1902. Considerable work was done during 1903, especially on properties between Short and Sand creeks.

"Where was Music City?" I asked. "I've read that the Music mining district was located on Short creek, a mile east of Liberty, and I was wondering if the camp was nearby?"

"Music Pass is the same as Sand creek, the next creek below Short creek, this side of the sand dunes. It got its name from the sighing sounds made by the shifting sand of the dunes. There was a camp called Music City, but I'm not sure that I've ever run across it. On a pack trip I remember finding a bunch of cabins high on the range. Maybe that was it. I don't know."

Returning down the overgrown trail close to the water, I could see glimpses of the San Luis valley, stretching miles away to the west.

Duncan   As we walked back to the car Jim told us of Duncan, a mile inside the grant, and of other small camps which were situated at the mouth of each creek that tumbled down the slopes of the mountains. Teton was all gone and Pole Creek had some buildings left, but it was a steep hot climb up to them.

The road to Duncan was worse than anything we had been over. At its best it was just wide enough for the car, and more than once rocks scraped the doors. At one place a deep arroyo had cut its way through the roadbed. Jim got out and looked the situation over, shovelled some dirt into the hollow and we dipped down to the bottom and up the other side. Just as we were congratulating him on his driving, he stopped suddenly on the brink of another arroyo, so deep and narrow that it stumped even him. As there was no way through it, we backed up and *backed* through the arroyo that we'd just struggled through. "Well," said Jim, "we won't try that road." We returned almost to Liberty and then took another trail to Duncan. Only John Duncan's cabin remains, now used as a Forest Ranger's fire station.

The first prospectors in this part of the valley were Spaniards who came in the seventeenth century and left traces of their crude mining equipment at various places along the base of the foothills. Governor Gilpin of Colorado was probably the next person to be interested in the area, for he found rich float, some of which assayed high in gold on the slopes of Milwaukee hill on Pole creek, at the time when he and General Fremont crossed the valley. Miners followed up his discoveries and dug feverishly trying to locate the ore chute from which the float came; but they were unsuccessful in their efforts, and the gulches were deserted until 1890, when another burst of prospecting began.

Duncan's camp was started in 1890, and although it was handicapped from the first by being within the Baca land grant and therefore outside the government's land and mining laws, it grew into a flourishing place. It had a daily newspaper, the *Golden Eagle*, a daily stage connection with the valley towns and a population of 1000. Five stamp and process mills were erected to handle the ore from the mines up Pole and Alpine creeks and on Milwaukee hill. As the camp prospered it constantly extended its boundaries, thereby occupying more and more land within the grant. Between 1889 and 1900 all its mines were working and enough miners' families lived there to warrant a school which forty pupils attended.

In May, 1898, the Supreme Court rendered a verdict concerning the grant which was of great importance to the miners of the region. The grant had been in litigation for twenty-five years, and both the miners and Mr. George H. Adams, agent for the estate (who had lived on it for twenty-three years and had started the cattle ranch there), were glad to have the issue settled. The court held that the presence of minerals found after the location of the land was not sufficient ground upon which to cancel the patent and therefore sustained the title to the land. The *Saguache Crescent* of May 5, 1898, states:

> We do not see in this decision a blow at the mining industry of the east range. We are informed that the grant will be thrown open to prospectors and that they will be given most liberal terms on a lease. Now that the uncertainty is over we expect to see renewed activities at Cottonwood, Duncan and Spanish Creek and believe that before another year rolls round, mills will be pounding away on the ores of the district and producing good revenues for the owners and operators alike.

"It seems superfluous to add that the future greatness of Duncan camp is assured," crowed the *Golden Eagle;* and then, just as its permanency seemed secure, Adams issued the following statement:

(305)

Leases will be granted to prospectors and miners now occupying the ground on a royalty ranging from one to ten percent; the land will be laid out as favorable to the locators as possible; it has not been determined how long the leases will run, nor what amount of work will be required. It will take sixty to ninety days to get through the vast amount of work required in considering and locating applications for a lease. I have waited twenty-three years for this decision and the miners can afford to give me a little time to systematize plans.

This sounded fine; but at the same time a half interest in the townsite of Crestone and all the mineral part of the grant were sold to an eastern company, who promptly stated that they would allow no business houses or mills on the grant and no saloons in Crestone.

In July, 1900, the San Luis Valley Land and Mining Co., which now owned the grant, sent a deputy United States marshall to serve a summons from the U. S. Circuit Court against a score of miners and settlers who, according to the company, were "withholding possession of the grant from the rightful occupants." The *Saguache Crescent* of July 12 said that if "trouble should break out it will be at Duncan. The grant is well patrolled. Practically all the squatters have been evicted" and have left. "The few that remain will be ousted by the company which has taken over the mines and is ready to work them."

"There is a great feeling of resentment among the settlers, . . . but the company is able to hold its own." General distrust and excitement exists but since the "blowing up of the cabins on Dead Man's creek on June 26 there has been no overt act of violence. The armed men of the company have been instructed to keep the peace. . . . Another batch of writs of eviction have been served in the settlement of Cottonwood and at Spanish Creek. . . . The company is willing to put friendly miners to work and four at Duncan have accepted.

"For the last year the miners have made every effort through the United States Land Office and the office of the U. S. Surveyor General to have the government make an authentic survey of the grant but without avail." The miners are convinced that "posts, boundary marks and fences have been moved, thereby increasing the grant to embrace several mining properties of value. Sufficient funds have been raised by subscription for a private survey . . . which it is hoped will establish the truth of what the miners claim."

They also assert that the "town of Duncan was not on the grant according to a correct survey and that the grant people changed the lines of the survey so as to take in Duncan without any authority of law. The case has been in the Court of Appeals once and is now sent back for another trial."

The survey found that nineteen of twenty-four section corners on the south side of the grant were correct, and although the miners were still unconvinced, they were helpless.

"I've heard people in Crestone talk," said Jim, "about when the miners were thrown off the grant. They say thugs were hired to run people out. I know a man whose father was killed by them. It was a case of having to

LIBERTY

↓ EMBARGO

BONANZA

run off or sell out. When the town folded up, houses were moved out to the valley."

Leaving Duncan, we followed a narrow, winding dirt road close to the base of the mountains, and crossed Pole creek, Deadman creek (so named because a dead Spanish soldier was found there) and Cottonwood creek. At the site of Spanish, Jim stopped the car and showed me where two or three old cabins still stood. At Cottonwood we passed the old smelter foundations and investigated the one cabin which is still in the trees. The rest of the way was down the old railroad grade to Crestone.

Back at the ranch we said goodbye to Jim, and I thanked Mr. Collins for making the trip possible for us. He showed us through his home, of which he was rightly proud, for it was full of the trophies of his big-game hunts in Africa. Stuffed animals were everywhere, and while he pointed out his treasure I sat on an elephant's foot and leaned against a tiger skin.

Two more years went by before I again saw Crestone. This time I went to get first-hand information about the camps which I had visited but about which I knew so little. I drove into Crestone one June afternoon and drew up in front of the two stores. Entering one, I asked about people who could tell me local history. The storekeeper was most cooperative and gave me a list of several names. He even took me across the street to introduce me to Miss Emerson, an elderly lady who had lived in Liberty years before, when the camp was called Short Creek and when only prospectors were there, for the real boom did not come until 1900. She still had her mother's diary, written while at Liberty, but she assured me that it was of personal rather than of historic interest.

Next I trudged up a side street lined with wild flowers until I reached the home of Mr. Handy. He had lived at Cottonwood in 1900, when the big one hundred-stamp mill had been running and when, in the election, 500 votes were cast from Cottonwood alone. While we stood talking on his front porch, the mosquitoes were making a killing; but I weighed historical evidence against a few bites, and history won. Mr. Handy suggested that I look up Mr. Noah Mayer and gave me directions to his house.

Mr. Mayer, his wife, his daughter and their dog were all at home, and as I sat in their parlor scratching the ears of their long-haired pet, they talked to me of Liberty. Producing a photograph album, they found pictures taken at Liberty and insisted upon giving me snapshots of Crestone and of the range in winter, and after a very pleasant and valuable half hour I left. They directed me to Mr. Marshall, who had lived in Cottonwood. He was an elderly man and his house was elderly, too. Offering me his rocking chair and hitching his chair up beside mine so as to hear my questions, he began to reminisce.

Cottonwood

"I've lived here over fifty years and I've seen lots of changes around Crestone. In 1898 all the mines were working as far down as Short Creek, and men were making new strikes all the time. When the Baca grant and the big mill at Cottonwood were closed in 1898 due to litigation, mining properties north of Crestone were developed and the camp of Wilcox sprang up.

"The Independent mine at Cottonwood was working in 1895 when I came here, and was the biggest property along the range. In 1900 a Philadelphia syndicate bought the Baca grant and began to develop its mineral resources. They built the mill which shipped $80,000 worth of gold bullion to the mint every month, with only seventy of its stamps running. The company also extended the railroad through Crestone to the mill, and as soon as the road was completed real estate began to boom and mining men swarmed into the district looking for good investments.

"When I was a boy I worked at Cottonwood, driving eighty head of jacks up to the Independent mine, waiting for them to be loaded with ore and then leading them down to the mill. There were mostly one-story log houses at Cottonwood then, but toward the end of the camp a few frame houses were put up. Some mining was done on the grant until the nineteen-twenties, when the mine was abandoned and many of the buildings torn down or moved into Crestone.

"There used to be a mill on Spanish creek this side of Cottonwood creek. The camp of Lucky was on Spanish creek, too, but it was a mighty rough place, built up and down the stream in one long, crooked street.

Spanish and Lucky

"Old John Hertzog came into Crestone once with his pockets full of gold nuggets. Some of them were the size of a grain of wheat and some were as big as marbles. He showed us chunks of quartz, too, with seams of gold in them from his claim on Spanish creek near the summit of the range. It was rough country, but he swore there were lots of outcroppings of free gold up near his diggings. Nearly every creek and gulch from Sierra Blanca north to Poncha Pass showed rich gold float, but the trouble was the ore was all at the surface.

"Two miles south of Cottonwood was Pole Creek, where they had a five-stamp mill. The richest strike was in the Esther mine whose ore ran $350 a ton. Half a mile up the creek were the Dexter and the Golden Gate, which had wire gold in galena, but most of the veins showed coarse free gold mixed with quartz. There were tie camps up the hill, too, cutting timber for poles and ties."

Pole Creek

When I rose to leave he insisted upon showing me his vegetable garden, which I admired row by row, and when I finally left he put a bunch of lilacs into my hand and said he was glad I had come.

Dan Slane, who came to Saguache in 1874 and who mined all through the region fifty-nine years ago, gave me the most information concerning Biedell and Crystall Hill. While in Saguache I inquired about these places at the courthouse and I hunted up individuals who remembered them, and from each one I gathered crumbs of information, which, when fitted together, gave a composite picture of the forgotten camps in the hills west of town. Dan Slane's adobe house was down by the highway and was half hidden by huge cotttonwood trees. Jumping across a narrow irrigation ditch, I pushed open the squeaking gate to his yard and rapped on the weathered door. There was no answer to my knock. The windows were dusty, the shades were drawn, and I doubted if he were at home; but to make sure,

Biedell and Crystal Hill

I walked around to the back of the house and there he sat on a box, leaning against the warm adobe wall smoking his pipe.

He was an old man, spare and dignified and a little deaf, but when I told him my errand he rose and ushered me inside. As we sat in his cluttered living room he began to talk of the days when he had worked at Biedell and at other camps of which I had heard. He showed me his collection of ore specimens, handling each piece with a nostalgic tenderness and identifying not only its composition but the mine from which it came. Occasionally his voice would trail off and his eyes would look far away as he recalled some incident of his youth. Then, collecting himself, he would pick up another specimen and begin a new story. I hated to leave him for he was an encyclopedia of mining history, but when I could think of no more questions to ask and he volunteered no more stories I left.

Mark Biedell, a French rancher and mining man for whom the mining camp of Biedell was named, came to the San Luis valley about 1865 and bought a ranch on La Garita creek. A few years later he sold the ranch and moved to the raw, new town of Del Norte, where he became a leading merchant. He became interested in the mines at Bonanza and invested heavily in them; he put money into the Shenandoah mine at Silverton, and in 1882, when the Saguache County Bank was incorporated as a state bank, he became one of its directors as well as assistant cashier.

Biedell was founded about 1881 on Crystal hill, southwest of Saguache, and thereafter both names are used in speaking of the camp and the mines of the region. By 1883 several mines were being worked and new strikes attracted one thousand men to the properties. The Esperanza was the oldest location in the camp and was still being worked in 1928. The principal mine was the Buckhorn, from which $80,000 in gold was taken. During 1886-1887 the Buckhorn-Alexander war raged. As usual the contention was over rival mining claims, and both properties were heavily guarded. By the time the feud was settled the camp was beginning to dwindle, and today little but its cemetery remains.

Carnero   Carnero, a carbonate camp twenty-five miles from Del Norte and seventeen from Saguache, was situated on Carnero creek. It was close to Biedell and Crystal Hill, and during the eighties several mines were found in its vicinity. To the irritation of the miners the post office was discontinued in 1886, just as the camp was beginning to boom. A hotel had just been built, a stage line connected the camp with Saguache and Del Norte, and the "Old Crow Literary Club" met every Saturday evening. According to the newspaper, "some of its members are apt to get full of enthusiasm and are liable to get spilt. Well, if they boil over, let their spirits waste."

The Spring Chicken mine, so named because it was discovered in mid-winter, was developed in 1886 and was worked for several years. The Humboldt, discovered the same year, was reported as being the "youngest claim in camp. It wears baby clothes, is now a good creeper and is expected to walk in six months." But in spite of the optimistic notes which appeared in the Del Norte paper, by 1887 "the boom was going the wrong way." Some mining was done in 1888, but before long the camp ceased to exist.

(310)

In the mountains southwest of Monte Vista was the Conejos mining district, of which I had heard; so early one morning we started out to look for Jasper, Stunner, Platoro and Summitville, all of which were minute dots upon the map and were reached by graded and unimproved roads. Some miles south of Monte Vista the highway was cut by a dirt road which we followed up Gato or Cat creek to the western rim of the valley, past the Terrace reservoir, and up into the foothills. After a drive of about eleven miles we came to some frame houses and cottages, all distressingly new and freshly painted. This was no ghost town but a modern resort. Feeling sure there must be more to Jasper (or Cornwall as it was once called) than what we saw, I began to explore back of the shiny new buildings, and less than four hundred feet away, down by the creek, found the old road and several decaying cabins with sod roofs and gaping doorways. These must have dated from 1874-75 when the town was founded. Prospectors, drawn to the region by the Summitville discoveries, combed the entire area and discovered the Perry lode at the foot of Cornwall mountain and the Miser, both of which remained the best properties in the camp.

The southern end of the Valley and the "Silver-Plated Mountains"

Jasper

Two and a half miles above Jasper was the Sanger mine. Its owners claimed to have found a mountain of "birdseye porphyry" that ran ten dollars to the ton. Having collected all the money possible from credulous investors, they proceeded to close down the mine and appropriate the funds. The unsavory reputation that Jasper received from this piece of wildcatting made other investors so skeptical that little money was put into the camp.

Partly because of its inaccessibility and partly because too little capital was invested in it, the camp never did boom. Instead, a jinx seemed to hover over it. In 1887 "Jasper had one more sad disaster for which this camp is noted." Ten tons of ore were shipped to Denver to be tested and before the run of the ore was completed and percentages tabulated, the Denver smelter caught fire, and "Jasper is still in doubt" as to the value of its ore.

Six miles further up the road was a government marker which read "Stunner," but we could find no town. There were no buildings at all, only rotting lumber, rusting machinery, and a few crumbling foundations. Completely disappointed, we drove away and started to climb the ledge road on the opposite mountainside toward Platoro. When we were about halfway to the top, we glanced across the narrow valley at some vermillion cliffs and looked down at the spot that we'd just left. There below us was Stunner! The town looked exactly like a great map, each street and foundation clearly discernible from above, whereas at close range they were swallowed up in grass and weeds.

Stunner

The first location of fissure veins was made in 1882, although as early as 1879 there had been a little prospecting in Cat gulch nearby. By 1886 the "camp was looking up," although very little attention was paid to it by the mining world. At that time Stunner, which is situated near the head of the Conejos river about forty-five miles from the towns of Conejos and Antonita, was reached by a toll road which followed the Conejos river the entire distance.

The usual confusion of names exists, Conejos Camp, Loynton and

Stunner all appearing as the post office designation in different years. In 1887 Loynton was changed to Stunner, yet in 1889 when there were one hundred and fifty miners there, both "Conejos Camp and Platoro asked for a post office."

"Several classes of ore were found, antimonial, brittle, ruby, native and sulphurets of silver, nickel, free gold and gold sulphurets found in white quartz from one to twenty feet in width in a porphyritic granite formation."

The Merrimac and Eurydice lodes seem to have been the best producers, although the Snow Storm and Log Cabin were also worked. Like all camps, the miners believed in its coming greatness, as this newspaper notice testifies. On the Fourth of July they admitted that although "we can get neither Robinson's circus nor Governor Adams to visit our camp . . . we will be prepared for the next (year) so that our roar can be heard all over the state."

Platoro

The shelf road squirmed up the side of the mountain toward Platoro, four miles east of Stunner. At the top it swerved around a corner, crossed a saddle and dipped into the next valley, where the camp lay spread over a mountain meadow. There were several well-defined streets and many empty log cabins, most of them with overhanging eaves and massive ridge poles. A mine dump peeped out from the edge of the timber, and the framework of an old store from which the outer lumber had been stripped stood like a skeleton sentinel. Cattle grazed over the meadow, and two or three cowboys watched us indifferently from the porch of the only newly-painted house in the place. Otherwise we saw no signs of life.

Platoro and Summitville are the oldest camps in the district and both are high, Platoro being 9700 feet and Summitville 11,300 feet. There were several good mines such as the Mammoth and Parole, in which gold and silver were found in fissure veins. Platoro was a camp of the eighties and attained a population of 300 by 1890 when rich ore was being shipped from several properties. Then the ore gave out and Platoro became almost as quiet as it is today.

The Mammoth mine was the most important property. It grew from a prospect hole held by Jim Walker and his two partners. When provisions ran low Walker, who was a shark at cards, went out to the valley to win enough to enable the trio to continue work, while his two partners remained at the mine, sinking the shaft. After some exploration they struck pay ore and then sold the mine for a large sum. With this sale the mining boom at Platoro began.

All of these camps were so inaccessible that as soon as mining companies began the development of their claims they begged for better roads to be built into the region. In 1888 a wagon road connected Summitville, which is on top of a mountain, with Del Norte, and an extention of the road was built to Platoro. Stunner and Jasper were reached by another extension of the Summitville road which branched off down the valley seven miles below that town. There was also a road from the valley up Cat creek to Jasper and Platoro but it was long, rough and narrow.

(312)

PLATORO   ↓ SUMMITVILLE

In 1901 and 1902 large veins and pockets of gold and silver tellurium were opened in the district, and Platoro and Stunner continued as the leading mining centers.

Gilmore

In the spring and early summer of 1913 Platoro received a temporary stimulus. Ore was discovered at the Gilmore mine on Klondyke mountain, about two miles west of the town. The ore was similar to that in the Cripple Creek district, and it was hoped that it would prove as rich and abundant. Although a townsite of Gilmore was laid out on a meadow between Klondyke mountain and Stunner and a tent and two wooden shacks, which housed a hotel, store and photographer's studio were hastily thrown up, the mine, which was on a steep slope, was more accessible from Platoro. Every house in that town was occupied, and so many tents were pitched along the streets that it looked like a tent city. The boom was short-lived, however, and by the end of the summer the tents were gone and Platoro was once more a lonely camp, roused only each spring by parties of fishermen or by cowboys grazing cattle in its streets. As the years have passed by the old shafts have become choked with snow and ice and the mine tunnels have caved in.

Summitville

We rolled down the shelf road to Stunner and on to the Summitville turn-off, where we began to climb again, up and up until the road's steepness, narrowness and series of hair-raising switchbacks left us gasping. At the top was a sight for which we were totally unprepared. Instead of a ghost town, we entered an extremely lively camp where mining was going full tilt. Ruined mills and mine buildings surrounded it like a fringe— ghosts of an earlier era. But the active place consisted of row upon row of identical houses covered with tar paper and a big community hall from whose top floated an American flag. It was a company town!

We talked to the postmistress and discovered that Summitville was a one-mine camp and that the mine had been operating for several years under the present management. Its output was not phenomenal but it was steady. "It's awful high up here," she told us, "and there's not much to do for amusement. Some of the men go over to Platoro to fish and weekends they go to Del Norte and Monte Vista, but most of us just stay here."

Not until 1870, when prospecting began in earnest in the San Juan country, was any effort made by the government to protect the rights of the miner as well as those of the homesteader. Finally the first Land Office was established at Del Norte, even though the first agent who had been sent out to the straggling little village for the purpose of opening it was so disappointed at what he found that he returned to Iowa and reported that the whole country was infested with rattlesnakes, prairie wolves and Indians. He did concede, however, that placer gold had been found on a high, bald mountain southwest of Del Norte, which by his description must have been the same South mountain on which we were now standing.

Hall's *History of Colorado* describes the first discovery of gold made east of South mountain in Wightman's gulch about the last of June, 1870, by a party consisting of James and William Wightman and others. As winter approached all but two of the group left the mountains, the two who remained continuing their sluicing until November. They then made their way out through waist deep snow and reached the Rio Grande after three days.

In the spring of 1871 people flocked to the district, hundreds arriving while the snow was still deep and work impracticable. All summer they tore at the mountain's crust with little success, and all but three left the district again. Peterson, Johnson and Wightman continued to work until fall, when they took the gold they had sluiced-out to Denver, had it refined in the mint and divided the $170 that it brought. During 1872 a new rush to the district commenced, and South mountain swarmed with prospectors.

John Esmond, who owned a ranch near the old Spanish town of Conejos, had been an even earlier prospector of the district. His neighbor, Barilla, had a daughter who, with another girl, ran away to the mountains. The following day Esmond and the girl's brother went out to look for them and discovered their horses in a "park where Summitville now stands." At first the girls refused to go home, though Esmond pleaded with them to do so. As he talked he noticed that the rocks all around were filled with free gold.

In 1873 Esmond returned to the mountain, intending to stake off and work some prospects there. To his surprise he found a cabin and a staked claim that was being worked on the site of his earlier discovery. He therefore staked two more mines, the Esmond (later called Aztec) and the Major. The Little Ida and Little Annie lodes, both of which were to make Senator Thomas Bowen wealthy, were also staked that year, as were all the best mines of the camp. The Little Annie became Summitville's greatest producer.

During the winter of 1874-75 the owners of the Little Annie, Del Norte, Margaretta, Golden Queen and Golden Star made arrangements to erect mills near the mines, and by the latter part of May machinery began to arrive at Del Norte. From there it was hauled over the summit of the mountain and installed in the mills. After that the miners began to build cabins and spend the long, cold winters near their properties. All supplies had to be laid in early, for during the cold months the camp was completely isolated, except for occasional horseback or snowshoe trips to Del Norte when weather conditions permitted.

The whole of South mountain was a mine; but of the twenty-five hundred locations that were made only a dozen or so were successfully developed. The several stamp mills pounded away, smashing the golden particles from the worthless rock and, in one instance, "producing a single gold brick worth $33,000," the result of a twenty-eight-day run.

By 1883 the district was the largest gold producer in the state, having nine amalgamating mills aggregating 155 stamps." By 1886 the population ranged from 300 to 600. Mail was delivered three times a week, news was printed in the *Summitville Nugget*, there were fourteen saloons, and the mines were booming. The rumor that a railroad might be built to the lofty camp caused some excitement, but the rumor died when, in 1889, there were only "twenty-five left in camp including three ladies," and no stores at all. By 1893 the district was deserted.

And then in the fall of 1934 the Summitville Consolidated Mines, Inc., which included over one hundred mining claims, began plans to rework the old properties on a big scale, and Summitville revived. New cabins "mushroomed up'' and new residents came in, bringing their families with them. In less than a year Summitville became the second largest mining camp in the state; but the miners with unusually good sense said, "It may yet equal Leadville. Again it may have its boom and then drop back into a ghost settlement."

Seventy modern homes were built for the miners on the new townsite, and all but one of the buildings of the original camp were taken down. A water system was installed, and a bathhouse, bunk houses and mess halls, as well as a two-teacher school house, a post office and an amusement hall were built. The road between the camp and Monte Vista was so greatly improved that trucks could rumble back and forth over it day and night loaded with ore. The population grew to 700 and the monthly output reached $70,000. Prior to World War II, when the government banned the mining of gold, Summitville was the leading gold producing district in the state. During the war it was converted to a copper camp and was operated on a limited basis, getting out strategic metal. In 1945, with the lifting of the gold ban, the camp resumed gold mining and is being operated in the old way today.

As we left Summitville and snaked our way toward the valley we ran into one of those sudden, torrential mountain showers which come so often in high country in the afternoons. It reminded me of a paragraph from a leaflet printed by the San Luis Valley Association in 1889 which mentions the "flanks of the great mountains, bathed by the embrace of the irrigating clouds." Now they were doing their best to irrigate the dirt road and turn it into a sticky pond.

Embargo   In 1948 friends in Del Norte invited me to visit them so that they might take me to several old camps in the region. The first place to which we went was Embargo, a gold and silver camp fourteen miles back in the hills. Long before we reached the gulch where the camp once stood, we could see the dumps on the hillsides, and after bumping over the road and driving a quarter of a mile up the bed of a creek, we came to the only cabin left at the site. The night before our trip, I had talked to George Bauchmann who used to work up there when the mines were operating, and he spoke of the place as familiarly as if it were alive today.

A little prospecting in Bauchmann Creek in 1878 had produced small quantities of gold, but not until 1882, when a large chunk of carbonate the "size of a water bucket" was discovered, was there any boom. Then the hills above Embargo creek were covered with prospectors digging holes, but the excitement didn't last and the miners drifted away. Later on there was another spurt of activity, and log houses were built all over the gulch. When the town was platted houses were put up on both sides of the main street, and those which were found to be right in the road had to be moved. The camp had no store, but one old man kept supplies in his cabin, mostly tobacco. There was a feed stable, a sawmill and a hotel run by Bauchmann's two sisters. Further up the gulch was a still smaller camp consisting of five or six cabins, called Mexican Town.

The Golden Income, over the crest of the hill, and the Tornado, on Tornado mountain, were the mines which shipped ore, as did the Little Ray until its rich lead deposits pinched out. In 1899 the camp was "experiencing no boom but was improving every day," and during the early 1900's considerable work was done on its claims. A slight flurry occurred in 1919 when new strikes were made: two mines shipped ore, and "everything pointed to a good-sized mining boom;" but it never came, and Embargo became another ghost camp. Until a few years ago old boilers and large pieces of machinery stood on the dumps and in the shaft houses, but nearly everything was hauled away during the scrap drives of World War II.

Across from the head of Embargo creek on Wanamaker creek is the *Sky City* site of Sky City, a gold camp established in the late eighties. Senator Tom Bowen named the camp, built a road to it and drove a tunnel into the mountain to cut the veins of ore. George Bauchmann told of working in this tunnel and of how the men wore overcoats even in summer, it was so cold in the mine. There was not enough high grade ore in the camp to justify its further development, so, like Embargo, it became deserted and joined the ranks of empty camps hidden high in the hills.

CHAPTER THIRTEEN

The Rio Grande Valley

Del Norte DEL NORTE is such a pleasant, live town today that it is hard to realize that it was started in 1870 as a supply point, when gold was found in Wightman's gulch, and that back in 1874, when it was the "gateway to the San Juan," it was a "rip-snortin', hell-raisin', gold-mad frontier town" on the banks of the Rio Grande. In front of its hastily constructed log and frame stores and saloons rolled long trains of freight wagons, their drivers covered with alkali dust, while equally long pack trains of jacks wound between the wagons and ploughed up the dust and mud of the street.

Every day stagecoaches rattled through town, filled with eager, impatient men, all hurrying to the new gold and silver fields. Road agents often held up the stages, especially in the mountains, hiding behind rocks or trees and halting the coach long enough to collect money and valuables from the passengers and to rifle the strong box which contained the gold dust and valuable express.

In 1881 Barlow and Sanderson's stage was held up by three highwaymen who robbed the mail, the express and some of the passengers. The holdup

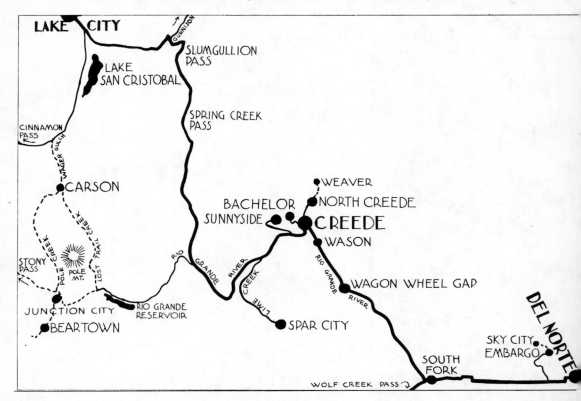

occurred not far from Antelope Springs, and during the commotion the robbers "fired a volley into the stage," injuring one passenger. When the stage reached Del Norte the people held a mass meeting and organized a posse to pursue the robbers. They also raised a good-sized purse as a reward for their capture. The posse found the robbers in the mountains and captured two of them, including the leader, Billy LeRoy.

News of the capture reached the town before the men were brought in and scores of people went up the road to take the prisoners from the sheriff. To prevent this he waited until after midnight to bring them into town and lodge them in the jail. Everything seemed quiet, and the sheriff went home to bed. An hour later he was awakened to find his house surrounded by armed and masked men, who, when he opened the door, seized his keys to the jail and put him under guard. The leaders of the mob then went to the jail, took the prisoners to a clump of cottonwoods on the bank of the Rio Grande and hanged them. "Half an hour later their lifeless bodies were cut down, taken back to the jail and placed in their cells," after which the men who had participated in the execution "passed noiselessly to their homes."

For several years the only bank in the San Juan was located in Del Norte, and its accounts came from Ouray, Mineral Point, Animas Forks, Eureka, Howardsville, Animas City and Parrot City, "all business being done by mail." Its newspaper, called the *San Juan Prospector,* is still publishing under the same title.

West of Del Norte, at South Fork, the highway branches, with the main thoroughfare continuing west over Wolf Creek Pass to Durango. The other road turns up the North Fork of the Rio Grande and follows the canyon past the rugged cliffs to Wagon Wheel Gap, where the rocks close in and form a gateway through which there is scarcely room for the river, the railroad and the road to pass. The origin of its name its usually attributed to the finding of a wagon wheel beside the road, discarded by some freighter or prospector as he worked his way through the cut. On the other hand, the Gap is known to have been the scene of a big Indian battle after which, according to one lurid account, the Indians stretched a rope between the cliffs over the river, festooned it with the scalps of the whites they had killed and weighted it with a wagon wheel dangling from the middle.

*Wagon
Wheel
Gap*

The valley widens into ranch and fishing country beyond the Gap. Further on, strange upthrust mountains border a narrow gorge, at the end of which is Creede, the fabulous camp of the nineties.

Creede

Here's a land where all are equal
Of high or lowly birth—
A land where men make millions
Dug from the dreary earth
Here meek and mild-eyed burros
On mineral mountains feed,
It's day all day in the day-time
And there is no night in Creede.

(319)

The cliffs are solid silver
With wondrous wealth untold,
And the beds of the running rivers
Are lined with the purest gold.
While the world is filled with sorrow,
And hearts must break and bleed,
It's day all day in the day-time
And there is no night in Creede.

Cy Warman

In the eighties the wagon route beyond Wagon Wheel Gap which led to Silverton or Lake City passed close to the future site of Creede. In 1885 a little prospecting was done in the vicinity, along Rat Creek gulch at Sunnyside, and a few mines, including the Bachelor, were located but not developed. Haskill Ryder built a cabin up Willow creek in 1887 and took an "extension" on the Bachelor mine, which was owned by John Mackenzie; but not until 1890, after Creede had discovered the Holy Moses, did scores of men come puffing up the crazy mountains at the edge of the Rio Grande valley in search of silver and gold.

One day in 1889 Nicholas C. Creede and his partner George L. Smith wandered through the high cliff gateway "to the junction of the Willows." There they found float, and Creede, tracing it to its source at the head of West Willow creek, made a location, sank a shaft and discovered a mine which he named the Holy Moses. The two men did some work on the claim that summer and then left till the spring of 1890.

David H. Moffat, President of the Denver and Rio Grande road, and other wealthy men heard of this strike and, after inspecting the property, bought it for $70,000, employing Capt. Campbell to act as manager of the mine and hiring Creede to continue to prospect for them. As soon as it was learned that these men were identified with the mine and had paid so much for it, prospectors were as thick as fleas on Campbell mountain, and a map of claims of the area looked like a patchwork quilt. Shortly after the discovery of the Holy Moses, Charles F. Nelson, who had prospected around Sunnyside with Dick Irwin a few years before, located the Ridge and the Solomon mines, which were later purchased by Ex-Senator Thomas M. Bowen.

In August, 1891, Theodore Renniger (or Rennica), who had worked down the Rio Grande valley for Ralph Granger, a butcher, tired of his job and started to prospect in the mountains. Granger grubstaked him. He and his partner would bring in samples of ore to be assayed, but none was of any value. One day he brought in some crumbling yellow quartz which was also said to be worthless. Renniger went back to the hills to try again, without telling Granger which way he was going. In a day or so the assayer rushed into Granger's market and told him that the yellow quartz was the richest stuff he had ever seen. "Close your store, and go find Renniger," he urged. "Get him to stake off the land where this came from and get him quick." Granger wasn't sure where the prospector was but he traced him

(320)

to Campbell mountain and watched him stake his claim, which he called the Last Chance.

That same summer Creede located the Amethyst mine from which a million and a half was realized. Within a year after the rush began, $6,000,000 in silver was taken from Creede. The mine yielded pay ore from the grass roots; the mineral resources were limitless. At first silver was the ore that was found, but later gold was discovered in increasing amounts.

With so many prospectors scratching at the "stony ribs of the mountains," a camp was the next necessity, and an embryo city called Willow sprouted along the gulch at the foot of Campbell mountain in October, 1890. By the end of the year there were houses and stores all along the gulch, and building continued all through the winter. As the population increased, houses were built anywhere they could be crammed—on pole foundations over the stream, crowded into the rock walls, or jammed along the one long thoroughfare, which was "rather straighter than a corkscrew." For six miles up and down Willow creek there was not a foot that had not been staked by somebody as a lot. One old timer remembers seeing big stocks of merchandise piled on the ice of the creek with a tent stretched over them.

There were really three towns. The original location was in the narrow gulch on East Willow creek, beyond the formidable cliff which guards the entrance to the canyon. When the population overflowed a half mile down stream to more level land, a second town sprang up in 1891 which was known under several names—Jimtown (or Gintown), Creedmoor and Amethyst. The third town of Upper Creede, now called North Creede, was a continuation up the gulch above the original location. In addition the suburb of Bachelor (or Teller), built after Creede's first fire, was up on the hill above Jimtown; that of Sunnyside was over the hill from Bachelor; and that of Weaver was beyond North Creede, on West Willow creek above the Black Pitch hill. Today only a few scattered cabins mark its site. The Creede post office was in the upper gulch, and the Amethyst post office was down in the business center of the camp in Jimtown.

As the town continued to grow, real estate speculators poured in. Zephyr Glen was platted, although everyone knew it was only another name for Windy Gulch. The best residential sites were on Capitol hill—the mesa overlooking the gulch. Locations were made in the morning, sold at noon and jumped at dark. If a man drove a stake into a lot, it held the ground a short time; but if he wanted to keep it, he had to lay a foundation. Four planks nailed together and laid on four stumps indicated the start of a building. Often, before it could be erected, the land was jumped by unscrupulous men. One woman stood on her lot while a carpenter built her cabin. "I'll stand here till I am frozen stiff but I'll hold my lot," she announced, the barrel of her six-shooter showing under her shawl. The next week she sold her property for $10,000. A freight load of lumber delivered in the morning meant a new place of business by night. At first the buildings were all tents or frame shacks. "Blacksmiths are needed. Painters are not called for because the decorative taste of the camp runs almost altogether to a severe style of plain board with nail-head dottings."

By October, 1891, a branch of the Denver and Rio Grande road was completed to Creede, but trains did not run regularly until December. Less than three months afterwards each trainload brought two to three hundred more people to the overcrowded camp. As a correspondent wrote to his paper, "The trains are jammed when they come in—men sit on each other and on the arms of seats and hang on the platforms." Fifteen to twenty cars arrived each day at the station below the Cliff, and the same number of cars filled with ore pulled out, bound for the smelters. The depot was half-buried under "bags, barrels, boxes, beer kegs, stoves, packing cases and furniture," and to lessen the hotel shortage all Pullman cars were left on the track, providing from three to ten sleepers for passengers.

Creede was a red-hot town in 1891 and 1892; everything about it was chaotic. There were 4000 rustlers in camp, and the total population was said to be 10,000. Every train brought more mining men, speculators, gamblers, bartenders, dancehall girls and tourists to the overcrowded city.

> I can hear the sound of saws and hammers, the tinkle of pianos, the scrape of violins, the scurry of flying feet in dance-halls, the clink of silver on gambling tables, the sharp bark of six-shooters as some life was snuffed out in the smoke of battle, and the maudlin laughter of a dance hall girl as she swung in the arms of some human form:

wrote the *Saguache Crescent* in "Dramatic Episodes in the Life of N. C. Creede."

There were dozens of hotels—"a board shanty sixteen feet square with a blanket for a door" was designated as "The Palace." Such a place might have twenty to sixty cots in its one room and would charge one dollar a night with blankets, and fifty cents without.

> Flour, bread, pork, etc., are twenty-five percent higher than in Denver. Whiskey is not much dearer if you're content to risk corrosion by drinking the ordinary article, retailed under the name of whiskey.
>
> . . . Now and then a ten-ton load of ore in a ponderous sled comes thundering down the steep road . . . with the driver pounding his horses lustily and shouting at the top of his voice. He is more afraid of its sticking somewhere than of smashing all creation by colliding with it. Behind him come two or three more. The sleighs whirl around with a tremendous swing when they reach the depot and unload into the cars. Down the trail from another direction has come maybe a train of fifty burros each with one hundred and fifty to two hundred pounds of sacked ores on his back. Now and then there's a new burro. An old one leaned over too far on some precipice and was overbalanced by his load, that's all.—From "Description of Creede Camp."
>
> Compliments of the Oxford Hotel, Denver.

Creede was a fabulous camp in which anything could happen.. Five days after ground was broken for an electric light plant the city was illuminated, and a light was placed high on the sheer cliff to mark the entrance to the canyon.

When the first baby was born the camp went wild. For days the cabin "was besieged with great, rough men, frenzied to get a peep at the 'barby.' Its father was king of Jimtown for a week," and a subscription was started for the father, the mother and the child.

CREEDE
PANORAMA

NORTH
CREEDE

To the father was given two suits of clothes, a mining outfit and a jug of Babb Bros. best Old Crow. The mother was presented with the most palatial residence in the heart of the four hundred on Capitol Hill, a blue silk dress and a monster bonnet with a huge ostrich plume on it that trails a foot beyond the rim of the headgear. But what was to be the baby's name? . . . three days of solemn deliberation were devoted to its discussion.

No name that the father suggested suited the camp.

As it was a girl, the mother considered it her privilege to choose the name . . . still the miners couldn't agree. A council was held . . . and after a lengthy debate someone shouted from the top of a beer keg, "How does Creede Amethyst McDonald sound?"

When Creede was told about it he said: "I'll do as much as any of you boys and maybe a little more. I'll give the baby the Daisy mine which is right close to the Amethyst and might turn out to be the same vein. Besides I'll send to Pueblo for $100 worth of togs for the little one, and give it a gold ring and a pair of earrings." This speech was greeted with three cheers and a tiger.

Although Creede's first newspaper was called the *Amethyst,* it did not survive long after Lute Johnson arrived with "a hatful of type, a hand press and brains," and started the *Creede Candle* as a weekly. Shortly afterwards Cy Warman, the "Poet of the Cochetopa," got out the *Creede Chronicle* as a daily.

Not everything printed could be reprinted in an eastern or family newspaper; the Chronicle was not a family but a mine camp paper, but the matter that verged on the obscene attracted attention to the camp more than any other matter.

The *Candle* became a permanent part of the camp and its files contain a complete picture of the vivid city, for as the editor said:

Of course if you are a miner or in any way interested in mining you will want the *Candle*. For two silver discs you can have a new one every week for a year and may be lighted to a prospect that will return you thousands for one.

It is supposed that you understand that it takes "tallow" to keep a *Candle* going and that is what I'm here for.

Lute H. Johnson,
Boss Trimmer

January 7, 1892

The camp was full of gamblers, fancy women and tin horns. As the *Candle* of April 29, 1892, puts it:

Creede is unfortunate in getting more of the flotsam of the state than usually falls to the lot of mining camps . . . some of her citizens would take sweepstake prizes at a hog show.

As another writer put it:

At night there are no policemen to interfere with the vested right of each citizen to raise as much Cain as he sees fit and . . . three-fourths of the population are of that kind that does see fit. . . . Drunken men empty their revolvers into the air or somebody's leg. . . . There are a few bad men . . . many who are reckless.

(324)

Three men were playing cards in a saloon and were sitting in front of a big window. There was some shooting going on outside, and in the fracas the leg of the chair in which one of the players was sitting was shot off.

Creede's most famous "bad men" were Soapy Smith, who with his gang ruled the city for a time, and Bob Ford who shot Jesse James. After the killing the paper announced:

> Bob Ford . . . is dealing Faro in one of the gambling halls, out of the range of any window and keeps a restless eye on the crowd about him, while ever near him lies the gun with which he brought down by a shot from behind, the much-feared Missouri Outlaw.

In June, 1892, Ford was killed by Ed O'Kelley, who had previously quarreled with him over a gambling debt. He was shot in the back, just as he had killed Jesse James. O'Kelley received a life sentence—Ford was buried in Boot hill.

At one gambler's funeral his friends drank champagne at the grave, and then joining hands, marched around the grave singing Auld Lang Syne. Creede had three women gamblers, Poker Alice, Calamity Jane and Killarney Kate, all of whom smoked big stogey cigars while playing. It also had its girls.

> Lulu Slain, a frail daughter laid aside the camelia for the poppy and passed into the beyond early Wednesday morning. She and the Mormon Queen had been living in a small cabin in upper Creede but the times grew hard and the means of life came not. They sought relief from life with morphine, the inevitable end of their unfortunate kind, a well-trodden path from Creede. Lulu's dead; the Queen lives.—*Creede Candle*, Sept. 15, 1893.
>
> Rose Vastine, known about camp as "timberline" became weary of the trials and tribulations of this wicked world and decided to take a trip over the range, and to this end brought into play a forty-one calibre pistol. With the muzzle at her lily white breast and her index finger on the trigger she waited not to contemplate the sad result. A slight contraction of the muscles caused the gun to empty its contents into Rose, the ball passing through the upper portion of her left lung.
>
> Medical attendants were at once summoned and the would-be suicide is in a fair way to recovery.—*Creede Candle*, Feb. 3, 1893.

Variety shows, melodrama and concerts, performed both by home talent and by road companies who made a circuit of the camps, provided entertainment for the miners. "The newsboy's song and rope skipping by Miss May De Rose made her a favorite with the audience" at the Theatre Comique.

In 1910 both the Daffy Darling Co., "Specialists in Real Comedy and Drama," and the Keogh Stock Co., played in Collins Opera House, the latter company presenting two plays: "When Women Rule, or A. D. 2011" and the "Great Labor play—'By the Sweat of the Brow.'"

The Knights of Pythias sponsored the historical drama "Pythias," "rendered by Mr. Philip Keene, supported by a strong company of local talent. 'Pythias,' is a copyrighted revision of the famous play, 'Damon and Pythias' . . . This drama expounds to the layman the true meaning of the term 'Pythianism.'"

(325)

By 1911 Creede had movies in the Gayety Theatre where:

Joseph U. Yeager promises that his shows will be free from all the vexations and delays due to accidents to his gas machine and that his film house has promised to send their very latest and best pictures.

The classics were also given. In 1912 Sheridan's "The Rivals" was advertised as:

A good clean play, full of episodes and amusing situations, well balanced in characters, each of which is the type of a great social class. The social truth taught in each incident is important and wholesome. . . .

Participants assigned and trained by Rev. J. B. Mather, pastor, Congregational church of Creede.

Religion came to Creede too. At first services were held in saloons and gambling halls. Then a large tent, donated by the Congregationalists of Denver and erected in Jimtown, served as a meeting place for religious gatherings. On Easter Sunday the tent was used for a place of worship in the morning and for a prize fight that evening. An extra supply of fresh eggs was shipped in for the hotels and restaurants, but they were all "converted into Tom and Jerry" long before noon.

The Rev. Joseph Gaston of Ouray received permission to talk for fifteen minutes in one "blub room," during which time the faro dealer left his chair and the preacher "mounted it for a rostrum. . . . The three hundred men within the sound of his voice stood with uncovered heads, paid rapt attention, a few joining in the recitation of the Lord's Prayer which closed the service."

Once when Parson Uzell preached in the camp, he stood on a pool table. The men listened, but that night one of them stole his trousers and the collection. Soapy Smith made the thief return the pants with more money in them than when they were taken.

Creede has had more than its share of fires. In 1892 a blaze which started in a saloon burned a stretch of the town a half mile long and an eighth of a mile wide, destroying most of the business section. In 1895 "the whistle of the D. & R. G. freight engine aroused the sleeping citizens, to the fact that fire was again in possession of the city." In 1902 twenty houses and two hotels in Upper Creede were licked up by flames, and in 1936 a third of the business section was again wiped out by the "red monster." There were fires at the mines too—a blaze at the Amethyst not only destroying all the surface buildings but killing four men in the shaft, when the cables of the "skip" burned through and it fell upon them.

Many old landmarks have disappeared through fire, the most recent being the frame county courthouse which was destroyed in 1946. It was a historic building which originally stood in Wason, four miles away, and was moved to the obstreperous new camp in a midnight coup shortly after an election.

In 1893 the new county of Mineral was organied from parts of Hinsdale, Rio Grande and Saquache counties, with its courthouse in Wason. The

CREEDE CLIFFS

ORE LOADING BIN, CREEDE

population of Creede resented this, saying that the county seat was "down in the Cow-Pasture at Wason" while the business of the camp was conducted in the "Heart of the City of Creede." Its removal was voted at an election, but there was talk of some legal delay in moving it; so, "as soon as it was dark, heavy transfer wagons began to rumble down the Wason road . . . At ten o'clock the wagons began to come back, piled high with huge docket books, and records." The vaults of the First National Bank were unlocked and the unoccupied rooms in the Wilcox building "were commandeered. . . Into these were piled the archives of the county and later came the furniture. By midnight not a vestige of the properties of Mineral county remained at the old county seat. . . Some said it was not legal and could not be done, but it was done."—*Creede Candle*, Nov. 10, 1893.

Not only fire but flood periodically destroyed parts of Creede. Willow creek is narrow and the gorge is deep, and when cloudbursts rush down, the water rips out everything in its way. In North Creede only a fringe of buildings pressed against the cliff wall have resisted repeated floods. Even now parts of the city are threatened each year by the torrents of water which tear through the middle of town, eating away banks, flooding streets and depositing a new layer of mud and debris.

A flood in 1917 left North Creede "in a deplorable condition," as it washed away not only the Cliff Hotel and the Holy Moses saloon but also the section known as Stringtown and left only heaps of rocks and driftwood. On a recent visit to Creede I noticed that the main highway through town had been re-routed and that in what used to be a street, surrounded by mud and rock, stands a yellow highway sign plainly marked "Stop!"

There is much to sketch in Creede, especially up Willow creek and in North Creede, where the ruins of mills and empty ore bins by the railroad track are dwarfed by the sharp pinnacles of rock which wall the canyon. Creede's population today is small as compared with the nineties, and it is not the wild camp of which Cy Warman wrote; but it is proud of its past and is preserving many relics of the early days in a historic museum. The Charles Davlins have gathered together, with the help of old families and civic-minded individuals, a priceless collection of "Creediana;" and in the log building which houses the collection, surrounded by old books and photographs, costumes and guns, ox-shoes and wagon wheels, is a Wurlitzer Musicbox from one of Creede's saloons. When it starts playing "The Spirit of St. Louis," its flat metallic jangle conjures up a glimpse of the Creede that has gone but which was once so vivid and uninhibited.

Bachelor

"Is there anything left of Bachelor?" I asked the post master in Creede.

"There are some wooden sidewalks but that's about all," he replied; but that was enough for me. The drive up Bachelor hill, although only three miles, was stiff. Partway up, the road passed the cemetery and nearer the top it ran beside a rocky gulch, down which tiny foot trails led to prospect holes and mine tunnels. The road wound on past the end of a meadow, and still there were no sidewalks. I drove another mile over a mere sliver of trail until it ended among some mine buildings. This wasn't Bachelor, and since there was no one around to question, I returned to Creede.

(328)

The next year I tried again. Victoria and I scanned every gully, meadow and patch of timber for the wooden sidewalks but found nothing. Parking the car where Bachelor should be, I climbed up one side of a hill while Victoria climbed up the other. On the edge of a grove of aspens was a government stake marked "Bachelor Mountain." This was encouraging, so I went on. Hearing a shout in the distance I hurried to an opening through the trees and saw, in the next clearing, two long rows of splintered planks—the sidewalks of the town. They bordered a gully which was once the main street. A few cabins were standing, though most were toppled over or completely flattened by the weight of successive snows. A few pieces of broken furniture, including a round-topped trunk, were strewn amidst the general debris. A table, its four legs in the air, lay half covered with the mud which had washed over it in the spring rains. Part of an old cupboard lay on its back, its doors gaping open. An occasional stone terrace or a fragment of picket fence showed where homes once stood. We walked the length of the town and back and, just before leaving, discovered a newly cut and recently installed post marking the corner of a mining claim. On it was printed: "S. E. Corner, No. 4, Ghost City No. 2."

There are conflicting statements as to who discovered the Bachelor mine, although all but one agree that it was located in 1885. John C. Mackenzie is known to have prospected near Sunnyside in that year and is said to have located the mine on Bachelor mountain. Another account claims that J. B. Burrett, (Burnett or Bennett) was the discoverer, and still another gives C. F. Nelson the credit for finding it. A fourth source states that it was found in 1884 by George Wilson, and a fifth gives his name as James Wilson. At any rate, in August, 1891, Theodore Renniger and others found outcroppings of rich mineral on Bachelor mountain similar to those found by Creede in the Holy Moses and thus located the Last Chance. Creede, who was prospecting near there at the time, also discovered the rich float and, recognizing its value, waited till the stakes were set on the Last Chance and then located the Amethyst directly to the north. Ore from both mines brought $170 a ton "from the first shovelful," and immediately, excited men rushed to the hill and staked hundreds of locations.

Soon after its discovery, the Last Chance was bought by the owners of the Holy Moses property for $20,000, and soon afterwards the Bachelor Mining Company was incorporated, with D. H. Moffat as one of the investors. A peculiarity of both the Last Chance and the Amethyst was that they needed no dumps, for the mineral was such that no sorting of ore was necessary.

"The latest townsite excitement is in the park on Bachelor Hill, around the Last Chance Boarding House," wrote the *Creede Candle* on Jan. 21, 1892.

> Yesterday there was a stake raid for lots and it is proposed to plat an eighty-acre government townsite to include the territory of the Last Chance mill site, a portion of the Quakenasp and Greenback claims and some vacant ground. . . . Two saloons and a female seminary are already in operation and other business houses are expected. It is to be called Bachelor.

The question of a suitable townsite became tense as squatters began to stake claims upon the land set aside as "school ground," saying that the land was "mineral and should revert to the government." As people began to build homes, sink shafts and open veins of ore, the clash between those usurping the school land and the others

> became so vigorous that noise of the wrangle reached the ears of the Governor and the State Land Board and early in January they proceeded to Creede in a body. . . . The advent of the governor was announced with such *eclat* as the limited means of the community could command. Everything that was capable of noise was brought into requisition and the salvos that the hills re-echoed made the huge pines tremble. . . . The leading citizen, in a woolen shirt, broke the trail for his excellency, whose short legs made sorry efforts in tracing the footprints.
>
> The largest edifice in the place was a general merchandise store into which the Governor was led. A beer keg upended was the rostrum and upon this the Governor was raised. The speech was not long . . . but it struck the spot. He would have said more but the physical exertion he made to maintain his equilibrium upon the keg consumed some of his reserve power.
>
> . . . The substance of his address was that the state would aid the camp . . . that lands would be sold to miners by lots and where minerals were present the state would exact a royalty. This solved the problem and the situation became pacific.
>
> Since the trip of the Governor's party, a greater impulse has been given the camp and arrivals vary from 50-100 per day.—*Sunny San Luis,*1889.

When a post office was granted to the camp in April, 1892, it was called Teller, not Bachelor, because there was a Bachelor in California. The following year the Amethyst post office was also recognized with a salary of $1700 for the postmaster and $150 for expenses.

In 1893 Bachelor was one of the liveliest camps around Creede, for such mines as the Bachelor, Spar, Commodore, Del Monte, Last Chance, Amethyst, Cleopatra and Sunnyside were all on Bachelor mountain. There were "eight stores and about a dozen saloons, several assay offices, boarding houses, hotels and restaurants in operation and more going up." Bachelor was considered one of the best suburbs of Creede. There was even talk of building a railroad from the Amethyst mine to Jimtown, below Creede.

Father Downey was active in sponsoring a Catholic Church for Bachelor. In August, the

> Merry miners, their dutiful wives and charming daughters cast aside for one memorable evening all arduous duties to participate in the mazy waltz and introduce the terpsichorean art at Bachelor; the occasion being a festival given by the ladies society of the Catholic church; the proceeds to go toward the erection of a church edifice in the thriving little town on top of Bachelor Mountain. Good music, courteous and competent reception and floor committee and the ladies' untiring efforts to make it pleasant for strangers, all combined to complete the evening's entertainment and make those present feel as though it had scarcely begun when the beautiful strains of Home Sweet Home were sounded.—*Creede Candle,* Aug. 19, 1892.

A benefit for the same project was held in the new opera house, where the "Bachelor City Dramatic Club produced 'The Wild Irishman' with acting declared to be much above the usual amateur attempt." The program continued with two recitations, "Shamis O'Brien" and "St. Peter at the Gate," and "Messrs. O'Leary and McWade performed in a double-dog act which brought down the house." There were songs and duets, "encores were frequent and enthusiastic," and a dance topped off the evening, which netted the church one hundred and sixty dollars.

Excitement and tragedy were frequent in the camp. A "distressing accident" occurred on the road down Bachelor hill when a hack on the way to Sunnyside Cemetery "with the remains of the six-year-old son of Capt. Hill of Bachelor, and with four ladies in attendance . . . was overturned and rolled over three times down the hill into Windy Gulch. . . . The casket was rolled almost to the bottom of the hill." Fortunately some freight wagons were going up the road and their drivers went to the rescue of the passengers.

Woodruff, a Negro, was shot and instantly killed in front of the Palace bar by Michael Sherry, proprietor of the Miner's Home saloon, in a quarrel over a turkey shoot. Woodruff had threatened to "do up" Sherry the first time .they met. By chance the two men collided and Sherry emptied his gun into the Negro, killing him. Woodruff, who had run a laundry and bath house at Bachelor since the beginning of the camp, was "buried with soldier's honors in Sunnyside."

Bachelor had its fires, the first in January, 1892, when the Free Coinage Hotel and Lundy and Sherry's saloon disappeared. Later that year another saloon went up in flames, and again the town was threatened. The *Creede Candle* of March 10, 1893, announced that:

> Bachelor is at the front. Her people know the danger from fire and her city council is not behind in taking the step to prevent the destruction of the town. A chemical engine to cost $600 has been ordered, together with a $75 alarm bell. A company to man the machine has been organized by the citizens and the town will be in shape to fight fire successfully. Creede is not doing anything in this line, but some day it will wish it had.

Again the *Candle* reports:

> Ten o'clock this morning word came down from the hill that the town of Bachelor was on fire, having caught from the timber fires, all around. In a few minutes, half of the population of Jimtown was headed up the hill to lend our neighbors all the assistance possible. Every available horse and vehicle was brought into requisition . . . many went afoot. . . '. The fire was exaggerated. . . . It burned to the edge of the town but a most dogged fight on the part of the citizens saved the town with the loss of only a cabin or two.—June 23, 1893.

Bachelor flourished between 1892 and 1908, the population at one time reaching 1000. But gradually the people moved down the hill to Jimtown below Creede, and the camp was deserted.

Over the hill from Bachelor is Sunnyside, an old camp where locations *Sunnyside* were first made in 1872 and 1873. During the middle eighties, long before there was any Creede, John C. Mackenzie camped in Rat Creek gulch and prospected the surrounding hills, locating the Bachelor, Alpha and other lodes on Bachelor and Mackenzie mountains. Dick Irwin and Charles F.

(331)

Nelson, who had previously prospected in Rosita and Irwin, hearing rumors of gold discoveries, reached the vicinity in 1885 and made some locations. After obtaining additional capital from some California investors Irwin developed the Diamond I lode, as well as the Nelson and the Hidden Treasure. The Sunnyside mine was located, and its owners refused $20,000 for it when it was only a prospect.

By 1887 a post office was established and some ore was shipped out. Although some of it had been worked in an arastra, most attempts to obtain gold by this method of reduction were unsatisfactory. In the nineties other mines were discovered and developed—the Corsair, the Yellow Jack and the Kreutzer Sonata.

Both Bachelor City and Sunnyside were flourishing camps in the nineties and were considered practically one camp, since their mines were located on the same mountain and a trail connected the two places.

The present road to Sunnyside turns off the main highway three miles beyond Creede and doubles back around the edge of the mountain to meander up the gulch to several old mine properties whose yellow dumps spill down the hillsides. One or two properties whose buildings are in the creek bottom are now almost hidden by willows and are falling to pieces, for Sunnyside like Bachelor is empty today.

Spar City   The first time I saw Spar City it rained so hard that I couldn't sketch, so on a bright afternoon in 1947, when the hillsides were a mass of rippling gold aspens, I went there again. The road branches from the main highway at the Seven-Mile bridge north of Creede, runs beside Lime creek at the base of vertical cliffs for a mile or so and then climbs the rest of the way over rolling meadows—past Robber's hill, where the road agents used to lie in wait for stagecoaches—and on up the narrow valley to the little camp. The last mile of road below the town is through a willow thicket. Beyond that is one long, wide street, on either side of which are rows of log cabins set well back from the grass-grown wheel tracks.

The camp, laid out in the spring of 1892, was known as Fisher City, after one of the first discoverers of float in the area, and also as Lime Creek. The mining district embraced three hills, and the best deposits were found at timberline in the Big Spar, Fairview and Headlight mines. A huge basin of ore was found, but the prospectors were unable to locate the "mother chimney," even though the ground was covered with boulders of spar and amethyst quartz, and assays at the grass roots ranged from 40 to 2500 ounces in silver to the ton.

By July, 1892, about three hundred people were in camp and as many more in the hills. Main street began to "assume business proportions, buildings going up solid on both sides of the thoroughfare." There were the usual stores, saloons and restaurants, as well as a sawmill and lumber yard. A hackline ran between the camp and Creede, and the *Creede Candle* opened a newspaper office to publish the *Spar City Spark*.

In August, 1892, a band of Indians was reported camping and hunting not far from Lime Creek. The prospectors' and settlers' attitude toward Indians is clearly shown by the "great indignation" that "was felt, both at

BACHELOR

↓ SPAR CITY

the unwarrantable wholesale slaughter of game and at the neglect of the Agent in allowing these red pests to be away from the reservation."

By February, 1893, Spar was lively, and had "daily mail communication with the outside world." It was even spoken of as "the coming camp outside Creede, all of which will be verified before the coming summer draws to a close." Then in June, when silver was demonetized and the panic came, Spar "flickered out," and its few remaining miners and their families were in actual want. In this emergency the people of Creede launched a novel plan for the relief of Spar City. The plan was explained in the July 21st issue of the *Candle:*

> Spar is peopled by honest, industrious Americans out of work and out of money. They are proud but they must eat. Having nothing to exchange for bread and meat, they propose following the plan of the N. Y. bankers and issue clearing house certificates backed by their brawn and industry and offer them in exchange for flour.

The plan was then outlined. A beef was to be butchered and sold to those who needed it, the "recipients promising to pay for same as soon as they can obtain employment."

Sam Hyde of Spar then wrote:

> People living in agricultural regions or large cities may find it difficult to realize how a community of people in this land of plenty can be placed in such a trying position, but, while a community may have untold wealth at its doors, it is not directly of a nutritive character. A power beyond our control has made our mineral valueless for the time being, our women and children must be fed, and in short, . . . assistance is necessary. Meat and flour we must have.—*Creede Candle,* July 21, 1893.

After the last few families moved away the camp dozed until about 1905, when a group of one hundred and fifty Kansans who "wanted to have good summer homes and to do a little mining" bought the townsite and remodeled the cabins for their own use.

We found the camp deserted except for the caretaker and his wife, who were closing the cabins for the winter. They pointed out the original meat market and the grocery, the log jail with its barred windows and the saloon and dancehall where the "girls" lived—the only two-story building in the place. They also told us that the Kansans who bought Spar were prohibitionists and that one of them, assigned to a large cabin with no partitions in it, found it contained a big pine bar and a poker table and that it had been the principal saloon of the camp! Some time later an old timer from Creede visited Spar, heard the story, and asked to see the bar.

"I remember it," he drawled, spitting tobacco juice accurately out the door. "It used to be in Creede, and Bob Ford who shot Jesse James was killed back of it. It was sold to a saloonkeeper here in Spar, and what a hell of a time they had freighting it in."

Beartown   When my Del Norte friends, the Colville's, offered to show me Carson from the Rio Grande side I quickly accepted their invitation, for Carson is on the Continental Divide, half on one side and half on the other. I'd visited the portion of Carson on the Western Slope, from Lake City; here was a chance to see the rest of it. It could be reached only by trail, and by the time I met my friends in Del Norte they had arranged the entire trip.

We were all to drive to Lost Trail Camp, at the far end of the Rio Grande reservoir, and from there on we were to be the guests of the Wetherills, who run that popular resort. Since I was hunting old mining camps they had planned a triangular trip, starting with a horseback ride to Beartown, then an over-night camp, and finally a ten-mile ride over a high trail to Carson. From there a trail led directly back to the home camp.

We arrived at Lost Trail Camp late in the afternoon and while the others worked I, the tenderfoot, watched Carol Wetherill and his daughter sort out food and utensils and pack them in saddle bags and boxes, ready for the morning start. Guests at the camp who knew of the proposed trip were as curious as I to visit the deserted places and asked if they might join the expedition. Therefore, early the next morning, after a tremendous ranch breakfast, ten of us were down at the barn watching the final preparations. Four of the horses were to carry packs, tents, and I watched the saddle-bags and other impedimenta skillfully placed and balanced on their broad backs and cinched with a diamond hitch. By eight-thirty we were off—our guide leading the pack-horses and the rest of us strung out single-file on the old road which we were to follow. A colt belonging to Cream, one of the horses, ran along beside us, nosing into the line and whinnying when too far from "mama" on a narrow stretch of trail.

The trip excited my imagination, not so much because of its difficulty nor because of its scenery, but because most of it was over the road used in the early days by the prospectors and freighters who went into the San Juan. For eight miles it worked its way up the narrowing Rio Grande valley, now in the open with the ragged peaks above it, and now in groves of pine and aspen so dense that the sunlight seemed far away. For awhile the river was far below us to the left, cutting its way through chalky, gray-blue cliffs, but when the trail started to climb Timber hill we lost it. Halfway up the steep hill, where even the horses took it slowly, was the big rock where road agents used to lie in wait for the Silverton stage or for loaded ore wagons from Beartown.

Once three wagons full of sacked silver were being brought down, escorted by scouts who rode ahead looking for robbers. They discovered the bandits hiding behind this big rock, and in the fight which followed all but one of the scouts was killed. The survivor galloped back to the wagons and reported what had happened, whereupon the drivers hastily unloaded the silver and hid it in a swamp not far from the road. Two wagons were emptied in this way, but before the sacks from the third could be cached in the water, the road agents appeared and killed all the men. They then took the third loaded wagon into Silverton and sold its contents. So far as is known they never returned, and the buried silver is still in the swamp.

After another mile the road leveled out, and just as we emerged into high, open country, Carol Wetherill rode back to where I was in the procession and pointed out a bare, rocky peak, to the left of which was a saddle. "Stony Pass is just to the left of that peak," he said, and with those words my excitement grew almost unbearable. For years I'd been reading about the hardships endured by the pioneers and the gold-crazy miners who had struggled over that rugged pass to reach the seductive San Juan.

Nothing but the craze for gold could have kept the stream of miners clambering over range after range without roads of trails other than those made by Indians or worn by animals. Even when trails were blazed by the impetuous men, they were almost impassable; and the first roads constructed were little better. During the seventies the chief route to the region was much the way we had come—from Del Norte up the Rio Grande valley, past Antelope Park to the headwaters of the river, over Stony Pass and down the gulch on the other side. Until this road on which we were traveling was built in 1879, people left their wagons in a park above Wagon Wheel Gap, packed their equipment on burros and fought their way up over the pass and down Cunningham gulch on the other side to Baker's Park.

For years W. D. Watson ran a "road house and stopping place for man and beast" at the foot of Grassy hill on this side of Stony Pass, and all summer long hundreds of pack animals were turned out to graze on the green slopes before sundown, while the weary miners and freighters rolled up in their blankets for a night's rest before tackling the difficult climb over the range. In winter "Grassy" was the end of the mail route, except for such pieces as could be packed over by a carrier on snowshoes. I watched that saddle below the austere peak as long as I could see it, for in my mind's eye I had travelled over it many times with the pioneers of whom I had read, and I knew that I'd never be so near it again.

Next, our road led along the edge of a mountain, so high that the stream was a mere ribbon below us and grazing cattle looked like toys. We could now look up another valley and follow the tiny sliver of trail to the far end, where Beartown lay. Dropping down to the creek we forded it, the horses sucking in great draughts of water after their pull over Timber hill. White-faced Hereford cattle were all around us, bawling in confusion at our presence and getting a slight respite from the horse and deer flies which settled on us in swarms and pursued us for the next two miles. The rest of our party were hungry and stopped to eat in a grove of trees, but I kept looking up the valley toward the invisible town, impatient to see what was left of it.

After another mile up the valley we passed a big cabin with its roof crushed in. This was once a stage station, and far in the distance was another building, a lone cabin in a big meadow. Just as we entered the meadow we passed the wreckage of a mill, and I realized with a start that this was Beartown. Near the lone cabin I saw some fragments of lumber, once part of a building, and riding close by I discovered the boards to be the remains of a toilet.

I tried to conjure up Beartown as it must have looked with its grocery and hardware stores, its blacksmith shop, boardinghouse, saloon, surveyor's and assayer's offices and other places of business. Merchants in Creede opened stores in the new camp, and stage lines operated between it and the larger town. Just as at Spar City, the *Creede Candle* was on the scene establishing the *Gold Run Silvertip*, a weekly, with A. W. B. Johnson as editor.

BEARTOWN

SYLVANITE MINE, BEARTOWN

Although as early as the seventies two men talked excitedly about gold they had found near the head of the Rio Grande and exhibited large nuggets as proof of their stories, no one seemed inclined to explore the area they described until the nineties. Then in May, 1893, about fifty prospectors began studying the rock formations near timberline on the range between Pole and Bear creeks and chose the meadow half a mile below the Sylvanite lode as a suitable place for a townsite. By June ninth, two hundred people were milling around, and still no town had been started and no name decided upon; everyone was too busy digging to bother with cabins. By the end of June four hundred "prospectors, not real estate boomers," were at work, and "more men were coming in than going out." "If this keeps up," crowed the miners, "this will be a respectable sized camp before the snow flies. In fact, in all likelihood it will be a Creede Annex."

At first the camp was called Gold Run, Bear Creek, and Silvertip. Hines Fork and Cub Town were also considered as possible names. A post office was opened under the name of Sylvanite, but by the time the postmaster received his commission he was unable to get to his office on account of snow.

"The camp needs a road," roared the miners, for in those days the last five miles from the mouth of Bear creek to the mines was only a trail. "A dozen men with a team could build it in a day and at the miners' meeting the other night it was decided to do this. Nothing has been done, however, and probably will not be until one of the mines wants an outlet for ore."

Leaving the Beartown townsite, we rode up to the Sylvanite mine, fording Bear creek below falls which have cut a deep gash in a rocky gorge. The horses climbed the far side of the bank, their hooves slipping among the loose rocks. Nearby stood a road grader, and we made bets on how recently it had been used. After a last stiff climb we reached the mine and its group of buildings. The assay office was full of equipment, and the hotel or boardinghouse was furnished with bedsteads and with a big iron range in the kitchen. While some of the buildings were fairly new (for the mine was working ten years ago), others dated from 1900, and still others from the nineties when the vein was first opened and when eight burro-loads of ore were taken from it over to Utah to be smelted. This mine, whose ore netted over $4000 a ton, is just below timberline, and above it, on the bare rock slopes, are the dumps of the Good Hope and the Yankakee, the Gold Bug and the Silver Bug.

Junction City

Leaving Beartown, we retraced our steps for five miles down the creek. As we neared the Forks, where Bear and Pole creeks join the Rio Grande, I looked for vestiges of Junction City, a camp laid out in the spring of 1894; but I was able to locate only one forlorn cabin.

The miners who had gone out for the winter and others who were arriving for the first time were eager to get to the camp as soon as possible and, rather than wait for the snow to melt in Gold Run Park, these early-comers laid out a townsite at the Forks.

A meeting of the settlers was held and it was decided that all prospectors and their grubstakers should have first choice of lots, and be entitled each to one business and

(338)

one residence lot. . . . Before this decision was reached there was something of a struggle between two outfits that had participated in the race to the townsite. One faction held out and seemed to want all. . . . It was a hot time for a few hours. . . . Finally the opposition weakened and all went merry thereafter.

John Doherty was not slow in getting up a saloon and a Salida man was not far behind in opening a real estate office.—*Creede Candle*, April 27, 1894.

Our guide now turned the horses across a slope near the foot of the hill, and after some climbing and sliding up and down over sagebrush and loose piles of rock, we forded Pole creek and rode along its bank looking for our camp. Soon we saw the pack horses grazing quietly in a meadow near the water.

Another quarter of a mile brought us to the camp that Carol had made while we explored the gold camp. He had pitched two tents and had unpacked everything and stowed it neatly away. Here we would spend the night in a little clearing beside the creek. I watched fascinated while he and Floyd, another guide, unsaddled the horses and turned them loose, hobbling those who were known to wander too far away. The saddles and blankets were placed in a long row over a fallen tree ready for the morning's departure. While Carol built a fire and made coffee for the party, the boys in the group forded the creek and climbed its almost vertical far bank, hunting for dead timber to be used for the campfire. Great limbs of trees came crashing down into the water and were then snaked to land.

By now supper was under way, and just at dusk everyone fell to, eating second and even third helpings of potatoes, onions, beans, ham, lettuce, coffee and cake. By the time the dishes were done and more fuel added to the fire there was a glow behind the mountains which made us watch for the full moon to burst from behind the black silhouette of the peaks. While we sat around the fire, washed in moonlight, I tried to outline in my mind the chain of events that led to the opening of all this country, especially that beyond Stony Pass, and I thought of the pioneers who in 1875 painted on the sides of their wagon sheets, "San Juan or Bust."

Charles Baker had heard from the Indians that there was gold to be found in the mountains in southwest Colorado; so in 1860 he and six other men started for the San Juan region. They searched for gold during the late summer and early fall and then, when snow prevented further prospecting, they dug in for the winter, living as best they could in rude shelters made of boughs and logs. Early in 1861 another party worked its way into the same area, looking for Baker and his companions, and found them in a gulch above the present site of Eureka. The new-comers began to prospect, but with as little success as the original party, and finally the men became abusive and told Baker that the area didn't look like gold country anyway and that it was about time to quit. The whole party then moved down the valley of the Animas to the site of Animas City, where they laid out a town and stayed until fall, continuing their fruitless search for gold. Not wishing to be caught again by snow, the men then abandoned the camp and separated, to work their way back to country they knew. When Baker reached Fort Garland he learned for the first time of the Civil War and, hurrying to Virginia, enlisted in the Confederate army.

After the war he returned to the San Juan. He was a captain now and he was still leader of a small party of prospectors. On this second expedition in 1868 he explored the valleys of the Gunnison, Animas and La Plata rivers, but again he found very little gold; and one by one the disgruntled and discouraged members of the party went back to their homes. Finally, when only two of the party were left, Baker gave up and started to leave the mountains; but on the way out he was killed by Indians. The small mountain-rimmed valley which he and his companions explored so extensively was called Baker's Park after the persistent but unfortunate prospector.

The next expedition was organized at Prescott, Arizona, in 1869 under the leadership of Jackson, an old Californian with experience in dealing with Indians. This group of twenty-two men expected to be joined by another party later in the season, but before the reinforcements arrived the men had had enough of Indian troubles and all but eight went back. The rest reached the San Juan, but their efforts to locate gold were as unsuccessful as those of their predecessors, and they gave up the quest.

Still another party set out in 1870 and struggled through the canyon of the Animas to Baker's Park, where they started to prospect. On this expedition, Miles T. Johnson discovered the Little Giant gold mine in Arastra gulch, the first profitable location made in the San Juan. He kept his discovery a secret and built a small arastra in the gulch one-half mile from the Animas river. With this he crushed his ore—performing the first milling operation in the region—and only when his pack train of mules "reached the outer world" two years later was his strike revealed.

Other men came into the valley in 1871, among them James Kendall, after whom Kendall mountain west of Silverton is named; and as the flood of prospectors continued, many claims were staked and Las Animas mining district was set up in June, 1871. This was done in spite of the fact that the land still belonged to the Indians.

To "effect a peaceful settlement," the United States authorities ordered that a council be held at Los Pinos agency in August, 1872, in order to induce the Utes to cede over some of their lands. Chief Ouray listened to the arguments advanced by the government men and then,

> with rare eloquence, demolished every detail of their carefully arranged program, putting them to shame by exposing the violation of their pledges, the injustice and wrong of their attempt to nullify a contract, which had been agreed to and ratified by the Senate of the United States, and the commissioners, worsted, fell back to Washington in anything but good order.

The following year Felix Brunot drafted a new and modified pact, which Ouray accepted, and with the signing of this treaty in 1873 a tidal wave of miners swept over the rich acres which had been torn away from the Indians.

"Time for bed," said Lucy Ann, and with a start I left Baker and all the other prospectors and crept into my tent to investigate the mysteries of a sleeping bag.

(340)

CHAPTER XIV

Lake City and Hinsdale County

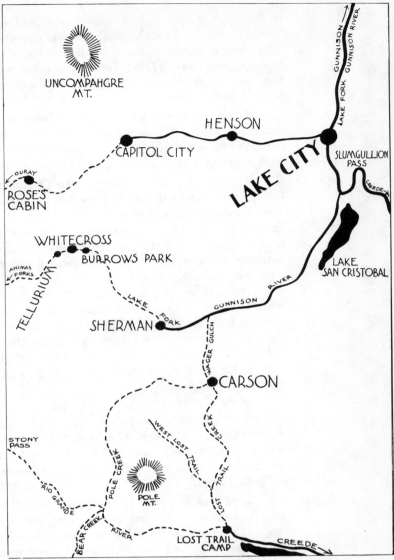

Lake City

PERHAPS because Lake City is tucked away in the mountains, miles from main highways, it has kept much of its early charm. Its wide streets, lined with huge cottonwoods, are shady and are bordered with trim frame houses. Except where fire has razed old landmarks leaving gaps between more substantial structures, its "business blocks," whether of wood or of the dressed bluish stone peculiar to the area, dot Silver street, almost to the bridge over Henson creek. Ever since 1875, when the townsite was entered in the United States Land Office at Del Norte, the city, named for Lake San Cristobal four miles away, has been a center to which men have hurried, first for work and recently for recreation. Mining brought them to the camp and now, since the interest in mining has declined, it is fishing and hunting that bring the tired business men, the Texas ranchers and the city dwellers to its resorts.

The road to Lake City from Gunnison turns south at Iola and winds across sagebrush hills, past Powderhorn and over Cebolla creek, until at Gate View it skirts the Lake Fork of the Gunnison river and follows it all the way in. A far more exciting drive is to come in from the south over Slumgullion Pass, preferably in the fall when the aspens have turned, and when much of the way is through groves so yellow that the sky, seen through the leaves, seems oppressively blue. The road from South Fork follows the Rio Grande up the canyon, past Wagon Wheel Gap and Creede, to the fork where it leaves the river and climbs over Spring Creek Pass. Then it winds through lonely ranch country and over the tops of rolling hills until it climbs again through forests of aspens and pines to the top of Slumgullion Pass, 11,361 feet high, from where, directly across the valley, the cruel and jagged silhouette of Uncompahgre Peak stands clean cut against the horizon.

At the foot of the pass is the lake, and as the road drops down the mountain one gets frequent glimpses of this sheet of water shimmering through the trees, and of yellow mine dumps with rusty shaft houses perched high on the rocky slopes or of others far below in the valley.

Until 1944, when it burned, the Occidental on Silver street, a two-story frame structure, half hidden by huge cottonwoods, was the leading hotel; and more than once I've sat in its parlor or close to the stove in the lobby on a cool fall evening, listening to the talk of old men who dropped in to smoke a pipeful and to reminisce with "Jimmy" Grant, the proprietor. There was the story of the man who rode a bicycle with hard rubber tires over Engineer mountain into Lake City, and then went on to Kentucky, covering 1800 miles in twenty days. And there was the story about a district judge who liked to play poker. Once during court session he spent the night playing with his cronies. The next day one of the players of the night before testified as a witness while drunk. This riled the judge, who fined him ten dollars. The witness pulled out a fat wad of bills and, as he "peeled off a tenner, he grinned at the judge and said: "That all you need? It's your money, you know.'"

"A friend of mine had an oxteam and freighted a load of bottled beer packed in barrels of straw to Lake City," drawled a man who had been a mule-skinner. "On the way here the load turned over and rolled into the gulch. Six bottles were broken. When he delivered it, the man who had contracted for it said: 'Forget it. I expected you to drink that much out of each barrel.'

"I had to go over to Tomichi creek once to get a load of coal," the man continued. "At one point there was a bridge with a loose pole floor which the oxen were afraid to cross. Another fellow was trying to get his outfit over, too, and was having the same trouble. When I got there he was standing on the bridge praying: 'Oh Lord, if you'll help me over this God-damned bridge I'll never ask you for anything again.' Both of us got across."

There were other tales, too, but no session was complete without the story of Packer the cannibal.

In the fall of 1873 a group of men in Provo, Utah, got the gold fever and started out for the San Juan. It was late in the season to venture into such high country, and after going a way the party split up, the bulk of the men giving up the project until the following spring. Six men, including Alfred Packer, the guide, voted to go on and pushed deeper into the trackless territory. Their provisions gave out, they were nowhere near Los Pinos Indian Agency toward which they were heading, and they accused Packer of being incompetent and of attempting to lead them through country which he did not know. No doubt hunger and cold half-crazed them all. Two months after the party had disappeared into the mountains, Packer walked into the agency, sleek and well-fed, telling a strange story about how his companions became demented through lack of food and died of starvation. His story, though "fishy," was believed at the time, and he left the agency.

In the spring of 1874 some prospectors ran across his camp and the mutilated bodies of his victims not far from Lake San Cristobal; four of the men had apparently been murdered as they slept, but the fifth had put up a struggle. In the meantime Packer had been persuaded into returning to the agency to conduct a searching party for the five men, and his suspicious actions and conflicting stories had landed him in the custody of the sheriff of Saguache.

After the bodies were found the evidence pointed to Packer's having killed them and eaten enough of the flesh to sustain his own life. He escaped from the sheriff and for nearly nine years was the object of a man-hunt which ended in Wyoming, where he was recognized, arrested and returned to Lake City for trial. A jury convicted him of murder and sentenced him to hang; but because of a legal technicality he got a new trial and was placed in the state penitentiary at Canon City at hard labor. Years later he was paroled.

About a mile above Lake City at the foot of Slumgullion Pass, on Cannibal plateau, is the grave where Packer's victims now lie buried, and rumor has it that this final burial, over which a properly inscribed tombstone rests, was combined with a community fish fry, staged by the sympathetic citizens of Lake City!

Precious metal was believed to have been found in the Lake City area in 1848 by members of Fremont's party; but their discovery was not followed up. In 1871 J. K. Mullen and Henry Henson prospected what is now Hinsdale County, locating the Ute-Ulay veins. Very few others explored the region until several years later, chiefly because the land belonged to the Ute Indians, who were distinctly unfriendly to intruders. In 1874, by the terms of the Brunot treaty, a strip of territory in the San Juan mountains was at last thrown open to settlement, and a headlong stampede of prospectors followed, with the result that many small camps made their appearance. Of these Lake City became the center and all through the mining era it alone served as a supply and provision point for countless numbers of prospectors, freighters and settlers.

It was Enos Hotchkiss' discovery in 1874 of a rich mine near the lower end of the lake which in a few weeks changed Lake City from a group of four or five cabins to a town of four hundred prospectors, all feverishly trying to locate other rich lodes. And it was the toll road from Saguache that he and Otto Mears built that same year which further helped to open up the region. Hotchkiss worked his mine, later known as the Golden Fleece, profitably for some time; but like most bonanzas it changed hands frequently, sometimes producing fabulous sums and at other times lying idle. One man who was working the vein got down to his last stick of powder and quit. His partner decided to use the stick, and "let off a pop shot in a bulge in one wall" which opened a pocket from which $1,000 worth of gold was taken.

The new owner found more pockets, but they, too, played out. Having put too much into the mine to stop now, he kept developing it and opened up a chimney of fabulously rich ore. Another big strike was made in 1891 when an almost solid mass of tellurium ore which needed no sorting was brought to light. The mine was sold that year for $75,000; it continued to produce through the nineties and has been worked intermittently ever since, for "the fitful old wonder opens up its heart" at intervals "and turns out thousands upon thousands in tellurium." In 1943 it was sold for taxes.

Three concentrators and smelters were built on the edges of the city to handle the local ores. Crooke's reduction works, built in 1874, were one mile above the city at Granite Falls and were worked by waterpower from the seventy-foot drop. As there was no coal in the region, coal and coke for the plant were brought in from Crested Butte by wagon. In 1882, two years before the plant closed down, fifteen charcoal kilns were built to furnish it with fuel. Van Geison's lixiviation works were erected at the mouth of Henson gulch, and after the opening of the Ocean Wave mine in 1876, a smelter was put up at the lower end of the city to handle its output.

From 1874-1876 mines were developed in the Slumgullion district, from the foot of Lake San Cristobal east for five miles, where the mountainsides were found to be covered with float. The first mining boom reached its climax in 1876 with the opening up of the Ocean Wave group and with the continued production of the Ute-Ulay and the mines on Hotchkiss mountain. In later years the Golden Ram and the Hiwasee-Black Crook group of a dozen gold-silver veins were also worked successfully. The region was so rich in minerals that the Lake City *Mining Register* of Jan. 1, 1881, spoke of the San Juan as "The Home of the True Fissure and the Field of the Cloth of Gold and Silver."

In the spring of 1875 the town consisted of three log cabins and a few tents, but it grew so rapidly that by summer a sawmill was needed and by fall sixty-seven finished buildings were ready to house a population of 500. In July of the first summer Barlow and Sanderson's stage line arrived from Saguache and thereafter established regular runs from the San Luis valley. In the same year the Lake City and Antelope Park toll road was completed. This made two wagon roads to the camp—the first open all year round and the second, over Slumgullion Pass, which was said to be a "villainous road," navigable most of the time. A stage road over Cinnamon Pass to Ouray was also constructed and this served the camps of Sherman, Carson and Whitecross as well. This road, which for years has been little more than a trail, is today being improved for auto travel in the hopes of once more making it a shortcut to Silverton.

A newspaper, the first to be **printed on** the Western Slope, was established in 1875 by Harry M. Woods. He published the *Silver World* "in a log cabin office whose roof was of saplings covered with mud, which permitted the dirt to sift down upon the editor and his presses in a never ending shower." On June 19th, less than two weeks after his equipment was delivered from the freight wagons, the first issue was on the streets. Since there was no post office in camp, in order to mail the paper the first three

LAKE CITY STORES (BURNED)

✝ CHURCHES, LAKE CITY

editions had to be taken on horseback to Saguache, seventy miles away. The editor took exception to this procedure and stated that:

> Probably no town on the continent similarly situated as we, living on the Pacific slope, are compelled to go to the Atlantic slope to reach the nearest post office. Our mails come in on bull teams and go out by chance and yet there are between 500 and 600 persons who receive their mails at this point.—Vol. I *Silver World,* June 19, 1875.

The *Silver World* was the leading newspaper of the city, although the *Mining Register* was also published in the eighties, and the *Lake City Phonograph* appeared briefly in 1891, followed in 1901 by the *San Cristobal Magazine,* which offered a premium of pressed columbines to each new subscriber.

Both 1876 and 1877 were big years in the camp, and the housing shortage continued. A second sawmill was installed, yet both working at their full capacity of 1500 feet per day failed to supply the demand for building materials.

The stage line by now was making tri-weekly trips from Canon City, carrying both mail and passengers, thus making Lake City the distribution point for the San Juan mines. By fall the company was forced to put on a daily service. During the entire summer "roads leading into town were lined with newcomers, pedestrians with packs on their backs, some riding burros and jacks, men on horseback or in wagons, a constant stream of humanity pouring into the San Juan through this metropolis."

In winter the town was often isolated for weeks due to heavy snows which blocked roads and trails. An eight foot snow late in 1879 caused all mail to be carried from Del Norte to the camp on sleds from November 25th up until April 8th. At Powderhorn the snow was so deep that even the trees were covered.

The population grew to 2500, the number of buildings to 500. Several lawyers "awaited the troubles that attend mining camps," yet at the same time there was not a physician in town, a fact that was attributed to the "healthfulness of the place." Property values soared. Lots which couldn't find purchasers at $250 in December sold for $500 in March. It was evident by now that Lake City was more than a camp, for its inhabitants, in spite of a large floating population, were substantial folk who had come to make their home in the mountains.

Indians were a constant menace, for the Los Pinos Agency was not many miles away, and "Indians roamed the country resenting the intrusion of the white settlers, especially the miners who offended their gods by digging into the earth and removing the precious rocks." Chief Ouray was the settler's friend, and through his intervention many tragedies were averted. Colorow on the other hand was a hostile Ute, and he and his band were constantly striking terror into the hearts of the miners and their families. As late as 1879 Lake City was surrounded by angry Utes under Colorow, and defenses were hastily constructed. Everyone was on the alert. One man remembers that day, although he was only four years old at the time. His mother put him in the attic of their cabin and passed up to him two loaded shotguns for him

BAPTIST CHURCH,
LAKE CITY

SILVER STREET, LAKE CITY

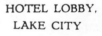

HOTEL LOBBY,
LAKE CITY

to watch. While everyone waited for the attack, Chief Ouray rode over from the reservation, calmed the ruffled Utes and averted the danger.

Lake City was proud of its four churches, Presbyterian, Catholic, Episcopal and Baptist, all of which are still standing. The Presbyterian, founded in 1876, claims the distinction of being the first church established on the Western Slope. Its bell, which came from New Jersey, was freighted across two mountain ranges in a wagon and was presented to the church in 1877. Rev. George M. Darley, the pastor, conducted services in Lake City and vicinity prior to the building of the church, preaching in any place he could find an audience, frequently a gambling hall. Once he was told by the proprietor "to wait until the games could be stopped when he would be given a chance at the boys." At such times a faro table might serve as his altar, and he often said that a more convenient one could not be found.

In his autobiography, *Pioneering in the San Juan*, he tells many stories of his experiences as a preacher in the camp. Once a pet deer came into the church during the evening service, walked down the aisle, looked about and then slowly stalked out. On a winter trip over the range to Silverton, where he was to preach, he slipped over a precipice and slid down the steep mountainside in the deep snow. Recovering himself, he struggled on until he saw below him a thin, dark line of timber and knew that he was away from the snow crests. He finally reached Animas Forks, still fourteen miles from his destination, but in spite of the danger of new slides he ploughed on to his storm-bound congregation.

The sporting element of the camp lived in Hell's Acre near Henson creek, and the pastor was sometimes called in to hold funeral services for the gamblers or for one of the "girls." He kept a register of names of those for whom he conducted services, from which the following entries are taken:

> George Elwood—saloon keeper—killed.
> Luther Ray—murdered in a gambling hall.
> Charles C. Curtis—killed by a snowslide while in his cabin.
> Alfred Shepherd—died from exposure.
> Harry Pierce—killed by a premature blast in Ule mine.

In 1881 the city had two banks, three smelting works, two drugstores, three breweries and a telephone line over the range to Animas Forks. It had a public library and a "newsstand where can be purchased all the eastern newspapers." The Illustrated Holiday Edition of the Lake City *Mining Register* for Jan. 1, 1881, "which can be sold in New York, Chicago, Rico, Silverton, Animas Forks, Lake City and Everywhere," summed up the city's progress by saying:

> Great is Colorado . . . grand in her infancy. Unlimited her possibilities. . . . We have room and opportunities for the coming thousands. . . . Our grand mountain canyons echo today with the music of the school and church bell, while the clatter of the busy printing press is heard in every camp and the smoke from the smelters and mills veil the snow-clad summits of our towering mountains and the hot breath from the furnace blast is forging links of silver and gold for the strong chain that binds us to the commerce of the world.

. . . The park or basin in which the city is built is guarded on all sides by mighty walls of mineral which look down upon it from the clouds like giant watchmen. . . . Its social status is far above the average of Western frontier cities and no mining camp in the world can boast of a more intelligent cultural peaceable citizenship. A street brawl is of the rarest occurrence and for months the log cabin that serves as a calaboose is tenantless.

Lake City had its culture in the form of concerts, lectures, readings and balls, to say nothing of the occasion on Sept. 20, 1877, when Susan B. Anthony addressed the citizens on the subject of Woman Suffrage. "The popularity of the speaker attracted a large assembly, the largest ever in Lake City. The Courthouse was secured for the occasion but a half-hour beforehand every seat was taken and all standing room occupied." The crowd outside was so large that the speaker was "unable to get to the rostrum;" so an outdoor meeting was held instead, at which the audience "stood for two hours in the cool night air and listened with rapt attention. . . There was a respectable sprinkling of the fair sex present showing they are interested in this question more than the opponents of the movement would have us believe."

In 1878 Mr. Wm. Penn Harbottle of New York City gave "a dramatic recitation of Shakepeare's beautiful Epic play, King Henry V" in which he "assumed the speaking part of forty different characters in four languages and five dialects in English . . . admission fifty cents."

A "Grand Musical Soiree" was held at the courthouse, November 23, 1882, to raise funds for a "public bell." This same firebell is still in use. By 1882 several stone and brick stores and residences had been built as well as the large schoolhouse at the end of the town, and the John S. Hough Fire Co. No. 1, had obtained a new hose cart.

In April, 1882, Sheriff E. N. Campbell was killed by George Betts and James Browning, saloon keepers. These men were suspected of robbing an unoccupied but furnished residence, and the sheriff and his deputies went to the house and waited for the thieves to return for more loot. Late that evening they were heard at the door, and as they entered the house the sheriff called out, "Throw up your hands;" but the robbers shot at the dark shapes within the building, instantly killing Campbell. As soon as this was discovered a posse was formed which rode in pursuit of the two men, captured them, and put them in jail. There was talk of forcing the building, and the Pitkin Guards were called out to protect it and the prisoners.

A parade and celebration by the Odd Fellows Lodge had been slated for the following day, but now all such festivities were postponed. Instead, the Hall and even the Hose House and apparatus were draped in mourning, and few business houses opened, even though the city filled up with "the boys from the mountains," who knew nothing of the murder but had come in to see the scheduled celebration.

During the day a vigilante committee was organized, "ropes, sledges and arms were secured and a rendezvous selected." At the request of the mayor all saloons and dancehalls were closed at sundown and an extra police force patrolled the streets. The city was as quiet as "the most isolated New

England village," but as the evening progressed "squads of men watched the progress of the moon toward the mountains" and "dark shapes moved toward a vacant lot on Silver Ave., near Sheriff Campbell's house."

The moon was now dipping toward the western wall and soon the shadow would creep downward. The veil of sweet, mellow moonlight would be replaced by a great, dark shadow into which the now great swarm of resolute men could plunge. One hundred and ten masked men were on guard. . . . A heavily disguised figure carried under his arms the ropes; another bore a heavy sledge hammer; others carried rifles and shot guns, . . . a hundred or more unmasked citizens were in waiting at the jail. . . . Then followed the dull thud of sledge hammers against the strong jail lock . . . the prisoners were marched to the bridge . . . a rope was thrown over a crossbeam and in less than a minute the two men were swinging. . . . It was now one o'clock. The dark shadows were creeping up the side of the western wall of the little city . . . the falls under the bridge gurgled and splashed mournfully—silence brooded painfully over the great court and jury and witnesses who stood with upturned faces looking at two figures swinging grimly at the end of the rope of Justice. . . .

At ten A. M. . . . Coroner Rapp, being notified of the hanging proceeded to the scene, lowered the bodies and summoned a jury who found that Betts and Browning came to their death at the hands of unknown parties.

A friend of mine who lived at Lake City as a child recalls this gruesome event and told me that the night of the lynching the town was too quiet, and that just as the moon sank behind the mountain and the men were hanged, she heard a great shout from the mob, followed by an awful stillness. Next morning school was dismissed, and all the children were marched to the bridge to see the bodies dangling over the water.

As more people flocked to Lake City and more mines were developed, the problem of shipping out ore became acute. A number of the larger mines worked part time only, and the floating population largely disappeared. This period of depression lasted until 1889, when the Denver and Rio Grande completed a branch railroad to the city from Sapinero, twenty-eight miles away. With the coming of the road, many of the old mines were re-opened. During the 1890's the road did an active business. At one time two passenger trains a day rolled in from Sapinero, "a good part of the town being found at the depot on these occasions to welcome the Flyer." The railroad is now a thing of the past; its rails were pulled up in 1937 and its trestles are gone, but the roadbed can be seen along the Lake Fork, now close to the stream, now high above on the cliffs. When mining decreased after 1893 the population shrank to 800 in 1897, and to about 150 today.

Where giant powder and mule shoes used to be stock in trade, today's visitors look for fishing tackle, gasoline stations, auto camps and dude ranches. In the fishing and hunting season Lake City is alive; but in the winter it is dormant, and old settlers swap yarns about the time when a man brought a burro from Mineral Point over Engineer mountain to the head of Henson creek on snowshoes which he had taught the beast to wear, or about the strike at the Ute-Ulay mine that was settled by the intervention of the Italian consul.

Henson   It was early June when I first drove up Henson gulch as far as Capitol City. "Some snowslides wiped out part of the roadbed, but the plough

(350)

has been up as far as you're going, so you can get through," said the garage man as he filled the car with gasoline. "There's a lot of mines up the gulch—the Hidden Treasure, the Ute-Ulay and the Ocean Wave, and up at Cap City there's a raft more."

The drive up the gulch was unexpectedly beautiful and varied. First the road lies almost in the creek bed as it winds around sheer silver grey cliffs. Then it climbs away from the water and passes the Hidden Treasure and its group of buildings, beyond which is the Ute-Ulay mine, the biggest property of all.

Joel K. Mullen, Albert Mead, Charles Goodwin and Henry Henson explored the region in 1871 and late in August located the Ute-Ulay (or Ule) mine. The men did enough work on their claim to assure them that it was a find, but since the territory in which they were prospecting was Indian land and since news of their discovery brought more prospectors to the vicinity, to the annoyance of the Utes, they willingly withdrew to wait for the ratification of the Brunot Treaty, by the terms of which the San Juan mountains were thrown open to settlement. With the signing of the treaty in 1874 the mineral development of the region began, and Henson and his partners were among the first to return to the gulch so as to develop their claims, which they worked so successfully that in 1876 Crooke Bros. of Lake City bought them out for $125,000. This company then erected a lead smelter, which operated on ore from the Ute-Ulay and the Polar Star mines.

The property was sold again in 1880 for $1,200,000, and as the mining operations grew, a townsite close to the mine on Ute mountain was laid out in 1880 and was named in honor of Judge Henry Henson. The gulch was so narrow near the mine property that there was barely room for the many buildings and for the houses of the employees. In 1882 concentration works were erected at the Ute-Ulay mine, and all during the eighties two to three hundred men were employed. By 1893 the mine was in full swing, and the plant was the largest in the San Juan. A tram brought cars loaded with glistening galena ore down the mountainside and delivered them to the huge mill by the stream.

The Henson Creek and Uncompahgre Toll Road, whose toll gate was at the entrance of the canyon, was completed to the top of the range in 1877 and, through private contributions made by the citizens of Lake City and the surrounding camps, was extended a mile and a half so as to connect with the Animas Forks road to Ouray and to Silverton. It crossed the divide at the head of Henson creek at an elevation of 12,200 feet. The first trip over the road was made by Oatman's six-horse coach from Lake City, which drew "a number of representative citizens to celebrate the event." For several years it was a single track highway, but as more and more turnouts were added it became one of the best mountain roads in the San Juan and today is "double track" as far as Cap City.

When the mines were all running, accidents were frequent and shootings were a dime a dozen. Dr. B. F. Cummings, who became company doctor for the Ute-Ulay and other mines, and seven other physicians were kept busy—eight to ten operations a day being a common occurrence. On one occasion the Ute-Ulay and the Hidden Treasure mines made connection un-expectedly through some miscalculation in tunneling, and the explosion of gas released in the passageway killed or injured twenty men from the Ute and sixteen from the Hidden Treasure.

A spectacular strike at the mine in March, 1899, sent the Italian consul scurrying to the mountain town. Eighty Italians, all members of the local union of the Western Federation of Miners, struck at the Ute-Ulay and Hid-den Treasure mines in protest to the company's order that all single men board at the company commissaries. Those miners who attempted to continue to work were driven off by the armed Italians or were beaten up.

The governor of the state, Charles S. Thomas, was appealed to and he acted promptly by sending four companies of infantry and two troops of cav-alry to Lake City by train over snow-clogged Marshall Pass. At the Sapinero depot stood another train which had brought Dr. Cuneo, the Italian consul, to the scene, so that he might plead with his countrymen to "lay down their arms."

Since it was rumored that the track into Lake City was mined, a "pilot engine, drawing a box car, ran at slow speed" ahead of the two sections car-rying the soldiers. At Lake City the troops were joined at the Armory by a group of men eager to join the expedition, but until plans were perfected they all "rested on their arms while a blizzard whitened the town."

Dr. Cuneo, the consul, and Charles Mairo of Lake City met with the colonel in charge of the militia, and the consul asked that Mairo be given a pass up the canyon to Henson. Cuneo then wrote a note to the strikers say-ing that "their government, through King Humbert, requested all its subjects at Henson to meet the officers of the militia, the county authorities and the royal Italian representative." Mairo started up the canyon road with the paper. Cuneo then put on a high silk hat, an overcoat with a fur collar, gloves, and patent-leather shoes and was driven in a buggy over the snow-packed road a little distance behind Mairo. Behind Cuneo came the officers, and the troops brought up the rear. Soon guards were seen on the cliffs, but as a white handkerchief was tied to the buggy whip the guards waved the delegation on. Half a mile below Henson a committee of six men waited for them, and after exchanging salutes and bows, the men cheered, the consul waved and kissed his gloved hands, and the procession rode on. Reaching Henson it passed along the silent street, lined with workmen and "their shawled womenfolk and children," until the buggy stopped and Cuneo went forward alone. Although it was bitterly cold he took off his hat, threw open his overcoat and stood before the surprised crowd in full evening dress, a red, white and green ribbon across his shirt bosom. The crowd cheered. He then addressed the men and commanded them to salute the officers of the state and county and to surrender to the sheriff. With their surrender a strange, silent stream commenced to wind down the snowy road toward Lake City, the women and children accompanying the men to prison. Three days after their arrest an announcement was made that the company re-fused to employ any Italians, and all single Italian miners were ordered to leave the county within three days and all married men within sixty days.

Cuneo and the strikers were dismayed at this decision, but they were helpless. Thanks to Dr. Cuneo's trusting innocence, the strike was settled without bloodshed and the militia withdrew.

It was hard to picture such turmoil in this quiet place as we drove along the road and looked down on the mine buildings, the long, curved flume and the high falls near the mill. We passed the few buildings left standing on the townsite and beyond them, half hidden in the trees close to the stream, saw the well-preserved frame school house.

Further up the canyon we came close to the snow. On some of the higher slopes were the scars left by many avalanches, and twice our road-bed was completely cut away by recent slides. At these spots we bumped over rocks, gravel, mud and debris, between snowbanks in which large trees were imbedded, their thick trunks snapped off as clean as a broken match stick. The force and destructiveness of the snowslide, seen even now weeks after the damage, were terrifying. We were closed in by walls of dirty snow full of ground-in rocks, some of which were of immense proportions. Passing the Ocean Wave property, we drove past a large red brick house at the lower end of the mountain park in which lay the site of Capitol City.

As we looked around the swampy, willow-grown flat with its few crumbling buildings and its ghostly white schoolhouse in the distance, I noticed an old man puttering around his cabin. He was old enough to know the history of the place, and since he was the only one living in the deserted city I asked him how long he had been there. *Capitol City*

"Only since the nineties, but I've heard tell about the early days in this camp," he said settling back in his homemade armchair. "It was a new camp in 1877 with a two-hundred acre townsite on this meadow, a sawmill, a post office and about thirty cabins. It was called Galena City then, but some of the boys were so sure it would be a big thing that they changed its name to Capitol City, in hopes that some day it might beat Denver.

"I've heard too of the grand ball they held here in May, 1877, in the Capitol Saloon. About fifteen couples went. My father was the fiddler for that dance and he kept the newspaper write-up of it. Here it is," he added, taking a tattered piece of paper from his frayed wallet. It was dated May 29, 1877, and read:

> The music of the violin and guitar swayed the feet of the gay dancers until the morning's light invaded the hall of revelry, and presented the claims of the coming day, when the happy crowd dispersed.

"This place was planned to be big, but it overbuilt itself," he went on, his eyes sweeping over the mountain-rimmed park. "The boys found silver near the surface and before they found how deep the veins ran they built on a big scale. Then when the ore or the money ran out, they were sunk.

"There were plenty of lode mines here on Majestic, Emperor, Sunshine, Capitol, Garbutt and Littlejohn mountains," he continued, pointing out the fourteen-thousand-foot peaks which surrounded the valley. "The population was all miners and prospectors and there was lots of paying properties too, but some of the best got tied up in litigation, and the owners got fighting over boundary lines and overlapping claims. Then the two smelting works went idle and everybody sat around for a while waiting for something to turn up.

"Did you see the big two-story brick house as you drove in to town? It was built by George T. Lee, who also built the smelting works a mile below town on Henson creek. He wanted to make a big thing of it and he wanted his home to be the best in the San Juan. Lee's saw and planing mill was right here in town too. He used to pack his hundred jacks with shingles and lumber and deliver as far away as Lake City. A mile above town was the Henson Creek Reduction Co. The city had a store which handled merchandise, several hotels and restaurants and saloons. See the big white schoolhouse up there? It was built in 1883 and it cost $1511. They tell me an architect designed it in what he called 'country cottage' style, but like everything else here, it was built too big after the boom was over.

"Some of the best mines were the Capitol City and the Yellow Medicine, both of which produced hundreds of thousands of dollars worth of ore. The Polar Star was good too and the Ocean Wave, but it got sewed up in litigation too. That's the dump of the Great Eastern up there, and there's the San Bruno, and the Incas, and the High Muck-A-Muck. The Morning Star lode on Sheep mountain was owned and worked by a bunch of niggers who were the most hardworking, industrious miners up here and everyone respected them.

"During the nineties there were nearly 700 people here and there was plenty of room for a thousand more. In 1900 when they found gold here there was another boom and a lot of prospectors began picking at the hills again or reopening the old properties. That's when the Ajax and the Moro lodes produced hundreds of tons of high grade gold and copper ore and shipped it. But there hasn't been much doing around here in the last twenty or thirty years."

To the old man's history of Cap City I was able to add only two items of interest, both of which were culled from old Lake City newspapers.

Telephone Concert.

Interesting experiment with telephone made last Sunday evening. Mr. Bates was at the Lake City instruments and Mrs. Lee at those of her residence in Capitol City. They sang several duets and then Mr. Bates called Rose's, Silverton and Ouray stations. From Silverton came responses and from Ouray Mr. Al Long said he would join . . . all sang several popular songs and so accurately too that it seemed as if all were singing by note from one book. Then an employee of Mr. Lee's saw mill up north fork of Henson Creek, played several airs on the accordian and later Mr.——————of Silverton played accompaniments to vocal music on the violin. The listeners were delighted with the music and complimented our Silverton and Ouray friends . . . upon their skill.—*The Silver World*, Oct. 15, 1881.

Election of Town Officers.

The election was unusually exciting. . . . No blood was spilt but several jaws were dislocated. Politics had no place in the contest which was centered on the distribution of town moneys, in improvement of the principal thoroughfares, Galena and Henson Avenues, the erection of a town hall and a calaboose. . . . A great deal of

CAPITOL
CITY

SHERMAN

opposition came from the west end of town as to the location of the latter. . . . After the election . . . the citizens of Capitol assembled in the public square and cried "Vive la President Messler." Most of the citizens of Capitol are French from Cork except Jock Henderson who is a Tipperarian. The new town officers spread an elegant lunch at Lee's, fascinatingly presided over by Mrs. Lee. Treasurer Lee closed the festivities with a speech on the future of Capitol City and President Messler pronounced the benediction and set 'em up at the *Creek.—Lake City Mining Register,* April 7, 1882.

Before leaving Capitol, we explored the huge, white frame schoolhouse, with its peeling blackboards and its plaster-cluttered floor. It stood at one end of the townsite and the Lee Mansion at the other—the sole survivors of the city's pretentious structures.

Rose's Cabin

Since the road had been ploughed only as far as Capitol City I could merely point out to my companions the road up the valley which led to Rose's Cabin, five miles away. I described how rough the road was the year before, when Dick Pillmore drove me over it. At the upper end of the park it turned to the right and followed the stream up a narrow valley, but the road or trail, for it was hardly more, climbed faster than the creek and was soon high on the mountainside. In one place a huge rock slide had covered it, and for nearly a quarter of a mile we crunched over boulders, the car at a crazy angle and the tires taking cruel punishment on the jagged stones. My desire to see Rose's Cabin kept me urging Dick to drive a little farther, while I pointed out the beauties of everything but the roadbed. The cabin was a bit disappointing for it had been recently enlarged and remodeled. Only parts of the square-hewn logs were visible behind tarpaper-covered additions, and the building was locked. I learned later that some time before the Golconda Mines Consolidated had used it as their office and that quite recently it had been bought by an individual who had further "restored" it.

Rose's Cabin was one of the first buildings constructed in the Lake City mining district and until 1874 was the "only place of entertainment this side of the range until Lake City was reached." The original one-story cabin of square-hewn pine logs was built by Corydon Rose, an early pioneer in the San Juan, soon after the Ute Indians ceded a strip of land sixty miles wide and seventy-five miles long to the United States. Prospectors and miners made it their headquarters in between their explorations of the nearby peaks, and travelers over the divide anticipated its "Hotel and Bar." The cabin, which stood at an elevation of 11,300 feet, was close to the fork of the trails which led on one hand to Mineral Point and Ouray, and on the other to Animas Forks and Silverton. As soon as a wagon road was built over the summit of the Uncompahgre range it became one of the chief stations on the stagecoach trail.

There was mining in the vicinity of Rose's Cabin between 1878 and 1882 when big strikes were found on Copper hill, on American Flats, and in the Palmetto and Frank Hough lodes on Engineer mountain.

Gradually a few miners' cabins were built near the combined restaurant, store and post office, and in summer nearly fifty men lived in the immediate vicinity. Large amounts of ore were packed to this place on burros and then freighted by wagon to the distant shipping points. By 1882 the cabin, which had been enlarged and "refitted," had become the headquarters from which trips could be made to all the mines in the San Juan. For the use of its patrons a pack train of sixty animals was kept in readiness for forwarding supplies to all the mining camps of the area, and meals were served at all hours from a "table that was always supplied with the best in the markets." The bar extended the entire length of the room, and the upper floor was divided into twenty-two cubicles which served as bedrooms.

Some years ago a United States revenue stamp was found tacked on the wall of the bar room. It read:

> Received from Charles Schafer the sum of five dollars for special tax in the business of Dealer in Manufactured Tobacco to be carried on at Rose's cabin near Capitol City, State of Colorado, for the period represented by the coupon or coupons hereto attached.

> Dated at Denver, April 26, 1878.

> J. C. Wilson
> Collector, State of Colorado

Even in its remodeled state Rose's Cabin is a symbol of the enterprise and determination of the pioneers, who let neither Indians nor mountain ranges hinder their progress into uncharted mineral territory.

"If you're going to Sherman be sure to drive on beyond to White- *Sherman* cross, and if you're a good hiker take the trail to Carson too," said an old timer of whom I asked directions. So armed with maps and lunch but with absolutely no knowledge about any of the places mentioned, Dick and I drove past Lake San Cristobal and from there continued on the dirt road which follows the Lake Fork of the Gunnison river into high country. About nine miles beyond the lake we found the deserted camp "cozily nestled at the base of giant mountains that pierce cloud land." Situated originally at the junction of Cottonwood creek and the Lake Fork, it was now literally in the streambed, its rows of cabins surrounded by sand and water-worn boulders, with little tricklets of water spilling from rock to rock or seeping from clumps of swamp grass. Only a few cabins at the lower end had escaped the torrent which, following a cloudburst, recut the streambed years after the place was deserted. At the upper end of the town was the stone foundation of a big, ruined mill, some of its machinery rusted and warped and overgrown with vines.

Back in Lake City that night I talked to several men who had lived in Sherman. They told me that it was a new town in 1877, located by A. D. Freeman and others, who laid it out in blocks, with streets sixty feet wide and alleys twenty. The town contained a big building at Main and Sixth streets which was used as a storage and forwarding house, a butcher shop and slaughter house, a bakery and grocery, and a tent where "a drop of the crather could be had for the small sum of twenty-five cents." Fifty votes were cast in the 1877 election, but in spite of the rich strikes found in Cuba gulch, the camp grew slowly.

There was little development of the mines until 1880, and it was 1881 before the Sherman House was open, offering "Good Accommodations for Travellers, Liquors, Wines, St. Louis Beer and Cigars," and before a store full of general merchandise "tempted the one hundred citizens to spend their money at home."

In spite of both placer and lode mines, the latter producing gold, silver, copper and lead, the little camp was dull by September, 1881, when most of the boys went out for the winter; and "Saturday evening prayer meetings and Sunday extempore concerts at Mrs. Franklin's and Mrs. Wager's" were the only activities. The miners, however, were sure that by spring "business will revive and rush ahead like a burro with a light load and a down hill trail." And spring indeed did bring the men hurrying back to work the George Washington, the New Hope, the Mountain View, the Minnie Lee, the Clinton, the Smile of Fortune and the Monster. The principal mine, however, was the Black Wonder, and its ruined mill was probably the one that we had seen beside the stream.

There was a strong spirit of rivalry between the miners of the Sherman and Whitecross district and those of the Henson district in regard to their representation in the Exposition to be held in Denver. According to the Lake City paper of June 3, 1882:

> Every effort is being put forth to make as creditable an exhibition as our sister camps. Ergo Henson Creek had better be looking after her laurels for they are in jeopardy as we are close behind her, and it will be no fault of our camp if we fail to pass her in the race for first premium of Hinsdale County.

Even poetry from Sherman filtered into the Lake City papers: a twenty-two-verse epistle signed "Oriole" was sent to the editor of the *Silver World* in 1883, of which the first two verses were printed under the heading, "Hang Him."

> The spring, the spring, the beautiful spring,
>   It's hurrying in like everything
> Today it shines, tomorrow it snows,
>   And that's the way the wide world goes.
>
> The mountain tops are clothed in white,
>   The old prospector still gets tight,
> The burro winds around the hill
>   A-carrying ore to Crooke's big mill.

22

Although Camp Sherman remained small, some mining was done there all through the nineties; and the Black Wonder was producing as late as 1897, when a Boston company spent $200,000 in developing the property and erecting a reduction mill.

"I put in a dam up there over forty years ago for a company who was working the mines," volunteered a miner. "The dam was to be one hundred and forty-seven feet high, but by the time I'd built it sixty-nine feet the company was broke. Another outfit took over and wanted the dam raised. They had the work done, and then a cloudburst took out the dam and most of the town and left it the way it is today. The last work done at Sherman was in 1925. Even then there were a good many more cabins there than now."

The ledge road to Whitecross switchbacks up the side of the mountain above Sherman and, when high above the Lake Fork, twists up the valley toward Cinnamon Pass. It had scarcely any turnouts and was full of ruts and boulders, some so big that Dick had to lift them or roll them out of the way before we could proceed. There were rocky stretches caused by slides over which the car crawled, and the corrugations and hazards of the road were so numerous that I had no time to look over the edge into the abyss where the stream looped far below. After two or three miles of this the road and the valley met, and the next stretch took us into Whitecross over a fairly steep meadow which sloped up toward timberline and the rocky, snow-capped peaks. Once we had to ford the stream, but the water was shallow and the creekbed rocky, and once we had to open a gate to enter fenced land where sheep were grazing, their persistent bleating coming faintly down to us from the rocky slope.

Whitecross was a disappointment, for although the country was magnificent, there was no town—just a couple of cabins beside the road and scattered mine dumps with rusty shaft houses and sheds nearby. For fear we hadn't gone far enough Dick, at my urging, drove a couple of miles farther through swampy land and through clumps of evergreens where the roadbed was spongy with tree loam and pine needles. The road kept on and so did we, until near timberline on Wood mountain we came to the skeleton of the Tobasco mill. It stood on the old road to Silverton almost at Cinnamon Pass, and from that height we looked back down the long valley up which we had slowly picked our way.

By now we were quite sure that we had climbed beyond the site of the camp, for even the white quartz cross on the mountainside, from which the place was named, was below us. We drove slowly back, stopping at the scattered cabins and mine shafts and looking for the sheep herder whose tent we had seen, in hope that he could tell us something about the country; but we could not find him or his dogs. As we returned along the narrow shelf road toward Sherman, we were conscious of the bigness and loneliness of the country, in which the only sounds were those of the wind in the trees and the mournful blatting of the sheep, now out of sight around a shoulder of the mountain.

Just before we dropped down into Sherman we had one birdseye view of that camp spread out below us—its streets and cabins were ranged in orderly rows except where the force of the water had moved one or carried it downstream and deposited it askew in among the boulders.

The exact locations of Burrows Park, Whitecross, Tellurium, Argentum and Sterling are difficult to establish today, since almost all signs of the camps have disappeared. The head of the valley in which the Lake Fork of the Gunnison rises was called Burrows Park in the seventies, after Charles Burrows who prospected the territory in 1873. A small camp of the same name was established in the valley, and another camp called Whitecross was laid out a quarter of a mile above it. A third camp, Tellurium, was situated just above Whitecross, and according to one informant a camp called Sterling lay just beyond Tellurium. Another campsite, Argentum, was six miles above the mouth of Cottonwood creek, but whether up Cottonwood or the Lake Fork I have been unable to find out. In 1882 the name of the post office was changed from Burrows Park to Whitecross.

That mining machinery ever arrived at the remote locations at which mills and smelters were built seems a miracle, and had it not been for sturdy "jacks" who packed or dragged heavy parts of boilers and stamps over tortuous trails, and determined men who also packed in such portions as they could carry, mining would have been at a standstill. The following notice in a Lake City paper of 1877 described the delivery of a mill at Whitecross:

> A portion of the machinery for the Gunnison Company's works arrived the first of last week and now lies at the foot of Cottonwood Hill. The freighters have returned to Antelope Springs for the remainder which they will bring up to the same point in the park, and thence with the help of the boys in the park, who have volunteered to shovel a road through, they will get the entire machinery in, probably by the tenth.

The Burrows Park ores were largely copper pyrites and argentiferous galena, although gray copper, ruby silver, sulphurets of silver, copper and iron pyrites were also found. There was plenty of waterpower for use in the mines, and the Bonhomme, Cracker Jack, Tobasco and Champion lodes began to produce extensively.

Nine families wintered in the park in 1878 and, in spite of severe weather, a few miners and their families spent successive years in the little valley. "Burrows Park Notes" for Dec. 27, 1881, printed in the Lake City paper, says:

Christmas in the Park.

> We were all invited out . . . to the Hotel de Clawson where Mrs. Williams and Mrs. Prentice prepared a generous feast. . . . Well filled tables stood there creaking, cracking, straining, while trying to hold up the precious burden of roast turkey, chicken, fruits, sauces, jellies, pies, cakes, pudding, sweetmeats, sure enough ice cream, sweet bread, and butter, also all the young ladies in town . . .
>
> At nine o'clock we sallied out to our gloomy, silent cabins.
>
> Yours truly,
>
> Snowball and Icicle.

In 1882 Burrows Park was a live camp with "Clawson still wielding the dish rag at the most popular hotel," but the development of the region was retarded by lack of transportation facilities. Even when railroads were built into the San Juan they were inaccessible. The one at Animas Forks was only five miles away to the west, but to get there one had to cross the divide over Cinnamon Pass at more than 12,000 feet. The railroad at Lake City was reached by a road down the valley, but it was nearly twenty miles away.

In spite of heavy snows "the adventurous Tom Byron crossed the bleak range daily on snowshoes, with the mail to and from Animas Forks and Mineral Point;" and in summer "four brand new horses were ready to run a daily buckboard from Lake City to Sherman, Burrows Park, and if business justifies, to Animas Forks, carrying the mail, express packages and passengers."

Between 1890 and 1900 Whitecross had a population of 300, the men and their families living in cabins and tents. In 1898 the Premier and the

CARSON

VIEW
FROM
STABLE,
CARSON

Tobasco companies "settled down to systematic work on two of the best groups of mines in the park;" and in 1901 the Tobasco outfit built a new hundred-ton mill, and the Bonhomme and the Champion were also working. Again in 1916 the Champion was reopened after fifteen years of idleness.

As we drove back to Lake City, I told Dick about the miner at Whitecross who wanted some coffee before going to work on night shift. There were two coffee pots in his cabin, in one of which four pounds of blasting powder were stored. By mistake he put the pot containing the powder on the stove!

Carson

After many inquiries, much correspondence and conflicting information as to the condition of the trail, the distance to the camp, and how much was left of it, Jane and I were finally off to Carson. The camp is located on the summit of the Continental Divide at an elevation of 11,500 to 12,000 feet, with most of the mines above timberline. It can be reached by two trails, one of which goes up Wager gulch on the Pacific slope side, and the other of which follows East Lost Trail creek to its head on the Atlantic side. Jane and I decided to take the shorter trail up Wager gulch; so in July, 1946, we hired horses from Vickers Ranch at Lake City and anticipated a pleasant and even an exciting horseback trip. As we had eleven miles to go before turning up the narrow, overgrown trail which leads to the lonely camp, the men at the ranch loaded our saddled horses onto a truck and drove us and them to the beginning of the trail. It was ten-thirty when we reached the turn-off where the truck backed up against the bank to unload the horses. Then the men helped us mount, waved goodbye and rattled off down the road.

"You're sure we can't get lost?" I asked before they left us.

"How could you? There's only one trail," they reassured me. "You might see elk or bear up there. It's pretty high."

We listened as the drone of the truck's engine died away, and then feeling very confident and excited we turned our horses up the trail and started the climb. In less than fifty feet the trail split two ways. We had noticed a man working near the road about a quarter of a mile back, so while I waited at the fork, Jane rode down to ask him for more explicit directions. Coming back with her he pointed out the proper trail, which proved to be neither of those that we had seen, but a third one which led off into the timber straight ahead of us and which was so overgrown and poorly defined that we hadn't noticed it. He, too, assured us that we couldn't get lost and went back to his work.

The first half mile was through trees and, looking carefully for all the landmarks that we'd been told of, we crossed the pipe line and started our rocky climb beside Wager creek. About a mile farther was a bridge and, although it didn't look very secure, we led our horses carefully over the log surface, avoiding the biggest holes and leaping across the last two feet, where the logs were completely rotted away, to the bank beyond. Next the trail led along the edge of a steep slope where there was just room for the horses' hoofs, and where the angle was about sixty degrees. A little farther on we came to beaver ponds and found the trail flooded and blocked with fallen trees, some rotted and some newly cut by the industrious little animals.

(362)

Dismounting again, we worked our way through the maze of tree trunks. On the far side of the pond we picked up the trail again, only to be stopped by another tree which crossed our path at an angle and was too low to ride under and too well rooted to drag aside. While Jane, who is considerably taller than I, lifted the trunk a few inches, I led first my horse and then hers under it, the saddles almost scraping the bark. The rest of the trail through the trees was well defined and easy to ride.

Near the top of the grade the trail widened into an old corduroy road, where the horses' hoofs cracked and powdered the rotten wooden logs with each step. By now we were almost on top and, leaving the trees behind, came out on a high meadow where the grass was tall and the wild flowers grew in great clumps. Ahead were jagged peaks with patches of snow caught in deep crevasses, and mingled with the rush of the wind was the bleating of sheep which we could not see. We passed some cowboys driving horses down the trail we had just come over, and when we asked them how near we were to Carson they shrugged and said, "One mile—two miles," and rode off. After another half mile we saw two things—the buildings of Carson and a black cloud! All the way up the trail it had been sunny; now, around noontime, the usual daily shower was gathering and it looked as if it would reach Carson about the same time that we did.

There were quite a number of buildings, most of them in pretty good repair. We dismounted to let the horses graze, and just as we started to look around the rain began. Taking my pad, camera and the lunch, I hurried to the biggest house and climbing in through a window sat inside, dry and comfortable, sketching the panorama before me. In less than five minutes Jane called that my horse had broken his bridle; so, leaving everything in the building, I climbed out onto the rickety porch to hurry to her assistance. In stepping out on the porch one foot crashed through the rotten boards and the other one doubled up under me, spraining the ankle badly. In spite of the accident I hobbled over to Jane across a little stream and helped her repair the bridle with some string.

While we worked, lightning flashed and thunder crashed around us, and the rain, which was driving by us in sheets, turned to hail. Leading the horses, we took refuge in an old stable. Of course our lunch and my sketching materials were still in the big cabin, but Jane dashed through the rain and rescued them. Then, while the storm spent itself above us, we spread our lunch in the manger and ate the flabby sandwiches and the bruised fruit with relish. One storm drifted down the valley, but another one hit just when we were about to leave the stable. Looking out the window, I sketched the old false-fronted store, the building with the porch and the tall, straight pines, in the midst of which some of the cabins were built. We could see the rest of the trail, a thin line along the mountainside, climbing to the top of the divide and over it to where the rest of Carson lay.

As most mountain showers are over in a few minutes we waited hopefully, tucking our cold hands in our pockets and keeping out of the way of the puddles and trickles that were gradually wetting the floor of our shelter. We waited half an hour, and still the thunder crashed and the lightning played around the trees. I recalled a chance remark made by one of the Vickers boys that "Carson was on an iron dyke" and that "people got killed by lightning up there!" It was now nearly two o'clock; we were fifteen miles from the ranch, and with my sprained ankle I could not trot nimbly down any road. Perhaps we had better start back; for the steady rain gave no indication of stopping, and I did not think it sensible to try to guide my horse, with his improvised bridle, any farther than necessary. Someday I'd return to Carson and see what was on the other side of the mountain.

The horses were not anxious to leave, but we ran them out of the stable and started down the wet trail. For nearly a mile we rode through the timber, wet pine needles brushing our faces and the rain drenching our wool shirts—we had forgotten to bring our slickers along! All the way down I was thinking of the knife-edge trail along the steep slope, and especially of the bridge with the rotten logs which by now would be mushy and water-soaked. Partway back the rain stopped and the trail dried out unbelievably fast. We crept along the steep ledge and came to the bridge.

Since the first few logs on this end were missing, both the horses and ourselves were forced to jump over the hole, and with each jump the bridge shuddered. The cowboys whom we had seen had driven their horses over it since we had gone up, and more logs were cracked or broken than before. Jane led her big horse over the better side, his weight splintering and cracking the logs with each step. That left me no choice—I had to take the other side, even though it had more holes in it through which I could see the raging creek twenty feet below.

I jumped onto the bridge, my horse following, and I picked the best spots left to walk on. Some of the logs gave with my weight and behind me I heard the crunching, cracking noise of other logs, which were splitting under the horse's hoofs. About halfway across there was a sudden loud crack and, glancing over my shoulder, I saw my mount's forefoot disappear through the bridge to the hock. Terrified, I tugged at the reins and ran the rest of the way, forgetting my ankle and reasoning that the horse was equally anxious to get off the rotten structure. Somehow we made it amidst an accompaniment of cracking timbers and snapping logs and, once on the bank again, we stood weak-kneed, trembling and thankful. The bridge was behind us and no one else would be able to use it again. Completely shaken but relieved, we mounted for the last time and rode the remaining mile beside the stream to the main road over ground so steep and rough that the horses had difficulty finding a place to set their feet among the big boulders.

The last eleven miles were taken slowly, for I found it impossible to bear any weight on my ankle and trotting was out of the question. Back at the ranch I slid, rather than dismounted from my horse, while Jane told the boys of our adventures.

"We wondered about that bridge," said one of them, "and if you hadn't come in soon we were starting up to look for you!"

Next morning Jane and I went home; but I was disappointed that Carson had eluded me. I wanted to see the rest of it, and especially the mines that were across the ridge on the far side of the divide. I'd heard that the St.

Jacob's was the big mine of the camp and that its buildings were still standing, and until I saw them I wouldn't be content. During the next two years I learned what I could about the remote sky-line camp.

Christopher J. Carson discovered traces of mineral in the vicinity several years before he staked the Bonanza King and several other claims on the rugged mountain top. The assays from the ore ran high in gold and silver, and he decided to stay near his claims and bring friends in to develop what he believed would be the biggest camp in the San Juan. The Carson district was organized in 1881 at the head of Wager gulch on the north and at the head of Lost Trail creek on the south, and in 1882 a camp, which was named for him, sprang up on both sides of the divide. Although some of the camp was situated at a 12,000-foot elevation and was completely above timberline, the lower parts of it were set in groves of tall white pines.

Before long more than a hundred prospectors were working over one hundred and fifty claims, "all staked on float," for mineral was found scattered over the entire area. During the eighties and early nineties the camp was active and there was much talk of the Chandler, the Legal Tender, the Kit Carson, the George III, Dunderberg, Cresco, Iron Mask, the Maid of Carson, St. John's and St. Jacob's mines. Some prospectors dug themselves in and spent the winter on the snowy mountaintop, but few were rugged enough to attempt it.

Because of its remoteness, the camp needed a road to facilitate the shipment of ore. During 1883 one was started from the Lake City side but it went so slowly that the miners asked:

> What has become of Overseer Wager? His road is growing so slow that the present generation will never have the pleasure of seeing it.

To the other side of the divide, however, they looked with a more hopeful spirit:

> Some parties with ample means are preparing to build a road up Lost Trail Creek to our camp and as they own some of the best claims in the camp, we think we are sure of a road.

The road was built, and by 1887 almost all supplies and most of the ore were shipped over it. Even so, a portion of it was bad and the miners still complained. They even threw out a hint that "a railroad up the Rio Grande would tap this camp," not realizing that in a few years Creede's sensational boom would bring trains up the valley to within fifty miles of Carson.

Expressing the sentiments of all prospectors in inaccessible camps is this item from the Lake City paper of Aug. 10, 1883:

> The trail from Carson is miserable . . . almost impassable on account of rain, for a loaded animal. Imagine a miner leaving his cabin, tent or perhaps the shady side of a tree, to hunt through brush for his faithful animal, the burro. . . . He finds him. Then he starts for Lake (City) to get supplies for him and his partner. He returns in two days tired out, to resume work, and starts with renewed vigor. About the third day he fears that the walls may cave in unless timbered. Then the burro must be hunted for and when found, a couple of timbers attached to him, and he started toward

the claim without wagon, road or trail, up the side of the mountain, winding his way through brush and rocks, and perhaps after you have taken off the timbers a time or two from rolling down the hill, you get there about exhausted. This is pleasant especially for the burro; these are the advantages a miner has in a new camp, but then capitalists always come along, just in time to reap the reward of a few years hard toil of nearly all prospectors in new mining camps.

By contrast, the *Creede Candle* printed the following notice, written in April, 1892, which shows the undying optimism of the miner:

Carson is a wonderful section. It asks no aid of capital. It is developing itself and says to the world—"I am the Eldorado of the Prospectors. I want no aid. The poor and rich fare alike with me. My mines will pay their way and do their own development." It is one of the best high camps in the world. It is 12,000 feet high, yet there is no danger whatever of snowslides, and the mines can work and ship their ore the year round. It has one mine that with only an average of forty men working, will produce the first year of its steady operation a net revenue of $250,000 and others are ready to begin a like record.

In the early nineties a traveler reported the whole country covered with prospectors and spoke of Carson as a first-class camp with four good, paying mines, the St. Jacob's producing over $300,000 in gold and silver and the Thor and Lost Trail working steadily. A new strike in the Maid of Carson in 1892 gave renewed interest to the camp, for the mine not only made one of the best showings that year but "will be a hummer next season."

After the silver crash in 1893 the camp was quiet until 1896, when more gold properties were discovered, and the Carson correspondent wrote to the *Gunnison Times*:

Every day is increasing the activity in the camp, houses are going up, new claims are opening, and more stock is being added to the already large pack trains. . . . The Thor people are putting up some fine buildings and thirty-eight jacks are packing ore from the Big Indian. . . . No doubt now exists as to the permanency of the veins or the gold and copper values.

By 1898 the St. Jacob's, the best gold property there, was still producing high-grade ore and working three shafts—a single year's record was $190,000. A new boardinghouse was added at the mine, a smelter was erected, and a "strong force of men" worked the various levels. Between 1900 and 1902 much of the mining was on the Lake City side of the range, and four to five hundred people lived in the camp. Yet by the end of 1902, according to the *Gunnison Times*, "Carson with its many promising properties is practically abandoned."

Bursting with all this information, I was more than anxious to return there but I saw no way to make the trip. Then in the spring of 1948 I gave a talk in Del Norte on Ghost Mining Towns, under the auspices of the University of Colorado, and after the lecture two people in the audience told me of having visited Carson from the "other side" and offered to take me there later in the summer.

So, hardly believing my good fortune, one cloudy morning in August I was one of a party of six who left the campsite below Beartown, which I

MINES ON THE DIVIDE, CARSON   ↓ SHAFT HOUSE, CARSON

described in the preceding chapter, and started on horseback over the sky-line trail to Carson. My two Del Norte friends, Lucy Ann and Alvin Colville were with me, and our guide was Carol Ann Wetherill, just seventeen and acquainted with every inch of the mountains. It was ten miles to the mining camp from the Forks, and at first we followed Pole creek, climbing higher and higher up the valley and crossing high moraines, edged with timber. Pole mountain with its ragged crags was on our right and other rocky peaks were ahead. The trail was just wide enough for a horse to travel, and whenever it crossed a meadow it was lost in the lush grass. On the far side it would appear again, and we would continue to pick our way up over the rocks and across dry gullies and "draws." After a couple of more miles the trail was marked only by stakes set at intervals, one on the right and the next one on the left, always just within sight of the last one. These, I was told, were government markers indicating a stock or sheep drive, and for nearly all the rest of our trip we guided by these posts.

Crossing the creek, we started up a steep slope where a misstep would have sent us tumbling a hundred or more feet down to the streambed. Working up this high valley above timberline, we rode for three or four miles over marshy grass or tundra, while gaunt peaks with snow patches on their sides towered above us. The farther we rode, the more overcast the sky became. Crossing the creek once more, we headed straight up a mountainside toward a pass between two peaks. High on this slope was a sheep herder's tent, and riding up to it we talked to the Mexican herders who were camped there with their dogs and mules while their sheep grazed the mountains above. At the top of the pass we rode beside a snowbank, one of the patches which never completely melts away, and once over the ridge, we looked down into a long, deep valley at the far end of which were yellow mine dumps among tall trees.

The rest of the trip was the most tedious and terrifying, for, avoiding the trail down to the floor of the valley, we kept high on the mountain's side, zigzagging up and down shale and rock slides, crossing gullies where the horses poised on the brink before they jumped over, and following a narrow trail for over a mile on the side of a very steep ridge. By now it was almost noon, and the clouds were boiling up around us. While we were still some distance from the mines, it began to rain and then to sleet, yet we plodded on, getting colder and wetter with every step. The trail finally wound up to the top of a little rise from which we could see the buildings in Carson, most of them half a mile away. There, near the top of the divide, was a large group of buildings, the St. Jacob's mine, I presume, and dotted over the entire surface of the mountain were shaft houses and dwellings. Alvin and Carol, who had been there before, pointed out the old hotel, the post office and certain mines, while rain ran in streams off our hat brims and down our horses' legs.

The storm was getting heavier, so we headed down hill toward a group of mine buildings hoping to find shelter for the horses and ourselves. The only building suitable for a barn had a broken plank floor, so the horses crowded close to its outer walls and turned their rumps to the storm. We climbed into the broken building only to fiind that its roof was a sieve and that the only dry floor space was a strip five feet wide along one wall. Sitting or standing in this partially dry area we ate our lunch. while we watched the ground whiten with hail and the lightning fork into the valley. While we ate, Carol pointed to a crumbling shafthouse and said: "There's a story about that mine. The men working it had packed seven sacks of silver ready to ship to the smelter but, at the end of their shift, they were too tired to carry them to the surface. Stacking them at the foot of the shaft, they left the mine, agreeing to get them out the following morning. During the night the pump in the mine broke down, and water flooded the lower parts of the workings and the bottom of the shaft where the sacks lay. There was no way to reach the pump and repair it, so the mine had to be abandoned with the seven sacks of high-grade still at the bottom."

We waited fifteen minutes, half an hour; but the rain continued. Although the center of the storm moved on, the sleet beat down. We waited another fifteen minutes, but as a new storm seemed to be gathering above us, in desperation I went out in it and made two or three sketches of what few buildings I could see across the rain-swept tundra. By now it was settling down to a steady drizzle; so, with a last look at the still elusive St. Jacob's property, we mounted our very wet horses and wetter saddles and started slowly down the mountain. This time there was no trail, and the grade was so steep that even the horses hesitated as to where to put their feet on the slippery bunch grass. I fully expected to turn somersaults with my horse before reaching the bottom, but we made it.

The mountain above the high pass over which we had ridden that morning was now white with snow, and it was still storming up at Carson when I looked back from the foot of the hill. By now we were out of the worst of the rain, the sky was blue ahead and East Lost Trail was under our horses' feet. Consequently we trotted nearly all the way back to the ranch, and except for the first half-mile out of Carson we were in sunshine. I talked to several people at the ranch who had been to Carson, and only one of them had found good weather there; even our guide admitted that eleven out of her twelve trips there had been similar to ours. If you ever go to Carson and get to the St. Jacob's mine, let me know what it is like; for I'm not going back.

CHAPTER XV

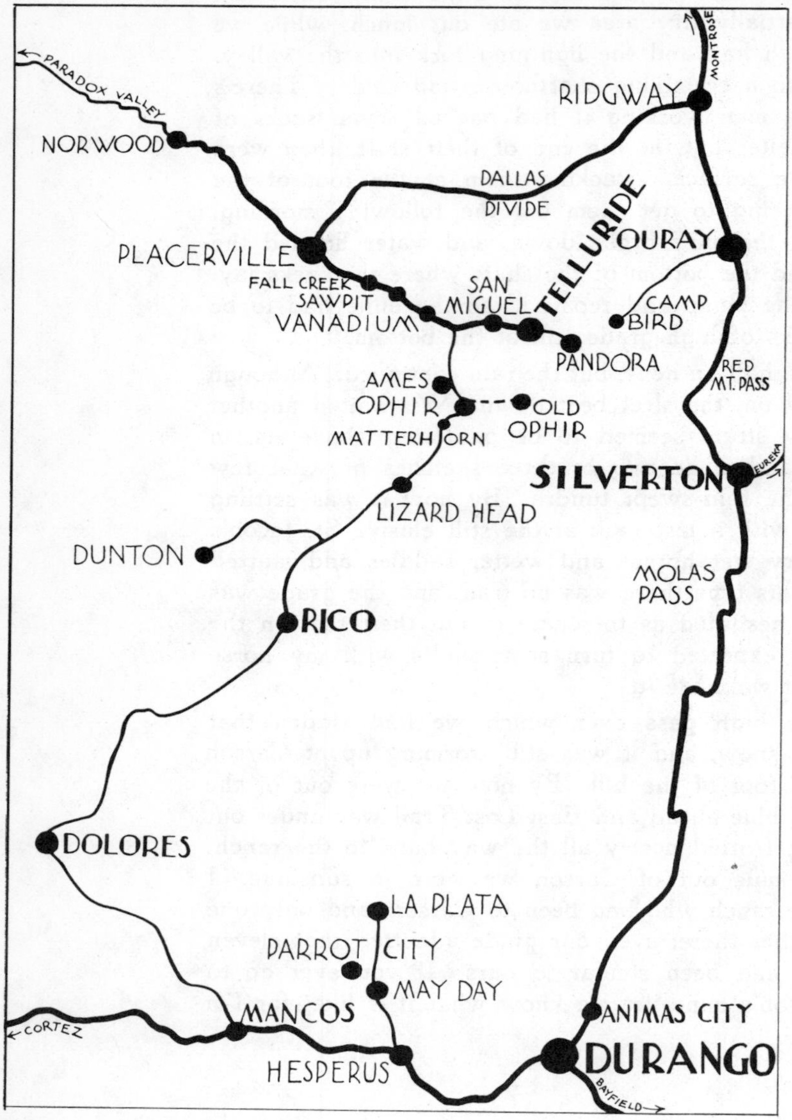

Ouray, Telluride and the Uncompahgres

MOUNTAINS are exciting and none more so than the jagged Uncompahgres whose white crests form a barrier between Ouray and the rest of the San Juan country. I had my first glimpse of them while driving toward Montrose. There on the horizon, miles away was a ragged wall of mountains with one great peak, Mt. Sneffels, towering above the others. Something inside me rose up at that sight, for these were the kind of mountains I'd always yearned to see—not the rounded, green slopes of the Catskills and the Great Smokies, but fierce, stark, uncompromising peaks that made one feel like an unimportant speck of humanity, even while they fired one to get amongst them and batter a way through them. Each mile travelled changed their hazy blueness to a sharper silhouette, until, as I drove down the red-cliffed canyon beside the Uncompahgre river, I was caught between them.

Ouray Ouray is caught, too, at the bottom of a bowl or ampitheatre of vertical cliffs which rim the city with strata of many-colored rocks, accented with patches of aspen clinging in the crevices. At the far end of the city, through a gap in the mountains cut deep by the river, curves a highway which seems to end against the rocky face of Mt. Abrams miles away. Ouray is a delightful place, with wide, shaded streets, comfortable homes and a general air of well-being. During the summer months many tourists select it as a center from which to make automobile or pack trips into the high country—over Red Mountain Pass or up the Horse Thief trail to Mineral Point.

In July, 1875, A. W. Begole and Jack Eckles crossed the Divide over Stony Pass and worked their way over the mountain ranges until they reached this horseshoe of mountains with its little park in the bottom. They did not stay, but went out over the mountains for more supplies. While they were gone A. J. Staley and Logan Whitlock from Mineral Point, who were on a hunting and fishing expedition along the Uncompahgre, discovered the Trout and Fisherman lodes at the mouth of Canyon creek. This was the first discovery in the district, and ore from the two mines was the first to be shipped out.

When Begole and Eckles returned in August with a load of provisions they prospected near the radium hot springs (where the swimming pool is) in Ahwiler's Park, locating the Cedar and Clipper lodes, whose veins run through the town. Their next find was the Mineral Farm, a group of extremely rich parallel veins which covers forty acres.

These discoveries brought a stampede of fortune hunters to the mountains, including Capt. Cline and Judge Long, who took up a townsite and drove stakes in the dense timber to indicate the location of streets and alleys. A few cabins were thrown together, and in October the Judge, the Captain and the Cutler brothers left with a team for Del Norte to lay in winter supplies. They had trouble with the Utes and were forbidden to cross Los Pinos Agency; but they did so, regardless of the orders of the agent or the threats of the Utes, and returned by December. Christmas, 1875, was celebrated by the boys at Long and Cutler's cabin on the hill. They had an excellent dinner, but as there was no liquor in camp they drank vinegar and "then and there christened the place Vinegar Hill."

At first the camp was called Uncompahgre City, but the name was changed to Ouray in honor of the chief of the Western Utes, who was the friend of all white settlers. A few years later he came to the camp while the White River Utes were on the warpath. The town was terrified when he appeared with his wife Chipeta and announced that he wished to speak to the citizens. The gist of his speech was that he was friendly to the whites and that if he had their cooperation he could guarantee their safety from the warring Utes. He spoke with such dignity and authority that the people believed him and, calling in their "scouts," relaxed.

By the spring of 1876 throngs of miners poured in from all the surrounding camps in the San Juan, and with their arrival Ouray began to grow. The first frame building belonged to W. J. Benton, and the nails used in its construction cost twenty-five cents a pound. For awhile it was the Star saloon, but when Ouray was made the county seat, it became the courthouse, with the county offices on the second floor and the city hall on the first. In this building the miners met to formulate "gulch laws" for the district.

For the Fourth of July, 1877, a "twenty-foot flag was made and formally presented to the town." While it fluttered from the pole near the courthouse, there were addresses and toasts—to the San Juan pioneers, to the ladies of the San Juan, to the burro and to the tenderfoot.

The forerunner of the Dixon House, one of the better hotels, was a cabin where Mrs. Dixon served meals and "the guests furnished their own bedding or curled up under the table." In July, 1879, Lt. Governor Tabor came unannounced to Ouray and stayed at the Dixon House. "During the evening large numbers of citizens paid their respects to the Governor" in the parlor of the hotel, and the Ouray band serenaded him.

Ouray is still surrounded by paying mines such as the American Nettie (which by 1900 had produced $1,500,000), the Chief Ouray Consolidated, the Wedge, the Khedive, and the Banner American, whose mill at the foot of Bachelor mountain handles ore from them all. Begole's Mineral Farm, which he sold in 1878 for $75,000, once produced quantities of ore both from the surface and from shallow shafts, and the Bachelor, whose vein was discovered in 1894, was said for a time to produce $30,000 a month. Its owners were three partners, one of whom was a mail carrier to the mining camps, another a camp cook, and the third a prospector. Every cent they made they put back into their mine, believing that deep inside was a vein worth opening. Seven hundred feet in they cut a "feeder," which led to the vein from which they realized a fortune. Until 1893 most of the mines were worked for silver, but after its decline in market value, gold was mined until two-thirds of the camp's output was in yellow metal.

During the first years the camp was retarded in its development by its isolation. As early as 1881 Crofutt wrote in his *Gripsack Guide:*

> If the miners of Ouray pray at all it is for the coming of the "Iron Horse." They consider the completion of a railway to the city the one thing of paramount importance.

But it was not until December, 1887, that a branch of the Denver and Rio Grande reached Ouray from Montrose, and it was three years more before the Rio Grande Southern was extended to the camp from Ridgway.

Ouray had three newspapers, two of which, the *San Juan Sentinel* and the *Ouray Times,* later called the *Plaindealer,* were established in 1877. But it was the *Solid Muldoon,* which appeared Sept. 5, 1879, that startled not only the community but all of Colorado by the "peculiar style and quality of its paragraphs" and by the "rich, racy and not infrequently scalding" character of its remarks.

David Frakes Day, its editor, came to Ouray in 1878 and for thirteen years printed the robust paper, which before long was being quoted all over the nation, "by word of mouth" when its remarks were too strong for the censor. Day never explained why he called it the *Muldoon,* although he twitted a rival editor who inquired about it by explaining that "Muldoon" is Zulu for "virgin." It is pretty obvious that the name came from the phrase in a popular song sung by Ed Harrigan in New York, one stanza of which ran:

For opposition or politician   23
Take my word, I don't give a d-n
As I walk the street each friend I meet
Says, "There goes Muldoon—he's a solid Man!"

(372)

In spite of his devastating practical jokes and his lusty vocabulary, Day fought fraud and dishonesty and made shrewd judgments concerning people and business transactions. At one time he had forty-two libel suits pending, but no one ever collected from him.

Day never cared for James Belford, Western Colorado's first congressman, and after listening to the congressman speak for an hour, he lay down on the grass at the edge of the crowd, waiting for the oration to be over. Belford saw Day's action and said he thought he had better stop as his audience was getting tired. "Don't mind me, Jim," called Day, "I can lie down here as long as you can lie up there."

Typical samplings from his paper include the following:

> A tenderfoot over in the Animas Valley ascended the Golden Clothes Pole last week; the ascension being caused by getting outside the wrong brand of mushrooms.

> Jim Vance reports that he had an engagement with a Ute at the mouth of Alder Creek. While the engagement is not discredited, the sex of the aforesaid Ute is seriously in doubt—pass the butter.

> One or two weddings are on . . . for next week. This weather kind of suggests two in a bed and spoon fashion.

Day, who was married and had a family, was not profane in his home, and those who knew him best were aware of his kindness to those whom he liked. After he brought his family to Ouray he published the following:

> There will be a falling-off in picnics and such. Reform is inevitable.

In 1892 he went to Durango, where he continued to publish his bombshell under the name of the *Durango Democrat* until 1914. It's too bad he couldn't write his own obituary!

Even the silver crash of 1893 did not daunt Ouray, for one year later she confidently announced:

> Mining, her chief industry, is yet in its infancy. . . . No greater diversity of natural resources did the Almighty ever plan on an equal area. . . . Perennial streams, as pure as crystal, come dancing down from the eternal snowbanks, and water and fertilize all the central valleys. . . . Men partake of the nature of the section of country they inhabit and if here they become as strong mentally and physically, as this region is rugged and grand, they will not be long dominated by the effete money kings and their political hirelings of the East.

> Ouray is peerless. She will be famous as a mountain resort when many of the now celebrated watering places are abandoned and forgotten. The flora of her mountain slopes is of great beauty and variety. Flowers adorn the mountains and make redolent the atmosphere. The helianthus with its golden face turned to the sun, and the lily with its spotted petals tinged with amber and gold, are seen on the grassy slopes and by the bounding waters. Daisies, buttercups, the meek-eyed violet, beautiful columbines, the verbena and other delicate blossoms, abound above timber line and nestle in the very borders of the eternal snow-drifts. Fruits and flowers, and grains and grasses bedeck the valleys of the mountain slopes, while the more lofty culminations wear their snowy caps in the very presence of the regal sun. Beauty and grandeur, and glory intermingle, and man stands appalled.—C. L. Hall, *Mineral Resources of Ouray County,* 1894.

Just before leaving Ouray on my first visit in 1938, I blinked. Could that be an elk slowly walking toward a back yard, making for some tender lettuce? It was; yet no one seemed surprised or excited to find the animal grazing inside the city limits. I learned that elk were frequent visitors and were even encouraged to wander up and down the streets as public pets. Years ago, bales of hay were placed regularly near the railroad station during the winter as feed for the bighorn sheep which came down from the high slope of the mountains.

A few miles from Ouray is the famous Camp Bird mine, and on my first trip I went up to see what was said to be the richest mine in Colorado.

The Camp Bird   The road to the Camp Bird leaves the main highway abruptly and starts straight up the mountain at an impossible angle. The map shows five miles to the mine, but what a five miles it is! Once past the top of the first steep hill, the road follows Canyon creek, passing some mines and then crossing the boiling stream below. Now the real climb begins up a road which looks only wide enough for one car until an ore truck comes grinding down the grade and somehow you squeeze against the inner wall until it grazes by. The canyon narrows and so does the road, which from now on is a rock shelf cut from a vertical cliff hundreds of feet high. There is no guard rail and no shoulder, just space as you look over the edge. The mountains close in until there seems no escape from this valley, and just when the grandeur of the scenery and the tension of driving become almost unbearable the road comes to an abrupt end in a colony of red-roofed buildings—the Camp Bird mine.

The story of the discovery of the mine is as strange as the gaunt but beautiful mountains which surround it. Bill Weston was in England in 1875 when he received a letter telling him of some rich ore that had been found on Mt. Sneffels and advising him to study assaying at the Royal School of Mines in London. After completing the course, he returned to the United States and hurried to the Uncompahgre country, where he met George Barber, an Englishman. The two men formed a partnership and began to prospect the steep slopes of Imogene basin, staking out seven claims, two of which were the Gertrude and the Una. The ore they found was not rich enough to warrant shipping to a smelter but it was promising enough to make them do their annual assessment quota on their claims. By 1880 they tired of climbing up the sheer face of the mountain to their workings and turned them over to H. W. Reed and his brother, with the understanding that they were to drive a cross-cut tunnel to intersect the Gertrude and Una vein one hundred and fifty feet below the outcropping. The tunnel was bored, but the vein was cut at a point where it pinched out, and the original owners gladly sold their property in 1881 for $50,000. Next a contractor agreed to tunnel fifty feet further into the Gertrude vein, but in the "late autumn of 1881, when slides of porphyry rock and snow began to run," he became terrified and quit, without even bringing any samples of ore away with him.

In 1895 Thomas Walsh, who was running a pyritic smelter in Silverton, needed some siliceous ores that could be used for flux and began to examine

CAMP BIRD MINE NEAR OURAY

dumps and old workings which might provide them. An old prospector, Andy Richardson, who knew the country well, offered to hunt suitable ore for him and ran across the Gertrude mine. Digging further into the old tunnel, he sacked samples of the ore and took them to Walsh to be assayed. Some of the ore was quartz-gold in telluride form which ran as high as $3000 a ton. As soon as Walsh saw the ore he bought the Gertrude and all the old claims in the vicinity for $20,000 and he let Richardson stake out a claim nearby. Andy called his claim the Camp Bird, the miner's name for the Canada Jay or "Whiskey Jack." Walsh also gave the name Camp Bird to his consolidated property, which by 1900 included one hundred and three mining claims and covered over nine hundred acres.

When the mine was less than four years old over $500,000 had been spent on surface improvements. The boardinghouse which accommodated four hundred men was:

> equipped with electric light, steam heat, hot and cold water, porcelain bath tubs, sewer connections, fire apparatus, reading room in which current literature, magazines, newspapers of the day and a library of standard works was provided.

In the lavatories the basins were marble-topped.

During the winter the mine buildings were covered with at least six feet of snow and the electric lights had to be left on all the time. Finally the boardinghouses at No. 1 and No. 2 tunnels were abandoned. One was destroyed by a snowslide, but the second although "in the path of the annual slide" was not dislodged. It was built into the side of the mountain in such a way that its roof conformed with the slope of the hill and

> offered no obstacle . . . except the smokestack, of which a supply were kept on hand. . . . At times the roof sustains the weight of ten to eighteen feet of well-packed snow. Entrance from the surface in the winter is gained by going down an opening in the snow like a ground-hog. The track from the mouth of the tunnel to the waste dump is covered by a shed. Every winter, for from two to four months, the only air which penetrates the building finds its way through this tunnel.—*Denver Post*, Feb. 7, 1904.

The employees at the mine were visited one June day by a number of ladies from Ouray, who rode up on horseback to visit. After inspecting the mine, they were taken to the dining room of the boardinghouse and served a "sumptuous repast," consisting of

> oyster soup, sliced cucumbers, young onions, lettuce salad, roast beef with brown gravy, boiled ham, fried chicken, potatoes, new peas, lemon and apple pie, snow-pudding, coffee and milk, fruit cake and cheese.

Visitors must have been frequent for:

> The mammoth boarding house is a veritable hotel, furnishing from fifteen to fifty transient people daily with free meals. It is "open house" for the native and stranger alike. All complacently walk in and partake of the hospitality of the Camp Bird Hotel, eleven thousand feet above sea level, as if paying $3 rates. All other mine boarding houses charge from twenty-five to thirty-five cents a meal.

(376)

In 1899 two masked men held up the afternoon stage between the mine and Ouray. The one passenger, the driver and the guard were ordered off into the road, while one of the robbers went through the coach looking for the gold shipments from the Camp Bird, which amounted to $12,000. Not finding the gold, the men took the guard's horse and then "ordered the driver to proceed." The coach dashed down the canyon to Ouray where a posse was quickly organized. That evening the posse caught up with the bandits and "exchanged shots with them" in the Yankee Boy basin, but the men got away and "headed toward Utah."

In 1902 Walsh, who was by now a multimillionaire and whose wife owned the fabulous Hope diamond, sold the mine, one of the largest gold mines in the world, to an English company which operated it until 1911. During those years it produced another $18,000,000. Of recent years the mine has been worked to some extent but never on the grand scale that Walsh established.

On my first visit to the mine I sketched the complex group of mills, sheds and tunnels and I noticed the unusual and picturesque architecture of the office and of the manager's home. These buildings had cupolas and turrets and steep-pitched red roofs, quite unlike any mine buildings I ever saw. Several years later I visited the Camp Bird again, and as soon as I started to sketch, a woman came out of the big house and called to me.

"I remember you. You've been here before. Would you like to see the inside of the house?"

Almost before she stopped speaking, I was on the front porch, eager to see if the inside measured up to the outside magnificence. It did—the woodwork was handsome, and although many of the original furnishings were gone there was a feeling of comfort and even of elegance about the rooms. As I was thanking the lady for the tour of inspection she beckoned to me, and throwing open a door to an outside pantry, pointed to the shelves on which stood seven complete china bowl-and-pitcher sets such as used to adorn washstands. These were part of the original trappings of the house, and never have I seen more handsome soap dishes and slop jars. While saying goodbye I noticed a road high up on the mountainside and I asked where it went.

"That's the road to Sneffels, where the Revenue-Tunnel is working," said the lady.

"Do you suppose I could drive up there?" I asked, eyeing the narrow ledge.

"Lots of cars make it every day," she replied. "It's only two miles."

With some misgivings I told Dan, who was chauffeur on this particular trip, to try it, and in less than five minutes we were crawling along the ledge, looking down on the intricate jumble of buildings that make up the Camp Bird property. Far above us and close to the jagged peaks was the mine, and between it and the mill a thin trail was just visible.

The road to Sneffels never stopped climbing, and had we met anyone, *Sneffels* one car would have had to back an unpleasantly long distance. After the first mile the road left the shelf and continued to rise toward the head of the high valley. We passed a couple of mines, and a huge deserted mill with a three-story boardinghouse. Occasionally there was a cabin, or the ruin of one, and when the road became too rough to drive, we hiked another half mile up its washed surface to an old shaft house, behind which the tops of the ragged serrated peaks stood like giant knife-blades. There was no town of Sneffels that we could find, so disappointedly, we crept down the slice of mountain which was called a road and returned to Ouray.

In 1945 I went again. This time I knew about the great Virginius mine and about the Revenue-Tunnel which penetrated Mt. Sneffels. Remembering the narrow road, I chose seven o'clock on Sunday morning as the best time to go there, feeling sure that no ore trucks would be on the way down and that no one else would be up at that hour.

Jane was my chauffeur, and just as the sun was creeping down from the top of the peaks into the deep canyon we started on our adventure. The air was cold and crisp and the weather perfect. Just as we reached the narrowest part of the shelf road we met a car, filled no doubt with good churchgoers hurrying to Mass, and after that we tooted before reaching every curve or blind corner. I had almost forgotten how steep the road was, until we reached the sharp corner hundreds of feet above the Camp Bird mine and, once around it, saw ahead another equally narrow, steep shelf leading up to the Revenue-Tunnel property.

On this trip I realized that the few houses I had seen before were the remains of Sneffels; but because the scenery was so exciting we drove as far as the Ruby Trust mine, and I hiked up the road again as far as the Governor to look at the knife-blade palisades behind it. Some men were working in muck and water at the entrance of the Ruby Trust, and from them I discovered that the empty mill and huge boardinghouse we had passed were those of the Atlas mine. On the way down I sketched everything in sight, for I vowed never to travel that road again and I wanted to miss nothing.

Prior to the founding of Ouray, a group of prospectors led by Quinn and Richardson established a settlement in the Sneffels district and opened a trail to the valley below, where Ouray now is. They located some mines which they worked all winter, "not knowing that the town of Ouray had been founded nor that there were any persons save Indians between them and Utah." Shortly afterwards, George Wright came over from Silverton on snowshoes and staked off a claim, which he called the Wheel of Fortune and which proved to be a very good property.

By 1877 the district was "beginning to assume a lively aspect. Shots can be heard at short intervals during the day and night and prospectors are beginning to come in." The Yankee Boy and the Virginius were discovered that same year, and as the district opened up, the Revenue, Ruby Trust, Atlas, Hidden Treasure, Humboldt, Governor and Senator mines were located and developed. Some of the ore assayed $40,000 to the ton.

Fifteen men worked all winter at the Virginius in 1877. They lived in cabins which became so buried in snow that the miners had to dig their way to daylight nearly every morning. The mine started as a silver property,

GOVERNOR MINE. SNEFFELS

but as it was developed its gold values were found to increase with depth, until "gold paid all the expenses of production and treatment, while silver is pure profit."

In 1884 the Thatcher Brothers, of the Mining and Milling Bank of Ouray, financed the construction of the Revenue-Tunnel, spending $600,000 on the venture before it was completed. The tunnel started at Canyon creek and was driven in to cut the Virginius vein. Since the tunnel tapped the vein 2900 feet below the mouth of the original shaft it "did away with pumping costs and simplified the problem of ventilation." The tunnel ran two miles into Mt. Sneffels, opening up ore enough to keep the mills running night and day for thirty or forty years. "No man alive today will see the supply exhausted," bragged the miners in 1897.

"The Revenue-Virginius is the great mine of the country, employing six hundred men," wrote a reporter in 1898. "A hamlet of buildings has grown up around the great tunnel's mouth" to which comes occasionally "a meek and lowly follower of Jesus . . . to talk to the boys about the great beyond."

According to a newspaper account of 1899:

Fully a mile of freight is handled daily both ways between Ouray and Sneffels . . . by hundreds of stalwart horses and mules, from six to twenty in a team.

Besides these, several hundred burros are employed as pack animals every day and the Ouray Sneffels road is a continual blockade from 7 A. M. until night. . . . Log teams start out and make double trips into the timber every day for the five months of the summer season and thousands of huge logs are hauled to the mine every fall where a complete sawmill and lumber dressing plant turns out the necessary material for underground workings and surface buildings. Two stages make daily trips, carrying passengers, mail and express and Brown's Dairy wagon delivers 150 gallons of milk and cream to the mine and mill boarding houses daily. There is also tourist travel . . . hundreds of visitors riding, driving and walking up the mountain road to view the scenery.

When we came to the entrance of the Revenue-Tunnel on the way down, I stopped to make a sketch or two. On my first trip to Sneffels there had been men and mules standing around the premises, but on this quiet Sunday morning the only sign of life among the mass of buildings was a line full of flapping clothes. It was a little hard to picture the Revenue-Virginius as such a steady producer that its gross output between 1881 and 1919 reached $27,000,000. In 1919 the Tomboy Gold Mines Co. of Telluride bought sixty claims from the Revenue-Tunnel Mine Co., twenty-one of which were located on the Ouray side of the range.

On the way back I tried to tell Jane about a newspaper item printed in 1881 which said:

For some time there has been a scheme afoot among the miners of this section in consideration of many acts of kindness shown them by Mrs. A. W. Richardson of this place . . . to show their appreciation of the same by making her a handsome useful and costly Christmas present.

A subscription was started and the miners responded in a very liberal manner. . . . An elegant Dolman was thought an appropriate gift and was purchased in Denver.

It was

the handsomest thing ever seen in this county, made of heavy black satin . . . the body lined with Siberian squirrel and the sleeves with quilted silk of rich crimson color.

It is trimmed with white feathers so arranged as to be smooth and compact. It is a perfect fit . . . with beautiful and costly ornaments which set it off in the most gorgeous style.—*Ouray Times*, Jan. 2, 1881.

After hearing that the Tomboy Company of Telluride was working lodes on the Ouray side of Mt. Sneffels, I looked at a map and found that by airline, Telluride was about four miles from where we had stood that morning.

"Let's go to Telluride," said Jane. "How far is it?"

"By road it's almost fifty miles, but it's grand scenery all the way."

Leaving Ouray, we drove to Ridgway, where a road branches off to the west. We drove through the quiet little town and commenced to climb the Dallas divide.

"There was a little flurry of mining around here in the spring of 1887," I told Jane. "Gold City was laid out on Unaweep creek, but the bars petered out and by August all the miners left. A year later the site of Gold City became Dallas, named for George N. Dallas, Vice President under James K. Polk. In 1890 Otto Mears and Fred Walsen bought a townsite two and a half miles from Dallas, and made it a junction point for the Denver and Rio Grande and for the new railroad which they proposed to build to Durango. Although the town was to have been called Magentie, it soon became known as Ridgway, and from the first it became a railway center in the midst of ranch country. After the new road, the Denver and Rio Grande Southern, was completed and built its machine shops there, Dallas dwindled away until it became only a flag stop on the D. & R. G." *Dallas and Ridgway*

The automobile road to the top of the divide was through fertile ranch country, so rolling and green that it did not prepare me for the view from the top. Only a few miles away stretched the solid barrier of the Uncompahgre range, the same wall of rock which had so stirred me when I first drove to Ouray, with Mt. Sneffels the highest, most wicked looking of all the rocky summits. The effect was indescribably awesome. The rest of the way the road circles this great mountain until, at Telluride, another rocky barrier stops any further progress.

At the foot of the Dallas divide is Placerville, a sleepy little place, especially so since the fire of 1919, which wiped out most of its business section. In March, 1876, nine men headed by Col. S. H. Baker, an experienced placer miner, left Del Norte and worked their way to the San Miguel river looking for gold. Reaching the river early in May, they began to wash its bars but at first found nothing. After about a week Baker discovered gold bearing sands in what became known as the Lower San Miguel Mining district, near the present site of Placerville. News of his findings started a rush to the placers, and in 1877 the town was laid out. In 1879 "a man named Smith located a ranch a mile and a half below Placerville" and built a log house. This became a general store and saloon. Gradually, other cabins were built near his store, and the town "drifted down river" to the new location. Even after the railroad was completed, it was nearly ten years before the town began to grow. In time it became the distributing point for supplies used by the people living along the San Miguel river and for those in *Placerville* the Paradox valley. From its tiny station hundreds of carloads of ore and of cattle and sheep have been shipped.

From Placerville the road follows the San Miguel river past Fall Creek, Saw Pit and Vanadium, tiny communities which owe their existence to mining.

Saw Pit   Saw Pit was only the name of a creek until July, 1895, when James Blake, a blacksmith, located the Champion Belle and shipped three carloads of ore which netted him $1800. A few days after his strike, hundreds of prospectors were at work, a townsite was laid out, and a few frame buildings were hastily constructed between the high red cliffs and the river. The following year, when the Commercial mine was found to contain high grade lead carbonates, the whole town celebrated with a champagne supper at the mine!

San Miguel   A mile from Telluride is the skeleton of San Miguel City, located in
City   1876 by Messrs. Lowthian, Mitchell and Brown. These men laid out a townsite in which "every street was supplied with an acequia." "Care was taken not to destroy the natural forest on the ground; . . . thus the townsite is already provided with shade trees," boasted the founders as they hammered a dozen buildings together and arranged supplies and provisions in tents. A herd of sixty dairy cows was put to graze on the meadow, and beef cattle were turned loose on the mesa south of town.

San Miguel City grew to a population of 5 women and 200 men in 1880, but Telluride grew faster, stealing its population away, until today San Miguel has only its trees and its cows. The land is now part of a farm, with nothing but barns and a few houses in the tall pines to suggest that a town once flourished there.

Telluride   When Jane and I drove into Telluride past the old stone brewery, the great mountains at the end of the valley looked pink in the afternoon light; but the most startling sight was the waterfall which dropped straight down the mountain at the end of the street and seemed to disappear just beyond the city limits. Telluride is a good-sized place, and, although some of its buildings are empty and certain blocks toward the edge of the city look dilapidated, the heart of town is full of stores, and the streets close to the main thoroughfare are full of homes surrounded by gardens and shaded by trees. But it was Telluride's past in which I was interested, and by poking about the older portion of the place I discovered certain landmarks of interest.

San Miguel City had a rival in 1876—a little camp called Columbia, a mile further up the valley, with a population of 100; and during the next few years both places eyed each other's progress. Columbia was closer to the mines, its streets were broader, it was packing ore by burro trains over the range to Ouray by way of Mt. Sneffels every day, and according to its citizens it was "full of high grade activity and enterprise."

In 1881 the name was changed to Telluride, and though the town grew slowly during the eighties, a brick county courthouse, large school buildings and several churches were built in that period. But like most of the mining camps it worked at a disadvantage until the Denver and Rio Grande Southern reached the city in 1890 and ore could be shipped by rail instead of by

(382)

TELLURIDE   ↓ MAIN STREET, TELLURIDE

burro and wagon train. From then on its development was rapid, and the mineral output increased until the silver ban of 1893 temporarily paralyzed the camp. Toward the end of the nineties gold values were found in increasing amounts in some of the biggest mines, and the camp boomed again. As I looked up at Ballard mountain and Ingram mountain and to the peaks beyond Savage basin and realized that mines high above timberline were responsible for the city's development, I became curious about its mining history.

Late in 1874 prospectors who had heard of the placers on the San Miguel river, crossed from Baker Park (now Silverton) into the Marshall basin. These men were looking for lodes, not placers, and in 1875 located several on what is now the Smuggler property. The Sheridan, called the most important lode in San Miguel County, was the first to be discovered. On it were located the Mendota, Smuggler and Union claims, all of which became fabulous mines when developed. John Fallon, a prospector, found the Sheridan in August, 1875, but did not develop it extensively enough to see what he had. In 1878 he leased the claim to two men who cut a drift and discovered richer ore, and the mine continued to change hands until eventually it became part of the Smuggler-Union property.

In July, 1876, J. B. Ingram was prospecting in the Marshall basin and "was inclined to measure the length of the Sheridan and Union claims, as they seemed to him rather in excess of the legal allowance of lineal feet." He discovered that each covered five hundred feet more than was allowed. Setting his own stakes on the "intervening ground," he named his claim the Smuggler.

Another vein discovered in 1876 was the Liberty Bell, two miles north of Telluride. W. L. Cornett, who located it, did little with the property, and it lay idle until 1897, when the Liberty Bell Gold Mining Co. began to develop it by building a mill along the San Miguel river and an aerial tram to the mine. The mine ran continuously for many years with but two interruptions—one in 1902 when a snowslide damaged the property, and the other in 1903 when labor troubles disrupted mining in the district.

By 1881 ore was being shipped from the Smuggler, Mendota, Cimarron and Argentine, and before the end of the eighties the Sheridan, Union, Cleveland, Bullion and Hidden Treasure were added to the list of big producers. As the Smuggler was developed, the company bought up other claims until its holdings and its plant were the biggest in the county.

Ore from the Smuggler-Union was found from the surface down, and even when freight rates on the nearest railroad were $60 a ton, smelter charges $35 a ton and miners' wages $4 a day it still made a large profit for the owners. The Smuggler-Union vein was worked for a mile in length and through vertical shafts for more than one thousand feet in depth. By 1900 it had thirty-five miles of underground tunnels and employed three hundred twenty-five men. In 1915 zinc obtained from concentrates brought still more profit to the company. From 1898 on, the greatest output of the district was from the Liberty Bell, the Smuggler-Union and the Tomboy.

The Tomboy was located in the Savage fork of Marshall basin in 1880 and "paid from the grass roots." It began to produce heavily in 1894, when it was bought from its owners for $100,000. In 1897 it was reported sold to Rothchild's of London for $2,000,000. The mine, which is situated 3000 feet above Telluride, is at the end of a county road, over which at one time a daily stage ran carrying passengers and mail. A little settlement, which contained a school, stores, livery stables and the cabins of the miners, grew up a few yards from the big mill and was called Savage Basin Camp. In 1899 the Tomboy Gold Mines Co. (the same company that in 1919 bought claims from the Revenue-Tunnel) took over the mine. Half a mile from the Tomboy were the Columbia and Japan lodes, the former an old location and the latter discovered in 1894.

On a previous trip to Telluride I had gone up to the Tomboy, after I had been assured that the road was good and that the miners drove it every day. To be sure it was narrow, but there were turnouts in case I should meet a car. Dan was driving for me; so, as we rose higher and higher above the city, I could look about at the superb mountain scenery. We hugged the bank when a car passed us, thankful that one of the "turnouts" was handy. About half-way the road turns a sharp corner and for the next quarter-mile climbs along the face of a vertical cliff, on a roadbed which seems to have been made by driving poles into the mountain, putting cribbing between the poles, and covering the resulting shelf with dirt.

The road was literally hung to the cliff, which swept down hundreds of feet to the new Smuggler mill at Pandora. To go ahead was terrifying; to look below, sickening. For the first time in my "mining career" I lost my nerve as I thought of driving out onto that hanging road over so much empty space, and I said weakly, "I don't think I want to go to the Tomboy. Let's go back."

"There's no place to turn; we can't go back," Dan replied practically, starting up toward the cribbing. I watched the next corner above us, praying that no car would round it until we were safely past and on rock and earth again. From the corner we could see both the Smuggler and the Tomboy mines, and since this was going to be my one and only trip over that particular road, I was willing to go on. The road was still a shelf and we climbed still higher, but underneath us was good, solid rock once more.

At the Smuggler mine we looked around, and I sketched it and the Tomboy, a mile away resting in a glacial cirque. The mountainsides were crisscrossed with trails and dotted with sheds and shaft houses. No sooner had we parked the car than several children and a friendly dog ran to greet us from a cabin perched crazily in a hollow of the cliff. They were followed by a woman who got her car out of a shed and started for Telluride to do her shopping. What if we had met her below that corner!

As I looked at the unfriendly, rocky summits above us, I remembered that the road over which we had come was originally part of the trail through Savage basin to Silverton and that hundreds of pack trains used to plod over it, loaded with ore on the way out and with coal on the way back. Below us was the long tram of the Smuggler-Union, dropping almost straight down the valley to the mill—the buckets on the cable wove rhythmically up and down between the spans of the metal towers.

. As we started down toward Telluride I recalled the words of a mine report which described this particular piece of road construction as "excellent and of uniform grade, can be traveled by horse, wagon or even automobile," and I knew that I was a coward. That evening I visited with several friends and listened to stories about the mines.

"The year 1902 was the worst ever for snowslides," began an old man who had lived in the county for fifty years. "We expect the snow to run every spring, but that year the slides began the first of March before we were looking for them. There were new slides every day, and the people of the county were almost in a state of panic—they never knew where the next one would strike or whom it would catch. The one that hit the Liberty Bell was the worst.

"There had been a terrible storm, during which the tramway at the mine was swept away and some of the men were lost. As soon as the storm was over, a search party set out to hunt for the bodies. A second slide caught them. The next morning as soon as it was light, a third party climbed back to the drift on the Liberty Bell, in spite of the danger of more slides from the hanging, heavy snow which threatened to come down at any minute. Before the rescuers could reach the bodies caught in the second slide, a third one came down, blocking their trail and forcing them to return to Telluride without the dead men and without any of those injured at the mine. It was another day before they could get back and cut a trail over the slide. None of the bodies were rescued for some time. As soon as a Cornish miner up at the Sheridan heard about it, he started to town to help with the rescue work. He'd hardly left the mine boardinghouse before a slide caught him too, and it was months before they found him at the bottom of the drift. Naturally Telluride was stunned by all this, and the day of the funeral all the business houses closed. Everyone went to the funeral and followed the bodies to the graveyard. It was the biggest turnout ever known in the San Juan."

One story led to another. "I remember Jim Clark, the town marshal. He was a good marshal but he was a very brutal man. He knew he had lots of enemies; so he kept a Winchester rifle in each of four stores just to have one handy in a hurry, and he carried two guns in his pants. He was a dead shot and kept in practice by shooting out the letters in the signs on the Lone Tree Cemetery fence. One night when he was walking his regular beat, a man who was hidden between two stores killed him with a Winchester."

"Jim was bill collector for my father," spoke up another old-timer. "A lot of Cornish miners traded at our store and when they owed us money they'd duck away from it as they went by. My father would tell Jim who they were, and he'd walk around town and spot them when they were drinking or gambling. All he had to do was tap them on the shoulder and mention father's name, and they'd hot-foot it to the store and pay up. Jim used to come into the store whenever he wanted a hat and he never paid for one either. I guess he thought he was entitled to them."

"Reverend Bradley used to hold Sunday evening services here. He didn't preach from the Bible but from articles in the newspapers. He sure could draw a crowd—even the highclass, gentlemen gamblers turned out when he spoke and they put plenty in the collection plate too. Once he announced that his subject was to be 'Gambling.' That night all the boys were there and he got more gold than ever."

That evening I also heard about Telluride's labor troubles. The first strike was called May 2, 1901, in order to abolish the "fathom" or "contract" system of work, an old Cornish method, introduced into the Smuggler-Union mine about 1899. A fathom was a body of ore six feet six inches long and as wide as the vein, whatever it might be. If a miner happened to get into a wide vein his pay was less than if he was working the same distance through a narrow vein. Under this system the men's wages were less, for many worked over eight hours a day and yet couldn't make the three dollar wage that was usual in the district. In spite of many protests the Smuggler-Union refused to give up the fathom system; so a strike was called.

Just after it began, the local union of the Western Federation of Miners asked the company to submit the question under dispute to the State Board of Arbitration, but they were told that there was nothing to arbitrate. After six weeks, the mine reopened with non-union miners, who were employed not in accordance with the fathom system but by the day at the regular wages for the district. This didn't set at all well with the union men, and in July about two hundred and fifty of them armed themselves and waited near the mine buildings for the non-union men to change shifts. When the scabs appeared, a committee of strikers ordered them to quit work immediately, threatening that there would be trouble if they did not. Some shots were fired and a union man was killed. After that there was a free-for-all, the strikers firing on the company buildings and the non-union men hiding in a mine tunnel and firing from its entrance. Finally, after three men were dead and six injured, the men surrendered. That afternoon the strikers lined them up, marched them up the trail to the top of the range, and ordered them to leave the county if they knew what was good for them. They emphasized their remarks by beating up a few.

On July 6 the strike was settled, and the non-union men who had been sent off were allowed to return and work beside the union miners. In November the mine manager and the Miners' Union agreed on a scale of wages and hours for the Telluride district; the eight-hour day was established and the fathom system was out.

The second big strike did not turn out so satisfactorily for the miners. On Oct. 31, 1903, one hundred men in the Tomboy struck because the mill had been started with non-union labor. On Nov. 5 members of the Mine Owners Association requested Governor Peabody to send troops to Telluride, assuring him that they could re-open their mines and mills with non-union labor if they were given military protection from attacks by union men. No troops were sent. On Nov. 17 another request was made to the

Governor by the mine owners, who admitted that the situation was peaceful at the time only because the mines were idle. They asked for protection so that when they reopened with non-union men trouble could be averted. On Nov. 18 Governor Peabody appealed to President Theodore Roosevelt for troops, but none were sent.

Eventually the state militia arrived under Major Z. T. Hill. In January, 1904, these troops arrested twenty-two men who were believed to be trouble makers and lodged them in the local jail. These men were deported to Ridgway by train and ordered not to come back. While this was being done Major Hill announced to all newspaper correspondents that all press reports were subject to censorship and that the telephone and telegraph lines were under his control.

On March 14 about a hundred men, members of the Citizens Alliance, armed themselves, searched the town, and took into custody sixty union men and sympathizers. The men were kept in a vacant store until after midnight, when they were marched to the station and loaded into two coaches. Some of the mob went with them as far as Ridgway, where they were put off and warned never to return. On April 5, the Telluride Mine Owners' Association issued the following statement:

> We do not propose to enter into negotiations of any nature with the Western Federation of Miners. We do not recognize a union in Telluride. There is no strike in Telluride. There is nothing to settle.

On the way back to the hotel that night I noticed a cluster of tiny, twinkling lights high above the town on one of the mountains—the lights of the Tomboy.

The first time I stayed at the Sheridan Hotel I made sketches of the lobby with its specimen case of minerals, its dried starfish, and the stuffed eagle on top of the phone booth. I also drew the unique staircase. The Sheridan is a three-story building, and the staircase cuts through the middle of it, starting at the front door and rising in one long flight to the back of the third floor. You just step off at the second story. While I was busily figuring out the perspective of the many steps, I heard someone behind me, and a voice said incredulously:

"You aren't drawing the stairs?" I nodded and kept on working. "Well," said the voice, with a scornful sniff, "if you lived on the third floor and climbed there as I do, you wouldn't."

One day while exploring the second story of the building I noticed a door ajar and discovered that it led on to the stage of the Opera House, next door. That evening just before dark I sat in the dusky auditorium of the theatre, while a friend of mine and the hotel bell-hop let down the drop curtain with its painted vista and elaborate scrolled border and afterwards showed me the scenery which was stacked on the shallow stage.

Before Telluride had a church building all kinds of meetings and festivals were held in the brick courthouse. One morning I asked the janitor if I might sketch the courtroom. "Can you work fast?" he inquired. "There's going to be a trial here in an hour, and you'll have to be out by then."

One evening I looked up my friend Eino, and after dinner he and his aunt said I must see the Finn Hall. The inside was one big room with a potbellied stove at one end and a stage at the other. On the stage was an upright piano, some bits of scenery, a table and festoons of crepe paper left from the last entertainment. The rest of the scenery was rolled up and lay either at the back of the stage or was hung above it. Behind the stage was a small room where refreshments could be prepared. On our way back we passed the Swedish Hall, which was similar to the Finnish one but larger. Both Eino and his aunt insisted that I go home with them for coffee and when at midnight I left for the hotel, they escorted me to its door.

Eino and an old whiskered gentlemen were my guides through the sporting section of the city. They showed me the Pick and Gad, once a notorious sporting house, and they took me through Pacific Hall, a decaying gambling establishment with a pool table and several game boards and gambling devices still cluttering the warped floor. As we left the sagging building with its broken windows and rotting porch, the whiskered gentleman left us. While we were investigating other old properties we ran into him again, this time with a wheelbarrow in which he was trundling a large cake of ice to a customer. As soon as he saw us he dropped his load, left the ice sitting in the sun and came over to us, saying that he'd just remembered something that I should see. Off we went again, through back lots and weeds to where a huge icebox such as storekeepers use stood rotting in the deep grass. He explained that Telluride had a big fire in which all the old sporting section with its twenty-one saloons and its eight houses of prostitution had burned down. This icebox and the double row of tiny one-story frame "cribs" where the girls lived were all that was left of it.

Telluride itself fascinated me, but whenever I glanced beyond the town toward the mountains I saw the waterfall and, below it, a trail which switch-backed from the valley to a group of mine buildings at the foot of the falls. The trail looked easy and I wanted to get close to it. The road out of the city led past the cemetery and the ruined Liberty Bell mill. Farther on was Pandora, a small settlement close to the huge Smuggler-Union mill. Hidden in the trees beyond the Smuggler property and its great settling pond was the beginning of the zigzag trail which fascinated me. From the gatekeeper at the Smuggler mill I learned that it led 3600 feet above Telluride to the Black Bear mine, whose buildings were in Ingram basin just below Ingram falls. Someday I hope to climb that trail!

The Pandora mine was located in 1875, and by 1876 a small group of prospectors had started a camp two miles south of Columbia. The camp was originally called Newport, after Newport, Kentucky; but in 1881, when the place was a good deal bigger than it is now, the name was changed to Pandora. The only houses in the little town today are those of the employees at the mill and their families.

As I looked at the steep slopes of the mountains which close in the valley and saw the long scars on their sides left by the snowslides, I thought of the item in the 1902 newspaper which spoke of a huge slide starting down the mountain just above Pandora which would have completely buried

Pandora

(389)

the town "had it not been turned by the Hidden Hand of God." On my last evening in Telluride I watched the Alpine glow fade from the high peaks and I thought of a quotation found in a publication prepared by the Colorado Western Slope Congress:

> His face can be discerned in the huge walls of His masonry, and His voice heard in the rushing cataracts that leap from their perpendicular sides. Nowhere is nature more beautifully adorned.

Ophir   One day while I was sketching the Telluride station the "Goose" came in. I had often wondered about the train schedule, but I was quite unprepared to see the converted auto-van with flange wheels which takes the place of the steam train. Back of the driver's seat is a seat for passengers, but the rest of the van carries freight. While I could not take the Goose to Durango or back to Ridgway, I could follow it by car through Ophir and as far as Rico and I could see the famous Ophir Loop.

Part of the road to Ophir runs through ranch country, part through the aspens, and the last portion skirts the canyon in which the Loop is built. With his usual ingenuity, Mears maneuvered his Rio Grande Southern through the mountains, crossing passes and gorges like this one by gaining elevation in a series of sweeping curves. The Ophir Loop with its hundred-foot-high, wooden trestle gives one a thrill.

There is little left of the town which clings to the foot of the Ophir Needles, except a station, an ore-loading bin, a store, an old hotel and a few houses lodged among the rocks. Near the trestle of the Loop is the Butterfly-Terrible stamp mill, its roof a mass of dormer skylights.

The first explorers to the region were Lt. Howard and his group of prospectors. The stream running through this valley was therefore named Howard's Fork, after the Lieutenant who had already given his name to Howardsville across the range. The first staked claim was made in 1875 by Lindquist, who uncovered the Yellow Mountain. All through 1876 and 1877 miners trickled in, staking claims and building a small camp which they called Howard's Fork. Even though the weather was severe, seventeen of them remained throughout 1878, working their lodes whenever they could. By 1879 the Osceola was producing gold, and ten sacks of surface ore from the Gold King brought $5,000. The miners also began experimenting with arastras and found them so successful in separating the free-milling ore that by the end of the year ten were in operation below the town.

Just when the town was settling down, rich carbonates were discovered a few miles away at Rico, and the population rushed over to the new camp, leaving Ophir temporarily deserted. But the Rico boom was short, and the miners hurried back to their Ophir properties and continued to develop their mines and to ship their ore by burro train to the Silverton smelter. In 1882 a small smelter was built at Ames, three miles away, but it was not successful and soon closed down.

The mines around Ophir improved with development; the Suffolk, the Carribeau, the Silver Bell and the Butterfly-Terrible turned out gold in gratifying quantities. One of the old mines, the Alta, located in 1878, is still

OLD OPHIR   ✔ SAN MIGUEL

working and its ore is brought by a two-mile tram to the loading bin at the Ophir station.

Until 1879 there was no regular mail service, but individual travelers to and from Silverton brought it in with them if they felt like it. In June of that year a semi-weekly service was established between Silverton and San Miguel by way of Ophir, but even the guaranteed delivery was far from satisfactory as was shown by newspaper comments in the *Ouray Times*:

> Nov. 15, 1879—McCann, the mail carrier from Silverton . . . has robbed the mail and left the country. The mailbag, cut open and with the registered matter rifled, has been found near Iron Springs.
>
> Dec. 13, 1879—No mail for four weeks. The Kansas tenderfoot says he wouldn't carry the mail for $5,000 a trip, after one trip.
>
> Jan. 3, 1880—No mail yet from Silverton. . . . No mail from Rico in ten days. The snow is nearly four feet deep and there are snowslides in every gulch on Silver Mt. "Scotty," the mail carrier from Ophir to Rico nearly froze on his last trip.

Two miles from the station of Ophir is Old Ophir. In 1898 it was a town of 400, with electric lights, waterworks, churches, a schoolhouse and "an up-to-date and alive spirit." From its mines two cars of concentrates were shipped daily the year round. Just when or why it began to fade I do not know, but by the summer of 1941 very few families were living in the houses which lined its several streets. Sheep grazed around the schoolhouse; tall, thin water-hydrants partly overgrown with bushes, stood like punctuation marks along the streets; and except for two or three frame hotels, on one of which the name "Colorado House" was painted, the town was made up of private homes. Beyond the houses in a grove of trees was the cemetery, and I spent some time examining the old markers and trying to imagine what Ophir was like when the men and women buried there made the life of the town. The mountains rise sharply on three sides, their slopes cut by mines, and at the end of the valley the old trail to Silverton is just visible as it disappears around a rocky shoulder. That was the trail over which the burro trains packed the ore for the smelters and on which Swen Nilson lost his life.

On Dec. 23, 1883, Nilson, the mail carrier, was lost in a snowslide and his body was not found for two years. It was storming when he left Silverton and he was warned against making the trip, but he wanted to deliver the Christmas letters and packages to the waiting families in Ophir. When he did not arrive, searching parties went out, but they could find no trace of him. During the summer as soon as the snow melted the search was resumed, but with no success. Not until August, 1885, did another searching party uncover his body at the bottom of a snowbank—the mailsack still strapped to his back.

Rico   Between Ophir and Rico is Matterhorn, a minute community at the base of Yellow mountain, which from certain angles resembles the Swiss peak. A little mining was done at Matterhorn and also at Dunton, another small place at the end of a side road some miles beyond Lizard Head. Until 1879 there was no town where Rico stands, although numbers of men had prospected in the immediate vicinity of the place.

The first gold was discovered in 1866 by Col. Nash, a Texan, who led a party of eighteen men up the Dolores river to the present site and began mining. In 1869 three experienced prospectors, Shafer, Sheldon and Fearheiler, started for Montana, resolving that nothing could stop them on their way but the discovery of mineral. They covered the same territory that Nash had, relocated most of his findings, and spent a year in the locality.

In the summer of 1870 R. C. Darling, while surveying along the Dolores river, ran across Shafer and Fearheiler and made some locations on what is now the Atlantic Cable lode. Darling then interested some army officers and some capitalists in the mines and got them to outfit a party to prospect the area more thoroughly. In 1872 he returned, bringing with him a party of men, mostly Mexicans, who not only located several properties but built a small adobe smelter in which to work the ores. Taking ore from the Atlantic Cable, Aztec and Yellow Jacket mines, the men produced a few bars of base bullion; but as their furnace was not very successful they abandoned it and the camp. Other prospectors who worked in the vicinity in 1878 organized a mining district and began to develop the lodes which had been located.

The boom came in 1879 after Col. Haggerty found lead carbonates rich in silver on Nigger Baby hill (so named for the large amount of black oxide of manganese found in the outcroppings). With the news of this discovery all the miners from Ouray, Lake City, Silverton, Ophir and San Miguel rushed in and began to dig.

> The town is in the midst of the greatest excitement. . . . Men are coming in and hunting locations for stores, whisky shops, meat shops and one man is looking for a brewery site. . . . All are wild as March hares over the prospect of having another Leadville in a few days. Already we have a milk ranch.
> Machinery is on the way for two smelters, and two sawmills will be turning out lumber in less than six weeks.—*Ouray Times,* Aug. 16, 1879.

Within a month there were twenty-nine buildings, seven saloons and four assay offices, and a sawmill which was being freighted to the camp was only sixteen miles away on the crowded road. People poured in until 600 were milling around the barely discernible streets. Until a printing press could be freighted-in in October, the *Rico News* was issued from the *La Plata Miner's* office in Silverton.

> This place impresses one as having gotten there before it was sent for. And yet everything is there, wine and women, cards and caterers, houses and horses, men and burros, moneys and mines, storms and stores, sawmills and gospel mills, busy boys and blowing bummers, working men and working women, pack trains and bull trains, carpenters and sign painters, assay offices and bunco steerers, Sunday schools and kino chambers.—*Ouray Times,* Nov. 29, 1879.

As usual so many names were suggested for the new camp that a committee was chosen to select one. From an assortment which included Carbonate City, Dolores City, Belford, Patterson, Glasgow, and Lovejoy, the name Rico was chosen.

Early that first fall the camp had an Indian scare. All the women were sent to a new log cabin without doors or windows and were "taken to the roof on a hastily-constructed ladder and dropped down." Guards were stationed nearby, and the rest of the men barricaded themselves in the upper floor of a store; but no Indians appeared.

In 1880, after the Grand View smelter blew in, the town began to build up, and more lots were covered with tents, cabins and frame houses than during the first year of the boom; but the camp was still isolated from markets and everything had to come in by "burro punchers." Beef cattle were driven to within six miles of Rico, slaughtered, and the meat taken to town on sleds. "Flour was $50 a sack, eggs $3.00 a dozen, boots $10 a pair and socks not to be had." Many men used old flour sacks in place of stockings. Whenever a pack train was due and the roads were bad, men went out to meet it and to shovel snow or break trail for the weary beasts. The arrival of such a train was always cause for celebration.

According to the *Ouray Times* of May 1, 1880:

Lent Is Over.

At nine o'clock this morning a long string of freight teams came rolling into town loaded with provisions for our merchants. Hungry men gathered with market baskets, empty syrup cans, sacks and buckets in their hands, telling how they liked bacon cooked, how they liked syrup and butter on slap-jacks, etc. Now and then you would see a man slap his hand on his side pocket and finger nervously at his empty bottle, spit and watch the whiskey kegs as they were rolled into the saloons. Drivers popped their whips around the ears of the off leaders, jerking their single lines, driving through the throng of men and boys who looked on at the performance with all the interest of a circus day in the paw-paw districts of Missouri.

In 1882 a second smelter was blown in, but not until the Enterprise mine with its abundance of rich ore was discovered on Newman hill were mining men with capital attracted to the camp, nor did Otto Mears begin to dream of a railroad north of Durango. The railroad did not reach Rico until 1891, the year the Enterprise mine was sold to an English syndicate.

David Swickheimer went to Rico after the first boom started and, while his wife kept boarders, he did hauling and other odd jobs. Like all men in a mining camp he dabbled in prospecting. In 1887 he located a claim just above town and named it the Enterprise. The couple put every dollar into its development until their money was gone and they were completely discouraged.

It was then that Mrs. Swickheimer spent one dollar for a lottery ticket and to her amazement won $5000. She insisted that the money be used to develop the property adequately, and the result was the uncovering of one of Colorado's richest mines. In 1891 the couple sold the Enterprise for $1,250,000, and the new owners made of it the biggest bonanza in the vicinity.

Many other silver mines helped to make the town—the Alma Mater and the Grand View, the Phoenix and the Pelican, the Diamond and the Electric Light; but in recent years lead and zinc deposits have kept the miners alive, and in 1903 tin gave the Atlantic Cable a new lease on life. As it was dark when I reached Rico I could not see its many mines on Nigger Baby and Newman hills nor its Grand View smelter. Only twinkling yellow lights indicated how big the place was.

LA PLATA   ↓ GOLD KING BOARDING HOUSE, LA PLATA

From Rico to Dolores and on to Mancos the highway runs close to the track over which the Galloping Goose rattles on its daily runs between Durango and Ridgway. Near Mancos and along La Plata canyon are mines and skeletons of old camps, and on one trip Vic, Jim and I hunted for those north of Hesperus. The map showed a road as far as La Plata City; so we turned up the canyon, looking for the old camp and keeping a sharp lookout for mine dumps, cabins, mills or other typical clues. The canyon road ran beside the river and climbed gradually but steadily toward the snow-capped La Plata peaks. After a drive of several miles we rounded a curve and saw ahead, in a meadow, a row of false-fronted buildings. Some had been stores and some homes, and altogether not more than half a dozen were left. The road went on another three miles to the Gold King property, where we found a big abandoned mill full of silent machinery. Its two-storied boardinghouse was across the stream and was connected with the mill by a long, swaying suspension bridge, high above the rushing water and just wide enough for a footpath.

After making several sketches we started back, passing an old stage station and stopping to talk to two prospectors camped near the road. Jim showed them a specimen of ore which we had collected a few days before, and the eyes of one of them lighted up at once.

"You got that in Creede, didn't you?" he asked. "That's amethyst quartz. You can't mistake that ore. Here's what the ore around here looks like. Even after all the years this district has been worked there's gold here, and we're after it. It was all placer mining in the seventies, and the boys didn't dream that there were lode mines in these mountains which could produce millions.

"Then in 1875 they began to find mines—first the Comstock, and then the La Plata and the Lady Eleanor and the Cumberland and the Snowstorm. There's a gold belt all through here, but for years there was so much more profit in silver mining that the gold fields were neglected.

"La Plata City had 200 people in it in 1882 and 500 in 1897. Stages ran between it and Hesperus every day. You saw the stage station, didn't you? When the camp was booming, freight teams were strung along this road night and day.

"The output was small around here until 1894, but it picked up after more mines were opened. You saw the Gold King, but you didn't get to the Red Cloud, the Neglected or the Swamp Angel.

"Down stream a ways are two of the richest mines in the district, the May Day, which produced from 1904 to 1907 and on and off ever since, and the Idaho. Both of them have production records of millions in gold. Too bad you didn't get here a year ago so as to see Parrot City."

"I noticed a sign, Parrot Ranch, on the way up," I said, "but I never heard of Parrot City."

"My partner's getting some grub together. You might as well stay and eat and I'll tell you about it."

Jim and Victoria were delighted at the prospect of food plus history and

(396)

signaled me to accept the invitation. I forget what we had to eat, but I jotted down the facts as he told them.

Capt. Moss and C. D. Posten pulled out of the California gold fields in 1856 and came gophering around the mouth of the La Plata river where they found good gold placers. Moss didn't return again until the summer of 1873, when he brought a party of prospectors from California to the mouth of the river and found not only gold but samples of quartz, which suggested that there might be some lode mining nearby. When their grub ran out they struck out for the nearest trading post, a hundred and thirty miles away. While they were on the road, one of the men accidentally shot himself in the neck. He couldn't go on; so the party divided, part going for supplies and the rest staying with the injured man. They called the place where they stopped Camp Starvation, and they lived for three weeks on nuts, roots, berries and game until the others got back with food.

While on this trip for provisions Capt. Moss made a private treaty with Ignacio, Chief of the Southern Utes. By its terms the men had the right to mine and farm in an area thirty-six square miles, with the center of the area at the spot where Parrot City came to be. In payment for these rights the Indians received a hundred ponies and a lot of blankets. A government treaty with the Indians was pending but it wasn't signed, and since the country which the men were in still belonged to the Utes, this move on the part of Moss was pretty shrewd.

Moss then took a copy of the treaty and some samples of gold quartz back to San Francisco and showed them to Tiburcio Parrot, a banker. Parrot was plenty interested and told Moss to outfit another party, take it back to the gold bar and draw on him for funds. Tiburcio Parrot never lived in Colorado but he spent a lot of dough in mining here through his agent, Capt. Moss.

In the fall of 1873 a party from Arizona started for these mountains and reached the bar of the river in November. The gold washed out well, and they were just about set for gulch mining when the snow drove them out. They were back again in May and began to dig ditches and build sluices for their work. Moss's party got as far as the Mancos river in April, 1874, but the snow on the range between there and here was too deep to cross; so they located ranches, built cabins and planted vegetable seeds which they'd brought with them. By the middle of May they reached the bar, only to find the Arizona party working it. The two groups held a pow-wow and agreed to work together, staking off twenty acres each. Moss and his outfit laid out Parrot City and put up the first building, a blacksmith shop. There were only about twenty-five people in La Plata county then, and most of them were in Parrot City.

As soon as the city was laid out a ditch company was formed and everyone started digging ditches or building flumes to carry water to the placers. One ditch was seven miles long and another a little less than two miles. The placers covered an area ten miles by two miles and were finally worked by hydraulics.

The first lode discovered was the Comstock, three miles north of Parrot.

After that over a hundred locations were made and twenty of them were developed. It was a gold section; but they found a lot of silver, too.

E. H. Cooper brought in the first sawmill in 1876. He had a lot of trouble crossing the San Juan river on account of high water. One of his wagons upset in the river, and everything spilled out. Some Navajos were watching him from the bank, and he got them to dive for the bolts, nuts and nails that had gone overboard. On the opposite bank was a band of Utes who didn't want him to land; but he did and went on, building his road through rough country all the way. He set up his mill at Parrot City and began to build the town. It took them four months to do it. There were two stores, a hotel and a raft of shacks for the fifty people who were living there.

I knew a man who carried the mail there in the early days. Once as he arrived some kind of a shindig was going on. One miner was carrying around a water bucket full of whiskey and inviting everyone to help himself. The whiskey must have cost plenty, too, for it had to be freighted in either from Fort Garland or Fort Wingate.

Although it had a post office in 1875, it was 1880 or 1881 before the population reached three hundred. Parrot was the county seat until Durango began to build up. After the Denver and Rio Grande reached Durango and the town shot up, Parrot lost out to the newer town. By 1883 the boom was over, and for years the post office was almost all that was left, except one old-timer who continued to live in his shack. Now it's a cattle ranch. The property changed hands recently and the last of the old buildings was torn down.

I looked with considerable disappointment at the Parrot Ranch as we drove back to Hesperus, wishing that I had started hunting in this area a year or two sooner. From Hesperus it is not far to Durango, the Smelter City, which was founded in 1880. The coming of the railroad the following year and the blowing in of the first smelter in 1882 caused the town to grow, until now it is the only city of any size in the southwestern part of the state. Surrounded by coal beds, lime rock and iron deposits, it is ideally situated for its great smelting industry.

Animas City, just north of Durango, is much older, for it was laid out by Baker in 1861. He had heard from the Navajo Indians that there was gold in the mountains north of their reservation, and while prospecting along the Animas river his party laid out a townsite which they called Animas City. From Durango the highway leads north to Silverton, climbing all the way to Molas lake and then sweeping down the side of Sultan mountain to the little park in which the city lies. From Silverton, trails lead to all the old camps of the region, and by visiting them it is possible to relive in part the early days of the San Juan.

CHAPTER XVI

The Silvery San Juan

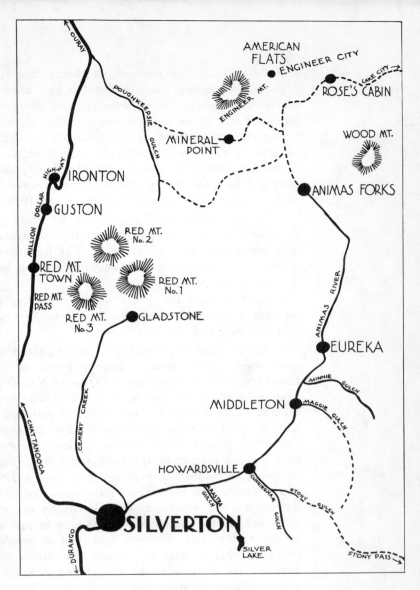

Cunningham Gulch

IN the seventies the main route into the San Juan was by way of Stony Pass at the head of Cunningham gulch. Major Cunningham, for whom the gulch is named, was the leader of a party of Chicago men who made some discoveries in Arastra and Cunningham gulches and who were among the first to put money into the development of the mines.

The trail crossed the top of the pass at an elevation of 12,090 feet, and the wagon road, when built, was 500 feet higher. The descent on the Howardsville side was very steep, dropping 2300 feet in the first two miles. Over this trail the prospectors came in and the pack trains of ore went out. Mail for Howardsville and supplies for the Highland Mary were often packed in on snowshoes by a Mr. Harwood, who thought nothing of carrying on his back sixty pounds of beef or any other provisions that were needed. The trail over the top was frightful, and everyone who traveled it clamored for a road.

From its mouth to its head, Cunningham gulch is full of mines and mills— the mines over a thousand feet above the road, and the mills close to the streambed. From each mill to the top of the mountain are rows of steel towers for the tramways which brought the ore from the mines in a constant stream of buckets.

The first property in the gulch on the way out of Silverton is that of the Old Hundred Company. On my first visit I saw a big, skeleton mill standing between the road and the stream. A few years later I returned to get a more detailed drawing of it only to find that it had been demolished by a mudslide.

Despite the fact that some of its claims date back to the seventies, the Old Hundred Company did not develop the mines extensively until the early nineteen-hundreds. The property was worked on levels which began a thousand feet above the mill and extended to the summit of Galena mountain, whose steep sides made it impracticable for the workmen to climb back and forth every day. Boardinghouses were therefore built at each tunnel opening, "especially designed to withstand the deadly snowslides." In 1906 the First National Bank of Silverton sent to the Denver mint a gold brick from this mine weighing fifty pounds and valued at $10,000.

A little further up the gulch is the Pride of the West property, one of the oldest in the San Juan. From this mine ore was shipped by pack train over Stony Pass as early as 1874. The mine has been a steady producer and is still in operation, its new one-hundred-ton mill at Howardsville handling the present output.

Next beyond the Pride of the West is the Green Mountain, which includes a group of veins—the Leopard, the Osceola, the King William, the Old Hammer and the Flat Broke.

At the head of the gulch is the Highland Mary, an old property and a great mine, whose strange history began in the early seventies when the Ennis brothers consulted a spiritualist in New York, asked her aid in locating a mine in the west, and paid her $50,000 for her advice. She designated a point on a map of the United States and told them that they would find a lake of gold waiting for them at that location. The two men traced the "point" to King Solomon mountain near Silverton and set stakes high on its side, naming their claim the Highland Mary. They not only spent large sums of money in its development but they built a $10,000 home near the entrance of the tunnel and furnished it lavishly. The course of the tunnel which was driven into the mountain was plotted by the spiritualist, who from time to time sent specific instructions as to how to proceed. She advised the brothers to dig first in one direction and then in another, until the main tunnel of the mine was a mass of "twists and turns, up and down." The brothers followed her directions with the utmost care, but the lake of gold was always around the next corner.

Everyone knew that a "medium" was directing the tunnel's progress, and before long the miners became superstitious and refused to work in the mine alone. While the tunnel's erratic path was being dug several good silver veins were cut and the ore was shipped to Del Norte by burro train. The ore tested well in silver, but it was molten gold that lay ahead, and the boring of the tunnel continued. The brothers never lost hope; but after spending over $1,000,000 and driving their tunnel nearly a mile into the mountain, their funds were gone, they were forced into bankruptcy and they lost the property in 1885. The new owners used practical methods to develop the mine and made of it one of the best producers in the region. Between 1893 and 1902 it lagged in output but by 1907 it was the second largest mine in the Silverton area. It was almost dark when I left the Highland Mary and drove slowly back to Howardsville. The mountain slopes had faded to gray silhouettes and everything was quiet. By now it was dark, but high on one rocky peak, like a star, was a pinprick of light from some mine.

As I approached Stony creek I thought of the story of the woman and her husband who in June, 1875, having crossed the summit of Stony Pass, were just entering the timber on this side when she gave birth to a baby. Her husband quickly made a shelter out of the wagon sheet and put some spruce boughs on the ground, and in this retreat she remained for several days until she was able to travel.

When I visited Howardsville in 1941 Henry Forsyth was alive, and from him I learned more about the town than from anyone else. He came out to the San Juan in 1874 and for nearly fifty years ran a store and acted as postmaster to the growing community. *Howardsville*

In 1874 Howardsville, the headquarters of the region, was a straggling little settlement, and its chief assets were a blacksmith shop and a store whose stock consisted mostly of rye. La Plata county at that time included the area now covered by San Juan and Ouray counties as well as parts of Dolores and San Miguel. When San Juan was formed in 1874 Howardsville became the county seat, the first one west of the Continental Divide. The two-room log cabin which was used as a courthouse is still standing beside the road at the mouth of the gulch—unless plans to move it to Silverton have been carried out. Howardsville did not retain the honor long, for within a year Silverton, a "growing town of a dozen houses," was voted county seat; and although Howardsville contested the decision, the county clerk moved the records to the new location. A post office was also established in 1874, whereas prior to that date the nearest was at Del Norte, one hundred ten miles away.

Although the town is said to be named for Lt. Howard, one of the leaders of the Baker party, old timers insist that it was George Howard, who built the first cabin in 1872, for whom it was christened.

Henry Forsyth, Dan McKay and the Bernard brothers packed in the first earthenware dishes and the first stove, which was very popular with the women folks who arrived in the camp. In 1876 a big livery stable was built, which kept fifteen to twenty horses and every spring bought a new string, thus avoiding the expense of feeding them through the long winter when the country was blanketed with snow.

Although mountain sheep were plentiful for food, the only beef available was the oxen who hauled freight over the passes and who, when past work, were butchered. John W. Waters, who later ran a butcher shop at Chattanooga, once drove eleven steers over the pass into Howardsville while the snow was deep. To prevent the cattle from sinking into the snow he would camp until the surface crusted and then drive the cattle over it. When it became mushy he would camp again and wait for a new crust. At Howardsville he butchered a steer, cut it up and sold it to the miners. He had no paper or string, so each man simply carried away his beef on a skewer.

Two miles above Howardsville, halfway between Animas Forks and Silverton, is Middleton. It is situated at the base of Middle mountain, and at the entrance to Maggie gulch. In the early days this gulch was neglected as "country that was useless" and for years it lay deserted. Then, Gottlieb *Middleton* and Konneker prospected it and located the Golden Nugget. In 1894 other prospectors began to swarm in, and by 1895 one hundred claims were staked along the four-mile stretch. The Kittimac in Minnie gulch and the Hamlet, both of whose mills stand beside the highway to Eureka, were among its big mines; but, as one mining man put it, "Wherever the pick has been intelligently driven it has exposed the yellow metal."

Eureka   The last time I saw Eureka it was a dead town; for it depended almost exclusively upon the great Sunnyside mine for its existence, and with the closing down of the mine in 1938, Eureka, which had been dozing, fell asleep.

According to one account, although Baker and his party spent the winter of 1860 in the little park where Silverton now stands, their "diggings were nine miles up the river at a point later known as Eureka." The next allusion to the site comes from a wanderer who wrote: "We came out into a thick clump of trees in which were several cabins bearing on a flaming signboard the word 'Eureka,' evidently intended for the name of a town that was to be."

The *Silver World* describes a dance held in one of the cabins in April, 1877, by saying: "Soon the damsels began to arrive, some on burros and some on foot." The music was provided by a fiddle and a banjo, and the ball opened with the San Juan Polka, "which resembled a Sioux War dance. . . . Soon the 'iron clads' of the miners began to raise the dust from the floor," so that "before long it was impossible to tell what was what. . . . Ground hog was the chief dish" at the late supper, which also served "big ox, gravy, bacon, coffee, tea, and a large variety of pies and cakes." After this light repast the dance was resumed till morning.

The town grew a little each year. By 1878 it had two stores, two meat markets, and one restaurant with a post office, but the "best building in town was a saloon." Before long the Eureka Town Company was busy surveying the city into lots and advertising that it was not only surrounded by mountains, one of which was "a mass of silver-bearing quartz," but that it was "protected on all sides from snow and rock slides"—a statement which, although true for the townsite, did not apply to the surrounding gulches where the snow ran with frightening regularity.

Typical of these slides is the story told by Al Bernard of the time he was working up Eureka gulch and had just stepped from his cabin to go to the mine a hundred yards away. It had snowed for a month, and the snow lay eight feet deep on the level. As he stepped out, a slide started at his feet and carried him to the bottom, dropping over a sixty-foot bluff on the way. He rode the slide all the way and climbed out of it with only a few bruises. The men at the mine came after him and took him to a cabin, where they found a bottle of whisky and some cayenne pepper, with which combination they rubbed him briskly. He swore he couldn't even feel the massage but he hated to see the whisky used externally.

A telephone message to the Silver Wing at Eureka in February, 1898, stated that the manager of the mine was dying in Silverton and requested Doolan, who was at the property, to come immediately. In less than fifteen minutes he was on the trail.

(402)

SUNNYSIDE MILL, EUREKA (DISMANTLED)

The Silver Wing bunkhouse was carried away in 1906 in a storm and one of the miners was killed. His two brothers came for the body to take it to Durango. The trail was piled high with snow, and after a struggle they were compelled to leave the body in the snow and go on to Elk Park. The next morning they found that a snowslide had swept over the place where they had cached the body. After a prodigious amount of digging they recovered the body and two days later reached the train which took them the rest of the way.

Although Otto Mears, the Pathfinder of the San Juan, began plans for his Silverton Northern railroad between Silverton and Eureka in 1889, it was not completed until 1896. The *San Juan Democrat* voiced the miners' impatience for the road by saying:

When the road was built it not only reached Eureka and Animas Forks, but a spur was run up Cunningham gulch as far as Stony gulch to serve the mines in that area.

The section of the road between Eureka and Animas Forks, four miles above, was the hardest to build and to maintain, for the canyon was so narrow and the mountain slopes so extremely sharp that slides were a common occurrence. Mears had already built a wagon toll road between the two towns, and when one of the engineers who was surveying for the railroad chanced to remark in Mears' hearing that the new road would be better situated if placed where the toll road ran, Mears is reported to have said: "Put it there. I built the other road. I guess I can build this one on top of it if I want to."

The road was built, and in 1906 Mears accepted a contract to ship ore from the Gold Prince mill at Animas Forks throughout the winter. To keep the road open and minimize the constant hazard of slides he designed an elaborate type of shed capable of resisting any amount of snow. Seven such sheds were to be placed between Eureka and Animas Forks where the worst slides ran.

They were to be made of the heaviest timber, reinforced and filled in between the logs with rocks, so that slides would glide over rather than damage them. A station was to be built in each shed where section hands would live all winter, who could keep the road clear between sheds. If the experiment was successful, it was thought that the Rio Grande Southern would adopt the same system in keeping the canyon of the Animas open. Mears was confident that the sheds could withstand any slides from above on the same side of the river—the only danger lay in slides on the opposite side which could push up the snow from beneath and loosen the foundations.

In October the first of the five-hundred-foot "snow breaks" was completed at the most dangerous location, near the Silver Wing mine. Its solid walls of cribbing, crammed ten feet through with rocks and "fortified with timbers of massive proportions lined each side of the track." Its "resisting power" was tremendous—it could even bear the weight of a slide above it. Mears prayed for a severe winter so that the shed would receive a supreme test. If it survived, "next year will see every danger point between Eureka and Animas Forks guarded." But before the season was over the impregnable shed was wiped out by a single slide! And the other six were never built.

On my first trips up the valley the tracks ran as far as Eureka, and I once saw "Casey Jones," the "Goose" which was equipped with cowcatcher, flange wheels and a Cadillac engine, as it stood beside the Sunnyside mill. The railroad was taken out nine years ago, and sand from the streambed has obliterated much of the right of way.

The Sunnyside was the mine that made Eureka. To be sure there were other good, producing mines in the vicinity—the Scotia, the Mastoden, the Toltec, the Golden Fleece, the Tom Moore and the Sound Democrat—but it was the Sunnyside and the Sunnyside Extension which ultimately paid off. To me the most exciting part of Eureka is the Sunnyside mill, the biggest I have ever seen. It is also the fourth mill built on the property; the first was above timberline and close to the mine on the shore of Lake Emma; the second at Midway, halfway between the mine and Eureka; and the third in Eureka, beside the site of the present mill. Ninety percent of the employees of the mine lived in Eureka with their families; twenty years ago there were still 300 people in the town.

The Sunnyside was located in 1873 and the Sunnyside Extension in 1874, and both have been worked since then with few interruptions and have produced millions of dollars worth of gold and silver.

Many names are connected with the complicated history of the mines— R. J. McNutt, George Howard, the Thompson brothers and several more— but two names stand out over all the rest. One is Rasmus Hanson, who in 1886 secured a lease on the Sunnyside Extension, and supervised its profitable development until he sold it to the Sunnyside Extension Mining and Milling Co. in 1893; and the other is John H. Terry, who staked his faith and his fortune on the mine and brought it through slim times to its peak of production. He died in 1910, and in 1917 his heirs sold a majority of the shares to a new company for half a million dollars with a promise of further loans. With one such loan the Gold Prince mill at Animas Forks was moved to Eureka and converted into one of the first flotation mills in the county. No sooner was the five-hundred-ton mill completed than it burned; but it was rebuilt and set in operation in 1919. The mine was reopened for the last time in 1937 and was worked unsatisfactorily for a year. In 1945 the United States Smelting Refining and Mining Co. bought nearly three thousand shares of stock at a dollar a share. By June, 1948, the property was $3,600,000 in debt and was sold at auction. The August, 1948, *Mining World* printed the following obituary:

> A $225 thousand bid submitted by the *United States Smelting Refining and Mining Company* has been accepted by a U. S. bankruptcy court for the *Sunnyside Mining and Milling Company* of Eureka, Colorado. . . . U. S. Smelting, which holds 12,000 of the 18,000 shares of stock outstanding, plans to close the mine and salvage what it can of the buildings.

All sorts of stories are told about the mine. One is about Judge John H. Terry, who believed so completely in the Sunnyside that, even when others abandoned it, he continued to work it until his money was gone. For six months it lay idle, and then he sold it to a New York syndicate for $300,000, with a cash payment of $75,000. The syndicate bought a mill-site, built a railroad siding, excavated for a mill and employed forty men to develop the mine; but at the end of six months they had found very little ore. A mining expert from New York came out to examine the property, and his report was so disillusioning that the company refused to continue its purchase. No second payment was made, but Terry was allowed to keep the $75,000, and the mine was turned back to him. The next day he started work again and "with the first explosion of powder opened a new vein." He continued to develop the mine until it was one of the biggest producers in the state.

Terry was never afraid of work. One day an Englishman who wanted to see him on business drove up from Silverton in a sleigh and inquired in the mine office for the Judge. He was told that they were having some trouble with the water pipes and that the Judge was at that moment standing in the middle of the creek fixing them!

Animas Forks   It was in Silverton that Dan and I met the mine inspector who invited us to his home one evening to talk to us about the camps nearby, and it was from him that I first heard of Animas Forks and of Mineral Point. He got out old maps, spread them on the dining table, and pointed out to us this gulch and that mine.

"You can drive as far as Animas Forks," he assured us; "but you'd better not try it to Mineral Point. I haven't been up there for years and I doubt if the road is open. You used to be able to drive all the way to Engineer Mountain and over to Lake City, but not anymore."

Next morning we went to Eureka and followed the road, close to the big mill, until it left the town and started its long, steep climb up the Animas valley. We passed the Tom Moore, the Toltec, the Silver Wing and other mines that I did not know, and after four miles of bumping and boiling over the railroad grade (which is a road once more), we swung up the main street of the deserted camp. Many well-built houses and stores were standing, and some tremendous stone foundations at the lower end of town, which I identified as the site of the Gold Prince mill. The houses, scattered over two or three street levels, were built in several styles of architecture from log cabins, through false fronts, to painted, gabled houses with dormer and bay windows.

While the radiator cooled off, I dashed about the town like a chipmunk, sketching houses and whole streets, all with a backdrop of gaunt mountain peaks. It was high, lonely country, 11,300 feet at least, and not far from timberline.

The mines in the district were first worked in 1875, and a mill was erected at the Forks to treat ore brought down from the Red Cloud mine at Mineral Point. The miners in the meantime pitched their tents in the dense timber which covered the future townsite, and as the mines were developed and more men moved in, the tiny camp became quite lively.

The first woman at the Forks was Mrs. Eckard, who got the men to build a cabin and a boardinghouse for her. As soon as she began to bake, the miners took their meals with her. After three months one of her boarders was missing at breakfast. When he did not appear for the next meals he was thought to be sick; but his tent was empty and he could not be found. One of the miners asked Mrs. Eckard if he had paid his board and learned that he owed for the entire three months. "Don't cry, ma'am. We'll see that you get your money. Saddle up, boys, and let's take a rope along." The boys went to Silverton, where they found their man in a saloon. As they surrounded him, the spokesman said: "Come back and pay your board or give us the money; if you don't we'll hang you. You have five minutes to fork over." The trapped man had no trouble finding the money and he did not return to the Forks.

Before there was any town, a man died a couple of miles down the valley near the site of the Silver Wing mill. The boys met around a campfire to arrange for his burial, and while everyone volunteered to dig the grave no one felt competent to conduct the service. As no nails or boards were available, the grave was lined with split logs and the bottom was covered with a layer of grass. The men wanted to give their friend a Christian burial, so they met again to try to decide what was best to do. The meeting grew silent as no one volunteered to handle the service. Finally a young man, John Davis, not yet twenty-one and a newcomer to the camp, said shyly that he belonged to a church back in Scotland. He was immediately appointed to do the task. In his own words: "That evening I tried to remember what verses of scripture I could and the committal service. I did not sleep. . . . We gave him a funeral." When the Silver Wing mill was about to be built, Davis told the manager about the grave and received his assurance that it would not be disturbed.

The townsite with its one principal street was not laid out until 1877. Lots were free to anyone who would "locate and build, parties selecting according to their own free will and choice." There was access to Lake City (then more important than Silverton) by way of Burrows Park; and with the completion of the Henson Creek and Uncompahgre toll road via Mineral Point, a new and shorter route was opened.

Animas Forks is the business center of Mineral Point and Poughkeepsie Gulch and always shows life, even in midwinter. Sundays are always lively days. The miners come sailing down from the timberline peaks to the snow-bound village, eager to get their mail and have a chat with neighbor miners on sunny sides of buildings; and around social card tables, mines and new mining enterprises are talked over . . . newspapers devoured and their contents thoroughly digested.—*Ouray Times,* Feb. 7, 1880.

By 1881 it was spoken of as the "Pivotal metropolis of the numerous camps which surround it," and it boasted that it was "without doubt the largest town in the United States at an altitude of 11,300 feet. Mineral Point may be higher but not as large." A ball given in the eighties was described as "a most creditable affair for this elevated mining camp." Even its twenty-mile telephone line from Lake City crossed the divide at a point 12,500 feet above sea level.

As the camp grew, a dozen business houses and two assay offices were opened to serve the "thousand miners and citizens" who used it as a center. The miners must have been a hardy lot for "there has not been a death in camp," wrote a correspondent to the *Lake City Mining Register* on Jan. 1, 1881, and since "there is but one cemetery in the county, it looks very lonesome." Crofutt of the *Gripsack Guide* visited the camp the same year and was impressed differently, saying "It is a wild and rugged country, where nothing but rich mines would ever induce a human being to live longer than absolutely necessary."

When the miners at the Forks ruled that patent notices of mining claims should be published in the nearest newspaper, Sol Raymond "saw the chance for a paper" and moved his plant there. He called it the *Animas Forks Pioneer* and sold the first copy for $500 to Bill Young, owner of the Bill Young claim at Mineral Point. Every copy of that issue brought at least one dollar, and many sold for as much as twenty-five dollars. As long as prospectors staked new mines, the paper flourished, but by 1866 subscriptions and patent notices fell off and the paper folded up.

The first community Christmas celebration was held in 1881 in the dining hall of the Kalamazoo House. Besides a tree and gifts for the children,

The ladies had done their best to satisfy the most sanguine expectations. You would hardly believe the display of eatables—turkeys, chicken, mountain sheep, fresh oysters and eggs, egg nog, etc.—when you take our isolated situation into consideration,

concluded the correspondent to the *Lake City Mining Register* with unusual modesty. In the evening everybody gathered in a hall for speeches and toasts. The one to Animas Forks was responded to by the mayor, who said that Animas Forks was incorporated as a town seven months ago. He mentioned that the streets since then had been somewhat graded and that a building committee was making plans to erect a church. He deplored the fact that "the timber south of us is being so rapidly destroyed as to endanger our town from sliding snows;" and he concluded by saying, "We need a public hall in connection with the jail . . . For a mining town I must acknowledge that we are exceedingly quiet."

As more and more timber was cut from the hillsides above the town the mayor's warning was fulfilled. One slide came down Wood mountain,

ENGINEER MOUNTAIN

↓ ANIMAS FORKS

jumped across Animas canyon and buried John Haw's cabin in fifty feet of snow. The slide burst in his door and filled the cabin in a moment. After three hours he succeeded in digging himself out. A still larger slide came off Cinnamon mountain and "after crossing the Animas River near the Eclipse smelter, ran up the other mountain and then folded over and fell back like an immense wave." During the winters, when twenty-five feet of snow fell at the Forks, no cabin was safe from December to March; and although sleighing was good all the way to Eureka, riders were always in danger from slides.

The railroad spur to the Forks, completed in the early nineteen-hundreds, enabled the mines to ship ore more easily and economically, but since 1920 the road has not run beyond Eureka, and all hauling has been by truck.

The biggest mining property was that of the Gold Prince at the head of Mastoden gulch. The group of mines was located on the Mastoden vein and was known as the Sunnyside Extension at the time Rasmus Hanson sold it to the Gold Prince Mines Company in 1903. (It is still popularly known by the earlier name.)

The Forks was at its peak during the late seventies and throughout the eighties, but when it began to fade "its decline was as rapid as its rise," and after the Gold Prince mill was moved to Eureka in 1917 its day was over. Although the Columbus property and the Early Bird were worked in 1939 and the Silver Coin is producing this year, there is no life in the town—it was deserted by 1923.

Several years after my first visit I went through Animas Forks again on the way to Mineral Point, and although most of the houses were still standing I missed some of them. As I made sketches of the town I noticed a large two-story, false-fronted building, with a wooden sidewalk in front and with shreds of paper hanging from its inside walls. It must have been a hotel, but whether it was the Mercer, the Flagstaff or the "newly purchased and refurnished Garrison House," which later became the Kalamazoo House, I could not tell.

One family was living at the Forks, and snuffling around their house were several pigs. One old porker eyed me suspiciously and every time I walked in his direction, looking for a new "composition," he started to charge me. Finally he won out, and I finished my sketching from the car. I've been stopped by beavers who dammed a road till it was unsafe to cross; and once deer flies cut my sketching trip short by their wicked bites, but never before had I been routed by pigs!

Mineral
Point

Mineral Point was inaccessible, and yet since the night the mine inspector in Silverton showed it to me on his big map I had wanted to visit the distant camp. I had been close to it several times. When in Ouray I looked at the towering wall of mountains, behind which lay Mineral seven miles away; when at Rose's Cabin, I knew that the trail over Engineer mountain wound out of sight to Mineral seven miles farther, and from Animas Forks I could see the beginning of the shortest trail of all, only four miles to the goal. Those last few miles, however, always meant hiking or riding horseback, and horses are not usually to be had close to ghost towns. Finally I persuaded two good friends, Charlotte and Gene, to try the trip with me.

We stayed in Silverton overnight and were wakened by jingling bells. I looked out just in time to see a string of twenty horses and mules trot by in single file on their way to work in the mines, their bells and harness tinkling and their hoofs clicking sharply against the cold ground. The drive to Animas Forks was simple, except when we had to climb the bank to let two ore trucks from the Columbus mine roll past; and while Gene drove, I pointed out the mines and told the story of Judge Dyes, who was once Justice of the Peace at Animas Forks. One of the boys was arrested for drunkenness and was brought before the Judge, who fined him ten dollars and costs. The miner refused to pay and threatened to take the decision to a higher court. "There is no such thing," stormed the Judge. "This is the highest court in the United States."

Just as we drove into the town we met a couple who were about to leave in their truck. I asked them about the condition of the road ahead and how far it was to the Point. The man was sure we could drive it, although he warned us it was rough and cautioned us about the two sections of shelf road, each a mile long, on which there were no turnouts.

"Go on and try it," he said as he drove off. "All you have to do if you meet a truck is back up a mile." We thanked him and decided to walk.

It was cloudy when we left the car so, besides carrying a thermos bottle of coffee, our coats, and my sketching equipment, we tied our slickers around us and set off up the trail. After a mile Gene suddenly remembered that the lunch and the map were still in the car, but none of us cared to go back for either item. It was a steady pull from Animas Forks for at least three miles. Part way up the first shelf road we met a man leading two pack horses, and a little farther on we found two crossed sticks braced in the middle of the trail, from which hung a heavy canvas bag. We did not examine it, but it appeared to be full of ore. Hours later when we returned both the sticks and the bag were gone.

The farther we climbed, the slower we moved, for the road gained altitude rather fast and breathing became more difficult. There was little to see except tundra-covered ground and the barren peaks which surrounded us. We rounded a corner, and at least two miles away saw our goal—a mountainside covered with yellow dumps and old shaft houses. " That's Mineral Point," I thought, "but it's still a long way off."

When we reached a fork in the road I longed for the map, but since I'd memorized the trails around Mineral Point for years I was fairly sure of where we were. Just ahead on the crest of a hill was a sheepherder's wagon and his two dogs, but the herder was not around. Up the mountain to our right was a truck and a man who disappeared into the mouth of a mine. "You stay here, and I'll go ask him directions," I called, starting over the tundra. It was steep climbing to the mine, and at the entrance I had to pick my way carefully over the broken rock which lay beside pools of iron-stained water. It was dark inside the entrance, and I could just see that the tunnel split in two directions.

(411)

"I wonder which way the man went," I thought, knowing that by now he would be at least a quarter of a mile inside. "I'll yell as loud as I can and maybe he'll hear me." So, braced against the walls of the entrance I shouted, "Hi," as loudly as I could and waited for a distant "halloo."

"What do you want?" said a low voice at my feet, and looking down I saw the man squatting just inside the entrance of one tunnel, tabulating notes in a report. Feeling extremely foolish, I explained what I was doing and asked where I was.

"No," said the engineer, going out of the tunnel with me and pointing to the mountain with the mine dumps, "that isn't Mineral Point; that's Engineer Mountain. Mineral Point is along that road to the left, but if you follow the right-hand road you'll come to the San Juan Chief mine and mill. There's more of it left than there is of Mineral, and from the Chief, if you climb up a little ways on an old road and get into a meadow, you'll see the site of the Point. The San Juan Chief used to be a heavy shipper. A good many thousand dollars worth of silver and copper were taken out of it, but they had trouble with water and then their concentrating plant didn't pan out, so they put in a J. J. Crooke process at a cost of $45,000 and that worked better."

"You wouldn't drive us over there in your truck would you?" I asked hopefully.

"No," he roared. Then he added more mildly, "Listen lady, I'm a week behind schedule now in my work, and my truck overheats, and I can't drive you there. If I could I'd do it for nothing."

I thanked him and went back to Charlotte and Gene with my assorted information. After a brief rest we started off briskly, for by now we were on top of a flat and the going was less tiring. In the distance were the ragged peaks near Ouray and the cup of mountains that surrounds the city.

Before long we noticed a mine high on a hill, and although the main road bore to the right, I had a hunch and left it, following a less travelled trail that seemed to lead nearer the mine. We puffed and plodded along until, at the top of a ridge, we looked down on the ruined San Juan Chief mill, its boardinghouse, and a handful of cabins. Scrambling over loose rock we reached the buildings, which we investigated thoroughly; they were all empty and pretty well dilapidated.

Next we looked for the site of Mineral Point, which the mine inspector had told us was a quarter of a mile west of the Chief. An overgrown wagon road led across another ridge, beyond which was a wide, swampy meadow bordered by stunted pine. In it were the remains of a few broken-down cabins. Across the meadow was the ruin of a small mill, but try as we would we could find no way across the swamp to it. Although I'd been told that little or nothing was left at the Point, I had hoped against hope that a few more buildings would be standing. There were such interesting accounts of the camp in its prime that it seemed impossible that it was so nearly obliterated.

Mineral Point may be called the apex of the continent, for the waters of the Animas and Uncompahgre rivers take their rise, and flow east and west from its summit, wrote C. A. Warner in 1876, in *San Juan, Its Past and Present Ways of Getting There*.

"The Point itself is a knob of quartz, fully sixty feet thick, from which several veins diverge," states the *Mining Scientific Press* of Nov. 27, 1915; while the *Silver World* of July 28, 1877, describes the area by saying:

> The entire mountain region . . . is a perfect network of veins . . . which . . . seems to be grouped about three great centers; . . . these centers being extinct craters, and toward them the majority of the veins center and dip. . . .
>
> The famous Mastoden vein stands up like a great wagon road and runs in almost a straight line over mountains and through valleys; upon it are some fourteen locations, the best developed and thus far the richest being the Bill Young lode.

As early as 1873 Capt. A. W. Burrows and Charles H. McIntyre spent several months at the head of the Animas river locating lodes and building a few cabins. Shortly afterwards two mining companies—the Dacotah and San Juan of which McIntyre was president, and the Buffalo and San Juan—were organized, and work in the mines really began.

The best mines were located during the first years of activity—the Burrows, Vermilion, Dacotah, and Yankton; and the Red Cloud, Ben Butler, Mastoden, Bill Young, and Old Lout. The company which developed the Old Lout sank a shaft over three hundred feet without finding anything valuable. As they were about to give up, one of the miners "put in a shot, more for curiosity than for anything else, and broke into a body of high grade." The first carload netted $8,000, and within a month over $86,000 was realized from this new ore body.

> Almost a decade before the air resounded with the shouts of the populace in recognition of the Red Mountain discoveries, the hardy explorer had traversed the country between Lake City and Animas Forks times innumerable and had left upon nature's handiwork the imprint of his visit by the familiar location stake, wherever indications of mineral existed.
>
> Long before the famous Yankee Girl or Guston were discovered . . . Mineral Point was a busy, bustling village of 600 or 700 population, and round it was heard the hum of industry, the music of the saw mill, the diamond and the hand drills, and the echo of the blast as it sounded through the hills.—*Silverton Weekly Miner,* Jan. 1, 1897.

In 1877, when burro trains packed "highgrade" every day over the trail to the works at Animas Forks, Mineral Point was the busiest camp in the San Juan. Unfortunately during these first years wildcatters squandered millions of dollars in mining operations. One promoter wasted $4,000,000 on the construction of a thousand foot tunnel and then abandoned it. Another had a fantastic scheme for advertising the district. He showed pictures of steamship navigation along the Animas river (which can be forded at any point), and of streetcars running along its banks between the camp and the Forks.

A group of newspaper items give a graphic picture of life during the seventies and eighties.

> The Lake City toll road is now at the foot of Engineer Mt. and I think a poll tax movement is now on foot among the people for the extension of the road to this

place, where we shall be semi-open to the outside world.—*Silver World*, Aug. 18, 1877.

Mr. Buell delivered a very able sermon in Mr. McIntire's cabin. A large number of our citizens were in attendance and seemed highly pleased with his clerical ability. He has been requested to preach again.—*Silver World*, Sept., 1877.

Mineral Point is blessed with regular weekly mail from Ouray, via this place to Animas Forks. Heretofore we have paid a man $4 a trip to bring the mail from Tellurium to Animas Forks.—*Silver World*, Sept., 1877.

In 1880 the Colorado Mining and Land Co. shipped over Engineer Mt. the first machinery used at the Point. It was freighted by wagon from Alamosa and dragged by cattle over a rough and rugged trail to Mineral Point.—*Silverton Weekly Miner*, Jan. 1, 1897.

Mineral City is held and carefully watched over by Ed Tonkyn, who is Mayor of the city, Street Supervisor, Post Master, proprietor of the Forrest House, and deacon of all the churches. Monday morning he takes up a collection of the poker chips and sweeps out cigar stubs.—*Ouray Times*, Feb. 7, 1880.

The camp is improving, McEntee Bros., put an annex to their store and will no doubt add terraces, bay windows and fluted chimneys. The most important improvement however is the

MINERAL POINT HOTEL

the enterprise of two Philadelphia gentlemen of "vim, vitriol and vinegar."—*Silver World*, July 14, 1882.

We the sporting men of Mineral Point have an unknown that we will match to fight the winner in the Strong Boy Jones and George Cooper contest for $500 a side (and winner to take gate receipts) London Prize ring rules to govern. We have this day deposited $100 with Sanford Harvey as a forfeit.—*San Juan Democrat*, April 18, 1889.

As I sat on this high, windswept meadow that had once been Mineral City I wished I could have been in town some evening while a work crew was building a road from Mineral toward Silverton and have seen the "little forest of camp fires" that glowed each night below the settlement. Some were those of the miners and roadbuilders, but others belonged to the "woodchoppers, coal burners, packers and teamsters" who were camped in the vicinity.

We decided to start back to the Forks, following the road at the base of Engineer mountain. A thin, half-obliterated trail wound up to the saddle of the peak, and in my imagination I climbed the rocky trail over the saddle and down the other side to American Flats, where Engineer City once stood between Mineral Point and Rose's Cabin.

Engineer City   Engineer mountain, "nature's grand monument on which San Juan, Ouray and Hinsdale counties corner," was the "grand pyramid of rich silver seams" into which H. A. Woods drove the first location stake in the summer of 1874, to mark the Annie Woods lode. While Woods, Burrows, and some other men were chopping a trail from Animas Forks up the valley to Mineral Point in order to get supplies in to the Yankton Company, Woods, who was always prospecting, climbed the high peak and located not only the Annie, but the Syracuse Pride and the Siegel lodes on Siegel mountain.

The following year he located the Polar Star near the summit of Engineer mountain, after a thrilling race in the dark, one cold April night. The story of the location of the mine begins with Captain Graham, who staked the claim but didn't work the location. Earle and Greene of Silverton, who were aware

(414)

CUNNINGHAM GULCH   ↑ GLADSTONE

that the assessment work on the claim hadn't been done and who considered the mine a good property, provided "Sheepskin Miller," a prospector, with food all winter, under an agreement that he locate the lode for them in the spring. The story as told by Woods, in the *Lake City Mining Register* of Jan. 13, 1882, continues:

I had gone out that winter but knew the claim was Uncle Sam's and that I had as good a right to it as anyone, so I hurried back in March, 1875.

I hired a man, C. Barret, and in company with Bob Cleveland, went in wagons to Antelope Park where we unloaded and made sleds, on each of which we packed 225 pounds, and each man dragging a sled, we started over Grassy Hill for Cunningham Gulch and Howardsville. . . . There we learned that the coveted claim on Engineer Mt. had not been staked. We decided to lay over a day to recruit. Meanwhile, the mail carrier passed down to Silverton and carried the news of the new arrivals. Earle, suspecting my intentions, came up that night to start "Sheepskin Miller."

I gave out I was going in another direction, but at midnight, while "Sheepskin" was in innocent slumbers, I and Barret slipped into our snowshoes and headed for Engineer Mt. We reached the summit about 6 A. M. and planted our stake just at daybreak. The weather being very cold suggested the name of Polar Star.

We returned to the Forks, went to bed and slept till 11 o'clock, when we were awakened by a terrible bustle outside, which proved to be "Sheepskin Miller," the Glatzenbergers and other parties, getting ready for a general race for Engineer.

When I got out Miller saw the fresh trail toward the mountain and asked what that meant. I was pleased to inform him that he had been scooped, and asked him if he saw anything green in my eye. "My God, Wood," he exclaimed. "You have ruined me, Earle and the company." And that was how I located the Polar Star, —April 19, 1875.

The Polar Star was a silver bonanza, but so also were the Syracuse Pride, the Palmetto, the Annie Woods, the Little Fraud and the Bill Young, all of them above timberline. Although the mines were inaccessible (the entrance to the Annie Woods was at 13,000 feet), first a trail and then a wagon road, built over the mountain between Animas Forks and Rose's Cabin, helped move the ore. The road over Engineer crossed the divide at 12,200 feet at Point of Rocks on a shelf barely wide enough for a wagon; yet over it went a continual stream of pack trains and teams.

When immense deposits of rich ore were reported in the Frank Hough lode on Engineer mountain in January, 1882, it was a foregone conclusion that American Flats, near the location of the mine, would swarm with prospectors by summer. The Flats, which were between the summit of the mountain and Rose's Cabin, looked like a military encampment as tents for the three hundred men who were working on the mountain were pitched close to Jack Davison's huge tent-boardinghouse with its monster stove. By the middle of July Davison was serving forty to fifty boarders, and to feed them thousands of pounds of grub had to be packed up the canyon every day.

Engineer City was the name of this new town on the Flats.

It can boast of more inhabitants than Mineral City, Animas Forks or Capitol City yet we have no saloon and the boys openly declare that with the grub put up at the Davison Hotel they can do very well without any. We believe this is the only city in the state that can boast of 300 to 400 inhabitants, without a whisky shop. . . .

Patience and perseverance only is wanted to make this undoubtedly the greatest camp south of the divide.—*Silver World*, July, 1882.

How long Engineer City lasted I do not know; the last entry mentioning it that I have found was dated Nov. 23, 1883, and it was headed:

MOUNTAIN SPORTS.

The boys on the Frank Hough mine enjoy themselves on moonlight nights and at the dinner hour, snow-shoeing.

American Flats, where the Hough mine is located, afford a magnificent field for the sport.

Dan and I started from Silverton very early one morning for Gladstone, about nine miles away. The road up Cement creek was narrow but not hard to drive, and after passing a few old millsites whose dumps were eroded and stained with iron-charged water, we reached both the deserted town and the end of the road, which stops abruptly at the Gold King mill. An identical row of frame houses formed a line on either side of the one street, and behind them were sheds and garages and outhouses. The sun had just come over the mountain and was picking out the tops of the ridges with shafts of yellow haze, and not a sound was to be heard. To our surprise, one thin blue column of smoke rose straight into the cold, clean air from what appeared to be a deserted cabin.

"Let's see what we can find out about this place," said Dan, knocking on the door.

A man, his face covered with soap and his hands dripping, came in answer to Dan's knock and just stared at us. Behind him stood his wife, peering wide-eyed over his shoulder. "Yes, this is Gladstone," said the man, and shut the door.

While Dan curled up in the car to complete the sleep he had lost by our early start, I wandered around town, sketching and taking pictures. On one front porch was an unfamiliar object which looked like an old-fashioned scale, such as drug stores once had. It stood about six feet high on a metal support and it had a big dial, below which was a leather cushion about a foot in diameter. Just as I stepped onto the porch with my camera focused to snap this unusual gadget, I heard footsteps in the boarded-up house, a bolt was drawn back from the inside, and the front door swung open. There in the doorway stood a young man, and while I stammered something about not meaning to intrude but being fascinated by the old scale, he interrupted me, saying, "That isn't a scale; it's a pneumatic punching bag," and giving the leather pincushion a blow, he sent the arrow on the dial spinning. He was very agreeable, and after watching me re-focus my camera he went back into the house and closed the door. No more "ghosts" appeared, but I did find an ancient automobile parked between two of the empty houses.

Just beyond the workmen's homes was the mine plant, which consisted of many buildings large and small and the huge half-demolished mill. Mine machinery was scattered everywhere, and it was impossible to tell from the

Gladstone

(417)

ground around the mill property which was earth and which was part of a dump. At the lower end of town stood the schoolhouse with a cupola and small porch, and behind it, ranged up the mountainside like giant steps, was the stone and concrete foundation of a great mill.

Olaf Nelson was working at the Sampson mine at the time he discovered the Gold King in 1887. The Sampson had been worked since 1882, but not until Nelson struck a "strong vein at a sharp angle" did he suspect that a better mine lay hidden nearby. He had no money; but he staked a claim over the vein, called it the Gold King, and managed to sink a fifty-foot shaft and to run a fifty-foot drift into the lode. From this he shipped several carloads of ore before his death in 1890.

In 1892, Cyrus Davis and Henry Soule were interested in the Harrison mine and knowing Willis Z. Kinney's reputation as a mine expert they made him superintendent of the property. For two years the owners poured money into their venture with little success. As it showed no signs of improvement they gave up developing it and instructed Kinney to try to find a better mine to take its place. Kinney, who had his eyes open, suggested the Gold King, and although it had shown nothing to warrant the purchase, Davis and Soule had such faith in his judgment that they ordered him to buy it.

Nelson's widow, who still owned the mine, sold it to Kinney in 1894 for $15,000, and within a year, under his skillful management, it began to produce. He was put in full charge and given an interest in the company, and before long "everything was humming with life and energy." A concentrating plant equipped with the Darrow process was built in 1894, but when it failed to handle the ore satisfactorily three Frue Vanners were substituted. In time the Gold King property consisted of forty claims, including the original Sampson lode and three thousand acres of coal land at Durango. Over five miles of drifts and tunnels were added to the original fifty-foot shaft, and at its peak the mine shipped between sixty and three hundred tons of concentrates daily.

Although the Gold King made Gladstone what it was, there had been some activity in Cement creek before it was discovered. A road from Silverton was built up the creek in 1879 to the head of Poughkeepsie gulch where considerable mining was being done, and chlorination and lixiviation works were erected at Gladstone at that time. In 1889 Fisherville was located one half mile below Gladstone, around Fisher's stamp mill, which worked ore from the Exposition mine, a gold quartz property. A few houses existed in Gladstone when the Harrison mine was working, and a boardinghouse run by a former hotel keeper from La Plata City accommodated the employees of the Harrison mill. But not until Kinney began to expand the Gold King property did a "veritable town" spring up on the flat below the mine, where 2,000 people milled around the main street and kept out of the way of the twelve draught horses which hauled concentrates from the mill to Silverton and returned with supplies for the town.

By 1897 several of the old mines were opened nearby, until it was rumored in Silverton "that with a few more mines and additional development, a branch railroad will be stringing along up there for the trade and traffic of these upper

(418)

elevations." In May, 1899, the following item in the Silverton newspaper settled the question:

The Silverton, Gladstone Northerly Road a Sure Go.
The Contracts Have Been Let—The Rolling Stock Purchased.

The assertion of Cyrus W. Davis, President of the Gold King Mining Co., on his departure from Silverton to his home in Waterville, Me., one year ago is being worked out. He said, "If the Gold King Mining Co.'s properties continue to improve in value and development progresses, I will return with a railroad in my pocket."

Mr. Davis has returned, bringing with him (engineers) from Boston for the building of the new road.

After much surveying and planning the Silverton, Gladstone and Northerly R. R. was built and reached the wildly excited settlement on August fourth. Thereafter it hauled the five cars of concentrates a day that the mill was turning out.

In 1907 fire destroyed the surface buildings at the mouth of the mine tunnel, and while only one man was injured three were trapped in the mine and were in danger of suffocation from the fumes and gases that accumulated in the workings. Volunteers from Silverton found the three men alive and uninjured when they entered, but "as the fumes began to tell on the rescuers, one by one became unconscious." More help was sent for, and "one hundred willing workers" arrived by special train but not before six men were dead from the fumes—four of whom were from the first rescue party.

Litigation among the heirs and stockholders for control of the company contributed to the mine's shutdown in 1910, but ore from other properties kept an occasional train rolling until shortly before the tracks were torn up in 1915.

Kinney became interested in the Gold Prince mine at Animas Forks in 1907, and for a few years he was connected with that property; but after the big mine in Gladstone was reopened in 1918 by a new company, he was back again as manager. By 1920 fifty men were at work in both mine and mill, and new ore deposits were adding to the mine's total production record of between eight and nine million dollars since 1895.

On a second trip to Gladstone in June of '42, I was turned back about halfway to the town by a swollen mountain stream which flowed over the road taking the roadbed with it. On my last visit in August, 1945, Gladstone had almost disappeared. I was prepared to find the mill gone, for in Silverton someone had said that "during the scrap metal drive they put a torch to it," but I did not expect to see only the walls of the company houses left. The schoolhouse, too, had gone, except for the facade which was standing half propped against a sagging wall looking very much like a piece of scenery for a Western movie. Most of the mine's offices and sheds were crumpled piles of lumber, and as I drove away I looked at the porch of the cabin for the punching bag. It too was gone.

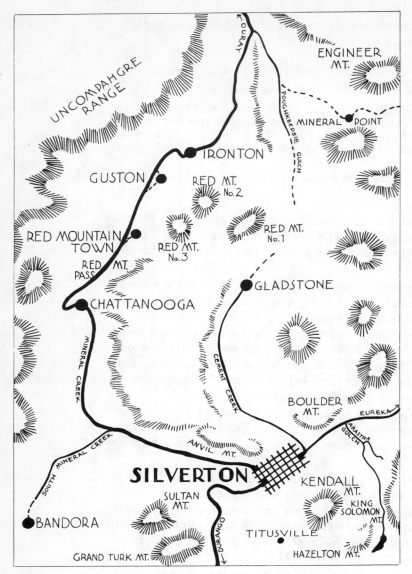

CHAPTER XVII

Silverton and the Red Mountain Mines

THE most spectacular automobile road in Colorado is the Million Dollar Highway between Ouray and Silverton. The scenery is tremendous, the shelf on which one drives is a marvel of engineering, and the mines which line both sides of the highway have poured thousands of dollars into the San Juan. On my first trips to Silverton I knew nothing of the history of the region and was only overwhelmed by the grandeur of the scenery, but now I have a fondness for the mines themselves — the Guston and the Congress, the Joker-Tunnel and the Silver Ledge. Red Mountain is incredibly vivid, especially in afternoon light; and Chattanooga, at the foot of Red Mountain Pass, is dwarfed by the great peaks behind it.

The approach to Silverton crosses one end of the level meadow which comprises Baker's Park and the highway becomes the main street which bisects the city. Silverton, the county seat, although not the oldest settlement in the region, dates from 1874.

It is no wonder that Baker and his party of prospectors were attracted to the green flat where Silverton now stands, as all the surrounding country was ruggedly inhospitable.

Outside of Baker's Park . . . level as the top of a table, and all of which is occupied by the city of Silverton, there does not seem to be enough level land in the whole county for one ordinary "ranch." God never made this country for farming purposes and man has, in that respect never attempted to set aside the will of the Almighty.

There is not a hill or a mountain in the whole county but what is gridironed with fissure veins of gold, silver, copper, lead or iron.—*Silverton Weekly Miner*, Jan. 1, 1897.

The little valley is only a mile wide and less than two in length, but it is watered by the Animas river, Cement creek and Mineral creek; and the mountains which surround it contain some of the richest mines in the San Juan. Anvil mountain "bounds" Baker's Park on the northwest, Boulder and King Solomon mountains lie at the north-eastern end, Kendall mountain protects the southeastern approach, and Sultan mountain, with the Grand Turk looking over its shoulder, forms the southwestern boundary.

The early prospectors looked for colors along the Animas river, following the stream out of the park up past Eureka, and they explored its many gulches —Arastra, Cunningham, Maggie, and Minnie. Later prospectors tramped the banks of Cement creek and its gulches and still others followed Mineral creek to the top of the divide. Everyone was in search of gold but no one found anything but silver. Once convinced, however, that silver was worth while, the miners opened the greatest mineral treasure chest in Colorado, one which produced between 1882 and 1918 alone, metals valued at more than $65,000,000.

Even before the Brunot treaty had been signed with the Utes in 1873, men like Baker and Howard had washed the streambeds and had tested samples of float rock; but most of them had been run off or killed by Indians. In 1871 and 1872, while the treaty was being negotiated, impatient miners worked their way over Stony Pass and began staking claims. By the end of 1873 nearly four thousand had been recorded and most of the big mines had been discovered. About $15,000 was produced in the district that year, of which $12,000 was from the Little Giant.

Real mining began in 1874, and by 1875 the whole region was full of men working feverishly and building the towns of Howardsville, Eureka, Animas Forks, Mineral Point and Silverton. Tom Blair's cabin, built at the mouth of Arastra gulch in 1871, may have marked the "genesis of the silver boom"; but his second cabin, built between Cement creek and the southern end of the valley, was the first in Baker's Park. The next cabin, the first within the limits of the present city, was built by Francis M. Snowden, one of the first pioneers to cross Stony Pass and settle in the new silver field. In his cabin many dances were held during Silverton's first years—the orchestra for such occasions consisted of a man and his wife, one of whom played the fiddle and the other a melodeon. If the couple were invited to play elsewhere, they "loaded the melodeon on a burro" and took him along to the dance.

Silverton

The first water provided for the town was delivered in barrels, which were hauled by a dog team on a wagon in summer and on a sled in winter. Pete Schneider, the owner, got his water from a spring at the base of Kendall mountain and sold it for fifty cents a bucket.

The first newspaper, *La Plata Miner,* was established in July, 1875, and was edited by John R. Curry. Its name was later changed to the *Silverton Miner* but not before the following friendly jibe at the editor of the Lake City *Silver World* appeared.

The *Register Call* (Central City) claims to be the only religious paper in the State. The *Silver World* will doubtless take exception to the claim for they have been giving their readers "Hell" for some time.—*La Plata Miner,* Jan. 11, 1879.

The *Silverton Standard,* Silverton's second paper, appeared in 1889, with Harry Smith and E. H. Snowden as its editors. It was printed on the press which had formerly pounded out the *Solid Muldoon,* and the press is said to be still in use in the *Standard* office.

The Reese Hook and Ladder Co., the first organization of its kind in the San Juan, was organized in 1878 and immediately bought equipment and ordered "neat and tasty uniforms" for its members. When the hook and ladder truck was delivered at Grassy Hill, "half of the male population of Silverton" was there to receive it and haul it by hand over Stony Pass and down to the town. The procession was led during the final stretch of the journey by the Silverton Silver Cornet Band, and in the evening, after the cart was safely lodged in the "handsome hall" provided for it, a big dance was given in its honor.

When in February, 1879, no mail had arrived from Antelope Springs for some time, Silverton's 3000 citizens were "aggravated," especially since the carrier's contract called for six deliveries each week. Finally in desperation the people hired a special carrier to go as far as the Lost Trail post office and bring back any mail that had collected there. He returned with three hundred pounds of it and reported to the incensed citizens that all the mail sent east for the past two weeks had been dumped at the Lost Trail office by his predecessor, and was still there.

Silverton is laid out on the gridiron plan. The streets in one direction are numbered and in the other they are named Animas, Cement and Mineral, for the creeks which flow nearby, and Blair, Greene, Reese, and Snowden for pioneers who contributed to the city's growth. Green Street is the main street, and next to it nearer Kendall Mountain is Blair Street—the "sporting center" of the city in the days when Silverton had thirty-seven saloons that never closed. In front of one of them Clayton Ogsbury was murdered.

A sheriff who came up from Durango with a warrant for two men, Wilkerson and Stockton, asked Night Marshal Clayton Ogsbury to help locate the criminals. Ogsbury saw two men standing on the sidewalk in front of a dance hall and crossed the street toward them trying to identify them. As he advanced both men "pulled their guns and fired," killing him instantly. The town went wild, and during the night a Negro who was completely innocent of the shooting was caught and lynched. Wilkerson and Stockton escaped. At the time of the killing the town was largely controlled by an unruly element which had no respect for law. After this murder a body of vigilantes was organized, and in a short time matters were under control. In addition, the town council hired Bat Masterson from Dodge City and put

SILVERTON
HOMES→

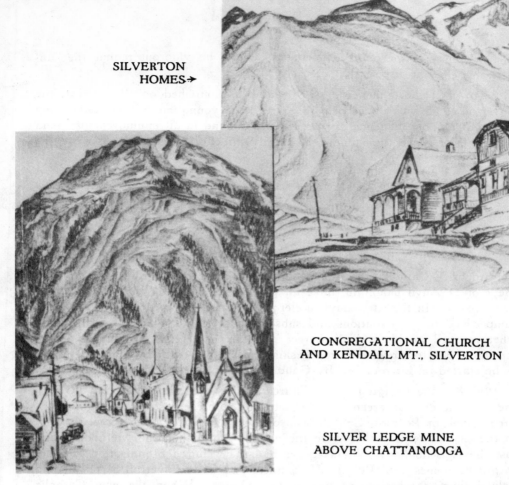

CONGREGATIONAL CHURCH
AND KENDALL MT., SILVERTON

SILVER LEDGE MINE
ABOVE CHATTANOOGA

him in charge of the police department. Under his vigorous regime the "undesirable element dispersed."

To offset the influence of such places as flourished on Blair street, the Silverton Club was opened in 1888 to "keep young men from frequenting places of ignoble influence of which many abound in all mining camps;" and to further improve the "tone" of the city an effort was made to close the gambling dens.

The good Lord has stepped in and helped the councilmen of Silverton to close everything up tight. The councilmen meant to stop all forms of gambling, but the Lord has almost stopped all sorts of business by laying down snow almost waist deep.—*Cripple Creek Morning Times*, Dec. 6, 1895.

Silverton is well supplied with churches—the tall-spired Congregational, the red brick Catholic, the trim Methodist and the rustic frame Episcopal at the foot of Anvil mountain, have all played an important part in the city's development. In the early days, a clergyman who was preaching in a nearby camp asked for contributions and subscriptions toward a $3,000 goal, which when reached would be used to erect a church in the city. He gave the subscription book to a good-natured Irishman who secured many pledges, saying as he started on his rounds, "By Gaud, we must have a church in Silverton."

In 1878 the Congregational Church Society was organized and in 1881 the first church was erected on the site of the present structure. The Congregational, or People's Church, also opened a public reading room, the first in the city. The Catholics were the next to build, then the Methodists and last the Episcopalians. The Negroes had their church organization but met in private homes until Rev. J. W. Sanders arrived in Silverton as pastor and helped them get first a lot and then a church. When the new Catholic church was built in 1883, the Negroes bought the old structure, moved it to their lot, and in a short time paid all their obligations and were out of debt.

Much of Silverton's social life centered around the many fraternal organizations which flourished, especially during the eighties and nineties. The weekly papers were full of notices of meetings and entertainments given under the auspices of the Masons, the Gem Chapter of the Order of the Eastern Star, the Woodmen of the World, Women of Woodcraft, Rathbone Sisters, Fraternal Order of Eagles, and the Silverton Miners' Union which had a membership of 1300. This organization's hall, built in 1901, is still standing. In 1889 the Silverton Jockey Club was organized, and at the driving park where the races were held, the "ladies were talking of having a stand erected for serving refreshments and a platform built for dancing."

In the late eighties Jack Sinclair organized a band. It became famous and gave many performances both in Colorado and in neighboring states—in 1891 it accompanied Gov. Routt's inauguration excursion; it played at Gov. Adam's inauguration; it attended the Cattlemen's Convention in Kansas City, and it performed at Pres. Harrison's inauguration. Jack, who was a showman, put his musicians into western cowboy clothes and called his band the Original Dodge City Cowboy Band, for no good reason except that cowboys were always a drawing card. He always carried a burro with him to demonstrate "how packing was done in a mining camp."

One night a prize fight at the old Walsh smelter drew an unusually big crowd, for it was known that one contestant was much better than the other. As the "professional" was anxious to get a return engagement, however, he made little effort to win. The crowd booed and hissed, and the infuriated referee entered the ring "with a gun strapped to his waist" and "seeing how things were going, pulled his gun and ordered the contestants to fight, not fool." The result was "a quick knock-out by the professional," who thereby lost any chance of being asked to return for another fight.

The people of Silverton celebrated the one hundred-and-thirty-eighth anniversary of the birth of Robert Burns by a program, the proceeds of which were for the benefit of the public school library fund. About $100 was cleared. The following comment appeared in the next issue of the paper:

> We have been told that the sensibilities of some were lacerated because (certain performers) appeared with bare knees at the Robbie Burns entertainment. . . . Such assumed modesty is characteristic of hypocrites. The boys personally informed us that they all washed their legs before the performance and suffered severe colds as the result. These same people who proffer their criticism on this occasion would break their necks in a front seat at some really obnoxious entertainment—a circus for example. Come off the perch, you are not so high in public estimation as you would soar.—*Silverton Weekly Miner and Red Mt. Journal*, Jan. 29, 1897.

The following obituary carries so many overtones of life in the nineties that it is printed here as it appeared in the *Silverton Weekly Miner* of July 9, 1897, except for the omission of names.

> The entire population of Silverton extend to S— S— sincere condolences. The loss of a wife robs him of a home and robs this community of one of its best characters of womanhood. No woman was more respected, more beloved by those who knew her than was Mrs. S—. Death resulted from child birth, and though the mother has departed the father can get some consolation from the little spark she left as proof of her existence. It was a life given for a life. Mrs. S—had given birth to four children in previous years but they all died. It seems it was not her lot to have a 'home well won and children by her side.' The deceased was twenty-eight years of age. . . It is too bad, Sam, but be brave and remember that 'while from a sigh,
>
> God's plans· go on as best for you and me;
> How, when we called, He heeded not one cry,
> Because His wisdom to the end could see.'

When the Denver and Rio Grande extended its rails in 1882 from Durango up Animas canyon through tortuous mountains and along rock ledges to the growing city of Silverton, it provided a much-needed outlet for the increasing mineral production of the entire district. The first passenger train entered Silverton on July 3, 1882, and in honor of the event "a wild, hilarious time was enjoyed by the populace for several days."

Silverton expects to be isolated for intervals during the winter and spring by slides which close the passes or bury the track of the D. & R. G. in Animas canyon under tons of snow.

The Silverton Railroad train with Nate Hunter's army of snow shovelers arrived in town Wednesday evening and opened the road. Nate promised the boys two kegs of beer if they got through (four small slides) 'that night, and they did.—*Silverton Standard*, Feb. 1, 1890.

Silverton Closed to the World.

Trains are stalled. . . . Five men were lost in a slide at the Sunnyside. . . . The last D. & R. G. whistle to wake the echoes was last Wednesday, the 17th. Snow fell for three days—then there were howling gales. . . . Eleven snowslides are down, seven to thirty feet deep and from fifty to four hundred and fifty feet long.

One of the larger slides plunged into the river bed, forming a dam. The river backed up several hundred feet, covering the railroad tracks, and then froze . . . . can't clear the track for another week. Mail is brought in by jack train.—*Silverton Standard*, Jan. 27, 1906.

In March, 1906, snow fell for more than a week, during which time nearly every slide in the county ran, and the week's toll was twenty deaths. Thirteen men were lost when a slide destroyed the Shenandoah boarding-house. Men from the mine wrapped the bodies in canvas, tied them on sleds made of two skiis, and then dragged them for miles through deep snow over the very drifts made by the slide which killed them.

Lake City's editor taunted Silverton on its over-abundant supply of snow, even as far back as 1877, by saying:

The citizens of Silverton turned out in force on the 5th instant to open the road to Antelope Park. While working in old snow twelve feet deep, two snowstorms occurred, depositing sixteen inches more of the beautiful . . . Come over into God's country and enjoy strawberries and cream and wear linen clothes.—*Silver World*, June 16, 1877.

By the end of the nineties Silverton prided itself on being the up-to-date city and county seat it still is.

Daily old landmarks are disappearing . . . and on their sites are being reared the majestic piles of progress.—*Silverton Weekly Miner*, Jan. 1, 1897.

When Silverton in 1899 objected to cows running loose on the streets and two years later became the "first city in the United States to own its public utilities," to quote a phrase from the *Red Mt. Mining Journal*, it "began to put on metropolitan airs."

In my search for early history I haunt the newspaper offices and the libraries, and in Silverton I found both places storehouses of information. The library had stacks of old papers, all bound and easily accessible, and the librarian was unusually gracious and helpful in digging up certain years and issues for me. I shall never forget my excitement as I opened a crackling, musty volume which I supposed was a Silverton paper and found instead that it was the *Red Mt. Mining Journal*, which I had discovered in no other collection. The library is one of the best that I have consulted and from the librarian I learned its history. In 1903 a group of citizens met to discuss ways of providing a more adequate free reading room for the city, and the pastor of the Congregational church told of his experience in establishing a public library in Indiana. It was found that "Andrew Carnegie would gladly contribute an amount sufficient to build and equip" a library if the town would arrange for its support. The striking building on Reese street with its thousands of volumes of up-to-date periodicals is the result of that civic effort.

On my first trip to Silverton I stayed at the Imperial Hotel with its mansard roof and battery of dormer windows, but not until last year when I was deep in historical research did I discover that the hotel, originally called the Grand, was built in 1882 by the Thompson brothers, who took pains to make it the "finest hotel on the western slope except La Veta at Gunnison." Nor did I know that the whole second floor was once rented by the county and used as a courthouse until the present structure was completed. In the hotel restaurant I was impressed by the massive mahogany bar and fine mirrors, relics of the days when it was the popular Hub Saloon, full of miners, gamblers and travelling men. One night a stranger was sitting in the saloon when the wife of a colored porter bounced through the side door from the hotel lobby, saying: "If I don't find that coon there will be a hot time in this old town tonight." Inspired by her threat the man took some paper from his pocket, and jotted down the words of the now famous song, "There'll Be a Hot Time in the Old Town Tonight."

The Courthouse was begun in 1907 but was not completed until the following year. It is a big structure, built of "pressed brick of gray color with gray lava stone trimmings," and it occupies the center of an entire city block. Inside I was shown not only many old maps but the original plat of the town of Eureka, beautifully drawn and hand-lettered with scrolls and flourishes. Outside on the lawn is a monument that tells graphically the story of Silverton's mines, and on each trip to the city I have studied its inscriptions. A bronze map shows the location of the surrounding mountains and creeks, and each side of the pedestal lists by name the mines in certain areas. To further identify them as well as ornament the marker, specimens of ore from the same mines are imbedded in the concrete base. Just to read the list of names made me more aware than I'd ever been of the part that mining played in the development of the San Juan.

The monument, which was sponsored by the Silverton Rotary Club and the County Commissioners, was erected in 1941 and is dedicated to the Mining Industry of San Juan County. The mines listed are:

Old Hundred	Toltec	Lead Carbonate
Highland Mary	Columbus	Mogul
Pride of the West	Polar Star	Henrietta
Buffalo Boy	Silver Wing	Joe and John
Black Prince	Treasure Mountain	Anglo Saxon
Molas	Little Ida	Brooklyn
Little Giant	Mountain Queen	Yukon
Little Fanny	San Juan Chief	Independence
Green Mountain	Frisco Tunnel	Robert Bonner
Shenandoah Dives	Lucky Jack	Bandora
Aspen	Tom Moore	Silver Ledge
Eyra R.	Ridgway	Champion
Silver Lake	Caledonia	Mystery
Royal Tiger	Hamlet	Little Dora
Iowa	Little Nation	Coming Wonder
London	Kittimac	Queen City
Sunnyside	Gold King	North Star Sultan

No sooner had I read this impressive list than I wanted to find some of the mines and their mills. Those up Cunningham gulch and Cement creek I knew (even to the Queen of Cement which is not listed); but those closest to town were unfamiliar to me. The next couple of days I spent sketching every old mill I could find, and as I drew I wondered about its history.

Just beyond the town along the bank of the Animas river stands a big empty mill with a whole battery of windows down its sides, but not until I had shown my sketch to a miner in Silverton did I discover what I'd drawn.

"That's the Silver Lake-Aspen mill," said the miner. "The Aspen was one of the first mines located here and from the time of its discovery and sale by Tom Blair it's been a shipper in the A1 class. Why, even after thirty or more years of surface scratching and gophering by leasers who took out $1,000,000, it's still a good mine. Now its part of the Silver Lake property and is worked through their big mill.

"When this mill was built in 1907 it was the last word in construction. Instead of putting the windows in the roof, Madge, the designer, put them down the sides, like steps, and after that, every new mill was built that way. There had been a mill on the property before, and this one was built on the old foundations."

"You've told me about the Aspen. Where did the Silver Lake come in?" I interrupted.

"I'm coming to that. The Silver Lake Basin, twelve miles from Silverton, is high on Solomon mountain and in it are many big mines all above 12,000 feet. The lodes are large and nearly all carry high-grade ore. One of the biggest is the Silver Lake—a constant producer since 1886—and its gross production was $11,000,000 from $17\frac{1}{2}$ miles of underground workings. Of course it had low grade ore, too, but they didn't bother with it until they built their first mill in 1890 and began to turn out concentrates. That mill operated all through the silver panic, and then in 1901 the property was bought by the Guggenheims for $250,000, and three months after they took over the ore ran out. Everyone thought they'd been rooked for once and talked about Silver Lake as the first big mine to be abandoned in the district, but the company kept right on working a hundred miners and a full force of men to develop the property. Then in December, 1902, the first shipment of ore was made and the mill started up again and by 1905 the Silver Lake had produced over 100,000 tons of crude ore and was employing three hundred and fifty men.

"Before 1902 the principal holdings of the company were the Silver Lake and New York City groups. Then in the summer of 1902, the Titusville group was added. It was over the crest of Kendall mountain from the Silver Lake and Iowa mines at an altitude of 12,500 feet. The mine had been worked from 1890-1893 and then shut down. The mill you drew was the one built in 1907 near the mouth of Arastra gulch. It had the first tramline in the county, too. I rode over it more than once."

"I read about a hair-raising ride in a bucket on the Silver Lake tram. Was it the same one?"

SILVERTON AND ROAD TO DURANGO, 1941.

"I don't know, lady. I don't read much; but if you look up Arastra gulch you can see the tram they use today. Maybe it's the same one."

That afternoon I went back to the gulch which is opposite the Shenandoah Dives mill and as I watched the buckets clicking overhead, I recalled the story told by Marion A. Spier in *Western Trails Through Seven States*. Spier, who was employed at the Silver Lake mine, describes the tram ride. Because of the broken character of the land, the tram-towers from the valley to the mine (which is close to the top of the mountain) varied in height and in location. Some were short, some tall, and where the tram crossed upper Arastra gulch the towers were far apart and the bottom of the canyon 3000 feet below. The grade at that point was seventy percent, or almost straight up! A long bucket, or "dead" bucket, was used to send sick men down from the mine, or the bodies of those who died in an accident, and it was in this bucket that Spier made his ride. He found it exciting enough even before the bucket reached the long span between towers. Here its gyrations increased until it was swaying rhythmically up and down with a variation of several hundred feet. One such ride was enough for him.

I had hoped to find another big mill like the Silver Lake-Aspen up Arastra gulch at the Iowa-Tiger property, but it was no longer standing. I knew about the North Star mine on King Solomon mountain with its entrance at 13,300 feet—said to be the highest operating mine in Colorado—and I knew that in 1874 John J. Crooke had purchased an interest in the then unpatented North Star claim. He and his co-owners did assessment work for that year, but as they did it "short," the mine was jumped. When Crooke, who still wanted the property, tried to buy it back from the new owners he had to pay $8,000 for it; but he made it a constant shipper. During the winter the ore collected on the mine dump, and to move it a toboggan sled was rigged up and run between the mine and the mill. Two thousand tons of ore were taken down the mountain on the sled.

While I sat beside the highway looking up Arastra gulch where so much of the early mining was done, I was almost blinded by the clouds of powdery rock which blew across the road from the huge settling ponds of the Shenandoah Dives mill, directly behind me.

The 10,000-foot tramway from the mine crosses the road at a height of fifty feet, delivering an endless line of buckets into the maw of the mill and returning with empty buckets which bob along on the cables till they seem to disappear up Arastra gulch. On the south slope of King Solomon mountain, at the far end of the gulch and so high on the sheer mountainside that it seems pasted against the rock, is the main portal of the mine and the other end of the tram.

The Shenandoah, the Dives and the Mayflower lodes date back to the early eighties; but according to mine reports the Shenandoah Dives Company was not formed until 1929 and the first mill was not built until 1933. The present holdings of the company include many other properties—the North Star, the Terrible, the Slide and the Silver Lake group. Some portions of the Shenandoah group have produced considerable amounts of ore since 1871. The present 700-ton selective flotation mill, which is operating to capacity, is equipped with the most modern processes and machinery and employs more people than any other mine in the southwest. It is also a custom mill, handling ore from other mines than those owned by the company.

Silverton had two North Star mines, one on King Solomon mountain and the other on Sultan mountain. Having seen the former, I drove to the far end of town to the base of Sultan to look for the other. The North Star mill was in ruins and did not look as if $7,000,000 worth of ore had ever run through its machinery. During the time when big companies were consolidating many small properties and combining many claims for more economical production, the Hercules Co. bought up the holdings of five companies and began to work twenty-six claims, which included the North Star and the Little Dora, whose mill was also nearby.

Another old building that looked interesting was the stone brewery at at the foot of the same mountain. Its owner was Charles Fischer, who came to the San Juan in 1873 and started a brewery at Howardsville on a small scale. He then moved his business to Silverton and built the stone structure, with its cellars and vaults cut into the solid granite at the base of the mountain. A well-known and popular feature of the building was the faucet and handy mug placed outside, at which all visitors were welcome to drink free of charge. "Mr. Fischer makes it a practice never to send a visitor away hampered with thirst." In 1907 a new firm operated the brewery and advertised:

> We use neither corn nor rice in our beer for intoxicating purposes, the beverage being a strictly A1 tonic.

On a flat across the road from the brewery was the black dump of the Walsh smelter, and, curious as usual, I began investigating Silverton's smelter history. In 1875, years before Walsh came into the picture, Greene and Co. blew in the first smelter, packing in the machinery on burros over Stony Pass before there were any roads. Consequently the cost of each brick used for the furnace and stack was $1.15! The smelter, which ran until 1881 when Greene removed it to Durango, was the first successful waterjacket type in Colorado. It was built, so far as I have been able to find out, down near the railroad yards.

The next year, 1882, the Martha Rose smelter was built across from the brewery, but it was unsuccessful and soon closed down. In 1894 Thomas Walsh opened a matte smelter at the old Martha Rose property, buying siliceous ore for flux wherever he could get it. In fact, it was while on a prospecting trip in search of such ore that he discovered the famous Camp Bird mine which made his fortune. His smelter handled a considerable portion of the ore of the region, especially that mined at Red Mountain.

In 1893, J. J. Crooke built a smelter, said to be the first in the United States which produced both gold and silver bullion.

> He is also the inventor of tin-foiling and receives a royalty on all tin-foil made and also a royalty on all ores treated by the Crooke copper process in use at the Pueblo smelter and at other points.—*Silverton Standard*, Dec. 9, 1893.

A smelter, built by Kendrick and Gelder, was placed near the mouth of Cement creek in 1900. In 1906 it became the Ross smelter and opened a home market for quantities of pyritic and sulphide ores. In addition to the smelters, D. Duyckinck & Co. and G. H. Stoiber ran ore sampling works down near the railroad tracks. Today only dingy dumps mark the smelter sites, for the buildings have long since been razed.

Silverton began as the heart of the Silvery San Juan, but by the time of the silver crash some gold had been found in certain properties and further developments revealed greater quantities of the precious metal. By 1897 half the mineral output was gold—silver, lead and copper made up the rest—and the region was renamed the Golden San Juan. During the nineties great strides were also made in mining machinery and methods of production. Aerial wire tramways were built between the mines and all the bigger mills, and the day of the burro pack-train was over. No attempt to concentrate low grade ore was made until 1890, but thereafter tremendous amounts of such ore were mined profitably.

> Between 1890 and 1891 there was so much mining that the railroad could not move the ore fast enough, so all kinds of concentration and reduction plants had to be established.
>
> Within the last six years there has been a revolution. The brawn and sinew of the husky miner has given way to the air drill; that faithful though lazy and indifferent animal the burro, has willingly given over to the Bleichert and Huson tramway system the burdens of freighting. . . Today if you go to Silverton, you hear no talk save of gold mines. White metal is out of fashion and is not searched for as eagerly as in the days before the late unpleasantness of 1893.—*Silverton Weekly Miner,* Jan. 1, 1897.

Typical of the miners' reaction to the Bryan-McKinley presidential campaign were the sixteen votes cast in the whole of San Juan county for McKinley. Bryan's campaign was based on the free silver platform, and "after the election, only two people were willing to acknowledge voting for McKinley—one of whom was the Republican postmaster."

In 1910, when autmobiles were a novelty, one of Silverton's county commissioners, Louis Wyman, invited D. L. Mechling of Denver and John A. McQuire, editor of *Outdoor Life,* to bring Mechling's car, a thirty-horsepower Croxton-Keeton, into San Juan county. The trip took five days and caused a great deal of excitement and interest all along the way. Wyman met the two men at Grassy Hill and "with the aid of the county team succeeded in negotiating Stony Pass." From the foot of the pass to Silverton the car ran under its own power, and as it rolled into the main street and drew up at the new City Hall its occupants were greeted by a welcome of the entire town. The next day, with further assistance from the county team, the car reached Ouray.

I always hate to leave Silverton, for no other part of the state has mountains which are so awe-inspiring and which rise so roughly and yet majestically from the high valleys at their feet; and each time I visit the mountain-bound city I am eager to learn more about the mines and the men who made them.

There is Titusville on Kendall mountain, which once had a population of 600 and now is marked, I am told, only by bits of broken machinery; and there is Arastra Gulch, so full of history. When I look at the Shenandoah-Dives mill and watch its endless line of buckets travelling so easily through the air I think of the days when Rocky Mountain "canaries" plodded over the narrow trails loaded with whisky, beer, boxes of dynamite or quarters of beef on the way up to the mines, and with sacked ore on the way down. I can almost hear the screech of the steel rails and heavy timbers that were tied to their backs in such a way that one end dragged on the ground, bumping and scraping over the rocks.

"Silverton used to have 3000 people. Now it has 1500; yet we move more ore than we did when the 3000 were in camp. The monthly payroll at the Shenandoah-Dives is about $40,000, and as Silverton hasn't a bank nowadays, the money is brought over from Ouray heavily guarded. Pay night is a big thing in Silverton," said one of its leading citizens to me on my most recent trip to the city. "It used to be that the mines needed three men where only one is needed now. That threw two out of work. Improved machinery and simplified milling processes have made it possible for three men to run a three-hundred-ton mill where many used to be necessary. In the old days there was one man to every ten or twenty crushing-stamps and there were men all over the mill. Sure, some of Silverton's houses are empty and some need a coat of paint. Renters don't spend money for improvements to property. If you own your own house you keep it up. In spite of the vacant houses we're more alive than ever. Remember that."

"What about Bandora? Should I go there?" I asked the garage man in Silverton who knew so much about the mines. *Bandora*

"They're hauling from there, but there aren't any old buildings left anymore," he replied. "I remember seeing a boardinghouse and a stable and a blacksmith shop near the mine, but that was years ago. They found some gold up South Mineral creek in 1882, and Bill Sullivan used to ship ore from the Little Tod before 1890. During the nineties some rich pockets were opened up at Bandora in the Ice Lake district. The Bandora ores were high grade but they could sure tangle up the smelters. Since 1940 the Blanco Mining Company (that's the old Bandora property) sends all its ore to the Shenandoah-Dives custom mill here in Silverton for treatment. They're working the Esmeralda, too."

Taking his word for it that all the old landmarks were gone, I crossed Bandora off my list of places to investigate. Whenever I leave Silverton for Ouray and pass the turn-off to South Mineral creek, I look up the road as far as I can see and I wonder what lies around the curve. Someday I'm going to find out.

The drive from Silverton over Red Mountain Pass to Ouray is always *Red Mountain* thrilling, for it and the Trail Ridge drive over the Divide beyond Estes Park *Pass* are the two most stupendous scenically that exist in the state. From Silverton to Chattanooga the climb is a steady one, and each mile takes one closer to the upthrust, towering peaks which overshadow the road. But it is beyond Chattanooga that the road really starts toward the top of the pass,

(433)

rising so sharply toward the goal that in a very few miles the 11,018-foot summit is reached. The great, snowy peaks seem to rise as you climb, until even on top they look just as high and far away as they did miles below in the valley.

The Red Mountain area is honeycombed with mines, all packed into a relatively small but rich area about eight miles in length and less in width, which occupies the heart of the Uncompahgre mountains. There are mines everywhere, to the right of the road and to the left, some perched so high above the highway that their shaft houses are barely discernible, and some below the level of the road which sweeps down through the mountain tops to Ironton Park, only four miles below in a series of switchback curves. Three towns laid out in this compact, rich, mineral area were Red Mountain Town, Guston and Ironton, with the big mines like the Yankee Girl, the Guston and the National Belle so conveniently sandwiched in between them that each town could claim the riches which they produced.

All along the highway from Silverton to Ouray are little ghost settlements close to the mines. Now that I knew the history of these places my desire to identify them made it difficult for me to keep my eyes on the road. On one old map I had found names of settlements or of stage stops of whose existence I had been ignorant. A short distance from Silverton was Burro Ridge; next came Chattanooga; then followed Summit, Guston, Red Mountain and Ironton.

On the morning that Francis and I started the climb out of Silverton, I looked as I always do, up South Mineral creek towards invisible Bandora, and I tried to identify the exact position of Burro Ridge. On a high meadow, just as the road swings left and heads straight toward the mountains before starting up the pass, stands the ghost settlement of Chattanooga.

Chattanooga   Mill creek rushes into Mineral creek at Chattanooga, and spotted along the entire gulch "in a string" were the Silver Crown group of mines—the highest at the head of the steep gulch and the lowest close to the town. The group was first located in 1878 before the Denver and Rio Grande Southern reached Silverton; so the shipment of ore meant a two hundred-mile wagon haul with a fifty-dollar freight charge. After the silver slump the mines were idle for years.

Chattanooga was a junction point at which freight was reloaded onto pack trains from teamsters' wagons if starting over Red Mountain to Ouray and from burros to wagons if the destination was Silverton. After Jim Sheridan opened his hotel, saloon and livery stable at Chattanooga, his place was spoken of as Sheridan Junction. Even when Otto Mears built and operated his famous toll road over the pass it was both narrow and very rough in places. The *Solid Muldoon* (April 13, 1883) took exception to it by saying:

> The wagon road from Silverton to Chattanooga is dangerous even to pedestrians . . . The average depth of mud is three feet. . . . The grade is four parts vertical and one part perpendicular.

When a gold strike was made near Chattanooga in 1893 in the Hoosier

(434)

RED MOUNTAIN TOWN

↓ IRONTON

Boy mine, prospectors rushed in; for the ore which was very rich, "lay in the quartz in wires and cubes," and the miners were sure they had found a good thing.

> Since the strike, there have been fifty-two locations in the district. Excitement is at fever heat—all are confident that Cripple Creek cannot show anything like it.—*Silverton Standard*, Nov. 25, 1893.

Unfortunately, their hopes were not realized, for the deposits played out and the boom was over.

The elements did their best to destroy the town on more than one occasion. Fire swept away a good portion of the place in August, 1892, and it was never rebuilt. Then a snowslide tore directly through what had been left, so that today hardly a dozen weathered, empty buildings mark the site of the once enterprising community. The Rev. J. J. Gibbons, in his *Sketches in the San Juan*, (1898), describes what was left after the slide:

> Ruins of roofs and sides of houses were strewn for half a mile over the valley and the population of this once flourishing hamlet dwindled down to two. One of these kept a saloon, which was a sort of halfway house between Red Mt. and Silverton. The other, who was a widow with many children, appeared to be in the laundry business . . . for the clotheslines were always full.

"That's the Silver Ledge mine ahead," I said when we left Chattanooga and started the long pull up Red Mountain Pass. "The mill was down at Chattanooga, but it's been in ruins for years. The shaft house at the mine was destroyed by an explosion in 1891. Just as the night shift sat down to supper in the boardinghouse the fire broke out. It was caused by a lighted candle igniting some waste, and in a minute the building was a furnace. The forty pounds of giant stored in the building caused the explosion that wrecked everything.

"At the time of the fire two men were down in the shaft, and the first they knew that anything was wrong was when the bell-cord came tumbling down at their feet. A few minutes later the bucket came down with a bang and all the rope after it, for the explosion had released the brake which held it. The men were now really frightened, but they managed to get out all right. From 1892 to 1898 the Ledge was in 'rich bonanza' and worked a full force of men. Then in the spring of 1898 it closed down for a while because of lack of water to run its boiler. There had been very little snow the preceding winter and the streams were still frozen solid and there was nothing they could do about it.

"The Silver Ledge mill was the first in the county to install magnetic machines which successfully separated the iron from the lead-zinc ore, thus rendering the zinc a marketable product. That was in 1904, and I don't know when the property was worked for the last time; but it has looked deserted since the first time I saw it."

Red Mountain Town

With all the times I've been over Red Mountain Pass I failed to find the town of that name until the fall of 1947. Both the highway and the mountain sides are lined with mines from the summit of the pass to below

(436)

Ironton Park, but the greatest concentration of buildings and dumps is in front of the incredibly red mountain with its iron-stained sides. As seen from the Million Dollar Highway, these mines cover an area about four miles in length and behind them Red Mountain looms up like a backdrop to some Wagnerian opera, with the mines and their buildings as the details in the setting. Two twisting dirt roads cross the valley from the highway to the mines—one "taking off" through the Treasury Tunnel property and the other from about a half mile further north.

The surface buildings of the mines in the Red Mountain district have been almost obliterated by more than one fire, and the town itself was partially destroyed in 1892. One miner to whom I talked remembered the night when fire broke out in the Red Mountain Hotel. "Everybody began piling furniture and bedding in the middle of the street. I can see them yet— men staggering out of the pool halls with billiard tables and roulette wheels, and women carrying silly things like lamps and quilts. Before they got them all piled up the wind changed, and the flames licked everything up."

In 1938, when I first wandered from mine to mine in this spectacular setting, there were many more buildings of all sorts than there are today. I remember in particular, climbing to the edge of a dump down near the Guston mine, and seeing below a large, two-story boardinghouse. On my next visit nothing seemed in the right location. In Silverton I learned that another fire, the year before, had destroyed most of the shaft houses and other surface buildings, leaving only crumbling dumps, charred walls, and the twisted, melted, blackened metal of old machinery.

The first flurry of mining was in 1879 when a little silver was found near the huge Red Mountain. "The excitement is intense; our streets are becoming deserted and he who cannot get a pack animal shoulders his blankets and grub and takes his way toward Red Mt. Park," wrote the *Ouray Times* on Aug. 23, 1879; but the severe winters and the lack of roads retarded any further boom in the region until late in 1882.

One of the first discoveries was the National Belle, which became a steady producer. The prospectors who located it broke into the knoll where the mine was hidden, and were amazed to find a giant cavern, filled with rich lead carbonates which glittered in the light of their candles. Masses of lead were imbedded in the walls and ceiling of the cave and were piled in a mound on its floor. In time, fifty to ninety tons per day were taken from the caves; but when they were exhausted and the mine was developed at deeper levels, the ore found was copper. The Congress and the Summit mines were discovered soon afterwards as well as the Enterprise, whose ore was "solid copper from the grass roots."

Although it was winter when these discoveries became known, "clouds of prospectors" drifted in and located their claims in ten feet of snow. By the end of January, 1883, the new town of Red Mountain was beginning to boom. Carpenters and loggers were going in every day, and a trail was being shoveled from Silverton over which boilers and heavy parts of machinery were to be brought in by tandem teams. Apparently the new camp was over-praised by the editors of two papers which appeared almost as

(437)

soon as tents began to dot the hillsides, and the *Solid Muldoon* with its customary frankness published the following blast:

> The *Red Mt. Pilot* and *Red Mt. Review* are both published in Silverton and are a tissue of falsehoods.
>
> There is but one tent and three bunches of shingles in Red Mt. City, they blow so much about, and the miners of Red Mt. refuse to patronize or tolerate such frauds. Both the enterprising editors have been ordered out of camp. Red Mt. needs neither gush nor exaggeration. We have ore enough in sight to attract capitalists and insure permanency and do not desire the services of journalists who are willing to do an unlimited amount of lying for a certain number of town lots. Curry and Raymond would kill any camp.—*Solid Muldoon*, Jan. 19, 1883.

In less than two months, however, the *Muldoon* admitted that progress had been made, by printing the following paragraphs:

> Five weeks ago the site where Red Mt. now stands was woodland mesa, covered with heavy spruce timber. Today, hotels, printing offices, groceries, meat markets, . . . a telephone office, saloons, dance houses are up and booming; the blast is heard on every side and prospectors can be seen snowshoeing in every direction.
>
> Everything has been packed or sledded over or under three feet of snow. . . We predict that by Sept. 1, Red Mt. will have a population of nearly ten thousand and a daily output surpassed by Leadville only.—March 9, 1883.

For months, according to the *Rocky Mt. Mining Review,*

> . . . the camp was accessible only by precipitous and dangerous trails. Every ounce of food, pound of mining implements and foot of lumber were transported by jacks through shine and storm. Today, the camp is reached from Ouray by what will in a few weeks be the grandest highway in the Rocky Mountains—covering a distance of seven miles and costing over $10,000 to the mile.

(This is the first mention of Otto Mears' Toll road, the predecessor of the present Million Dollar Highway.)

There were several routes to the Red Mountain district, but none of them was easy. One was from Lake City to Mineral Point, then by trail to the head of Poughkeepsie gulch, and down Cement creek on a good wagon road to Dela Mino, a new camp built since the Red Mountain excitement. From Dela Mino a trail went to Red Mountain town, making a total distance of thirty miles. Dela Mino was simply an unpacking point for burro trains, and from it the ore was carried in wagons into Silverton. Another route was up Dry gulch, between Gladstone and Dela Mino, and then up a trail to the camp; and a third way was from Mineral Point partway down the Ouray trail and then north to the mines. In the autumn of 1883, as the mines of the district became steady producers and large amounts of eastern capital were invested in them, Otto Mears, always alert to transportation needs, began to build his famous toll roads. One led from Sheridan Junction to the Yankee Girl mine and another ran from Ouray to the skyline camp, 11,300 feet high, at the top of the pass. Over this road the pack trains and freight wagons moved in an endless stream.

Because of conflicting accounts it is difficult to determine the exact location of Red Mountain town prior to 1886, when it was moved to the place it occupies at present. The original townsite was on Congress hill, near the Congress mine, and it was later referred to as Old Congress Town; and Upper Red Mountain town was also mentioned as well as the towns listed below in a clipping from a paper of 1883.

> Could it be that this town was built in from two to six feet of snow? It was and Congress also. . . . The architecture of the buildings is not at all attractive. Many of them stand on uncertain footing, are wapple-jawed or bias and one of the grand hotels at Congress looks cross-eyed out of many a miss-set window frame. Red Mountain Town has an unsteady look, after the boom, but there is still a healthy glow.

And to further confuse the issue, in April, 1883, a Lake City paper wrote:

> Red Mt. City is halfway from Chattanooga to Red Mountain Town. Red Mt. City is on the Silverton side of the mountains. . . . We then cross the divide and travel one mile on the Ouray side to Red Mt. Town. At present this seems to be the future great of the Red Mt. Mining Region.

In the fall of 1886 the town was moved bodily to a new location, a flat at the head of Red Mountain creek—and sixty substantial buildings were erected to accommodate the population. Some say that the townspeople wanted to be close to Mears' new toll road, which was built through the flat, and others say that when Slover and Wright, the largest liquor dealers in the district, built the first and largest building at the new location, the rest of the town just naturally followed. These two men not only built their saloon and club rooms, "which were an honor to a town . . . much older than this," but they put up other buildings which were occupied at once. By Nov. 11, 1886, according to the *San Juan Democrat*, "The town of Red Mt. is putting in waterworks and assuming other metropolitan airs," such as the Red Mt. Hook and Ladder Co. Hose House. The "Hose house is completed and ready for the implements of deluge. Hose, reel, hooks and ladder, buckets, etc., are ordered and as soon as they get here the honored chief will call a meeting of citizens to organize a company."

All during 1887 the town continued to grow, and a new newspaper appeared—the *Red Mountain Mining Journal*—which was published every Saturday in the "Mineral Hub of the Universe."

"Gid R. Propper, the 'rolling stone' of San Juan journalists, yanks the lever, wields the scissors and is the brains of the concern and it is apparent to us that is a venture in the direction of success," wrote the editor of the *Rico News* in October, when the paper appeared. In the very first issue is this tidbit copied from the *Telluride Republican*:

> Red Mountain is prolific in weddings. It is a lonesome place to live in and the young people are not to be blamed for doubling up. A man who will sleep alone during a winter in Red Mt. either has no affection for the fair sex or they have none for him. Besides, Red Mt. needs an increased population.—*Red Mountain Mining Journal*, Oct. 1, 1887.

Not all the miners spent the entire year in the lofty camp which drowsed under a blanket of snow most of the winter, but those who stayed wanted no sympathy. A well-organized musical society, the Knights of Labor, and the Odd Fellows were all "prepared to make camp pleasant during the winter in numerous ways of enjoyment."

> As a class all are united and nothing intervenes to mar the happiness of all who have cast their winter lot in the camp, and a silver lining and plumage of hope and prosperity are now assured.
>
> The mines are on all sides. The men have but a short walk to work and the whistle for meals and shift time breaks the gloom of what may seem an isolated or desolate camp. It is a town of happiness unconfined the year round.—*Red Mountain Mining Journal,* Nov. 26, 1887.

Yet on November 29th the editor complained that Thanksgiving is the "day set apart by the President for giving thanks. That's all right but who are we going to thank for our turkey that we haven't got?"

Early in 1888 the following comment appeared in the paper:

> The town is five years old and as yet there is no graveyard. Two children have died from unnatural causes. We should be contented.

By 1889 English and American capitalists had invested millions in the mines of the region, Red Mountain was the liveliest it had been since 1883, and every mine in the vicinity was working. Such activity caused the *San Juan Democrat* of Feb. 14, 1889, to remark:

> Red Mt. is destined to become a great metropolis, as one of these days it will take into its corporate limits such suburban villages as Sheridan Junction, Ironton, Guston and the high line trail.

In the meantime, Otto Mears' toll road was in constant use, but it was not enough—a railroad was needed.

> Instead of waiting for a newly discovered camp to grow and develop the need for roads, he at once utilized the old trails, constructed roads and thus helped to make the camp. When he saw that the Silverton and Red Mt. districts had outgrown the roads he had built, he commenced the construction of a railroad winding its iron arms around the mountains with its rainbow curves tapping every principal mine in the Red Mt. district.—*Mines and Mining Men of Colorado.*

The road was begun in June, 1887, and was completed to the Red Mountain mines by September, 1888, and to Ironton by November of the same year. The people at Red Mountain watched each day's progress with the greatest of interest, for the arrival of the road in town would give an even greater spurt to mining.

> It has been casually suggested that when the graders begin moving dirt through Red Mt., a day be set apart by a number of our citizens and leisure hour people and that they make 500 feet of grade for the railroad. At the same time we should arrange to have a silver spike driven in the most central part of the track. The people of Chattanooga are to have a ball; the people of Silverton, at the instigation of the Jockey Club, raised $500 to celebrate the first train down from Red Mt. Now, we must certainly do something to show our appreciation of the coming event.
>
> The graders are between Chattanooga and Old Congress Town.—*Red Mountain Mining Journal,* Oct. 1, 1887.

The road was

> A unique and daring piece of railroad engineering. Originating at Silverton where it connects with the D. & R. G. system, it runs north twenty miles and ends. Half of the distance it ascends the mountain at an average grade of 212 feet to the mile, crossing the pass at an altitude of 11,650 feet. From this point, surrounded by the snows of centuries, it descends to Ironton, at about the same grade, making a bow over the mountains, hence the name the Rainbow Route. . . .

> Otto Mears built it contrary to the advice of capitalists, but the result has demonstrated his wisdom.

> It carries from 20,000 to 25,000 tons of ore out of the district annually and 15,000 tons of coal into it. Receiving its silvery traffic from the realms of eternal snow, on bands of steel, it passes it down through the drifting clouds to add to the sum of the nation's wealth.—*Silverton Weekly Miner*, Jan. 1, 1897.

When Mears issued passes on his railroad, he gave out not the usual flabby strips of cardboard, but filigree-bordered plates of gold or silver bearing the recipient's name. Passes issued to less important persons were made of buckskin. The railroad grade through Red Mountain town ran just below the houses, barely missing the lowest row. It then made a long switchback from the National Belle to the flats and back to town again. From there it dropped on down the valley to Ironton.

Winter always meant almost constant work on the railroad. After every heavy snow large gangs of men had to dig out the track—fifty men starting from Silverton, forty more from the Junction and another fifty from the Yankee Girl and Guston on Red mountain.

The town never lacked entertainment, although on account of its isolation it was forced to furnish its own talent. The first performance of the Red Mountain Lyceum and Dramatic Association was given on Feb. 8, 1888, one week after its organization. A song by the club, "Dipped in the Golden Sea," was given with gusto; one of the members rendered a guitar solo, "The Siege of Sebastapol." This was followed by O. K. Franklin, who "held the audience spellbound while delivering his excellent oration—the soliloquy of King Richard III," and at the conclusion a debate—"Resolved: That land be a free heritage to mankind"—was hotly contested.

The Knights of Labor ball, which was held in a store from nine P. M. to six A. M., was a gay affair. Ten couples came over from Ouray and ten from Silverton. The program of twenty-four dances was "repeated a second time with extras." "The Knights of Pythias Ball was the grandest affair the Sky City has witnessed for many days. Everybody was there and all the babes, too. . . . The supper was beautiful; . . . confections were furnished by the Vienna Bakery of Ouray." More than once a special train from Silverton carried guests to a ball at the Free Coinage Dancing Club or at the Sky City Miners' Club. On such occasions not only was the regular coach "filled to overflowing, but a box car was cleaned out and filled with seats, and in this the "males took passage." Other sports included horse races and drilling matches, "both single and double-handed." One horse race was a "spirited contest between Ironton and Red Mountain for supremacy."

Although by 1893 the population dropped to 400, the region was doing a business of "hundreds of thousands of dollars annually," and a new newspaper, the *Silverite Plaindealer,* was published in the "High Line Camp," or "Sky City" as the town was now called. When a member of the Sky City Lodge of the Federation of Labor died, the whole order "turned out in full force and accompanied the remains in sleighs to Cedar Hill cemetery." The winters were one perpetual battle with snow.

> Five feet of snow. The inhabitants of Red Mt. are buried neck deep. There are ten men and two women in town and only nine families at Ironton.—*Silverite Plaindealer,* Jan. 6, 1899.

The nineties were the best days of the camp—the lights never went out, the gambling halls never closed, and armed guards rode the ore trains all the way to the Denver and Durango smelters. The Yankee Girl, from which a total of $8,000,000 was taken, was still the best mine. It had been developed on twelve levels and at its peak was employing 2300 men. From the Red Mountain and Ironton mines more than $30,000,000 had been added to the "imperishable wealth of the world" in comparatively few years.

Today, the Idarado Mining Co. is operating many of the old mines through the Treasury Tunnel, built only a few years ago under the Works Progress Administration, and already over 11,000 feet in length. Through it, mines as far away as the Black Bear at Telluride are being tapped. The tunnel was bored at a staggering cost of $1,500,000 but within the first two years of its operation it paid for itself. The Red Mountain region is still active, but while its mines are worked by big companies who operate many consolidated properties, its towns are dead.

Although I had looked for the town of Red Mountain every time I came to that high, wild country all I had been able to find were mine buildings, an occasional boardinghouse and a few scattered miners' cabins.

In 1947 I spent much time in Denver doing research on the history of the towns and one day I found an old photograph of Red Mountain Town, but nothing looked familiar. The mountains were on the wrong side, and the houses lay in a valley I'd never seen. So when Francis and I were in Silverton in September, 1947, we began to question people who knew the territory intimately. One was "Highland Mary," who ran a liquor store on the main street, and who once lived in Red Mountain. "It's in a hollow back from the highway. It had a schoolhouse but no church. The railroad ran through the town," were her comments. Mr. Maxwell, the City Clerk, was even more helpful, and following his explicit directions we found the elusive little town.

Just beyond the crest of Red Mountain Pass, where the road runs for a short distance beside a marshy meadow, the bed of the old railroad can be seen, as well as a faint dirt trail which leads to the right and curves around the edge of a knoll. Leaving the car on the highway, Francis and I hiked along this road for a quarter of a mile and as it dipped around a corner there, below us, was the town that I'd seen in the photograph. To the left, against the knoll, was the National Belle mine, with its huge dump topped with a shaft house. On the flat were what few houses remain—barely enough to

(442)

MINE AT GUSTON

BUILDINGS AT GUSTON (GONE)

mark the location of the several streets—and through the town ran the railroad grade just as Highland Mary had told me. No matter how many old ghost camps I see, the discovery of a new one is always exhilarating. I darted here and there from one end of the town to the other, sketching, and clicking my camera in a perfect frenzy of excitement. After all these years here was Red Mountain!

Ironton

A short distance north of Red Mountain Town is Ironton, a camp which materialized during the winter of 1882-83, as part of the Red Mountain excitement. A double row of houses flanking the highway used to mark its site, but year by year I have watched the town crumble, house by house and store by store, as the false-fronted shells crushed to the ground during a high windstorm or after an unusually heavy load of wet snow. By the side of one gaping store whose walls careened at a drunken angle stood a cast iron coffee mill. The next time I went past, it was gone. The town's iron waterplugs are gone, too.

During the summer of 1881 John Robinson and several others discovered the Guston mine, and although the surface ore was not worth shipping, the men worked the property till fall and then left for the winter. In the spring when they returned for a second season's work, an agent for the Pueblo Smelting Company, who was on the lookout for lead ores, persuaded them to further develop their mine in the hope that it might produce such ore as he needed. They did find such rich lead-silver ore that the mine became one of the best in the region, paying dividends of hundreds of thousands of dollars; and then in 1894, when it was thought to be worked out, it came to the front again with another big strike.

Guston

Not far from the Guston mine, but more accessible by the dirt road that meanders away from the highway half a mile north of the Treasury Tunnel, is a little church. The first time I ran upon it set on a low hill and half hidden by aspens it was beginning to sag, and the shingles on its roof were weathered into dry curls or were missing altogether. The building had a cupola, which I presume once supported a bell. The door was ajar, and I squeezed in and picked my way over the plaster and glass-strewn floor. The inside was depressing, for long rafters and boards which had broken loose from the roof hung down into the building or leaned rakishly against the walls. A few pews and a bench or two were all that was left in the big room—even the windows were without panes of glass.

Two years later I looked from the highway across the narrow valley toward the little knoll to see if the church was still there or whether the weight of snows had flattened the frame building. Just above the aspens was the belfry, so I knew it was still erect. In 1945 I again stopped on Red Mountain road and wandered down toward the Guston mine looking for the church. At first I could not find it, but when I located the yellow aspen grove I saw it, or rather what was left of it; for the entire structure was awry and was gradually settling to one side, supported insecurely upon its disintegrating foundation. In 1947 I did not walk over to the grove, but looked through binoculars and could not find the belfry among the aspens. The church fascinated me and I wondered what was the story behind it. Last year I pieced

(444)

together part of its history from three sources—a man, a book and a newspaper.

During the summer of 1891 the Rev. William Davis, who had just arrived in this country from London, was sent from Denver to Red Mountain by the Home Missionary Board of the Congregational Church. He was told that Red Mountain was a place where there was a fertile field for work and, filled with enthusiasm for his task, he brought his family to the mountain town and began to look for a place in which to hold meetings. Red Mountain was polite but too busy to bother with such matters, and when he could find no room in which to conduct services and hold a Sunday School, he and his family went over to Guston where they received a more cordial welcome. The rest of the story is taken from the *Silverton Standard* of Nov. 14, 1891.

In a short time $300 was pledged by the people at Guston for the erection of a church. "Thinking that Ironton ought not to be uncared for he went over there and tried to find room for a Sunday School." Some of the ladies of the camp went to the school board and asked if they might have the schoolhouse; but the Board members said, "No. Why don't you build a house of your own for a Sunday School?"

"We have no money," replied the ladies.

"Here's ten dollars apiece. That's thirty dollars," said the men. "Start your Sunday School with that." And in a short time more money was raised and the church was built.

Davis had been a contractor and builder in his younger days so, as the people brought him the lumber he did the work. The church site was given by Lt. Gov. Story and the pews by the Rev. Gaston of Ouray. Both Ouray and Silverton contributed money for the building, and when it was completed and the debt was only $159, Silverton raised an additional $100 to help cancel the deficit.

Then some of the Cornish miners, of whom there were many in the community, insisted that it should have a bell to call the worshippers to service. A belfry was built and a bell installed; whereupon another miner, used to the shrill toots that announced the change of shift in a mine, said that "there ought to be a bloody whistle on it." A whistle accordingly was added.

The church was formally opened in November, 1891, and all during the years of mining activity it was the only church in the Red Mountain district. Perhaps its isolated location on the aspen-covered hill had something to do with it but, at any rate, through fires and winter storms years after the towns and congregations which it served had disappeared or moved away, the church remained, until it too slipped closer and closer to earth and the mines and by now is perhaps just another pile of lumber.

Yet in the early nineties a little community called Guston was located at this spot. Its population was 300, it had daily mail service from Ouray, and it was

> blessed with a little church that sits on a hill and cannot be obscured. Quite a delegation of young ideas go to school there. . . Guston and Red Mountain are only two miles apart and if they ever become great cities they will have to pull together like St. Paul and Minneapolis. What do these miners care for cities if the riches of

(445)

the mountains only hold out? Cities may do for gold bugs to live in, but not for miners. Miners and gold bugs will never harmonize in this world and probably not in the next. Hall,—*Mineral Resources of Ouray County*, 1894.

Only three hundred yards from the Guston was another great mine, the Yankee Girl. Two conflicting stories exist about its discovery. One version tells that while Robinson was deerhunting in Red Mountain park he found a piece of ore that was pure galena and, realizing its value, prospected for the source of the vein from which it came and discovered the Yankee Girl mine. On the twentieth of September, when the shaft was only twenty feet deep, he sold the claim for $125,000 cash. Not being able to determine in which direction the vein lay, he then staked off mines on either side of the Yankee Girl. These he called the Robinson and the Orphan Boy, both of which turned out to be valuable. The second version of the discovery of the Yankee Girl insists that the ground where the mine was found had been worked for three years unsuccessfully without "one ounce of mineral being found." Finally a prospector and his two partners began to work an old prospect hole and struck the vein.

The Yankee Girl became one of the most widely known and productive mines in the district but it was expensive to operate because of the "irregular form of the four separate ore chimneys and the abundance and corrosive activity of its waters." Any iron and steel left in the water became coated with copper, and iron pipes and rails were so rapidly perforated and destroyed that constant replacement was necessary. This expense and the low market price of silver caused the mine eventually to shut down.

By January, 1883, during the boom in the area, three hundred tents had been pitched on the snowy flat of Ironton. A campsite was surveyed on March 4, and five days later the *Solid Muldoon* announced:

> Three miles north of Red Mt. town . . . is the new town of Copper Glen or Ironton, which was surveyed Sunday, and on Monday evening had thirty-two cabins under headway and the ever ready lot jumpers on hand.

Soon there was not a vacant lot to be found, and the townspeople had decided to drop the name Copper Glen in favor of Ironton. Before the end of March the

> outlook for business was enough to cause several Silverton merchants to abandon that village and move to the new Eldorado. Each day brings scores from the outside, notwithstanding two feet of snow.—*Solid Muldoon*, March 23, 1883.

By June 1 word from Lake City predicted that:

> Ironton promises to become the town of the Red Mountain district, because of its superior location. Though less than three months old it has . . . ten saloons and two or three hundred houses.

Besides the Guston, Yankee Girl, Robinson and Orphan Boy, such mines as the Saratoga, Candice, Silver Bell, Paymaster and Genesee-Vanderbilt added to the camp's fame and, since the mines at Red Mountain were

CHURCH AT
GUSTON. 1941

INTERIOR OF CHURCH

CHURCH IN 1945

equally productive, the two towns were described as "two little camps that claim the World's Mineral Badge and Trophy of Fortune."

> Like a diamond in a beautiful setting lies the little village of Ironton in a picturesque little park surrounded by treasure laden mountains. A number of God's own people inhabit this beautiful dell, sorrow and strife do not exist there, while peace and plenty reign supreme.—*Red Mountain Mining Journal*, Dec. 31, 1887.

During 1887 there were but one hundred of "God's own people" in the town, but by 1889 the railroad was extended from Red Mountain to Ironton and the town perked up. Ironton's level park was chosen for the terminus of the Rainbow Route, and coaches from Ouray met each train.

> The stage road from Ouray to Ironton is one of the marvels of the region. In places it is merely a notch carved into the vertical rocks that wall in the Uncompahgre river. Mountains hang overhead and a thousand feet beneath is the River. In places it is like looking into the jaws of death.
>
> Rarely does an accident happen on this, the most remarkable highway in the world. The Ouray Stage and Bus Co. is prepared to transport 200 passengers daily with celerity, certainty and safety over this eight and a half miles of mountain trail.
> —*Western Slope Congress of Colorado*, 1893.

In the busy season two trains ran daily to and from Silverton, filled largely with tourists who revelled in the superb scenery and who were duly impressed by Ironton's system of waterworks and its electric light plant.

Between 1893 and 1898 many of Ironton's mines were idle, but in the latter year gold was discovered and a new boom was on.

REVIVAL AT IRONTON.

> The search for gold is a success. . . Perhaps a hundred and eighty people have gone in there this season. . . Several families are living there. . . Ironton used to have two thousand and the two thousand made it a howling wilderness, and men joined the long train of the ages on a shutter. That was in the palmy days of silver, before the country went into mourning for a dead industry. The pick and drill are again clicking . . . in the solitary places. . . Whatever they lost in silver they are trying to recover in gold, copper and lead.—*Silverite Plaindealer*, July 29, 1898.

As the mines were developed and the shafts and drifts ran deeper into the mountains, the character of ore changed from lead to copper, and also with greater depth came the problem of underground water. Most mines are hampered by water which seeps and flows from hidden sources and has to be constantly pumped out so as to permit the men to work at the deep levels; but in the Red Mountain district an added problem had to be faced, for the waters were impregnated with sulphuric and other acids which "quickly destroyed bolts, rails, candlesticks, picks and other iron and steel tools" by its corrosive action and coated them with copper. The acidulous waters came from bodies of iron and copper ores, but below a certain depth the acids in the water disappeared.

George Crawford, a mining man familiar with the district since 1882, decided the problem could be solved by unwatering the mines through a tunnel which should start fifty feet below the collar of the Yankee Girl mine shaft.

(448)

Work on the tunnel, now known as the Joker tunnel, began in July, 1904; and after it was opened in 1906, the main shaft of the Yankee Girl, which had not been operated for twelve years, was emptied at the rate of twelve hundred gallons a minute. Since then other properties have been successfully drained through this tunnel.

Leaving Ironton, we continued down the highway toward Ouray, past the mouth of Poughkeepsie gulch above which the Micky Breen mine is working, and down the corkscrew curves to the head of Uncompahgre canyon and the beginning of the shelf road.

In 1889 it was rumored that Mears intended to build a "cogway," similar to that at Manitou, between Ouray and Ironton the following spring, but although there was great excitement over the prospect, the road never materialized.

At Bear Creek Falls, with its parking place and observation platform, I recalled the photograph taken at the toll gate at this point on Mears' old road, where there was hardly room for one team to travel along the muddy, rocky ledge that served as a highway. The present grade is six percent— the old one was twenty-one percent; the present road cost $20,000 a mile— the old one $10,000. Mears never traveled over the Million Dollar Highway, but it is a road of which he would have approved and, but for his vision of a shelf along this vertical canyon, it might never have been built.

Save for him the steeply towering Uncompahgres might have remained an impregnable barrier between Ouray and the rest of the San Juan; but now even their rocky sides have been notched and blasted, and roads rim or cross the uncompromising peaks that form the range. The road from Ridgway to Ophir and then to Dolores and Durango forms one-half of the big circle. From Durango to Silverton and over Red Mountain Pass no way was found to skirt the peaks; so the road simply scrambles over them and then drops straight down Uncompahgre canyon to Ouray, completing the loop by cutting across the circle's diameter.

We hated to leave the San Juan with its incredibly steep and ragged mountains and its little travelled trails, for the rest of Colorado seems so tame by comparison; but vacation was over, and it would be another year before we could return to the rugged country across the Pass.

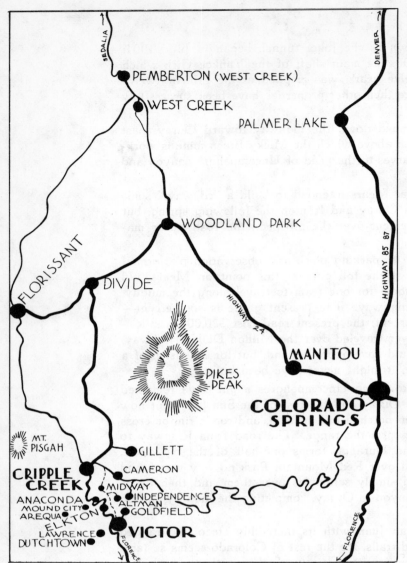

Cripple Creek

CHAPTER XVIII

Pikes Peak Country

THE Cripple Creek mining district is close to Colorado Springs, and were it not for Pike's Peak which looms up behind the city, it could be reached by a short drive. The great mountain separates the city from the gold camp, and to reach the latter one must drive around three sides of the peak, taking the Ute Pass road out of the Springs as far as Divide and then turning south toward Cripple. The latter part of the drive is up an interminable hill full of hairpin curves until, once on top, the road runs over the mountain for miles with the peak to the east, rows of hills and valleys in front, and the white-topped Sangre de Cristo range, like a gigantic mirage, on the horizon.

Some miles outside of Cripple Creek the first signs of mining appear— a broken down shaft house, yellow dumps or the foundations of a mill—and just as you begin to wonder where the city is, a turn in the road opens up a whole new panorama, with Cripple Creek right below sprawled over the mountainside. The city looks big, with block after block of buildings, some flanking the streets east and west and others sliding down the gulch toward the creek.

Cripple Creek is built on the side of a hill so steep that one block of Bennett avenue is built on two levels, traffic west taking the upper roadway and traffic east taking the lower. The side streets race down hill, pausing at the intersections just long enough to level off for the width of the avenue and then tearing on down another block. Bennett avenue runs the length of the town, and on it are located the main business houses, the city hall and fire station, and the Teller county courthouse. Above it the residential section of the city is full of small frame houses, in the midst of which stand the hospital and the Catholic church. Below Bennett avenue is the site of the rest of the city—the still empty blocks, full of foundations left by the disastrous fire of 1896.

On one visit to Cripple Creek four of us planned to spend the night and part of the next day in the city painting and sketching. Not knowing where to stay, we asked the advice of a local storekeeper, who recommended some rooms on the main street. We went there, but as we could not find the landlady we returned to the storekeeper.

"Oh, that's right," he said, as he wrapped a parcel for a customer. "She went to the Springs for a couple of days. I don't know just when she'll be back, but she left the keys up the street at a cafe. You look up Mamie and ask her for them."

Mamie was on duty when we entered the dark cocktail lounge where she worked and she wouldn't be off for another two hours. "You take them," she said impulsively, handing me a huge ring full of keys of assorted sizes and kinds. "I think one of the front rooms is vacant, and No 5 is, too. You try these until you find the ones you need, and then bring the keyring back here. If the lady isn't home before you leave tomorrow, just leave the money in an envelope in the hall. It'll be all right," and with a smile she turned back to her customers.

Armed with the keyring, which was as big as a jailer's, we returned to our lodgings and settled ourselves in two rooms that we hoped were vacant. That evening other lodgers tramped by our doors and at daylight the next morning tramped out again, but the landlady never appeared. When we left we put our money and keys in an envelope in the mailbox and left the first "self-serve" rooms we'd ever encountered.

At breakfast, as the four of us were perched on stools at the counter of a restaurant eating the usual meal of orange juice, coffee and toast, we noticed to our left a fine-looking, elderly man who ordered three whisky straights and nothing else! All morning I explored the town, from the three-story railroad station at one end of Bennett avenue to the edge of the city at the other, and from the reservoir to the crumbling foundations on Myers avenue. I discovered a garage over whose portal was lettered Butte Opera House, and I was shown the building where Jack Dempsey once worked.

Cripple Creek sprang up in the early nineties, at the same time as Creede, and like Creede it resulted from random prospecting in cattle country. The first discovery of gold was made in 1874, when T. H. Lowe, one of Hayden's surveying corps, picked up some rich float on a meadow near the present site of the city and, becoming excited over his discovery, organized a prospecting party to examine all the nearby gulches. The men found a little gold but not enough to warrant mining, and with their departure mining was forgotten for ten years.

Then in the spring of 1884 word of a new gold field got around. It was said that a prospector known as Chicken Bill was taking nuggets out of the ground by the fistful; and lest he get too many, over three thousand men started on a dead run for the slopes of Mt. Pisgah (west of Cripple Creek) where the excitement was centered. An express messenger on the South Park railroad loaded a burro into the express car, rode to the hilltop nearest the strike, and then "dumped the beast out, jumped his job, and struck across country to the place."

At the gold field everything was in confusion. Men "hitched their horses to trees, threw a blanket over their grub and made a run for the country." Each person drove his stake which entitled him to three hundred feet by fifteen hundred feet. By night the entire region was covered by stakes.

Dan O'Connell was one of those who rushed to the scene, and excerpts from his account of the excitement as told to Thomas Dawson are given here:

> The crowd was good natured. Most of the men had brought along their demijohns. But if they had not been so foresighted they would not have been compelled to suffer from thirst. Louis Liverman was looking after that. Louis was in Alma when the news came. He'd been through such excitement before and he knew quicker and surer returns were received from other sources than new mines. . . . He loaded his wagon with whiskey and beer and hurried across the Park with the cargo. . . . Liverman sold his beer by the bottle—when the bottles were empty he filled them with whiskey which he brought in barrels, and sold the bottles at $2.50 each. . . . Long before sunrise next morning Louis exchanged his refreshments for cash and an early hour saw him headed for home. He had done so well . . . he determined to continue his operations by bringing in another load. There is where he miscalculated . . . . when he returned there were no customers . . . . He was absent four days. When he arrived the tents were folded and gone. . . .
>
> The revelation came early in the second day. We found no outcroppings and no other evidence of mineral. . . . Only one hole, owned by a man named Butters. The hole was not even new but had been sunk by someone who preceded our party probably a year before. It was ten feet deep, showing that it never had given much promise.
>
> At first Butters refused to let anyone enter it, but the demand was so overwhelming he could not long resist. Denny Carter was one of the first to descend. He returned with a panful of dirt . . . . barren of gold as a Missouri cornfield. . . . When the fraud was made apparent there was general silence for a moment. After this a voice was raised. It simply said: 'Let's hang the s-n of a b-h!' Then we all started to hunt him, but we could not find him. . . . The crowd scattered almost as fast as it gathered . . . . at any rate, information of the supposed strike spread in all directions and the railroad company sold hundreds of tickets, being the only person or institution to get anything out of it except Louis Liverman.

After this hoax men were suspicious of new discoveries in the region, fearing another salted mine. Some prospectors from Leadville came into the region in 1887 by way of Canon City and are said to have found the first gold in paying quantities at the head of Squaw gulch. They put up a location stake but apparently did not recognize what they had found, for they left soon afterwards and did not return.

William W. Womack came to Colorado from Kentucky in 1876 and filed on a homestead where Cripple Creek now stands. In 1884 he sold his land to the Pike's Peak Cattle and Land Co., and they in turn sold it the following year to the cattle firm of Bennett and Myers. Bob Womack, the son of the original owner, rode this range during the eighties and was always on the lookout for pieces of float rock in hope that they might contain gold. He took his best specimens to the Springs and showed them around, but no one paid any attention to him or his discoveries. Finally he pegged out a claim which he called the Chance, and he proceeded to work it for nearly six years without bothering to record it. In December, 1890, Womack got E. M. De la Vergne and F. F. Frisbie sufficiently interested in his gold samples to go with him to the pasture land and see for themselves. After inspecting his shaft in Poverty gulch, they too began to prospect and soon afterwards located the El Dorado lode. By the summer of 1891 Womack had found good float that assayed $25 to the ton and several days later, when he struck the vein "which glistened with sylvanite," he hurried to Colorado Springs to celebrate. In his drunken excitement he disposed of his mine, which he had relocated as the El Paso, for $500 in cash. As soon as his discovery became known, men flocked to the cattle land and began staking claims all over the area six miles square. Womack was never able to cash in on his discovery and got nothing out of his work, but he is credited with being the discoverer of the district.

Cowboys had already named the creek which flowed through the cattle land Cripple creek, because so many cattle were lamed or broke their legs while crossing it on rocks; but Cy Warman of Creede embellished the story by explaining that five men and their burros came to the creek and that one of the burros became lame while crossing the stream. While the beast rested, its owner started to prospect and when he had washed out the sand from his pan and had discovered gold in the bottom, he decided to continue placering. While building a cabin one of the men with him fell from the top of it, lit on the dog, and broke the dog's leg and his own arm, making three cripples in the camp; so they called it Cripple Creek. The creek was about one yard wide!

A straggling settlement of tents and cabins grew up on the present site of the city, and a mining district was organized in the fall of 1891. In the meantime, Bennett and Myers had discovered that gold was being found on their land and "being shrewd, they platted eighty acres for a townsite," called it Fremont for John W. Fremont, the pioneer explorer, and began to sell lots which were eagerly snapped up by the crowds which poured in. Hundreds of wagons lined the only approach to the camp (from Florissant) and emptied their loads of men and supplies at the new placer fields. The post office officials would not accept Fremont as a name for the camp since there was already a town of that name in the state. Morland was then suggested, but E. M. De la Vergne proposed the winning name—Cripple Creek— which, by its selection, christened not only the embryo camp but a whole new era in Colorado's mining history.

> Cripple Creek became a real mining camp in the latter part of June or the forepart of July, 1891, when 'Pete' Hettig and 'Bob' Work reached the infant camp.
>
> Hettig brought a tent, two barrels of beer, two jugs of whisky and a few cigars, and opened the first saloon in camp by laying a board across the top of two barrels in front of the tent. Work also brought a tent and a barber chair and opened a barber shop.—*Victor Record*, Feb. 3, 1902.

The year 1892 was called the "year of expectancy." Most of the mining was from placers; and had it not been for them the camp might have failed, for the great lode mines were not discovered until the next year. Two stage lines—one from Divide on the Colorado Midland and the other from Canon

City on the Denver and Rio Grande—carried people to and from the camp; and the population quickly rose to 4,000 in spite of a slur by Cy Warman of Creede, who contended that "people were crazy over Creede and went there by the hundreds and by two and fours to Cripple Creek."

Warman describes the early days of Cripple Creek with color and atmosphere in the *Review of Reviews* for February, 1896.

His stage ride to the camp was

> A sixteen mile ride through wild gorges . . . where even the mail coach had to side track for the heavy freight wagons laden with ore. Nine miles out we exchanged our tired bronchos for six fresh horses, heavier than the others to take us over the long high hills. . . Away we dashed never slacking our pace until we swung round and came to a quick stop at the door of the big wooden hotel. Stage coaches always arrive that way. It's one of the 'theatricals' of the camp.
>
> From then till midnight it seemed the swinging doors between the lobby and the bar would never come to rest—either open or shut for a single minute. . . . Everywhere could be seen signs of the life, *that* nervous sort of life peculiar to mining camps and all the people had about them an air of suppressed excitement.
>
> 'We ain't got time to change forks at this station' said the tired looking table girl replacing the fork which I had left on the fish plate for her to take away.

The first newspaper was published by E. C. Gard, who moved his plant up from Palmer Lake and established his office in a log cabin. He called his sheet the *Cripple Creek Crusher* and printed the first issue with a flourish in gilt ink. The *Cripple Creek Prospector* which appeared in December, 1891, was printed under that name until January, 1895, when it changed hands and became the *Cripple Creek Morning Times*. Even when its plant was destroyed by fire the paper continued to appear, for the editor sent the forms for each issue to Victor six miles away until a job press could be rigged up in the still smoking city. The following request for advertisements which appeared in its columns should have brought results:

> Cripple Creek has a few concerns who do not advertise. You may not know them. Very few people do.—*The Morning Times,* Cripple Creek, Jan. 22, 1896.

During the winter of 1892 the brokers arrived and sold shares of stock with amazing rapidity. Most people had a little money to invest and thought the best way to do it was through the mining companies which were organized by the hundreds. Some of them were reliable, but others had "no more claim to a piece of land than the location stakes and a ten-foot hole that the law required." The entire country was staked for miles around and nearly everyone had at least one claim. "All the trading was curbstone and the streets were crowded with excited people. Gold King stock was put on the market at twenty-five cents. Twenty-five thousand shares sold immediately. Soon it went to sixty cents a share." Buena Vista stock went from $1.75 to $5.00 a share in a single day.

The next year marked the turning point in the camp, for during 1893 the big mines of the district were discovered and developed, and after the demonitization of silver thousands of miners who were thrown out of work by the closing down of the silver camps flocked to Cripple Creek to dig for gold.

Among the first lode mines to be discovered prior to 1893 were the El Paso, El Dorado, Hub, Blue Bell, Ironclad and Marguerite, and as more mines were located "the erstwhile grass-clothed hills" were "thickly dotted with buildings of assorted designs, scarred by shafts, tunnels, open cuts and trenches, while ore roads and trails" ran in all directions. The mines of the district were located on many hills—Gold, Globe, Tenderfoot, Mineral, Carbonate, Frink, Raven, Ironclad and Beacon, and on Battle mountain, Big Bull mountain, Squaw mountain, Grouse mountain and Straub mountain.

From the very first the ores of the district were an "enigma and a paradox." Gold should not have been present at all in the rock and when found it should have been on the surface only; yet the deeper the mines were developed, the richer the veins became. The first authentic account of the complicated geological structure of the region resulted from the field work done by Dr. Whitman Cross of the U. S. Geological Survey, assisted by Prof. R. A. F. Penrose, Jr., who was in charge of economic geology. He was the first man to suggest that the veins would continue to improve to considerable depths and still maintain their values. At first the gold ore was sent to Pueblo and Denver for reduction, but as chemical processes of treatment were perfected a large portion of the ores were handled in cyanidation and chlorination plants which were built in the district and thus permitted the profitable handling of ore yielding as low as $6 per ton in gold.

Each year the mineral output increased until "as a high-grade camp Cripple Creek is without a peer in the world today." By 1895 the camp was in its stride, and it was distinctly annoyed by criticisms from other camps not so fortunate.

> It is rather amusing to read in papers from other camps in Colorado notes of warning against the present era of mining excitement and the disgrace resulting from over booming. It is not a boom brethren, it is Colorado rising to her natural. Cripple Creek is not alarmed and if this camp has no fear there is certainly little for others to be alarmed about.—*The Morning Times,* Cripple Creek, Dec. 4, 1895.

> Base envy withers at another's joy
> And hates that excellence it cannot reach.

> Thompson.

> Respectfully commended to numerous newspapers that would belittle Colorado gold mines because they are not east of the Mississippi.—*The Morning Times,* Dec. 11, 1895.

> Tis a heavenly delight for a fellow to possess a comfortable share of this world's goods and it must surely be more than heavenly to be walking on streets paved with gold. Recent development in the city of Cripple Creek indicates that the New Jerusalem must be located somewhere about within its confines.—*The Morning Times,* Dec. 10, 1895.

> Go to church today and thank the Giver of all good for guiding your footsteps to Cripple Creek.—*The Morning Times,* Dec. 15, 1895.

Yet with all its bravado, Cripple had to admit that while its best properties were in the mining district they were not adjacent to the city but were from three to six miles away at Victor, a new camp which sprang up in 1893.

> It is a lamentable fact that while all the paying mines are all in and about Victor, the hurrah has gained an echoless location at Cripple Creek. Can't be helped. Cripple

Creek was on the map first. But there is a good show still for Victor.—*The Morning Times*, Dec. 10, 1895.

Aside from the further development of the mines, the biggest event in 1894 was the completion of the railroad to the city. Both the Midland Terminal from Divide and the Florence and Cripple Creek railroad from Canon City were racing toward the same goal, and the latter won, sending its first train puffing into the expectant camp on July 2. The road, which cost $800,000, was built by David H. Moffat, largely to provide an outlet for ore; but shortly after it was opened, the miners went on strike for several months, and few shipments were made until after the strike was settled.

Years before making Colorado my home, I visited Colorado Springs and took one sight-seeing trip to Canon City and back to the Springs by way of the old railroad grade through Phantom Canyon to Victor and Cripple Creek. At that time the watertanks and stations stood beside the right of way, and the narrow but high trestle bridges with no railings were thrilling to cross. About nine years ago I drove that road again, but much of its charm was gone. New bridges replaced the rickety trestles and all the tanks and stations had disappeared; now it is just another road to the mining camps.

As the town grew its business "blocks" became more numerous and more pretentious, although most of them were frame structures.

> In response to invitations prepared in the highest style of the Printer's art, hundreds called on Carberry and Hanley to participate in the festivities attending the opening of their saloon at 114 Third St. Music, mirth and song, intermingled with solid and liquid refreshments, constituted the program that . . . sent every one away with a conviction that the proprietors have started out with a purpose to treat their trade in a most gentlemanly and clever manner."—*The Morning Times*, Cripple Creek, Dec. 12, 1895.

Bennett avenue was the business street, but Myers avenue, one block south, was equally busy with a different type of trade. It consisted of a half-mile of "one-storied cell-like cribs, false-front saloons, dancehalls and Parlor Houses." The author, Julian Street, visited Cripple Creek for the purpose of writing an article for *Collier's* about the fabulous gold camps; but when the story appeared it was not to Cripple Creek's liking, for Street had overlooked the city's civic and economic achievements and had instead written a highly colored account of life on Myers avenue. The citizens were both angry and disgusted and passed a city ordinance whereby the name of Myers avenue was changed officially to Julian street.

DEATH OF RUTH DAVENPORT HERE AT DANCE HALL, WHERE SHE MADE HER LIVING. PNEUMONIA THE CAUSE.

> One of the saddest scenes that has occurred in the camp for some time was witnessed last night in a little room over Mernie's Dance Hall. It was a death bed scene and the surroundings were what made it so affecting.
>
> On a bed in a little dingy room lay a woman, an unfortunate woman. Around her bed stood other unfortunate women who shed a few tears and administered to the sick woman's wants as well as their untrained hands and minds could do.
>
> The sick woman was young—only nineteen—and exceedingly handsome, but the dreaded disease pneumonia had driven her to her bed and was slowly but surely

closing her lungs and making each breath more difficult. Only a week ago this same woman had been on the floor below, as merry as anyone there, laughing, drinking and joking. On the same floor, while her life was slowly ebbing . . . the caller was yelling out in his usual, loud manner the different figures, and the shuffle of the feet of the dancers was heard. . . . The music seemed louder and the talk in the bar room was more boisterous than usual. . . . The sick woman realized that she was about to die and asked for a drink of water. Just as her attendant reached the pitcher of water, the caller on the floor below called out, 'Promenade to the bar,' the sick woman's muscles relaxed, her head lay motionless on the pillow and she was dead.

The music in the dance hall below was dismissed, the lights were turned out and the undertaker's wagon bore the remains of Ruth Davenport to the cooling room.— *The Morning Times*, Cripple Creek, Jan. 21, 1896.

On January 21, 1896, the Cripple Creek Stock Exchange was opened:

BAPTIZED IN WINE.
OPENING OF CRIPPLE CREEK STOCK EXCHANGE.

The Cripple Creek Stock Exchange started into business last evening in its own building on Bennett Avenue, next door east of the Bi-Metallic Bank. . . .

Colin Munro of Chicago, who has been chosen caller of the exchange, then took his appointed position and stated that his voice had not as yet become acquainted with the altitude, and called on Mr. Berry of the Gold Mining Stock Exchange to take his place for the evening. Mr. Berry ascended the platform and after being provided with a box so his chin could come above the rail of the desk, he started on the call, which continued for over an hour and resulted in the sale of 402,800 shares. . . .

It was shortly after 9 o'clock when Pres. Chew stayed the work of the brokers by announcing that the Cripple Creek Stock Exchange would now request a suspension of the call, that the guests might partake of a light refreshment solid and liquid. The suggestion was heartily accepted and in a jiffy the pit was transformed into a banquet hall—a table was spread with delicately prepared sandwiches, a huge block of ice with a spacious cavity filled with cut fruit was hoisted on to it and behind this, with beaming countenance, and confident that he alone could serve up champagne punch to the queen's taste, was Jack Condon.

As if one touched a trailing fuse, began the pop and fizz of champagne bottles, and the buzz of the hundreds of voices soon ripened into the consequence of trading in gold stocks and drinking 'gold seal' champagne. When the participants became well impregnated, the tongue of the erstwhile crier of fractions loosened up.

Cripple's outlook for 1896 is best expressed by an open letter written by the Mayor to the *Times*:

CRIPPLE'S FUTURE.

Not one century nor five centuries will see the Cripple Creek mines exhausted. Our greatest, our richest and largest mines will be found in the granite and the grandchildren of our children's children will not see the end of gold mining in the hills that belt the Cripple Creek district.

A century from now will see Cripple Creek the metropolis of a great mining district, extending twenty-five miles north and south and ten miles east and west, with blocks of magnificent brick and stone fronts lining its thoroughfares, with palatial and royally furnished residences dotting its suburbs, with its splendid electric street car systems, with its gorgeous electric lights . . . with its lofty church spires lifting into the blue ether of our mountains—with its five hundred mills grinding and pounding away upon the daily product of the mines, and finally with its quarter of a million of energetic, progressive, law-abiding people . . . It will cause the "tenderfoot" of that day to exclaim in the language of the Queen of Sheba, "The half had not been told to me."

Mr. Editor, I trust that the foregoing picture of the future great mining city will not cause your readers to dub me an enthusiast, as holding visionary views.

Hugh R. Steele
Mayor of Cripple Creek.

The Morning Times, Jan. 2, 1896.

The National Hotel, the largest and the tallest structure in the city, was completed in February, 1896, complete with Turkish baths, an elevator and its own electric light plant. It contained one hundred and fifty rooms, forty suites provided with baths, and as a special favor to its guests number thirteen was omitted from the list of rooms. Its accommodations and fine cuisine made it:

Possible for the refined tourist or the health-seeking invalid to see the wonders of a mining camp and receive the benefits experienced by all invalids who remain in Cripple Creek a short time.—*Evening Star*, New Year's Edition, 1904.

In spite of such buildings as the National Hotel, a large portion of the city was built of wood, and fire was a constant menace.

On account of the heavy winds that prevailed yesterday Chief Allen of the fire department had the town team hitched to the fire engine all day ready in case of fire. All the carts were brought out and stood in front of the different stations in order that no time would be wasted. . . . Luckily there was no fire.—*The Morning Times*, Feb. 7, 1896.

Then on April 25, 1896, the staccato blasts of the whistle at the Mocking Bird mine sounded an alarm as clouds of black smoke began pouring from a building on Myers avenue. The fire, which wiped out nearly half of the city, started in a "den of vice" where Jennie Larue, a dancehall girl, and her lover, while quarreling, accidentally upset a gasoline stove. The flames quickly ignited the flimsy structure and spread to adjoining buildings. The following day the *Denver Republican* carried a timely headline:

JENNIE LARUE GOES INTO HISTORY WITH THE CHICAGO KICKER.

As the fire spread, buildings in its path were blown up in a vain effort to stop its advance. Each explosion "threw the debris high in the air, which in its falling felled men right and left." The fire departments of Victor, Florence, Colorado Springs and Denver dashed to the city's aid, but there was little that could be done; and before the flames could be gotten under control the greater portion of the city was in ruins. The fire occurred on Saturday, and all over the weekend the people stared dazedly at the smoking ruins of the camp. And then on Tuesday the twenty-ninth the fire alarm shrieked again and, exhausted as they were, the citizens turned out again to fight an even bigger blaze than the first one.

This fire was believed to have been deliberately started by firebugs, for although it broke out in the Portland Hotel on Myers avenue, other fires were discovered simultaneously in other parts of the city, and "one or more men were lynched for spreading the fire." Myers avenue was a furnace, and

ROOM, CRIPPLE CREEK

VINDICATOR HILL
ABOVE GOLDFIELD

EL PASO MINE, CRIPPLE CREEK

to add to the terror the cartridges in Wright's hardware store in the Portland block began "firing a fusilade." In this fire eight blocks of buildings
were consumed, several lives were lost, and nearly four thousand were left
homeless. When the smoke cleared away less than ten buildings were left to
mark the site of the city which a week before had boasted a population of
ten thousand.

The town was in a serious plight, for "all the stoves are in ruins and the
town is out of bread." One man paid twenty dollars so that his wife might
sleep in one of the few remaining houses. Leadville immediately sent $200 in
cash to the stricken city as well as 5000 pounds of flour, and Victor and
Colorado Springs sent tangible aid to the helpless citizens. Almost before
the ashes were cold, rebuilding commenced; and in a few months another
bustling, well-built city, thoroughly modern and with all the business houses
of brick or stone, rose on the foundations of the former camp. Once again
it became:

> A town of 10,000 without a tree. As one looks down one thousand feet on the
> vividly painted city, set like a toy village on the dull, gray slope, this is what most
> impresses. The streets are regular. Brick buildings, succeeding those destroyed in
> the fire six years ago are shining red. No fences, no waste lumber, few sidewalks and
> not a tree on the townsite.—*Denver Times,* Sept. 15, 1902.

Each year the mines yielded greater amounts of valuable ore. In 1898
production jumped to $16,000,000, and during the year large shaft houses were
built and railroad spurs were constructed to the principal mines. In Cripple
Creek a combined city hall, jail and fire station was built on Bennett avenue;
and the Sisters' hospital as well as the Catholic church was completed. Total
production for the year of 1899 reached $21,000,000. All the mines were de-
veloped at greater depths, double-deck cages were installed, and electricity
replaced steam for power. As water was encountered at the lower mining levels, great pumping and compressor plants were installed. Many mines were
consolidated under a single company, which ran drifts still further into the
hollow hills.

By 1900 the year's production was $23,000,000. The Colorado Short Line,
a standard gauge road, reached the district from Colorado Springs, and with
its arrival Cripple became a tourists' paradise, to which "wide-eyed excursionists armed with lunch baskets, cameras and notebooks" swarmed. In 1903
two electric lines connected Cripple Creek and Victor—the High Line over
the hilltops that separate the two camps, and the Low Line around the edge
of the same hills.

Labor troubles in 1894 and again in 1903 closed the mines, but since
most of the strike activities centered nearer Victor they are described in connection with that town.

Having survived the fire, the city continued to prosper as its mines produced in ever increasing amounts; and while the city flourished financially,
its cultural life was not forgotten. The Butte Opera House had been remodeled for Louis James' production of *Othello* as early as Oct. 6, 1897. Dances
given in the early years of the camp were rough affairs sponsored by the
local politicians, and although they were open to the public the better class

seldom attended. Later on, when the many lodges and clubs gave dances, they were well patronized. When the Corbett-Fitzsimmons prize fight was held, movies of it were shown to a crowd as curious to see the moving pictures as to see the record of the fight.

> The audience was composed in much larger part of ladies than on Monday night. . . . The pictures which flash past the light at the rate of 48 each second form on the canvas a life-like moving picture. . . . There is no blood seen, and nothing to shock the nerves. The life-size pictures flit back and forth as silent as shadows; but every motion of the big fighters is plainly seen.—*The Morning Times*, Sept. 15, 1897.

Between 1894 and 1900 new camps appeared in the Cripple Creek mining district—Victor, Goldfield, Gillett, Anaconda, Independence, Cameron, Altman and two or three smaller ones—and the people felt that their needs and their combined population of 20,000 warranted the creation of a new county with Cripple Creek as county seat. Victor, which was next in size, protested violently, but Cripple not only invited the state legislature to come and look things over but chartered three special cars on a train for the dignitaries. The train pulled into the Victor station first, and when it left for Cripple Creek the legislators were still in Victor, as the cars had been cut off by the jealous citizens of that city. The train proceeded to Cripple where a delegation met it, ready to welcome the legislators and to conduct them to a special breakfast that had been prepared in their honor. Hours later the amazed law-makers, who in the meantime had been feted by the citizens of Victor, were driven to Cripple Creek in carriages for a delayed tour of that city. In spite of Victor's trick, Teller county was created with Cripple Creek as the county seat.

From Cripple Creek to Victor one is never out of sight of the mines. The broad shelf of road cut into the mountainside is the only interruption to the ore dumps, shaft houses, hoists and railroad tracks that belong to the big properties which cover the entire six-mile stretch. Look up, and the mountain is terraced with dumps and latticed with mine roads and railroad tracks; look down, and mines fill the gulches.

One of the biggest although not one of the oldest of these is the Cresson, which is still operating. Years ago a Chicago man named Harbeck bought some mining property in Cripple Creek. He knew nothing about mining, and when it paid no dividends he believed that it was worthless. After his death his son inherited the property and decided to go to Colorado to look the mine over before disposing of the stock. In Cripple Creek he met Richard Roelof, a geologist and mineralogist, and from him and others he learned enough about mining to realize that his property, which he called the Cresson, was worth developing. Returning to Chicago he organized a mining company and hired Roelof to manage the mine. Not long afterwards a chimney of gold was discovered and a vug of high-grade ore was opened up, "gleaming like a jeweler's shop" with gold hanging in crystals from the walls of the workings. The Cresson, which was "gold all through," was soon paying $400,000 a year in dividends, and Harbeck found that he was a millionaire! In 1914 one carload of ore, valued at $1,000,000, set the world's record for production, and it was whispered that even richer deposits were known to exist in the fabulous vein. In 1916 A. G. Carlton bought the mine for $4,000,000 and developed it still further. The Cresson Consolidated Gold Mining and Milling Co. operates it now, and its ore shipments are steadily increasing. A lateral from the Carlton tunnel is being bored to the Cresson to drain water from the lower workings, and upon its completion the entire mine should be emptied.

Around a bend where the road cuts back in a long loop to reach the opposite side of the gulch, not more than an eighth of a mile away, is the Mary McKinney, whose huge yellow dump rises beside the highway and spills down to the base of the ravine. Its big shaft house, which used to top the dump like a cupola on a roof, has burned down, but the rest of its surface buildings on Raven hill remain. Cribbing lines both sides of the highway to keep the dump from sifting down over the road, and thus forms a deep cut through which one drives past the property. The Mary McKinney was a mere prospect in 1898, but only a year later it was a "mine of the first magnitude," shipping quantities of high-grade ore which totalled over $11,000,000.

Anaconda   Almost adjoining this mining property is the Anaconda group on Gold hill, where the ore was so rich that it was "ploughed out with ox-teams in the early history of the camp and shoveled up as if a railroad were grading a right-of-way along the hillside." The entire gulch below the Mary McKinney property was once full of houses—the camp of Anaconda, which was supported not only by the Anaconda mine but by the Mary McKinney, Doctor and Jack Pot properties.

> The activity of Anaconda and the crowded condition of the switches, attest the fulness of the city's claim of being the chief producer of the district. . . . Her warrants are at par. Her people are out of debt. . . . The class of homes is of the best— nice cottages, dotting the hills, on either side of the stream.—*Cripple Creek Morning Times,* Jan. 1, 1899.

When I inquired from a friend if anything remained of the once prosperous place which had a population of 2,000, he replied that only the "jug"
Mound City was left. He drove back from Victor to show me the jail and also the site of Mound City, farther down the ravine, where, around the Rosebud and Brodie mills, another small camp had once stood. A couple of more hairpin curves brought us to the Elkton mine, another big producer which is still working. A cluster of workmen's cabins line the highway and the road to the mine entrance, but few of them are in use today. In the gulch below was the site of Arequa, where a big cyanide mill used to treat the low-grade
Arequa ores of the district. Arequa townsite, which had its scattering of buildings —long since gone—was close to the spot where the Leadville prospectors drove a location stake in 1887 but, ignorant of what they found, went away disgusted.

In the next gully, below Squaw mountain, are tier upon tier of foundations of what must have been a tremendous mill. What had it looked like when in operation? One day, while working at the State Historical Society in Denver, I found two pictures which showed the property. One was a photograph of the Economic Gold Extraction Company's mill—the enormous building which once rested on the foundations covering a good part of the hillside—and the other was a diagram of the Columbine Victor tunnel which was bored through Squaw mountain in 1899, from the Gold Coin mine in Victor to the big chlorination mill in the gulch. Ore from the Coin with its many levels was loaded in cars and was shuttled through the tunnel direct to the mill.

Once around the shoulder of Squaw mountain the road heads for Victor, *Victor* entering the city suddenly through a rocky cut beyond which is seen a startling panorama of mines, dumps, city streets and buildings, all clinging to the side of a steep hill. In Victor the mines are both above the city and under it, with tier upon tier of shaft houses and terraced dumps filling the mountainside and spilling into the backyards and alleys behind the houses. I have friends who live on top of the Mt. Rosa Placer land and who pointed out men digging in a backyard across the street on part of the Gold Coin property.

> Here you find mining operations carried on in backyards. . . . Gallows frames rearing their heads away up above the roofs of the houses, thundering detonations of giant underground which shake the floor on which you stand and the constant rumble of heavily laden ore wagons through the streets, alleys and vacant lots, each seeking the shortest way to the railroad.—*Denver Republican,* Jan. 1, 1899.

Victor with its backdrop of mines is as full of material for the artist as is Jonny Hill in Leadville, and on many occasions I have sat on its hillside streets drawing and painting. The first time I drove into the town through the rocky gates it was late afternoon, and the city was suffused with a golden haze that made the dumps pure gold and the houses rosy in the soft light. On another trip I was sitting on à curb sketching a hillside with its wavy stripes of houses, when a man stopped to watch me work.

"You're another of these artists, aren't you?" he asked rather bitterly. "There have been a lot of them here lately. One fellow came up a few weeks ago from the Springs. He painted all over town, and then last week a picture that he painted here was printed in the *Denver Post* and was called 'Ghost Town.' We didn't like that. We're no 'has been' place. We've a population of 1200 and we mine more ore than Cripple does; and say, you should hear our high school band! Ghost town, indeed," and he went off muttering.

Although the Victor and other mines in the vicinity were located in 1891 and 1892, it was not until September, 1893, that the Woods Investment Company promoted the town of Victor and located it on the Mt. Rosa Placer property on the south slope of Battle mountain. At first a white city of tents interspersed with a few log cabins, it grew slowly until March, 1894, when the Woods Company, while excavating for the Victor Hotel, uncovered a vein of ore, and the usual stampede to a new gold field commenced. Not long afterwards such important mines as the Portland, Independence, Gold Coin and Strong were discovered, some within the city limits. The Gold Coin buildings were in the center of the city itself, the

Strong mine was behind the railroad station, the Independence was nearby, and dominating the top of Battle mountain were the Portland and the Ajax. A large portion of the city was covered with mining claims, many of which were worked beneath the streets and residences.

As the big mines were developed, Victor became the shipping center of the district and the rival of Cripple Creek, and shortly after Cripple's fire it out-ranked it for a time.

When the Semi-Centennial Celebration and Pioneers Jubilee was held at Salt Lake City from July 20-25, 1897, Victor was represented by a float and Cripple Creek was not. Several young ladies competed for the honor of representing their city, and the winner was sent to the celebration to ride in the parade.

> Victor did the nice thing by Cripple Creek when our representative at Salt Lake invited Miss Gulley, the Cripple Creek queen, to ride on the Victor float. We might say that Cripple Creek took a ride in Victor's band wagon, but Cripple has often done that commercially and the habit is growing.—*Victor Daily Record,* July 20, 1897.

The float was:

> a glittering crystallization, an allegorical epitome of the wondrous mineral riches which have made the Core famous throughout the broad expanse of two worlds. . . . It represents Victor—the predominating colors being silver and gold. A mass of silver pierced on either side by the bore of the Uintah tunnel—In front is the reproduction of a stamp mill in operation. In the rear an ore car moves on its iron tramway. On the four corners of the float are miniature reproductions of the Independence, Portland, Gold Coin and Strong mines. On the summit of the float lies a ton of shining gold and on its apex rises the throne from which Victor's queen held sway during her triumphal progress through Zion's streets in the Jubilee pageant.—*Victor Daily Record,* Aug. 1, 1897.

When in 1897 the Fourth of July fell on a Sunday, certain of the people of Cripple Creek took exception to a celebration being held on that day. Victor had no such scruples and voiced its protest in the press as follows:

> The goody-goody people of Cripple Creek mean to suppress all sorts of patriotic doings on the Fourth (Sunday). Patriotism must be below par with our neighbors for didn't she close up gambling on Friday and reopen the games on the following Sabbath? And are not the gambling halls, bagnios and saloons of Cripple running wide open on Sundays? Is it more a desecration of the Sabbath to have a drilling match than to go on a Myer's Ave. debauch? Is it worse to play baseball than faro or roulette? Oh, consistency thy keepers are not the divines of Cripple.—*Victor Daily Record,* July 3, 1897.

Part of the festivities consisted of a parade in four divisions—the first consisting of the mayor and other dignitaries, the second of the unions, the third of the secret societies and the fourth of the "Ore Haulers Union, with citizens on horseback and carriages" bringing up the rear. Later in the day a miners' drilling contest was held, as well as a wheelbarrow race, a ladies race in bloomers, a burro race and an ore shovelers' contest. Prizes consisted of a horse and buggy, a lady's hat; and a screen door.

Victor was spoken of as the "Core of the Rich Cripple Creek Mining

District," and with its two railroads—the Florence and Cripple Creek line and the Midland Terminal, its $30,000 opera house which seated 1200, its new city hall and "commodious jail," and its "reliable waterworks," it felt secure. But on Aug. 21, 1899, fire broke out in a dive, and in two hours fourteen blocks of the city were smoking ruins. The damage was estimated at $2,000,000; but almost before the fire was out, the city began to rebuild, this time with "pressed brick" and stone.

As mining increased and the population of the district grew, three more railroads were built. The Cripple Creek Short Line from Colorado Springs was financed by the mine owners at a cost of $5,000,000 and was completed in 1901. When Theodore Roosevelt visited Victor that same year he traveled over the Short Line and was so impressed by its scenery and engineering that he described it as "bankrupting the English language." Over its serpentine roadbed a scenic highway, known first as the Corley highway and now as the Gold Camp road, was built after the railroad ceased operation and its tracks were removed. It is full of thrills, for it drops nearly four thousand feet by a series of sweeping curves, loops and ledge grades which shoot through tunnels or out over high trestles, until it reaches the Springs far below.

In the early 1900's "there was thrown around the camp a network of lines, with electric trolley service which connected nearly every town and had depots within easy reach of practically every mine. Both a 'High Line' and a 'Low Line' service was conducted," and these two roads alone ran fifty-six trains daily through the city. The district was unique, for as the local Promotion and Publicity committee of 1904 said:

> Cripple Creek is the only mining district in the world where the miner can go to his work in an electric street car, descend to the mine in an electric hoist, do his work by electric light, run drills operated by electric air compressors and fire his shots by electricity, from a switchboard remote from the point of explosion.—*Colorado Mining Resources.*

While Victor has several churches today, there was a time when

> The Gospel pursued in hot haste the immigration of the people. In those days the Masons, Elks, Odd Fellows, the unions and churches would hold meetings in the same humble frame structure, but on different nights. . . . Obstacles to religion were work . . . the never-ending toil on the Sabbath.—*Victor Daily Record,* March 16, 1905.

Every time I visited Victor I stopped to see my friends, the Ripleys, *Cameron* for Bessie and Don were as interested in the history of the region as I was and could tell me much about it. Don drove me all over the hills, pointing out the location of Cameron, where the Short Line swung across Grassy meadow into the district after its long climb up the mountains from Colorado Springs; showing me the El Paso-Gold King in Cripple Creek where Womack sunk his shaft; taking me up Bull hill to Altman, where so much violence occurred during the Cripple Creek labor war, and from its summit indicating the location of Independence and Goldfield, two other camps that were active during the strikes, and of Dutchtown and Lawrence, two suburbs, south of the city.

(465)

"There's nothing left of either of them," said Don on one of our jaunts. "The Woods Investment Company started Lawrence right after they'd laid out Victor and commenced mining there. Then Tutt, Penrose and C. M. MacNeill put up a chlorination mill in 1894 and began to treat the low-grade ores of the district. Until then only high-grade was considered worth mining, but after their mill started moving, ore that carried as low as $10 to the ton in gold could be treated at a profit. Their experiments at Lawrence revolutionized milling, and when their mill burned they went to Colorado City and started up there.

"Until production costs went up sky high, millions of tons of low-grade were mined; but sometimes it's cheaper to let the ore go than mill it. You've ridden over roads made of gold. There's a stretch of highway near here surfaced with ore from the Portland dumps which assayed $12,000 a mile in gold; but the cost of extraction made it cheaper to sell it to the highway department."

From Don, too, I learned a good deal about the history of Victor's great mines. The formation on which Victor was built was solid red granite, in which were imbedded vast quantities of gold. The ore appeared in the rock in the form of crystals, geologically known as sylvanite and calaverite. Because this was refractory to extract, intricate firing and chemical processes had to be developed; and as the mines were sunk deeper and the ore improved in quality, many sampling and reduction plants were built.

The Victor mine, which was discovered in 1891 on Bull hill, was one of the first producers. A few months later, "when D. H. Moffat and his associates signed an agreement to pay $65,000 for the mine, the price was declared to be sky high;" but before long under his able development it was paying upwards of $1,000,000 in dividends and "had ore enough in sight to pay three or four times over." The mine was well known on two continents and large blocks of stock were held in London and Paris.

The Pharmacist, located by two druggists, was the first dividend payer in camp. Neither of the men who found it knew anything about mining, and since all places looked alike they threw a hat into the air and dug where it landed, striking a jack pot. The Strong mine, which was discovered in 1894 and later sold for $50,000, is credited with having produced over $20,000,000 and is still a shipper.

On my first visit to Victor I noticed a large group of substantial brick buildings (which looked to me like an electric sub-station) just off the main street, and as I walked past the barricaded doors and windows and looked at the broken and charred ore bin I wondered what they had been. "That's the Gold Coin property," shouted a boy in answer to my question, as he sped by on a bicycle; but I was not wholly satisfied until I saw some old photographs of the Coin, which showed its stack belching smoke and its surface buildings covering a somewhat greater area than they do now.

The Gold Coin mine, located in 1891 by J. R. McKinnie, was the one accidentally tapped in 1894, when a blast into solid rock for the foundations of the Victor Hotel opened a vein, which upon development paid over a million dollars in dividends. The Woods brothers, promoters of Victor,

RUIN OF CHURCH, GILLETT

VICTOR HILLS

↓ BENNETT AVENUE, CRIPPLE CREEK

secured a bond and leases on the Gold Coin property for $55,000 and offered stock to the public for seven cents a share. Little of it was bought, so they raised the price to $6.50 a share; whereupon it was snapped up.

The Coin was the chief mine in the heart of the city and each year, as its output increased, its property was improved. On New Year's night, 1898, the Hotel Victor was formally opened

> With a grand ball and banquet given by the Gold Coin Co. and its employees. The entertainment really began in the shaft house of the Coin where the reading room was gracefully tendered to the men by Warren Woods, president of the company and accepted on behalf of the miners.
>
> Over the engine room in the shaft house, a bath room and lockers for 125 men have been constructed and in the adjoining room there are tables containing all the latest periodicals and best books, so that the employees in quitting work can bathe, change their clothing and acquaint themselves with the latest thing in literature before leaving the mine.
>
> The presentation of the reading room was followed by a reception held by Mr. Woods in the parlors of the Hotel Victor, which was attended by fully 400 people, including all the Gold Coin employees.
>
> The hotel was a beautiful spectacle, being decorated throughout with green and yellow bunting, palms, potted plants and leaves of lycopodium.
>
> At 11:30 the doors of the big dining room were opened and 350 guests were seated at once. No prince ever sat down to a banquet more delicious or served with more perfection.—*Victor Daily Record,* Jan. 2, 1898.

By 1899 the mine, whose ore bodies increased as depth was gained, produced 30,000 tons a year and paid $120,000 in dividends. Even Victor's fire, which destroyed the frame shaft house and the other surface buildings, delayed production only forty days. A new shaft house of brick was then erected. Theodore Roosevelt and his party visited the Coin in 1901 and were taken down to the 800-foot level, where they were shown a streak of high-grade ore. The Colonel was greatly interested and when he was handed a pick and invited to help himself he "peeled off his coat and started to grab hold of the pick, but they told him it was simply a demonstration; that there were ample rich specimens available for him up in the shaft house."

That same year the Woods people developed the Economic Gold Extraction Co.—"the largest ore reduction plant in the United States"—whose huge mill foundations lie in the gulch below Squaw mountain. They also built the United Mine tunnel through the mountain to connect the Coin with the Economic mill.

The two greatest mines of Victor were the Independence and the Portland. Winfield Scott Stratton came to Colorado in 1872 and, to fit himself for prospecting, took a short course in assaying and mineralogy. He then tried his luck in virtually every camp in the state but never struck a bonanza. During the winters, when the mines were covered with snow, he earned his living as a carpenter; but mining was in his blood, and in the spring of 1891 he walked to Cripple Creek so as to save stage fare, carrying his prospector's outfit on two burros. He talked to Bob Womack, prospected on the nearby hills, and wandered over to Battle mountain, six miles from the area where most of the digging was being done. In the middle of June, while most of

(468)

the prospectors were scouring the surface of Bull hill, he came upon a big outcropping of granite at the base of Battle mountain. Though it looked worthless, he took samples from the surrounding ore and tested them with his blowpipe. The results showed some gold in the float, but he was positive that he had not found the vein. He staked out a number of other claims but kept returning to the immense granite dike which he felt sure must contain the mother lode; for his knowledge of mining told him that "where the ledge protruded, he would find the contact of porphyry and granite" which was bound to contain it. Consequently, on July 4, 1891, he rode back to the spot and staked out the Independence and the Martha Washington claims; and almost as soon as he began digging he struck a rich vein.

By discovering and developing the Independence mine Stratton did more than any man to make the camp known. The mine proved incredibly rich from the first, and before long Stratton found himself a millionaire—the first in the district.

> Stratton had barrels of luck when he came into possession of the property which he has successfully developed With him it is gold, gold, gold. He has more gold than he has any earthly use for, hence he took out from the Independence last year only the ore which was met with in prosecuting development. . . . Chambers of sylvanite running from $25-$5,000 a ton were passed by with not a regret and only 6,000 tons were shipped from the great mine during the year.—*Denver Daily News*, Jan. 1, 1899.

In 1899 Stratton sold the Independence to an English company for $11,000,000, and during the next fifteen years the new company continued to develop the phenomenal property. Then on July 1, 1915, the Stratton Independence, Ltd., became part of the Portland estate. At three o'clock on June twenty-ninth all the deeds to the property were signed at Colorado Springs. At the same hour in Victor the transfer was made a reality by Philip H. Argall, the general manager of Stratton's Independence, Ltd., presenting to the manager of the Portland Gold Mining Co. "a tuft of grass with attached soil, a piece of ore and a key." These emblems, according to an old English custom, symbolized the transfer from one company to another of soil, buildings and underlying ores.

Between 1891 and 1915 the total gross production of the Independence was $23,621,728. After it was consolidated with the Portland Gold Mining Co., workings from the Portland were extended under the Independence workings with the intention of mining the Portland group through the Independence shaft.

John Harnan, the discoverer of the Portland, was an experienced miner, who, having prospected in Idaho and Montana, drifted to Cripple Creek with the gold rush but found no work. Just as he was preparing to leave the district after several unsuccessful weeks of job-hunting he met Stratton, who immediately hired him as a cook. For several months he worked both as a cook and miner until he accumulated a little money and decided to try mining on his own. Near the top of Battle mountain he met James Burns and James Doyle, who owned a little triangular piece of ground, not more than a sixth of an acre in size, on which they had staked a claim in January,

1893, which they called the Portland. The men had built a cabin on their claim and were working the ground but without success. Both of them were completely discouraged when Harnan came along and chaffed them by saying, "Why don't you make a mine out of this claim?"

"We'll take you in as a partner and give you a third of the holdings if you uncover any pay ore," grunted Burns. Harnan set to work and ten days later, having driven a crosscut from their shaft six feet below the surface, he struck the Portland vein.

The claim was not patented, and fear of claim jumpers made the partners keep the mine a secret. They worked at night, two sacking ore underground while the third stood guard at the entrance to the shaft. While it was still dark, one of them would pack as much as he could carry on his back and start on foot for Colorado Springs, thirty-five miles away. When enough ore had accumulated at the Springs it was taken to the smelter, where it brought as much as $1,000 a ton. With this money the men paid for supplies and tools and a much-needed wagon in which to transport their ore. The wagon broke down on its first trip and, although they successfully hid the ore by covering it with sacks, the wheel tracks revealed the location of the shaft.

Prospectors on adjacent claims immediately began to make trouble, and the mine was tied up in litigation. Stratton, who by this time was making money, urged the three partners to form a company, promising to take stock in it up to $75,000 and to supply the money they needed to fight the jealous claimants. Together in 1894 they formed the Portland Gold Mining Co. and were able to buy off desirable claims and contending interests, even though at one time there were twenty-six lawsuits on the records against the mine. Their holdings soon comprised nearly two hundred acres, with an equal underground area of mineral territory honeycombed with tunnels, drifts and cross-cuts. As years went by both the Portland and the Independence mines were developed until the properties adjoined. More consolidation followed until the value of the entire group rose to $4,000,000.

The ore was so rich that occasionally carloads were worth $50,000. By 1911 the mine had produced over $30,000,000 and the grand total of all properties owned by the company was estimated at nearly $100,000,000. The mine was one of the richest in the world—its yield being one-eighth of the whole return of the district. During World War I increased costs of operation put the company nearly a quarter of a million dollars in debt and caused payments to be suspended; but by 1928 the debt was wiped out and dividends resumed. The Portland is still producing. To cite but one example: After World War II a G. I. made $25,000 from a lease within six months after his discharge.

Rich ore is always a temptation to miners, and it is not unusual for some to carry away small quantities of it hidden on their persons; but in the Cripple Creek district, where so many of the mines were bonanzas, high-grading reached an all-time high. A High-graders Association was formed, and organized bands of ore-stealers operated through twenty-seven assay offices, whose owners took a cut of the proceeds and asked no questions as to the origin of the ore. Even when the assayers took more than their share of the profits the men dared not squeal for fear of discovery. It was estimated that $5,000 of stolen ore was brought to these exchanges in a single day. Finally several of the places were dynamited, either by members of the High-graders Association who knew that the owners were keeping more than their share of the ore, or at the instigation of the mine owners who were anxious to break up the illegal practice.

Members of a gang would work at the same mine and would manage to carry away several pounds of ore a day. The men often made midnight raids on shafts where night shifts were not working, or they would go into unused shafts where there was known to be valuable ore and drill at night, working by candlelight and making small blasts that could not be heard outside.

In one mine the high-grade was carried out in hollow pick handles. When a pick was taken to the blacksmith shops to be sharpened, the blacksmith, who was on the "inside," would unload it. At the Last Dollar mine the thieves held up the engineer and stole $1500 worth of ore; at another mine they drove up in a wagon just at dawn and loaded it with all the high-grade stored in the mine office.

To protect their property, mine owners sent ore to the sampling works and to the smelters in sealed cars accompanied by armed guards who rode on the car roofs. The Independence mine alone was said to have lost $1,000,000 through high-grading; so the company ordered all men leaving the property each night to strip and change their clothes. This was modified to an inspection of each miner clad only in his underwear; yet even so "under-grounding" went on. One night mine guards surprised three men at work in the portion of the Independence known as the Jewelry Shop. The men blew out their lights and the battle was fought in the dark, except for the spurts of flame whenever a revolver was fired. One man was shot, and another fell eighteen feet down a shaft.

Labor troubles which upset the camps of the district in 1894 and again in 1903 were caused by clashes between the mine owners and the Western Federation of Miners. The first strike was caused by inequalities in wages and working hours and "excelled in desperation and disaster any conflict between employers and employees that had ever been fought out in the metalliferous mining camps of the country." Forty mines were working under an eight-hour schedule and were paying $3 a day, and nine were working under a nine-hour system. In January, 1894, a notice was posted at the Pharmiscist mine stating that hereafter only $2.50 would be paid for an eight-hour day, and a few days later similar notices appeared at the other large mines. The only explanation given was that production did not warrant the three-dollar wage; yet dividend figures disproved this statement.

In February, as a result of a meeting of the miners, all managers who were working men nine hours a day were notified that unless they complied within ten days with the union law of $3 and eight hours, the men would be called out on strike. No attention was paid to this threat, the strike was called, and pickets were placed around the offending properties.

The first violence occurred at Altman above the city of Victor, where on March 16th six deputy sheriffs who were on their way to the Victor mine were attacked and "arraigned before a Police magistrate on the charge of carrying concealed weapons." At the same time rioting miners visited other mines and beat up the guards. As a result of this disorder the sheriff of El Paso county (there was no Teller county then) appealed to Governor Davis H. Waite for troops, and two days later three companies under Brig. Gen. E. J. Brooks arrived. That evening a delegation of union men from Altman met with Gen. Brooks and assured him that there was no disturbance in the district "beyond the ordinary offenses constantly occurring in mining camps." When this word was reported to the Governor, the troops were withdrawn.

Next, a committee of strikers met with the mine owners; but as no agreement could be reached the strike continued, while the mines operated with non-union labor. To protect the men who were working the mines Sheriff Bowers swore in a large number of deputies and placed them around all the properties in the district. The strikers were afraid that this large force of men would run them out of the county or that the sheriff would serve warrants on them at the first opportunity.

Defiantly they constructed a fort on Bull hill near Altman and awaited an attack from the deputies. When more deputies arrived (making the total number 1200), the miners waited no longer but marched down Bull hill to meet them and in the ensuing skirmish took possession of the Strong mine above the city of Victor. The following morning the two groups clashed again, both sides losing men and taking prisoners as hostages.

To attempt to settle the trouble Gov. Waite went to Bull hill and met the strikers at a meeting held at Altman, in which he assured them that they had nothing to fear from the deputies. Delighted with his fairness and understanding, the strikers made him their sole arbitrator and authorized him to settle all differences between them and the mine owners. At the next conference the Governor represented the strikers, and J. J. Hagerman and D. H. Moffat the owners, and as a result of the meeting the eight-hour day with $3 wages was agreed upon, as well as the policy of the open shop. The settlement of this strike in favor of the miners ushered in nine years of industrial peace in the district. All during these years the miners had a strong organization—most of the civic officers of the camps (especially those at Goldfield) were union men—and although none of the towns was completely unionized, non-union men were kept out of key positions.

The strike of 1903 was called in protest to the treatment given certain workers in two Colorado City mills. Certain unfair and discriminatory practices were said to have been investigated and rectified, but the Western Federation of Miners claimed that the mills had not lived up to their contract. Therefore, when a protest strike in the Cripple Creek district was ordered on Aug. 10, 1903, "an almost general close down was affected," and thirty-five hundred miners were out of work. The mine owners declared that since the men were not asking anything of them they would run their business to suit themselves, and they promptly filled the mines with non-union workers and surrounded their properties with armed guards.

During the rest of the summer occasional fights occurred between the miners and the men who were replacing them, but violence did not become general until September. After a justice of the peace from Anaconda was attacked while walking down a street in Altman, and several non-union men were badly beaten up at the Independence mine, and a train was wrecked, and two men were killed by an explosion in the Vindicator shaft, Governor Peabody ordered out the National Guard and "proclaimed Teller county in a state of insurrection and rebellion."

The militia patrolled the streets in place of the local police and began to arrest men who threatened them or who were considered dangerous characters. These men, many of whom were members of the Western Federation of Miners, were thrown into the local "bull pens" and held there without definite charges being made against them. Even with the soldiers on guard, tragedies occurred. On Jan. 26, 1904, just as the night shift at the Independence was leaving the mine, the cage in which sixteen men were being brought to the surface was dropped down the shaft and all but one were killed. Early in the spring the Governor met with the Mine Owners' Association and, after putting the responsibility back on them, removed the troops in April.

At 2 A. M. on June 6 the station at Independence was blown up while twenty-five non-union men from the Findlay mine were waiting for a suburban train to take them home. Some were in the waiting room and some on the platform when the train whistled. Immediately afterwards a terrific explosion blew up the depot and killed thirteen of them. Others were mutilated and injured. No clue was found except seventy-five feet of wire leading from the wrecked station and part of a revolver.

Next morning the managers of the mines ordered them closed; all saloons in Victor, Cripple Creek and Goldfield were shut, and the idle miners gathered in the streets of Victor or visited the scene of the explosion. During the day the mine owners took over by forcing the sheriff to resign and appointing their own man in his place. While the secretary of the Mine Owners' Association was haranguing the crowd in Victor and denouncing the Western Federation of Miners as a breeding ground for agitators, a riot broke out in which several men were shot—two fatally.

The Colorado National Guard was immediately put in complete control of the Cripple Creek district, and squads of soldiers and deputies began to round up members of the federation and throw them into the bull pens at Victor, Goldfield and Independence. Twenty-eight men were deported from Cripple Creek by train, accompanied by deputy sheriffs, and were released upon reaching Denver. On June 10th Adjutant Gen. Bell, who was in charge of the National Guard, issued a more drastic deportation order saying: "It is a military necessity. They are men against whom crimes cannot be specified but their presence is regarded as dangerous to law and order."

That afternoon seventy-nine men, heavily guarded, left Victor on a special train and were taken to within one-half mile of the Kansas-Colorado border. They were ordered to enter Kansas, but not more than half a dozen had crossed the line before a Kansas sheriff and his posse arrived and forbade the rest to enter. There was nothing for them to do but to walk back four miles to Holly, where the local authorities permitted them to spend the night. Later in the month thirty-three men were similarly deported to the New Mexico line, and with all the union leaders removed, Governor Peabody thought it safe to withdraw the troops on July 26, 1904.

As a result of the strike all the unions in the district were broken up and the card system of employment was instituted by the Mine Owners' Association. Under this system all applicants for work were required to answer certain questions on a blank form, and if the answers were satisfactory the applicant was given a card authorizing that he be employed. He kept the card until he found a job and then surrendered it to his new employer. The next time he looked for work he was issued a new card by his former employer, but if he had been a trouble maker, his card was withheld; and without the card he could not obtain work in other mines. By this system the mine owners successfully prevented any member of the Federation from securing work in any mine in the district. The sympathy strike was over, but the miners had lost.

A short time before this strike was called, the mine owners had agreed to start work on a drainage tunnel which would unwater the lower levels of the big mines. Work had scarcely begun, and the El Paso mine, unwilling to wait for the settlement of the strike, put armed guards on its property to protect the men whom it hired to carry on the 5000-foot-bore; and through their efforts the work was completed. On the day the tunnel was opened, the whistle at the mine "announced that a torrent was pouring from the tunnel's mouth," and as soon as its insistent screech was heard the whistles at every other mine in the district took up the chorus.

A still larger project was then proposed—the Roosevelt Drainage tunnel—and was completed in 1910. From its terminus laterals were later run to tap various hills, so that by 1914 the "general water level of the district had been lowered about 700 feet vertically." After that the big mines continued to dig until they were below the level of the Roosevelt tunnel, and water collected in the deep shafts of these properties. To cut pumping costs the Golden Cycle Company then decided to bore a new and deeper drainage tunnel, known as the Carlton tunnel, which would connect with the Portland shaft and ultimately with the Cresson, Ajax and Vindicator mines. The seven-mile bore, which cost $1,500,000, was completed in 1941, and in less than two days the properties tapped were dry.

Most of the mining in the district since 1901 has been done under the leasing system, by which a man or a company obtains a lease which permits the working of some portion of a mine where ore is believed to be present but where the owner of the property has not yet explored. Since each leaser finances his own area and discovers new veins and pockets, the mine is developed with little outlay of capital.

On my last visit to Victor, while I sat at breakfast with the Ripleys, Don fired bits of information at me between sips of Bessie's excellent coffee. "Did you know that Lowell Thomas graduated from the Victor high school and that Jack Dempsey worked in the Portland mine?" When I shook my head he went on, "His name wasn't really Jack; but after his brother, who was named Jack, was killed in an accident at the mine, he took his brother's name. He came from Manassa, Colorado, you know, way down by the New Mexico line.

"Lots of millionaires were made here and in Cripple Creek. Verner Z. Reed of Denver and Spencer Penrose of Colorado Springs made their money through investments; D. H. Moffat, through his mines and his railroads; and Stratton, through the Independence.

"You remember the morning that we drove up on Battle mountain and watched the ore trains switching below the Vindicator dump over near the Golden Cycle property? Last June the officials of the Golden Cycle Corporation decided to junk the Midland Terminal road, which has been hauling ore from their mine here to the mill in the Springs. Now they plan to move that mill right up to this district where the gold is mined and they won't need the railroad any more."

One day as I left Victor and climbed out of the city past the Portland and Ajax properties and on up the hill toward Altman, I looked down on the huge dump and the group of buildings at the Vindicator mine and back at a neat village far below on the flat. The place was Goldfield and, although only part of its buildings are standing today, its streets still form a perfect gridiron dotted with low frame buildings and a few larger structures, such as the fire station and the church. Both because of its proximity to the big mines and its comparatively level terrain the freight yards of the Florence and Cripple Creek railroad were located at Goldfield, and stations were built both there and at Independence.

Goldfield and Independence

In 1894 Goldfield was "naught but a cow pasture given up to the undisputed possession of herds of cattle and the omnipresent gopher" and was "surrounded by the eternal hills, green with sweet-smelling grass . . . almost the year round." All about it were mines—the Victor, the Vindicator, the Golden Cycle, the Independence, the Findlay and the Hull City Placer. Goldfield has been variously described as the "City of Homers," as the third city in size in the Cripple Creek district, and as the one with most sidewalks. It was entirely covered by surface locations of mining claims;

> The very dust of the streets of Camp Goldfield is impregnated with the precious metal, and is not the ground beneath honey-combed and seamed with drifts and stopes and cross cuts and veins and deposits of gold?—*Cripple Creek Evening Star,* New Year's Edition, 1904.

> The familiar rough shanty of the average western mining town and its narrow, squalid streets, are here replaced by well-kept lawns and neat, comfortable residences.— *Cripple Creek Morning Times,* Jan. 1, 1899.

Close to the Vindicator mine, a good paying property which shipped over 20,000 tons of ore a year, was the Hull City Placer, whose activity caused the town of Independence to spring up in 1895. As the town spread in the direction of Goldfield, the two communities were consolidated, bringing the combined population to 3,000. Next to the Portland and Gold Coin mines, the Hull City Placer produced more than any other mine in the area.

(475)

Goldfield was in the heart of the labor struggles both in 1894 and in 1903. Between it and Victor was the Strong mine, which was captured by the strikers in the first clash, and in both strikes the militia camped close to the city, which was a hot bed of Unionism. All the city officials were members of the Western Federation of Miners, and not until the strike was in the hands of the militia in 1904 did a mere handful of non-union citizens oust them from office. The Federation members left the district, and by the time the new civic regime began nearly half the population was gone and almost half the buildings were empty. Even so the new city fathers optimistically asserted: "That Goldfield has a bright future even the most pessimistic will agree." But in 1947 Goldfield's streets were almost empty, and at Independence little but a station and a water-tank are left.

Altman   I heard about Gillett while talking to a Forest Ranger at Steamboat Springs. "It's right behind Pike's Peak," he told me; "and it had forty-one assay offices and ninety-one attorneys during boom days. It's the only town in the United States that ever staged a bull fight. You'd better look it up." A year later I drove toward Cripple Creek from Divide, looking for it.

Gillett was harder to find than I had supposed, for the road which the map showed as leading to the town, wandered across open ranch country toward two large white buildings—the only ones visible for miles. "That can't be Gillett," I told my companion. "Old mining towns don't have freshly painted white buildings. Let's go to Victor by way of the High Drive and ask some questions about it there."

From the High Line road the entire mining district is spread out below like a great map. Close by are Globe hill, Ironclad hill, Bull hill and Battle mountain, all covered with hoists, shaft houses, transformers, sheds and dumps. Some properties are large and some small; some are working and others are idle. We drove over the tops of the hills until we reached Midway and stopped to get our bearings. While we were trying to identify certain properties below us, a miner came out of his cabin and began to talk.

"You ought to go to Altman on top of Bull hill," he said, pointing to a twisting road which disappeared among the pines and aspens near a shaft house. "It was the world's highest incorporated city—11,000 feet. During the big strike in 1894 there wasn't any town there. You can still see the location of the old fort on Bull cliffs where the miners barricaded themselves. The place was named for Sam Altman who ran a sawmill and built the first stamp mill in Cripple. He used some of the steam from his saw mill to operate the stamps. You should have seen Altman when it had hotels and restaurants and its main street was full of buildings. It was incorporated in 1896, and four days afterwards warrants covering the cost of incorporation were redeemable at par. Two thousand people lived there in 1900, two-thirds of whom worked steadily in the mines in the vicinity. There wasn't any water up there, so they piped it from Grassy gulch two miles away and had to raise it a thousand feet to get it to the town."

We thanked him and went to Altman, where we found piles of rock and debris, the skeletons of mine buildings, a rusty fireplug, three or four frame cabins and a herd of cows grazing on the sparse grass of the hill

GILLETT AND PIKES PEAK

↓ PEMBERTON (WEST CREEK)

top. "And this is the place of which the *Denver Daily News* said: 'From the summit of Bull hill the lights of Altman twinkle on dark nights like stars in a firmament,' " I murmured, surveying the dismal townsite. I noticed a dirty fragment of lace curtain flapping at the broken window of one of the cabins as we drove away, and I recalled a photograph taken in 1900 which showed the whole hill top covered with buildings and the town surrounded with shaft houses from whose smoke stacks smoke and steam were pouring Looking at the dreary waste that marks the site of the once active community I quoted one sentence from the 1899 New Year's Edition of the *Denver Republican*: "A breezy place is Altman, but it has no slums and no hospitals, for the people will not have the one and have no use for the other."

"We still haven't found Gillett," said Ruth, my companion on this trip. "When we get back to Midway, I'll ask the miner if he can direct us to it."

Gillett

"It's Gillett now, is it?" he inquired in answer to our knock on his cabin door. "It's back a ways, down on the flat. You must have passed it coming up here," and beckoning to us to follow him, he led the way to the edge of the hill and pointed down into the valley toward two familiar white buildings!

"That's Gillett," he said. "One of those buildings belonged to the Midland Terminal railroad which used to run through there. You can just see the dump of the old Reduction Works, too. It used to handle one hundred tons of ore a day. It was a chlorination plant and employed close to a hundred men the year round. Gillett was a one-man district; that is, each man worked his own property. There was never enough outside capital invested in the mines to make them come to the front.

"The Lincoln mine was the best property. It was located in 1892 and paid from the grass roots, with surface ore that averaged $114 a ton; but it got tangled up in litigation, and that stopped production. There's still ore that was never found waiting to be mined, and the hills and gulches for miles around are full of prospect holes and miners' cabins.

"They used to call it the Gateway City, because it was the first town you came to on the railroad as you entered the Cripple Creek district. Did you ever hear about the bull fight?" he asked, and sitting on a rock he lighted his pipe and between puffs told us the following story:

During the summer of 1895 "Arizona Charlie" Wolf arranged for a bull fight to be held in the race track at Gillett. Mexican bulls and matadors were imported for the affair and the event was widely advertised. On August twenty-fourth, the day of the fight, fifty thousand people poured into the little city "from all parts of the United States and from Mexico" and not only packed the arena but crowded the sides of the nearby hills. Some say that the bulls didn't put up a fight and that several were killed, and some insist that so many protests were made to the authorities on the grounds of cruelty to animals that the fight was stopped after the first bull fell. Whichever is true, the rest of the three-days celebration was called off, and the slaughtered bulls were distributed to the poor.

The half-mile race track on the north edge of the town where the fight was held, was for years the pride of the Cripple Creek district, and many

(478)

a thorough-bred horse pounded its turf. It was therefore a shock to the old-timers when in 1911 the track, which was by then part of a ranch, was ploughed up and sown in oats.

Filled with the miner's stories we started back to the dirt road and drove to the two white buildings beyond which were the remnants of the town. A row of water hydrants careened along the ditch at the side of the main road, several houses were scattered over the meadow much as they had been at Pearl, and the ruins of the reduction plant could be seen a quarter of a mile down the railroad track. What fascinated us most was a brick and stone building with a barrel-curved roof surmounted with a cross which stood in the middle of a ploughed field, and scrambling through the barbed wire fence we hurried over to it.

"I believe Gillett had an Evangelical, a Congregational and a Roman Catholic church, and this must have been the latter," I told Ruth as we stepped into the frame vestibule and peered into the building. The interior was a depressing sight, for everything had been removed, broken plaster littered the ground, and nothing but cattle had found shelter in it for years. We saw no one in town to talk to, so after making some sketches of the church we drove away. Gillett was a disappointment until five years later when I accidentally ran across a copy of the *Gillett Forum* in the State Bureau of Mines and from its issue of December 31, 1898, gleaned the following:

THE GATEWAY TO GOLD.

> Gillett is well-named the "City of Destiny" for Aphrodite-like She Spread Her Wings and from Her Exalted Position Overlooks the Entire District.

The city was regarded as the "natural residence town" as well as the summer resort of the district.

> Gillett has admitted thousands of tons of food and clothing to the brawny miners who delve in the bowels of our many hills and produce that which enriches the world at the rate of sixteen millions in gold annually. . . . After climbing the hills of our sister cities the entire week, the citizen wishing to give his family a day of recreation brings them to Gillett and here enjoys the benefits of . . . sitting at the foot of one of our many crags, that tower away up into the clouds or by the side of one of the many waterfalls, and after looking from nature to nature's God, leaves for his home the better man.

The people have

> Pride in their homes and like the beaver, whose home they have destroyed in order to make room for a higher order of creation, they have never rested until the town was supplied with all the modern conveniences.

The city had a water system supplied from the "melted snow of Pike's Peak" and an electric light and power plant of its own.

> Supt. Smedley must certainly have sold his blankets, we are certain he never takes time to use them. Here, there, everywhere, the man is always busy, and constantly improving the light and making it more convenient for the users in private offices and homes.

(479)

The Midland Terminal railroad ran through the town, and because of its level location the company's railroad yards, roundhouses and shops were located there. The road, which was broad-gauge, ran two trains a day to Cripple Creek and to Colorado Springs and handled all the outgoing freight of the district.

When Cripple Creek was gunning for a new county seat Gillett announced modestly that it was

> Not in the fight but would accept the temporary county-seat until the balance of the district made up its mind as to its ultimate location. If in the wisdom of the legislators, Gillett should be designated as temporary county seat she will furnish adequate buildings for county purposes.—*Cripple Creek Morning Times*, Jan. 1, 1899.

I always hate to leave the Pike's Peak area, for it conjures up so vividly the ghosts of a fabulous mining era. So on this trip to Gillett before returning to Colorado Springs I drove back to the hill above Cripple Creek and stopped to look down over the district that was once so full of excitement, violence and gold. The first two have disappeared, but the gold is still there.

West Creek and Pemberton

"Whether there's anything left of the mining days at West Creek I don't know, but let's go and find out," I said to Francis one October morning as we started from Colorado Springs for a day's drive into the hills. At Woodland Park we left the paved highway and drove for miles northwest through forested areas and through ranch country looking for the mining town.

The mining excitement in this district began in 1895. That August, Capt. George F. Tyler sent his son to Denver with samples of outcroppings he had found on his ranch and told him to show them to mining men and to persuade some experienced man to come out and make a thorough investigation of the country round about as a mining proposition. An investigation was made, and although the samples found were not promising they warranted further prospecting, and with Tyler's help a mining company was formed. Early in 1896 about five hundred square miles of public land were thrown open to prospectors, who were soon scratching at the lime belt east of where Pemberton was to be located and at the porphyry belt west of the present site of West Creek in the hope that the formations were an extension of the Cripple Creek field.

Prospectors and investors poured in, and as men pitched their tents or hastily ran up log cabins several small campsites were laid out and called Tyler, Pemberton, West Creek, North West Creek, North Cripple Creek, Ackerman, Trumbull and Given.

Some ore was found but nothing sensational, so the miners held a meeting at which a novel but practical plan was proposed for the development of the most promising claims. According to the proposal:

> Each man is to work so many days for nothing, with the understanding that he has no claim against the property worked upon, unless paying mineral is found, when his claim shall be a lien on the mine. The idea is to demonstrate what the camp is, by shipping ore as soon as possible, and all hands will turn in and aid in a movement which is for the benefit of all.—*Silverton Standard*, Dec. 28, 1895.

In March, 1896, when the first carload of West Creek ore was shipped, the miners said loudly but to rather deaf ears: "Now is the time for Denver people to take hold of West Creek to the advantage of both places." Without waiting to see what Denver would do they launched another community project under the auspices of the Miner's Protective Association. The plan was to drive a tunnel five hundred feet into the most promising vein in the camp. Subscribers to this project "will put in their work at the rate of three shares of stock for each shift and three shifts are to be kept at work constantly and until the completion of the tunnel."

In May, 1896, a strike was made at Pemberton and another at Given. Nick Miller made his strike in the Last Chance mine southeast of Pemberton and excitedly showed specimens of the roasted quartz "covered with globules of gold" to everyone. He even invited the mayor to come out to the mine, get some rock and test it for himself. This the mayor proceeded to do, returning to town with a bucketful of samples which he took to the assay office. When the tests were made, "gold came to the surface, with one piece as large as a grain of wheat."

When the strike on Given's ranch was known, everyone dashed across country to the new site, where a tunnel was being driven and a town had been laid out. Upon their arrival the newcomers found the camp deserted, for all the miners had gone to the hills where the strike had been made to stake out new claims.

In 1897 the West Creek district, in which there were now five thousand prospectors, was spoken of as a "promising infant which may develop into a full-sized mining camp of lusty proportions." More people were pouring in every day by stage from South Platte, or across the hills from Palmer Lake. There were two women in Pemberton and they were "reaping fortunes baking bread at fifteen cents a loaf." The entire country was so staked out that it resembled a "forest of stakes," and newcomers did not even attempt to look for new locations but bought claims from those who were already there. Pemberton was the largest camp, with forty buildings, ten saloons, telephone and telegraph facilities and a newspaper.

"We must be nearly there," I said, after we had driven for miles without seeing anything but trees and rocks.

"It must be at the foot of this long hill," said Francis as we dropped down into a little rolling valley walled with grotesque rocky knobs covered with pines. He was right, for by the time we had reached the bottom of the grade we were in West Creek. Its buildings were all fairly new cabins and barns, and there seemed to be nothing that suggested the days of its mining boom. Just as I was suggesting that we leave, I spied a false-fronted store of weathered timber. It was obviously older than the other buildings, and while I made a drawing of it Francis tried to gather data about the town from a young woman who came over to watch me work. Nothing else in the place was old except two cabins facing the store; so in a short time we drove off, expecting to take a back road to Florissant.

The road leading out of West Creek toward Florissant was narrower and less travelled but "possible if it's dry," the young woman had said; and since it was a beautiful day we thought it safe to take it. After travelling about a mile we came to a fork in the road marked by highway signs, one of which said "Florissant" and the other "West Creek;" but the latter sign, instead of pointing toward the town we had just left, pointed in exactly the opposite direction. As the Florissant road was shaded by trees it was deep in snow and ice, and we decided not to try it. But the other road baffled us —how could we go ahead and reach West Creek when we had just come from there? Still, as it was the better road, we ventured down it through farmland and woodsy country, and the farther we drove the less we knew where we were. All at once I saw another false-fronted, deserted store standing in the middle of a field where no store should be, and excitedly I called a stop.

A few hundred feet beyond the empty building was a modern cabin from whose chimney curls of smoke rose into the crisp air. In order to get our bearings we walked over to it to ask some questions. A pleasant-faced woman, two children, and a sheep with a bell around its neck greeted us at the door, and in answer to our inquiry as to the store in the cornfield the woman said:

"Oh yes, that was the hardware store in West Creek."

"But we've just come from West Creek," we replied.

"You were in Pemberton," she continued, "but now they call it West Creek. My husband grew up here in West Creek and this was part of the main street. There were lots of cabins and tents here, too, but they're all gone now."

So, leaving West Creek, and old Pemberton which is now the new West Creek, we drove back to Woodland Park, utterly confused as to the logic of the names and convinced that research takes one to strange places and produces proof from unexpected sources.

CHAPTER XIX

Boulder County Camps

(For map see inside of back cover.)

IN THE hills back of Boulder in a relatively small and compact area are some of the first mining camps of the state. Some are mere names today, some are tiny villages, a few are "ghosts," and the rest are towns which drowse through the winters when snow nearly isolates them from the valley but which wake each year when summer visitors fill their cottages and resorts.

All the histories agree that the first discovery of gold in the county was made early in 1859 on Gold Run by the first party of "immigrants" who made camp at Red Rock, at the mouth of Boulder canyon. Arriving in October, 1858, the party established itself in shelters and prepared for a long, hard winter. Instead, it was an unusually open winter, and the impatient miners were able to do some prospecting, first at Red Rock where they found enough color to excite them, and then at Gold Hill, where after following the ridge between Four Mile and Left Hand creeks, they discovered in January, 1859, a little gold in a streambed twelve miles up the canyon. The stream, which they christened Gold Run, was shallow and narrow and the placer deposits were small, but the men scanned the surrounding hills for float rock, sure that in them would be found the lodes from which the placer gold had washed down.

Gold Hill

The first quartz vein was discovered by J. D. Scott and was named for him; but a far more important lode was the Horsfal, located in the spring of 1859 by Wm. R. Blore, M. L. McCaslin, and David Horsfal. The Twins and the Alamakee lodes were also found and were developed from surface workings, and as a result of these discoveries the top of Horsfal mountain and the nearby gulches were soon swarming with prospectors.

Although George Jackson had already found placer gold on Chicago Creek (in Clear Creek county), his good fortune was not known until four months after the Gold Run diggings had been discovered and after both placers and lodes had been opened in the Gold Hill district. In July, 1859, the Gold Hill Mining district was organized and laws to govern it were drawn up. The land on which the miners were prospecting was part of Nebraska Territory, so the record of the event was headed, "Miners Meeting of Mountain District No. 1, Nebraska." The fortieth parallel (now Baseline road in Boulder) is the state line between Nebraska and Kansas, and since some of the mineral discoveries were made considerably south of the Gold Hill area, a few of the early claims were recorded as being in Kansas Territory.

By the fall of 1859 a small quartz stamp mill had been hauled by oxteam across the plains and up Left Hand creek, where it was set up at the base of Gold Hill. In this mill, said to be the first of its kind in the state, the first milling was done in the spring of 1860—the ore handled being surface quartz from the Horsfal lode. The placers, several of which were worked by arastras, paid well but by 1861 they were washed out, and although many veins had been located, no one knew how to work any but the rich surface ores. One by one the fifteen hundred miners who had come so eagerly to the diggings left, and the gold field became almost deserted. The Horsfal continued to produce, even after its surface ores were exhausted, yielding $30,000 by 1862. In 1863 its owners erected a six-stamp mill, which worked even though other properties were idle.

Gold Hill was quiet until 1869 when, with the blowing in of the Hill smelter at Black Hawk, ore which did not respond to stamps could be packed over the mountain to it on burros. Since gold was the only metal for which the miners were looking, silver, copper and lead were completely ignored and not until 1872 was tellurium ore considered worth while. Then, with the discovery of gold in combination with tellurium in the Red Cloud mine, mining revived and a second rush to Gold Hill commenced. Other discoveries followed in the Cold Spring, the Slide, and the Cash, until the hills were again swarming with men and cabins were going up on every side.

The camp was still small, for until this new boom not more than fifty men had been in the entire mining district since 1861. A few cabins on top of Horsfal mountain, a boardinghouse close to the Horsfal mine, two or three cabins strung along Aikins gulch (later called Lick Skillet gulch) and a few more at the base of the hill in Left Hand canyon had more than supplied the dwindling population.

With this second boom the townsite was moved from the mountaintop to its present location at the head of Gold Run, and by 1880 over one thousand people were living in the little valley overlooking Lick Skillet or were busy building homes along Gold Run as far down as Salina.

The Wentworth Hotel and the Gold Hill House were popular, but the most celebrated hostelry was the one immortalized by Eugene Field in his poem "Casey's Table d'Hote." In this sturdy log building the round table at which Field wrote his poem is still preserved and is shown to guests. In 1921 Mrs. Jean Sherwood, founder and president of the Holiday House Association of Chicago, purchased the building as a summer resthouse for business and professional women and rechristened it Blue Bird Lodge.

Like most of the mountain towns Gold Hill had two bad fires—the first in 1860, when a forest fire swept the camp, forcing the people to take shelter in prospect holes until the flames had passed by. The second occurred in November, 1894, and for nearly twenty-four hours the town was threatened. The fire started in timber near Ward, and leaped from ridge to ridge borne by a terrific west wind until it reached the ranch land west of the camp. The entire population left the town, which was directly in the path of the fire, and taking whatever possessions they could carry with

OLD POST OFFICE, GOLD HILL (GONE)

ORGAN,
GOLD HILL

HORSFAL SHAFT HOUSE
FROM BIGHORN MT. (GONE)

them climbed to the top of Horsfal mountain to watch the progress of the flames. Many people buried their household treasures in mine shafts or in the sandy sides of the gulches away from the timber. The one piano in town was carefully buried in a hole in the front yard of its owner's cabin and after the danger was past was dug up again. Late in the afternoon the wind subsided, and as snow began to fall the hissing flames were extinguished.

On one trip to Gold Hill I stayed in the home of a woman whose parlor contained a small organ which had been brought across the plains by oxteam. She told me about the days when wild raspberries grew in abundance on the hill above the town, of how all the women went out to the berry patches with their wagons loaded with jars and sugar to put up the fruit, and of how they made camp and stayed a week or more if necessary until the year's crop was canned. She was good enough to go all over town with me, pointing out old landmarks and telling me what they were. From her I heard the story of the piano which was brought to Gold Hill in the nineties and which furnished the music for many a dance. As she talked I could see the six young men who once a month carried the instrument from Mr. Lee's home to Forester's Hall where the dance was held, and at the end of the evening carried it back again.

One summer afternoon Boyd Brown drove me all over the Gold Hill area, which he knew intimately, and after we had explored old trails to forgotten mines, he drove down Lick Skillet gulch to Left Hand canyon to show me more old mills. The road down the gulch is old, not kept in repair, and unbelievably steep; and as we picked up speed while descending it even in "low," I could easily believe the vivid stories of the men who drove stages, ore and lumber wagons down it, especially in winter, when ice and snow coated the surface. At such times they rough-locked the wheels and kept the horses at a trot so as to keep the vehicle from sliding over the outer edges of the roadway.

I have driven home from Gold Hill to Boulder many times down Gold Run past Summerville, Salina and Crisman, but until I knew the mining history of the gulch, the groups of buildings that constitute each of these tiny towns looked alike. At the south edge of Gold Hill and across the stream from the highway is the cemetery, with its old stones half buried in long, unkempt grass. Below it the road swings around the edge of the hill *Summerville* and loops down upon Summerville. Yellow mine dumps cover the hillside beside the road and across the narrow valley. The Victoria, the Cash, the U. S. Bank, the Hoosier Ledge, the Black Cloud and other mines caused a tiny hamlet to grow up close to their shafts and tunnels. The Black Cloud was first worked in the seventies, but with the limited reduction processes then in use ore averaging $50 a ton did not pay. By 1902, because of new methods of treatment, ores averaging $20 a ton were a "source of delight and profit.

Salina　　The most picturesque building left in Salina is the white community church which stands beside the road not far from the town well. Although it has been closed for some years, plans are underway to restore it and open it again. The gulch is narrow and steep at Salina and the mines and the houses cling to the hillsides on either side of the steep, winding main street.

While color was first spied in the waters of Gold Run in 1859, it was not until 1873 that O. P. Hamilton led a party of six to the spot and helped them pitch their tents beside the streambed below the old placer workings. He called the place Salina for the town in Kansas from which they had emigrated and was pleased that in less than a year thirty families were living in the little pioneer colony.

The mining boom lasted from 1874 to 1876, during which time many claims were located and developed. The Black Swan and the Melvina lodes on the summit of Salina mountain were considered the big mines of the camp. By 1875 one hundred mines had been opened, and the reduction works built by Capt. West were running to capacity with ore from his own Shamos O'Brien and from other properties.

According to the *Golden Globe* of Aug. 14, 1875, the camp contained "sixty-nine voters, twenty-five women, and eighteen children." The same year a school house was built in which a six months' school session was held. There were "not many children, but if the citizens are diligent I think we will be able to keep the school marm busy before a great while."—*Sunshine Courier,* Nov. 1, 1875.

Mr. Crofutt of the *Gripsack Guide* visited Salina in 1881 and spoke of its "one hotel, the Salina House, three mills, several stores and saloons and a *high priced toll gate*" as comprising the business portion of the town. In those days the entire region was full of cabins, and according to one optimist Gold Run "must eventually become a close succession of mountain villages."

A little below Salina is the Black Swan property, and for a mile or so *Crisman* below it the road is still lined with mine dumps, old mills and new settling ponds. The next cluster of buildings is at Crisman, a tiny place of a few houses, which even in 1875, when G. A. Kelley was storekeeper and postmaster, had a population of but thirty-five. Obed Crisman, who preceded Kelley to the gulch, erected an ore concentrating mill through which fifty to four hundred pounds of high-grade ore were run and sold direct to the Mint in Denver.

The gulches in the vicinity were full of mines and mine tunnels, but none were better than the Yellow Pine mine in Sunbeam gulch and the Logan which was discovered in 1874 and was "stoped up to the grassroots." While the Yellow Pine was rich in silver and copper with only a trace of gold ore, the Logan, named for Gen. John A. Logan, was said to be the richest gold mine in the county. It was developed through four tunnels one on top of the other, and its free gold was so pure that it was put in a strong box and taken separately to Denver. The rest of the ore was amalgamated at the mill on the property and sold direct to the mint.

A. S. Coan was superintendent of the mine in 1908 when the manager came around to inspect a new tunnel which was being driven into the hillside. It had been bored 2200 feet without finding ore, and the manager ordered the work stopped. He even offered Coan a lease on the mine, and Coan had selected the breast of this tunnel as the portion of the property he would develop. One last round of powder was put into the tunnel, and the blast uncovered $1500 of high-grade ore! The manager hastily withdrew his offer of a lease and ultimately took out $200,000 for the company.

Orodelfan
From Crisman to Boulder the road squirms down the hillsides to the valley, where it joins the Boulder Canyon road at the junction of Four Mile and Boulder creeks. Nothing but a meadow and the charred remains of a resort mark the site of Orodelfan today, but at one time Hunt and Barber's smelting works, a sawmill, a post office and a store covered the little delta between the two streams. The place was known by several names—Maxwell's Mill, Hortonville, Hunt's Concentration Works, and finally Orodelfan. Between 1895 and 1900 a small group of Chinese placered the gravel of the stream for gold, cleaning up their sluices every two weeks and making a modest living from the gold flakes which they painstakingly extracted.

Wall Street
At Salina a faded roadsign at a fork in the road reads "Wall St. 2 miles," and not only the enticing name but the knowledge that an old camp lay ahead lured me up the narrow road which skirts Four Mile creek. Until recently the Boulder mill stood in Salina at the forks of this road, and fortunately I once took time to sketch it; for now that it has been razed, it is difficult to conjure up its size or appearance from the broken foundations and rubble that mark its site.

The two-mile drive to Wall Street was pure adventure. The road was woodsy, and during the first mile I passed only two or three cabins pressed close against the narrow canyon's sides. Suddenly around a curve, framed by the overhanging branches, was a medieval fortress. At its base were cabins and barns, but above these flimsy buildings the stone battlement rose sixty to seventy feet high.

Not far from the massive stone foundation stood a stone house with tall chimneys, which was surrounded by an attractive flower garden in which stood an old lady who smiled at me. I pointed to the stone fortress and asked excitedly, "What is that?" She replied placidly, "That is the foundation of the Wall Street Gold Extraction Company's mill that was built in 1902 to work the Nancy Tunnel. It was a chlorination mill, specially designed to handle the ore of this district in the most economical way. They say it cost $175,000 and was a pioneer of its kind in northern Colorado.

"The Nancy Gold Mine and Tunnel Company was organized early in 1902 to take over the Nancy Mining and Milling Company and to combine and develop all the properties held by that company. I always like to say the names of the mines—they're pretty. Not only the Nancy lode, but the Last Chance, the Gray Copper, the Grand View, the Freya, the Wedges, the Gillard, the Lion's Roost, the Southern Slope, the Gold Eagle, the Silver Eaglet and the Golden Rule were worked through that tunnel, and one-third of the tonnage needed to supply the big mill was provided by this group of mines. New England capital built the mill, and after its completion Wall Street camp came to the front for awhile—1903 was one of its best years.

(488)

"Of course the Nancy and most of the other mines were worked for years before this mill was built. Back in 1893 when Wall Street was called Delphi, the South American, the Wood Mountain, the Forest, the Great Britain, the Star, the Mountaineer and the Tambourine, between here and Salina were all working." She laughed as she said, "I talk like a book, but my people lived here and I grew up with the mines. If you drive up the road a little farther you'll pass the schoolhouse and then an old boarding·house close to the road. Beyond it you'll pass several mine properties be-fore you reach the Wood Mountain mill on the right. The Wood Tunnel was located by G. P. Woods in 1879 and was intended to cut the summit of the Phillips and several other lodes. It's one of the oldest properties here and has been worked on and off for years."

Eager to see all of Wall Street I thanked the white-haired lady and drove on past the huge foundations, past the frame schoolhouse set high above the road and reached by a flight of steep steps, past the dormer-windowed boardinghouse which has since been razed, and past a group of mine buildings whose elaborate stacks and vents made it look like a gigantic still. Finally, at a bend in the road I saw one of the biggest mills that I've found in this county. It was sway-backed and its lower walls bulged, but the glass panes of its many windows caught the noonday light, and a steep trail up a gully beside it invited me to investigate its upper levels. The climb was stiff, and by the time I reached the old mine road which passed the uppermost doorway into its interior I was out of breath. Inside was the usual skeleton-like framework of girders and beams, ladders and stone plat-forms, over which the sunlight made fantastic patterns of light and shade as it shone through holes in the broken roof or penetrated the dusty window panes. Metal-bound vats, a boiler, and the rest of the paraphernalia of a gold mill stood surrounded by the grit of pulverized ore and stained with chemicals. The damp, slightly sour, earthy, acid smell of old ore dumps was all around. While I was drinking in the aura of mining I heard foot-steps, and a couple of men entered the mill on a level lower than the one where I stood. One of them told me he had a lease to work the property and that he was showing the mill to the other mining man.

"This is an old property," he said. "The mill never claimed to save over sixty percent of the ore run through it but it paid big dividends for awhile. If you want to see a real plant, climb up over those big foundations that you passed. The surface buildings of that plant went away up the mountain to the mine road which led to the Nancy Tunnel."

"Have you been beyond this mill?" asked the older man. "A little ways up the road was a small gold camp called Copper Rock which mushroomed in '91. There's nothing there now, but maybe you can locate it by the green copper stain on the side of the cliff.

Copper Rock

"The railroad ran up through here on the other side of the creek, you know. It went on to Sunset and from there over to Ward. Before the trees got so thick you could see the right-of-way from this mill. The Dirigo Tunnel of the Colorado and Northern Gold Mining Company had property

(489)

close to the railroad, as handy as a pocket in a shirt when it came to shipping ore."

Sunset "If you drive another mile still you'll be at Sunset. There were a lot of people there in 1893. I remember the Columbine Hotel where, after the railroad came through, they had fifty people for every meal and tourists were thick as bees all summer. My brother worked in the Poor Woman and the Free Coinage mines and at the Scandia up above the camp. You won't find much at Sunset today—just a couple of houses and some foundations. And come to think of it, you might be interested in the old cemetery, too."

Wall St.
Cont'd. "Was the stone house down by the big foundations the railroad station?" I asked.

"No, that was the mine office and pool hall, if I remember right," said the old man. "I think it was built about 1898 and was used as a kind of club house by the miners. The big mill was dismantled and all the machinery taken up to Sugarloaf, where it was installed in the U. S. mill there. The mine adjoins the Wood Mountain property and is above the Wood Mountain Tunnel, you know."

I drove on past Copper Rock to Sunset, but there was little left to see. Back at the big foundations I left my car by the stone house and started up a trail toward the deserted property. The top of the biggest foundation was level and overgrown with grass, but near the outer end was a large circular well, lined with brick and as deep as the structure itself. Turning my back on the circular pit and looking up at the mountain, I saw another series of foundations that cannot be seen from the level of the road. These rose in terraces, thirty to fifty feet above those on which I stood. As I retraced my steps down the trail, the tremendous area covered by the mill was plainly visible, as terrace upon terrace of stone walls marked the site of other portions of the great mill which had stood beside the solid battlement.

Sugarloaf South of Wall Street is Sugarloaf mountain, on whose southern slope are the remains of the United States Gold Corporation's great mill. Having learned that the machinery from the Wall Street mill was installed in the Sugarloaf property I decided to visit it, by way of the road that turns north from Boulder canyon.

The district was first prospected in 1860, and some of the first ore discovered was worked in an arastra. When the surface gold was worked out the district was abandoned. Like Gold Hill and Salina, the next spurt of mining came in 1873 when tellurium was found in the vicinity and many mines were located and developed.

In October, 1902, a prospector named Niles saw some float in a potato patch a few hundred feet from the shaft of the Livingstone mine. This mine had been worked for some time and had produced over $300,000 in gold. Niles got a team, scraped off the top soil of the patch, and found quantities of rusty gold several feet in depth. After a week's work with his scraper he uncovered a ten-foot vein of rich ore, which was believed to be a continuance of the streak on which the Logan mine near Crisman was located. In a short time $20,000 was taken from this new hole in the ground, and as the

(490)

BOULDER COUNTY MILL, SALINA (razed)

FOUNDATIONS OF MILL, WALL STREET

fame of the Potato Patch shaft became known the Livingstone mine's value was greatly increased.

In 1915 the United States Gold Corporation began to construct the one hundred and fifty-ton cyanide mill, whose carcass still stands on the side of the hill near the center of the camp. In 1940, when I first visited Sugarloaf, the mill was idle but in good condition; during World War II its obsolete machinery was removed for scrap metal, and this past summer as I drove past I noticed that its walls were bulging and that its roof listed heavily to the south. A few mines in the vicinity are worked by leasers, but most of the territory attracts only ranchers and summer visitors, whose cabins dot the hillsides or stand beside the streams.

Magnolia   Almost opposite the Sugarloaf turn-off from Boulder canyon is the one to Magnolia.

The road is a test for any car, for from its take-off beside Boulder creek until it reaches the tiny ghost camp two miles above, it climbs steadily and sharply, with no level stretches on which to gather momentum or to stop to cool the engine. Near the top of the two-mile corkscrew, dumps and ruined hoists and shaft houses begin to appear, some on the open rolling hillside, and some hidden in the bottom of the gulch or screened by pine trees.

In 1875 when Magnolia was a new camp, it was said to be in the Big Hill district, and although the once lively camp is gone, the big hill remains. The first ore was found in June, 1875, by Hiram Fullen, who is also identified with the mines at Sunshine camp. During the telluride boom of the seventies, Fullen and other prospectors discovered ore at Magnolia similar to that which existed at Sunshine, and while excitement ran high the Keystone, Mountain Lion, Washington (formerly the Downs lode), Little Maud and Lady Franklin mines were located. Rich float was found on the surface and in open cuts, and shallow shafts were made along the veins.

The camp was in two parts, the main portion situated on the ridge dividing two canyons, with a fairly steep main street "gently undulating" from one end of town to the other. Further down the hill was another group of buildings and below it a third group, known as Jackson's Camp.

In 1898 all the mines were working, and four or five teams were making daily trips to the mills and sampling works in Boulder. Lessees began working old properties in the early 1900's and succeeded in finding some high-grade ore. In 1915 gold in the form of telluride was again found in rich pockets, but until the Redemption Mines Company built a fifty-ton cyanide mill at Magnolia the great bodies of low-grade ore remained untouched.

I am glad I did most of my sketching at Magnolia over ten years ago, for most of the buildings drawn then are gone now. After exploring this place with Gene, I decided to visit Hiram Fullen's other camp, Sunshine, in which he really uncovered a bonanza.

Sunshine   To reach Sunshine I had to return to Boulder and start back into the hills up Sunshine canyon. After climbing for about seven miles up another long, steep hill, I found the fork in the road and the faded sign on which the word "Sunshine" was lettered against a sunburst painted with yellow radiating rays. Another two miles through timber brought me to an open hilltop dotted with houses—the present town of Sunshine.

Prospectors visited this area in 1859, and as one writer says, "kicked the rotten rock around as if of no value," not realizing that the outcroppings were good tellurium ore. After the discoveries at Gold Hill in 1872 the tide of prospectors swept over the whole area, and in the fall of 1873 D. C. Patterson located the Little Miami lode. Shortly afterwards the Sunshine, Inter Ocean, Grand View, and White Crow lodes were found; but it was George Jackson and Hiram Fullen who discovered the bonanza of the camp, the American mine. After the men had taken out $17,000 in gold they began to fear that the vein might pinch out; so they decided to sell it while it was still producing. When Hiram Hitchcock of New York City became interested in the property they sold with great alacrity, for they were sure that they were getting the better of the bargain.

Hitchcock, who was the proprietor of the Fifth Avenue Hotel, had made and lost fortunes in mines, but with a gambler's instinct he authorized his Colorado agent to buy just one more gold mine for him. In less than two years Hitchcock realized $196,000 from it, sending the ore by burro pack trains to the nearest smelter at Black Hawk. This time Hitchcock had picked a winner, for his mine not only yielded enough gold to recoup his earlier losses but financed his Fifth Avenue Hotel as well.

In 1876 great chunks of ore loosely bound together by wires of gold were sent from the American mine to the Centennial Exposition at Philadelphia, where they aroused great interest. In time the vein pinched out, but not before its output totalled $1,500,000.

The first pioneer who brought his family to settle in the new camp in 1874 was Peter Turner, and his daughter, Sunshine Turner, was the first child to be born there. The camp was situated in White Crow gulch below the site of the present town, and its main street was crowded with buildings. By the spring of 1875 the camp was still growing, and carpenters' hammers were "beating time to the progress of the town."

The *Sunshine Courier*, edited and published by J. B. Bruner and J. W. Cairns, made its appearance May 1, 1875.

The Sunshine Courier
is strictly a
Miners Journal
and the only paper printed in Colorado
that keeps its columns
Free From Politics
and aims to be an
Organ of the People
striking fearlessly at all times in defense of
Right, Truth and Justice.
We will be found always ready with our coat off and sleeves
rolled up to vindicate and battle for the most sacred
Interests of the People.

The paper carried "News from the Rich Free Gold Calaverite Telluride and Sylvanite Regions of the Rocky Mountains" which would be of interest to miners, who were defined as "a kind of cross between a ground hog and a beast of burden—rarely a success at either."

The Grand View Hotel and the Howard House advertised in the paper, as well as the Forest House, which opened in June, 1875. Shortly afterwards a dance was held in the new building, attended by "some of the loveliest dancers that ever fed on mountain air." It lasted

> Till the barnyard choristers were heralding the fast approach of the 'round rosy morn.'—*Sunshine Courier*, June 5, 1875.

In 1876 Commodore Decatur, State Representative to the Centennial Exposition at Philadelphia, visited Sunshine to arouse interest in sending a mining exhibition to the fair. While in town he made a speech, from which an excerpt was printed in the *Courier* of May 20.

Commodore Decatur
What He Thinks About Sunshine.

> The outlook to the east is one of great interest. See how the hills from this wonderland filled with rich ore channels of surprising richness gracefully slope down and kiss the great plains with fond and loving embrace. . . . There are our brothers, the grangers, who struggle with the brown dust of the "Great American Desert."

Later in the year Governor Routt spoke at a Republican meeting held in the Sunshine schoolhouse. The building was "surrounded for many rods in front and on either side by anxious hearers." The meeting

> Ended with a campaign song, when three of the loudest cheers that have ever greeted the grand old hills surrounding Sunshine were given to Gov. Routt and the Republican ticket, and that cheer sounded like a death knell to the ranks of Democracy.— *Sunshine Courier*, Sept. 23, 1876.

Sunshine was notable not only for having "as fine a shaving saloon as can be found in the territory" but also for having "no saloons or tippling places open on Sunday."

The camp reached its peak in 1876, when its mines were all producing and its population rose to 1200. By 1877 the population had dropped to 800, and a paragraph in the *Golden Globe* of Nov. 17, read:

> Our town is not so lively as it once was but we who are here and know what ore is in the mines and what is shipped monthly to the smelting works at Boulder, do not apprehend the danger that many of our croakers do of the future of our town and the permanency of our mines. It is true that the excitement that we once had has passed away and things are now brought to an actuality in our camp. We have 2 grocery stores, one dry goods store, 2 saloons, 3 hotels, 1 drug store and a blacksmith shop and a great many empty houses that were built during the excitement of the place.
>
> Flicktus.

In 1904 gold ore from the Inter Ocean mine won first prize in the Mineral Exhibit at the World's Fair at St. Louis, but although a few mines are worked by leasers and a few families still live there, Sunshine is a sleepy little place. Its tiny cemetery is above the town alongside the present road which climbs toward Bighorn mountain. Trees shade the graves, and mountain winds rush through the tall grasses which half hide the stones.

The first view of Nederland is always a surprise. For miles the drive up Boulder canyon has been through pine forests and between rocky walls, following the stream the entire way. Below the town of Tungsten the canyon widens, and the road cuts through one or two small ranches before climbing the last hill to the breast of Barker Dam. Then, suddenly, as you reach the top, a striking panorama opens before you. At your feet lies the lake of the Barker Reservoir, stretching to the cluster of houses in the distance which is Nederland, while behind and beyond rise the snow-capped peaks of the Continental Divide.

Nederland grew up in 1870 around A. D. Breed's mill. Breed owned the Caribou mine four miles away, and because of the abundance of water in Middle Boulder creek he built his concentrating mill beside the stream. The mill, which stood on the site of the present Wolf Tongue mill, handled the silver ore from his mine, concentrating it and turning out silver bricks, which were then freighted to Denver. A load of these bricks was sent to Central City in 1873 when General Grant visited that town. They formed a pavement in front of the Teller House, on which the General walked as he entered the famous hotel. Gold was so common in Gilpin county that it was not considered good enough for the occasion.

The first settler was N. W. Brown, and for a short time the new camp was called Brownville. It grew slowly and was spoken of as a "struggling village" in 1873, by which date it was known as Middle Boulder.

In 1874, after a company from Holland purchased Breed's mine and mill, the name of the town was changed to Nederland and all during the seventies, eighties and nineties the little community grew steadily, becoming the chief trade center of the entire region. In 1900 it had its first real boom, when tungsten ore was discovered by Sam P. Conger, and during World War I it had a second tungsten boom.

Prospectors and miners in the region became used to finding a heavy dark mineral float, but as they were unfamiliar with it they gave it several names, "heavy iron," "black iron," "hematite" and "barren silver." Conger and his partner. W. H. Wannamaker, took samples of the ore to Denver for analysis and when they learned that the ore was wolframite or tungsten, a rare metal, they quietly secured a lease on a tract of land on the Boulder County ranch and began digging. They discovered the Conger and the Boulder County mines, but at first kept their find a secret. As soon as the news leaked out, however, the rush was on and the hills were black with prospectors.

Conger concentrated his ore at the Midget mill in Nederland and sold the concentrates at from $60 to $97 a ton. During 1901 sixty-five tons of tungsten were mined; during 1903 two hundred and forty-three tons had been extracted, the ore bringing $5 a unit. Until 1904, when the Wolf Tongue Mining Co., who were heavy producers of tungsten, acquired the Midget mill and remodeled it to treat ore from their properties as well as custom ore, nearly all tungsten concentrates had been purchased by the Primos Chemical Co. of Primos, Pa., and had been shipped by them to Pennsylvania, where they were refined into a marketable product. The entrance of the Wolf Tongue Company into the tungsten field opened a competitive market which brought the price of ore up to $12 a unit.

By 1907 the tungsten ore of Boulder county was well known and buyers from Europe began to visit the field. In 1908 several properties were consolidated to form the Primos Mining and Milling Co. with C. F. Lake as manager, and the annual output shot up to five hundred and eighty-four tons of black ore. About this time the steel companies began to clamor for more tungsten to use in hardening their products, and the Primos Co. in 1909 felt justified in building a huge mill at Lakewood, three miles from Nederland. The big mill handled the ore successfully, shipping in 1916 close to $1,000,000 worth of tungsten concentrates. Late in 1914, during World War I, a second rush to the region began, and men mined feverishly for the black metal that was needed in the making of high-powered guns and high-speed tool steels.

As the price paid for tungsten rose from $6 to $36 a unit for high grade ore, the population of Nederland grew overnight. Prospectors slept in barns and tents and paid a dollar a night for the space. Beds in hotels and rooming houses were rented in eight hour shifts, and patrons at restaurants were allowed only twenty minutes for a meal. Nederland had three bars and six bartenders, and to accommodate the trade in one saloon, two extra doors were cut so that the men could enter faster. The stages brought in one hundred passengers a day. Miners from the nearby camps of Crisman, Sunshine, Salina and Eldora headed for the tungsten belt and began haggling for leases on promising properties. Fabulous prices were paid for properties that showed the thinnest streak of tungsten ore. Still the price of tungsten soared until, for a brief two months, it brought $75 a unit. Because of such high prices, big producers imported ore from South America and China where ore was cheaper, and as a result the market broke. After 1918 tungsten brought $25 a unit. but with the end of the war the demand for the metal decreased, and by 1919 the Boulder county companies were forced to close down their mines.

The big Primos mill at Lakewood has disappeared, but the Conger mine and a few other properties are still producing. Nederland has remained a trade center for a mining area, and in summer its cabins are filled with tourists, who revel in the cool nights and quiet charm of the mountain town.

Tungsten   Just below the breast of Barker dam is a little town called Tungsten. The new highway by-passes it, sweeping up above the streets and houses and barricading a few properties at the upper end of town behind its high embankment. In 1926 when I first went there, a good-sized mill stood at the lower end of town beside the old road. It was built during the tungsten excitement of World War I by the Boulder Tungsten Production Co. and so successful was mining then that, although it cost $30,000, it paid for itself in thirty days. At first the town was called Stevens' Camp for Eugene Stevens who was developing the Rogers patent, and it was also called Ferberite, but in time it was known by the name of the only metal mined in the vicinity— Tungsten.

One sunny day I took the Nederland bus and got off at Tungsten so as to have several hours of sketching before its return. It was nearly noon when I alighted, and the only place that seemed as if it might provide a lunch was a store over whose door was a sign, "Ted Green N'Everything."

"Sure, we can serve you," said Ted genially, when I inquired about food. "Just go in the back room and sit down at the table. The boys will be in soon for chow."

Nearly filling the back room was a table covered with oil cloth and set for a meal. At each place was a large, thick plate, face down on the oilcloth. I sat down, turned my plate over and waited. In a few minutes several men tramped in, filled every seat around the table and fell upon the food which was served us. They were all mining men who were working at the mill, and their talk was full of terms that I did not understand. One man older than the rest began to reminisce, and to him I listened eagerly.

"Up to 1900 when the first 'black iron,' as they called it, was found by Sam up at the Conger, this land around here was thought to be worthless. It didn't have silver like Caribou and it didn't have gold like Wall Street; but Sam found us something better.

"After the boom started you should have seen this road, chock full of rigs, wagons and even Stanley Steamers, which were the only cars that could make the grade up through the Narrows of the canyon and up this hill by the dam.

"During the war when the big boom was on, there were 5,000 people in this district and a year before there'd been less than a thousand all told. So many men were bound for the tungsten belt that they had to put an extra car on the interurban from Denver to Boulder, and five big steamers' met the early morning train each day at the Boulder station ready to bring the folks up here.

"When old Charlie Buckingham donated several acres of land below here to the city of Boulder, he said he wanted it called Boulder Falls Park. During the tungsten boom in 1915 he agreed to let them work the tungsten veins on the property, provided the profits went into developing Boulder's parks and recreation areas, and he recommended that the tunnel method of mining be used so as not to ruin the landscape. You've seen the mine up above the falls, haven't you, and the Blue Bird tunnel on the road near the trail to the falls?"

When we had finished our lunch and stacked the dishes, I still had an hour before the bus was due, and sitting on the hillside below the dam I sketched the schoolhouse and the mines within sight.

Three miles beyond Nederland is Eldora, a prettily situated little town *Eldora* in a wide, U-shaped valley. In winter it sleeps, but in summer its cabins and attractive cottages are filled with visitors, many of whom know nothing of its picturesque history.

The Grand Island Mining district was organized in March, 1861. It was sixteen miles long and four miles wide and extended from Castle Rock in Boulder canyon to the Continental Divide. The name Grand Island seems to have been inspired by the imagination of the prospectors, who spoke of a mountain-like island in North Boulder creek a few miles below Caribou, but no such phenomenon existed.

A little prospecting was done nearby on Caribou hill in the early sixties, but so little gold was found that the district was abandoned until 1869 when Sam Conger located the Caribou mine. Even then no other sensational discoveries were made until May 21, 1875, when C. C. Alvord located a mine some miles to the northwest, which he named the Fourth of July; and on Dec. 29 of the same year he staked out the Alvord Placer about halfway between the mine and Eldora. A few locations were made between 1875 and 1892, but until the latter date no real activity was evident.

John H. Kemp, who had been living in Central City, visited the area in 1883 on a hunting trip and was so attracted with its mineral possibilities that he returned frequently to investigate it further. In September, 1891, Kemp and seven others from Central City located the Happy Valley Placer— five hundred acres along Middle Boulder creek and its north fork. As a few settlers built cabins within the placer territory and a camp grew up, it was also called Happy Valley.

Trouble developed when another town company appeared and laid off a new townsite within the Happy Valley Placer grant, claiming that the land did not contain minerals and could not therefore be included in the original grant. The case was heard in Denver before the Register of the General Land Office and a decision was given in favor of the newcomers. The case was then appealed and the decision was reversed. As more settlers arrived, the promoters of the placer laid out a townsite and sold lots, and before long the growing population had renamed the settlement Eldorado Camp. Since there was a camp of the same name in California, mail for the two places was constantly being delivered in the wrong state. Once the payroll for the Terror mine went gaily to the coast while the angry miners waited for their pay envelopes in Colorado. To prevent other such embarrassments the citizens agreed to change the name of the town by dropping the final syllable and calling their camp Eldora.

Other camps sprang up at about the same time. Three miles northwest of Eldora, on the north fork of Boulder creek was Grand Island; two miles west, where the north and south forks meet, was Hessie, named for the wife of the first postmaster; and one mile below Eldora was Sulphide Flats. The town company which platted the Flats was confident that it would outlast Eldora, chiefly because it was situated beside a small lake, a feature that the other camp lacked. Consequently they built a two-story hotel, a store, and a few cabins and waited hopefully for the stampede for town lots which never came.

In 1892, when lode mines were discovered on Spencer mountain, which forms the south side of the valley, the Clara, Virginia, Village Belle, Bird's Nest, and especially the Enterprise mines attracted prospectors to the district. Other mines were located, until by 1896 Eldora was a hustling gold camp and by the spring of 1897 was in the throes of a boom. Seven grocery stores catered to the "solid" needs of the population and nine saloons to the liquid,

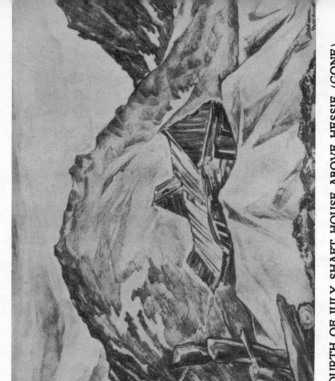

FOURTH OF JULY SHAFT HOUSE ABOVE HESSIE (GONE)

BOARDING HOUSE, WALL STREET (GONE)

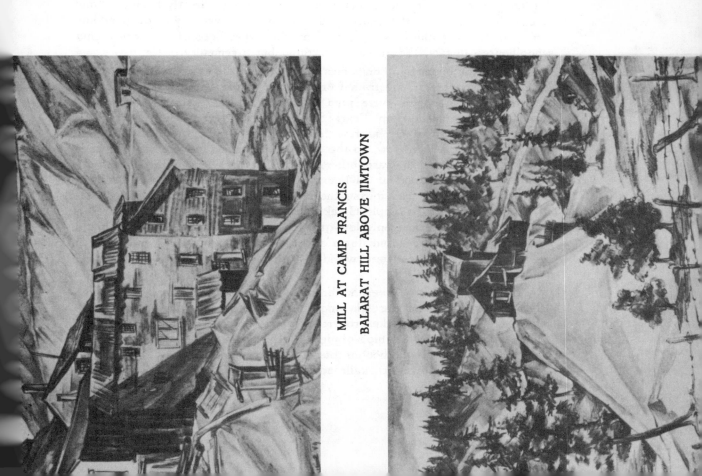

MILL AT CAMP FRANCIS

BALARAT HILL ABOVE JIMTOWN

while dancehalls and gambling houses ran day and night. During the winter of 1897-1898 fifteen feet of snow lay in the streets, and sleds replaced the coaches that continued to bring men to the thriving camp.

When John A. Gilfillan saw mine after mine opened on Spencer mountain he decided to provide more economical removal of the ore from the best properties by driving a drainage and transportation tunnel, called the Mogul Tunnel, into the mountain, to cut below the surface veins that were being worked. Other prospectors were endeavoring to find methods of treating the ores from their mines. Two stamp mills were built and successfully operated, one at Mary City below Eldora and one near Lake Eldora; but when the surface ores were exhausted and complex tellurides and sulphides were found these mills proved useless. The Eldora Mining and Milling Co. was then formed, and a seventy-five-ton chlorination, custom mill, known as the Bailey mill, was erected just west of the town to produce concentrates which could be sent to the Denver smelter. This, too, ran for awhile but was not a success. When the manager at the Bailey mill skipped a pay day his employees set fire to his house and shot him.

In 1898 a big strike in the Enterprise brought a stampede to the camp, and the town mushroomed almost over night. Claims were staked anywhere by the optimistic prospectors who were convinced that all the land must contain riches. Spencer mountain was covered with stakes as were Eldora, Mineral, Klondyke, Chittenden, Guinn and Bryan mountains.

The Gold Miner was the leading hotel during boom days, and many dances were held in its big dining room. The jail was directly behind it, and across the creek was the sporting district, where every type of gambling went on. Social gatherings were held on the upper floor of the two-teacher schoolhouse—in fact, Eldora had everything but a cemetery.

During the boom four companies ran stages to the camp, making up their loads of passengers on the train from Denver before it reached the Boulder station. The passengers were then hustled from the train to the waiting coaches, which dashed up Pearl Street, each driver racing to be first to reach the mouth of the narrow canyon road. Traffic was heavy on that road and turnouts were few, so the drivers of lumber and ore wagons hung bells on their horses to warn other vehicles of their approach. Freighters' outfits were on the road at all hours hauling everything from "a needle to a hoist." Eldora was gay during the boom, and some went so far as to say it would be a second Cripple Creek! But when the rich surface pockets of gold were exhausted and only low-grade ore and refractory ores were found, one by one the mines closed down and the boom was over. Finally, late in 1898, only three mines were working—the Bird's Nest, the Village Belle and the Revenge.

But the promoters were not through and for several years they advertised the district in the most glowing terms. Mines were salted, and gullible investors bought low-grade properties which had been lavishly sprinkled with sparkling samples of high-grade. Real estate agents shamelessly promised the moon to any who bought lots in the once happy valley. But even the Colorado and Northwestern railroad, which was extended from Sunset to

Eldora in 1904 and which provided cheaper transportation rates for the shipment of ore, could not revive the dying industry. After 1917 hardly any mining was done.

Promoters overboomed Eldora; the miners never did. They had proved that there was ore in the mountains but not in the quantities and qualities so loudly proclaimed by the writers of the elaborate brochures that were dangled as tempting bait before the eyes of unsuspecting investors. And yet, Eldora has survived, with old timers sunning themselves in front of a log cabin and with summer visitors returning year after year to spend a season in the mountain valley.

I have never climbed the Arapahoe glacier, but each year I've listened to glowing accounts of the trip and of the trail up the Fourth of July valley that leads to the base of the peak. "You should go as far as the mine shaft house," said friends who had made the climb. "You'd like to sketch it, and if you go in June or July the valley will be full of wild flowers."

It all sounded tempting; so one Sunday morning two friends and I drove to Nederland and on through Eldora to Hessie. Years ago there were a number of buildings at this small camp, but less than half a dozen mark the site today.

From Hessie a narrow road turns up the mountainside to Fourth of July valley, climbing through aspens and pines until the valley opens out and the road comes to an abrupt end at a camp ground. Leaving the car in the shade, Rebecca, Francis and I started up the trail toward the mine. It was a steady pull all the way, but the trail was broad and well built and the meadows above and below were carpeted with flowers. There were pentstemon and golden pea, little elephant and gallardia, lupin and loco weed and an occasional mariposi lily. Patches of meadow where masses of blooms were concentrated appeared from a distance as wholly blue or rose-colored. The air was spicy with the scent of the pines, and when the wind blew in the right direction we could hear the gurgle of the stream far below.

Just as the trail branched toward Arapahoe peak and started up the shale slope above timberline, I spied the shaft house on top of a dump less than an eighth of a mile away. It was made of huge logs, some of which had fallen away from the walls, so that one could look through the building and see up through the broken, sway-backed roof large patches of blue sky. Some rusty machinery stood inside amid debris of rocks and fallen timbers, and the wind whistled through the ribs of the broken building. After making two or three sketches I was ready to leave this high, lonely country and started back on the trail over which we had come.

"Don't go that way," called Francis, scrambling down the mountainside over rocks. "There should be an old road down here that led from the mine to the mill."

We followed him, picking our way from rock to rock and clinging to sturdy branches and roots as we let ourselves down the steep slope into the valley. A shout from below told us that Francis had found the road, and before long we reached the mill. It was full of machinery and sunshine, the latter making a pattern of broken stripes of light and shade, as it pierced the slatted roof, whose boards and shingles had blown off in storms and gales. There were also a boardinghouse and a blacksmith shop and all the other surface structures necessary to a property which once produced appreciable quanties of ore.

The mine was discovered by C. C. Alvord on May 21, 1875, and was worked for silver alone, although it did not contain enough of that metal to pay for mining it. The property was therefore shut down for twenty years, until in 1900 it was found to contain copper ore similar to that at Butte, Montana. The Consolidated Copper Mining and Milling and Smelting Company was then formed to develop the mine, and three million shares of stock were sold at a dollar a share. Though the ore was rich, it was hard to mine because of the underground water that filled the workings and had to be drained out through a tunnel driven into the mountainside.

We left the mill and made our way back to the car over an old corduroy road half covered with boggy moss and muddy ooze. In 1947 a photographer friend brought me a picture of the shaft house which he had taken that summer. It had collapsed on the dump like a house of cards. For once I had gotten my sketch just in time.

Cardinal   From Nederland to Caribou is a steady pull up a steep mountain road that years of neglect have not improved. About halfway up, at a fork in the road, stands a group of frame houses, and almost out of sight is a big mill. Curious as ever, I stopped to look at the mill and the other buildings that covered the property. From an old miner, who was tramming an ore car to the dump, I found that I was at the Boulder County mine and that the houses I had passed were those of New Cardinal.

"Was there an Old Cardinal?" I asked.

"Oh, yes; it was called Cardinal City and was located on the first flat below Caribou. I've heard that the town plat, which was made in 1870, showed five main streets, called Fountain, Gold, Silver, Quartz and Foundit, and that they'd planned for a courthouse square, smack in the middle of town. Of course it was never built, for the town never got big enough for a courthouse. Even in 1872 there were only two hundred people around, and the city consisted of a post office, a few stores and saloons, and some miners' cabins. The boom came between 1878 and 1883, and during that time there were perhaps fifteen hundred in camp. The people lived in the houses on the north side of the present road, and the business section was on the south side.

"In 1881 Caribou got pious and ran the loose women out of camp. They came down here to Cardinal and lived in little shacks down by the saloons. At night the streets were full of miners, woodchoppers and teamsters whooping it up. Some of them drifted down from Caribou for the fun. The women stayed here for two years and then a few of them went back to Idaho Street, in the lower end of Caribou; but they didn't get to stay long. First thing you know they'd been shooed out again, and back they came.

"Old Cardinal's all gone—you'd have to be shown the site to find it, and there's not much left of New Cardinal except the Boulder County mine which is still a steady producer. When the railroad was built to Eldora, Cardinal was the station halfway between Caribou and Nederland."

The road above Cardinal is increasingly steep and rough. Most of the way it skirts the edge of the mountain, with Caribou Flats and the old Coon Trail road to the railroad below it on the left and with mines and shaft houses above and below on all sides. At the head of the gulch is all that is left of Caribou—a few windswept houses widely spaced over the once-thickly populated hillside.

Crumbling stone and plaster walls, a house or two, and depressions filled with rubble mark the locations of stores and homes. The hilltop is bald as an egg, but on the edge of the meadow on which the town once stood are fringes of timber, survivors of the forest fires which have swept the area.

In 1860, years before he discovered tungsten ore near Nederland, Sam Conger, while elk hunting, found silver float on Caribou hill. Eight years later in Laramie he noticed a carload of ore which was being shipped over the Union Pacific. Unconsciously, he picked up a piece of the rock and was examining it, until a shout made him drop it.

"Keep away from that ore," yelled the trainman. "That's high-grade silver from the Comstock lode in Nevada."

"If that's silver, I know where there's a whole mountain of it," replied Conger and, although it was autumn, he hurried back to the high hill near the Continental Divide, where he had seen the flow of blossom rock. Snows hampered his prospecting, but he found one vein which he called the Conger and which he proceeded to work all winter.

In the spring of 1869, as soon as the snows had melted, he found the spot he had remembered and thus uncovered the Caribou, the greatest silver vein of the region. In August he took five partners, William Martin, George Lytle, Hugh McCammon, John H. Pickel and Samuel Mishlee, two of whom had also been gophering around in the region, and together they worked the mine. The nearest road was four miles away, but the men hacked out a trail, carried in provisions on their backs, and before the winter built a cabin near their property. They took one load of Caribou ore all the way to Prof. Hill's smelting works at Black Hawk, where it assayed high in silver. Working through the winter, they piled up their ore and waited for the snows to melt in order to pack more of it to the smelter. Word of their strike leaked out, and by June, 1870, the woods were full of men and the rush was on.

Conger subsequently exchanged his share in the Caribou for his partners' interest in the Poorman, leaving them sole owners of the Caribou. Later on he sold the Poorman to Neil D. McKenzie for a good sum. Next to the Caribou and the Conger, the Sherman and the Poorman were the most productive mines. That summer many more lodes were located: the Idaho— from which the owner took $6,000 from the first twenty feet of his shaft— the Trojan, Boulder County, Sovereign People, No-Name, Spencer and Seven-Thirty. A. D. Breed became interested in the Caribou mine in 1870 and paid, some say $50,000 and some $125,000, for a half-interest in it. That

(503)

year the mine produced $70,000 and in later years it yielded even more. In 1873 it was sold to a Dutch company for $3,000,000.

As more mines were developed, the owners began to dream of a railroad which would move their ores cheaply, and the following statement appeared in the *Golden Globe* of June 14, 1873:

> Dear Globe,
>
> Over twenty mines are producing. . . . Ex-Gov. Evans has been here. Caribou people are looking for a railroad to run through the mines and on to Salt Lake with a grade not exceeding sixty feet to the mile. Golden will then be blotted from the map of Colorado.

A mine railroad was eventually built into the region but it never reached Caribou. Instead, a station at Cardinal served the hilltop camp, and between it and Caribou ore wagons rumbled along "Coon Trail," the most direct route from the camp, delivering silver to the waiting freight cars.

Caribou City was organized in September, 1870, and by the spring of 1871 had sixty houses and a population of four hundred. A newspaper, the *Caribou Post*, appeared the same spring and was published until August, 1872, by Collier and Hall, editors of the Central City paper. During boom days the town grew until its several streets were lined with houses and stores and its population rose to three thousand. Its exhibit of silver ore at the Philadelphia Centennial Exposition attracted "the attention of the whole world" and brought more men to the already crowded district. Mining continued to flourish, but the peak of the boom was past and slowly the town began to quiet down. The silver crash in 1893 further paralyzed it, and fire in 1900 leveled its buildings. A little leasing kept mining going sporadically, but the town was dead.

In 1946 the Consolidated Caribou Silver Mines Co. completed the 3500-foot Idaho Tunnel which had been abandoned for fifty years. When the tunnel was opened on Nov. 20th, a special telephone connection was made from the mine to the office of the company's president in Rockefeller Center, New York City. At the president's order to "Go ahead," a blast was set off which not only inaugurated the extension of the tunnel but also was heard in the eastern office.

Caribou was swept by two epidemics, scarlet fever and diphtheria, both of which took a frightful toll and populated the cemetery on top of the hill. Cold weather and exposure also caused many deaths among the miners. Some of them had no relatives, but the bodies were brought down from the mines by the boys to one of the two little churches for a service and then were carried up the hill again to the lonely graves. I had heard so much about the Caribou cemetery that it was one of the first spots I looked for. I found it up a winding road away from the windswept hill where the town once stood, partly sheltered by aspens and evergreens and partly exposed to the elements, which have taken their toll of the marble stones by cracking and splitting them and by wearing away the carefully-cut letters. A few of the markers have survived year after year of frost and ice but many stand awry or lie broken on the mound they once marked. Some graves are enclosed in wooden or iron fences, which by now are almost hidden by lusty new evergreens or aspen saplings. I read as many of the inscriptions as I could decipher and was shocked to find so many of the graves those of children and young wives.

SARAH COLLINS
WIFE OF
JAMES COLLINS
BORN IN CORNWALL, ENG.
DIED
Oct. 5, 1875
aged
36 yrs.

> Gone before us O our sister
> To the Spiritland
> Vainly look we for another
> In thy place to stand.

Over the grave of a three-year-old is the verse:

> Thy pale cheeks
> Decked for thy silent tomb
> Soon like roses,
> Fair in heaven will bloom
> Though like the angels in the skies
> Thou should unfold thy wings and fly
> Oh why so young must you leave us here
> So kind and dear to my mother.

Another child's grave dated June 27, 1879, is that of "DARLING TOMMY, son of J. G. and M. A. COSGROVE," who died when "3 yrs. 5 mo. 26 ds."

One marble shaft, the most pathetic of all, was inscribed on three sides with the names of children who died in the diphtheria epidemic of 1879. Anna, aged ten, died on July 5; Willie, aged eight, on July 6, and Alice May, aged three, on July 8. On the fourth side of the monument is the verse:

> Gone before us
> Oh our children
> To the better land.
> Vainly wait we
> For others in your place to stand.

And below this is the text: "Suffer little children to come unto Me for of such is the kingdom of heaven."

As I walked from mound to mound, I read the same verses that have been carved on tombstones all across the country, such as the one beginning:

> Remember friends as you pass by
> As you are now so once was I
> As I am now so you must be
> Prepare for death and follow me.

and I felt that there was a certain kinship in all pioneers, whether in New England burying grounds or on this stark mountain top where storms break and where snows rebury the white stones every winter.

Caribou is high, 9800 feet above sea level, and it is located on an iron dike that attracts violent summer thunder storms. Its barren hilltop, denuded of trees by fire and by the woodchoppers who provided cord wood for fireplaces, stoves and boilers, is buried deep in snow for nearly nine months of every year, and old-timers tell of keeping a shovel just inside the house door with which to clear their way outside each morning. Because of danger to the children during the severe winters, school was held during the summer months.

Snowdrifts were often so deep that even at the two-story Sherman House on the main street the guests entered and left through the upstairs windows. One man bought a house in the fall and then left camp for the winter. In the late spring he returned and hunted for his cabin among the melting drifts of snow but could not locate it. On the Fourth of July he tried again and finally managed to reach the roof by pushing a long pole through the snowbank which completely covered the building and the surrounding hillside. Another resident recalls that the drifts back of the houses eventually joined, making one huge wall of snow which reached the entire length of the town.

Besides snow and electric storms Caribou had plenty of wind. Even sturdy buildings were braced on their east sides against the terrific gales which blew almost constantly from the Divide. Old-timers who called Caribou the "town where the winds were born" learned to lean against the gusts which whipped around corners or scurried across the treeless slope where the city stood.

Twice fire raced through the camp, in 1879 and in 1900. The first big blaze started from a forest fire and roared in from the west, destroying everything in town below the Sherman House, including the rows of wood all corded and piled for winter use. People fled to Nederland to get away from the flames, taking with them whatever they could carry. Though the town was immediately rebuilt it never "came back" entirely. By 1886 there were only a thousand persons in camp, and from then on families began gradually to move away, a few at a time, but enough to be missed. The town never did recover from the second fire in 1900, which virtually wiped Caribou off the map. Today only a few crumbling cabins and many old foundations mark its site, leaving the winds to blow unobstructed across the barren hilltop.

Left Hand Canyon

Left Hand canyon, named for Chief Ni-Wot (Left Hand), an Indian who was friendly to the early settlers and prospectors, was once full of mines and mills and little camps. The mines are there still but they are idle; the mills, long empty, are gone—razed in the recent scrap metal drive—and the camps are memories.

Altona

Almost at the mouth of the canyon are the remains of Altona, never a mining camp, but a trading center for both the prospectors and the quarry men who worked the red sandstone deposits along the front face of the range. The site of Altona is covered today by a ranch, and all but one of its

CARIBOU   TODD HOUSE, CARIBOU

frame buildings is gone; but to miss nothing of the past, I crossed the foot-bridge over Left Hand creek one day and entered a barnyard full of inquisitive chickens, to peer into the one old cabin that dates from the settlement's heydey, when Pete Haldi ran the place and catered to the needs of the whole canyon. The post office was maintained until 1918, and then, since no mail had arrived for sometime, the postmaster shut up the cabin and Altona's chapter was closed.

Jamestown Whenever I drove up Left Hand canyon I looked up the woodsy road, at the junction of Jim creek with Left Hand creek. Jamestown, the town from which Douglas Fairbanks came, lay up that road, and one day I turned right at the fork and visited the place. A three-mile drive along a narrow canyon, dense with trees and always within sight or sound of the creek, brought me to the outskirts of the town. All the way up the canyon there had been signs of early mining days—dumps, tunnel openings into the cliff face and one big foundation which I learned later was that of the Golden Age mill.

Jamestown, or Jimtown as it is usually called, is a pretty little place, full of life, and supported by its still active mining industry. Several times on the drive up there big trucks loaded with ore ground slowly by on their way to the new mill built on Valmont butte, east of Boulder. Jamestown's store, school, and community hall and church are all active, and its weekly dances are advertised in the local papers. But it was not the town's present prosperity that held my interest so much as the fact that it is one of the oldest mining camps in the county, and I wanted to know its history.

George Zweck, the first settler, built a cabin in 1860 and prospected for gold while his cattle grazed where the town now stands. In 1864 a few galena veins were uncovered, and about four hundred persons settled in the valley near Big and Little Jim creeks. A year later a camp, at first called Elysian Park, was founded, and less than six weeks afterward six hundred prospectors were panning the stream, working arastras, digging up the gulches and building cabins along the two streets.

A letter written at Jamestown and quoted by Ovando J. Hollister in his book, *The Mines of Colorado*, describes life in the raw, new camp:

> There is great excitement about town lots just now. All the front lots, or lots near the gulch, are pre-empted for about three miles along the stream; also all mill-sites. And now as there are some coming in and threatening to jump the lots not built on, it creates some excitement. Miners meetings are in vogue and we are having a good many. I attended one not long ago, which was conducted after this fashion: When the crowd had gathered, the business was introduced by the singing of "Sweet Betsy from Pike."

A sawmill worked night and day turning out lumber for the hundred stores and houses, and by the time two stamp mills were constructed to handle the gold the town was big enough to petition for a post office. This was officially called Jamestown, although the miners had indicated that Jimtown was the proper title. For three years mining was active, but then the boom collapsed and most of the people left.

In 1875 Frank Smith and Indian Jack found surface float of unusual value, which assayed as high as fifty per cent in gold. They located a claim, the Golden Age, which they later sold for $1500, not realizing that their discovery would become the best mine in the district. From the start the property produced quantities of high-grade ore, and its owners announced in 1902 that it had been in continual operation longer than any other mine in the state.

The Buena (now called Wano) gold mine was discovered the same year as the Golden Age, and it, too, has been a steady producer with a yield of over a million dollars worth of ore.

In 1882 a new boom began and buildings were thrown up in a day. Anything served for shelters for the swarming crowds that poured into the overflowing town. The two hotels, the Evans House and the Martin, the thirty-three saloons and dancehalls were all well patronized, and still new-comers arrived. A toll road built from Left Hand canyon to the camp made money for its owner, for traffic was heavy—while men and supplies rolled in, wagons filled with ore rolled out again.

As men brought their families to the town a schoolhouse was needed and built, and "One church pointed the orthodox pathway to the proper destination over the range."—*Jamestown Whim,* April 21, 1883.

The big flood of June, 1894, tore down Jim creek and washed away part of the town. Men still remember the torrential rains and the gulches full of snow water that preceded the flood. And they tell stories of the night when the flood struck, when cabins and sheds were sucked into the stream and soggy banks crumbled into the boiling waters, already full of debris, and rushed down the valley.

George W. Chesebro began working a high-grade spar streak in 1916 and by processing it got ninety percent pure fluorspar concentrates a day. Then came World War I, when

> Industrial activities in the Jamestown district . . . turned largely to mining, milling and marketing of fluorspar, from great dykes of this mineral known for years to exist there but never before having proven as attractive as the silver and gold mines.— *Mining in Boulder County, Colorado. Silver Semi-Centennial Edition,* 1919.

In 1918 the Golden Age Mining and Milling Company "turned for the war period to the fluorspar business, then booming as a war minerals industry. Large contracts were made . . . and the company took over options and leases also on spar mines."

J. F. Barnhill, the manager of the Golden Age, noticed that a thin black streak was left on the edge of the Wilfley tables in the mill on which fluorspar was separated. Realizing that this indicated the presence of some metal heavier than lead he had the black streak tested for platinum but the tests revealed no such metal. The Bureau of Mines then ran samples, which showed the presence of uranium and radium in amounts averaging 1/10 of 1%. When this was known, many old properties were bought up and worked for these rare metals; but the amounts found were commercially negligible.

Up until 1915 the Jamestown district produced over $5,000,000 in gold, silver, lead, copper and fluorspar ores, with some gold being found in such pure form that it was sent direct to the Denver mint. The Wano mine was operated as a gold mine until 1940, when it was closed by the government. At the request of the War Production Board the mill was remodeled, however, and equipped to produce both metallurgical grade and acid grade fluorspar concentrates, and as a fluorsspar mill it is running today.

Camp Providence, Camp Enterprise and Gresham

In the seventies two or three small camps grew up around mines which were found in the vicinity of Jamestown. Balarat was the largest and most lasting, but Gresham, Camp Enterprise, and Camp Providence had their day.

Camp Enterprise was four and a half miles west of Jamestown and was said to be a "Swede camp." Camp Providence, first known as John Jay Camp, was three miles southwest of Jamestown on Big Jim creek and was started by a group of prospectors from Central City, who discovered telluride veins on Overland hill in 1875. The John Jay was its leading mine. Sometime in the early thirties I was driven over the old ledge road to the site of Gresham, a few miles beyond Jamestown; but nothing remained of the camp except the postoffice with its empty pigeon-holes.

Springdale

One day while I was sketching up on the hill near the Jimtown schoolhouse and looking down over the town, a man came up the hill, and when he approached I asked him about Springdale, the little camp that once stood halfway down the creek toward Left Hand canyon.

"The camp was new in 1874 and it became as well known for its mineral springs as for its mines," he said, leaning on his stick and placing his bag of groceries beside him while he visited. "The gulch above and below Peabody's Mineral Springs, as they were called, used to be full of houses where about three hundred people lived. The land near the springs was developed into a summer resort, and a hotel, the Seltzer House, and eight or ten cottages were built for summer tourists. They say the water resembled that of the famous seltzer springs in Germany. Anyway, it was very popular and was bottled at a little plant close to the water. It sold pretty widely too. Most of the buildings at Springdale were caught in the big flood which struck in 1894 and a couple of those that escaped have burned since. There are only two or three left now, up above the road. You look for them on your way home.

"I never cared about the mineral water myself but I did some prospecting down that way. There were good mines near the springs, and I used to know them all and the men who worked them." He looked off across the canyon and began reciting a list of names, each of which had a special meaning to him but which to me were only interesting and imaginative designations given to black holes in a mountainside.

"There was the King William and the Grand Central, the Big Blossom, the Gladiator, the Rip Van Dam and the Copper Blush. They weren't as good as the Wano and the Golden Age and the Longfellow, but the ore was there, some of it in blanket veins. When it was gone, you were through."

Balarat

The name "Balarat" appeared on old maps of Boulder County, but I'd never tried to find it. The day before our trip there I chased around Boulder collecting data. The road was said to be narrow but "all right if you don't meet anyone," and I was advised to telephone to Ellery Cruthers, who lived on a ranch close to the townsite and who knew its history, and to tell him we'd be up in the morning. I visited the county courthouse and consulted an old map, and I talked to a man who had lived in the camp for forty years but who hadn't seen the place since 1930.

We drove up Left Hand canyon to its junction with Jim creek and turned up the fork that led to Jamestown. After questioning three people we found the wife of the man who was to give us more specific directions. He wasn't at home but was working at the Wano mill; so our next stop was at the big mine property which produces fluorspar concentrates. Inside the big building several men were at work, but the noise of the machinery was so great that no one noticed us until we stood close beside one of them and tapped him on the arm. He took us to the man whom we had been sent to find and, sure enough, he did know all the answers. After I had explained what I was doing and why I wanted to go to Balarat he said: "You should talk to Grandma Mason. She used to live there and she lived here in Jamestown until a week ago. Now she's over at Lyons. Her husband wrote a record of the camp, and if you can get a gander at it you'll find out a lot of facts. You're on your way to Balarat now and you don't know the way there? I'll write you a picture." And wiping his wet hands he led the way to a sort of office at one side of the mill. Leaning over a rough board desk he began making a diagram of the roads we were to follow and the landmarks for which we were to look. Armed with this we left the mill and drove on up the draw till we reached a fork to the right, which took us up Balarat hill. It was just as narrow and steep as we had expected, with deep ruts which the car straddled. Fortunately no ore trucks were coming down, and we made the top with no more difficulty than a slightly over-heated engine. On the flat at the summit were some signs, and we stopped to consult our map. In the distance, two miles away, was the Golden Age dump in the midst of a circle of timber which crowned the next ridge. On the way back from Balarat we would climb up to it.

The next two miles were over a dreadful road, which bounced us down-hill, over rocks and ruts to a gate which our "picture" showed was the entrance to the Cruthers ranch. Another half-mile drive across meadows brought us to the ranchhouse. Here we found Mr. Cruthers expecting us. He ushered us into his kitchen and gave us chairs. While we sat around an oilcloth-covered table looking at a map which he brought out of an old trunk, he talked about the days when Balarat's mines were producing.

The Smuggler was discovered in 1875, and the camp grew up below it along a narrow gulch, stringing out for a length of two blocks. The Bindago and Eldorado lodes were located on the fourth of May, 1876, by two prospectors named Smith and Mason, and news of these lodes hastened the formation of a mining district, which was organized later in the same month. The following year a road was built from Jimtown to the camp by the Smuggler Mining Co., and fifty log houses and two large boarding-houses accommodated the population which was said to be "almost entirely

American." One of the boardinghouses was run by the McClancy family who later opened a hotel at Ward. With the exception of a meat market and a saloon, there was but one other store, called the Chipmunk store possibly because of its small stock. It was owned by two men who worked in the Smuggler during the day and ran their store only at night.

The Smuggler's total output reached two millions, the ore being taken from a group of mines which included the Careless Boy, Waumega, Little Eddie and Eldorado. By 1877 the mine was employing sixty men, many of whom worked in the twenty-stamp concentrating mill constructed on the property. The ore was then shipped to the smelter by freight wagons, which took two days to reach Boulder over the rough, difficult road. Later on the mine was tangled up in litigation; but in 1918 it was taken over by a group of capitalists who formed the Smuggler Mine and Milling Co. and operated the property successfully for a number of years, developing new ground at various levels and producing ore which ranged from $200 to $5,000 a ton.

"I can take you over the hill and show you where the mine stood," said Mr. Cruthers; "but there's nothing there to see. All the buildings are gone and most of the dump was reworked and shipped to Denver during the depression."

Thanking him for his information and helpfulness, we retraced our steps and drove back over the bad road to the top of Balarat hill. We parked the car under a big tree and started on a long two-mile hike to the Golden Age dump.

The trail was an old wagon road, from which at intervals wheel tracks led off through the timber to other mines. After a long pull uphill we reached the dump, one of the biggest I have seen, and sitting on the crumbling yellow rock which formed it we looked around. To the west was a white-topped semicircle of mountains which stretched from the Mummy range at the north to Arapahoe glacier at the south. To the east as far as the eye could see was an endless pattern of plains, and to the south were the Flatirons and Flagstaff mountain at Boulder looking tiny and far away. Except for an old windlass and one small building higher on the mountain beside a tunnel opening, there was nothing visible of the Golden Age property but the dump. While my friends started back down the road toward Balarat hill, I made a sketch or two and then scurried after them.

The next afternoon I drove to Lyons, a valley town over the ridge from Balarat, to interview "Grandma Mason" of whom I'd been told. The telephone operator at Lyons directed me to her trim, white house. Mrs. Mason was at home and was very gracious.

"I just bought this house and I moved in from Jamestown last week," she said with pride, glancing around the neat, comfortable room. "After seventy years I got tired of pumping and carrying my wash water. Yes, I remember Balarat. I lived there many years and I also remember the dances that were held every week. Most of the men had cabins, but some who didn't live closeby used to ride to and from their work at the Smuggler on horseback.

"The camp was just one long row of houses on the south side of the gulch. In front of them was the wagon road and below it was Balarat creek. Across from it was the Smuggler, with its big ore house at the mouth of the tunnel. The only way to get from the mine to the houses was by a foot-bridge over the stream. The big flood of 1894 washed away most of the buildings, so you wouldn't know the place now."

I asked her if I might see the book with the history of the camp which her husband had written. She had lent it to the real estate agent uptown. Leaving her house after thanking her, I looked up the agent, whose office was in the stone bank building on the main street. He was kind enough to stop his work and show me the book, and when I couldn't read the fine penmanship without my glasses, he read aloud the account of the Golden Age, the Balarat and the Smuggler mines which it contained.

While I was talking to him the phone rang and to my surprise the call was for me. Mrs. Mason had gone across the street to her daughter-in-law's as soon as I left and had told her about my visit and that I was from Boulder. Whereupon the daughter-in-law called to give the names of several people in Boulder who were acquainted with the deserted camp. Seldom have I had more friendly and helpful cooperation in tracing clues than in Lyons, and never have I been paged in a town in which I was a stranger.

Less than two miles beyond the Jamestown turnoff in Left Hand canyon was a small camp called Glendale, which was connected with the town of Sunshine by a hair-raising road which clung to the south rim of the canyon. The camp was in existence in 1881 but today it is only a site, save for half a dozen cabins near the highway. Less than a mile beyond Glendale was Rockville, better known as Rowena, a once lively camp where numbers of miners and their families lived in the days when the Prussian, the Gold Nugget and other paying mines were being worked. Several large mills were located at Rowena, but now nothing but stone foundations mark the place where the Prussian mine produced $175,000 in two years and where the Gold Nugget and Cold Spring mines poured a steady stream of pay ore into the mills.

Glendale and Rowena

Further up the canyon the mines become more frequent, and dumps and prospect holes pit the hillsides. The big mills which used to line the canyon have been razed, and bushes and underbrush grow over the stone walls that remain, hiding the weathered stones and stained concrete supports, the twisted iron and the broken rubble. The dumps and the settling ponds, with their flumes balanced casually on thin wooden stilts, are too big to hide, and show up sharply against the thick stands of pine and spruce which cover most of the hillsides.

Close to Ward other small camps materialized, centered around a particularly successful mine or a rich lode which promised well. Quigleyville, northeast of Ward was located near the Mellor mill; and Camp Tolcott, below Ward, in Left Hand canyon at Hanging Rock was laid out by Col. Wesley Brainard of Evanston. For twenty years Brainard, who is credited with first realizing the "strength and value of the mineral veins of the district," prospected the area north of Left Hand canyon and east of the steep hill which leads into Ward, persistently developing claims in the immediate

Quigleyville, Camp Tolcott, Puzzler, Gold Lake

area. Puzzler gulch was full of mines and had its own school, post office, and telegraph and railroad station, as well as a group of miner's cabins. I knew that the Puzzler schoolhouse was standing and that some of the old desks were piled up outside of it. One October day, two of us explored Puzzler gulch, passing the schoolhouse and flushing a covey of grouse from the underbrush as we hiked to the site of the Puzzler mill. The railroad grade was above us all the way up the gulch until it crossed the road at the big millsite and disappeared in an aspen grove.

Some of the camps that were laid out by ambitious prospectors or town companies never got beyond the paper stage. One of these was Gold Lake, situated in the Gold Lake district, east of Ward. A plat of the town, drawn up in 1861, showed the main street, Lake Street, circling a small body of water three hundred feet back from its shoreline. The land between it and the water was reserved for millsites, while from its other side building lots radiated like a sunburst.

Camp Francis Several of us drove along the Peak to Peak highway near Ward one afternoon looking for Camp Francis, a small community whose broken-down cabins at the head of a gulch I had seen from the road. Leaving our car, we hiked through fields of Indian paint brush and golden pea to the weathered buildings ranged on either side of the gulch road. Some of the cabins were in good repair, but others were caved in; and one, whose walls had fallen outwards like the sides of a water-soaked box, was full of empty medicine bottles. This must have been the remains of the store, which in 1895 served the camp of two hundred. In those days fifty cabins and a schoolhouse filled the gulch and a railroad station stood just below the Dew Drop mine dump.

Farther down the gulch was the Big Five property—a group of buildings operated in the nineties by a syndicate which worked several of the best mines in the Ward district. The company employed one hundred men, held eight hundred acres of mineral land, and worked the Adit tunnel, and the Adit, Columbia, Dew Drop and Ni-Wot mines—"old million-dollar properties." They brought the ore through the tunnel and processed it in the mill which stands beyond their big powerhouse with its tall, black smokestack.

The Big Five mill was built up the side of the gulch, extending from the streambed to the height of the dump where we stood. Before climbing down to its lowest level, we wandered all over the top of the dump, past empty ore cars, rusty cables and pools of iron-stained water. We saw the stone powder house high above the dump in a grove of trees. Also hidden in a grove of trees was a small frame building—the mine office—on whose side was painted a "5" large enough to cover one entire wall. Inside, I found a weather report for the month of October, 1912, in which some conscientious employee had reported twenty-one inches of snow and had written under the heading, "Remarks":

5th, rain and hail. 8th, snow and rain. 10th, snowing a little all day. Melting. 28th, flurries of snow all day. Wind blowing a hurricane.

(514)

CONGREGATIONAL CHURCH, WARD

WOOD MT. MILL, WALL STREET

TOWN
OF
WARD

At the bottom of the gulch, which we reached by means of an over-grown and badly washed road, was the foundation of the mill, a tall, gaunt structure which in the low, afternoon light cast long, grotesque shadows across the narrow ravine. Its interior was dark, but as we became accustomed to the dim light that filtered through the boarded-up windows and the holes in the roof, we saw the massive machinery and the maze of platforms and ladders which led from level to level of the silent building. I can never quite reconcile myself to the silence of these camps, for in boom days they were so full of sound—the thud of stamps, the clank of machinery, the pulse of engines, the scream of whistles, the boom of exploding powder and the shouts of men.

Back at the dump again we discovered the railroad grade and, looking down the narrow valley, could follow the cut along the face of the mountain up which the little narrow gauge trains ran on their way to Ward, the terminus of this branch of the Switzerland Trail. Snow often blocked the tracks and filled the cuts along the right of way, thereby causing the train crew to spend hours bucking the drifts and shoveling the track clear.

On April 24, 1901, a snowslide caught a train engaged in bucking snow and killed several of the crew. The train as it steamed up from the valley to a point near Francis had encountered more snow with every mile traveled. Finally, huge drifts blocked the way; so the train crew un-coupled the one coach and left it standing on the track while they took both engines and started butting against the heavy, packed obstruction. The drift was big, and they made little progress. "We'll try once more, and if that doesn't do it we'll quit," they called, backing up to get a good running start. Whether the push started the snow running or whether a slide swept down from above and caught them is uncertain, but in a minute both engines and their crews were shooting down into the gulch below, cutting a wide swathe through the snow as they slid to the bottom. Two firemen, the brake-man, and the conductor were killed and several other persons were injured. Hours later another engine puffed up the grade from Boulder to bring relief to the survivors and to take the stranded coach back to the city.

Camp Albion It was getting dark when we left Camp Francis and returned to the car. Driving back toward Nederland, I looked toward the west where Mt. Albion stood silhouetted against the fading light. On its slope the Snowy Range mining district was laid out in 1861 by prospectors who found indications of ore in the high country near the Divide. The only settlement in the district was Camp Albion, named after the mother lode of lead and silver found there. In the eighties the camp, which was in the vicinity of Albion lake, north of Silver lake, had a population of 200. Nothing is left of it today.

Ward Ward's mines were among the most productive in Boulder county. They were nearly all gold mines, but a few like the White Raven showed values in lead. Calvin M. Ward located the first claim in the district, the Miser's Dream, in the spring of 1860; but a more important discovery was made the following year by Cy Deardorff. His pick uncovered the Columbia vein from which $5,000,000 worth of gold has been taken. The properties

(516)

located on this vein include the Columbia, East Columbia, Central Columbia, Ni-Wot, Utica, Baxter, Boston and Idaho mines.

With the discovery of free gold in the Columbia, the district began to attract the attention of other prospectors. One of these was C. H. Merrill, who paid fifty dollars for claim No. 10 on the Columbia vein and who was laughed at for his purchase. Two years later he sold it for fifteen dollars to W. A. Davidson and Samuel R. Breath, who had a hunch as to its worth. The following season they took $50,000 from the mine with the aid of a six-stamp mill; but for further development of the property, which they called the Ni-Wot, they needed money. The two men therefore went back east and organized a company with a paid up capital of $500,000. They also bought machinery for a mill and enough wagons and five hundred oxen to carry it across the plains. They hired men to drive the wagons, who when they finally reached the mouth of Left Hand canyon, had to hack a road all the way to the claim. A sawmill cut lumber from the solid mass of timber that covered all the hills, and before long a mill was completed. Almost as soon as it started operating it burned down and a second one had to be built.

The mine changed hands several times, Davidson and Breath selling it for $300,000 to a company which later received $500,000 for it. Yet by the time the Big Five Syndicate acquired it—after it had been in litigation and after its second mill had burned—they were able to get it "for its encumbrances" which ran into several figures. Although it had yielded an estimated $1,250,000 in gold, an equal amount was said to have been lost or wasted within its thirty to forty years of production.

> With it has been associated names well known in financial circles of the East, London has given it a whirl, H. A. W. Tabor has thrown over it the glamor of his name and to every old-time miner and operator in the state the Ni-Wot, its history and its riches is a familiar tradition.—*Ward Camp. Its History, Mines and Resources. What to See, How to See It.* 1898.

With the opening of the Ni-Wot mine and the building of its mill to treat the surface gold ores Ward began to boom, until by 1865 six hundred people were living in or near it.

Sniktau, a "poet of no mean pretensions" according to the *Burlington Gazeteer*, visited Ward in the fall of 1867, when two hundred people were living in "good class frame houses in a thickly settled portion known as the Columbian district." He found five steam quartz mills and one small water-power mill, and he mentions the "mat of raspberry bushes bearing fruit enough to supply the whole population" which grew on the slopes over which forest fires had swept. After his tour of the camp he wrote in the *Rocky Mountain News* of Oct 30:

> Did it ever strike you very forcibly that Dickens would derive definite satisfaction from a tour through the mining district of Colorado? Why? Because it would enable him (to realize) he (had) NOT (made) a caricature of a human family by giving us a portrait of Wm. Micawber, Esq.
>
> W. M. lives and breathes hopefully, waits for something to turn up "and falls

back for a spring of gigantic magnitude" in every mining locality in Colorado. Even up in Ward I saw him just as I left him six years ago.

He took comfort then in eating his slap-jacks and sow-belly, garnished with a dessert of dried apples, hopefully awaiting the day when a fortune would jump into his lap from between the walls of rock; and I have seen him now, the same cheery, happy, hopeful Wilkins, scant of stamps but flush with "great expectations."

Sniktau

E. H. N. Patterson

then at Ward district

The Utica, also discovered on the Columbia vein by Deardorff, became the leading mine of the camp; it began to pay dividends in 1888 and had "a million dollars to its credit" by 1898. Its stone mill, one of the oldest still standing, is beside the road just below town. It was originally run by waterpower, the water being brought five miles over the hills to the mill through an iron pipe. Fire destroyed the main shaft of the mine in 1898, forcing a shut down for a short time and suspending the average monthly profit of $10,000. Its gold ore averaged $200 a ton, and more than one carload was worth $5,000.

The early stamp mills were equipped to crush oxidized ore and when that was exhausted the mills were useless. Many experiments were made with mining methods and with new types of equipment, and Ward is credited with constructing the first successful chlorination mill used in the territory and with designing the first bumping table.

Although the town grew all through the seventies and eighties, it was not incorporated until 1896. That same year the Congregationalists started work on their frame church on Modoc street, and the Catholics had a church higher upon the hillside. During the nineties the town was active, the mills ran night and day, and "the monotonous sound of dropping stamps filled the air."

Ward's only connection with the valley before the railroad was built was by a stage road which ran over Sawmill hill to Gold Hill. From Gold Hill two roads descended to the valley town of Boulder, one following Four Mile canyon and the other climbing around the edge of Big Horn mountain before entering Sunshine canyon.

Early in 1897 a company was organized to build a mine railroad from Boulder to Ward. Money for its construction was subscribed by seven men, who thereby owned all the stock. During 1897 the road was surveyed by engineers who were remarkably successful in finding ways through the mountains, and the grading of the twenty-six-and-a-half-mile right of way was begun. To reach Ward a climb of 4100 feet was necessary, ending "just below the eternal snowbanks, at an altitude of 9,450 feet." The road was officially named the Colorado and Northwestern but it was popularly called the Switzerland Trail. Another name was the Whiplash Route, for on a map its twistings resembled the long, flexible lash of the whip used by all drivers of the six and eight-horse stages and freighters' wagons.

The road ran up Boulder canyon to Four Mile canyon, which it then followed past Crisman, Salina and Wall Street to Sunset. There the road divided, one section (built a few years later), turning left and passing by

Sugarloaf and Cardinal to the terminus at Eldora. The original section turned right at Sunset and climbed in long, horseshoe curves past Mount Alta which was not far from Gold Hill. A hotel and dancehall were built on the mountain and picnic grounds were laid out by the railroad company, which was anxious to make a playground that would attract excursionists during the summer months. It became a popular place for tourists who rode the cars as far as the resort and frolicked under the trees until a later train took them back home again. I was taken to Mount Alta by some friends who often drive over the old railroad bed, which has been a rough but possible roadway since the rails and ties were removed. We picnicked there, just as hundreds had before us; but the pavilion was gone, and only its big stone chimney was left standing gaunt and smoke-stained among the pines. The fountain which stood in front of the building was also gone, except for a stone pedestal surrounded by a circle of cement and rocks, inside of which the grass grew knee high. From Mount Alta we could see one of the big sweeping curves of the road, but no plumes of steam and smoke announced the approach of a train. Mount Alta is another landmark which is almost obliterated and forgotten.

Mount Alta

From Mount Alta the roadbed crossed the ridge into Left Hand canyon and then cut along the south side of the canyon, crossing the Sawmill hill road and looping around the head of Puzzler gulch, to skirt other hillsides until it reached Camp Francis, just below Ward, and then entered the town itself.

On June 23, 1898, the first passenger train ran over the tracks, and on June 28 a formal opening to "passengers, traffic and business" was celebrated with an excursion from Denver which brought officials and special guests to the mountains. This event was advertised as the "Formal Opening of the Whiplash Route from the Verdant Valley of Boulder to the Cloud Kissed Camp of Ward," and it was the occasion for great festivities.

Ward Cont'd.

As the train approached Camp Francis it was greeted with a salute of guns and whistles and one hundred shots of giant powder. A stop was made at the Big Five tunnel and a trip into the mountainside was arranged for the guests. Boards were laid over the wet places, candles were lighted along the entire line of tunnel to be explored, and more than a hundred visitors enjoyed the unique experience of entering a mine. To further thrill them, the miners set off some shots in the breast of a branch tunnel in the old Ni-Wot mine. The result of the blast provided a greater thrill than had been anticipated, for at the first shot every candle in the tunnel was blown out by the concussion and the guests found themselves in total darkness until rescued by the amused miners. From Francis the train proceeded to Ward "amid the thunder of miner's artillery."

The streets of Ward were decorated with evergreen and floral arches, and every window was hung with bunting. An evergreen decked booth was prepared for the speakers, and a procession was organized to meet the delegation at the station and conduct it to the center of town where the speeches would be made. The train was in two sections with Governor Alva Adams riding in the first coach of section one. As it pulled into the station, a salute of thirteen guns was fired and the "hills echoed and re-echoed with a hundred thousand cheers."

"Ward feels the stimulus of the greedy hunt for gold and is roused into activity by the locomotive whistle," wrote a newspaper reporter, shortly after the opening of the road. "The town has quadrupled in size," he continued, describing the mining boom which Ward enjoyed in the first few years of the century. During this boom the railroad carried an average of two hundred and fifty passengers a day and one hundred tons of ore, the little narrow gauge trains chugging up hill and coasting down grade over the serpentine route.

With the coming of the railroad in 1898, thousands of tons of mill dirt or low grade ore, which had been accumulating on the dumps for over twenty years because shipping costs were prohibitive, became "negotiable into dollars, when only a short time ago it was worthless." But the ores of the mines became increasingly refractory, and lack of economical methods of treatment ultimately broke the boom which in 1904 had made Ward the largest camp in the county.

On Jan. 24, 1900, a fire which was believed to have started in an ash-can behind the McClancy Hotel destroyed almost the entire town.

> Not a store, hotel, saloon, restaurant nor a business house of any sort escaped the flames. . . . If the life of the old town depended wholly upon the profits that are taken over the counter and bar, its destruction would be complete, and the little basin in which its business houses once stood might be abandoned for the home of the chip-munk and coyote.—*Ward Miner*, Jan. 26, 1900.

Fifty-three buildings were consumed, with a total property loss of $85,000 and an insurance coverage of less than $7,500. Due to the untiring efforts of the townspeople, the schoolhouse which was kept drenched with water and was hung with wet quilts and blankets, the Congregational church, and a stone building in the middle of the business district were only scorched. The schoolhouse on one side of town and the church on the other served as firebreaks for the residential sections behind them, but nothing could save the business section and the blocks adjacent to it.

The fire broke out in the middle of the night and burned for six hours unchecked, fanned by a strong wind which made any attempts at extinguishing it futile.

> When the sun rose Thursday morning the burned district looked like a miniature sea dotted with miniature icebergs, the water poured upon the debris having frozen and formed into beautiful encrustations.—*Ward Miner*, Jan. 26, 1900.

The following day the Boulder county commissioners sent to the stricken town several thousand pounds of provisions, which the railroad carried free of charge and which the city officials distributed among the families who had lost everything. An editorial comment in the *Miner* expressed the sentiment of the camp by saying: "We're still here. Disfigured badly of course, but you can't drown the 'Miner' . . . we expect to stay in Ward."

I have been to Ward many times and have had some interesting experiences in the little mountain town. There was the cold winter day when, as an enthusiastic but tenderfoot member of the Colorado Mountain Club, I gingerly tried out skis on the milder slopes above the town and found the sport a decidedly sedentary one. I recall how we sat in the sun in front of the big general store, which even then was propped up with timbers on its east side, and ate our lunch, and how a thin film of ice formed on the hot coffee as soon as it was poured into the tin cups. That afternoon when we started home the pine trees in the canyon were covered with powdery snow and cast long shadows down the hillsides almost to the frozen creek.

One spring vacation Gwen, an artist friend of mine, and I spent three cold days in the unheated C. & N. Hotel, of which Mrs. Thompson was proprietress. The hotel was closed for the winter, but she agreed to let us stay in the big building if we would agree to cook our own meals and not expect her to heat our bedroom. Except for the big front room which Mrs. Thompson occupied and in which she kept a stove crackling hot, the hotel was so cold that we had to wear our coats even when we went to the kitchen. Behind the hotel a trail through the snow led to the outdoor toilet which was full of drifted snow. Each night we slid into sleeping bags laid on the floor of our room and gradually thawed out. The room was directly above the one with the stove, and the stovepipe, instead of entering a flue in the room below, came up through the floor into our room and disappeared through the ceiling like a sheet-iron column. One night the noise of wind hitting the building wakened me, and in the darkness I was fascinated and a little scared to see that the pipe glowed a dull red from the heat of the banked stove below and that it vibrated back and forth whenever a particularly strong blast of wind struck the building.

The days were spent in sketching and painting, in tramping all over the quiet town which must have had less than twenty residents, and in fighting the wind from off the range, which ripped paper from my pad and whipped powdery snow over freshly painted, damp watercolors, set to dry in the clear, cold air. Gwen solved her painting problems, first by hanging a rock to the tripod of her easel to keep it from blowing over and, when that failed, by nailing her canvas to a tree trunk and daring the wind to touch it.

In summer Ward is a livelier place, and the artist is not irritated by the wind, though sudden showers spatter finished sketches or turn pads to soggy pulp before shelter can be found. Vacationists fill the cabins, and one or two stores do a steady business in groceries, postcards and pop. The old railroad station above the town is now a store, and from the high level road in front of it, where the trains used to stand puffing, tourists buy gasoline and ask questions about roads and trails, as they drink cokes and look down over the town in the cup-shaped pocket below.

In the store is a large framed photograph of Ward, showing street after street packed with houses, few of which survived the fire of 1900. Around the edge of the picture is a border made of more photographs, each showing an important building, and in addition, a column of text gives a brief history of the town itself. During one visit to the store I stood on a chair in front of the picture, copied the history and sketched certain of the buildings in the border. Few people who stop at the store may notice the big photograph in its massive frame, but to those who do Ward takes on added interest.

(521)

When I first went to the town the Catholic church was surmounted with a cross and its interior was filled with pews and other church furnishings, but the building was empty and unused; now the cross and the pews are gone and the place, alas, is used as a garage. The Congregational church, now the Community church, has fared better, for even on my last visit I found it completely furnished with hymnals, a piano and a vase of dusty dried flowers. As one drives into Ward from Left Hand canyon, the church is the building that dominates the town's panorama. The C. & N. and the Columbia hotels, though bigger structures, melt into the landscape, while the church stands out like a sentinel watching over the town. Not far below the church is the old jail and firehouse, in which stands a hand-drawn hosecart.

Above and behind the town are the mines, with their dumps—all of which look alike to the uninitiated—rising one above the other on the hilltops. Most of the shaft houses have disappeared, and over only a few holes a windlass stands guard; but point to one of the piles of rock which cascade down the mountainside and any old timer will identify it and eagerly tell you the story of the mine from which it came. To him Ward has never changed; it is not the quiet little settlement where thirty or forty people live the year round but remains the great Sulphide Camp of the county where one thousand people made their homes and dug much gold and some silver from the throats of the mines.

CHAPTER XX.

There's Always One More

IMMEDIATELY upon my return from an old camp or townsite not previously visited, I have placed a red dot in front of its name on a key chart which I have compiled of all such places in the state, and I have marked with another red dot its location on a large map. As the red dots increased in number I began to look toward the day when the record would be complete and I could stop traipsing over impossible roads in search of invisible towns. But no sooner had I returned home from a trip than some one would say, "Have you been to ——?", and mention a place of which I'd never heard; and away I'd go again to record it and check it on my list.

A botany professor had been on leave from the University for several months, and shortly after his return I saw him on the other side of the street. He called across to me. "Have you been to Busk?" "No," I shouted back, "Where is it?" He told me that it was below the mouth of the Carlton tunnel, on the old Colorado Midland road; and for two years I fretted until I bribed some friends to take me to it.

We left Leadville by the cemetery road and, once past it, were on the old railroad grade which for years has been an auto highway of sorts. After crossing the main line track of the Denver and Rio Grande in the Arkansas valley, the road began its long climb up the side of Mount Massive. The railroad had been built to Basalt by tunneling through Mt. Massive. At Basalt it turned and followed the Roaring Fork river to its terminus at Aspen. On the Leadville side of the divide there are no towns, and not even any houses, except a few close to Turquoise lake. Somewhere near the lake the road crosses a bridge, and just beyond is a big roadsign marked "Warning. Road Closed. Proceed at Your Own Risk," or words to that effect. We "proceeded" and were soon on a ledge overlooking a deep valley. Turquoise lake was now far below us but Mt. Massive was ahead, and we continued to climb. Since the road is not kept in repair, its surface was washed and rough. It was such wild, lonely country that we were not surprised to see a deer come up from below the road and walk toward us for several yards before bounding up the mountainside. Marmots whistled and chattered at us from their secure hide-outs among the rocks. We began to see patches of snow beside the road, but still no sign of Busk or of the tunnel's mouth. Another half mile and a deep snowbank covered two-thirds of the road, making further progress impossible.

I left the car and hiked around a curve in hope that the tunnel was near or at least in sight, and though I looked closely at the pine-packed valley below, at the bottom of which must lie Busk, I saw nothing but tree tops.

Although we felt certain we were close to our goal, we could not explore further—we had been foolish to try such high country so early in the season before the snows had melted. It was even difficult to turn the car on the narrow ledge, but we finally edged it around and started back.

By the time we had reached Leadville, even its roughest side streets seemed marvels of smoothness compared to what we had been over. The others were relieved to be back in civilization again; but Busk is still a black dot on my list, and someday I shall go back, find it, and change the dot to red.

Now that I have been to as many of the historic mining towns as I have been able to visit, I should be content; but instead I am anxious to revisit many of them, especially since I have learned so much of their history. A return visit would reveal so many things missed before through ignorance, such as the location of certain mines, and of certain old, forgotten trails over the hills.

I should like to go again to Whitecross and look for traces of the camps of Argentum and Tellurium, and I want to know just where Tellurium in Boulder county was located. It is described as near Hoosier hill and two miles from the camp of Sunshine. Another source mentions a mine "a little below Camp Tellurium at the mouth of Gold Run," and another item refers to Camp Lyon at the head of Sand gulch, "one mile from Sunshine and a half-mile from Tellurium!" Some day I shall try to find Manhattan, near the Cache le Poudre canyon.

Where was San Juan City? I have never found it on any map, yet I read that it was "twenty-five miles southeast of Lake City on the Rio Grande," that Antelope Springs was a little below it, and that Lost Trail was west of it. On my next visit to Silverton I shall try to find the site of LeMoyne City which was laid out at the foot of Boulder mountain in 1883. Although the plat showed four blocks each way, only five or six cabins were ever built, "about 200 feet up the hill from where the present road crosses the creek." Within the last month I have run across the only allusion I have found to Hughesville (near Black Hawk), which describes it as the "seat of the silver belt on the ranch claim of Patrick Hughes" and further states that in 1878 the Hard Money mine was found on the ranch property. The extreme northwestern portion of the state is still to be explored, especially the territory northwest from Placerville and on into the Paradox valley, where radium bearing ores have been found. The country up Cache le Poudre way contains traces of camps which I know only by hearsay and which I hope to explore; and the history of Golden and the prospecting up Clear creek between there and Idaho Springs deserves further investigation. Good Coloradoans from all parts of the state continue to bring to my attention facts and anecdotes about many places; and all this material I file for future use. I am sure I have been to the sites of Poughkeepsie, near Ironton, and of Adelaide and Birdseye, on the hills above Leadville, but no trace remains to allow me to make positive statements about them.

Most of the places that I have not visited are mere sites and all are inaccessible—except to the hardiest climber—probably I shall never reach them. Yet I do not consider my research ended; there will always be one more fact or one more picture to add to those already collected. Accurate pictorial data has often been hard to obtain, for unless one was familiar with sites or buildings, or had some one along who knew every idiosyncracy of the landscape, it was easy to drive by an important link in the historical chain I was trying to create. Nevertheless, I have succeeded in finishing some nine hundred sketches for my record, and still have as many more "made on the spot" drawings to bring to completion. I do not expect, therefore, even if I were prevented from again visiting the old mining towns in the heart of the Rockies, to be out of intimate touch with them for years to come.

Other bits of information, invaluable but hard to obtain, are the tales and historic facts remembered by citizens who lived in the mining towns when they were new. Their stories relate colorful anecdotes which never made the papers, but they are also, at times, inaccurate. Each town has several such persons who must be looked up and interviewed, and I have never found one who was unwilling to reminisce; but often the reminiscences were irrelevant, and the results of a morning's chat could be reduced to a few sentences. These elderly pioneers are gradually passing on, and unless their stories can be saved now they will be completely lost. My most fortunate break was last summer when, through the kindness of a friend, I was able to interview an old gentleman who told me facts that I had been unable to find elsewhere. Less than two weeks after our interview I received word of his death.

The most valuable sources of information, files of old newspapers, were also difficult to find in anything like complete form. Even those offices which have preserved the material, rarely have it bound or arranged chronologically. A few files are intact in the towns where they were originally printed; but some are in private hands, and some have been moved to other states. And worst of all is the confusion of information—disagreement as to dates and locations, and discrepancies about names and other important items. To sift the conflicting evidence so as to establish the real fact or facts is often well nigh impossible. Since I am not a historian I make no pretense to having found all the printed matter available. I have consulted as many sources as possible and from each have culled only such material as is pertinent to this book.

The journalistic style of the old newspapers has fascinated me—it is so florid and so full of words and phrases that sound quaint if not amusing today. Snow is spoken of as a "fall of the beautiful;" and the miners at Mineral Point once commented that Animas Forks "too has a goodly thickness of the niveous cloak with which her sister city up the creek is blessed." One entry is entirely unintelligible to me but it is certainly startling:

A Pointer.

Red Mt. Mining Journal

If Christ was out with a shot gun killing damn fools he would inevitably begin on Red Mt. Town. This is a Pointer.—*Central City Register,* June 1, 1888.

Advertisements are good reading too:

About 60 head of golden jacks, will trade for real estate in Telluride or Ouray. The train is composed of all native animals, who have been packed for one season in the mountains. Address C. R. Clark, Red Mt., Colo.—*Red Mt. Mining Journal*, July 14, 1888.

T. B. Bond's Fashionable
Hair Dressing Saloon and·Bath Rooms

All who are desirous of cultivating a luxuriant growth of whiskers, or having a most fashionable cut on their hair, can be accommodated by calling on me at my rooms. Hair and whiskers dyed a beautiful black or any color desired. . . .

Celebrated Hair Tonic

It also removes rancid smells from the hair caused by the use of oils, etc.

For Ladies' Toilet

It is the only preparation that will give a rich, glossy appearance without soiling the bonnet or hat.—T. B. Bond—*Central City Miner's Register*, April 30, 1863.

Having met Mr. Forsyth on my first visit to Howardsville I was interested in finding the following item·in the *Silverton Standard* of Sept. 1, 1894:

The citizens of·Eureka crowded into two lumber wagons and all the inhabitants of Middleton, assisted by a few Silverton friends, made life a burden to Henry Forsyth and his wife last night. The chivari was all in good nature and the guests all had a very enjoyable time. Lunch and refreshments were served.

And to show how times have changed read this:

Hunters Attention.

There are 1500 head of Mountain Sheep just opposite Minnesota Gulch.—*Silverton Standard*, January, 1890.

If you too are anxious to take trips similar to mine you will need faith in the Almighty and a sense of humor. If you are convinced that any road, no matter how impossible, can be travelled by some means, and that in spite of weather and spikes in the roadbed lying in wait for your inflated tire, you can make your objective; and if you do not get giddy on ledge roads, and if you have car brakes that work (although all of your driving on grades will be done in gear), and if you don't mind leaving your car when the road peters out, and hiking the rest of the way, no matter how steep the trail nor how high and rare the air, you can have as much fun as I have had.

Just as important as faith is a sense of humor. Sometimes the situation is simply amusing, as it was on the day when I entered a newspaper office in a town on the Western Slope and asked the editor if I might make a sketch of his office. He seemed surprised at the request but he grudgingly consented, saying, as he looked at my sketch pad, "Sure, you can make a picture if you want, but I warn you I won't buy it."

Sleeping accommodations frequently call for a sense of humor. Do not be surprised to find "No Vacancy" signs on every type of lodging at the opening of the fishing season, over the Fourth of July, or if you are unfortunate enough to drive into some town or city on the weekend when they are celebrating their Strawberry or Lettuce Festival. On such a night you may find but one room for your whole family, or some hospitable citizen may put you up in his living room on the davenport. No two nights are alike, and something always "turns up;" but don't expect Beauty-Rest mattresses or a private bath.

There is also the problem of food. Aside from taking an occasional lunch along I have preferred to eat wherever I happened to be, for I have learned many valuable facts from waitresses, or from customers to whom I have talked over a bowl of chili. There was the man in Central City who absently put butter in his coffee and stirred the brew with the handle of his fork while he told me about the baseball games that used to be played at the park which is now hidden under the big mine dump. And there was the old man in Victor who sat across the table in the Gold Coin Cafe and talked about the days when Victor had an Opera House and Cripple Creek didn't!

Every trip is full of unexpected incidents, most of which are fun; and once you have surrendered to the lure of the mountains, nothing can keep you out of them. I hope that some of those who read this book will remember some camp or some bit of history which I have missed, and that they will be good enough to let me know about it, that I may make an even more complete record of the towns which helped to make the state. And finally, I hope that there will always be just one more site, or mine, or camp to visit, and that I will be able to drive or ride or hike or hobble to it; for like the prospectors of '59 I shall continue to search, not for float and colors, but for the history and pictorial matter which to me are the ingredients from which my "gold in the hills" is made.

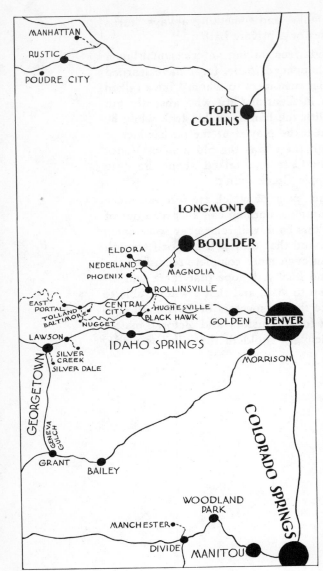

CHAPTER XXI

Twenty-Five Years Later 1949-1974

Twenty-Five years have brought me much more information and many more trips. Some of the questions I was left with when I originally finished this book have been answered. And many changes have been wrought in old familiar sites.

Since *Stampede to Timberline* was published in 1949, many persons have written me informative and friendly letters retelling anecdotes and giving facts and dates connected with the specific place that each knew intimately. Perhaps the writer had grown up there and was eager to reminisce about local activities. Others had revisited places that they had not seen for many years and helpfully described the current appearance and economic condition of the town. I too have gone back to certain of the towns and watched slow deterioration as well as occasional rebirth; and I have explored a number of places unknown or inaccessible to me in the thirties and forties. From these varied sources my store of information has been greatly enlarged and enriched. In this chapter I share with you interviews and portions of the contributions and experiences of my correspondents, as well as my own research.

Beartown San Juan County pp. 334-338

E. L. Bennett, author of *Boom Town Boy: In Old Creede, Colorado,* wrote me in 1969 from Mesa, Arizona:

No one who reads paragraph 3 on page 336 of *Stampede to Timberline* can doubt that you went to Beartown. The stock grazing on Grassy Hill could change from black-

---

Page number cited with marginal notation of town indicates original discussion of that town in the previous chapters.

face sheep to whiteface cattle and the once populated towns of Junction City and Beartown could settle into the ground but the horseflies and deer flies would carry on so industriously they would win a place in every history of the upper Rio Grande.

In answer to my question as to where San Juan City was, Mr. Bennett replied:

San Juan City Mineral County p. 524

> Surely someone wrote to tell you you went through its remains when you went to Carroll Wetherill's camp on Lost Trail Creek. On page 119 of their *Colorado's Century of Cities* the Griswold's mention San Juan City. . . . There's a picture of one of its cabins on page 103. When I first knew the place in the neighborhood of 1900, there were several cabins similar to that one mentioned above. . . . The place is now a combination cow ranch and dude cabin area.

A summer visitor to Colorado in 1966 wrote that the road to the site of Gresham (above Jamestown), in Boulder county, had been improved, presumably because the land higher on the mountainside was to be developed; it had been subdivided into lots, and streets were carved into the hillside.

Gresham Boulder County p. 510

Skiers in Aspen who ride the lift to the top of Aspen Mountain (Ajax Mountain to oldtimers) may not realize that they are passing over the site of Tourtelotte Park, a small camp which grew up around the mines located by Henry Tourtelotte in the early eighties. One of the first prospectors in the area, he worked his way up Castle Creek and then up the mountain until he found outcroppings in a natural park near its summit. At its peak the camp had a store, a schoolhouse, several dozen cabins, and a voting place. Mule trains carried the ore to the valley. As the mines were developed, additional facilities for hauling the ore to the smelters were needed; but soon after a tramway was completed to Aspen, a disgruntled muleskinner, whose business was thereby wrecked, cut the cable with a hacksaw and no repairs were made.

Tourtelotte Park Pitkin County p. 233

Mining camp architecture is governed by available materials and practicality. Ore mills, if possible, are built against hillsides so that the ore, which is fed into the topmost section, falls by gravity from level to level and emerges at the bottom ready to be hauled to a reduction plant or smelter. The day in 1950 that friends drove us in their jeep from Hillside, in the Wet Mountain Valley, up the east slope of the Sangre de Cristo Range to the Cloverdale mill, we saw an interesting construction. The mill, which stood on a steep shale slope above timberline, was well-preserved and extremely sturdy, because it was built of two-by-fours laid flat one above the other. Such an arrangement made the walls both thick and strong enough, it was hoped, to defy destruction by snowslides. I have seen the same method used in jails in Ashcroft and in Animas Forks.

Cloverdale Fremont-Custer Counties

When I originally visited Hillerton, two miles north of Tin Cup, I was greatly disappointed, for none of it remained. Then in November, 1949, I received a helpful letter from H. L. Curtiss of Paonia, Colorado:

Hillerton Gunnison County pp. 181, 182, 186

> Hillerton, when started, had no sawmill and no lumber [except] possibly a few boards they had whip-sawed, therefore the houses were all cabins with dirt roofs. I

can show you where the buildings stood and an occasional bottom log. . . . When the buildings were gone the . . . dirt on the roof, two or three times deeper than the [top] soil was, sank to the ground. Consequently, the sagebrush grew two or three times taller than anywhere else, and you can pick out where practically every house stood, to say nothing of pieces of glass turned purple, broken dishes, old cut nails, etc.

Thanks to this information I can "read" sites better than I could before.

Montgomery
Park County
pp. 81, 82

In 1953, Everett Bair, Deputy County Treasurer of Fairplay and local historian, spent an evening with me before the fireplace of the Fairplay hotel and told me old tales of the region, one of which concerned Montgomery.

A man named Austin (or Ashton), his wife and children, and another man came in their covered wagon drawn by oxen into the valley northwest of Fairplay to search for a mine. They went first to Buckskin Joe which was booming, but not making a strike there they left. Climbing over the ridge to the north they continued prospecting and discovered a mine. By then it was September, and Austin put up a tent for his wife and children before he and the other man went back to Denver for supplies. They were gone a month and on the return trip they battled their way through a blizzard in South Park. Worried about his family, Austin went on the next day, but because of the storm could not get farther than Alma. As soon as conditions permitted, he set out for the place where he had left his family. He found the tent blown down and his wife and children frozen.

When bodies were exhumed from the Montgomery cemetery a few years ago, just before the dam was built, the skeletons of a woman and two children were found in one grave. She must have been young because the skull had all its teeth, and buttons in the grave were similar to those worn by women in earlier days. No one knows for certain, but it may have been the Austin family's grave.

Today the town of Montgomery is only a memory, for a rock-face dam blocks the narrow end of the valley, and real estate developers are advertising lots on the flat at the foot of Hoosier Pass.

Crystal
Gunnison
County
pp. 218-226

In 1957 another tale was told me, of the strange preparations made by a fanatic several years earlier, who took his wife and young stepdaughter to Crystal along with "thousands of cans of food, bolts of cloth, and a sewing machine." Having arrived and cached his supplies, he blew up the bridge at the entrance to the town. Convinced that the world was going to be destroyed and that everyone living below 9,000 feet was damned, he and his wife would survive and repopulate the world from Crystal City.

Since this catastrophe did not occur, and since the road from Marble to Crystal has been improved, it is not surprising that in recent years the camp has become popular with summer residents, who occupy the old cabins and even bring small housetrailers over the shelf road above the Crystal River.

Not only camps but source material disappears or gets lost or damaged through ignorance or neglect. Old newspaper files are gold mines of information, and while they may not always contain the most accurate material, their reporting has flair and gives a human flavor to the most prosaic subject matter. The loss of such records is a real calamity.

In 1950 I wrote to the newspaper editor in Ouray and asked if he had files of the early papers, planning to combine a sketching trip with additional research. His reply was prompt but distressing: "I am sorry to report that most of the old files of the *Ouray County Herald* were destroyed by a former publisher who, we understand, used them for making the morning fires. There are some, but only a few."

An unexpected find was made some years ago in Breckenridge, when a stack of old papers was discovered in a shed into which rain and snow had drifted. The papers, when first seen by Miss Ina Aulls and Mrs. Alys Freeze, librarians of the Western History Department of the Denver Public Library, were completely frozen, and the task of thawing and separating the fragile sheets was overwhelming but challenging. The project was successful, and now the library has on microfilm the *Summit County Journal* for the years 1883-1888.

Whenever possible I obtained a driver or guide who knew the area so well that he could supply me with facts and anecdotes that only a native would know and could also point out all manner of sights along the way that I would have missed if alone.

Bandora San Juan County pp. 433, 434

In 1950, while staying in Ouray, I made arrangements with Mr. Davis, who ran a jeep service, to be taken to several locations in the Silverton area, some of which were new to me. The first of these was Bandora, which I first heard about in 1942 from Henry Forsyth of Howardsville. He had told me that a few buildings were still standing and that for several years trucks had been hauling ore from the mine.

One September Mr. Davis and I whisked up the Million Dollar highway in the open jeep that I had requested. Early fall temperatures at that altitude at seven in the morning in a fast-travelling vehicle are bone-chilling, and long before we reached the summit of Red Mountain Pass I was shivering but ecstatic, for the mountains had never looked so dramatic nor the air, though bitter cold, been so invigorating. Down the Silverton side of the pass we rolled to the South Mineral Creek turnoff, which followed the stream several miles through a steep, mountain valley, where aspens covered the slopes and bare peaks loomed ahead. At the Mineral Campground, five miles from the highway, was a large pack outfit with at least 100 sleek horses and mules all tethered to ropes or tied to trees. Cowboys were watering them at the stream. We learned that the outfit was being taken up to Ice Lake to finish some filming for MGM.

To reach Bandora we turned through the campground and then drove ahead up a narrow, steep road to a 10,500-foot elevation. At the head of the valley were some cabins and mine dumps and a truck beside a tent. When we stopped, a woman came from the tent and eyed us curiously, but to my delight she could answer my questions. The mine we'd passed, she said, was the Bandora. Nearby on the valley floor were the foundations of its mill. Higher on the mountainside were other mines, whose dumps and the trails leading to them we could see from below.

On the way back to the highway, we passed a sheepherder's wagon and saw the Navajo Indian herder, his wife, and their sheep on the hillside above.

Titusville
San Juan
County
p. 433

Our next stop was Silverton, where I inquired about Titusville, a deserted camp on the west shoulder of Kendall Mountain at the end of a four-mile, abandoned trail. Its peak population was said to have reached 500. Its mines, including the Montana, were at 12,500 feet or higher, and to take out the ore a two-mile tram was built down to Silverton. "Don't even try to go up there," one miner said to me. "No buildings remain, only broken machinery and a boiler."

Eureka
San Juan
County
pp. 402-406,
427, 526

I hadn't seen Eureka in years, so when we left Silverton, Mr. Davis suggested that we return to Ouray by way of that deserted camp, Animas Forks, and Poughkeepsie Gulch. As we passed the mouth of Cunningham Gulch he asked if I'd ever been to the Highland Mary mine at the head of the valley. When I nodded "yes," he told me that the telephone line to the mine for the entire length of the valley had been strung up the middle of the canyon to avoid destruction by snow slides. Guy wires anchored on either side of the canyon supported the live wires which ran up the center.

Eureka in 1941 was the perfect ghost town. Its main street was lined with falsefronted stores and its back streets contained many homes. The Sunnyside Mill, seven-stories high, was well-preserved though inactive. By 1950 Eureka was almost erased. Only one falsefronted store and the fire station remained on the street. Most of the houses had been moved up Red Mountain Pass to the Treasury Tunnel. The schoolhouse was on skids ready to be hauled away, and all the wooden surfacing of the big mill was stripped off, leaving only a metal skeleton.

While I looked with amazement at the townsite, Mr. Davis suggested that we eat the lunch his wife had prepared before we climbed over Engineer Pass. As we sat on old mine timbers and hugged our coffee cups for warmth, a strong wind was blowing, and low, ominous clouds were scudding above us. Before we finished, flakes of snow filled the air, and all the way to the top of the pass we were enveloped in the swirling flurry of a "niveous cloak" so dense that when another jeep, on its way to Silverton, loomed up in front of us we were completely unprepared for it and scuttled to the right like a frightened rabbit.

In 1965 I saw Eureka again. Almost every building was gone, some torn down for their lumber, much of which lay in untidy piles like scattered jackstraws. Even the metal carcass of the Sunnyside mill had been removed and its concrete foundations alone, terrace upon terrace, testified to its size.

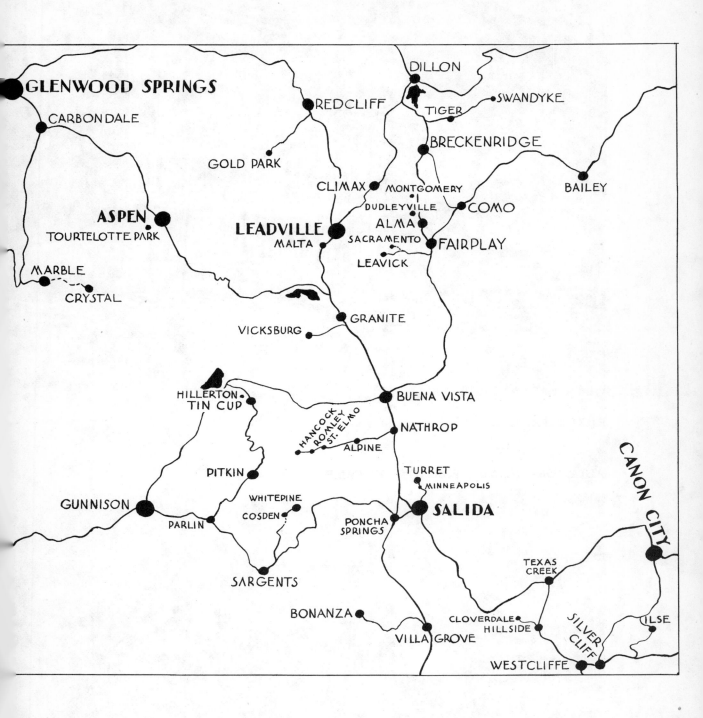

RICO CAFÉ, 1950.

ALTA, 1964. NEWER PORTION OF CAMP.

On the way down Poughkeepsie Gulch, Mr. Davis pointed out the portal of a tunnel across the canyon, high on the mountainside. The mine was that of Elmer Eggleston, who mined it alone for forty years, even persuading the county to build a road up to the tunnel. Although he never got more than a few tons of lead ore from it, he worked it steadily. Davis knew him and drove him to and from Ouray several times, though usually he walked. He died in 1949 at age ninety-five.

Poughkeepsie Gulch Ouray County pp. 407, 418, 438, 449

People's hospitality and helpfulness never cease to amaze me. In 1950 I planned a brief stop at Rico, in western Colorado, partly to sketch and partly to learn more of its history. It would also be a base from which to visit Dunton, a camp I had not yet seen.

Rico Dolores County pp. 390, 392-394

Rico, which is on Highway 145 between Telluride and Cortez, has no hotel; but at the grocery store I learned that Mrs. Engel sometimes took roomers. When she opened the door the most wonderful odor of pickling spices and fruit greeted us, and even though she was in the midst of canning she graciously prepared rooms for Russ and me.

"There's no restaurant either," she said. "Even the Bar isn't serving short orders. There's a man who might fix sandwiches for you, but I'm not at all sure. I'll point out his store." Fortunately the man agreed to feed us and said to return later. This gave me time to do some sketching. At the store Russ and I dined on canned soup, sandwiches, and ice cream cones, and by the time we returned to Mrs. Engel's she had called up a neighbor, Joe Stampfel, who knew lots about Rico and who had mined at Dunton. "You should meet Mrs. Pellet," he told me. "I'll call her up and take you to her home. She's just back from Denver." I knew that Mrs. Pellet was a Colorado State Representative and that she and her late husband had mining properties in Rico. "I wish I'd known you were in town," she said when we met. "You could have had dinner with me. I cooked a roast. I know your drawings — have seen them in the *Denver Post.*"

As we sat in her living room filled with art treasures from a trip around the world, she told me that her husband died in 1949 and that she continued to run their mining interests. She identified mines and mining properties for me, and when Joe said he'd have to leave, since he went to work at eleven P.M., she replied, "That's all right Joe, I'll take her home," and continued her narrative. As he left she called to him, "Go over to Mary's and tell her I want the book back that I loaned her. And see if Hartley Lee has a copy of that other old book." Joe Stampfel was back in no time with the proprietor of the cafe where we'd eaten. When Mrs. Pellet introduced him to me, he replied: "Oh yes, my customer." Handing me a series of newspaper articles about Rico, he offered them to me overnight and said he'd open his cafe an hour earlier in the morning so we could get an early start to Dunton. Laden with this material, I returned to Mrs. Engel's and read until after midnight. When I thanked Mr. Stampfel for doing errands and taking me to Mrs. Pellet's he replied: "I'm glad to do it. It's the least one can do when someone is interested in Rico."

Next morning I rose early and went out to sketch. At the cafe Russ and I were the only customers. Hartley Lee had brought old newspapers and a book of mine claims for me to look at and set out our breakfast in the adjoining booth. "It didn't rain last night so you can get to Dunton. It's only twenty-two miles," he called to us as we left. Before starting off I went to the store where Mrs. Engel was serving on the election board. "I'm glad to see you," she said. "If you are going to Dunton will you take these pamphlets over there and deliver them to the clerk for us? They should have been there yesterday." Bidding her goodbye, we drove back six miles up the highway toward Lizard Head Pass to the Dunton turnoff, a narrow shelf which climbed the face of the ridge and crossed an open park, called Montezuma Meadows, where sheep were grazing. Another shelf road slid down a hill through timber with a gurgling stream beside it, and finally we were in Dunton. Not much of it was left, only one group of cabins and a two-story bunkhouse, an indoor hot springs pool, run by three brothers to whom we delivered the pamphlets, and below the town, the Emma and Smuggler mine properties — a jumbled assortment of dumps, tunnel portals, rusting ore cars, and a few surface buildings. We met but one car on the return trip to the highway.

Some mining camps that I have visited in recent years have almost disappeared. Such a town is Bonanza, in the northern part of the San Luis Valley. Because I hadn't seen it since 1938, I made a special trip in 1965 to see what was left of it. Jeff, who was with me, had never been there, and I was eager to show him how well-preserved it was with its mills and its main street lined with stores and homes.

The fourteen-mile drive off Highway 285 to the west was easy, for the road was now wide and well-maintained. But Bonanza was virtually gone. Broken beaver dams below the townsite, dead trees, and old, eroded settling ponds should have prepared us for what we found. No big mill loomed beside the road; only its concrete foundations marked the site. And instead of the row of buildings along the main street, only a handful of empty cabins and stores was left. A few of the houses have been fixed up for summer people, but little of the Bonanza that I had seen remains. As we were leaving I noticed a faded sign that dated back to Bonanza's prime. It pointed up a side gully and read: "Slaughterhouse Gulch."

A little-known place is Baltimore, between Rollinsville and Tolland, one-quarter of a mile south of the graded highway that continues west to the east portal of the Moffat railroad tunnel. Its opera house, which I discovered in 1934, had scenery on its stage; upstairs there were more flats from other sets which had been used to make partitions and turn the building into a rooming house for a while. In 1953 I visited the camp again. The opera house was a twisted mass of sagging lumber, snow-flattened. The Baltimore Club's door was wide open, its fine mahogany bar was gone, (reinstalled in Central City, I've been told), and its only furnishing was an old icebox.

There wasn't much left of Bachelor in 1942, so when I planned to revisit it in 1972 I thought I had better stop in Creede to get up-to-date information about the camp and the condition of the road to it. The first three people I questioned were in the kitchen of the hotel in Creede. The young waitress had never heard of it. The busboy thought that although the road up the mountain might be driven in a passenger car, there were two places where we could get in trouble. A woman who lived in Creede said the road up to the cemetery was all right but very rough beyond that point, and that even if we got all the way only parts of two houses remained in the townsite. All the sidewalks and scraps of lumber had been carried off.

I thanked her and crossed the street to talk to the postmaster and his wife. Both agreed that the three-to-four miles of road to the ghost site were hard on cars and advised us against trying it. "Bachelor's gone," the postmaster concluded. "Forget it. When you were there before, there was something to see."

Russell Gulch (southwest of Central City) means more to me than it did before I met Mr. Hinkley. The town has few year-round residents, and many of its buildings are empty; but on a sketching trip in 1953, I was fortunate to find two people who pointed out many spots that I would otherwise have missed.

When I parked my car just off the main street and started to draw, an old man came out of his cabin and walked over to watch me work. We talked and he introduced himself and invited me into his home, where he showed me old photographs and stereoptican views of the town in its prime. As we walked to his door he pointed out the skeleton shafthouse of the Jefferson-Calhoun mine on top of the hill to the north. While I climbed the rough terrain to the shafthouse, I left a copy of *Stampede to Timberline* with him to look at. Upon my return he offered me a glass of spring water and, standing at the door, showed where the ballpark was and where the Welsh church had stood.

"That big schoolhouse," he said, pointing to a two-story brick structure beside the roadway, "is the third one that was built. The first one is way down the gulch near the old stone building and off the road. The second one is the big stone-walled ruin below on the main street. Go see Mrs. Waggoner before you leave," he urged. It was from her I learned that the old cemetery, which I'd seen while descending the hillside from the shafthouse, was almost gone except for a few markers. "When the Odd Fellows' Cemetery was established in Central City," Mrs. Waggoner said, "most people moved their dear ones there or took them to Denver cemeteries."

Leavick was another of the well-preserved ghost towns when I first saw it in 1942. Its empty houses and abandoned mills covered the hilltop close to timberline, and from one of its mills a tram with ore buckets dangling from its cables rose to the top of the mountain and disappeared in a clump of twisted, timberline trees.

Returning in 1966 from a trip to the southern part of the state, I asked my driving partner if she'd like to see Leavick, knowing that she was as much of a fanatic as I when it came to visiting old camps.

At the Fourmile Creek Road south of Fairplay, we started our side trip. This was a new road to me, wide and built to accommodate trucks. From Highway 285 it ran west, then south, and finally climbed steadily to Leavick. After six miles of driving, a government marker in an open meadow on our right read "Site of Horseshoe, 1879." (In 1942 there were still two cabins and a stretch of railroad track at this location.)

Beyond the townsite our road headed straight toward Horseshoe Mountain, a glacial cirque, with Sheep Mountain on the left or south side of the high, exposed valley. Beaver dams, mine dumps, debris, and a few weathered, disintegrating structures, half-hidden in underbrush, were all that indicated former activity. As we neared Leavick, the best-preserved cluster of buildings — a mill with two cabins behind it and a tram tower surrounded with tangled cables — was on our right. Beyond these the road swung up to the summit of a low, bare hill where the camp should be. I waited eagerly for my first glimpse of the place. But no houses appeared, only another marker — "Site of Leavick, 1880." Piles of lumber that had been buildings dotted the ground, and faint trails marked former streets. Beyond the townsite the present road continued for another two-and-a-half miles to the Hilltop mine, which has been worked sporadically since its shutdown in 1930. Another landmark gone. What had once been a true ghost town is now a windswept slope.

Dudleyville
Park County
pp. 82, 83, 85

Just north of Alma is the site of Dudleyville. As late as the 1940's the ruins of a smelter and several frame buildings and cabins marked the place. Even after the smelter was torn down, its black slag heap was visible from Highway 9, but by 1970 underbrush along the river obscured the slag pile and Alma Park Estate Realtors were selling 5-acre lots where buildings once stood.

Gold Park
Eagle
County
pp. 246-250

Gold Park, companion camp to Holy Cross City, is eight miles south of Highway 24 on the west side of Tennessee Pass. It is also at the end of the drivable road that skirts tumbling Homestake Creek. I hadn't seen it for thirty years, and I doubted if any of the old cabins that had dotted the tree-studded meadow remained. The roadbed seemed rougher than ever, with long stretches of sharp, loose gravel that slowed our progress. Rugged peaks capped with lowering clouds closed in the head of the valley, while rumbling thunder urged us to look around quickly and leave.

I recognized the meadow (now called Homestake Campsite) where the cabins had stood and the narrow steep trail that led up through the aspens to Fancy Pass, Hunky Dory Lake, and Holy Cross City; but I could find only one of the old, chinked log structures, half-hidden in a thicket of young trees. The Community House was also missing. On the way out we met a number of cars carrying campers or fishermen. Thirty years had made a vast difference in the place.

Two of the old towns I found almost unchanged in appearance. One was Magnolia and the other was Whitepine.

Magnolia
Boulder
County
p. 492

Magnolia is perched above Boulder Canyon, at the end of a steep two-mile grade. Many of its early buildings are gone, and of those remaining most are remodeled into private homes. I visited the camp in the late 1930's and by following a side road was soon descending a steep gulch into a valley south of the main town. At the bottom of the grade were many evidences of earlier mining activities — dumps, machinery, sheds, stone foundations, an assay furnace or small smelter, and a large mill. I made several sketches before leaving.

In 1967, Boulder friends who had a summer cabin at Magnolia invited me to explore with them some of the old mine sites in the vicinity. We pulled up the long hill; before reaching the heart of Magnolia we turned to the left on a narrow road past several dumps and collapsed shafthouses and drove to the top of a steep hill where we left the car. The rest of the way was on foot down an old mine road into Keystone Gulch. As we neared the bottom I recognized through the trees the dumps, foundations, and big mill I'd seen in 1938. Excitedly I drew more sketches, and after reaching home compared them with those drawn thirty years earlier. Except for the height of the trees that were growing out of the ruined foundations and two fallen smokestacks, nothing had changed at the Keystone-Mountain Lion mining properties.

Whitepine
and Cosden
Gunnison
County
pp. 161,
168-176

During the 1940's I visited Whitepine twice and found it a most satisfying ghost town — a theater, the town well, a store, a hotel, a schoolhouse, and many other buildings in a fair state of preservation. On my second visit most of the cabins were occupied, and my driver and I were offered vegetables from small garden plots and even a couple of freshly caught trout. My third trip to the camp came in 1972.

Since cars are lower slung than they were in the 1940's, Joel and I stopped at Sargents to inquire about the road. The young attendant at the filling station looked critically at my Ford but said, "Sure, you can drive it up there. It's only ten miles from here and the first six are paved. You can't get to North Star at all unless you have a four-wheel drive vehicle."

As we rolled along the paved road north of Highway 50, I said to Joel, who was driving, "We must see if we can locate the site of Cosden, which should be on the flat at the edge of this valley just before we start to climb up to Whitepine. A small smelter was built there about 1900. I brought with me a letter I received in 1950 from David H. Campbell of Iron River, Michigan. Here's what he wrote:

> Cosden was at the opening of the gulch, about three miles below Whitepine. There was nothing there when we started operations, and we built the smelter, office, bunkhouse, stables, two boarding houses and nearly a dozen small residences. . . . Two years ago there was no trace of the smelter and but few houses."

Keeping a sharp lookout we did spot a small, black slag heap, a few sheds, one two-story house, and one square log building. The slag identified the site.

Next we looked for the Whitepine cemetery, to the left of the road on the way to town. The picket and cast iron fences around the graves were buried deeper in underbrush and new trees than on my last visit, but as we drove by I got a glimpse of one marble or granite gravestone and a few wooden markers.

Just before we pulled up the last steep pitch onto the main street of Whitepine we passed several large dumps and concrete foundations of a good-sized mill. A sign at a road fork that branched off to the right and disappeared among dumps and trees read "No-Name Gulch — 4-wheel vehicles only." I am positive that the road led up Galena Gulch to North Star.

Whitepine looked much as it had in 1945, except that many of the log houses and frame cabins on the south side of the street were boarded up and roofed with shiny, corrugated iron. The store facade had been slightly modified and the schoolhouse had been painted dark red. Only two buildings were missing: the theater and the big rooming house below it. Some homes on the north side of the street were apparently occupied, but we saw no one during our brief stay.

On the way back to the valley we noticed a campsite below the road beside Tomichi Creek. When I saw that the sign read "Snowblind Campsite," I remembered reading that the first prospectors, after making the initial discovery, had to leave the district for the winter and on the trek out went snowblind.

Chalk Creek
Chaffee
County
pp. 146-158

A delightful short drive on an old railroad grade up Chalk Creek begins at Nathrop, on Highway 24, and climbs the eastern slope of the Divide, past the sculptured Chalk Cliffs to Hancock. The roadbed over which trains climbed to the Alpine Tunnel and burrowed through the Divide to descend to Pitkin is gravelled and suitable for most cars. The narrow ledge section with its blind curves is now one-way up to the Cascades, beyond which the roadbed is wide enough for two-way traffic.

Alpine
Chaffee
County
pp. 149-150,
152, 154, 179,
185

To revisit Alpine I turned right at Kullman's Ranch, dropped down to the creek and crossed it to the old main street. Of the smelter, only the assay office and the stack remained, both almost completely hidden by the aspen grove that surrounded the property. The log stage station with its sod roof stood at the upper end of the town close to the lake. The Chaffee County assessor, C. E. Rathbun, wrote me in 1972 that "this building, which records show was built in 1889, is now recreational and in good shape."

St. Elmo
Chaffee
County
pp. 145,
149-154, 156,
185, 187

On my 1950 visit to St. Elmo the one store was open as usual and Miss Stark was waiting on a swarm of tourists. During the summer of 1971 I was in St. Elmo again. Most of the buildings were still there but showed the effects of weather and neglect and many were boarded up. After the death of Miss Stark (the last of the family) over ten years ago, the store was closed; because the property has since been in litigation, it has not been reopened. The frame schoolhouse across the bridge at the edge of the forest is well-preserved, as are a few falsefronted buildings and cabins that line the ap-

(540)

proach to the foot of Tin Cup Pass. The steep, narrow trail looks inviting, but a marker warns that it is navigable to four-wheel vehicles only.

Since writing this book, I learned from Robert R. Knowles of Sterling, Colorado that Romley was named for a distant cousin of his, Col. B. F. Morley, the first three letters of his name having been reversed to produce Romley. The Morleys lived in Buena Vista by the end of the nineteenth century, having moved there from Chester, Pennsylvania, where the Colonel was head of the Pennsylvania Military Academy. Their son became the noted archeologist Sylvanus Griswold Morley.

Romley Chaffee County pp. 154, 155, 157

For many years Col. Morley, a man of considerable means, had large interests in Chaffee County, one of which was the Mary Murphy mine, which he operated on a paying basis. He also built and ran a smelter in Buena Vista, the county seat, and served two terms as mayor.

On page 155 of this book, the founding of Romley is dated 1897; this is incorrect. Subsequent research has shown that Romley existed at least a decade earlier. (*Colorado Postal History* [1917] lists the establishment of a post office at Romley in 1886, and a March 1887 *Denver Republican* mentions Romley as a new town.)

In 1903, Col. Morley, who was general manager of the Mary Murphy mine, died while inspecting the workings. Just before leaving for a planned business trip to the East, he and his superintendent, Adolph Aberson, and Archie Ackerson, superintendent of the Four M Company, descended to the fourteenth level and failed to reappear. A party went in search of them, fearing they had been overcome by bad air. When found, Morley and Aberson were dead; Ackerson recovered.

On previous trips to Romley I saw only the portion of the community adjacent to the railroad. In 1953, while on an outing with the Gates Rubber Company of Denver, I camped overnight in Pomeroy Gulch where the Mary Murphy mine is located. Here were the main mine buildings and dumps, as well as the tram that carried the ore down to the railroad. Near the mouth of Pomeroy Gulch the tram with its buckets crossed above the steep downgrade of the roadway to the loading station.

In 1971 I revisited Romley. The railroad station roof was askew and the sides bulged and sagged. Nothing but debris marked the site of the mine office. The post office had caved in, and at least half of the buildings on the flat were either leaning or merely piles of broken boards. The schoolhouse and the "teacherage" next to it were there, but the desks were gone. I could not find the building that bore on its two doors (so I had been told) the names of girls and their price.

The loading stations between Romley and Hancock have disappeared or are approaching collapse. The trestle over the road at the Flora Bell is gone, and the biggest building at the Allie Bell is split in half like a great gaping beast hovering over the roadway. The watertank at Hancock disappeared years ago, and it took some close scrutiny in 1971 to find the stone founda-

Hancock Chaffee County pp. 153, 155-158, 181

tions that once held it. Tacked to the wall in an empty cabin was a full page from the *Denver Post* dated 1896. Under a large portrait was the caption: "Our Next President, William J. Bryan."

Ilse
Custer
County
pp. 286-287

In 1968 I revisited Ilse, a small lead-silver camp on the east side of the Wet Mountain Valley. It was even quieter than when I'd seen it in 1941. We approached it from the south, having driven east from Silver Cliff. Near the top of Hardscrabble Pass we turned north on a county road which rambled through ranch country over rolling hills covered with sagebrush and chamiso. From the crest of one hill we saw ahead the rusty, red tailings of the Terrible mine and its empty, disintegrating mill. Across the road from the mill was the big glory hole left from earlier mining activity — golden-brown and deep, the bottom filled with water.

Mrs. Lorena Wolfe of Silver Cliff, who accompanied us and who had lived in Ilse, told us of a fire in "The Mine," as it was called locally, and how the men escaped through a tunnel. Later, when her husband was in charge of retimbering the burned shaft, which was 200 feet deep, she went down it with him in an ore bucket. The shaft was twelve feet wide in some places, but at the foot they had to slide down a bank of earth to reach the bottom.

As we left Ilse she pointed out the ruins of the post office and the store and the sites of the schoolhouse and the house where she had lived. The only modern touch was a new trailer home where the caretaker of the mining property lives.

An early resident of Silver Cliff had long ago told me about Joseph Raphael De Lamar, who had unsuccessfully attempted to develop the Terrible mine and thereby went so heavily into debt that he had to leave Ilse without paying his creditors. I was curious about this prospector from Holland. While traveling through the western states collecting data to be used in my book, *The Bonanza Trail*, the name of De Lamar kept cropping up in connection with mining ventures in Idaho, Utah, and Nevada; further research revealed that it was indeed the same person and that he had become immensely wealthy through his enterprises. What I lacked was proof of his transactions in Ilse and the dates of his stay in that place.

Newspaper entries in the *Silver Cliff Miner* of 1879 mentioned his business trips to New York and Chicago and conferences with eastern partners and capitalists. When the citizens of Silver Cliff organized a campaign to halt the ruthless tactics of mine jumpers and printed a resolution, drawn up by ninety-three of the Cliff's "truest and best citizens," which was sent to "such parties as are known to be doing the dishonest and dirty work," one of the signatures was that of J. R. De Lama. [sic] Mrs. Bertie L. Bauer, treasurer of Custer County, Colorado, searched old records for me and found his name on many mining deeds, tax rolls, and ownership papers of lots in the Cliff between 1879 and the late 1880's.

The Denver Westerners *Brand Book* of 1968 (published 1969) contains an article of mine about De Lamar called "The Midas Touch"; it outlined his fabulous career and the facts about his life. Since its publication, I have heard several times from his daughter, Alice, who reminisced about her father and the mansion in New York in which she grew up. De Lamar died in 1918 at the age of seventy-five. The *Rocky Mountain News* of Denver, October 17, 1895, describes the man:

> At a time when the possibilities of low-grade gold-silver mines were not understood, and when the war on silver threatened loss of all producers of that metal, Captain DeLamar became known to the miners and capitalists of two continents as the purchaser and organizer of a large, idle property in Idaho. . . . There are in Colorado dozens of gold-silver mines of a higher grade than the Idaho property, but they are yet waiting for their DeLamar.

In recent years it has been hard to find oldtimers to talk to about the early years of a camp. In 1950 Russ and I were fortunate to find one in Vicksburg. We left Highway 24 south of Granite and turned west onto the rough, gravelly Clear Creek road that climbs eight miles to the lonely town. As on my previous visit, I admired the canopy of aspen trees that lined the main street and surrounded many of the cabins. This time the only signs of habitation were three cars, but no people were visible. Since I wanted to learn more about the camp, I began knocking on doors in hopes that someone was about. At a cabin with the sign E. J. LEVIN & SONS my knock brought a response. The elderly man who opened the door was E. J. Levin, and when I stated what I wanted he smiled and said, "I guess I can tell you everything. I came here in 1881 and I raised four sons here. Sit down," he added, making room for me on an old car seat on his porch.

Vicksburg Chaffee County p. 146

"The trees along the main street are beautiful," I said by way of beginning.

"I planted them," he replied. "There was a big fire in the gulch in 1872. No quakies in Clear Creek after the fire. Two miles up the road is Rockdale and beyond it is Winfield. Rockdale had a smelter on the creek, but it was never used. Vicksburg and Winfield were booming at the same time. Vicksburg was gold and silver. They had a five-dollar dinner dance in Vicksburg in 1881. That's when the population here was 600 and the mines were the Tip Top, up Missouri Gulch, and the Argus. Beaver was another camp, a mile below here. There used to be lots of séances at Beaver. They'd make the tables talk and then dig according to the results of the séances. Beaver Smith, we called him Whiskey Smith, was the last man down there. He killed himself. The Columbine mine was up the mountain from Beaver. There's no minerals below Beaver."

"Do you stay here all year?" I asked.

"Not any more," he told me. "I usually go out in December to California where it's sunny and warm. Then in May, back I come — when the fishing season opens."

(543)

Carson straddles the Continental Divide. On my first two trips there cloudbursts prevented exploration of the camp and curtailed my sketching. On my third try in 1950, I arranged to be driven there in the morning by jeep, hoping that I could explore both sides of the Divide before the clouds let down.

Early in September Russ drove me to Vicker's ranch in Lake City where we stayed overnight. Purvis Vickers agreed to take us to Carson leaving at seven A.M. There was frost on the grass when we walked across the road to Purvis' home to eat the hearty breakfast served by his wife. It didn't take long to whisk through Lake City and up past Lake San Cristobal to Wager Gulch. The air was nippy but clear, and fresh powder snow covered the peaks.

The Wager Gulch trail was much better than when Jane and I rode horseback up it in 1946. According to Purvis, it had been bulldozed only a month before so that some mining men could get their equipment in. We soon reached the bridge with the splintered, broken boards. It is bypassed now and vehicles ford the stream instead. The road winds up through yellow aspen groves, past beaver ponds and forests, until it breaks into a high, open meadow, at the far end of which stands New Carson. On up the grade we went past this camp, where Jane and I sat out the cloudburst in the stable. Then two miles farther, watching the vegetation dwindle to tundra, up to the saddle of the Continental Divide, about 12,300 feet, and across it to the steep, rocky slope where the big mines lay.

We were now at the head of Lost Trail Valley, which stretched for miles down the Rio Grande side of the mountain. It was spotted with dumps and empty shafthouses, but none so imposing as the St. Jacob's property from which over $1,000,000 had been taken. Beside the big ore dumps are the remains of its shafthouse, a smaller building which may have been the office, a boarding house with dormer windows, and a dilapidated barn. Inside the shafthouse lay a large bellows, and in the assay furnace lived a family of mink.

Farther down the mountainside was another mine and also the shafthouse with the leaking roof where I took shelter on my second trip (1948) to the nearly inaccessible camp. At one time there had been eleven properties, all with mills, on this barren, east face of the Divide. According to the engineer who had given me the information, they had all been "wildcatted to death." Lost Trail or Carson City (they were the same place) was an older camp than the group of buildings at the head of Wager Gulch, known as New Carson.

By now it was nearly noon, and storm clouds were boiling up over Carson Peak. While Purvis started the jeep, I made a hasty sketch of the Hamilton mine which was close by, and then we were off, over the saddle and down the steep trail to New Carson. This time we stopped to give me a chance to investigate the buildings that I'd seen before. Because it is partly protected by tall trees and is a newer camp than Carson, high on the eastern side, it is better preserved.

Back at the mouth of Wager Gulch, we stopped at Child's ranch to see a sign that formerly hung in a nearby stage station. It read:

RATES: LAKE CITY AND SHERMAN TOLL ROAD

Each Wagon and Pair of Mules, Horses or Oxen	.75 cts.
Each Additional Pair	.25 cts.
Loose Cattle, Horses or Mules, Each	.10 cts.
Saddle Animals	.25 cts.
Pack Animals	.10 cts.
Trail Wagons (short tongues only)	.50 cts.

The best preserved (although deserted) company town that I visited in 1942 was Gladstone, eight miles up Cement Creek outside of Silverton. One or two streets of identical houses were situated below the big Gold King mill and its subsidiary buildings. Many of these as well as the belfried schoolhouse were boarded up, while the majority of the mine buildings leaned or bulged, with window frames askew.

On my second visit in 1945 more havoc was noticeable, much of it due to the ravages of wind, snow, and neglect. The schoolhouse no longer had a cupola, and the roofs of the company housing units were broken in or completely missing.

I did not see the camp again until June, 1972, and before attempting to drive to it, Joel and I inquired at a Silverton gas station as to the condition of the road.

"You'll have to watch out for trucks. They're mining up there now. The road's rough, but it's wide, and you won't have any trouble," said an attendant. Reassured by his description we set off.

At first we were above the stream and occasionally saw dilapidated shafthouses and dumps almost choked by dense forest growth, but as we neared Gladstone, Cement Creek was beside us and more signs of former mining activity were visible such as loading stations and dim roads and trails winding out of sight up the sides of the mountains.

"We've come eight miles," said Joel. "Where's the town?"

There were no rows of houses in sight, and where the big, ruined mill should have been a shiny new one blocked the way. Huge trucks loaded with crushed ore passed us as they started down the canyon. According to a sign, Standard Metals Corporation was responsible for this new burst of life. Between the noise from the mill and that of the truck motors, it was hard to get the attention of one of the drivers to find out whether we were really in Gladstone. "Sure, this is it," he shouted as he shifted gears and swung around to roar down to Silverton.

At first nothing looked familiar except the mountains and the big, flat terrace that is now the loading area. The old sheds and shops that stood on it have been torn down. Looking down the canyon, I did discover the concrete foundations of the Mogul mill, built against the hillside near the site of the old schoolhouse. Above the creek to the north of the new mill was a small shafthouse that I also remembered. These I later verified from sketches I had made in the 1940's.

Several empty mine trucks passed us as we returned to Silverton. At the county jail (now a historical museum), we inspected the barred cells as well as local exhibits. Just as we were about to leave the town, the narrow gauge train from Durango puffed up the street and pulled to a panting stop to disgorge its swarms of passengers.

La Plata City
La Plata
County
pp. 395, 396

One place I was eager to see again was La Plata City. In 1942 the meadow on which it stood had a row of falsefronted stores and homes, and three miles farther up the valley was the Gold King property with its big mill full of machinery and its two-story boarding house overlooking La Plata River. Now, thirty years later, what would be left?

It was midafternoon when Joel and I left Durango and drove west on Highway 160, looking for the turnoff north to May Day and La Plata Canyon. To my surprise the first four miles, as far as May Day, were paved, but beyond that the gravel road grew steadily narrower and rougher.

We found considerable activity in the canyon — new cabins, mobile homes, and occupied campsites. At least a dozen cars full of young people passed us coming or going, driving with more abandon than we dared to try. I kept looking for the wide meadow edged with buildings that I had seen before, and finally I saw it ahead — but no, it couldn't be, for there were no buildings. "Drive farther," I told Joel, peering around each curve to find what I was looking for. After a mile of rocky driving with no success, we reached a sign that warned: CARS ARE ADVISED NOT TO PROCEED BEYOND THIS POINT.

As we were turning around, a jeep full of young women rolled down the road toward us. I hailed them and asked if we were near La Plata City. "You drove through it," the driver replied. "Are there any more buildings above here within a mile?" I asked. "No," they shouted as they sped on. Defeated, we started the drive back and within a short time reentered the wide meadow which still looked familiar. At its far end the road swerved left, but a trail ran straight ahead up a little rise and there, among the trees, stood the schoolhouse (or church) that I'd sketched before! The meadow was the townsite and this building the only recognizable landmark left.

Parrott City
La Plata
County
pp. 396-398

Parrott City no longer exists. The last of its buildings was torn down around 1942, and the townsite near May Day is part of a private ranch.

Thanks to correspondents, let me correct mistakes found on the map on page 370 and pages 396-398 of this volume. "Parrott" is correctly spelled with two "t's," and "Tiburcio" should be "Tibercio." In 1962 Myron H. Broomell of Durango wrote that "the site marked 'Parrott' on the U.S.G.S. topographic map (La Plata Quadrangle) is the site of what is known as May Day and the actual Parrott City was a mile or so south and a little west of that."

GLADSTONE SCHOOLHOUSE, 1944.

GLADSTONE
SCHOOLHOUSE, 1941.

GLADSTONE TOWNSITE, LOOKING DOWN CEMENT CREEK, 1972.
MOGUL MILL (RIGHT).

SWANDYKE, 1950.

MANHATTAN, 1950. STEVE PRENDERGAST GOLD MINING CO.

An old prospector, Clarence Reckmeyer of Black Hawk, told me about Hughesville. "The mines were discovered in 1870 or before," he said. "At one time two hundred lived there and a small schoolhouse was built. There's nothing now but a couple of old shafts and a log shack. It's two-and-a-half miles from Black Hawk up the Dory Hill Road, or you can come down from the top of Dory Hill past the cemetery till you see a ranchhouse on your right. The people there can tell you the way."

Hughesville
Gilpin County
p. 524

In 1953 a friend and I took the steep grade down Dory Hill until we reached the ranchhouse. The woman who answered our knock told us that the area was once the seat of a silver belt that grew up around the ranch claim of Patrick Hughes. She pointed out a narrow, dirt road "by the two trees" and we drove on it until it split. A man leading two horses talked to us and identified the proper fork. From there on it was a stiff climb on foot for nearly a mile through an aspen grove to a meadow. Looking ahead we saw prospect holes, small dumps, and what had been roads branching off toward them. Farther on were more shallow diggings out of which aspens were growing. I hurried on, squeezed under a barbed wire fence, and climbed to the top of a hill from which I could look down on several large dumps and a small shed in another meadow. To the west were more trees and behind them distant mountains. Hughesville was a true ghost site.

It was also Clarence Reckmeyer who, in 1952, gave me the most specific information about Nugget. Knowing that I was familiar with the road between Apex and Tolland and that the dirt road to Nugget branched off to the west at American City Junction, he wrote:

Nugget
Gilpin County
p. 38

> You'll remember the Mackey mine, a little west down the hill from the American City Junction? As you get to the bottom of that hill, a side road turns down Elk Creek. Nugget was less than half-a-mile west of where that Elk Creek road turns off. Only three foundations mark the site. A post office was established in 1895 and discontinued in 1901, when the mail was sent to Apex.

For years I'd seen a cascade of gray dumps near the top of a mountain south of Lawson, in Clear Creek Canyon, and wondered about them, but not until two oldtimers told me they were from mines in Silver Creek did I look at them longingly. According to the men, the small camp in 1890 had a saloon, one store, and two producing silver and lead mines, the Seven Sisters and the Joe Reynolds. By 1942 only broken coffins lay scattered where the undertaker's cabin had stood. "You couldn't drive your car up there anyway," they said. "It's too rough and steep, and you wouldn't know which of the turnoffs dead-ended. It's about four miles and you climb over 9,000 feet."

Silver Creek
Clear Creek
County
pp. 112, 114

My next informant was Fred Mazzulla of Denver, who told me that Silver Creek was first known as Chinn City. He also gave me an old photo which showed a few cabins, the Reynolds mine and mill, and the schoolhouse. Then in 1964 Theora Hoppe drove me to Silver Creek, and I found more left than I expected. The townsite appeared to have been in two parts, the lower site identified by the flattened wrecks of two or three cabins on a meadow, and the upper townsite dominated by two big dumps between which ran the road. The view seemed to coincide with Mazzulla's photo of the Reynolds property.

A couple of weathered cabins and a stone fireplace of a third were below the dumps. We drove above the townsite and out onto one of the Seven Sisters dumps. From there the view north across the Clear Creek Valley was awesome. Opposite on the north side of the canyon were the dumps of the Red Elephant mine. Below, in the bottom of the canyon, Highway I-70 looked like a twisted gray thread and cars like moving specks upon it. On the way down we saw through the trees the Nabob shafthouse, and as we neared the highway there stood the shell of the Red Elephant mill; but in all of our searching we found no trace of a coffin.

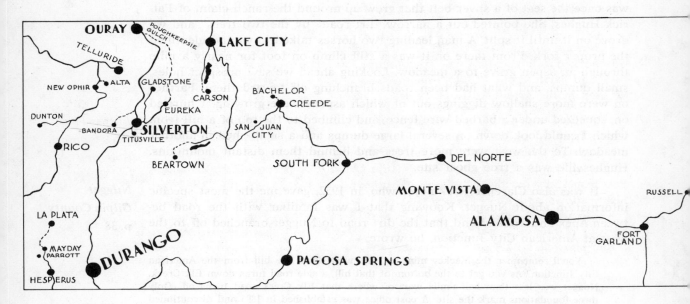

Silver Dale
Clear Creek
County

A former student, Betty Criley Carmen, took me in the fall of 1949 to the site of Silver Dale, a little camp south of Georgetown between the Public Service Co. reservoir and Green Lake. The townsite, where fifty families once lived, was an overgrown meadow where only broken stone foundations, rotting timbers, and old bedsprings remained. The aspen-shaded cemetery at the lower end of the reservoir was so well-hidden in underbrush that we really had to search to find the few marble stones and the one wooden marker within its picket fence.

When we drove into Silver Dale from Georgetown on the old road, the first foundations seen were those of a small smelter, worked originally by Negroes. At the upper end of the reservoir were more foundations and the dumps of the Colorado Central mine. Beyond it and across the South Fork of Clear Creek were the Equator mine, two cabins, and the foundations of the Equator mill.

Mrs. Hazel McAdams, former owner of the Hotel de Paris in Georgetown, told me that when the mines were working, the women of the town shopped on Saturday mornings and then went home, "leaving the streets to the men that afternoon." Later the miners from Silver Dale came into town on foot or with pack jacks to do their weekly buying. As she put it, "It was a constant, single file of men and animals, like a funeral."

In the mid 1960's two of my dreams were realized. One was to find the smelter in Geneva Gulch and the other was to cross Boreas Pass. The road to Geneva Ski Basin and Guanella Pass leaves Highway 285 at Grant and skirts Geneva Creek (named by Swiss prospectors), past Tumbling River Ranch, up to a long, wide, high valley where a smelter was built many years ago to handle the ores of the area. Today only a pile of rubble marks its location; even the smoke-stack is gone. When it fell, the heat-resistant bricks were carted away and re-sold.

*Geneva Gulch
Park County*
p. 103

Beyond the smelter site, at the head of the valley, is an iron mine that was worked as late as 1963. The strip mining has left terraces of stained orange rock and earth, really "rust," much of which was shipped to New Jersey to be used in the manufacture of paint.

While I was gathering material for this book in the 1940's, I received letters from W. C. Rupley, chief train dispatcher for the Colorado and South-ern Railroad's South Park Division. He wrote reminiscenses and exciting ac-counts of keeping the trains moving from Como to Breckenridge over Boreas Pass, especially during the winters. Although not a high pass, only 11,482 feet, heavy snows and high winds made railroading a constant battle. Tales of trains marooned in snowbanks, of crews shoveling out cuts while standing on tops of box cars with drifts above their heads, and of other obstacles to traffic showed how vitally important the railroad was in moving supplies across the Continental Divide to the remote mining camps on the western slope.

*Boreas Pass
Park-Summit
Counties*
pp. 76, 101

After the railroads ceased running in 1951 and the tracks were torn up, an Army battalion and the Forest Service made an auto road out of the right-of-way. It was my good fortune to have Gordon Tripp, who knows that sec-tion of Colorado intimately, drive me over the pass pointing out landmarks all the way. The roadbed is solid, traffic is slight, there are frequent turn-outs, and passenger cars can navigate it with ease.

From Como a dirt road crosses the dredge dumps in Tarryall Creek and heads west up the valley to Peabody Switch before starting the climb onto the railroad grade. The first part of the drive is through groves of aspen trees. These replaced other species that burned in fires often started by sparks from the locomotives. Davis Overlook offers a panorama of South Park, while directly below the scenic point the undulating mounds of waste rock, spewed from the stacker of the gold dredge that worked the Tarryall, look like a great snake wriggling out onto the valley floor. Beyond the lookout the road swings west and climbs to the pass, with views of Mt. Silverheels and of the Tarryall Valley below to the south.

Since South Park has an elevation of 10,000 feet and Boreas Pass is a scant 1,500 feet higher, the summit is reached in a short time. On top is a shed and a two-story sectionhouse. In June the shed was still full of the winter's snow. Behind the buildings, to the north, rises Mt. Baldy with a mine shafthouse on its barren slope. On the opposite side of the road are the stone foundations of the roundhouse, and beyond it, curving across a marshy meadow, are rotting rows of ties that indicate a former switching area. Two long snowsheds once stood at the summit, one of which contained the station, but neither has survived the fierce winter storms. Even the snowfences on the west side of the pass are shattered.

Farther down the western side is the Farnham Spur loading station for the 7:30 mine, whose rotting tram towers retreat into dense timber. Straight ahead above the trees, the Ten-Mile Range comes into view; and as we drop lower, Baker Tank, one of the few watertanks that have been preserved, stands at the entrance to a small picnic area. Beside the tank is a marker:

BAKER TANK: MILEPOST 102.16

SERVED SOUTH PARK & PACIFIC NARROW GAUGE R.R. (LATER COLORADO & SOUTHERN) FROM COMO TO LEADVILLE.
R.R. HAD 63.03 MILES OF TRACK AND 435 CURVES. LONGEST STRETCH OF STRAIGHT TRACK WAS 1.6 MILES.
THIS LINE BEGUN OCT. 2, 1880 AND COMPLETED FEB. 5, 1884.
ABANDONED APRIL 10, 1951.
TANK RESTORED BY SUMMIT COUNTY, 1958.

Beyond the tank, the grade slices through one or two narrow cuts and then is once more among the aspens. Below is Breckenridge, no longer the quiet county seat with buildings dating back to boom mining days. Now it bristles with condominiums and lodges, restaurants and real estate offices. The ski area on the Ten-Mile peaks across from the town has transformed it.

Swandyke
Summit
County
p. 81

A letter dated September, 1950, from Kermit Matthews of Granada, Colorado, mentioned Swandyke as a true ghost town. In the late 1890's it had 400 to 500 people, enough to justify a hotel, the Summit House. He also said that mail was brought in two or three times a week. Naturally, I was eager to get there.

Swandyke was a gold camp, and during its brief span of activity a good many mines were opened and worked. Some of the oxidized gold was found close to the surface of the ground, but other deposits necessitated tunneling into the steep mountainsides above timberline. Miners boasted that the ore was the richest in the Breckenridge district and described the decomposed sulphide as "fairly glistening with free gold." Eight properties, including the Three Kings mine, were owned and operated by the Swandyke Gold Mining and Milling Co., which predicted a great future for the camp by 1901.

The high elevation of the camp, the steep slopes of the mountainsides, and the heavy snows discouraged attempts to work during the winter months. Avalanches during the winter of 1898-1899, one of which swept away a mill and deposited the wreckage across the gulch, closed the camp to those who had gone out for the season and prevented their return until June. On one

(552)

occasion, when snowdrifts closed the railroad across Boreas Pass, the miners hand-shoveled a road over Georgia Pass down to Jefferson in South Park in order to obtain needed supplies.

At Dillon I asked a storekeeper about getting to Swandyke. He had been up there and said that a stage barn and a two-story cabin (once a boarding house) were still standing, that an iron bed was upstairs in the cabin, but that the place was infested with rats. "Talk to Max Bunker at the Lucky Horseshoe Inn," he suggested. "He has a truck and could get up there." So I looked up Mr. Bunker, who agreed to take me if I let him know in advance. Early in September I parked my car by his Inn, and away we went.

Bunker's truck was old and the cock on the gas tank was loose. Gasoline sloshed on the running board as we swayed and bounced over ruts and rocks, and I was enveloped in fumes all the way.

We drove up the Swan River through Tiger and beyond for several miles on the middle fork of the Swan. The road was not only rough but very steep in places. Finally Bunker stopped at a fork and suggested that I get out and look for car tracks to see which branch was the more traveled. The road I chose led up an extremely stiff grade, and I continued walking until it leveled off at a high meadow. There, surrounded by spruce trees, stood the barn (half fallen down), a cabin with lace curtains and old newspapers dated 1901, and the two-story hotel with the bed. By this time Bunker had followed me up the grade and parked the truck. The elevation must have been over 11,000 feet. Together we examined Swandyke, finding foundation hollows on all sides and the remains of streets. Prospect holes and mining stakes set in piles of stones marked the corners of old claims. A brittle flight of steps led nowhere, and bits of broken furniture were strewn over the ground. The mine dumps were above timberline, the nearest being that of the White Swan, according to Bunker, who added that the cabin with the lace curtains was the White Swan Mining Company's office.

Before we left the townsite, Bunker told me that the road we had come up continued beyond the camp to the head of the gulch. "There are more mines up higher and some cabins too at Upper Swandyke," he said. "If we took the road that circles around Missouri Gulch and crosses the summit of Georgia Pass, we'd be on the eastern slope and would drop down to Jefferson in South Park."

On the way back to Dillon I learned that logging was still being done in the region and that during dredging days much timber was cut for the dredge boats which used wood as fuel for their boilers. He also mentioned that Keystone (now a ski area) was the end of the railroad that crossed Boreas Pass from Como. It formerly carried all the ore shipped from Montezuma and Sts. John to the smelters on the eastern slope.

According to Richard M. Pearl, geologist, mineralogist, and author (*Exploring Rocks, Minerals and Fossils in Colorado*, plus over two dozen additional books) the site of Manchester, west of Colorado Springs, is about eight miles

Manchester
Teller
County

(553)

north and west of Divide, in what was the Little Westcreek mining district. It had a post office, a general store, a sawmill, and a few houses. The claims were patented in 1885.

My driver asked directions at a gas station in Divide (on Highway 24) and was told that Manchester was just over the hill; so we started off to the north. When within a quarter-of-a-mile the road forked by the cemetery, we drove back to the nearest house to inquire further. "Take the road straight ahead," the lady told us, "but I warn you, you won't catch any fish at the lake."

We drove nearly eight miles, following Pearl's detailed directions, crossing a cattleguard, entering Pike National Forest, and finally reaching a road with a dim sign "Manchester Creek. Wagon Road Only." It led down a steep draw, through an aspen and pine forest and beside a creek for nearly two miles before reaching Manchester. Nothing is left but flattened cabins, piles of lumber where houses had stood, and a few dumps. Cattle grazed on the site, and when we left a cottontail rabbit bounced ahead of us up the road.

Minneapolis
Chaffee
County

On my two trips to Turret I must have passed the site of Minneapolis without knowing it; for in 1950 my friend, Richard M. Pearl, wrote me that it was located on the road between Turret and the Calumet mine and that a few years earlier two or three buildings were still standing.

Russell
Costilla
County

On the western side of La Veta Pass on the north side of Highway 160 is Russell, a placer camp located on the Trinchera Grant. In its prime it had one main street and smaller back streets, two general stores, a saloon, schoolhouse, a hotel run by Mrs. Margaret Sutton and her sister, and a post office, according to Charles Guhse, a miner whom I interviewed in 1956 when he was over seventy years of age. He had a mine up Grayback Gulch which he worked in the early 1900's, and his memory of the camp was clear.

Originally called Placer because of its gold-bearing gravels, it was worked from the early 1870's into the 1900's when placering ceased. Next, the mouth of Grayback Gulch was hydraulicked; later, dredging was carried on. At one time the C.F.&I. had an iron mine in Grayback Gulch.

The narrow-gauge railroad that crossed La Veta Pass from Walsenburg into the San Luis Valley ran past Russell, and oldtimers point out the hole where the turntable stood. Russell's cemetery was up the hill from the post office, and Guhse said that its graves included those of a few "sluice box robbers who were planted there."

In August, 1972 I drove past Russell on my way to Fort Garland. A signpost marks its location, and two or three frame buildings and a small schoolhouse stand back from the highway. That people live there was revealed by washing on a line and by a car and a truck parked in front of the houses.

Manhattan
Larimer
County
p. 524

Harry S. Thayer, a mining engineer, wrote me in December, 1949:

> In 1904 I carried the mail route from the old camp of Manhattan to the post office called Home (which was a summer resort run by Zimmerman, about eight miles west of Rustic in the Cache le Poudre Canyon). . . . The road to Manhattan branched off at the top of Pingree Hill. . . . The camp was about two miles west. The only

mine operating there . . . was the Forest or Forster, about two miles south of Manhattan in a small park. The mine was operated intermittently for a number of years and produced a small amount of high grade gold ore.

Here was the clue I was waiting for. In the spring of 1950 I left the Cache le Poudre Highway 14 at Rustic, in northern Colorado, and took the old Pingree Hill stage road two miles to its summit. There were vestiges of a side road nearby, but I drove to the next fork to the west, where a marker pointed toward Red Feather Lakes, and within a mile was at the site of Manhattan.

A number of cabins were scattered among the trees. One big cabin and a barn edged a grassy meadow fringed with aspen trees. A small stream cut through the meadow in front of the big cabin over whose door was a sign: STEVE PRENDERGAST GOLD MINING CO. Back at Rustic I inquired how to reach Prendergast and was given a Fort Collins address. I had heard the name before through a letter from a man in Nebraska who wrote: "I can refer you to a gold miner, now in his late eighties, who spent his summers at his mine in Manhattan. Steve A. Prendergast is his name." So I wrote to Mr. Prendergast, and in September, 1950 received a long and informative letter from which I quote:

> Prospecting for minerals in Manhattan started in 1886 but not much was accomplished until 1887-1888 when Fort Collins businessmen mobilized a few prospectors to search for minerals in the camp. It was gold ore, some of it assaying high . . . which caused an excitement, and many claims were located. Considerable work was done for several years. . . . Probably 200 or more miners and mine owners were there at its peak which lasted up to 1895 when the excitement died out. . . . I went there in 1910 and have been there [most] every year ever since. There will be mines there some day but not in my time.

In October I drove to Fort Collins and talked with several Fort Collins businessmen who were acquainted with Manhattan, and with a Mrs. Prendergast, believed to be related to Steve. From them all I learned much of interest and of value. Grover Griffith was in Manhattan in 1906 when there were many buildings there. He drew a diagram of the town on a cardboard carton and told me the hotel had been called The Ace of Clubs. At the Pioneer Museum, Clyde Brown got out old photos of the place and a copy of the *Manhattan Prospector*, from which I copied certain data. My last call was upon Mrs. Prendergast who lived south of town where her family had homesteaded. Upon my arrival she told me that Steve had been buried just the day before.

In 1962 Robert K. Wattson, Jr. of Wichita, Kansas, wrote me of his recent visit to the ghost town. According to him:

> No sign of any sort marks the town. . . . Perhaps a quarter-of-a-mile east, up the hill north from the road [is] the tiny cemetery, perhaps as big as my living room, fenced in by chicken-wire. Half-a-dozen wooden headboards and one wooden cross, as I recall, are within the enclosure, but only two boards have decipherable inscriptions.

Poudre City
Larimer
County

The same day that I investigated the townsite of Manhattan, I drove farther up Cache le Poudre Canyon, looking for the site of Poudre City. Late in 1949 I had learned about the place from Harry S. Thayer. Of Poudre City he wrote:

> During the 1880's, some five or six mines were operating, a mill was built beside the river and a surface tram connected the mines with the mill. Besides company buildings, some fifteen or more miner's cabins stood on the flat by the mill. All mining operations ceased before 1891. The mill and the cabins were dismantled by ranchers in the valley and if anything remains it is only a foundation.

Two miles west of the roadhouse at Rustic I spied a marker, "Site of Old Poudre City," and scrambling under a fence and across a field, found one fireplace and a chimney big enough to have belonged to a small mill.

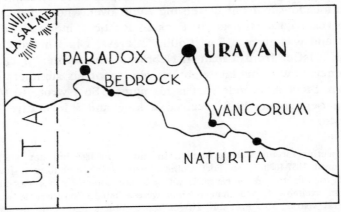

Paradox
Valley
Montrose
County

Just as Manhattan is close to the Wyoming line in northern Colorado, the Paradox Valley mines almost touch the Utah line near the western boundary of the state.

Paradox Valley is long and wide and flat and walled on three sides by high, red mesas. The surface is covered with sagebrush and stunted cedars, and in the distance the La Sal Mountains of Utah keep their snow crests most of the year. At Bedrock the Dolores River bisects the valley and provides irrigation for green meadows which provide good grazing land. At the head of the valley is Paradox, a small town with a handful of homes, a church, and one store which serves the surrounding ranches and mining properties. Mines can be seen near the top of the cliffs and mesas surrounding the valley, but few are active.

In the Paradox store I learned that most of the mines were a few miles away, but if I drove up the rimrock beyond the town and down into the next valley I'd see some of the properties including the Cashin, of which I had heard. "Yes," said a woman in the store, "you look down on the Cashin from the highway and you can drive down La Sal canyon to the mine, but you won't be able to get up the road again."

The paved road looped up the steep hill beyond Paradox to the top of the rimrock. Crossing the ridge, the road dropped into a new valley where

(556)

the rock formations were yellow rather than red, and there at the bottom of the canyon was the Cashin copper mine. John Constantine of Boulder, who lived in the Paradox Valley while working with the Vanadium Corporation of America, told me in 1950 that the mine was in litigation. "It's such pure copper that you can't get it out. When you dynamite it," he said, "it blows all to pieces."

When I was sketching the one store in Bedrock (near Paradox), a big car drove up and stopped, and a man and his children came over to watch me work. After a minute he said, "You should read the book that woman wrote." "I think I have," I replied. "I thought so," he answered, and drove off.

My introduction in the 1960's to Alta, a deserted camp in the San Miguel Mountains, was by jeep up Boomerang Hill, a forest-service road a mile or so west of Telluride; it climbs through evergreens and aspens and passes the three Alta Lakes, which are favorites with campers and fishermen. Alta lies below the lakes on a high, sloping meadow from which one gets a spectacular view of Sunshine Peak, Mt. Wilson, and Lizard Head.

Alta
San Miguel
County

Alta was basically a one-mine camp, with its best property the Gold King, which was discovered in the 1870's. This mine produced gold, silver, lead, and copper throughout the 1880's and well into the twentieth century under a succession of owners and developers. From 1917 to 1938 it was owned and operated by John Wagner. He sold it to H. F. Klock, who worked it until his death in 1945. Following Klock's death, the mine reverted to Wagner. When Wagner became ill and realized that he was dying, he married his housekeeper, leaving the property to her. Though she had several offers for the mine, the poor lady became senile before any settlement could be made.

In June, 1972 my Telluride friend Dick Wagner (no relation to John) drove me to Alta in his Scout, since he knew my car couldn't make it. This time we approached Alta via Highway 145 and left the pavement just before reaching New Ophir. The steep five-to-six-mile climb on the narrow, rough, forest road brought us to a ruined mill surrounded by broken machinery and rusted, twisted tram cables. The base of several tram towers above the mill were buried in lupines and underbrush. While I sketched the empty mill, Dick told me that Alta had once had three mills but that all had burned, the last in 1945.

It was only a short distance up the road to the townsite, and once again I saw the boarding house with its separate cook house, the schoolhouse, the tram-operator's office, and the newer cabins that were at the head of the slope. Behind this cluster of buildings in a wooded hollow were a number of cabins and sheds slowly crumbling into dust. These were older than those we had just seen.

Leaving Alta we crawled down Boomerang Hill to Highway 145, getting momentary glimpses of the famous Ophir Loop with its narrow-gauge right-of-way and wooden trestles.

Within a mile we reached New Ophir, which was built close to the Loop station. The new highway, constructed in the late 1950's, sweeps past its few buildings, but the station and the hotel are gone, and a big fill replaces the trestles.

The narrow road to Old Ophir leaves the highway and passes a few new houses and trailer homes hidden in aspens before climbing two-and-a-half-miles to the original settlement. Of it D. F. Holaday of Midwest City, Oklahoma, wrote me in 1962:

> There are some company houses, five or six built in 1952 along the right side of the road. One or two of the buildings you sketched lay in the path of a snowslide in 1960 and were pushed around or broken up.
>
> Old Ophir, even with a population of two in 1950 . . . is my hometown. My folks left there before I could walk and I didn't see the place for forty years. Just for fun I took the family there in 1953.

Up beyond the town in the trees is the cemetery, and ahead, at the end of the valley, is the narrow shelf road cut into a shale slope which crosses 11,789-foot Ophir Pass — thrilling but scary. Jeeps go over it now, but it's the same trail from which Nilson, the mail carrier, slipped during a blizzard in 1883. His body was recovered from the foot of the pass the following July.

Good friends have within the past two years driven me to Phoenix and to Sacramento, camps that I have not been able to reach by myself.

In July, 1971 two Boulder companions took me to Phoenix. Driving south from Nederland, George left the Peak to Peak Highway (72) for a wide, unpaved road on our right and continued for one-quarter of a mile south and then right again, until we left it for a narrow dirt track which wound westerly through woods to Phoenix. The roadbed was rutted and boggy in spots but passable for cars with four-wheel drive. What few buildings remain at Phoenix seem to date from the nineties. Most prominent is a fallen shaft-house reclining on a dump; near it are two wooden structures, one of which encloses some machinery. As we left, I noticed prospect holes, overgrown dumps, a few ruined cabins, and tracks leading in among the trees. Back at the roadfork we read the sign —2 miles left to the Peak to Peak Highway and 1½ miles right to Rollinsville. We took the latter and drove through a forest on a very narrow road down a steep pitch all the way, past the Rollinsville Ranger Station into Rollinsville.

In spite of many inquiries, to date all I have been able to find out about Phoenix is the following news item of 1902:

> Boulder County: In the Phoenix district the Champion is producing a large amount and good grade of ore, and eastern people are about to start up the German and Phoenix No. 2, which have large bodies of low grade ores and also a good-sized streak of smelting ore. — *Mining Register*, June 5, 1902, p. 538.

SHAFTHOUSE ON MINE DUMP, PHOENIX, 1971.

TOMBOY MINE ABOVE TELLURIDE. STAMP MILL RUINS, 1972.

SMUGGLER MINE ABOVE TELLURIDE IN SAVAGE BASIN, 1972.

SMUGGLER RUINS WITH TOMBOY PROPERTY IN DISTANCE, 1972.

When I heard that a big ski development was slated for the Telluride area I knew I must go to the quiet mining town before "progress" caught up with it. I particularly wanted to see what was left of the Smuggler and Tomboy mining properties close to timberline above the camp.

Telluride San Miguel County pp. 380-390, 442

In 1941 I almost got to the Tomboy, but the narrow shelf road and the sheer drop into the valley below so unnerved me that when we reached the Smuggler mill I drew *it* and insisted that I could sketch the Tomboy, a mile away, from where I stood. I have always regretted this decision; so, when Richard Wagner, an artist friend who makes his home in Telluride, promised to take me up there in his Scout, I immediately agreed. The shelf road was no better in 1972 than it had been before and if anything was rougher; we bounced and swayed much closer to the edge of the 1000-foot drop than I cared for, but Dick is an excellent driver, and by the time we were past the most treacherous stretches I began to look for landmarks that I'd seen before.

At the Smuggler the houses to the left of the road were gone and the mill itself was badly deteriorated. Another mile of shelf road brought us to the Tomboy property, but where years before I'd seen the "Tomboy lights" from the valley, only foundations, a couple of houses, and scattered debris remained. We were now 11,300 feet above sea level; the highest shacks and ruins were at 11,400 feet. By searching, I found where the big stamp mill had stood, and I located part of an old brick-faced furnace. Timberline was close and patches of snow on barren peaks surrounded the property. The view toward the valley was breathtaking. On the nearest mountain, with its incredibly steep slant over which many an avalanche had shot, was the shelf road we had inched along from the Smuggler mine. Straight ahead, as far as one could see, were mountains, including Little Cone. Behind us the jeep road continued to the top of Imogene Pass, 13,365 feet. On the way back to Telluride we met a jeep on its way to the top of the pass, and by adroit maneuvering passed it safely. When we were back among the aspens, Dick pointed out a blue grouse that was fluttering about in the nearby trees.

Telluride was more alive than I'd ever seen it, with old stores refurbished and new shops preparing to open, good restaurants planned, and condominiums being hastily built to accommodate skiers during the first winter season.

That evening, Dick and Evelyn took Joel and me for a drive just at sunset. Beyond the town we climbed for miles on an old ranch road over high, mountain meadows until we reached the topmost one. On three sides were rugged snowcapped peaks. Far below in the valley was the winding San Miguel River. It was absolutely quiet. We stayed until the shadows crawled up the mountainsides and the lights of Telluride sparkled below. I'd always suspected it, but now I *knew* which of the mining camps drew me the most. I'm glad I revisited Telluride before it changes, as it inescapably will.

Sacramento had eluded me for years. I knew approximately its location but no way to get to it. Drivable roads ended three-to-four miles short of the camp, and the remaining distance meant climbing on unimproved trails al-

Sacramento Park County

SACRAMENTO CABIN WITH TWO-LAYERED ROOF, 1972.

RUINED SHAFTHOUSE, SACRAMENTO, 12,000-FOOT ELEVATION,
LOOKING DOWN 2,000 FEET ACROSS SOUTH PARK.

most to timberline. What little I could find written about it mentioned a brief but successful boom period and a fair amount of preservation of its buildings because of the remoteness and the protection offered by a dense surrounding forest.

It was in October, 1878 that three prospectors who had unsuccessfully gophered in the hills above Fairplay all summer started out of the mountains for the winter months. While still close to timberline, they were caught in a snowstorm and holed in among the pine trees in Spring Valley, about six miles west of Fairplay.

To keep from freezing, the men — Charles W. Dwelle, Napoleon P. Le Duc, and W. M. Tobie — built a campfire from fallen pine boughs that littered the ground. One piece of timber they were about to throw on seemed too heavy to be wood, and when they examined it they found they had picked up a slab of wire silver. Their journey was forgotten, and next day the men searched until they found the outcrop. As soon as the weather permitted, they filed a claim which covered seventy acres and began digging. Considerable silver ore was discovered near grassroots, and by means of open-cut methods and tunneling they developed a paying property, which they named the Sacramento. Next they opened two tunnels: the October, and a lower adit, the Lark, through which they removed "three flat veins of blanket deposits."

For five years the mine was steadily worked, first by the men who discovered it and then by a New York group which formed the Sacramento Mining Co. Dwelle continued to be identified with the property, both as owner and director, until his death in 1895. During the early 1880's, the Sacramento is said to have produced a million dollars in silver, much of the ore averaging 214 ounces per ton.

. At its peak the camp consisted of about twenty cabins and other buildings which housed the sixty-nine workers and their families. In 1883, just as prospects looked favorable for a productive and stable community, the vein of silver was lost, due to a fault running laterally through the ore body. Further exploration revealed only an "underground cavern filled with stalactites and stalagmites," and all further development ceased. The miners began to leave and the camp faded, though in the same year an English company obtained control of the mine and operated it until 1886, depending chiefly on ore that was recovered by sorting the dumps. Some years later the Sacramento reverted to Park County for unpaid taxes. In 1951, according to Lee Olson, it was owned by Redman and Associates of Denver.

In July, 1972, through the efforts of a Denver friend, Dennis Smith, I reached Sacramento. Smith, his neighbor Fern Schertfeger, and I left Denver at seven-thirty A.M. in Fern's Blazer and headed for the hills west of the city. We scurried through Turkey Creek on Highway 285 and over Kenosha Pass into South Park, the 10,000-foot high mountain valley that stretches for miles in all directions until stopped by foothills. Just beyond Fairplay, we turned west onto the Four-Mile Creek road and drove six miles to a still higher meadow marked by a government sign which read: "Site of Horseshoe, 1879."

Here we took a narrow, unimproved side road that led directly into the timber. Within a mile it forked, and we took the left-hand trail. From there on it climbed steadily all the way to Sacramento.

"This is the stretch my wife and I hiked earlier this summer," Dennis remarked as the Blazer picked its way around rocks, straddled ruts, and climbed over dead branches. "How far was it to the town?" I asked eagerly. "About four miles," said Dennis, "but my wife insists it was ten."

We soon entered an open space, identified by Dennis as Spring Valley, where the first prospectors encountered the snowstorm and built their fire. One large, roofless log cabin is settling into the marshy bog at this place. Beyond the meadow the road crept close to the edge of shale cliffs, from which we looked straight down several hundred feet into Sacramento Gulch. Next we squeezed through another grove of evergreens and then caught sight of cabins ahead. We were at Sacramento!

There was more left of the place than I had expected. I'd read that in 1951 fourteen buildings were still standing. Five or six remained in varying states of decay when I was there in 1972. The tall trees were so dense that it was impossible to see more than one or two buildings at a time. One cabin had a rock terrace in front of it, and the largest log structure had a two-layer roof, such as I'd never seen. A few cabins near mine dumps were broken down and roofless with splintered window frames and gaping doorways. Vestiges of what had been streets led off at angles among the trees. One group of dumps supported a crumbling shafthouse.

"That reminds me, I saw a shafthouse above timberline the last time I was here. Could we go and see it today?" Dennis inquired of Fern. With no delay we set out again in the Blazer, crawling past dwindling timberline vegetation up to the 12,000-foot summit. The mountain top was a level expanse of tundra from which the view was magnificent. Below and in front of us stretched South Park, while behind and on either side of us were snowy peaks. Farther away, distant ranges were silhouetted against the horizon.

We found the shafthouse pancaked on a dump, with a crude ladder leading down into the open shaft. The entire summit was pitted with shallow prospect holes, as well as with mine shafts. Dumps and rusting machinery testified to the extent of development of each property. "I can't identify these mines," Dennis told me, "but there were five important claims besides the Sacramento. Two of them, the October and the Lark, were near the initial strike. The other three were the Annibody, Ada, and Watacka."

It was late afternoon when I left my companions in Denver and drove home, exhausted physically and emotionally, for it had been a long, exciting, and satisfying day. I could now cross Sacramento off the diminishing list of camps that still beckon me.

A Selection of Mining Terms, reprinted by permission from

A GLOSSARY OF THE MINING
AND MINERAL INDUSTRY

by

ALBERT H. FAY

WASHINGTON PRINTING OFFICE, 1920

Adit.	A nearly horizontal passage from the surface by which a mine is entered and unwatered.
Amalgam.	In gold metallurgy, an alloy of gold and mercury, usually obtained by allowing gold-bearing minerals, after crushing, to come in contact with mercury in stamp batteries, sluices or mercury-coated copper plates. The alloy (amalgam) is collected and the mercury is driven off by distillation, the gold remaining in the retort.
Argentiferous.	Containing silver.
Arrastre (or arastra).	Apparatus for grinding and mixing ores by means of a heavy stone, dragged around upon a circular bed. The arrastre is chiefly used for ores containing free gold and amalgamation is combined with the grinding.
Assay.	To test ores or minerals by chemical or blowpipe examination. Gold and silver require an additional process called cupelling, for the purpose of separating them from the base metals.
Assessment work.	The annual work upon an unpatented mining claim in the public domain necessary under the United States law for the maintenance of the possessory title thereto.
Ball mill.	A short tube mill of relatively large diameter in which grinding is done by steel balls instead of pebbles. The discharge is usually through a screen.
Bar.	Accumulation of gravel along the banks of a stream, and which, when worked, by the miners for gold, are called Bar diggings.
Bedrock.	The solid rock underlying auriferous gravel, sand, clay, etc., and upon which alluvial gold rests.
Blanket vein.	A horizontal vein or deposit.
Blossom.	The oxidized or decomposed outcrop of a vein.
Breast.	The face of a working.
Calaverite.	A telluride of gold and silver.
Carbonates.	Ores containing a considerable proportion of carbonate of lead.
Chimney.	An ore shoot. A natural vent or opening in the earth as a volcano.
Chlorination process.	The process in which auriferous ores are first roasted to oxidize the base metals, then saturated with chlorine gas, and finally treated with water, which removes the soluble chloride of gold to be subsequently precipitated and melted into bars.
Clean-up.	The operation of collecting all the valuable product of a given period of operation in a stamp mill, or in a hydraulic or placer mine.
Concentrate.	That which has been reduced to a state of purity or concentration by the removal of foreign, nonessential or diluting matter.
Concentration.	The removal by mechanical means of the lighter and less valuable portions of ore.
Cribbing.	Close timbering, as the lining of a shaft.

Crosscut tunnel.	A tunnel driven at approximately right angles to a main tunnel, or from the bottom of a shaft or other opening across the formation to an objective point.
Cupel.	A small, shallow, porous cup, especially of bone ash; used in assaying to separate precious metals from lead, etc.
Dredge.	A scoop or suction apparatus, operated by power, and usually mounted on a flat-botttomed boat. Extensively used in mining gold-bearing sand and gravel.
Drift.	A horizontal passage underground. A drift follows a vein, as distinguished from a crosscut, which intersects it.
Face.	The surface exposed by excavation.
Fault.	A break in the continuity of a body of rock, attended by a movement on one side or the other of the break, so that what were once parts of one continuous rock stratum or vein are now separated.
Fissure vein.	A cleft or crack in the rock material of the earth's crust filled with mineral matter different from the walls and precipitated therein.
Float.	Pieces of ore or rock which have fallen from veins or strata, or have been separated from the parent vein or strata by weathering agencies.
Frue-vanner.	An ore-dressing apparatus consisting essentially of a rubber belt traveling up a slight inclination. The material to be treated is washed by a constant flow of water while the entire belt in the meantime is shaken from side to side.
Galena.	The commonest lead mineral.
Gash vein.	A mineralized fissure that extends only a short distance vertically.
Giant.	A large nozzle used in hydraulic mining.
Giant powder.	A form of dynamite.
Glance.	Minerals having a splendent luster, as silver glance, lead glance, etc.
Horn silver.	Chloride of silver.
Hydraulic mining.	A method of mining in which a bank of gold-bearing earth or gravel is washed away by a powerful jet of water and carried with sluices, where the gold separates from the earth by its specific gravity.
Lixiviation.	The separation of a soluble from an insoluble material by means of washing with a solvent. Used in certain metallurgical processes.
Location	The act of fixing the boundaries of a mining claim according to law.
Lode.	A tabular deposit of valuable mineral between definite boundaries.
Matte.	A product obtained in smelting sulphide ores of certain metals, as copper, lead or nickel. It is crude metal combined with more or less sulphur and requires to be further purified.
Mill.	Any establishment for reducing ores by other means than smelting.
Mining district.	A section of country usually designated by name and described or understood as being confined within certain natural boundaries, in which gold or silver (or other minerals) may be found in paying quantities.
Mother lode.	The principle lode or vein passing through a district or particular section of country.
Nugget.	A lump of native gold, silver, platinum, copper, etc.
Pan.	To wash earth, gravel, etc., in a pan in searching for gold.
Pinch.	The narrowing of a vein or deposit.
Placer claim.	A mining claim located upon gravel or ground whose mineral contents are extracted by the use of water, by sluicing, hydraulicking, etc.
Pyrite.	A hard, heavy, shiny, yellow mineral, . . . generally in cubic crystals.

Pyritic smelting.	The fusion of sulphide ores by the heat generated by their own oxidation, and without the aid of any extraneous heat.
Quartz mill.	A machine or establishment for pulverizing quartz ore, in order that the gold or silver it contains may be separated by chemical means. A stamp mill.
Reduction works.	Works for reducing metals from their ores, as a smelting works, cyanide plant, etc.
Riffle.	The lining of the bottom of a sluice, made of blocks or slats arranged in such a manner that chinks are left between them.
Roasting and reduction process.	The treatment of lead ores by roasting to form lead-oxide, and subsequent reducing fusion in a shaft furnace.
Ruby silver.	(Proustite). A silver-arsenic sulphide mineral.
Sampling works.	A plant and its equipment for sampling and determining the value of ores that are bought, sold, or treated metallurgically.
Skip.	A large hoisting bucket.
Slumgullion.	A muddy, usually red deposit in the sluices.
Smelt.	To reduce metals from their ores by a process that includes fusion. In its restricted sense, *smelting* is confined to a single operation, as the fusion of an iron ore in a shaft furnace, the reduction of a copper matte in a reverberatory furnace, and the extraction of a metal from sweepings in a crucible, but in its general sense it includes the entire treatment of the material from the crude to the finished metal.
Stamp mill.	The building or apparatus in which rock is crushed by descending pestles (stamps) operated by water or steam-power.
Sulphuret.	The undecomposed metallic ores, usually sulphides, chiefly applied to auriferous pyrites.
Sylvanite.	A gold-silver telluride.
Tailings.	The worthless slimes left behind after the valuable portion of the ore has been separated by dressing or concentration.
Tellurium.	A rare element analogous to sulphur and selenium, . . . usually combined with metals as with gold and silver in sylvanite.
Telluride.	A compound of tellurium with another element or radical. Often rich in gold or silver.
Tramway.	A suspended cable system along which material as ore or rock is transported in suspended buckets.
Vug (or vugg).	A cavity in the rock, usually lined with a crystalline incrustation.
Wilfley table.	A side jerk table used in ore dressing. It has a riffled surface which separates the light and heavy grains into layers by agitation, and the jerking action then throws the heavy grains toward the head end, while the light grains are washed down over the cleats into the tailings box.
Wire silver.	Native silver in the form of wire or threads.

Index

(569)

(571)

(574)

(576)

Erratum: Camp Frances is the correct spelling for Camp Francis (pp. 514, 516, 519; inside-back-cover map).